The Comp
PRIVACY
&
SECURITY
Desk Reference

Volume One: Digital

Michael Bazzell

Justin Carroll

The Complete Privacy & Security Desk Reference
Volume One: Digital

First Published: May 2016

Due to the use of quotation marks to identify specific text to be used as search queries and data entry, the authors have chosen to display the British rule of punctuation outside the quotes. This ensures that the quoted content is accurate for replication. To maintain consistency, they continued this format throughout the entire book.

All examples of privacy techniques in use have been slightly edited to protect the individuals' details. While the general methods and outcomes of the examples are accurate, details such as names, locations, and employment have been modified.

ISBN-13: 9781522778905
ISBN-10: 152277890X

Contents

ABOUT THE AUTHORS

Michael Bazzell

Michael Bazzell spent 18 years as a government computer crime investigator. During the majority of that time, he was assigned to the FBI's Cyber Crimes Task Force where he focused on open source intelligence and personal data removal methods. As an active investigator for multiple organizations, he has been involved in numerous high-tech criminal investigations including online child solicitation, child abduction, kidnapping, cold-case homicide, terrorist threats, and high level computer intrusions. He has trained thousands of individuals in the use of his investigative techniques and privacy control strategies. He currently works and resides in Washington, D.C., and also serves as the technical advisor for the television hacker drama *Mr. Robot* on the USA network. His books *Open Source Intelligence Techniques* and *Hiding from the Internet* have been best sellers in both the United States and Europe. They are used by several government agencies as training manuals for intelligence gathering and securing personal information.

Justin Carroll

Justin Carroll is a veteran of 15 years in the service of the United States Government. He is a plank-owner in the elite Marine Special Operations Command (MARSOC), has worked on a contractual basis with another government agency, and has deployed to some of the world's most dangerous and inhospitable places. After completing his last overseas deployment, he spent five years teaching digital security and identity management to hundreds of soldiers, sailors, and Marines of the United States Special Operations Command (USSOCOM) and was instrumental in the development of a highly technical surveillance program currently in use abroad by US Special Operations Forces. Justin resides just outside of Miami, Florida and is the author of *Your Ultimate Security Guide: Windows 7* and *Your Ultimate Security Guide: iOS*.

INTRODUCTION
THE COMPLETE PRIVACY & SECURITY DESK REFERENCE

This book is a culmination of numerous written works, both published and unpublished, by us, the authors. We revisited all of our content, ideas, and experiences in order to provide a single source of reference for the reader. We have learned a lot from our successes and failures while testing every facet of privacy and security. We hope that these experiences will help you gain the knowledge that you desire on this topic.

The content of this book fits within these two distinct categories. For the purposes of this writing, the privacy material will focus on your personal information. We will attempt to not only remove any undesired details from public view, but also make changes to your daily habits that will prevent repopulation of this data. The content of this writing that focuses on security will have a strong emphasis on digital protection. While an entire volume will be released on physical security, this book will be restricted to the best practices for securing your electronic surroundings. We believe that you cannot have privacy without digital security, and vice versa.

Target Audience

This book is for normal people that care about privacy. We will not instruct you to break ties with friends and family, flee the country, stop going to your favorite places, or move to a cabin in the woods. Both of us lead normal, active lives and are fully integrated into society. We both live near major US cities. We pay taxes, have friends over, know our neighbors, travel, and use cell phones and the internet daily. We do not talk about privacy to strangers, we do not rant about government conspiracies, and we do not wear tinfoil hats. We do care deeply about our privacy and security, and both have strong reasons for doing so. We dislike defining our entire audience into categories, but do believe that our readers have strong reasons to care about their privacy. Most of our audience will fit into one or more of the following categories:

Victims of Domestic Violence

Seventy-five percent of domestic homicides against a battered partner occur after she leaves the relationship. If you are thinking of leaving or have recently left an abusive spouse or partner, this book is the perfect resource to hide and protect yourself and your children. This book will give you the tools and knowledge you need to start a new invisible life.

Victims of Identity Theft

Identity theft is a serious and increasingly common crime. In fact, one of us has been the victim of aggravated identity theft. This book will give you the information to make yourself impervious to future instances of this fraud. If you have not yet been the victim, it is reasonable to assume that you may be in the future. Some sources estimate that one in every three Americans will be impacted by identity theft at some point in their lives. There is no need to wait until it happens to do something about it.

Government Officials and other Targeted Subjects

There are many professions that are often targeted for personal information such as law enforcement, federal agents, judges, attorneys, prosecutors, public officials, and other members of the government. These subjects should put extra effort into protecting their details from the general public. Law enforcement officers across the country have been doxed in the wake of incidents like those in Oakland, CA, Baltimore, MD, and Ferguson, MO. Prosecutors and judges have historically been targeted by sophisticated criminal enterprises and drug organizations. Members of the judicial system at all levels have been threatened by parolees. Members of our nation's criminal justice system should not wait until they face a personal threat to begin securing their lives.

Special Operations and the Intelligence Community

As former members of the government and military, we have a strong desire to keep our information private. Unfortunately, we no longer believe that we can rely on the government that we served to protect our information and guarantee our own safety at home. During the writing of this book, large breaches occurred against the Office of Personnel Management. This is the government entity that houses background checks and security clearances. Both of us have held high-level clearances within the intelligence community. Personal information about us was stolen in this breach including Social Security numbers, financial information, and sensitive family details. If you work in one of these communities, it is in your best interest to protect your own information before it is too late. This information may make you vulnerable overseas or compromise your safety or that of your family here at home.

Celebrities, Executives, and the Wealthy

Celebrities, executives, and the extremely wealthy are common targets of stalking, extortion, scams, and sometimes physical violence. Members of malicious groups like Anonymous target individuals in this category. Paparazzi and journalists hound celebrities and executives. This book can help these individuals opt-out of the public view and recapture a private life.

Dedicated Privacy Enthusiasts

This book is also for those who care enough about their privacy and security to pursue it, even though they do not fall into one of the aforementioned categories. Individuals in this category are much like us. They already understand the dangers to privacy and security and need no convincing. These individuals understand the risks to personal finances, reputations, and safety of their families and will actively make efforts to secure them.

Regardless of which of these categories you fall into, the sooner you begin this process the bigger the benefits will be and the faster you will begin to see them. Even if you cannot do it all now, do what you can as soon as you can. It is also highly recommended that parents begin to implement these techniques on behalf of their minor children. How much easier would it be to demand your privacy back if most of the information available had never been put there in the first place?

Levels

This book is presented in four levels: Basic, Intermediate, Advanced, and Expert. These levels were designed to be implemented individually or as a whole. You do not have to complete this entire book to reclaim your privacy and achieve a strong level of digital security. You may also pick and choose from each section as it fits your scenario. We leave it to the reader to choose his or her path.

Basic: If you are an average user who has little knowledge of personal privacy and digital threats you will probably see the most substantial increase after completing the steps in these chapters. This section will not make you "invisible", nor will it make you completely digitally secure. However, if everyone took these simple steps, computer crimes like identity theft would be far more difficult to perpetrate and far less common. This level is recommended for everyone.

Intermediate: If you have purchased this book you are very likely already a member of this category. Completing the steps presented in this level will require only very modest expenses, and a small amount of time. You will be very difficult to locate using public databases and openly available online resources. You will be more digitally secure than 98% of the population. This level is a recommended minimum for victims of identity theft.

Advanced: This part of the book is for those who are truly serious about privacy and security but not yet ready to commit to the expert level. After completing these steps, you have created a messy trail of disinformation, your new alias has a greater internet presence than your real name, and all of your communications will be encrypted with the latest technology. Most readers will not progress beyond this level and most will have no need to. Readers at this level are very elite among the privacy and security conscious. This level is recommended for victims of domestic violence, members of law enforcement and other targeted occupations, and special operations and intelligence community personnel.

Expert: This level is not for most of our readers. It is primarily for those under extraordinary threats and/or who are determined to become as private as possible. These techniques require much time, patience, and some financial investment to fully implement. They are not feasible for many, but the reward for accomplishing this level is total privacy. Individuals at the expert level are truly invisible. Their homes and utilities are not tied to their true names, their license plates and driver's licenses do not lead back to their physical locations, and they have taken additional extreme steps to hide their presence. It would cost tens or hundreds of thousands of dollars for a private investigator to track down an individual that has successfully executed the expert level techniques. This category is recommended for anyone with the willingness to pursue it.

Some portions of the expert level may pertain to individuals who have not made the full commitment to live the expert lifestyle. Chapters covering Major Life Changes and Data Leakage Response may be useful to all serious users of this work.

Will this make you completely "invisible?"

Yes, and no. Eliminating your personal information from the internet will make it much more difficult for someone to locate you, but not impossible. If you reach the expert level you will be all but impossible to find by any private entity including private investigators, journalists, and the like. However, a determined adversary with a sufficient budget can find anyone. This book cannot completely hide you from the government.

If you are a fugitive running from the US Marshals, this book will not help you. If you have pending warrants, we recommend that you turn yourself in now. If you owe back taxes or child support, we recommend that you pay in full as soon as possible. This book cannot protect you from license plate readers, facial recognition, informants, cell phone tracking, and other tools at the government's disposal. This book can provide no help when the IRS places liens against your property or your wages are garnished.

This book is not intended to help you commit any unlawful act, nor are we especially worried that it will. While there are those who will undoubtedly say that encryption and privacy tools enable criminals and terrorists, we would counter that so do automobiles, smartphones, and occasionally hammers. Any tool can be applied to either side of the law, and the applications and techniques presented in this book are merely tools. While much of our live training sessions have been for government and military groups, we understand the need for the private sector to become more secure. We believe that this information should be available to every law-abiding citizen. How you apply it can only be determined by you.

But I have nothing to hide!

One comment we frequently encounter is "I have nothing to hide". Individuals employ the logic that they have done "nothing wrong" to justify an indifferent attitude toward security generally and to privacy specifically. Obviously we do not agree with this logic. Though we are completely law-abiding and theoretically have "nothing to hide", we still believe in the individual right to personal privacy. We also strongly believe that just because you think you have nothing to hide doesn't mean it is so. There are over 27,000 pages of federal criminal laws, not including many thousands more pages of regulatory law. Each state in the nation, and each county, city, and township within it has a similarly huge library of recorded jurisprudence. It is very likely that even if you think you have done nothing wrong, you have.

Despite their protests to the contrary, most of those who claim they have "nothing-to-hide" actually do have something to hide, and on grounds that lean much more toward the ideological than the legal. We will borrow Glenn Greenwald's technique here. If you truly have nothing to hide, we ask that you put your money where your mouth is. Send us the username and password to your personal email account to the email address listed below. We will log into your email at will, read through your old sent messages, your inbox, your folders, and view your photos and videos. You should have no problem with this because you have nothing to hide, right? We don't expect to receive any emails containing usernames and passwords, nor do we really want to. We respect everyone's right to privacy and believe each individual should fight for it. It is equally unlikely that anyone who would make this argument would purchase this book. However, if you believe you have nothing to hide, our email address for this purpose only is privacyandsecurity@protonmail.com.

What will you need?

This book will provide all of the instruction that you will need to remove your personal information from the internet, generate new privacy-focused protocols, and secure your data and devices. It will explain the methods of living a normal life, but one that is invisible on paper. While the book is a one-stop shop for your privacy needs, you must bring three things. **Initiative**: There was a time when you could be a relatively private person by requesting that your landline phone number be unlisted. This is no longer the case. Privacy is no longer a passive process. A lack of participation in the digital world does not make you private. If you wish to be private, it is still possible to opt-out of the standard model, but you must be willing to pursue it, to make it happen yourself, and to demand it. This book merely provides the knowledge. You must have the willingness, determination, and discipline to make it happen.

Patience: Though we recommend that you start on this path as soon as possible, understand that you will not disappear overnight. Both of us are completely invisible but it took years to accomplish in both cases. Both have experienced successes in finding ways to protect their privacy, and both have experienced significant failures when executing new techniques. There is much you can do right now to make yourself less visible and safer. Do not become discouraged if you experience a setback.

Vigilance: Attaining your desired level of privacy and security is only the first step in a lifelong process. You will constantly be asked to give out your telephone number, email address, and even home address by parties that wish to market your information. You will also sometimes have to give out this information to take advantage of a product or service. To achieve and maintain your privacy, you must be prepared with alternate information that does not compromise your real information. After investing a great deal of time and energy into reclaiming your privacy, you should guard it intensely.

A special page has been created on both of our websites to help with the process. Navigate to **IntelTechniques.com** (Michael) or **YourUltimateSecurity.guide** (Justin) and click on the "resources" section. Along with other helpful categories, there is a page titled "**Privacy**". This page will have every link that is presented in this book, without the instruction. As links change, we will update these pages to reflect the changes. As new services arrive, we will include new links to protect your data. The pages are divided into sections for each chapter. You will also find related posts on the blogs at these websites.

Finally, we should very clearly state that we are not attorneys and this book contains no legal advice. Please consult with an attorney before attempting the advanced techniques outlined in this volume. This writing shares our experiences with executing basic and advanced methods for achieving complete privacy and security. Your results may vary. The entire content of this work was accurate to the best of our knowledge as of January 2016. Technology constantly evolves, and you may identify outdated content. Please refer to our websites for any updates. Further, many of the educational theories in this work would require you to violate the terms of service of various online providers. On rare occasion, the government has claimed that violating a private agreement or corporate policy amounts to a Computer Fraud and Abuse Act (CFAA) violation. While we believe that this should not be the case, always proceed with caution and at your own risk.

Whatever led you to this book, your interest in the topic indicates that you are ready to begin a journey into total online privacy and security. Anyone can do this, but few will. Will you?

Let's get started.

LEVEL ONE:
BASIC

We believe that this first level of privacy and security applies to every individual reading this book. It starts with basic computer security that will harden your devices and secure your web browsers. It will protect you while navigating to the websites required for searching and removing your personal details. A detailed guide to preparing for your privacy adventure will make sure that you have any documentation that you will need for the remainder of the book. Anonymous email addresses and telephone numbers will make you ready for intrusive requests when trying to eliminate information. A pre-assessment of your current online exposure will identify areas that need addressed. It will then lead you through a self-background check that will identify additional areas of exposure that may have been previously unknown to you. It will help you take action against your personal details being leaked on social networks, and will prepare you for the vast undertaking of making yourself truly private. You will learn how proper online authentication protects you and your online accounts. It will walk you through the process of demanding removal of sensitive information from websites and data brokers and will end with important instructions for securing your credit.

This is just the beginning.

Chapter One
Basic Computer Security

With the inconvenience and time investment inherent in securing a computer, many wonder why to bother. Both of us hear frequently "Why would anyone want to get into my stuff?" or "why would anyone care about me?" The honest answer is they probably wouldn't. But what if your computer was stolen from your home, hotel room, or rental car? What if your computer is borrowed by your child and lost or forgotten at school or on the bus? What if you were mugged and your briefcase was stolen? What if your landlord, babysitter, housekeeper, or dog walker decided to sit down at your computer and see what they could find? What if you were in an automobile accident and your laptop was left at the scene in your car? What if any of a thousand scenarios occurred that resulted in you losing physical control, whether permanently or temporarily, of your computer? In any of these instances the new "owner" of the computer may try to take a look at your data. What will they find there?

On our fully encrypted Windows, Mac, and Linux laptops they would find nothing but a blank screen prompting them for a boot password. Our entire hard drives, including the operating system, are encrypted and the devices will not boot without the correct password. Replace our computers with that of most home, business, and government users, and the answer is likely to be credit reports, medical documents, résumés, job applications, family photos, saved logins, credit cards, financial information, internet browsing history, hobbies, sexual affinities, and more. All of this information may be used to harass, blackmail, extort, or further exploit you. It could be used to steal your identity, open lines of credit, or commit crimes in your name, leaving you to clean up the mess. Though it is almost a certainty that no one is after you specifically, it is very possible that under the right circumstances you may become a target or victim of opportunity.

When deciding what material should be covered in this book, we agreed without reservation that basic computer security should be included. Though basic security is boring, without it we cannot rely on the more "advanced" security measures we discuss later in this book. Further, even though these measures are "basic" they are perhaps the ones with the greatest potential payoff. Even if you are reasonably certain that you are already doing everything right, this chapter should serve as a good review of your baseline digital perimeter. All of the techniques that will be presented in successive chapters rely upon the assumption that you have a desktop computer that is reasonably secure and free of malware. If your computer is infected with malware, or is at risk for malware infection, you should fix this before continuing. Conducting simple Google searches on an infected machine can open you up to further infections. Literally millions of viruses, Trojans, worms, and other exploits exist to take advantage of security holes. Some of the most damaging categories of malware include the following.

Spyware: Malware falling into this category is designed to harvest information off of your machine. This information may be your internet browsing habits, contact lists, login information, credit card information, online communications, or other highly sensitive data. Hijacking software that can surreptitiously enable your camera and microphone are particularly frightening examples of spyware. Some spyware may interfere with your computer directly by redirecting your browser or providing an opening for other malware to be installed.

Key Loggers: A key logger is a piece of malicious software that logs all the keystrokes that are entered on your keyboard. The keystrokes are stored to a text file which is then transmitted over the internet to the controller of the malware. This type of malware can defeat many of the privacy and security measures we will put into place such as encryption and strong passwords. Further, anyone with a full record of your keystrokes may be able to see your full home address, your true name, and any aliases you use.

Ransomware: Malicious software that takes an action and then demands payment before undoing that action falls within this category. The most commonly seen form of ransomware is also sometimes called "cryptoware". Cryptoware installs itself surreptitiously, and then quietly encrypts your files. Once the files have been encrypted, you are informed that you must submit a payment in exchange for the decryption key. You can save your files by purchasing the password to unlock them, for a nominal fee paid in Bitcoins.

If this seems unrealistic, consider the following. Several law enforcement agencies in the United States have fallen prey to ransomware and have paid hackers' ransoms to avoid losing massive databases of reports and investigations. If you do fall victim to ransomware, and have to pay, you may further compromise your privacy by giving up your name, credit card information, billing address, and a great deal of information about your computer and operating system. Because most of us would be very hesitant to pay such a ransom, even with our important files at stake, malware designers have also added a countdown to many of these programs. If you don't submit the payment within a certain number of hours, that you can watch ticking away, your files will be deleted.

Scareware: Scareware is malicious software that attempts to leverage the success of true ransomware by manipulating users into downloading other applications, purchasing rogue antivirus applications, or taking some other action that is beneficial to the malware's author. One commonly seen example of scareware is a popup with an FBI logo that solemnly informs the user that he or she has broken an online piracy law. The popup goes on to explain that an immediate payment of $50.00 will result in the charge being dropped.

The types of malware listed above are only the tip of the iceberg. While annoying, they are those that we fear the least. The most dangerous types of malware, in our collective opinion, are implants that are very quiet and whose job relies on remaining undetected. Malware falling into this category can persist on your computer for years and give its master unrestricted, remote access to your computer. This would allow the attacker to see everything you do on your machine, view all of your online accounts, and activate your camera and microphone at will. Exploits like these can disable your antivirus's ability to update and modify the antivirus definitions to allow their own activity. Exploits of this nature were once available solely to nation-state actors but are becoming more common and popular in the criminal underground.

Despite the dangers presented by malware, we are frequently informed that "no one would want to hack my computer". Again, this may be somewhat true. It is unlikely anyone would want to hack your computer specifically, but a hacked machine can take on a life of its own. Though the threats listed above are scary, there are dozens of other ways that infected computers are used to serve the needs of hackers. Some infections, like the Conficker worm, may sit silently on your computer for months or years until activated by their master. Once activated, your computer may be used as a bot to send out spam, accessed as an anonymization proxy, as a CAPTCHA-solving zombie, or as a node in a distributed denial of service (DDoS) attack. Your machine may be used as a web server to host a spam site or a malware download page. It may even be used as child pornography server. In this case you would probably prove that you are innocent of downloading and viewing child pornography but only after countless hours in court and thousands of dollars in legal fees. And it is doubtful that your neighbors would ever fully trust you again.

All of this happens without the owner's knowledge and your computer's hidden activities may persist for months or years. This enables cybercriminals and makes much of this illicit activity possible. Having an infected computer impacts society at large and, like immunizations, we all benefit from "herd immunity". Even if one cares little whether his or her own files are hacked, securing a computer is in the best interest of all of us.

This book will cover the three major operating systems Windows, Apple's OS X, and Linux. For Windows, we will cover Windows 7 and 10, but not 8.1. Windows 7 is still in very wide use in the corporate world, is used by the U.S. Government, and is almost universally employed among law enforcement agencies. Due to the relatively unpopularity of Windows 8/8.1 it will be omitted, but we will cover Windows 10 as it is already proving to be the next widely adopted Windows version. For Mac, we will cover OS X, specifically working with OS X 10.11.2 (El Capitan), as it is current at the time of this writing. Linux is a bit more complicated, and we will not cover specific steps for Linux operating systems. We have an assumption that if you are a Linux user, you are already ahead of the security curve and have a fairly strong technical grasp on using a computer. However, this book will mention Linux frequently. The distributions that we most frequently use are Elementary, Mint, TAILS, Ubuntu, and Whonix.

Choose Your Operating System

Choosing your operating system is an important step in security. Sometimes users may have little control over which OS they use. Government, law enforcement, and military users are frequently burdened with grossly outdated or even unsupported operating systems. Corporate users are at the mercy of their IT departments. Even on personally-owned equipment there may be a need for software that is only compatible with one operating system. If you do have some level of choice, you should consider the privacy, security, and convenience benefits and drawbacks of the following operating systems:

Windows 7/10: Windows 7 is the most widely used operating system in the world and Windows 10 is poised to quickly replace it. This is both boon and bane to its users. The bad news is Windows has an enormous attack surface and malicious hackers and software engineers are constantly writing new exploits numbering in the thousands every day for Windows. This is precisely because of its popularity and near-ubiquity. The more machines that may be affected by an exploit increase the value and desirability of that exploit. Windows is popular because it is available on hardware from dozens of manufacturers. Because Windows is so popular, it is also compatible with the widest array of applications.

Both of us have been committed Windows users for many years until the release of Windows 10. Windows 10 is Windows' newest version and was released during the writing of this book. We anticipate it enjoying a level of popularity and acceptance similar to that of Windows 7. Many of the same security applications that are available for 7 are also available for 10. However, Windows 10 collects a staggering amount of data about its users that they cannot opt themselves out of. There is no choice with Windows 10 but to accept the fact that your information is being collected. This has revealed Microsoft's increasingly heavy-handed data collection strategy and made us distrustful of the Windows 10 operating system. We neither use it as a primary OS, nor in good conscience recommend its use.

One major factor in the security of Windows operating system is the architecture (32-bit vs. 64-bit). Though most modern computers ship with a 64-bit operating system, some do not. You should determine which version you have in the "System" area of the Control Panel in Windows. The 64-bit versions of Windows have many more security features enabled than the 32-bit versions. These versions natively incorporate features like address space layout randomization (ASLR), mandatory driver signing, kernel patch protection, and data execution prevention. These functions are not incorporated into 32-bit versions of the operating system. Additionally, 64-bit OS's are generally capable of much greater computer power, including utilizing far more RAM.

OS X: Apple's OS X series of operating systems is renowned for being very secure and it does boast some impressive security features. However, the primary claim made about OS X is that it is immune to viruses and other malware. This is a fallacy. Many OS X users do not use antivirus at all, and the vast majority get away with it. The reason for this widespread belief is that very few malware applications are ever written for OS X because of its shallow market penetration. There are exploitable flaws in all operating systems and OS X is no exception. One other consideration is that Apple's iCloud ecosystem captures and stores a large amount of information from iPads, iPhones, and Mac computers. Though this data is not scraped or sold to data marketers, we deeply distrust cloud storage. The good news for Mac users is that they can opt themselves out of this collection almost completely. Mac computers enjoy enough popularity that they are well-supported by aftermarket applications. They are also very convenient to use.

Linux: The hundreds of open-source Linux operating systems are perhaps the least popular among those listed here. This is not to suggest they are unpopular. Linux operating systems are very popular in the IT and security communities. They are also immensely popular in the freeware community. Many of the expensive programs available for Windows and Mac computers are nearly replicated by free software that is available on Linux machines. Many Linux distros, short for distributions, are also often very lightweight and can be used on older machines that would otherwise lag with more resource-intensive mainstream operating systems. Because they are so small, sometimes as small as 100 MB, they can also easily be run from USB flash drives or optical media.

If security is your primary concern, we strongly recommend you consider a Linux-based operating system. Computers running Linux can be made incredibly secure, and very few viruses exist to take advantage of the Linux OS. There are even Linux distros like JonDoym, Liberte, TAILS (The Anonymity Incognito Live System), and Whonix that were constructed entirely around the ideas of protecting privacy, providing built-in security, and creating anonymity. Some of these operating systems will be discussed in more detail in Chapter 22. If you are adventurous, you can build your own custom Linux distro fairly easily with open-source plug and play tools. The only real disadvantage to using Linux is compatibility. Because of the free nature of Linux, many popular programs are not available for computers running it.

Common to All

The very basic best practices listed here should be employed by all users, regardless of hardware or operating system.

Operating System Upgrades: Upgrading to a new OS as soon as it is released can be tempting. In the weeks leading up to an iOS update, the news will be abuzz with amazing new features that users cannot live without. Though we certainly believe you should upgrade, we recommend doing so with caution. Running an old version of any operating system can be problematic, especially when support for it is dropped. Updates, including security patches, will no longer be released and the OS will become very insecure.

There is a balance to be found. Upgrading to a new operating system when it is only hours or days old is also a somewhat fraught proposition. Though software is tested thoroughly before it is released, there is no test protocol that can find issues like giving it to millions of people who use it daily. The first few weeks following a major software release are typically followed with hasty updates and security patches. We recommend waiting a decent interval before upgrading. For a mobile device such as an Android phone or iPhone, we recommend at least two weeks. For a desktop computer OS, we recommend at least three months after the initial release. Waiting to install a new OS is no guarantee you will be safe, but it will allow the easily-discovered security issues to be found and patched.

Our Recommendation

There are a number of factors to consider when choosing your primary operating system. These include familiarity and comfort, requisite software, cost, performance on a given system, and privacy and security concerns. We also strongly believe that brand loyalty is not one of these factors, whether this misplaced loyalty is for a certain brand or against it. We prefer to leave all options open to ourselves and feel the need to point this out due to the polarization between some Mac and PC users. The companies themselves are the real winners when it comes to brand loyalty. Using only one option, or refusing to use another, fills a company's pockets while needlessly limiting your own options.

Both of us use Windows, Mac, and Linux on a regular basis, sometimes all three in a day. But all three are run from Apple hardware, and OS X is our primary operating system. This is partially due to Microsoft's frighteningly aggressive new policy of data collection that was ramped up with the introduction of Windows 10. However, Apple does not monetize data at all. This decision was partially driven by the more user-friendly nature of OS X compared to many Linux distros, and the fact that OS X enjoys a wider array of mainstream software than Linux. It is also partially due to Mac computers' lack of bloatware applications and privacy-compromising applications such as "Superfish". It comes with good security software pre-installed such as full-disk encryption and secure file deletion utilities. Macs are currently a much smaller and less lucrative target to the malware authors. Finally, with a Mac and a virtual machine utility (discussed later) a user can run all three OS's from the same hardware.

OS Updates

Keeping your operating system up to date is one of the most important steps in securing a computer. As software ages, security holes are discovered in it, and attacks are written to take advantage of these holes. Though software updates are occasionally released to add features and to deal with bugs, they are often written specifically to patch security holes. If your software is outdated, it is vulnerable to holes that are, in addition to everything else, well-publicized by virtue of the fact that a patch exists to fix them.

Windows 7/10: Microsoft releases updates to Windows on "Patch Tuesday", the second (and occasionally the fourth) Tuesday of each month. If a serious security vulnerability is discovered, critical updates may fall outside of this cycle. There are several options for how you update Windows. You can allow all the updates to take place automatically in the background (the easiest option), download all the updates and individually choose which you will install and when you will install them, or download and install fully manually. There are some advantages to fully automating and some to doing it yourself.

When installing updates automatically, you enjoy several advantages. This is the method we recommend for most users. First, all of the updates will be installed at the earliest possible opportunity, meaning the computer will spend the minimum time running outdated software. We also like the idea of fire-and-forget solutions where updating happens on its own and you don't have to worry about it. Alternatively, downloaded updates that install automatically will install the very next time you turn your computer off. If this happens to be an inopportune time (i.e., moments before you leave work) and these updates take a great deal of time to install, you may be stuck for a while waiting for them. Also, not all of the updates may be necessary or desirable for you; one such example is several Windows 7 updates that duplicate much of the privacy compromising "features" from Windows 10.

The downside to searching for, downloading, and installing updates manually, is that important updates may not be installed in a timely manner or may be missed altogether. Further, we like the idea of the computer doing things for us when possible. However, we like the freedom of being able to choose which updates we install and when. The solution we prefer for Windows operating systems is to split the difference. We have Windows check for updates, download them all automatically, and then we can choose which ones to install. If an update is questionable to us, we will read the bulletin and decide whether or not we need to install it. We will always install security updates, and you should, too. Once they are downloaded, we can choose to install them at a convenient time.

To change update settings, navigate to the Start menu, Control Panel, System and Security, Windows Update, and select Change Settings from the left sidebar. Open the dropdown menu. If you want to go fully automatic, where Windows downloads and installs updates as soon as they are available, choose "Install updates automatically (recommended)". If you prefer to go with our technique, choose "Download updates but let me choose whether to install them".

OS X: As with Windows, we like to have the opportunity to review updates prior to installing them. We also like downloads to install in the background so that when we do choose to install them they are immediately available. The following steps will walk you through setting up this process.

All modern versions of OS X can be updated through the App Store. Before visiting the App Store to check for updates, open the App Store settings. There are six check boxes in this menu. Ensure that the following are checked.

- Automatically check for updates

- Download newly available updates in the background

- Install system data files and security updates

These settings will ensure that important security updates are installed automatically while still allowing you to install app updates and OS X updates at your convenience. Helpfully, the App Store icon will display a badge informing you of the number of updates you have available at a given time. If updates are available and indicated, open the App Store by clicking on its icon. It will display a list of updates you have available. You may select "Update All", which will install all updates. Alternatively, you can install each update individually which may be preferable if you do not wish to install a certain update.

Superuser Accounts

Superuser accounts are those that allow you access to system-wide changes such as installing programs or enabling and disabling features. While every computer must have an account with these abilities, it is inadvisable to use a superuser account for day-to-day operations in most cases. Though it is a phrase that is normally applied to the corporate or government sectors, computer users should also employ and adhere to the Principle of Least Privilege (PLP). The Principle of Least Privilege is a concept stating that any user should have only the permissions necessary to do his or her job. In the corporate world, this prevents users from "privilege escalation", or performing tasks that are not within their scope of work. On a personal device, this means that accounts that are routinely used do not have superuser privileges.

Windows 7/10: Windows has two different types of accounts titled Standard User and Administrator. A Standard User account has all of the necessary privileges for most of us to do the jobs we do on home PCs. Even if you work at a computer daily, you should rarely need to log into an Administrator account. User accounts have the privileges necessary to do most day-to-day tasks including creating, opening, editing, and saving documents, and browsing the internet. There are a very small handful of things a User account does not have the privileges for, the most important of which is installing programs.

Because Administrator accounts have the necessary privileges to install programs, executable files may be able to run on an Administrator account without having to ask permission. If permission is required, malicious executables are sometimes capable of tricking the user into agreeing to install the program. Standard User accounts have fewer permissions, and the most important permission this type of account lacks is the ability to install programs without permission from the Administrator. When a malicious program attempts to install itself on a Standard User account, a prompt will appear asking for permission from the Administrator (and the administrator's password if the account is password protected). Seeing a password prompt alone should be enough to make a user question whether he or she really wants to allow the executable to run.

When you install a new version of Windows, the only account that is enabled by default is an Administrator account. Many home users will never create another account, choosing instead to work only inside this account. This is problematic as it makes the computer more susceptible to malware and viruses. To set up a user account, navigate to Start > Control Panel > User Accounts > Add or Remove User Accounts > Create a New Account.

Both User and Administrator accounts should be password protected. To set up passwords for these accounts, navigate back to Add or Remove User Accounts, then click on the icon for the selected account. When the expanded menu for that account appears, select "Create a Password". The passwords for administrator accounts and user accounts should be different, and passwords will be discussed at length in Chapter Six. Though we recommend using long complex passwords in most cases, we recommend (and use) easily memorable passwords that are quick and easy to type for the Administrator and User accounts. This is because the password protection on these accounts offers very little actual security, but having a password can hinder anyone attempting to install malicious software on your device.

OS X: OS X has several different types of accounts including Standard, Administrator, Managed with Parental Controls, and Sharing Only. Like Windows, the only two with which we work are Administrator and Standard. A Standard account has all of the necessary privileges for most of us to do the jobs we do on home computers. Even if you work at a computer daily, you should rarely have to log into an Administrator account. User accounts have the privileges necessary to do most day-to-day tasks including creating, opening, editing, and saving documents, and browsing the Internet. There are a very small handful of things a User account does not have the privileges for, the most important of which is installing programs.

Because Administrator accounts have the necessary privileges to install programs, executable files may be able to run on an Administrator account without having to ask permission. If permission is required, malicious executables are sometimes capable of tricking the user into agreeing to install the program. Standard accounts have fewer permissions, and the most important permission this type of account lacks is the ability to install programs without permission from the Administrator. When a malicious program attempts to install itself on a Standard account, a prompt will appear asking for permission from the Administrator (and the administrator's password if the account is password protected). Seeing a password prompt alone should be enough to make a user question whether he or she really wants to allow the executable to run.

There is also a very compelling reason to use at least two administrator accounts on OS X. The FileVault II full disk encryption utility relies on user passwords to unlock the disk. You can allow any or all of your users this privilege but we recommend creating one Administrator account with a very long password solely for this purpose, and another through which you actually administer the computer. This prevents you from having to type a very complex administrator password into the machine each time you wish to install an application or make some other global change to your computer. This will be discussed in more detail in Chapter Thirteen (data at rest).

User and Administrator Account Names

There is a tendency to give Standard User and Administrator Account distinctive names. As an example, a family of four might name their accounts Tom, Tina, Chris, and Jack. Unfortunately, these unique account names associate themselves with many things. For example, Microsoft Office identifies the creator of a file by recording the user account name under which it was created in the metadata. If you send out files of any type, this may leak information about you or your family. For this reason, we strongly encourage using bland generic names such as Administrator, User 1, User 2, and so on.

Application Updates

Just as vulnerabilities in the operating system may be exploited, security holes in your installed programs can be used as attack vectors. It is important to keep all software up to date. It is also extremely important to limit the number of installed applications on your device to an absolute minimum. Each application represents potential undiscovered security flaws. We recommend scrubbing your list of installed applications every three months and uninstalling anything you have not used during the previous three-month period.

Windows 7/10: Secunia PSI (Personal Software Inspector) is a program that scans all of your installed programs to ensure they are up to date. Simply open the application, enter your Administrator password (Administrator privileges are required to run it), and click "Scan Now". Similar to Windows Update, Secunia allows the user some discretion in downloading and installing updates. The options are to "Update programs automatically (recommended)", "Download updates but let me choose whether to update", and "Check for updates but let me choose whether to download and update (not recommended)". Again, we prefer the flexibility of the second option. Any necessary updates will be downloaded, but we still have the option to choose when to install them. Secunia PSI is free and available at **http://secunia.com/vulnerability_scanning/personal/**.

OS X: The App Store will automatically display a badge when applications that have been downloaded through the App Store have updates available. To update these applications, simply open the App Store and click the Update All button. Alternatively, if you only wish to update certain applications and not others, select the applications you wish to update and click the update button for each one individually.

Antivirus and Anti-Malware

We strongly advocate the use of both a real-time antivirus application (yes, even if you use a Mac) and an on-demand anti-malware scanner. The two programs we recommend here should be sufficient for your needs on both platforms. At this point, it seems that nearly everyone, and certainly everyone with an interest in computer security, is aware that a computer should run an antivirus application. Literally thousands of viruses are written and deployed on a daily basis and the consequences of your computer becoming infected with one are potentially dire. Viruses and malware come in all degrees of severity. They can range from merely annoying to posing serious threats to the user's personal privacy, financial information, data integrity, and more.

Antivirus: Antivirus tools are primarily preventative in nature, detecting viruses and other malware programs before they have a chance to be installed on the host machine, and there are various paid antivirus tools on the market. Though paid antivirus applications do a good job and some have very comprehensive suites that perform many functions, we still prefer free antivirus software. Fortunately, there are numerous, free antivirus options available that compete very well against the premium, paid suites. Whether using a free or paid solution, antivirus definitions (the list of malicious software and behaviors it scans for) must be kept up to date for the program to be effective.

Avast is our preferred antivirus program and is available for both Windows and OS X. Avast is easy to set up, offers excellent real-time scanning, and consistently performs at the top of independent tests for detection of viruses in the wild. Although Avast is feature-rich and allows power-users a good range of settings to modify, it is still amply capable in the default configuration and requires very little intervention, which is perfect for inexperienced or disinterested users.

Avast gives users real-time protection against viruses, and is very responsive in handling those threats. In addition, Avast offers on-demand scanning of specific files, drives, or devices. It also offers network scanning that will examine your home wireless network to alert you to vulnerabilities within it. Avast works on a freemium model. Paid versions of Avast offer a number of other features including a VPN service. Avast is free and available at **avast.com**.

Anti-Malware: We frequently get asked by friends and family members to "take a look" at a computer because they think it might have a virus. The symptoms are usually the same. The computer is running slowly, they get tons of pop-ups, or instead of their internet browser going to Google.com, it goes to some other search engine homepage. While the computer may actually have a virus, what it much more likely is that it has some other forms of malware. Malware is a general term, and though a virus is technically malware, not all malware is a virus.

Anti-malware differs slightly from antivirus. While antivirus software scans in real-time for viruses and other malware and is primarily preventative in nature, anti-malware scanners are primarily reactive in nature and scan for a broad array of threats that may have slipped through the antivirus suite or were inadvertently installed. Once the infections are discovered, these programs also have the capability to fully remove them from your system. Anti-malware scanners typically scan through an on-demand basis. Whenever you elect to run a scan, simply open the anti-malware application, update its definitions, and allow it to scan your system. We recommend running one of these scans at least once a week. Although the program mentioned below offers premium paid versions with real-time scanning, the free version is capable for our needs. These programs are not standalone and should always be used in conjunction with a real-time antivirus software like Avast.

Malwarebytes Anti-Malware (MBAM): The anti-malware application that we employ most commonly and have the most trust in is Malwarebytes Anti-Malware. Malwarebytes is perhaps the most user-friendly anti-malware application we have found, and it has an excellent, well-deserved reputation. Malwarebytes is consistently at or near the top of every independent test of anti-malware scanners. Malwarebytes Free Anti-Malware and Malwarebytes for Mac are free and available at **https://www.malwarebytes.org/mwb-download/**.

Firewall

A firewall is an application that monitors and restricts the incoming and outgoing traffic to and from your computer. There are various free and paid third-party firewalls on the market, but very capable application firewalls are built directly into Windows 7/10, Mac OS X, and almost all modern Linux distros.

Windows 7/10: Windows 7 and 10 come with a very flexible and capable built-in firewall called Windows Firewall. Conveniently, Windows Firewall is usually turned on by default. The Windows Firewall blocks incoming connections by default when you are connected to a public network. For this reason, we set up all Wi-Fi networks as Public as explained further in Chapter Fourteen. The Windows Firewall is extremely adaptable and can be heavily modified to block outbound traffic and force all traffic for certain applications through a virtual private network. For most users, the standard firewall settings should offer an acceptable level of security. To access the Windows Firewall and ensure that it is turned on navigate to Start > Control Panel > System and Security > Windows Firewall.

Mac OS X: To enable the application firewall, open the Apple menu and choose System Preferences. Next, click "Security and Privacy". Click on the Firewall tab, then click the padlock in the lower-left corner and enter your administrator username and password to unlock the pane. Once the pane is unlocked, click "Turn On Firewall" or "Start" to enable the firewall. We recommend leaving the OS X firewall in its default settings unless you have a compelling reason to do otherwise. Rather than rely on the native firewall to restrict incoming and outgoing transmissions we will use another application called Little Snitch to manage this traffic, which will be discussed in Chapter Fourteen.

Camera and Microphone

Though perhaps not practical for handheld mobile devices, you should consider physically disabling the camera on your computer. On machines that permit opening of the case, we prefer to physically disconnect cameras and microphones to ensure they are not being eavesdropped upon. In the case of laptops, this means opening the case and physically severing connections to the camera and microphone. This may sound like an extreme measure, but software protections like disabling the microphone or turning on a light when the camera is on can be overridden by sufficiently sophisticated spyware. Disabling the hardware is the only sure defense, but we realize that the vast majority of individuals will not take it this far. At a minimum, we recommend blocking the camera with tape, a post-it note, or a dedicated sticker. The Electronic Frontier Foundation sells very reasonably-priced, completely un-hackable stickers for covering webcams that leave no sticky residue behind. They are available at **https://supporters.eff.org/shop/laptop-camera-cover-set**. We have no financial interest whatsoever in any sales through the EFF.

Physical Security

If you follow the suggestions listed in this chapter, it will be very difficult (we would never suggest it could be impossible) for the vast majority of attackers to install malware on your device remotely. However, with physical access to your device, there are a number of attacks that may be carried out successfully against your computer. This includes the "Evil Maid" bootloader attack to capture your full disk encryption password as explained in Chapter Thirteen. USB or optical media attacks work by bypassing your OS password, or the installation of hardware key loggers that cannot be detected by antivirus applications. Though this volume does not cover physical security measures in depth, we do offer some basic suggestions.

We strongly recommend that you carefully control the physical access to your computer, especially when traveling. Though it would be possible for someone to covertly enter your home and exploit your computer, it is not very likely. It is much more likely when traveling, so be especially cautious in hotel rooms. Even though you have locked the door, hotels doors and locks are susceptible to dozens of defeats, not to mention the fact that management, housekeeping, and maintenance all have operating keys to your room. Do not walk away from your computer to go to the restroom in a coffee shop. Do not leave it in your rental car, and do not leave it sitting in the conference room when you break for lunch. If you must leave it unattended in a hotel room or elsewhere, take the following physical security precautions:

- Turn off all interfaces including Wi-Fi and Bluetooth.

- Ensure your computer is full-disk encrypted and completely shut down as explained later.

- Remove all external media including CDs/DVDs, SD cards, USB drives, external HDDs, etc.) and take them with you.

- Take any transmitting devices, such as a wireless mouse and its dongle, with you when you leave.

- Store your computer in your hotel room's safe. Though the management will always be able to access the safe and this does not guarantee its safety, it does protect you somewhat against certain threats.

All of these precautions give you a fighting chance. However, against a very skilled adversary, they cannot guarantee your computer's security. Again, the absolute best practice is to avoid relinquishing physical control of your devices.

The previous section covered topics that are vital to the security of computers regardless of operating system. The following sections of this chapter will cover specific security precautions to take with Windows 7, Windows 10, and OS X.

Windows 7/10

Removing Bloatware: If you purchased your Windows computer from one of the major manufacturers, there is a very good chance that it is clogged with bloatware. Bloatware is the almost universally useless third-party software packaged with Windows by hardware manufacturers. Though all of this software is intended to at least appear helpful, there are a number of disadvantages to bloatware. The first is system performance. More applications running at once require more processor power, leaving less processor power to do what you really want to do. Superfluous programs also create system "clutter", slowing your computer and its startup process by adding thousands of lines of code to the registry.

The next disadvantage of bloatware, and the one we find most abhorrent, is its effect on privacy. Many of these programs are intrusive, constantly prompting you to register your device or send information to the manufacturer. Registering the computer is unnecessary as your receipt is legally acceptable proof of purchase for warranty purposes, and sending information back to the manufacturer is just a marketing scheme that benefits only them.

A shocking and frightening example of invasive bloatware was revealed in late 2014. A prominent PC manufacturer named Lenovo had shipped computers between October and December of 2014 with ad-serving software called Superfish. Superfish automatically and quietly breaks all HTTPS connections made over the computer (more details on HTTPS vulnerabilities are available in Chapter Fourteen). This program was purportedly included in the OEM software load to allow the manufacturer to serve advertisements on encrypted web pages, which by necessity allows them to see the page. As if this weren't bad enough, it also exposed the user to potential third-party, man-in-the-middle attacks. Superfish is not limited to these particular machines. Your computer may contract it or another app like it elsewhere as well. This is an incredibly shocking example of a machine that has shipped from the factory with what amounts to pre-installed malware.

Bloatware can be avoided altogether through a couple different methods. Computers purchased through small companies that custom build computers typically don't package bloatware into the OS. Another option would be to purchase a clean, OEM version of Windows 7 separately. This is the surest, though costliest option, as operating systems are not inexpensive, especially when added to the cost of a computer that already has an operating system. The third, and most cost effective option, if you already own or are purchasing a laptop from a major manufacturer, is to remove the offending applications yourself. Though you may not get all of them, you should try.

Applications can be removed manually by navigating to Start > Control Panel > Programs > Uninstall a Program. Each application can be culled individually, allowing you to selectively remove them one at a time. When doing this, it can sometimes be difficult to tell which applications are bloatware, and which are required by your system. When in doubt, do some research before uninstalling a program that may be necessary for the operating system to function correctly. If it isn't critical to the OS, get rid of it. This is not our favorite method of cleaning. It is difficult to catch everything. Some programs resist being uninstalled, and it can be difficult to sort the necessary from the unnecessary. However, it doesn't all have to be done manually. There are some programs out there that can help.

Decrap My Computer: Decrap would be my choice for cleaning a brand new computer. Decrap is a very simple, intuitive program that scans your computer for all unnecessary software. If run in fully automatic mode, it will remove everything that is not critical to the function of the machine. Even when running on a brand new computer, we would still use Decrap in the manual mode, allowing us the opportunity to select programs to remove rather than having it done automatically. Decrap is free and available at **www.decrap.org**.

Revo Uninstaller: Some programs simply do not want to be uninstalled. The programs that make uninstallation purposefully and exceptionally difficult usually do so for a reason. They are probably some form of malware. When we find programs like these, we use a Revo Uninstaller to remove them. Revo is a powerful, dedicated uninstaller. Not only does it remove the unwanted program, it also gets rid of the remnants of the program that are typically left behind by the Windows Uninstaller. Revo is also much faster than the Windows uninstaller, has a clean interface, and is simple to use. Revo offers a more feature-rich, paid professional version as well. The basic Revo Uninstaller application is free and available at **http://www.revouninstaller.com/revo_uninstaller_free_download.html**.

Autorun and Autoplay: These are features in the Windows operating system that automatically start accessing and playing content when a removable hard drive, flash drive, or CD or DVD is inserted into the computer. This is a convenience feature designed to allow the operating system to record your preferences for various types of media. For example, if you insert a music CD, Autoplay allows music to begin playing from the CD with no further input. Unfortunately, this also introduces a vulnerability. If the CD in question (or SD card, flash drive, hard drive, or any other type of removable media) contains a malicious program, AutoRun and AutoPlay can allow the code to execute without asking for permission first. Disabling this feature is the first line of defense against this attack vector. AutoRun and

AutoPlay should always be disabled by default. This is especially important if you use removable media across multiple devices.

To disable AutoPlay and Autorun, navigate to Start > Control Panel > Hardware and Sound > AutoPlay. This will open a Windows Explorer dialogue allowing you to choose what action the OS should take for various types of media. The first action you should take within this dialogue is to uncheck the box at the top that states "Use AutoPlay for all media and devices". Next, in the drop-down menu for each type of media, select "Take no action" and click Save. Your computer should no longer AutoPlay, but may ask you to make a decision if a form of media that the computer has not previously encountered is connected.

It is important to note that disabling AutoPlay does not completely eliminate the threat of a USB device executing malicious code. It is still possible that malicious files can execute automatically upon the insertion of a USB device. For this reason, caution is strongly recommended when using USB devices. We personally recommend never using a USB device that you do not personally own and control. Hot-swapping USB devices is a significant cause of infections and helps them spread.

Displaying File Extensions: By default, Windows hides the file extensions of most files from its users. The filename extension is the three or four letter appendage at the end of most file names, such as .pdf, .jpeg, or .docx, and it is there simply to inform Windows of the encoding of the file which is commonly used to determine which program will be used to open it. We are not sure of the reason Windows hides these, other than out of a likely correct assumption that most of its customer base doesn't care about the file extension or need to see it. For security reasons, it is a good idea to keep file extensions visible.

An attacker who wants you to open a file containing a malicious payload will likely wish to make the file look like one that you would usually open. For example, assume an attacker wants a malicious file to look like a text file created in Notepad. The usual file extension would be .txt, so he or she could simply name the document Innocent_File.txt. If file extensions are not displayed on your computer, you cannot see the real file extension and may only see the "fake" one that is part of the root name of the file. The full filename, including the extension, would make clear that something was wrong with this document such as Innocent_File.txt.exe. Further, attackers can easily make the malicious file's icon appear to be a standard Notepad icon (even though the file is an .exe), making it reassuring to the recipient, and increasing the likelihood it will be opened and run.

Displaying file extensions is an important step, but it does little good if the user does not take the time to verify the file extension before opening a file. Pay close attention to the file extension, especially when opening a file downloaded from the internet or received from a questionable source. If the file is questionable, consider scanning it with antivirus and anti-malware software as described in the next section. To display filename extensions, open any folder on your computer and at the top right side of the folder are several drop-down menus.

Click Organize, and within this menu click Folder and search options. This will open a new dialogue called Folder Options. In this dialogue, click on the View tab and scroll down to Hide extensions and uncheck this box. Click "Apply" in the dialogue before closing it.

Windows 10

As we have mentioned previously, we have serious reservations about Windows 10. The new flagship OS from Microsoft collects significantly more user data by default than any one previous and users have little choice but to accept this collection. As a result, we advise remaining with Windows 7 for as long as possible. In Windows 7, it is possible to opt out of Microsoft's new collection strategy by uninstalling the following updates from Microsoft.

KB3022345
KB3068708
KB3075249
KB3080149

If you still decide to install and use Windows 10, we recommend all of the best practices we have outlined in Windows 7, plus the following.

Installation: When upgrading to Windows 10, you may be tempted to use the "Express settings" option. This option will choose default settings for you to make the install or upgrade process faster and simpler. Most of the defaults are not in the best interest of your personal privacy. Instead, choose "Customize settings". This will allow you much more choice in the installation options. You will be presented with two screens allowing you to choose from a long list of features that you wish to be enabled or disabled. These include two settings for "Browser and protection", three settings for "Connectivity and error reporting", three settings for "Personalization", and one setting for "Location". All of these should be toggled OFF.

The next screen you see will be titled "Make it yours". On this screen you will be encouraged to log into your Microsoft account or create one. We strongly recommend against doing so and working with a local account instead. By signing into a Microsoft account, you are sharing much more information with Microsoft. Click "Skip this step" and proceed with the installation or upgrade.

Privacy: Thankfully Windows has included a fairly comprehensive and intuitive menu of privacy settings. To access it, open Settings and click "Privacy". There are thirteen pages of options listed down the left side of the Privacy settings page. They are Location, Camera, Microphone, Speech, Inking & Typing, Account info, Contacts, Calendar, Messaging, Radios, Other devices, Feedback & diagnostics, and Background apps.

Open each of these pages. The General page will give you a list of options that can be toggled on or off, such as "Let apps use my advertising ID for experiences across apps". Obviously, we recommend turning all of these apps off. Some of the settings, such as Location, will have both a global setting that allows you to turn off the feature for all apps, and settings for individual apps. If the global setting is turned off, individual app permission settings will be greyed out. In the interest of redundancy, our recommendation in cases like this is to turn on the global setting temporarily and then go through each app individually and toggle its permission setting off. After you have turned off each app individually, go back to the global setting and toggle it off. This ensures that if the global setting is inadvertently enabled the number of apps that have access to this data will be somewhat limited. Repeat this process for Location, Camera, and Microphone.

At the "Speech, inking, and typing" page click "Stop getting to know me" and confirm this decision in the pop-up by clicking "Turn off". This will stop Cortana, Microsoft's "digital assistant" from passively listening to your voice and everything within earshot of your computer. It will prevent the collection of dozens of other pieces of information from your machine and activity on it. Ostensibly, this information is collected so Cortana is more familiar with you and it can provide you with more personalized results and services. The amount of information collected, as listed by Microsoft, is shocking:

> "To enable Cortana to provide personalized experiences and relevant suggestions, Microsoft collects and uses various types of data, such as your device location, data from your calendar, the apps you use, data from your emails and text messages, who you call, your contacts and how often you interact with them on your device.
>
> Cortana also learns about you by collecting data about how you use your device and other Microsoft services, such as your music, alarm settings, whether the lock screen is on, what you view and purchase, your browse and Bing search history, and more".

On the "Feedback & diagnostics" page, open the first pull-down menu labeled "Windows should ask for my feedback". Select "Never". In the next pull-down menu, "Send your device data to Microsoft", choose "Basic". It is not possible to opt out of this information entirely, so choose to send the smallest possible amount of information. After you have completed these changes navigate back to Settings and then to Update & Security.

Update & Security: On the Update & Security page open Windows Update. Click the Advanced Options button. In this dialogue you have the option to choose how your updates are installed. We recommend having Windows download them automatically, but letting you choose when to install them. At the bottom of the page click "Choose how updates are delivered". This will open a dialogue titled "Updates from more than one place". This enables a peer-to-peer function that allows you to get updates from computers on your local network or from PCs on the internet. We do not trust the security of this option and recommend toggling this setting off entirely.

Next, open the Windows Defender tab. We do not recommend using Windows Defender. It performs poorly in independent tests, so our preference is for Avast. However, if you choose to use Defender, you should disable "Cloud-based Protection". We also recommend turning off "Sample submission" which sends malware samples from your machine to Microsoft. Cloud-based protection and Sample submission both provide some of your data to Microsoft. Though Microsoft offers a stated benefit to the user, we question how beneficial transmitting data to the cloud truly is.

Network & Internet: Next, back out to Settings and open Network and Internet and select "Wi-Fi". Click "Manage Wi-Fi settings" to display Wi-Fi Sense settings. Wi-Fi Sense is a feature in Microsoft that allows you to share Wi-Fi passwords with your contacts, through Microsoft of course. This sharing also means that you have to provide your Wi-Fi passwords so your friends can connect to your networks. There are two settings that should be turned off titled "Connect to suggested open hotspots" and "Connect to networks shared by my contacts".

This is the majority of the settings that are clearly available in the Settings menu. There are some other changes you should make to Windows 10 but they are made elsewhere in the interface. The first of these is disabling Cortana and Web search.

Search Bar Settings: Open the Search bar and click the gear-shaped icon, which will open Settings. Toggle Cortana off. Turning Cortana off will also delete any data stored on the device but not in the cloud. If you have been running Windows 10 with Cortana active, you will also want to click "Manage what Cortana knows about me in the cloud" and delete all data possible there.

The next setting is "Search online and include web results". This means that anything you search in the Windows search bar will also be searched on the internet. This could reveal the names of sensitive files you search for.

Disabling Telemetry: This setting is not available through the graphic user interface and must be done through command line. This setting is for slightly advanced users. If you are unfamiliar with command line you may wish to seek some guidance before executing this step. First, open the Command Prompt as an administrator by pressing Win+X or opening Command Prompt (Admin) in the programs menu. Commands entered into the Command Prompt must be entered EXACTLY as show here. When the command prompt is open enter the following:

sc delete DiagTrack

sc delete dmwappushservice

```
echo "" > C:\ProgramData\Microsoft\Diagnostics\ETLLogs\AutoLogger\AutoLogger-
Diagtrack-Listener.etl

reg add "HKLM\SOFTWARE\Policies\Microsoft\Windows\DataCollection" /v
AllowTelemetry /t REG_DWORD /d 0 /f
```

If You Are an Existing Windows 10 User: If you have been using Windows 10 for some time you should take all of the steps listed here. If you have been logged into a Microsoft account, you should also take the time to switch to a local account instead. Open Settings and go to "Accounts". Under "Your Account" click on "Sign in with a local account instead". If this option is unavailable, you may first have to go to "Sync your settings" and turn it off. You should now be able to revert to a local account.

Mac OS X

There are not many settings in OS X requiring attention, but there are a few. First, and most importantly, if you are running an outdated version of OS X, update it as soon as possible. The latest version, El Capitan, offers some very good security upgrades, one of which is a complete overhaul of OS security design called system integrity protection. This protects the privileged root access by making it unavailable while the system is running. This means that malware installing itself below the operating system cannot modify the system while it is in use. Though few users will ever notice this, it is a major upgrade. These settings can all be accessed through your computer's System Preferences, which are accessed by clicking on the grey gearbox icon on the dock.

General: There is one option under General to consider, which is the default internet browser. For now, we will recommend you leave this as Safari. However, once you have completed Chapter Two you may wish to change this from the default to Mozilla Firefox or Google Chrome.

Privacy & Security: The first set of settings here will determine some basic password strategies. The user who is currently logged in can change his or her password from this menu. A user can also choose the interval between the screen dimming and the computer locking. We recommend the shortest interval possible which is immediately. If you desire, you may also choose a custom message to display when the computer is locked. If you work in an office environment with dozens of laptops that look exactly the same it may be useful to set the custom message to something you can quickly and easily identify.

Gatekeeper is a native service in OS X that is designed to prevent software from unknown sources from executing. Below the password settings option to "Allow apps downloaded from:" there are three options. The safest of these options is the first, "Mac App Store". This will only allow apps that have been downloaded through the Mac store to be executed and installed on the machine. This is not always the most convenient option. There are many apps that are perfectly safe and necessary that are not available on the Mac App Store. The next option is also the default and reads, "Mac App Store and identified developers". This is a much more flexible option that allows you to install apps from trusted sources. The final option will allow you to execute applications from any source. It is the least secure option.

We recommend leaving your Mac computer set to "Mac App Store" only. At some point you may need to install an application from a non-App Store source or even an unidentified developer. If this is the case, opening the Security and Privacy settings will allow you to make a one-time exception by entering your administrator password. This is only a slight hassle for a huge potential payoff. We should disclose that the Gatekeeper service is not one-hundred percent secure. Vulnerabilities have been discovered. It does offer some measure of protection, and in this cat-and-mouse game of computer security, you should take all the protection you can get.

Spotlight: Spotlight is an Apple service that will recommend apps and services to you based on the usage of your computer. The privacy policy located in the lower right of the Spotlight menu will plainly state that your information will be sent to Apple. The information sent will depend on the app you are using, location services, etc. Regardless, we prefer that this information not be transmitted beyond our control. Disable every category displayed under "Search Results". Additionally, at the bottom of this menu uncheck the box for "Allow Spotlight Suggestions in Spotlight and Lookup". Next, navigate to the privacy tab. Here you may assign locations on your computer that will not be indexed by Spotlight. We recommend doing so for any folders containing sensitive information, and certainly for the drive locations of mounted encrypted volumes (encrypted volumes are discussed thoroughly in Chapter Thirteen).

iCloud: iCloud is Apple's native cloud server that allows you to back up critical data. This is integrated seamlessly into the OS X/iOS ecosystem. Though we do admire Apple's strong stance toward security and privacy, we are still wary of cloud storage of any kind. It exists on hardware we do not control and it is transmitted over the internet where it must be secured. It is a complex system and there is much that could go wrong.

In the iCloud configuration, the most important settings are the list of items that are backed up to iCloud. The only one that we choose to use is Find My Mac. Without enabling this setting here, it will not function. Uncheck as many other options as you are comfortable with.

Network: The Network settings are extremely important and will be covered thoroughly in Chapter Fourteen, Data-in-Motion).

Bluetooth: Bluetooth should be turned off when not in use.

Sharing: This setting is a very important one. Sharing can allow others on your local network to perform a number of functions on your computer remotely. These services are listed on the left side of the menu and clicking on any of them will display a description of that service. The services listed by default are screen sharing, file sharing, printer sharing, remote login, remote management, remote Apple events, internet and Bluetooth sharing. Because of the potential for abuse we recommend disallowing all of these services.

After unchecking each of these options we also recommend looking at the expanded options for each. For example, when clicking on "Screen Sharing" a description of screen sharing appears, as well as a button labeled "Computer Settings…". You should open each of these additional dialogues and make sure all of the options are turned off.

This screen also allows you to change the name of your computer. If you have given your computer a name that leaks information about you, we recommend you change it.

Users & Groups: As we discussed in the common-to-all settings earlier in this chapter, setting up user and administrator accounts is incredibly important. In OS X this is done through Users & Groups which is a category under System Preferences. In Users & Groups you may add or delete user accounts, create groups, and create or change passwords. Under the second tab in this setting you can also access Login Items. This will display a list of sites or applications stored in your Keychain that you will be automatically logged into when you visit or access them. We recommend storing nothing here.

This first chapter may seem very basic to some and overwhelming to others. It contains the principles of computer security that will provide a foundation for the remaining content of this work. Digital security is only as strong as its weakest link. Applying every method discussed in the expert section would be meaningless without executing the basic requirements outlined here. This chapter does not need to be tackled overnight. We hope that it assists in the creation of the most appropriate basic computer security strategy for you. Once your computer is secure, it is vital to protect your web browser.

CHAPTER TWO
WEB BROWSER SECURITY

Your internet browser serves as your computer's ambassador to the internet. How it presents itself to the websites you visit and their third-party advertisers will, to some extent, influence how those sites and advertisers will behave in return. More importantly, the setup of your browser will certainly dictate what browsing information your computer stores. Your browser's settings can also limit annoyances like pop-up advertisements and prevent some security threats like the installation of malicious add-ons. Setting up your browser is an important step in controlling your virtual security perimeter and protecting your personal privacy.

This chapter will be presented in two parts. The first part of this chapter will focus on "standard" browsers such as Firefox, Chrome, and Safari. We will discuss hardening these browsers to limit the amount of information that may be collected by the sites you visit. We will also attempt to make your browser more secure and limit opportunities for encounters with potential malware. The second part of this chapter will delve into browsers that are designed around privacy and security. Because these browsers can be inconvenient and can break websites, we recognize the need for both types of browsers. Before getting into specific techniques we will first discuss the things we are trying to avoid.

The Threats

Most people are at least passingly familiar with the concept of "Google tracking me". Knowledge about how users are actually tracked online is perhaps less common though. This section will attempt to explain the threats that can be mitigated through good browser setup. These threats include tracking, malware installation, and hardware exploitation.

Cookies are perhaps the most common means through which your browsing sessions are tracked. Cookies are small pieces of data placed on your computer by the websites you visit. They are placed there to be helpful. Cookies remember which links you have clicked, the products you have looked at, and sometimes your login information. You may be already logged in when you visit the page again. Accepting cookies is almost always required to complete a purchase or other transaction on a webpage. If your browser won't accept a cookie, the site you are visiting cannot remember what items are in your cart. For this reason, we recommend accepting cookies from the sites that you visit, at least for the duration of your browsing session.

Unfortunately, cookies are capable of doing much more than remembering which videos you have previously viewed on a website. Cookies can also be used to spy on you. Third-party cookies are not placed on your machine by each site you visit, but by a third-party that is partnered with the "host" site. These cookies are purely for analytical purposes and track your browsing from site to site. Some popular websites may allow as many as 40 third party cookies to be installed when you visit their site. Each one of these can record your username, account name, IP address (which can be resolved to your physical location), and each site that you visit. All of this can be used to create a comprehensive picture detailing your online activity.

Making matters worse, these cookies are also very persistent. Cookies are usually designed to last 90 days before they expire (some last longer). During the entire 90-day period the cookie may be used to track you. If you revisit the site where you got the cookie, a new one is installed and the 90-day clock resets. In this way cookies can be used to track users more or less over a lifetime unless steps are taken to get rid of them. We recommend clearing cookies frequently and never accepting third-party cookies. This is why the book will spend so much time explaining how to ensure cookies are deleted upon closing the browser.

Browser fingerprinting is the process of identifying enough specific characteristics about a browser so as to make it unique or nearly unique. Though this fingerprint may not positively identify you, it can be used to create a very comprehensive picture of what content you frequent. If you have been, or subsequently are, positively identified, this information can be directly correlated to you.

The factors used to fingerprint a browser are many, and most of the reasons they are requested are legitimate. The sites you are visiting must know some of this information to allow sites to present and function properly with your device. These factors include your screen size and resolution, the fonts you have installed on your device, the time zone to which your computer is set, any add-ons that you have installed, cookie settings, and your browser and operating system details.

Browser fingerprinting is an extremely dangerous form of tracking because it is very difficult to defeat. While you can refuse to accept cookies it is very difficult to change your screen resolution. In the sections on Firefox and Chrome we will discuss some methodologies that offer some light protection against this form of tracking. The Electronic Frontier Foundation has an excellent browser fingerprinting tool that will tell you how unique your browser is, as well as an excellent white-paper on the topic. It is available at **https://panopticlick.eff.org**.

Malicious websites will attempt to lure you into downloading and installing viruses and other malware. There are several ways this may occur. It could be from a site attempting to automatically install a browser add-on when you visit it or pop-up advertisements enticing you to click them. Though the best practices discussed in Chapter One will prevent almost all applications from installing without your explicit permission, you still want a sound defense-in-depth. The browser is the front line of that defense.

Malvertising is a relatively new and dangerous attack vector. Malicious advertising is the insertion of malicious software into seemingly legitimate ads. Many prominent and reputable sites have inadvertently served malware-laden advertisements because true malvertising is much more sophisticated than the annoying, ostentatiously-blinking popups that most of us have come to loathe. These ads are designed to be indistinguishable from non-malicious ads and may appear in widget bars along the sides of webpages, hidden iframes, and banners. Once a malicious ad is clicked the host computer becomes infected with the malicious payload.

This chapter will cover some steps to take that can limit pop-up, pop-over, pop-under, rollover, banner, and other forms of annoying advertisements. Advertisements can be attack vectors for malware as mentioned in the previous paragraph. Ads also slow your internet connection by consuming precious bandwidth. The content of the advertisement is competing for bandwidth with the content you actually want.

Your computer stores a vast amount of information about your browsing sessions, such as what sites you visit. These sites reveal your interests, dating and relationship history, sexual proclivities, items you purchase, places you visit, usernames, and the email and social media services you utilize. All of this information can create a vast privacy compromise. This information can be taken physically if your device is lost, stolen, or accessed while out of your physical control. It can also be extracted off the device remotely with malware.

Though we will discuss some methods of securely removing this and other information in Chapter Twenty-One, proper browser setup will prevent much of this information from ever being saved. It is far easier to avoid saving such information in the first place. It is also much more secure. If you forget to delete it with a third-party application, it will not matter much since it won't be there anyway.

Firefox (Windows, Mac OS X, Linux)

We do not equivocate on our choice of browser. If you wish to set up a browser for maximum security and privacy, we recommend Firefox. This is not to suggest that Firefox is inherently more secure than other browsers, though it might be. This is also not to say that Firefox is an inherently security or privacy focused browser more than other mainstream options, though it probably is. The reason we like Firefox is that it offers the greatest control over security and privacy settings, and there are numerous add-ons for Firefox that can harden the security of the browser. Firefox is free and available at **www.mozilla.org/en-US/firefox/new/.**

The first and most basic step you should take is to ensure your browser is up to date. Outdated browsers with security holes are an extremely common attack vector. Browser updates are issued frequently to patch these vulnerabilities as they are discovered. You can check your version of Firefox by clicking on the "Menu" button. The menu button appears as three horizontal lines stacked on top of each other, aka "the hamburger", and is located on the top right of the Firefox interface. Go all the way to the bottom of this fly-out menu, click on the Help button (question mark icon), then choose the very last option labeled About Firefox. This will open a new window that will display the version of Firefox you are running, or a warning that the version you have is out-of-date. If yours is out-of-date update it immediately.

Once you have ensured your browser is the latest stable version, some settings must be modified to ensure the greatest possible privacy and security. To access the settings again go to the Menu button, open the menu, and select "Options" (the gear icon). The Options dialogue consists of eight categories: General, Tabs, Search, Content, Applications, Privacy, Security, Sync, and Advanced.

General: The first item under the General category that should be changed is the homepage. You may choose any website you like to be your homepage, or you may choose to use a blank page. For maximum anonymity, https://google.com is a good homepage. Millions of people use this as their homepage and it is completely non-alerting. The next setting that should be modified under this category is Downloads. By default, Firefox saves downloaded files to a "Downloads" folder but this is not ideal because files are not immediately visible to the user. They may be forgotten, unencrypted, in the Downloads folder. Instead we prefer to have Firefox always ask where to save files and let us make the decision for each file we download. If you download a large number of files and prefer to choose a location to which they automatically save, we recommend creating an encrypted location to which they save. This prevents the files from being written to your hard drive in an unencrypted format.

Privacy: The privacy category is where you will do much of the real work of deciding what information Firefox stores and what it does not. The first section under Privacy is "Tracking", which has three options. Users can choose to tell sites they do wish to be tracked, do not wish to be tracked, or tell the sites nothing about their tracking preferences. Because sites have no obligation to honor your requests not to be tracked, and because we will take more aggressive steps to limit online tracking, we leave this site at the default "Do not tell sites anything about my tracking preferences". You may elect to tell sites that you do not wish to be tracked.

History: Under the "Firefox will:" option, select "Use custom settings for history" from the pull-down menu. This will allow you to choose everything that is stored or forgotten when you close your browser. Next, uncheck "Always use private browsing mode". Even though this probably removes everything, we like the granularity and control of choosing these settings and seeing exactly what items Firefox will delete. Next, uncheck "Remember my browsing and download history" and "Remember search and form history". This will prevent Firefox from remembering any history after your browsing session has closed.

Next, check the box that says, "Accept cookies from sites". This will allow cookies from the sites you visit. Without cookies, it is very difficult to make purchases, use online streaming services, or enjoy many of the other potential benefits of the internet. Though accepting cookies is not ideal, we will take steps to get rid of them upon closing Firefox. Next, under the "Accept cookies from third party sites" drop-down, select "Never". Third-party sites are sites that you have not visited but that are still attempting to track internet usage for marketing purposes. There is no need to accept their cookies since you have not visited these websites. Under "Keep until" (which refers to how long cookies are retained), select "I close Firefox". By default, cookies may last 30, 60, or as long as 90 days, and may track your browsing sessions throughout that entire period. This option will ensure they are not saved after your browsing session has ended.

Finally, check the box that says "Clear history when Firefox closes". This will delete remnants of your session that Firefox has retained. Before moving on click the "Settings" box to the right. This will bring up an entirely new dialogue that gives you very granular control of the items that Firefox clears upon closing. They are Browsing and Download History, Active Logins, Form & Search History, Cookies, Cache, Saved Passwords, Site Preferences, and Offline Website Data. Select all of them and click OK to close the dialogue. Finally, under "Location Bar" uncheck History, Bookmarks, and Open Tabs.

Security: Under Security check the "Warn me when sites try to install add-ons" box. This will require you to approve or deny a site when an add-on attempts to execute. This affords you some level of protection against annoying add-ons or semi-malicious add-ons that would track your browsing history. Next deselect both the "Block reported attack sites" and "Block reported web forgeries" options. Both of these options could allow Firefox to track your web activity by sending the sites you visit to Mozilla for vetting against a whitelist. Though we don't distrust Mozilla or Firefox, we still prefer to send them as little information about our browsing sessions as possible.

Finally deselect the "Remember passwords for sites" and "Use a master password" options. When Firefox stores a password, it does not do so in the most secure manner. Additionally, when you visit a website for which Firefox has a stored password, your credentials may be automatically transmitted to that site. This is not ideal if you are working on an insecure or untrusted internet connection. If you have saved passwords within Firefox in the past, transfer them to your password manager (to see them click the "Saved Passwords" button). Once you have transferred the passwords, delete them all from Firefox by clicking "Remove All" in the Save Passwords dialogue.

"Private" Browsing Modes

Do not rely on Firefox's native "Private Browsing" mode (or on other browsers' analogs like Incognito or InPrivate modes). Though these modes are designed to prevent any information from your browsing session from being stored on your computer, researchers have proven that they are not always fully effective. Controlling all of these settings manually allows you to define exactly what Firefox does and does not store and gives you confidence that all your browsing history and associated data is deleted when you exit the browser. Also, do not be confused about the nature of these private modes. In fact, we consider the term "private" slightly misleading. Any browsing you do in these modes is private only on your device. Your traffic is not encrypted or otherwise protected from interception or exploitation, and your IP address (which can reveal your physical location) is not obscured. To achieve true privacy one must also use of a Virtual Private Network (VPN) or Tor. VPNs will be covered fully in Chapter Fourteen: Data-in-Motion. Tor will be covered later in this chapter.

Advanced: Under the Advanced tab there are five additional tabs: General, Data Choices, Network, Update, and Certificates. Under the Data Choices tab, we recommend unchecking all three of the options. Telemetry, the Firefox Health Reporter, and the Crash Reporter all collect data about your usage on Firefox. While most of this data should be anonymized and only consist of metadata about your browsing, we still prefer not to transmit it.

The most important option in the Advanced options is the Update tab. This will choose when and how Firefox is updated, and keeping your browser up to date is incredibly important for security reasons. We recommend choosing "Check for updates but let me choose whether to install them". This option makes you aware that an update is available, but lets you choose the time and place to install it, and gives you time to research the update and understand how it will impact your security and privacy. If you choose this option, do not ignore the notifications that an update is available.

WebRTC vulnerability fix. There is one final setting we recommend you adjust in Firefox. The ability to adjust this setting is one of the reasons we choose Firefox over other browsers. A relatively recent vulnerability was discovered in Firefox and Chrome that allows websites to see your true IP address despite the use of a VPN (see Chapter Fourteen). When using a VPN any site you visit should only see the IP address of the VPN's exit server, preventing them from correlating you with your visit with your geographic location and building profiles based on your IP address. With the WebRTC vulnerability this protection can be bypassed and reveal your true IP address and physical location.

Thankfully this vulnerability is very easy to correct but it cannot be corrected through Firefox's Options dialogue. To correct it go to your URL bar in Firefox and type "about:config". This will open a menu where power-users can make many adjustments to the application (some of these adjustments can be made through the Settings, but many cannot). Bypass the warning and scroll down to "media.peerconnection.enabled". This setting is "true" by default. Double-click this line which will toggle the value to "false". This is all that is required to turn off WebRTC and secure this vulnerability.

Unfortunately, it is not completely possible to mitigate this vulnerability in Chrome. Chrome does offer an add-on that corrects the vulnerability but it is easily bypassed and do not recommend it. This is a huge privacy concern and the reason we recommend Firefox as the most private of the browsers listed here.

Firefox Add-ons: Add-ons are small programs that can be added to Firefox. There are thousands of add-ons for Firefox and most of them are not designed to enhance your privacy or security. In fact, many of them allow you to be tracked more easily. Some add-ons hurt security and privacy in more concrete ways. The add-ons listed here make Firefox more private and more secure, make it more difficult for your browsing history to be tracked, and reduce the possibility of certain types of malicious attacks successfully targeting you.

With the exception of NoScript, each add-on in this section is more or less "fire and forget", meaning that once installed they require no interaction with the user to perform their intended functions. Again, with the exception of NoScript, they are also unlikely to "break" (i.e. render inoperable on your machine) most websites. Because of the low maintenance these add-ons require, they are suitable for beginner or non-security conscious users. If we are asked to "fix" a friend's computer, we install these add-ons for him or her and have yet to receive a complaint. These applications provide a good baseline level of security and hardening for the browser as well as limiting the ability of websites and ISPs to track your browsing habits.

"Malicious" Add-Ons

There are a myriad of add-ons for Firefox and many of them offer convenience as their primary selling point. They will make websites easier to use, remember information for you, or make shopping on ecommerce sites more convenient. Unfortunately, many of these add-ons can compromise your security and privacy. Some of these add-ons will actively track your browsing sessions, some may insecurely store data, and others may be vectors for malicious code. Further, the more add-ons you have the more unique your browser is. This makes you more susceptible to browser fingerprinting. Think twice and do your due diligence before installing and trusting an add-on.

During the writing of this book a popular proxy app called Hola! was found to be conducting some very questionable practices. Users installed the add-on to be able to bypass geographical content restrictions. Unfortunately, the app was selling the bandwidth of users with the app installed, through which some malicious attacks were perpetrated. Before installing any add-on ensure that you read the privacy policy first. We also recommend uninstalling any pre-installed add-ons or default extensions that you did not personally install and research for trustworthiness.

These add-ons are not presented in either an ascending or descending order of importance or utility. They are presented merely in alphabetical order. We feel that each is important and have trouble narrowing this down to a shorter list. Some of the functionality of these extensions overlap. If this is the case, we will attempt to clarify the need for the redundancy. Unless otherwise indicated, all of these add-ons are free, and most are available at **https://addons.mozilla.org/en-US/firefox/.**

Better Privacy: Better Privacy is a simple, transparent add-on that performs a very important purpose. It deletes resilient "Flash" cookies which are sometimes referred to as locally stored objects (LSOs). LSOs are not formatted as, and may not be recognized as, cookies. Because they do not look like standard cookies to Firefox, they may not be deleted when Firefox closes and may track your internet browsing from session to session. Better Privacy detects these cookies and upon closing Firefox will delete them for you. We like Better Privacy because there is no icon in the upper toolbar, it requires no interaction from us, and it consistently performs its function.

Disconnect: Though we have used a number of add-ons over the years in an attempt to defeat tracking, the one we prefer now is Disconnect. Disconnect detects and blocks trackers and shows a graphic display indicating how many advertising, analytics, social, and content requests are made when you visit a site. It also shows how many of these are blocked and which ones are not. Disconnect also saves both bandwidth and time by not allowing advertising content to be served to you.

Though NoScript (discussed below) can help prevent tracking like Disconnect and may be considered redundant by some, Disconnect is a dedicated anti-tracking app. We believe what redundancy does exist between these two add-ons is necessary because NoScript frequently is too heavy-handed and will not allow a site to work properly. In these cases, we have to allow the page (whether permanently or temporarily). When this occurs and a page is allowed to run, we still want some protections in place. Disconnect does not replace NoScript (and vice-versa), but they do complement each other well.

Disconnect Private Search: This is one of our favorite Firefox extensions. Disconnect Private Search can replace the default search engines in Firefox and route all of your searches through a "light" VPN via a Disconnect server. This allows you to search semi-anonymously because the search provider does not see from whom the search is originating. Additionally, if you set Disconnect Private Search as your default search engine, all your searches (whether from your homepage, Google.com, the address bar, or the search bar) will be routed through Disconnect Private Search.

When you search through Disconnect Private Search your search terms are sent to your preferred search engine and those are the results that are returned. If you don't like those results, there is a drop-down menu within in the search page that allows you to search through any of the other search engines supported by Disconnect Private Search: Bing, DuckDuckGo, Google, and Yahoo. Disconnect Private Search will warn you that because they trust DuckDuckGo, search requests are sent directly to that search engine. We like Disconnect Private Search if for no other reason than the convenience of having four search engines immediately available through a dropdown menu.

HTTPS Everywhere: HTTPS (HyperText Transfer Protocol – Secure) is intended to encrypt data-in-motion between two devices using the SSL and TLS encryption protocols (the SSL and TLS protocols are discussed in Chapter 14: Data-in-Motion. Though vulnerabilities exist in HTTPS it should be considered the first line of defense for your data-in-motion. The HTTPS Everywhere add-on can help ensure you establish and maintain HTTPS connections throughout your browsing sessions.

Unfortunately, many sites have the ability to offer HTTPS connections but only do so during "sensitive" portions of the session such as login or financial transactions. During the rest of your session, many sites will revert back to plaintext HTTP. The HTTPS Everywhere add-on was designed to force any site with the HTTPS capability to encrypt the entire session, and it works very well. Encrypting your entire session will ensure that anyone sniffing your Wi-Fi, or otherwise inspecting your traffic, will encounter much more unusable, encrypted information. HTTPS Everywhere was developed and is maintained by the Electronic Frontier Foundation (EFF). HTTPS Everywhere is free and available at **https://www.eff.org/https-everywhere**.

NoScript: NoScript is the nuclear option of security-focused browser extensions. NoScript blocks all scripts and plugins, including Flash, Java, and JavaScript, from executing except on websites that you approve. It also performs a number of other browser-related security functions. Unfortunately, the security of NoScript comes at a cost. NoScript has a very steep learning curve. Because it blocks so many scripts, NoScript tends to "break" many websites. In many cases, this may be desirable as NoScript prevents videos from automatically playing, stops animations, prevents pop-ups and other advertising, and generally makes busy pages much more manageable. For sites that you need to work, this can be quite frustrating initially after installing the add-on. For this reason, the application allows itself to be customized to whitelist certain sites permanently or temporarily. Clicking the NoScript icon on a page will display all of the scripts that are running on the page. It will present options for enabling or disabling each script individually, as well as settings that apply to all scripts on a page and globally. These options are:

- **Allow scripts globally (dangerous):** This setting basically removes all protections afforded by NoScript and lets all scripts on all pages run. Unfortunately, this option is not reset when you close and reopen your browser. There are some occasions where using this option is desirable. For example, if we are creating a new account or making an online purchase, and may be redirected to a page where scripts blocking may interfere with password input fields, we will allow scripts globally, but only for that transaction. As soon as we are finished, we will enable script-blocking again.

- **Allow all of this page:** This setting permanently whitelists the entire page. Be aware that permanently whitelisting a site on NoScript will place the name of the site in a list on your computer. This list is unencrypted and may be viewed by anyone with access to your computer, allowing him or her to see what sites you visit frequently.

- **Temporarily allow all of this page:** This setting allows the page you are visiting and all the scripts on the page to run for the duration of the browsing session or until permissions are revoked. This setting will be reset when you close your browser.

- **Allow…:** This allows you to whitelist an individual script on a page permanently.

- **Temporarily Allow…:** allows you to whitelist an individual script on the page you are visiting. This permission will be revoked when you close the browser. This may be desirable if you are visiting a page that needs a Flash script to run to play a video, animation, or other graphic that is broken by NoScript, but only desire it for a single visit.

- **Make page permissions permanent:** If you frequent a site and have allowed the minimum number of scripts to permit that page to function properly you may wish to use this setting. It will add those permissions permanently to your whitelist so you do not have to manually allow scripts each time you visit the site.

- **Revoke Temporary Permissions:** This option allows you to immediately revoke any temporary permissions and stop the scripts associated with them.

- **Forbid…:** Forbidding a given script allows you to stop any script to which you have granted temporary or permanent permissions. When visiting a site, you may wish to allow all the scripts on the site, then forbid them one by one until only the desired functions on the site are running and nothing else.

- When you no longer wish to allow scripts on a given page NoScript also gives you the ability to revoke permissions. Additionally, each script on the page will have an "Allow" or "Temporarily allow" option, so you can fine tune each page to make the content you desire visible while blocking everything else. Though using NoScript can be frustrating at first, once the sites you primarily use have been whitelisted and are working well, the add-on requires little intervention except when visiting new sites or sites that are not permanently whitelisted.

This section has only covered the tip of the security iceberg that is NoScript. In addition to preventing scripts from executing, NoScript also prevents Cross-Site Scripting attacks, allows you to force sites to use HTTPS connections (where available), prevents clickjacking attempts, and provides automatic boundaries enforcement (ABE). NoScript is free and available through the Firefox Add-Ons menu. For more information on the capabilities of NoScript visit: **https://noscript.net**.

Chrome (Windows, Mac OS X, Linux)

While we like Firefox for its malleability in regards to privacy and security, we also recognize the need to use multiple browsers at times. We also have noticed that Firefox (when setup in the manner we advise) can be difficult to work with on certain websites. When NoScript is running in Firefox it may break certain sites that you need to access and an alternative browser may be necessary. There may be times that you need to be logged into more than one account with the same service (multiple Gmail accounts, for instance) and cannot do so from a single browser. Our second favorite "standard" browser is Google's Chrome which is available at **https://www.google.com/chrome/browser/desktop/**.

Chrome is an excellent browser that is known for being very lightweight and low-impact.

Chrome is also very secure by nature. Chrome sandboxes each tab. Sandboxing restricts the content in that tab to that tab only, preventing it from "touching" other tabs in the browser, or the computer's hardware. This is a very important feature in preventing malware from being installed when you visit a malicious website.

Unfortunately, Chrome is also a Google product, meaning by default it collects a lot of information about the people who use it. Because of this we use Chrome only in a very limited capacity. We use Chrome to log into certain accounts. While logged into those accounts we do not conduct searches, don't open links in other tabs, and do not log into other accounts. After accessing these accounts, we close Chrome and clean our system as detailed in Chapter 21. The other occasion for which we turn to Chrome is when Firefox's security precautions "break" a website. The most common reason for this is connecting to Wi-Fi hotspots in hotels that require a login on a webpage. Frequently Firefox will not allow this page to function correctly and a lighter, less secure browser must be used.

We believe that using Chrome only for these very limited purposes is a good privacy practice. We also believe that there are some technical steps that you can take to increase the privacy and security of Chrome. To manipulate the settings in Chrome, navigate to the settings menu. Like Firefox this is the "hamburger" icon in the upper-right of the interface. In the fly-out menu scroll down to and click "Settings".

Sign in: The very first setting in Chrome is perhaps the most important one: Sign in. By signing into Chrome you are positively correlating all of your internet activity with your Google account. This information is collected and stored by Google and used for advertising purposes. If you are signed in you should disconnect your Google account, but not before deleting the data that has already been collected about you.

If you wish to remain signed into Chrome, we strongly encourage you to encrypt the information you store with Google. This can prevent Google from accessing the data that it stores about you, though very few people take advantage of this option. To do so you must be signed in to Chrome. Click the Advanced Sync Settings tab. This will open the dialogue that allows you to choose the information that Chrome stores about you. Again, we urge you to store nothing with Chrome, but if you do, you should reduce the amount of information to the bare minimum. The Advanced Sync Settings dialogue will also allow you the option to encrypt this data, either with your Google Credentials or with a different password. We recommend using a different password. This password is not sent to or stored by Google.

Privacy: In the Chrome settings menu scroll down and click the "Advanced settings" hyperlink. The first set of options that will open is "Privacy". The first set of settings in Privacy is the button labeled "Content Settings". Clicking this button will open a dialogue that allows you to change the way Chrome handles certain content. Most of the defaults in this section are acceptable from a security standpoint.

You will notice that these settings allow many more privileges than those allowed in Firefox. This is because we are setting Chrome up to be a more inherently usable browser. Important precautions are still taken, but this setup is less robust which is why we recommend limiting usage of Chrome to a few specific tasks. You will also notice that in many instances when there is an option between always disallowing an action and having Chrome ask when a site requests to take that action, we choose to be asked. We recommend this because it gives you some situational awareness about the sites you visit by showing you the actions they are attempting to take.

The settings within Content Settings that we prefer are as follows:

Cookies:	Keep local data only until you quit your browser, and
	Block third-party cookies and site data
Images:	Show all images
JavaSript:	Allow all sites to run JavaScript
Handlers:	Allow sites to become default handlers for protocols...
Plugins:	Let me choose when to run plugin content
Pop-ups:	Do not allow any site to show pop-ups (recommended)
Location:	Ask when a site tries to track your physical location...
Notifications:	Ask when a site wants to show notifications (recommended)
Mouse Cursor:	Ask me when a site tries to disable the mouse cursor...
Media:	Ask when a site requires access to your camera and microphone
Unsandboxed...:	Ask when a site wants to use a plugin to access your computer
Automatic Downloads:	Do not allow any site to download multiple files automatically
MIDI devices...:	Do not allow any sites to use system exclusive messages...

Beside the content settings button is a button labeled "Clear browsing data..." This button will open a dialogue that allows you to clear any or all of the following: Browsing history, Download history, Cookies and other site and plugin data, Cached images and files, Passwords, Autofill form data, Hosted app data, and Content licenses. You may erase information for a period of time ranging from the last hour to "the beginning of time". Though we will discuss system cleaning options in Chapter 21, you may wish to use this function to clear all of your browsing data now.

The remainder of the options in Privacy are simple checkboxes. We recommend unchecking all of these boxes. This may seem counterintuitive because some of the options, like "Enable phishing and malware protection" seem to improve security. These options are detrimental to privacy, however, because they require that information about the sites you visit be sent to Google for vetting against white and blacklists. We also recommend disabling the "Send a 'Do Not Track' request with your browsing traffic". As we have discussed previously in this chapter, sites have no duty to honor Do Not Track requests and they make your browser more distinctive and easily fingerprinted.

Passwords and forms: We recommend disabling these features by unchecking both boxes: "Enable Autofill to fill out web forms in a single click", and "Offer to save your web passwords". Instead we strongly recommend using a dedicated password manager. If you have stored form-fill information or passwords in Chrome we recommend moving it to a secure location and deleting it from Chrome.

Chrome Extensions: Extensions are available for Chrome that improve the privacy and security characteristics of the browser. Because our goal with Chrome is to create a middle-of-the road browser that compromises some privacy and security for usability, the add-ons included here all require very little interaction from the user. Additionally, none of these extensions should "break" websites.

To install add-ons in Chrome, navigate to the settings menu. Click "Extensions" on the upper left side of the Chrome interface. You will be presented with all of the add-ons that are currently installed in Chrome. We recommend uninstalling any add-ons that you did not personally install or research for trustworthiness. Scroll to the bottom of this screen and click "Get more extensions".

Adblock Plus: This is a content-filter add-on that does an excellent job blocking advertisements. Once installed and running Adblock Plus requires no user interaction. Adblock Plus is available on the Chrome Extensions page. For more information, visit **https://adblockplus.org**.

Disconnect: See the previous section about Firefox.

Disconnect Private Search: See the previous section about Firefox.

HTTPS Everywhere: See the previous section about Firefox.

Internet Explorer (Windows)

Internet Explorer is the browser packaged with all versions of Windows through Windows 8/8.1, and is our least favorite. The privacy and security settings in Internet Explorer are neither thorough, granular, nor self-explanatory. We strongly caution you against using this browser for anything other than those very rare occasions when it is absolutely necessary. The only reason we would ever use Internet Explorer is when it is the only browser that a certain site will work with. For this reason, the changes we make to it will be minimal. To manipulate the security settings in Internet Explorer, open the "Internet options" menu by clicking the gear icon at the upper-right of the screen. This will open a new dialogue with seven tabs. Click on the Security tab. This tab has four "zones": Internet, Local intranet, Trusted sites, and Restricted sites. You can select a security level for each of these zones via a security slider that allows you to choose from Low, Medium-low, Medium, Medium-high, or High levels. We recommend setting the sliders to the following levels:

Internet:	Medium-high
Local Intranet:	Medium-high
Trusted Sites:	Medium-high
Restricted Sites:	High

We also recommend checking the "Enable Protected Mode" box on all four tabs if it is not checked. Next, click on the Privacy tab. We find the Internet Explorer security options to be incredibly confusing and misleading. Though a "Custom level" button is available that allows you to customize each zone it is also non-intuitive and intimidating.

After you have selected a security level for each zone, click the Privacy tab. In this tab we recommend checking the first two boxes: "Never allow sites to request your physical location" and "Turn on pop-up blocker". The third box, "Disable toolbars and extensions when InPrivate browsing starts" is irrelevant as we will only use this browser sparingly and not with InPrivate mode.

Microsoft Edge (Windows 10)

Edge is Microsoft's new browser that is phasing out the aging Internet Explorer. We recommend only using this browser when absolutely necessary, such as when Chrome and Firefox are both too heavy-handed and break a site. To access the privacy and security settings in Edge navigate to the menu which is accessed by clicking the three horizontal dots in the upper-right of the page. When the fly-out menu appears click "Settings". An expanded menu will appear. Scroll to the bottom of this menu and click on the button labeled "View advanced settings". In the menu that appears scroll down to "Privacy and services" and make the following changes:

Offer to save passwords:	Off
Save form entries:	Off
Send Do Not Track requests:	Off
Have Cortana Assist me…:	Off
Show search suggestions…:	Off
Cookies:	Block only third party cookies
Let sites save protected…:	Off
Use page prediction…:	Off
Help protect me from…:	Off

Because Windows 10 has many data collections built into it, we recommend against the use of this browser. With the release of 10, Microsoft has been more open and upfront about its collection of personal data and we do not trust the privacy settings in Edge (or Internet Explorer) to offer much protection. We do recommend making these adjustments so the browser is as private as it can be if and when you should need a completely "clean" browser.

Safari (OS X)

Safari is the default browser for Apple products. Safari offers the user some flexibility in modifying privacy settings and we recommend using it only when other browsers will not work with a particular website or service. However, we do recommend this browser over Chrome We still like Chrome because we can use Disconnect Search to bypass much of Google's collection effort. Both Alphabet (Google) and Microsoft have made a business of collecting and marketing your personal data while Apple has not. To modify Safari's settings, visit click on "Safari" in the tool bar and select "Preferences". This will open a new dialogue with ten tabs. The first tab we will visit is General.

General: There are several settings here to which you should pay special attention. The first is "Remove history items". Change this setting to the minimum time allowable which is "After one day". If you forget to manually clear your history after using Safari this will take care of it for you within 24 hours. The next setting is "File download location". You can change this to any location you wish, but we recommend choosing an encrypted location so files are not inadvertently stored on your machine in plain text. The next setting that we will modify is "Remove download list items". Change this to "When Safari quits". This will ensure that Safari does not maintain a list of items you have downloaded that could later be forensically exploited. Finally, uncheck the box that says "Open 'safe' files after downloading". This will ensure that files do not automatically execute after being downloaded.

Autofill: This tab allows you to select elements of information that you would like to be automatically populated into appropriate fields on websites. We recommend unchecking all four of these boxes. This will ensure that sensitive information is not transmitted to websites without your consent.

Passwords: This tab will allow you to view usernames and passwords that have been saved by Safari. There is also a check-box that will allow you to "AutoFill usernames and passwords". Ensure this box is unchecked.

Search: Change the default search engine to DuckDuckGo.

Security: There are five check boxes under this tab but only two that you need to be concerned with. The first is "Warn when visiting a fraudulent website". Ensure this box is unchecked as it will send every website you visit to Apple for cross-referencing against a whitelist. The next checkbox that you should be concerned with is "Block pop-up windows". Ensure this box is checked.

Privacy: The privacy tab offers several options but far less flexibility and choice than Firefox. Under "Cookies and website data" select the "Allow from websites I visit" radio button. Directly below the radio buttons is a single button labeled "Remove All Website Data…" that can be used to clear your browsing history. The next option here is "Website use of location services". We recommend never allowing a website to track your location. Our recommendation is to select "Deny without prompting". The last option is "Website tracking" where you can send a Do Not Track request. We recommend leaving this at the factory default, as few Mac users change this setting and changing it can make you more distinctive.

Extensions: Under this tab you can add extensions to Safari. Because there are relatively few privacy and security related extensions we recommend installing Adblock Plus.

Privacy and Security Focused Browsers

The browsers in this section are designed with privacy and security as the primary focus. These browsers may be less user-friendly, but they require no setup to be private or secure. We have carefully selected the Epic Privacy browser from a very long list of competitors that claim to offer privacy and security but fail in one way or another. The second browser listed here, the Tor Browser, is the only one of its kind.

Epic Privacy Browser

If you want a very secure browser, but do not want to take the time to set up Firefox (or if you prefer Chrome's interface low system impact, and tab sandboxing), consider using Epic Privacy Browser. Epic is a privacy and security focused browser out of the box and is based on Chromium (the same foundational code as Google's Chrome). Unlike Chrome, Epic Privacy Browser does not track or store any information about you.

Epic also blocks third-party trackers and does not allow third-party cookies. Further, Epic offers a built-in proxy, the enabling of which masks your IP address which may be used to reveal your physical location, internet service provider and other sensitive information. The proxy also encrypts your traffic and routes all searches through the proxy, whether it is enabled or not. Epic even features "Encrypted Data Preference", a built-in function similar to HTTPS Everywhere that attempts to always force an HTTPS-encrypted connection where available.

Due to privacy concerns around most browser extensions Epic does not allow any add-ons to be installed except a few curated add-ons (one of which is the LastPass password manager add-on). This is a good thing for users who would install privacy-compromising extensions but it does hamper the ability of the security-conscious user somewhat. Epic Privacy Browser is free and available at: **https://epicbrowser.com/**

Tor Browser

The Tor Browser Bundle is a secure, anonymous web browser. Though it is nearly impossible to be completely anonymous online, Tor is as close as you can get. No discussion of online privacy would be complete without a thorough discussion of Tor. Both of us use Tor frequently and advise others to do the same. Tor prevents your internet service provider, third-party advertisers and trackers, and even governments from seeing what you're up to online. Tor is free, open source, heavily audited for security issues, and frequently patched. Tor is typically demonized in the media as a tool for terrorists and criminals but it was originally developed by the US Navy. The US military continues to donate money to the project to the tune of $1.8 million in 2013. This is the last year for which figures were available. It is currently operated by a non-profit called the Tor Project. For the disproportionate amount of privacy Tor offers, it is incredibly simple to use.

Simply visit the site at **https://www.torproject.org/** and download the Tor Browser Bundle appropriate for your operating system. This will extract a folder called Tor Browser. Within this folder is a file called "Start Tor Browser". Installation is now complete. Because Tor runs as a portable application you simply double-click this file each time you wish to access the internet through Tor and Tor will begin constructing your circuit (the set of servers through which your traffic will be routed for the duration of your browsing session). Once your custom circuit has been built Tor will open its own browser. The Tor Browser is a highly customized version of Firefox and has the HTTPS Everywhere and NoScript add-ons already built in. You can then begin browsing with the closest thing there is to true online anonymity.

At this point a brief explanation of the more technical aspects of how Tor provides the anonymity it offers may be necessary. When using the Tor browser, the traffic you request is not sent straight to and from the website you wish to visit. Instead, Tor makes your traffic anonymous by routing it through three intermediary servers (called "nodes") prior to sending the request to the desired site. When you first open Tor Browser, a connection is made with a server (called a directory server) that receives your request. This server will then build your custom network. Figure 2.1 illustrates a Tor circuit; traffic is encrypted from the user device, through the network, and is only fully decrypted when it leaves the network en route to its intended destination.

Your traffic is heavily encrypted within the Tor Network, which also contributes to your anonymity. When your request leaves your computer it is encrypted three times. The first node at which it arrives (called the "entry guard") can see that it came from you. Upon removing the first layer of encryption, it can "see" the next node in the network to which your traffic is to be sent. When your traffic arrives at the second node, it can see the node it was sent from and the node it will forward to, though it cannot tell that the request originated with you, or where the request is ultimately being sent. When your request arrives at the exit node the last layer of encryption is removed and your request is transmitted to its final destination. When your traffic is returned it is routed through the same network.

Tor disadvantages: Even though we believe strongly in both the philosophical mission of Tor and in the technical implementation of the browser bundle, we would be remiss if we did not mention the disadvantages of using Tor, and its vulnerabilities. The first disadvantage to most people is Tor is inconvenient. By routing all your traffic through three intermediate servers prior to sending it to its destination Tor traffic is much slower than "normal" traffic.

Each of the computers through which your traffic is routed may be much slower than your own, and so may be their individual internet connections.

Another major disadvantage is that some sites disallow logins, account creation, or other transactions from the Tor network. Further, many sites will require multiple captcha entries and are generally unfriendly to Tor. As we will say many times throughout this book, convenience and security are inversely proportional. We believe the slight inconveniences of Tor are more than made up for by the privacy and security. Even though Tor is very secure it is still not invulnerable.

Finally, Tor creates a very distinctive signature. Packets sent over the Tor network look very different from "normal" internet traffic. We believe this elevates your profile and makes you more "interesting" than non-Tor users. If you are trying to remain anonymous or non-alerting Tor may not be the best tool for you to use, but sometimes it may be the right choice. You should carefully consider your adversary and its capabilities.

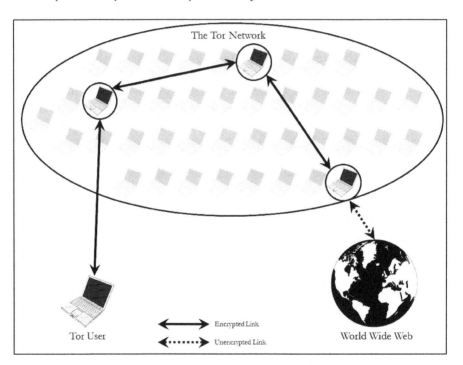

Figure 2.1: A typical Tor circuit. After the directory server creates the network the user's traffic is routed through three intermediary servers, each of which can only see one node in either direction. This prevents any one node from seeing both the requested website and the requestor, and prevents the destination website from seeing who made the request.

Tor vulnerabilities: All the Tor servers used to re-route communications are hosted by volunteers. The host of the final server your communications are routed through can monitor any transmissions that exit Tor in plaintext though it would still theoretically be anonymous. This is why Tor places such emphasis on the HTTPS Everywhere add-on. When your traffic leaves the exit node it will still be encrypted with the TLS protocol if so supported by the site (for more information on TLS see Chapter 14). This will prevent your traffic from being monitored by a malicious exit node.

You should also be aware that because of the anonymity provided by Tor it is used extensively by the "dark web", the criminal element that deals in child pornography, online drug sales, etc. Because of this, Tor is extensively monitored by law enforcement and intelligence agencies (both domestic and foreign) that may, under some circumstances, be able to observe your traffic. Tor is not a perfect solution and is vulnerable to some types of exploits. Your anonymity can be compromised on Tor in any of several different ways. For example, if you make a purchase on Tor using your credit card or other financial information that is linked to your true identity your anonymity will be breached. Further, Tor may also raise your profile. If your threat model dictates that you maintain a low signature, using Tor may be very alerting and not the appropriate tool for you.

Likewise, if you log into an email, social media, ecommerce, or other site that is associated with your name, your true identity will be associated with that entire browsing session. If you open an application on your computer that has the ability to communicate with the internet (e.g., Microsoft Office or Adobe Acrobat) your anonymity may be compromised by information leaked through those applications. Opening a downloaded document while still connected to the internet is one of the most prevalent ways in which the anonymity of Tor is broken.

Further, if you make any modifications to your version of Tor Browser it may be fingerprinted. This fingerprint can track you around the internet and eventually reveal your true identity. The default Tor Browser is designed to prevent browser fingerprinting. It discourages you from installing add-ons, and it makes all versions, regardless of download location, exactly the same. It even warns you not to maximize the browser which can reveal your computer's full screen size and resolution. Any modifications can make your version of Tor Browser absolutely unique and make you trackable. There are many other ways that the veil of anonymity Tor provides can be pierced. To be truly anonymous takes extraordinary effort.

The Tor Browser also features the "Tor button", an onion-shaped icon placed just to the right of the URL bar. This icon summons a fly-out menu that gives you several important options, including the ability to check for updates. It also has "New identity" and "New Tor circuit for this site" options. These options will change your IP to make you appear to be a different user, and construct a new, unique Tor circuit. If you desire maximum anonymity, we recommend against using these features. Rather, close the browser and start a brand new session. This is the only certain way to ensure that one website or session does not contaminate another.

Even if you are using Tor "perfectly" and adhere to all best practices, your anonymity may still be compromised by adversaries with worldwide reach. Such adversaries can correlate the time between a Tor connection being established and the location from which it was established to determine a user's true identity. Very few adversaries have this capability but the ones who do can be very dangerous. For more information on how to use Tor to achieve the maximum level of anonymity possible, we suggest that you visit the Tor Project's website at **https://www.torproject.org/download/download.html.en#warning**. The Tor Browser Bundle is free, open source, and available at **https://www.torproject.org/**.

Browsing Privacy Best Practices

Don't stay logged in: When you are logged into your email or social media account, these services monitor everything you do on the internet. Not only do social media accounts log your "likes" and "tweets", they also record other sites you go to, accounts that you create, things you purchase, videos you watch, songs you download, appointments you make online, and a wealth of other information. Many people like to remain logged into their Gmail or other accounts constantly because of the convenience it affords. This convenience can be compromising to privacy.

While it is much more work (privacy is neither easy nor convenient), we recommend the following. If you need to check your Gmail, Facebook, or other account that is associated with your name, close your browser and clean it as described below. After you have done this, open your browser, log in, and conduct your business. While you are logged in do not visit any other sites or log into any other accounts. When you have finished, log out of the site, close your browser, and clean your system again.

Close and Clean: We strongly recommend closing your browser between sessions. It is especially important to close your browser after visiting a site to which you have logged in, such as an email or social media account so that all browsing history and cookies are deleted. Simply logging out of the site will not delete the cookies it placed on your computer, and the site will still be able to track your movements around the internet. Though this is not an absolute measure of protection from tracking it does break your data down into smaller pieces. If you never clear your system you are creating a month or year long record of every site you have visited on the internet, and sharing it with hundreds of third parties.

We also recommend cleaning your system between sessions. We recommend using Bleachbit or CCleaner as described in Chapter 21. These programs will thoroughly delete all browsing history including your internet cache, cookies, download history and location, session history, compact databases, and much more. Though it is an extra step this ensures that absolutely no data is carried over between browsing sessions. Instead of one long browsing session, your sessions will be broken up into thousands of very small pieces that are much more difficult to assemble into a thorough profile about you.

Don't "Like", "Tweet", Comment, etc.: Interacting with a website via social media informs the social media account of your interests and forever links your name to an interest in that site. It also allows the website you "liked" to gather information about your social media presence and profile, and allows both to build comprehensive marketing profiles about you. You should also be cautious about commenting on blogs and other websites. Even if the website doesn't track you, comments often contain your IP address and other identifying information.

Browsing Security Best Practices

All the security settings and add-ons in the world will not protect you if you practice poor internet browsing hygiene. The best protection is the human element of security. Thoughtfulness, awareness, and patience are better than settings, add-ons, and antivirus. Below are some browsing best practices that will make you much less likely to encounter malicious sites and make it much less likely that your machine will be compromised if you do.

Be Careful What Sites You Visit: The beauty of the internet is that it puts the world at your fingertips. Any interest you have can likely be explored and expounded upon on the internet. Many (the vast, vast majority) of these sites do not have your best interests in mind and care little about your security or privacy. Websites are commonly used as attack vectors for malware, to track your browsing habits, or to get personal information from you. Thoughtfulness is required when browsing the internet. Pornography sites are notorious as being attack vectors for malware. Clicking on the wrong link on a porn site can quickly lead to adware, nagware, ransomware, or worse. Pornography sites are not alone in this. Be careful about the sites you visit. Pause and ask yourself two questions when any site is full of pop-ups. Does clicking a link on the site cause a new, unrelated window to open? Does the site cleverly conceal links that end up opening lots of new windows? If the answer to either of these questions is yes, the site is probably one you should avoid.

Do Not Click Ads: In the introduction to this chapter we mentioned malvertising, an extremely sophisticated attack vector. This threat alone should be enough to dissuade you from clicking on online advertisements. If this isn't enough to convince you, also consider the fact that even the most benign of these ads will still track your browsing session. If you are in the market for a product or service we recommend searching directly through a reputable site like Amazon or Google, or better yet navigating directly to the manufacturer or service provider's website.

Do Not Ignore Warnings: If you visit a website and receive a warning from your browser, your antivirus software, or from a browser extension like NoScript, it is probably a good idea to skip that site. There are a variety of warnings you may receive. If Firefox gives you a grey page letting you know that a site's SSL/TLS certificate is invalid, this could mean the site has a forged certificate, in which case the connection is not secure but is trying to make you think that it is. It could mean that someone is interfering with your secure connection, also indicating that your visit is not actually secure and any credentials you transmit could be intercepted in plaintext. Take these warnings seriously.

Your browsers may also warn you that a site is attempting to install an add-on. This may be a "drive-by download", which is a site attempting to install a malware application without your knowledge. Unless you specifically visited that site with the hopes of downloading an add-on, do not allow it to be installed. As discussed earlier, even seemingly benign add-ons that are presented as a way to enhance your experience with a website often harvest a great deal of data about your browsing habits. You may also receive warnings from NoScript that will warn you when a Cross-Site Scripting (XSS) attack is detected. Avast Free Antivirus will also warn you that a site presents a potential threat to the well-being of your system (alarming you with a siren sound if you have not disabled these audible indicators). While it may be tempting to ignore warnings and continue to the site, you do so at your own risk.

Do Not Download from Untrusted Sites: Be very careful about the sites from which you download files and applications. Though torrent sites are fun and many people use them to get free media, they are also rife with malware. If you download a free version of Microsoft Office, you have saved yourself a few dollars, but the risk of also downloading malware with it is very high. You should scan any files that you download from the internet with your antivirus and anti-malware scanners before attempting to open or execute them, even when downloading from trusted sources. This is no guarantee of protection, as the file(s) may be infected with a zero-day vulnerability that is not yet in your antivirus software's definitions, but it does provide some level of protection.

Use Care When Downloading Applications: When downloading applications, you should always use extreme care. Applications can contain extensive malicious payload, and attention should be paid to the quality of the download you are getting. If at all possible, attempt to download programs directly from their source (the original developer's site). All of the applications in this book are accompanied by a link to a reputable site through which they can be downloaded. In almost all cases these are original developer pages.

Also be aware that some sites may prompt you to download an application to enhance your experience on that site. One example was a recent client who fell victim to a shady website that convinced visitors they needed a special application to watch videos hosted on the site. The page displayed the message "The video won't play? No problem, download 'our' video player". Beware of such enticements to download applications. If a video cannot be posted on a reputable video hosting site like Vevo, Vimeo, or YouTube, it is probably an attempt to get you to install a malicious program.

Now that you have applied the basic security measures required to protect your computer, it is time to start thinking about your personal privacy. Much of this book will encourage you to remove or alter sensitive information available about you in digital form. Before we can approach any of this, we need to prepare ourselves and our digital communications.

CHAPTER THREE
PREPARATION

Before you attempt to remove any of your personal information from the internet, you must take several steps to prepare yourself for this journey. While most of this book can be read in any order, this chapter should be read in its entirety before proceeding. Failure to have these preparations in place will cause some of the methods described in this book to take longer than necessary. Even worse, it will make some of the methods ineffective. Before you prepare to start removing your personal information from the internet, you should evaluate how your information became accessible to the public.

Rule # 1: Stop Giving Out Your Information!

The first obvious thing to discuss is how you provide your personal information to the world. Every month, you provide many personal details about you and your family that get sold to numerous companies. Large databases are created that include a profile on you that is passed around and updated continuously. The following are three examples of the information that you provide unknowingly.

Reward Cards & Loyalty Programs

As frugal people, we love these money saving cards. As privacy advocates, we hate them. Many grocery stores, cafes, restaurants, and discount clubs offer them to save you hundreds of dollars every year. When you use these cards, everything you buy is associated with your name, address, and credit card. When companies contact the rewards card provider looking for new customers, your information often gets sold if you fit a certain criterion.

For example, a shoe company wants to know all of the customers of a specific grocery store that purchased magazines associated with running or fitness. That grocery store can easily conduct a search and create a list of reward program customers that fit the criteria and sell that list to the shoe company. This list could include your name, home address, telephone number, email address, and shopping habits. Now, you may get bombarded with unwanted advertisements in the mail, spam in your email inbox, and telephone calls offering fitness-themed vacations. This same information may then get passed on to another company. In one extreme scenario, The New York Times reported in February of 2012 that the department store Target began sending advertising for expectant mothers to a female high school student in Minneapolis. The package included coupons for baby items addressed to the minor. The father was furious and complained to the store. He accused Target of encouraging minors to become pregnant. He later was informed by the minor that she was indeed pregnant. This automated package was sent to her after analyzing her shopping habits.

We are not against the continued use of the loyalty cards and programs, but users should change the way they apply for the program. The first step is to simply stop providing accurate information. Very few of these programs verify the information provided. If you sign up for one of these programs, change the spelling of your first and last name. If your last name is Laporte, use Lepurt. It is enough to confuse the system but still be accepted by you. More importantly, never provide your home address and telephone number. This chapter will discuss what to use as an address and phone number if you want to receive information from the company.

Many people use a completely false name. For programs that rely on the use of a physical card, such as a grocery store, there is no harm in providing a false name. The only purpose of the card is to save you money immediately at checkout. Be aware, however, that the debit or credit card you use will be associated with that loyalty card. Cash is king and cannot be associated with your name or address. For those programs that demand to see your identification before issuing a card, tell them you recently changed your address.

Utility Bills

When you have your utility bills mailed to your residence, you are announcing to the world where you live. Your utility company will obviously know your address, as they are providing a service to the structure such as electricity or water. They maintain a database of the utility bills sent to the customer including home address and phone number. This is often passed around to other companies that may have an interest in providing other services, and you will be targeted with advertising. These details are also made available to data mining companies that can be searched online. If you have a utility bill in your name mailed to your home address, internet searches will eventually announce the location where you and your family sleep at night.

Removal vs. Disinformation

Much of this book will focus on the techniques to permanently remove your information from internet searches and data mining companies. There will be moments that will require you to provide information to companies in order to add or remove their products or services. Sometimes you will need to provide details about you that will be verified by the company. This may include utilities that insist on a working telephone number for you and your date of birth with Social Security number. It could also be a website that requires your mailing address, email address, and mother's maiden name before granting you access to the website. These situations can be handled in two extremely different ways.

You could take the standard approach that most people take and supply all of your real information and allow those details to be passed on to dozens of companies that will pass it on to dozens more. Alternatively, you can use a combination of anonymous information and disinformation. In this chapter, you will learn how to create an anonymous email address and telephone number that can be provided to companies without jeopardizing your privacy. As for the other information requested, we prefer to use disinformation. Disinformation is basically falsifying or manipulating the data in order to cause so much inaccurate information that it becomes difficult for companies to know the real details. Chapter Sixteen will identify many ways to fool every data mining company in existence with disinformation.

Any time that someone requests your home and work address, you should evaluate whether that information is really needed for that scenario. If you are turning on water services at a building, that seems like a legitimate reason to disclose the address. You should not disclose your work address though, as it is not needed for that situation. If you are completing a membership form to join an association of bird watching enthusiasts, a post office box would be more appropriate. If you are making a purchase at a store that wants your address to add to the purchase history, you should be prepared to provide disinformation. One approach is telling them that you do not want to provide that information. This is usually met with hostility, and on rare occasion, refusal to sell the item or service. Instead, consider having a fake address ready to provide from memory. This should be an address that does not exist since you should not cause someone else to receive unwanted advertisements and mailings. Eventually, databases will start to associate you with this fake address, which is better than having no record in the database.

Many companies will want your date of birth and Social Security number for their records. Unless you are requesting some form of credit from the business, there is no need for them to have these details. Again, simply refusing often results in a difficult situation. Instead, consider providing a different date of birth. If it is something you will need to remember, reverse the month and day of birth and add 10 to the year. If your date of birth is 5/9/1970, provide 9/5/1980. Most people will avoid questioning your age, especially if you look older. The Social Security number is a little stricter. Usually, the company does not have anything in place to verify if the number is valid or assigned. Using someone else's number can be a crime. Instead, use one of the ten numbers reserved by the government to be used in advertisements. None of these special numbers will ever be assigned to a human and they do not look false as does 000-11-2222. Here is the complete list.

987-65-4320	987-65-4324	987-65-4328
987-65-4321	987-65-4325	987-65-4329
987-65-4322	987-65-4326	
987-65-4323	987-65-4327	

A recent client had an ideal scenario to use this technique. He was self-employed and paid for high deductible health insurance. He did not have any sort of dental plan. He visited a new dentist in order to have his teeth cleaned. He completed the paperwork requested, but left the line for a Social Security number blank. When questioned by the receptionist, he politely informed her that he does not have dental insurance and will be paying cash for his cleaning.

Because of this, he felt it was unnecessary to disclose his SSN. She resisted and eventually told him that he could not be treated without providing this information. Fortunately, he was prepared. He finally gave in and provided one of these numbers to the receptionist. She added it to his form and proceeded with his appointment.

If he had given someone else's SSN, he would have committed a crime. If he had given 123-45-6789, she would have immediately detected it as a fake. Instead, he legally provided a number that bypassed her scrutiny and compromised no one. Obviously, this would never work at a doctor that was billing your insurance or Medicare. Some will say that this is overkill. We disagree. If, or more likely when, the records at this office are breached, our client will have very little to worry about. We will later disclose the method for an anonymous physical address that could be used on these forms.

One scenario that provides a unique situation is when applying for employment. We do not recommend providing any disinformation on the application. Instead, use a post office box, the anonymous email address you will learn about here, and your real date of birth. The risk of this data being entered into a public database is minimal. Providing your Social Security number will probably be safe, but you could also fill in this space with "Upon hiring".

Whenever a company wants your personal details, stop and consider where this information may be copied or sold. In order for the rest of the techniques in this book to work, you must change the way you provide your personal information. You could take every step in the book and eliminate everything out there, but signing up for a great credit card offer or filling out a form to win a new car with all of your information will reintroduce the details to the web based companies. You must change your habits.

Providing disinformation is not identity theft. Providing these small "errors" is not the same as creating a new account under another person's name. The disinformation that you provide will only be enough to meet the collection requirements while masking your true information. It should never cause any fraud or financial gain to you.

Anonymous Email Address

Many of the websites that will be discussed throughout this book will require an email address to remove information. The email address provided to them will be stored by the company that it is submitted to and possibly sold to other businesses. If you use your real personal or business email address, this is counter-productive to the idea of eliminating personal information online. Therefore, you should never provide your current personal email address to any online website from which you want your information removed. To get around this, you will create two anonymous email addresses.

Gmail

First, you should create a new account with a free email provider. Personally, we have many Gmail accounts from Google. Most privacy advocates hate Gmail and refuse to use their services. We agree that Gmail is invasive and scans all of your email for advertisement delivery. They are very open about that. However, we will not be using them for our personal email. For the purposes of this book, we will only use Google services as part of our effort to remove personal information and provide disinformation. We will not be using Google for personal messages or "real life" content. Therefore, we recommend Google services for some of the methods discussed in this book. The services are reliable, free, and very secure from outside public intrusion. After you have completed the removal process, you never have to use their service again if desired. Alternatively, you could choose any other email provider.

Navigate to gmail.com and click on "Create an Account" in the upper right corner. Provide any name that you want and create a password. For the gender and date of birth, you can also provide any data that you want, including false information. This will not be verified by Google. Gmail will ask you to pick an email address. We recommend choosing something with your real name in it. This address will be used to request removal of your personal information from select companies that demand an email response. If your real name is Mike Smith, but your email address is BillJohnson@gmail.com, this looks suspicious. It may delay your request for removal. This email address should only be used during the removal methods described in this book. It should never be used for any other personal or business communication. This book will refer to this account as your new removal email address.

Many services that allow for information removal from their systems do not require you to email them. Instead, they will ask for your email address and will send an email directly to you. For these situations, you should use a completely anonymous forwarding email address that cannot be associated with you. You could create temporary forwarding accounts online, but after a short period of time the email account is automatically terminated. Our preference is to forward email from a permanent anonymous account to a personal account. This is different than the many providers that will give you a temporary account that works for a limited time. The next technique will give you a permanent email address that will always forward to any real email address of your choice.

333Mail

This is our favorite email forwarding service. Similar to Not Sharing My Info, which is explained in a moment, it will transfer any incoming email from your anonymous account to your real personal email address without the sender knowing. However, this service provides three additional features that make it superior to other email forwarding companies. It provides unlimited forwarding email addresses within one account, the option to reply from these addresses, and the ability to disable a forwarding address if desired. The following steps will explain how to create your new account and use the free service.

- Navigate to **33mail.com** and create a new account at the "Get Started!" button.

- Provide your personal email address, choose a username, and provide a password when prompted. Your username should not have any association with you. It will be visible on all of your new forwarding email addresses. Somehow, we were able to obtain "NSA" as a username.

- Choose the "Free" service plan when prompted. This is not selected by default.

- Check your personal email account and confirm the email from 333Mail to verify your personal email address.

- You now have a new domain that you can use for any email address. Any email sent to that domain will be forwarded to your real email address. If an email was sent from anyone to removal@nsa.33mail.com, it would forward to our real email address.

- The next time you visit a website that asks for your email address; do not give it to them. Instead, make one up especially for them. For example, if the website spokeo.com demanded an email address for removal of your content, give them spokeo@yourcustomdomain.33mail.com.

You do not need to create any alias addresses on the 333Mail website. This will happen automatically when incoming mail is received at their server. In order to demonstrate the service, we sent an email message to the following three accounts.

test@nsa.33mail.com
spam@nsa.33mail.com
removal@nsa.33mail.com

We immediately received the three messages in the inbox of a personal email address. Additionally, 333Mail created the three aliases of Test, Spam, and Removal. If we were to start receiving a lot of unwanted email addressed to spam@nsa.33mail.com, we could click the "block" link next to that account, and that address would no longer be forwarded to our real account.

We are excited to see this new service and have been using it successfully for several months. Many social networks and other services have begun blocking addresses that end in notsharingmyinfo.com and 33mail.com. This limits their usefulness somewhat but we are sure you will have many opportunities to use these services. We encourage you to create, test, and maintain addresses through both services.

Michael's Experience with 333Mail

This service helps you identify how companies share your personal information. While writing the book *Hiding from the Internet*, I encountered a service that required an email address before I could access any potential personal information about me on their website. I provided the email address of shady@nsa.33mail.com. I received an immediate email verification link at my personal email address that was forwarded by 333Mail. One week later, I began receiving several spam messages from various clothing retailers. They were all addressed to shady@nsa.33mail.com. I now know that this web service shares their email database with online marketers. In one click, I could block all future email from that address. You can use this technique to monitor how your information is shared. I recommend a unique email address through 333Mail for every removal process mentioned in this book.

As a free user, you can reply to one message per day from the anonymous address that you created. This is still in beta, and not extremely reliable, but worth testing. If you reply to this message, it will be delivered to a unique email address only used once for each message. In this case, it was 0735c09e9b0001a31dd6bbcba1f669a72f31a9dd@reply.33mail.com. When 333Mail receives your reply, it will forward your message back to the original sender. However, instead of your real email address being visible, the recipient will see your 333Mail address.

Not Sharing My Info

This is an anonymous email forwarding service. Not only does it provide instant email delivery and a superb privacy layer, it is also free. Obtaining a permanent email address is immediate.

Navigate to **notsharingmy.info** and type in your actual personal email address. This can either be the new Gmail account that you created earlier, or a personal account that you check frequently. This may be the free Gmail, Yahoo, or Hotmail account that you use for your everyday email. We do not recommend using your business account since you probably have very little control over the account and access. When you click on "Get an obscure email", the site will give you your permanent forwarding email address. One of our addresses is dhd9j@notsharingmy.info.

From now on, any time a person, automated service, or verification procedure sends an email to the address dhd9j@notsharingmy.info, the email will be forwarded to the address test@computercrimeinfo.com. This is all done behind the scenes and the original sender of the message will have no idea of what your real email address is. However, if you respond to an email received from this account, the email will be sent from your actual personal account, not the anonymous account. This method should only be used for receiving emails.

For people you correspond with, you should not use this type of address. Instead save this type of address for use with verification techniques during information removal. Many websites that require a profile on the site also require a valid email address. As an example, when you sign up for Facebook, you must provide a valid email address. Once you do, Facebook will send an email to that address which you must read and click on a link within the email. Clicking on this link verifies to Facebook that they have an email address that belongs to you. By using the anonymous method described here, Facebook would only know your anonymous address, and not your real personal address. This also allows you to continue to receive messages from them without disclosing your personal account. Facebook occasionally restricts new accounts from Not Sharing My Info addresses, but the next service that will be discussed is always allowed.

The email address that is created for you from this service is rather generic and may be hard to remember. If you want a more custom email address, such as a vanity account similar to MikeBazzell@notsharingmy.info, you can do that as well. This will require you to sign into your Facebook account and convince a friend to sign up for the free service. We do not recommend this for two reasons. First, attaching this service to your Facebook page eliminates a layer of privacy that this service provides. Also, picking a custom address, such as your name, helps attach you to your anonymous account. For the purposes of this book, both are a bad idea. We recommend accepting the default address created for you. It is wise to write down the address immediately for future use. If you do decide to create a custom address, the instructions are on the same page as your new address.

According to the notsharingmy.info website, after an email message is delivered to the recipient, the message is not stored on their servers. This means that if you are using a service such as Gmail, Yahoo, or Hotmail, this company only has the content of your message for a short period of time. The site states that they do collect your IP address when you create your account, but that it is not associated with the email address or kept permanently. It should be noted that the service will always know your real email address, there is no way around that. The only way that this would be disclosed is through a legal request such as a subpoena or search warrant. For the scope of this book, the only concern is keeping this information away from the general public.

Over the past few years, readers have advised the Not Sharing My Info would occasionally not work reliably. They reported outages for short periods of time. For a brief period, they were not accepting new accounts. At the time of this writing, the service appeared stable. We believe that you should have accounts at both 333Mail and NotSharingMyInfo at your disposal.

Blur

Blur (**abine.com/index.html**) is one of our favorite new privacy enhancing services. The service is available through a web-based login or through a dedicated mobile app. Blur offers a free trial that allows use for thirty days. Unfortunately, this trial does not include access to many of Blur's features. The options offered by the full version of Blur include password storage, password generator, masked email addresses, masked telephone numbers, and masked credit card numbers. This section will only discuss the masked email option while later chapters outline the masked phone numbers and credit cards.

Masked email addresses allow you to use email addresses that will forward to your "real" address but appear randomly generated. An example of a Blur-generated email address is: a049b2d21@opayq.com. Blur allows you to create as many of these email addresses as you wish. When you no longer desire to receive email from a given address you have the option to turn forwarding off, similar to 333Mail.

These "masked" addresses allow you to give out an email address that does not leak information about you, and does not give up your "real" address which could be used as a starting point for an attack against you. It also allows you to create unique usernames for each online account you have. Again, this greatly reduces your visibility and attack surface. More details about this premium service will be explained later.

A Word of Caution on Mail Forwarding Services

Both of us use 333Mail and notsharingmy.info extensively. However, you should approach these services cautiously. Using mail forwarding services gives these companies access to the content and metadata of your email. Because of this, we recommend never using these services in conjunction with your real name, email addresses that are personally tied to you, or for messages containing personal content.

Anonymous Telephone Number

Having an anonymous telephone number to provide to various sites and services that demand one is very important. Years ago, this would be difficult and expensive. Today it is easy and free. There are several services that will issue a telephone number to be used over the internet. This is called Voice Over Internet Protocol (VOIP). Some of these services have a small fee, and some are free and advertiser supported. One of the most common is Google Voice.

This free service will assign you a new telephone number in your area code and let you make and receive calls. Although this service is free, it has many drawbacks. You must associate the account with an actual telephone number and email address. All of your incoming voice mail will be transcribed and analyzed. You will then see advertisements based on the conversation recorded by the service. We believe all of this is invasive. As privacy advocates, we do not recommend daily personal use of the Google Voice service. However, it is the most stable free option currently available. Later chapters discuss non-Google apps that will also generate new anonymous numbers. Google Voice is adequate for the techniques described in this book. However, the way that you create the account is very important.

Google Voice

Most users of Google Voice (**google.com/voice**) create an account on their home computer, provide their real name, associate their cellular telephone number with the account, and use the associated Google Mail account for all of their personal email. We will do none of that. You should have already created a Google Mail (Gmail) account. When you log into this account and navigate to google.com/voice, you will have the option to create a new telephone number. You will be prompted to enter a valid telephone number before you can choose your new number. This must be a number where you can receive a text message or telephone call in order to verify your access to the number. This can be tricky. You do not want to associate your real cellular or landline telephone with this service. If you do, your new "anonymous" number is not anonymous at all. Instead, you only need a telephone number where you can receive one telephone call. There are many options.

- Many hotels allow guests free unlimited incoming calls. If the hotel you are at provides a direct line to your room, you could use this. Google must be able to dial a ten-digit direct number, and not dial an extension.

- Your place of work probably has several direct telephone lines that you have access to. You can tell Google to contact you at one of them.

- Your local library probably has a fax machine for patron use. The direct phone number of this device is likely written on the machine. These machines are usually set to not accept an incoming fax. Therefore, if it rings, you could answer.

Use your imagination and position yourself at a location that provides both wireless internet access and an incoming telephone line. You can use a laptop computer to complete the setup. Provide the telephone number that you have access to and allow it to call you. When you answer, you will be given a two-digit code. Type that code into the Google Voice window that is requesting it. You have now activated your Google Voice account and can choose your area code and new number.

By default, Google will want to forward all incoming calls from your new number to the number associated with the account. In the settings menu, under the phones tab, uncheck any options for call forwarding. This will force any incoming calls to go straight to voicemail. You can create a custom voicemail message, but we recommend leaving the default generic message. In the "Voicemail & Text" tab, you can choose to have all messages forwarded to your anonymous email address. You now have a new telephone number on which you can receive incoming calls and the caller can leave you a message. That message will be forwarded to your email inbox.

Blur

In addition to providing masked email addresses and a number of other services, Blur also offers masked telephone numbers. Only one number is available per account but it can be changed for a fee of $7.00. If you choose to use your Blur number for opt-out purposes we recommend using it only for this, and changing it once you have completed your opt-out journey. Blur will be discussed in greater detail in Chapter Ten.

Mailing Address

Most services, memberships, and publications that you sign up for are going to want a mailing address. Using your personal residence is one of the worst practices when trying to stay private. For much of this book, you will focus on removing any trace of your home address from several databases. Occasionally, you may need a real address where you can receive mail. We recommend a PO box at your local post office. These are associated with your real name and personal address, but only the post office will have access to that information. It will not be passed on to any public databases. I like to have a post office box address available for various services such as utilities, medical, or any organization that needs to send a bill or invoice.

You can print an application from the USPS website or receive one in person at your local post office. Later chapters discuss how to start sending all of your mail to your PO Box, and eventually no mail designated for you and your family will arrive at your residence. This may sound like overkill, but all of those magazines, coupon packs, and advertisements sell your information to many online services. You will never eliminate this information from the public internet until you stop receiving items at your home. The only mail that should continue to arrive will be generic items addressed to "Current Resident".

Driver's License Image

In order to complete the data removal process with some companies, they will want to verify that you are indeed the person requesting the removal. Most companies do this by demanding a copy of your driver's license. Many of you are probably skeptical of this request, but there is no way around it. Fortunately, you can mask most of the personal content on the license before you send a copy.

The first step is to create a digital image of your license. There are two ways to do this. The easiest way is to use a digital camera or the camera on your cellular telephone to take a close-up image. Try to get good detail and fit the license perfectly into the border of the photo. An alternative to this method is to use a scanner connected to a computer. After you have created the image, use photo editing software to mask some of the information. For those of you that use Microsoft Windows, there is a free tool for this already installed called Paint.

This program will allow you to manipulate the digital image that you created of your license.

The only information that the companies need from this image is your name, address, and date of birth. Therefore, you should give them nothing more. You could use the paintbrush feature of this program to mark over the additional information, but that looks messy and is more time consuming. Instead, use the "Shapes" tool to easily draw filled blank boxes around all other sensitive information. Mac users can execute the Preview application and use the Line Selection tool to block any sensitive data. Figure 3.1 shows an example of a masked driver's license image.

Opt-Out Request Forms

You are now ready to prepare your generic Opt-Out Request Forms that will be used for submission to several companies. By creating one form that has all essential information, you will not need to create a new form for each company from which you want your information removed. We recommend using Microsoft Word for this, but you can use any word processing program you prefer. If you do not use Microsoft Word, you will need to save your document as a PDF file, which will be discussed later.

The first form will be referred to as the "Basic" form, which will contain the following information.

Date: This should be the date of the submission of the form.

Company: This should be the official company name that owns the database containing personal information.

Request: A brief statement identifying the request. We recommend "I request to have my name removed from your public and non-public databases. Here is the information you have asked me to include in my request".

Name: Your full name as it appears in the online database. This should reflect any shortened or misspelled names as they appear online.

Mailing Address: Any addresses that appear in the database that you want removed.

Social Security number: This should only be included when specifically requested. The few sites that demand this will be identified in this book.

Date of Birth: This will be necessary for all requests that require this form.

Direct URL(s) of personal information: This will be direct links to information that you find online that you would like removed from the internet. A "URL" is the "Uniform Resource Locator". It is the address of a web page. Examples of URLs are google.com, facebook.com/user/johndoe, and pipl.com/opt-out. It is the information that you type into the address bar to get to a specific web page.

Driver's License / State Issued ID: This is a copy of the masked image that you created in the previous step.

The second form that you should create will be referred to as the "Extended" form. This form will only be used for a small number of companies, and will not be necessary for everyone reading this book. These companies include data brokers such as Westlaw, Accurint, and LexisNexis. The data here can contain several dozen pages of information about you including every place you have lived, every car you have owned, your SSN and DL number, all of your family members' names and locations, your neighbors' names and phone numbers, limited financial information, marriage and divorce information, court cases you are involved in, and much more. Law enforcement relies on these companies for information, but the data is not limited to the government. This information is also shared with businesses that are willing to pay for it.

The profile created about you includes information from both public and private sources. While the government customers get access to all of the information available, private businesses are issued a redacted view. This usually only removes a person's SSN and DL number. The rest of the personal details are available to any commercial customer with a few bucks. This can include lawyers, private investigators, hiring firms, and anyone else that has an affiliation with a business. Most organizations pay a monthly premium for unlimited data requests about individuals. The wide scope of people that can access these personal details is disturbing. Removing your information from these databases is more difficult, but possible.

Since this data is much more valuable than public information from websites, the removal process is stricter. The companies that sell this data are bound by the rules of the Fair Credit Reporting Act (FCRA). All companies must allow people to have their information removed as long as the person requesting the removal meets any of the following criteria:

- The person is a judge, public official, or member of law enforcement; or

- The person is the victim of identity theft; or

- The person is at risk of physical harm

At first glance, you may read this and think that you would not meet these requirements. The criteria are actually quite broad and will be explained in Chapter Eight. The only instances that you will need this form will be during the removal processes explained in Chapter Ten. You will learn how to complete this form there and do not need this step completed until then.

Once your basic form is complete, save it and have it available when needed throughout the rest of the book. Each technique in this book that requires this form will explain which information to complete on the form and where to submit the completed form. Note that the printed version of the driver's license in this book masks the name, address, and date of birth in grey. This information should be visible on your copy. The information masked in white should also be masked on your version. Figure 3.01 displays an example form.

Facsimile (fax) Service

Several companies demand that requests for removal from their databases be sent via fax. This outdated and wasteful technology is seldom used by the general public. Fortunately, several online websites assist with this function free of charge. We believe the best free service is Got Free Fax at **www.gotfreefax.com**.

When a section of this book instructs you to send a fax to a company, navigate to this site. Enter your name and new email address into the "Sender" section and the company details provided into the "Receiver" section. This should also include the subject line of "Data Removal".

The next section of this website will allow you to send a free fax using two different methods. The first method allows you to enter text directly into the site and send that text. The second option will allow you to upload a document to be sent. You should use this second option to send the Opt-Out Request Form mentioned earlier. This site will only accept documents with a DOC or PDF extension. If you are using Microsoft Word, the DOC extension is usually the default. If your version of Word is newer that 2007, this default extension may be DOCX. You may need to open the form and select "Save as" and change the file type to DOC. If you are using a free word processor such as Open Office, you will have the option to save any document as either DOC or PDF.

Select the option to "Upload a PDF or DOC file to fax". This will display a "Browse" button. Click on that button and select the document you created from the window that opens. In the section directly below this option, choose the "Send FREE Fax Now!" button. You will receive an email that will include a confirmation link. When you click this link, the fax will be delivered. Each time that this method is required in this book, you will have complete instructions on what information to include with the fax.

If you followed all of these steps, you are ready to begin eliminating your private data from the internet.

Date_____   Company_____

I request to have my name removed from your public and non-public databases. Here is the information you have asked me to include in my request:

Name: _____

Mailing Address: _____

Social Security Number *(If Required)*   _____

Date Of Birth *(If Required)*   _____

Direct URL(s) of personal information online:

http://_____

http://_____

Thank you for your prompt handling of my request. I have also included a redacted copy of my driver's license below to prove identity.

Figure 3.01: An example of an Opt-Out Request Form and masked driver's license.

CHAPTER FOUR
SELF PRE-ASSESSMENT

Before you embark on the adventure of removing your personal information from the internet, you should take a moment to identify the types of personal information present. Everyone will have different types of content visible about them. Each situation will require a unique strategy for removal. A person who owns a home and has a property tax record will find much more personal details online than a person who rents a home with included utilities. Also, a person with several social networks will see many more details than a person that has none. This chapter will help you quickly discover the amount of work that you will have ahead of you.

Search Engines

The first basic step is to identify the standard information available about you within search engines. In order to properly search for your information, you will need to do more than a standard Google search. Search engines will help you tremendously, but you will need to provide specific instruction when conducting your queries. For the first group of searches, assume that the following information describes you.

John Williams
1212 Main Street
Houston, TX 77089
713-555-1234

Searching "John Williams" will likely not be productive. Even if it were a unique name, the results would include spam and websites that provided no valuable information. Instead, conduct the following search including the quotation marks.

"John Williams" "77089"

This query instructs the search engine to locate web pages that have exactly John Williams and 77089 on the same page. This will eliminate many unwanted pages that do not contain relevant information. If your name is generic, such as John Williams, you may still be bombarded with unwanted results. Try the following search.

"John Williams" "1212 Main"

This query instructs the search engine to locate web pages that have exactly John Williams and 1212 Main on the same page. This will likely display pages that announce your home address to the world. These will be the pages that you will target for information removal. You should also search the following example to locate pages that display your home telephone number.

"John Williams" "555" "1234"

This query instructs the search engine to locate web pages that have exactly John Williams and 555 and 1234 on the same page. The two sets of numbers were searched separately in case the target websites did not use a hyphen (-) when separating the numbers.

If you live alone, these searches will likely suffice. However, your listing may be displayed in the name of your spouse, a parent, or roommate. Alter the searches to include any appropriate names. If you have a unique last name, such as Bazzell, you could try the following searches to catch all family members.

"Bazzell" "1212 Main"
"Bazzell" "555" "1234"

These queries will locate online content that references you and your home. Additional searches should be conducted based on your name and associations such as your employer, interests, or organizations. Create your own custom queries based on the following example searches.

"Michael Bazzell" "Accountant"
"Michael Bazzell" "software programming"
"Michael Bazzell" "International Police Association"

The quotation marks in the above searches are vital to the queries. They inform the search engine to only look for exactly what is presented. This will prevent Google and others from adjusting your search in order to "help" you. Each search engine that you use will likely give different results. You may want to try variations of your name. If your first name is "Michael" you will also want to search "Mike". If you do not receive any results, you may want to repeat the search without the quotation marks.

Every engine has its own algorithm for search and also its own sneaky ways of collecting information during your search. Later chapters explain many ways to protect you while searching. For the purposes of this chapter, you only need to apply two policies.

First, never conduct these searches while you are logged into an email or social network account. If you are conducting queries on Google while logged into your Gmail account, Google stores this information about you. If you are searching on Bing while logged into your Facebook page, Bing now associates your queries with your profile. Overall, you do not want any companies to store your searches and associate them with you.

Second, you should not conduct these searches while using a web browser that knows a lot about you. All browsers store "cookies" that record the sites that you visit and the activity that you perform on the sites. Ideally, you should eliminate all of your cookies within a web browser before you conduct any searches. The procedure for making your browser as private and secure as possible is described in Chapter Two.

Alternative Search Engines

There is no lack of search engines that could be used. While Google and Bing are the two main players, there are many other specialty engines that display results the others miss. The following is a list of recommended engines for your self pre-assessment.

Google	Google.com
Bing	Bing.com
Yandex	Yandex.com
Exalead	Exalead.com
Google Groups	Groups.google.com
Google News	News.google.com
Google Images	Google.com/images
Bing Images	Bing.com/images

Duck Duck Go

There are many people that do not trust Google due to their policies on data collection and advertisements. If you would like to conduct a query within a search engine that does not track you or record your actions, consider Duck Duck Go (**duckduckgo.com**). This engine combines several sources to give you a collection of search results. None of your actions are recorded and the search engines that supply the content do not see your search information. This can be a great search engine for daily queries. However, we believe that you will be missing many results if you do not use engines such as Google directly for the searches in this chapter. Later chapters outline additional steps that you can take in order to protect your privacy while on the internet.

Start Page

If you want to take advantage of Google's search abilities but insist on hiding yourself from their intrusive monitoring techniques, you can use Start Page (**startpage.com**). Start Page searches Google for you. When you submit a search, Start Page submits the query to Google and returns the results to you. Google only sees a large amount of searches coming from Start Page's servers. They cannot associate any traffic with you or track your searches. Start Page discards all personally identifiable information and does not use cookies. It immediately discards IP addresses and does not keep a record of any searches performed.

All-In-One Search Tool

The website IntelTechniques (**inteltechniques.com/osint/user.html**) maintains a page that will allow you to conduct a single query across multiple websites in one click. This is our preferred method when conducting a pre-assessment on someone. The website listed above will present many search fields that will allow you to execute a query on various services. The last search field at the bottom will allow you to execute any query on all of the listed services.

Figure 1.01 displays this page. Clicking the "Submit All" button will open a new tab for each service. This currently requires Firefox or Safari web browsers. Chrome and Internet Explorer may block the required code to perform this action. However, any browser can conduct individual queries through the listed services. This utility will search the following services with associated descriptions. Use the following box to document your progress. Knowing the date searched and whether you found a result or not might be useful later in the removal process.

Date:	Result:	Engine:	Description:
_____	_____	Google	Google Results
_____	_____	Google Date	Recent Results
_____	_____	Bing	Bing Results
_____	_____	Yahoo	Yahoo Results
_____	_____	Yandex	Russian Results
_____	_____	Exalead	Business Results
_____	_____	Google Groups	Newsgroups
_____	_____	Google Blogs	Blog Entries
_____	_____	Google FTP Search	FTP Documents
_____	_____	Google Scholar	Documents
_____	_____	Google Patents	Patents
_____	_____	Google News	Online News
_____	_____	Baidu	Chinese Search
_____	_____	Duck Duck Go	Anonymous Search
_____	_____	Qwant	Social Networks

Figure 1.01: A custom search page on IntelTechniques.com.

Ancestry Records

Most readers will know someone in their life that collects information about the family's history. In previous decades, this meant writing relatives' names and lineage onto a piece of paper and distributing copies at the next family reunion. Today, this means uploading all of the data to a public website. These websites do not display Social Security numbers of the living, but the information can be quite intrusive. If you are listed in an online family tree, it is likely that the following information is available about you.

Full Name
Date of Birth
Parents' Names
Siblings' Names
Children's Names
City of Current Residence
City of Birth

With this information, a private investigator could quickly hone in on your actual address. He or she could obtain a copy of your birth certificate and would know your mother's maiden name. There are several financial institutions that still mistakenly rely on this piece of information for identity verification. Knowing your child's names could help answer security questions and jeopardize their safety if you are a targeted individual. We believe this type of personal information has no place on the internet. Identifying this exposure can be difficult. Visit the following websites and conduct a preliminary search on your name or your parents' names.

Date:	Result:	Service:	Website:
_____	_____	Ancestry	ancestry.com
_____	_____	Family Search	familysearch.org
_____	_____	Mocavo	mocavo.com
_____	_____	Roots Web	rootsweb.com
_____	_____	Geneanet	en.geneanet.org
_____	_____	My Heritage	myheritage.com
_____	_____	One Great Family	onegreatfamily.com
_____	_____	World Records	worldvitalrecords.com
_____	_____	My Trees	mytrees.com
_____	_____	Find My Past	findmypast.com

If you find information about you or your immediate family, document the results with a "Yes" or "No" in the results column and keep this in mind when data removal is discussed later. The majority of the content on these websites is user submitted and can include sensitive information. Fortunately, you will be able to remove most of the personal information that you locate.

Some of these services will require you to be a paid member in order to conduct a full search. We do not recommend purchasing a subscription for the sole purpose of looking for yourself. Instead, we encourage you to search these specific websites through a search engine with your details included. Consider the following example. You want to search any ancestry.com services for your name and address. For this scenario, assume that your name is George Bluth and you reside in Alton, Illinois. Submit the following search to several search engines.

site:ancestry.com "George Bluth" "Newport Beach"

This informs the search engine that you only want to search ancestry.com, but also that you want to search every indexed page at that domain. Your name within quotation marks mandates that your exact name is present on the page as well as the term Alton. This may display results that you cannot find manually by searching the actual website.

Email Addresses

After you have identified the various websites that display your residence and telephone information, you should identify services that are connected to your email address. In years past, providing an email address to a company or service did not seem too alarming. Today, this unique identifier can be used to create a detailed record about you and your interests. To obtain accurate results of your email search, quotation marks must be used before and after your email address. Figure 4.02 displays a Google search result for an email address. The listed websites are present because that email address is associated with a website. Notice the blue "Sign in" button in the upper right corner. That is an indication that you are not logged into any Google account which provides a small layer of privacy.

It is important to know what information is associated with your email address. Many people will conduct a quick search on your address when you contact them. If you locate embarrassing or inappropriate content, you may want to use a different email account when corresponding about business or other important matters. The information found during this search will be very difficult to remove. You may consider switching to a new email address.

Figure 4.02: A Google search result from an email address within quotation marks.

Usernames

You may wish to search for any social networks that you have visible on the internet. You probably remember your Facebook and Twitter pages, but how many networks did you create and abandon when they lost popularity? We often forget about MySpace, Friendster, and other profiles that we no longer use. Often, those profiles are still visible and may contain personal information. Consider identifying any accounts that you wish to delete. The easiest way to discover any accounts that may still be lingering is to search by your username. Since we usually use the same username for numerous accounts, you may look at known social networks for a hint. You may want to search your Twitter name, Facebook profile name, or the first part of your email account. If your email address is "michaelb911@yahoo.com", you may want to search for only "michaelb911". Locating your old network profiles can be a daunting task. Fortunately, we have services to assist us.

KnowEm

KnowEm (**knowem.com**) is one of the most comprehensive search websites for usernames. The main page provides a single search field which will immediately check for the presence of the supplied username on the most popular social network sites. In the main page, a username search provides information about the availability of that username on the top 25 networks. If the network name is slightly transparent and the word "available" is stricken, that means there is a subject with a profile on that website using the supplied username. When the website is not transparent and the word "available" is orange and underlined, there is not a user profile on that site with the supplied username. For your purposes, these "unavailable" indications suggest a visit to the site to locate your profile. The "Check over 500 more" link in the lower left corner of the page will open a new page that will search over 500 social networks for the presence of the supplied username. These searches are completed by category, and the "blogging" category is searched automatically. Scrolling down this page will present 14 additional categories with a button next to each category title stating "check this category". This search can take some time. If you had a unique username that you liked to use, the search is well worth the time.

Location Based Searches

You have now likely located the publicly available content that we will attempt to remove from the internet. This will often be easy to find because it is searchable by your name, address, or telephone number. However, there is often social network information that is defined by the location from where it was posted. Many services such as Twitter and Instagram embed the GPS coordinates of the user along with the posted content. This can quickly identify where a person lives or works. It is likely that you are not uploading this type of detail. However, your children, friends, and family may not think about this type of technology and unintentionally compromise your privacy. You should consider conducting searches based on location as well as text. The easiest way to do this is through Echosec.

Echosec

This simple website allows you to zoom to any location and query social network posts that were submitted from that location. Conduct the following steps to search your targeted area.

- Connect to app.echosec.net in your web browser.

- Either navigate through the interactive map or type your address directly into the search box in the lower left.

- Click the "Select Area" button in the center bottom portion of the page. Draw a box around the target area and release the mouse.

- Navigate through any results displayed below the map.

The square icons within the map identify Twitter and Flickr posts by the location they were uploaded. This type of sharing can quickly disclose your home address, your employer, or your relatives' addresses. After searching your home, consider a query for your workplace, relatives, or child's friends' houses. You will likely locate personal information that would have been difficult to find based on keyword searches alone. This can be a useful technique to find a child's account when they are unwilling to share it with you. This will only search recent Twitter posts. You may also consider the following services which will allow you to search Twitter archives by location.

MapD: MIT (http://mapd.csail.mit.edu/tweetmap/)
MapD: Harvard (http://worldmap.harvard.edu/tweetmap)

Instagram

Echosec will no longer display Instagram results in the free version. While not as pretty or user friendly, we do have a solution for locating these posts by location. Navigate to the following website and enter the GPS coordinates of your desired location on the last line.

http://inteltechniques.com/OSINT/instagram.html

Be sure to use either Chrome or Firefox as your web browser. Click the "GEO View" button in order to display any posts with geo-tagging enabled from your target location. Clicking on the Instagram hyperlink will open the post. If your result looks "garbled", you are missing a browser plugin that allows you to display XML/JSON files. We recommend installing the plugin "JSON View" to your browser of choice. If you need the GPS coordinates of a location, search the address within Google Maps, right click on the building, and select "What's Here". This will display the coordinates in the upper left corner of the map.

Now that you have identified the basic types of information that is publicly visible about you through search engines, consider the content that you would like removed. Most privacy seekers want to eliminate any reference to their home address and telephone number. Some people just want to remove those embarrassing photos posted in college. Regardless of your situation, the later chapters in this book assist with erasing this data. This assessment was only a first step in establishing the scale of information available about you. It is recommended that you conduct the following self-background check to identify more details.

CHAPTER FIVE
SELF-BACKGROUND CHECK

At this point, you have completed the basic steps to identify your personal information visible in public view from search engines. You are now ready to conduct a complete self-background check. This will be done in two phases. The first phase will include only public internet websites that anyone could use to find you. The second phase will involve you requesting personal reports that will identify information stored about you in private databases not visible from the internet. The entire check should be completed at least once every five years.

Phase One: Public Websites

Later chapters outline the removal processes for the majority of the websites that display your personal information. Before attempting removal, you should identify those sites that have a record visible on you. Navigate to each of these websites and conduct a search on your name, address, telephone number, or username as appropriate. Be sure to take note in the accompanying worksheet of which services possess information that you wish to remove.

People Directories

People directory website removal will be explained later. Before you can target these websites to remove your information, you should identify which services contain information about you. You should also consider searching for your children's information. If personal information is located, conduct the removal process for that specific website.

Telephone and Address Directories

While these are not technically people directories, searching your home address or telephone number on these websites will likely display your name as an association. Some of these will not allow removal. However, a strategic disinformation campaign will often mask the results. Use the following table to thoroughly identify any compromised information. Attempt searches by name, address, and telephone number as appropriate for each site.

People Directories

Date:	Result:	Engine:	Website:
_____	_____	Spokeo	spokeo.com
_____	_____	Pipl	pipl.com
_____	_____	Yasni	yasni.com
_____	_____	ThatsThem	thatsthem.com
_____	_____	Zabasearch	zabasearch.com
_____	_____	Intelius	intelius.com
_____	_____	ZoomInfo	zoominfo.com
_____	_____	InfoSpace	infospace.com
_____	_____	PeepDB	peepdb.com
_____	_____	Radaris	radaris.com
_____	_____	WebMii	webmii.com
_____	_____	Genie	reversegenie.com
_____	_____	PeekYou	peekyou.com

Telephone Directories

Date:	Result:	Engine:	Website:
_____	_____	411.com	411.com
_____	_____	WhitePages	whitepages.com
_____	_____	YellowPages	yellowpages.com
_____	_____	Addresses	addresses.com
_____	_____	InfoSpace	infospace.com
_____	_____	SuperPages	superpages.com
_____	_____	411.org	411.org
_____	_____	SearchBug	searchbug.com
_____	_____	Genie	reversephonelookup.com
_____	_____	Detective	phonedetective.com
_____	_____	Reverse Genie	reversegenie.com
_____	_____	Phone Tracer	freephonetracer.com
_____	_____	Privacy Star	privacystar.com
_____	_____	TrueCaller	truecaller.com
_____	_____	PeekYou	peekyou.com
_____	_____	WhoCalld	whocalld.com
_____	_____	ThatsThem	thatsthem.com
_____	_____	NumberGuru	numberguru.com
_____	_____	MrNumber	mrnumber.com
_____	_____	10 Digits	10digits.us

Social Networks

If you use social networks, you should occasionally look through your profiles for any sensitive data that reveals personal information. Even if you no longer use social networks or deleted your account completely, you cannot ignore these sites. Your family and friends are still likely to post sensitive information about you. It could be a photo identifying your home address, vehicle license plate, or the location of your child's favorite hangout. It could also be a family member posting your telephone number to other family members, intending to be helpful. Searching the publicly available information on these sites is easy. The websites listed here will display a search option to find the most common information. Some services require you to be logged into an account in order to search their data. If you do not already have an account on a service, we do not recommend creating one for this purpose.

Date:	Result:	Network	Website:
_____	_____	Facebook	facebook.com
_____	_____	Twitter	twitter.com.com
_____	_____	LinkedIn	linkedin.com
_____	_____	Google+	plus.google.com
_____	_____	Tumblr	tumblr.com

Facebook

The Facebook data visible about you may extend beyond the content that is visible on your main profile page. There is often additional personal information leaking into other areas of the network. Use the following techniques to locate further details about your own profile and those of your family. This may help you decide if deleting your entire account is the way to go.

Facebook collects a lot of additional information from everyone's activity on the social network. Every time someone "Likes" something or is tagged in a photo, Facebook stores that information. Until recently, this was very difficult to locate, if not impossible. You will not find it on the target's profile page, but the new Facebook Graph search allows us to dig into this information.

In order to conduct the following detailed searches, you must know the user number of your account. This number is a unique identifier that will allow you to search otherwise hidden information from Facebook. The easiest way to identify the user number of any Facebook user is through the IntelTechniques website. While you are on your main profile, look at the address (URL) of the page. It should look something like Figure 5.01.

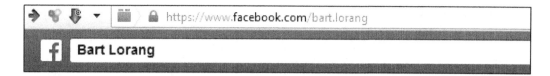

Figure 5.01: A web address (URL) of a Facebook Profile.

The full address of the page is https://www.facebook.com/bart.lorang. This identifies "bart.lorang" as the username of the user. In order to obtain the user number, place this username into a Facebook Custom Search tool located in the resources section of the Intel Techniques website at **inteltechniques.com/OSINT/facebook.html.** Figure 5.02 displays this search tool that translated this username into a user number.

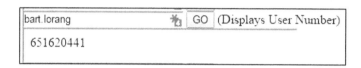

Figure 5.02: A Facebook user number.

The number that you see in this result is the person's user number on Facebook. This data will allow us to obtain many more details about the account. Repeat this process on your own Facebook page. If we want to see any photos on Facebook that you have "liked", we can type the following address into a web browser. Replace 651620441 with your own Facebook user number as in the example https://www.facebook.com/search/651620441/photos-liked. This basic structure contains the website (facebook.com), the action (search), the user number (651620441), and the requested information (photos-liked). Since these are photos that were "liked" by you, the results will include photos on other people's pages that would have been difficult to locate otherwise. If we had asked Facebook for this information with only your name, we would have been denied. If we asked within the search filter options mentioned earlier, we could only search by general name and could not identify a specific user. If you have a common name, this would not work. The method described here works because we know your user number. There are many other options with this search. We can navigate to the following addresses to see more information about you (user number 651620441). Explanations of each address will be explained after the list.

https://www.facebook.com/search/651620441/places-visited
https://www.facebook.com/search/651620441/places-liked
https://www.facebook.com/search/651620441/pages-liked
https://www.facebook.com/search/651620441/photos-by
https://www.facebook.com/search/651620441/photos-liked
https://www.facebook.com/search/651620441/photos-of
https://www.facebook.com/search/651620441/photos-commented

https://www.facebook.com/search/651620441/videos
https://www.facebook.com/search/651620441/videos-by
https://www.facebook.com/search/651620441/videos-of
https://www.facebook.com/search/651620441/videos-liked
https://www.facebook.com/search/651620441/videos-commented
https://www.facebook.com/search/651620441/apps-used
https://www.facebook.com/search/651620441/friends
https://www.facebook.com/search/651620441/events
https://www.facebook.com/search/651620441/events-joined
https://www.facebook.com/search/651620441/stories-by
https://www.facebook.com/search/651620441/stories-commented
https://www.facebook.com/search/651620441/stories-tagged
https://www.facebook.com/search/651620441/groups
https://www.facebook.com/search/651620441/relatives

The "places-visited" option will display locations that your profile states you have physically visited and allowed Facebook to collect the location information. This is often completed through a smartphone, sometimes unintentionally. This can be used to disprove alibis or verify trips.

The "places-liked" option will display any physical locations for which you have clicked "like". This will often identify vacation spots, favorite bars, and special restaurants. This can be priceless information for an investigator or skip-tracer.

The "pages-liked" option will display any Facebook pages that you visited and clicked "like". This will often display your interests such as a favorite sports team, musical group, or television show. These results will include a button labeled "liked by". Clicking this will identify everyone on Facebook that liked that item. This can quickly identify the people that visit the same hole-in-the-wall bar that you frequent.

The "photos-by" option will display Facebook photos that were uploaded by you. These will likely already be visible on your photos page. However, this search could potentially reveal additional images.

The "photos-liked" option was explained on the previous page. This can be beneficial by showing photos that you have liked, most of which you have probably long forgotten. If the photos of interest are on someone else's profile that is not private, you will be able to see all of them.

The "photos-of" option will display any photos that you have been tagged in. This search has already proven very effective in many investigations. This will immediately locate additional photos of you that are not available on your profile. This is helpful when the photos are private on one person's page, but not others.

The "photos-commented" option will display any photos on profiles where you left a comment on the photo. This can be important because you may not have "liked" the photo or been tagged in it. The option may produce redundant results.

The "videos" option will display videos visible on your profile. These may or may not be directly connected to the target. They could also be videos linked to the original source with no personal ties to the subject.

The "videos-by" option will display videos that were actually uploaded by the target. These will be much more personal to the subject and will usually include more relevant content.

The "videos-of" option is similar to the "photos-of" filter. This will display videos that supposedly contain images of the target within the video itself. It could be compared to "tagging" someone inside a video.

The "videos-liked" option will display any videos that the target clicked "like". This can also be used to establish personal interests of the target and are often of interest to parents.

The "videos-commented" option will display any videos on profiles where the target left a comment on the video. Again, this can be important because the target may not have "liked" the video or been tagged in it. The option may produce redundant results, but it should always be checked.

The "apps-used" option will display the apps installed through Facebook. These are usually games that can be played with other people. Many of these specify the environment that they work with such as "IOS". This would indicate that the target is using an iPhone or iPad instead of an Android device.

The "friends" option should display a list of all of the target's friends on Facebook. This will be the same list visible on the main profile page. If you receive no results, the target likely has the friend's list set to "private".

The "events" option will display any Facebook events that your target was invited to attend. These often include parties, company events, concerts, and other social gatherings. This will usually display events that are not listed on the target's profile.

The "events-joined" option will only display the Facebook events at which you acknowledged attendance. This could be in the form of a "R.S.V.P". or confirmation by the target that they are currently at the event. This has been used to question the alibies of suspects.

The "stories-by" option will display any public posts you have made. This can often identify posts that are not currently visible on your profile.

The "stories-commented" option will display any public posts by any users on which you entered a comment. This could be useful in identifying communication between you and a private profile. The standard privacy options do not prevent a search of your comment history on public posts.

The "stories-tagged" option will display any posts that you tagged. This tagging is usually performed because of an interest in the post.

The "groups" option will display any groups that you are a member of. This is beneficial in identifying your stronger interests. In our experience, an individual must only have faint interest to "like" something. However, the interest is usually strong if a group related to the topic is joined.

The "relatives" option will display a list of people that you have identified as a relative. Often, this will display relatives even if you have your friends list set to "private".

Custom Facebook Search Tool

You may now be wondering how you are going to implement all of these searches in an easy format. Navigate to the following website in order to access an all-in-one option.

http://inteltechniques.com/osint/facebook.html

This page will allow you to conduct all of the Facebook Graph searches that were mentioned in this chapter. Copy and paste your username from the profile address into the second option to identify your user number.

The next group of searches will display the "liked", "tagged", and "by" information that we previously discussed. Make sure you are logged into a Facebook account for this to function. We also recommend using the Firefox browser. Chrome occasionally blocks the script required to make this work.

Phase Two: Private Databases Reports

The websites and services in this section can be queried at any time. Most of these businesses do not publicly share your information and do not offer opt-out methods. The data stored is shared with other businesses and can affect your credit score, insurance rates, and ability to obtain a line of credit. While you cannot remove your profile from these databases, you can correct any errors in the reports. These corrections could save you money if you find yourself paying rates that appear to be higher than normal.

Free Credit Report

There are several websites that offer a free credit report. Most of these will try to convince you to sign up for premium offers and never offer a free credit report. The only official government supported free credit report website is at **annualcreditreport.com**. This website allows you to view your credit report without any fee once yearly from each of the three credit bureaus. This means that you actually get three free credit reports every year. Instead of viewing all three reports at the same time, create a schedule to spread out the viewings. We recommend the following:

- In January, connect to **annualcreditreport.com** and request a free Equifax report.

- In May, request a free report from Experian.

- In September, request a free report from TransUnion.

These months can be adjusted. The important element is that you are viewing your credit report throughout the year. The process for viewing your report varies by state. The website will explain every step. When you receive your report, pay close attention to the entire document. Further, we believe that the following sections deserve extra scrutiny.

- The inquiries section of a credit report will identify any companies requesting a copy of your report. This will usually be creditors verifying your details for a loan request.

- The non-impact section of a credit report includes requests from employers, companies making promotional offers, and your own query requests.

- The address information of a credit report will identify any addresses used for current and previous lines of credit. If you see an unfamiliar address, report this.

- The open accounts section of a credit report will identify any unused open accounts and a contact number to close the account if desired.

- The closed accounts section will verify that an account was closed.

LexisNexis

Chapter Eight will explain how to conduct an advanced removal from LexisNexis. This includes instructions to opt-out of non-public databases. Whether or not you apply these techniques, you should request your personal file from this company. Even if you requested information removal, you will find that the company maintains a file on you. This does not mean that your information is available to the public. The steps below will allow you to review the data LexisNexis stores about you.

- Navigate to **personalreports.lexisnexis.com/pdfs/CD107_CP-File-Disclosure-Request-Form_pg-3.pdf** and print the form.

- Navigate to **lexisnexis.com/privacy/for-consumers/CD307_Accurint_Person _Report_Info_Form.pdf** and print the form.

- Print a redacted copy of your driver's license as discussed in Chapter Three. Mail it and both forms to the address listed in the upper right corner of each form.

Westlaw / Clear / Thomson Reuters

This is another large company that was discussed earlier. The detailed content of your personal report will probably surprise you. This report can often identify attempted fraud or identity theft conducted in your name. Follow these instructions to obtain your free report:

- Navigate to s**tatic.legalsolutions.thomsonreuters.com/static/pdf/ info_request_form.pdf** and print the form.

- Complete the document with your real information. The information is only used to verify you for the report. New information is not added to any databases. Print a copy of your redacted driver's license (Chapter Three). Mail it and the printed form to the address listed.

Acxiom

Acxiom offers two types of personal reports. The first is a fraud detection and prevention report. This report exists if you have returned a large amount of merchandise to retail stores. It is used to identify fraud and probably does not apply to the audience of this book. This report costs $5.00 to obtain and can be found at **isapps.acxiom.com/rir/rir.aspx**.

The second option is the background screening report. This is provided to potential employers that request the product. Inaccurate information in this report could explain difficulty in obtaining employment. This report is free.

- Telephone 800-853-3228 and select option 3. State the following to the customer services representative.

- "I believe that there are errors on my background screening report. Per the rules of the Fair Credit Reporting Act, I would like to request a free copy of my report".

Sterling Infosystems

This is another service that provides employment related consumer reports to potential employers. An online or mail request can be conducted.

- Navigate to **sterlingbackcheck.com/About/Fact-Act-Disclosure.aspx** and then complete the online form. Provide a valid email address to receive your digital report.

Innovis

This is another consumer credit information company that is similar to Equifax, Experian, and TransUnion. One big difference is that you cannot obtain your Innovis credit report through the free website annualcreditreport.com. Innovis encourages mailed requests for a personal credit report, but the automated telephone system is easier and more efficient.

- Telephone 800-540-2505 and listen to the recorded message. Choose "1" for the first two menu options. You will then be asked to enter your Social Security number, date of birth, zip code, and numeric portion of your home address to verify your identity.

- You will be informed that you can obtain a free credit report if you are unemployed, on public assistance, or suspect that you may be the victim of identity theft. The first two choices are obvious, but the third is open to interpretation. If you believe it is POSSIBLE that you are a victim of identity theft and want to verify this through a credit report, select option "4" as instructed.

Michael's Experience

Approximately one month before I requested credit reports from Equifax, Experian, TransUnion, and Innovis, I contacted my bank and changed my telephone number to an anonymous forwarding number. The only credit report that obtained this new number was Innovis. The number is now associated with my name and will be shared with several companies. This intentional form of disinformation will help mask my real telephone number from the public.

Core Logic

Core Logic is a consumer information powerhouse. If you complete the opt-out process described later, the company will no longer share your information. However, they still maintain your profile and will allow you access to the report.

- Use your personal anonymous email account explained previously and create an email message with the subject of "Opt-Out" to **srumph@corelogic.com**. State the following and include your name, home address, and date of birth.

- "Per your policy as published at corelogic.com/privacy.aspx, I would like to request my consumer report maintained by Core Logic".

CoreLogic Credco is one of the largest credit-related credit reporting agencies and is often used by mortgage lenders. Your consumer file can contain previous homeownership and mortgage information, rental payment history, any reported delinquencies, and other debt obligations such as child support. You are entitled to a free copy once every 12 months.

- Print a written letter stating "I would like a disclosure copy of your consumer file in my name". Include your full name, Social Security number, current and previous addresses, and date of birth. You will need to send a copy of one of the following.

Valid driver's license
Social Security card
State identification
Military identification

- You will also need to send one secondary form of identification which can be any of the following.

Valid driver's license
Utility bill with your current address
Rental lease agreement
Mortgage statement
Bank statement
State identification

- Send everything to the following address.

CoreLogic Credco, LLC
PO Box 509124
San Diego, CA 92150

SageStream

SageStream, LLC, formerly known as IDA Inc., is a credit reporting agency that produces credit reports and scores from their repository of consumer information contributed by a wide array of companies. If you believe that information contained in your report is not accurate, you can take steps to dispute it. To obtain your free personal consumer report, you will need to submit a signed, written request to SageStream with the information listed below. For security purposes, they must verify your identity by receiving a minimum of two copies of verification documents that match the information you provide with the request.

- Create a written request with signature that includes your full name, home address on file, anonymous phone number, Social Security number, and date of birth. Include copies of at least two of the verification documents listed below that substantiate the personal information that you provided.

Driver's license or Government ID
Recent utility or phone statement, produced 60 days ago or less
Social Security card
Birth certificate
U.S. passport picture page

- Mail your request to the following address.

SageStream, LLC Consumer Office
PO Box 503793
San Diego, CA 92150

Safe Rent

If you currently rent your residence or plan to seek rental housing in the future, you should request a copy of your consumer file maintained by Safe Rent, a Core Logic company. You must complete a form and submit via fax or postal mail.

- Print the form located at **corelogic.com/downloadable-docs/nbd03-104-disclosure-request-web-packet.pdf.**

- Complete the form with your real information and submit via postal mail to the address on the document.

- There is a fee to access a report. However, there are certain situations that allow for a free report. If you meet ANY of the following conditions, the fee will be waived:

Denial of your housing application
Required to have a deposit not required by others
Required to have a cosigner
Assessed a higher rental rate than others
Denied employment or promotion
Reassigned or terminated
Unemployed or filing for unemployment within 60 days
Public welfare recipient
Have reason to believe your file may contain errors

We believe that practically everyone can qualify through one of these conditions. The last option can apply to anyone that believes "typos" are POSSIBLE on their report. Follow the instructions on the form and expect your report within two weeks.

Insurance Services Office

Your vehicle and home insurance rates can be influenced by your loss history report. Inaccuracies in this report can cause unnecessary rate increases. The Insurance Services Office will provide a free copy of your report. Included in this copy are any losses reported to your insurance company in the past five years.

- Place a telephone call to 800-627-3487. Provide the information requested for verification purposes. Your report will arrive via postal mail in about one week.

Tenant Data

This is another rental data agency that reports resident history and a tenant profile of rental prospects. If you do not rent a home, this would not apply to you. If you would like to see the data collected about you and your rental history, complete the following.

- Navigate to **tenantdata.com/downloads/AuthorizationforFileDisclos_new.pdf** and print, complete, and send the form.

Experian Rent Bureau

Experian maintains their own database of rental history and creates profiles of renters.

- Navigate to **experian.com/assets/rentbureau/brochures/request_form.pdf** and print, complete, and send the form.

Chex Systems

If you have been the victim of identity theft or any type of financial fraud, criminals may be attempting to write checks against your accounts. Many automated systems will stop this fraudulent activity, but may not notify you of the issues. You can request a report of any negative impact on your checking accounts from two sources.

- Navigate to **consumerdebit.com/consumerinfo/us/en/chexsystems/report/index.htm**.

- Click "Agree" to begin the online form submission. Complete all required fields and click "Submit". You should receive your report via postal mail within five days.

TeleCheck

The second company to request a checking report is TeleCheck. The request process is more demanding than the previous report, and the submission must be sent via postal mail.

- Open a copy of your custom opt-out form created in Chapter Three. Include your anonymous telephone number and your Social Security number. All other information can be removed from the document except the driver's license.

- Package the previous form, a copy of any utility bill or tax statement, and a voided check. Send the documents to the following address.

TeleCheck Services, Inc.
Attention: Consumer Resolutions-FA
PO Box 4514
Houston, TX 77210-4514

Retail Equation

When you return a product to a retail or online store, your information is recorded and shared with several companies. This includes the location, product, amount, and reason for return of the product. This database was created to combat exchange fraud, and you are likely in it. If you are curious about the information being shared about your shopping habits, you can request a copy of your report.

- Create an email addressed to returnactivityreport@theretailequation.com. Include your name and anonymous telephone number in the message.

- You will be contacted by the company to process your request. If you are asked for a transaction number, state that you do not have that information.

Medical Information Bureau (mib.com)

When you apply for medical insurance, the provider will seek your report from the Medical Information Bureau. This report will include information such as height and weight, and identify any noteworthy gains and losses. Depending on your medical history, the additional information will vary. This report can influence the amount of money that you pay for medical insurance. Verifying the accuracy of this report is important when seeking new coverage.

- Navigate to www.mib.com/disclosuretransfer/disclosureservice/formrequest and complete the online request form. Select "For Yourself" on the first screen and click "next". Provide only the following information. The additional fields are optional.

Name
Gender
Mailing address (PO Box)
Anonymous telephone number
Birth date
Social Security number

- Confirm the information and expect a report within two weeks.

Milliman IntelliScript

This company stores information about your prescription drug history. These reports are shared with insurance companies that determine your insurance rates. If you are seeking new insurance quotes, inaccuracies in this report can be devastating. You may obtain a free copy of your report.

- Telephone 877-211-4816. Be prepared to disclose your name, mailing address, telephone number, date of birth, and last four digits of your Social Security number. Expect a mailed report within ten days.

National Consumer Telecom and Utilities Exchange

This database is managed by Equifax. It provides fraudulent activity and delinquencies involving utilities and related services. These reports are obtained by companies before utilities are authorized for a building. If someone has fraudulently used your personal information, this report will disclose the details.

- Telephone 866-349-5185 to speak with a representative. State that you want to request a free copy of your "data report". Be prepared to disclose your Social Security number, name, and date of birth. While we usually never recommend providing this information, it is only used to verify your identity to the company. If you have ever had any utilities in your name, they already have this information. Supplying the details does not put you at additional risk.

- You will be placed on hold while your report is retrieved. After the report is generated, you will receive a confirmation number. The actual report will arrive within three business days.

- Visit **www.nctue.com/Consumers** and complete the Opt-Out request.

Social Security Administration

Beginning in 2012, the social security administration no longer sends reports via postal mail. This cost savings measure requires you to view your statements online. If you plan to conduct a credit freeze, be sure to complete this process first. The account creation on this website cannot be completed with a credit freeze in place.

- Navigate to **ssa.gov/myaccount** and click the button labeled "Sign in or Create an Account". Click the "Create an Account" button and provide the requested information. Choose a secure password and view this statement yearly. If anyone attempts to use your Social Security number for payments, this statement will disclose the fraud.

The reports in this phase of the chapter are optional and none of them will help you hide from the internet. Many will not apply to you. Only you can determine which companies are likely to possess information about you. If you find yourself continuously trying to figure out why you tend to pay more for various services than other people, your answer may be in one of these reports. Generally, requesting a copy of your own consumer report does not adversely affect your credit score since it is not considered to be a "hard" inquiry that a potential creditor would make when you apply for credit or open an account.

CHAPTER SIX
ONLINE ACCOUNT SECURITY

It has been suggested that the strongest password is the one you don't know. Humans are notoriously poor at developing effective passwords because we are limited largely by the constraints of memory and the desire for convenience. Later in this chapter we will discuss how to create effective, difficult-to-crack passwords that are still memorable and usable. We will further recommend, and explain why it is a good idea that you use a different username and password on all your online accounts. This may seem terribly difficult, exceedingly inconvenient, and impossible to remember, and generally we would agree. With only the benefit of human memory it would be nearly impossible to remember and use more than just a few passwords of the recommended length and complexity. For that reason, we have chosen to begin this chapter with a discussion of password managers, one of the single biggest and most important tools you can employ to strengthen your digital security posture.

We have both been using password managers in one form or another for years, and neither can even consider the possibility of going back to not using one. A password manager is a purpose-built application that creates an encrypted database for storing and organizing your usernames and passwords. Password managers solve many of the problems inherent in password development and use by "remembering" your passwords for you so that you don't have to. This allows you to easily implement the online account best practices of using a different username and password on every one of your online accounts, using passwords that are randomly generated and of the maximum allowable length and complexity, and changing them as often as you deem prudent without fear of forgetting them.

Because password managers store all your passwords in one place, they create an "eggs-in-one-basket" situation. It should go without saying that a password manager should be protected by an extremely strong password, and if at all possible, two-factor authentication (see successive sections of this chapter on passwords and two-factor authentication). If you can only take the time to remember one very strong, very complex password, you should do so for your password manager. Be especially careful not to lose or forget this password. Password managers are designed to not let you back in without the correct authentication credentials. This could result in the loss of all passwords for all your accounts, an unenviable situation in which to find yourself. It should also go without saying that your password manager should be backed up. If you are using a host-based manager and your computer crashes, you must have a way to recover the information the password manager contained. Otherwise you risk being locked out of, and potentially losing, hundreds of accounts.

There are two basic categories of password managers, host-based and web-based. Although this section will discuss both, our recommendation is to only use a host-based password manager. While web-based password managers are strongly encrypted, they are significantly riskier because they store your passwords in the cloud on machines that you do not personally control. Further, online password databases are a natural target for hackers because of the wealth of information they contain. Though a certain amount of confidence is placed in all online account providers, an extraordinary amount is required to entrust your passwords to all your accounts to an online service. We have not yet found an online service to which we are ready to give this level of trust for our extremely sensitive accounts.

Host-Based Password Managers

A host-based password manager is an application that runs locally on a single device. All the information that is stored in a host-based password manager is stored only on that device and is not sent to the cloud or otherwise transmitted. This is somewhat less convenient than a web-based password manager as your passwords are only available on your computer or device. As a result, you may not be able to log into your online accounts from computers other than the ones you own and that store your password database. This is not an issue for us since we are reluctant to log into an account from a computer that we don't control and therefore don't trust. However, there are good reasons to use a host-based password manager. The biggest advantage host-based managers enjoy over web-based password managers is security. We have an instinctual, inherent distrust in cloud storage, and prefer to keep our passwords stored safely on devices that we physically control.

The password manager that you choose will depend on your unique computing environment. The combination of operating systems, number, and type of devices that you use will doubtlessly drive your decision. The recommendations here cover most modern desktop and mobile operating systems and should allow you to choose the password management system that is right for you.

Windows: Password Safe

Password Safe is our favorite host-based password manager for Windows operating systems, and we cover Windows specifically because of its prevalence and popularity. The vast majority of our readers are Windows users. Developed by cryptographer and security and privacy icon Bruce Schneier, Password Safe is free, uses very strong Twofish encryption, and is widely known for its simplicity and ease of use. The first step is to download the application and install it on your machine. Password Safe is free and available at the website **https://www.pwsafe.org**. Upon first opening the application you will be required to build a database, which is the file that stores your passwords. By default, Password Safe will build a folder called "My Safes" in the My Documents folder on your computer. To increase the security of your Password Safe database and its backups, we recommend you store them in an encrypted volume (encrypted volumes are covered in Chapter 13). To do this, simply navigate to the location of your choice when creating your Password Safe database.

Once you have created your database (it will save *.psafe) and created a "Safe Combination" (what Password Safe calls the master password), you will be allowed to create entries in the database. Each entry, when opened, contains several tabs. The "Basic" tab is displayed by default when an entry is opened and contains the login information for the account. It also has several fields to allow you to customize the entry. These fields are the group or subgroup into which the entry is to be placed, such as title, username, and password (with a build-in password generator). The Basic tab also contains a field for the URL, the email address associated with the account, and notes.

Though it may be tempting to only fill in the basic information, we recommend filling in all of these fields as thoroughly as possible. We use the Title as an organizational tool and typically number our accounts to order them efficiently for day-to-day use. Filling the URL field allows Password Safe to open your browser to the desired webpage when clicking on the "Browse to URL" button at the top of the application. Filling the URL field with the exact URL may also provide some protection against redirect attacks or look-alike sites. We also recommend filling in the email account field. If you maintain and use a very large number of email addresses it is helpful to remember which account is associated with which email address. Finally, you can use the Notes section for any additional information relevant to the account. If the account in question is a Gmail account, for instance, you can use the Notes section to store the phone number associated with the account, recovery email address, and the backup two-factor authentication codes. If it is an account that requires password reset questions, you can use notes to record the answers to these questions. This places all the relevant information about an account in one single, easy-to-access location that is heavily and safely encrypted.

The "Additional" tab allows you to make several customizations to the shortcuts in Password Safe. These options give you the ability to change mouse and keyboard shortcuts and the ability to choose how many legacy passwords are stored for the entry. In our opinion, it is a good idea to store at least two or three old passwords, especially if you change passwords frequently. There may be occasions when you change a password on a website and update the entry in Password Safe, only to realize later that the entry was not saved on the website. In this case you will still need access to the old password and the Additional tab is where you can go to get it. The vast majority of these old passwords will never be used, but it is nice to know they are there should you need them.

The "Dates and Times" tab allows you to set password expiry which will remind you to change the password on a specific date or after a set period of time (which may be recurring or not). We recommend changing all of your passwords periodically and Password Safe's expiry can serve as a good reminder to do so. We recommend every six months under normal circumstances. The icon beside each entry that is due for a password change will change from red to green when a password reset is due. This tab also provides some statistical information about the entry, including the dates and times it was created, last accessed, and the last password change.

Double-Click and "Shift" Double-Click

One of the most convenient features of Password Safe is the ability to copy a password just by double-clicking the entry. By default, double-clicking on an entry will copy the password to the clipboard, allowing you to paste it into the necessary field. Double-clicking while holding "Shift" will then copy the username, allowing it to be pasted, greatly speeding the process of logging into a site.

You should always copy and paste in the order of password then username. This is a very small measure, but ensures that your password is stored in the clipboard only for a few seconds before you copy the username. This reduces the risk of inadvertently pasting a password in an insecure location such as the body of an email or in a Word document. Should someone else gain access to your computer, this also ensures that a password is not readily available in the clipboard.

Finally, the "Password Policy" tab allows you to select from a very comprehensive set of parameters for password generation for each account. The first option allows you to choose a password policy (see Password Safe Options below). You can create as many policies as you like, allowing you to quickly and easily switch between very long and complex policies to shorter, simpler policies for logins that restrict password length or complexity. If you choose not to use a pre-defined policy, you can set up a custom policy for each entry.

The details you can assign when creating a custom policy are password length, character sets (allowing or disallowing upper and lowercase letters, numbers, and special characters), and the minimum number of each character type to be included in each password. These options also allow you to exclude ambiguous characters, create pronounceable passwords, or use hexadecimal digits only, though we don't recommend any of these for day-to-day use. Reducing the pool of potential characters from which passwords are constructed inherently weakens them.

Password Safe Options: Password Safe is highly customizable to the needs of its users. There are a number of options you can customize to make Password Safe work better for you. We will cover only two of those options here: Security and Backups. To reach the Security options, open the Manage drop-down menu and navigate to Options. In the Options dialogue select the Security tab. The Security tab allows you to adjust certain security measures in Password Safe. The settings that we recommend are the following.

- Check the boxes for Clear clipboard on minimize
- Clear clipboard on exit
- Lock password database on minimize
- Lock Password Safe after __ minutes idle

We recommend setting this last option at no more than 15 minutes idle, after which you will have to restore Password Safe and reenter your authentication credentials to access your database.

The other tab that deserves some attention is the Backups Tab. Password Safe will automatically save backups of your database in the same location as your database. For this reason, the folder containing your database may appear cluttered with a bunch of unsolicited *.ibak files. These are the backup files and should be kept. Should you change a password that is unsaved in the database, you can revert back to one of these backups. By default, Password Safe will only save the most recent three backups, deleting the oldest one when a new one is added. If you desire more backups (we save the last 10) or want to change the location to which the backups are saved, go to Manage > Options > Backups.

Global Password Policies

Regardless of which password manager you choose, we recommend defining global password policies. These policies allow you to quickly choose from a predefined length and character set for given websites. There may still be occasions when you have to build a custom, per-entry policy but these instances should be rare. We recommend building the global policies listed in the table below.

RECOMMENDED POLICIES FOR PASSWORD MANAGERS			
Policy	Length	Character Set	Uses
Standard Policy	60+	All	Most websites and logins
Long Policy	99+	All	Sites allowing very long passwords
Short Policy (or policies)	12-32	Customized to site restrictions	Sites disallowing very long passwords; sites disallowing the use of certain characters in passwords We recommending creating a custom policy for each site with such restrictions and using it ONLY on that site
Username Policy	24	Uppercase letters and numbers only	Creating random usernames for sites where user-selected usernames are allowed (see section below on Usernames)

Keepass (Windows, Mac, Linux)

Keepass and its variants are completely open source solutions for password management. One advantage is the availability for all platforms. While Windows is the only official port of the software, options for OS X, Linux, iOS, Android, and Windows Phone exist. KeePass stores all data within any entry, including notes, within an encrypted database. The default actions are stored only locally to your computer, and not on the internet. Additionally, KeePass can import from over 30 common password management programs. The following represents our recommendations by platform if you are looking for a single password solution on all of your devices. A single KeePass database can be read and modified by all of these options.

Windows - KeePass 2.x Professional Edition: This is the standard version available on **keepass.info**. In the downloads area, you have a secondary option of a portable version. We like this because installation is not required, removal if desired is complete, and transport to another device is easy.

OS X - MacPass: This is an unofficial port of KeePass for OS X available at **github.com/mstarke/MacPass**. We have defaulted to this version for several years due to KeePassX (another OS X version) not supporting the modern 2.x database format. While KeePassX has recently adopted this format, we still like the feel of MacPass better. The same encryption standards are in place and the databases can be utilized by other variants of KeePass.

Linux - KeePassX: This version of KeePass is the only option for Linux users and is available at **keepassx.org**. It is stable and functions identically to the official Windows port. As stated previously, the latest edition now supports 2.x databases that contain enhanced storage features.

iOS - Keepass Touch: This iOS version works with the same KeePass databases but has a look and feel similar to other iOS apps. It can be found by searching KeePass Touch in iTunes.

Android - KeePass Droid: This staple for Android can be found at the Google Play store. Again, it will read and write to the most recent database versions created in any KeePass version.

Web-Based Password Managers

A web-based password manager is a cloud-storage application that stores all of your passwords online and allows you to access them from anywhere. Web-based password managers are very convenient as they allow the user to access them from any computer or device with internet access and the appropriate browser add-on or app installed. Though web-based password managers do offer robust encryption, two-factor authentication support, and other security features, they are primarily focused on convenience. While this convenience is nice, we remain unconvinced that being able to access our passwords from anywhere on any device is always a good thing. One benefit of web-based password managers that cannot be denied, however, is the inherent safety in having them stored offsite. If your computer crashes, is destroyed, or rendered otherwise inoperable, you will still have access to your passwords and the accounts they protect.

We offer a warning here about accessing your web-based password manager from an untrusted computer. If you do not have control of the computer, it is possible for the owner of the device to capture your master password. This would necessarily grant access to all your passwords unless two-factor authentication is enabled. Even if the owner of an untrusted device is not intentionally logging your keystrokes he or she may not have taken the necessary pains in securing the device. As a result, it may be infected with keylogging software or other malware that could compromise your password. Because we trust neither computers that we do not personally control, nor cloud storage, we are very cautious about web-based password managers and you should be, too.

Both of us use or have used LastPass in a very limited capacity. In both cases we use LastPass to access some special accounts, the breach of which would not reveal sensitive information. These accounts are not associated with our real names, banking information, travel accounts, or other personal data. The credentials for these accounts are stored with LastPass because the convenience in accessing them outweighs the security risks should they be lost.

We also include web-based password managers here because we do wish to encourage maximum participation. Using a web-based password manager for extremely sensitive credentials, while not acceptable to us, is in all likelihood a perfectly good option for some. In fact, using a good web-based manager like LastPass would be a vast security improvement for most individuals, the majority of whom use the same two or three poorly constructed passwords across dozens of accounts.

LastPass (Windows, Mac OS X, Linux, Android, iOS)

LastPass is our preferred web-based password manager. LastPass has a strong, well-deserved reputation for being very secure. In early 2015, during the planning stages of this book LastPass was breached and some encrypted master passwords were stolen from LastPass servers. Though this is alarming, LastPass is the only password manager we recommend because of how they handled this incident. LastPass immediately notified every one of its users and urged them all to change their master password. Next, LastPass required email verification upon initial, post-breach login for all users who did not have two-factor authentication setup. It is this type of responsible incident handling that eases some of our fears about LastPass. Even so, we still recommend cloud-based password managers only reservedly.

LastPass offers the user the ability to utilize a number of two-factor authentication schemes including the app, hardware, and paper-based systems, all of which are described in detail later in this chapter. Passwords stored in LastPass are encrypted locally on your machine, and then uploaded to the LastPass' cloud servers. From there they can be accessed from any Windows, Mac, or Linux system with a simple browser add-on for the Chrome, Firefox, Opera, Safari, and Internet Explorer browsers, or from an Android, Blackberry, iOS, or Windows mobile device via the LastPass app.

In addition to being very secure (which is certainly a prerequisite for cloud-based systems), LastPass is also very user friendly. LastPass has auto-fill and auto-login functions that will automatically fill the login fields and log the user in as soon as you browse to a site requiring a login. In addition to this, and storing all usernames and passwords, LastPass has a secure notes function that allows you to record small bits of information securely.

One problem endemic to web-based password managers is that they are sometimes difficult to use with logins consisting of more than a username and password. For example, some logins require a username, password, and some other identifier before allowing access. When working with sites like these, LastPass can usually fill two of the three fields, but often does so poorly. If LastPass consistently has a problem with a site with three or more fields, you can usually work around this by placing the login credentials in a secure note with LastPass, and copy and paste each one individually.

We believe that the following configurations will create a LastPass account that is extremely secure and would be very difficult to compromise. If you are looking for a cloud-based solution that will sync all of your passwords, LastPass is the way to go.

- Do not use the "remember master password" feature. This will eliminate the possibility of a digital attacker exploiting a stored password on your computer.

- Install the binary version of LastPass instead of simply adding a browser extension. This will give you better security. Navigate to "Tools", then "About". If binary status is "false", use the button to activate it, or use the full installer to download LastPass.

- Setup two-factor authentication through either SMS recovery or YubiKey. This adds an additional layer of protection by requiring another verification step before the master password can be reset on your LastPass account.

- Increase your password iterations to 5000 or more. Navigate to "Account Settings" panel from your LastPass vault, and ensure it displays 5,000 or more in the iterations field. You can increase the number of iterations. This also happens automatically if you update your master password. You may increase the number of iterations up to 200,000. The number of iterations drastically slows the time taken to test passwords in a brute-force attack. The downside to this is that the higher the number of iterations you have, the longer it will take LastPass to open the database and LastPass may have some compatibility issues with certain browser integrations. If you are willing to sacrifice instantaneous access, we are comfortable going as high as 25,000 iterations. This should cost you no more than five additional seconds on login.

- Disable account recovery. Turn it off in the Preferences menu of the LastPass browser extension within each browser.

- Restrict access to trusted countries. In your Account Settings, ensure you restrict access to only the location(s) where you regularly access LastPass.

- Disable TOR access. TOR is used to communicate anonymously on the internet, so it is often used by hackers. Disable access from TOR in your LastPass Account Settings.

- Remove any "Trusted Devices" in the account settings. This will force you to enter your credentials upon each use of your browser. It prevents others from accessing your password while on your computer.

- Use a unique, strong master password and never reuse your master password.

Overall, we have two main opinions about password management solutions that sync with the cloud. The first is that these accounts should be overly inconvenient. Password reminders, stored devices, and "remember me" type options should all be disabled. This is the most vital account to protect. Do not create unnecessary attack surfaces. The second opinion is that we must all remember that our information is stored somewhere out of our control. No one knows the exact server, or even the state, where their data is located. We also do not know exactly how our information is handled during transit to their servers. While services such as LastPass are the best option for online storage, they still possess security concerns. Please consider our upcoming password management strategies before you commit.

LastPass is a freemium service. LastPass on any single device is totally free. LastPass Premium costs $12.00/year and allows you to access LastPass from unlimited devices, share a folder with up to five other people, and use a YubiKey for two factor authentication. LastPass is available at **https://lastpass.com**.

Usernames

With password managers to keep up with all of your login information, it is now possible to elevate your security posture significantly without a corresponding increase in the amount of work required. Generally, usernames are completely overlooked in the discussion of online security. We think this is a mistake. We believe that usernames should be considered the very first line of defense for such accounts. Most websites require at least two things to log in: a username and a password. If the attacker cannot find your username, your account is significantly more secure. To launch an attack against your account would require first finding your account and an obscure username greatly reduces the chances of this happening.

Michael's Password Management Strategy

Local Storage Solution: MacPass database based in KeePass 2.x format. This stores every password that I own. The database is stored on a TrueCrypt container within my full disk encrypted laptop. The password to the KeePass database, TrueCrypt volume, and disk encryption are all unique from each other.

Online Storage Solution: LastPass installed to the OS. This stores all accounts that are not extremely sensitive. Alias social network profiles, forums, secondary email accounts, and any "junk" sites are stored here. Two factor authentication is enabled via YubiKey. Only my primary email and financial accounts are not stored here. The password for LastPass is unique, account recovery is disabled, binary version is installed, and there are no trusted devices associated with the account.

Justin's Password Management Strategy

Local Storage Solution(s): My favorite password manager for years has been Password Safe. This was ideal when using Windows machines; the only "official" version of Password Safe is the Windows version and if you are a Windows user, this is the only manager I recommend. After switching to OS X it took me a while to find the ideal solution. I finally bit the bullet and paid money for Codebook Password Manager. I like Codebook because it lets me sync a vault with my device without storing anything in the cloud. The ability to transmit passwords to my device securely is very important to me. I should point out that I ONLY put passwords on my phone that are used on my phone: the email accounts I have, my VPN, and a couple other functions; I do not carry around my entire password database in my pocket. Why is this so important? If you are manually entering passwords on your device (any device, really) they probably aren't great passwords.

Online Storage Solution: None

A predictable username has several problems, the first of which is susceptibility to guessing. If an attacker is targeting an attack against a specific individual, he or she will attempt to guess the target's username(s) to various sites. The attacker will base guesses on known information about that person. This information can be gathered online from social media sites, personal blogs, people search sites, and public records. Predictable usernames are most commonly generated from a combination of first, middle, and last names. For example, if your name is Amy Schumer your username might be "ABSchumer". Sometimes they are combinations of monikers or initials and dates of birth such as "chumer81". Once the username has been discovered the attacker can now target that account and attempt to break the password. Conversely, the attacker can never begin targeting the account if it cannot be located.

The second problem with predictable usernames is that they are typically used across multiple sites, especially when the email address associated with the account is used as the username. Using the same username across several of your accounts correlates those accounts. This makes them easier to locate and leaks information about you such as your social media presence, interests, the online services and commerce sites you use, etc. This can expose a great deal of information about you. After locating your username, the attacker in this scenario may user a service like KnowEm (**http://knowem.com/**) to locate other accounts you have. If a common username and password combination are used across multiple accounts, hacking one account can very quickly lead to the compromise of multiple accounts with disastrous consequences. Though you may not care if your throwaway email account or an old social media profile is hacked, it could lead to your bank account or an active e-commerce account being hacked if they share a username and password.

The third major problem with predictable usernames is that when breaches occur, the username and password combinations are usually sold or posted online in massive databases. If you use a username or email address that correlates to your name, a breach can reveal personal information about you, especially if you have an uncommon name. As an example, let's assume your name is Harrison Tang and your username to a site is harrisontang83, an obvious and easily guessable username based on your name and year of birth. Let's also assume that a large password breach occurs at a given site, and the usernames and passwords are posted online. Anyone seeing this database would easily recognize your name and with some research could probably confirm that user is you. This reveals information about you and your personal interests. This could be a dating site (like Adult Friend Finder or Ashley Madison), a bank, an ecommerce site, or an online service of some sort. This would reveal to anyone seeing this database that you use this dating site, bank, online retailer, or service, leading to further avenues of exploitation.

To combat this, you should consider the username a security measure. If the usernames on your accounts happen to be obvious, change them. If a particular site does not allow you to change your username, consider closing your account and opening a new one using a non-obvious username. There are several ways to create difficult-to-guess usernames.

Random Generation: When setting up an account that lets us choose any username we want, we will use a random string of letters and numbers in the maximum allowable length, generated by a password manager. An attacker may know a great deal of personal information about you and use it to guess your username if it is personally relatable to you. More commonly, your username will probably be your easily-guessed email address. However, it is unlikely that an attacker will guess a randomly generated username. A string of characters has several advantages beyond being difficult to guess. First, it will not be easily memorable to anyone should they happen to see it. Second, if someone did find this, the likelihood that they would even recognize it as a username is low. Finally, if that username was leaked in a breach, it would not point directly back to you because it is not personally relatable to you.

An ideal username would look something like this: 532T4VYL9NQ54BTMDZI1. Though this would be extremely difficult to remember (especially if the account bearing it was used only on an occasional basis), a password manager solves the memory problem. Some online accounts will allow you to choose a username up to 60 characters in length and you should consider this wherever it is allowed. Unfortunately, many online accounts do not allow you to choose your own username, and will use your email address as the username by default. If this is the case, there are several ways in which you can still have a difficult-to-guess username.

Gmail Address Modifiers: One technique creating unique usernames for multiple accounts, while still having all emails go a single inbox is available through Gmail. Though this is not our preferred method since we do not have Gmail accounts for personal use, it is very reliable and does not rely on a third-party service. Gmail allows you to add a "+" in your email address, immediately before the "@gmail.com". After the "+" you can add a modifier to make this email address unique. Gmail will disregard anything between the "+" and "@gmail.com" and you will still receive your emails as normal. For example, if your Gmail address is completeprivacyandsecurity@gmail.com, you would add the "+" and an additional modifier after "completeprivacyandsecurity", like this:

completeprivacyandsecurity+example@gmail.com

The modifier can consist of letters and numbers, and can be unique for each online account you wish to associate with that email address. To reap the maximum security benefit from this technique, we recommend making the modifier a random set of characters rather than something easily guessable. For example, if we were going to set up an Amazon.com account using this Gmail address, we would add a short, random, modifier like this:

completeprivacyandsecurity+3xc8i@gmail.com

Though "+amazon" is easy to remember, it is also easily guessable, which defeats the whole purpose for using this technique.

With a single Gmail address, a user has an infinite array of email addresses at his or her disposal (we have successfully used modifiers as long as 40 characters), and can use a unique email address for each online account owned. Be aware that these should not be considered anonymous, as a human seeing these addresses could very likely be aware of this technique and quickly figure out your "real" email address. It should also be pointed out that some services do not recognize an email address with a modifier as valid.

Multiple email addresses: Though this is the most time-consuming method of setting up multiple usernames, it is perhaps the most secure. See the section later in this chapter for more information on structuring these accounts. For more information on email forwarding services see Chapter Three.

Passwords

Though password managers provide most of the memory you need, there are still a handful of passwords that you will need to manually enter on a day-to-day basis. Not only do you want these passwords to be memorable, you also need them to be incredibly strong as the compromise of these passwords could lead to the compromise of all of your sensitive data. For this reason, you still need to know how to develop a strong password that you can remember and enter manually.

Password Basics: Before we discuss how to build a good, strong password it is critical to understand what comprises one. There are two factors that make (or break) a password: length and complexity. Added length and complexity both exponentially increase the difficulty in breaking a password.

Password length is uncomplicated. With today's computing power, 20 characters is a prudent minimum length (if your site does not allow a longer password). When passwords are cracked using brute force techniques, powerful processors run through hundreds of millions or billions of possible passwords per second. Every possible combination of a very short password could be tested in a matter of minutes with strong enough computing power, and computers are growing faster every day. Password length is the single most important factor that increases the strength of a password.

When using a password manager, we will use passwords that are much longer than 20 characters, sometimes exceeding 100. If this seems like overkill, consider the following. Regardless of whether a password is 1 character or 100, both require the exact same amount of effort when using a password manager. Why not go with the longest allowable password? If a site with which you are registering does not allow a longer password, think twice before registering with that service.

Complexity can be a bit trickier. Password complexity is created by following some basic rules. Ideally a password will contain characters from the full ASCII suite, including upper and lower-case letters, numbers, special characters (!@#$%^&*_+=-/.,<>?;'":[]}{\|), and spaces. Spaces are very important as they are not commonly used in passwords, and as a result are not commonly searched for by password-cracking programs.

Password Vulnerabilities

You may be wondering why such extreme measures are needed to develop an effective password. The reason complexity is desirable is that passwords are not typically cracked by "dumb" brute force methods alone, like starting at lowercase "a" and going all the way through "ZZZZZZZZZZZZ", and testing everything in between. Though brute force attacks exist, they are not the most popular or effective method of cracking a password, as they can take an immense amount of time. Time is the enemy of the password cracker, and your goal in designing a password should not be to make it unbreakable. Nothing is truly unbreakable given enough time, but you should aim to make it take an unacceptable length of time. Passwords are typically cracked in a much timelier manner by understanding how people make passwords and designing a dictionary attack to defeat it. Dictionary attacks rely on specific knowledge of the target and heuristics.

Knowledge of the target is useful when cracking a password because personal information is frequently used as the basis for human-generated passwords. An individual may use his or her birthday (or birthdays of a spouse, or children, or a combination thereof), favorite sports team or player, or other personal information or interests. This information can be input into programs like the Common User Password Profiler (CUPP). This application takes such tedious personal data as birthdays, names, occupation, and other keywords, and generates thousands of potential passwords based on the data. This list of passwords can then be programmed into a custom dictionary attack against the target machine or account.

Justin's Experience

Passwords are a phenomenon much like keys. We all carry them and use them daily, but few realize the threats against them or the concepts underlying a good one. As an example of how poorly understood passwords are, I recently had a new television installed in my home. The television is internet-capable and required my Wi-Fi password for setup. After the installer typed my very long, very complex password into the television he remarked in a frustrated tone, "You really should change that". I replied that although it's an inconvenience now, once all my devices are set up I rarely have to enter the password. He responded with reasoning that left me speechless: "Well, if you have guests over it's easier to give them a shorter password…" Needless to say, I changed the password immediately after he left, though not to a shorter one.

The television installer mistook the point of a password, considering it a convenience feature rather than a security measure. Passwords aren't very exciting, but good passwords are an absolutely crucial component of digital security. The ability to design and implement strong passwords will be extremely important to the proper execution of many of the techniques discussed in the remainder of this book. The password techniques that I recommend here produce extremely long, complex, and difficult to crack passwords. Unfortunately, this makes them somewhat inconvenient to input and slightly more difficult to remember, but the security they provide is well worth it.

Dictionary attacks work through a trial and error approach. First, a list of passwords is entered into a password-cracking program. This list might be customized against the target (through applications like CUPP as described above), or it may be more generic. Even though "generic" lists are not tailored to a specific target, they are still far more successful than they should be. These lists are based upon the heuristics of how people develop passwords. These lists are developed with the knowledge that many people use the techniques explained in the following list of password pitfalls.

- Never use a dictionary word as your password. Almost all dictionary attacks will include a list of dictionary words in a number of languages.

- Do not use a dictionary word with numbers/characters at the beginning or end (e.g. password11 or 11password), and do not use a dictionary word with simple obfuscation (p@ssword). These are the most common methods of adding complexity to a dictionary word-based password, and combinations such as these would be tested in any decent dictionary attack.

- Never leave the default password on your devices (Bluetooth devices and wireless routers are notable offenders in the retail market). Default passwords for any device imaginable are available through a simple web search, and would absolutely be included in an attack against a known device.

- Never use information that is personally relatable to you. As we have discussed, information that is personally relatable to you can be used in an attack that is customized to target you specifically.

The inherent problem with complexity is that it makes our passwords difficult to remember, though with creativity it is still possible to create passwords that are very long, very complex, yet still memorable. Below are two of our favorite techniques to develop strong (and memorable) passwords.

The Passphrase: A passphrase is a short phrase instead of a single word and is our preferred technique. Passphrases work like passwords, but are much more difficult to break due to their extreme length. Additionally, if appropriate punctuation is used, a passphrase will contain complexity with upper and lower-case letters and spaces. A shrewd passphrase designer could even devise a phrase that contains numbers and special characters. An example of a solid passphrase might be the following.

"There's always money in the banana stand!"

An even better example might be:

"We were married on 07/10/09 on Revere Beach".

Both of these passphrases are extremely strong and would take a long, long time to break. The first passphrase contains 43 characters, including letters in upper and lower-cases, special characters, and spaces. The second is even longer at 46 characters, and it contains numbers in addition to having all the characteristics of the first. Additionally, neither of these passphrases would be terribly difficult to remember.

A variation on the passphrase is the "XKCD method". Rather than inventing an actual phrase, you simply choose four, five, or six (the more the better) random words. Like passphrases, this is a good method for developing passwords that are long, though it eschews the use of numbers and special characters. The example in the infamous comic (which can be found at http://xkcd.com/936/) is "correct horse battery staple". Other examples are nearly infinite, but be careful not to use information that could be easily guessed about you. Further, hackers have noticed the uptick in popularity of this method in recent years and have designed dictionaries and heuristics-based attacks that take advantage of this.

Diceware Passphrases: Diceware is a method of creating secure, randomly-generated passphrases using a set of dice to create entropy. To create a diceware passphrase you will need one die and a diceware word list. Numerous diceware word lists are available online. Because of the way the passwords are created, these lists do not need to be kept secret. These lists consist of 7,776 five-digit numbers, each with an accompanying word and look like this:

43612	noisy	43616	nomad	43624	nook
43613	nolan	43621	non	43625	noon
43614	noll	43622	nonce	43626	noose
43615	nolo	43623	none		

After you have acquired a die and a world list, you can begin creating a passphrase by rolling the die and recording the result. Do this five times. The five numbers that you recorded will correspond with a word on the diceware list. This is the first word in your passphrase. You must repeat this process for every additional word you wish to add to your passphrase. For an eight-word passphrase you will have to roll the die 40 times. Diceware passwords are incredibly strong but also enjoy the benefit of being incredibly easy to remember. A resulting diceware passphrase may look like the following.

puma visor closet fob angelo bottle timid taxi fjord baggy

Consisting of ten short words, this passphrase contains 58 characters including spaces and would not be overly difficult to remember. After you have completed this and compiled the words from the list into a passphrase you can add even more entropy to the passphrase by capitalizing certain words, inserting numbers and special characters, and adding spaces. Experts currently recommend that six words be used in a diceware passphrase for standard-security applications, with more words added for higher-security purposes. You should never use a digital or online dice-roll simulator for this. If it is compromised or in any way insecure, so is your new passphrase. Wordlists are at **world.std.com/~reinhold/diceware.html**.

An enterprising sixth-grade student in New York City creates and sells diceware passphrases in her spare time. Each passphrase contains six words, is handwritten by her, and no copies are stored. The passphrases are sent to you sealed in a security envelope and sent via US Postal Service which, as she points out, cannot be opened in the United States without a search warrant. One passphrase costs $4.00. For more information, visit her website at **www.dicewarepasswords.com**.

The "First Letter" Method: This method is a great way to develop a complex password, especially if it does not have to be terribly long (or cannot be because of site restrictions on password length). For this method select a phrase or lyric that is memorable only to you. Take the first (or last) letter of each word to form your password. In the example below, we use a few words from the Preamble to the Constitution of the United States.

We the people of the United States, in order to form a more perfect union, establish Justice, insure domestic Tranquility

WtpotUSiotfampueJidT

This password contains 20 characters, upper and lowercase letters (the letters that are actually capitalized in the Preamble are capitalized in the password), and does not in any way resemble a dictionary word. This would be a very robust password. The complexity and length of this password could be increased greatly by spelling out a couple of the words in the phrase, and more complex still by replacing a letter or two with special symbols as in the following example.

We the People of the United States, i02famPu,eJ,idT

Containing 51 characters, this is the strongest password yet, but would still be fairly easy to remember after taking some time to commit it to memory. The first seven words are spelled out and punctuated correctly, and the last fifteen words are represented only by a first letter, some of which are substituted with a special character or number. This password is very long and very complex, and would take eons to crack with current computing power.

The Concept of Gradual Complexity

Creating long, strong passwords can be a pain, especially if you implement them all at once. If there is a particular application for which you actually need to place a password into human memory, gradually increasing the process will help you retain it. Start with a short password that you can remember fairly easily and gradually increase its length and complexity by adding three or four characters every couple of days until it has reached sufficient length and complexity.

One application for which Justin has used this technique time and time again is when creating a passcode on his smartphone. Every week he adds four characters to the passcode until he has reached what he believes to be an acceptable length (and everyone else thinks is ridiculously long). Such a long string of characters would be impossible to commit to memory all at once, but by adding only a few to an already familiar sequence it becomes ingrained in small pieces. It should go without saying that when using this technique, you should never store sensitive information behind the password until it has reached an acceptable strength. This requires some consideration and planning on the part of the user but is, in our opinion, worth it in the long run.

Other Password Issues

Even if all your passwords are strong, there are some other issues to be aware of.

Multiple Accounts: Though this is covered elsewhere in this book it is worth reiterating. Each of your online accounts should have its own unique password that is not used on any other account. Otherwise the compromise of one account can lead quickly to the compromise of many of your accounts. If a password manager is doing all the work for you there is no reason not to have different passwords on every single online account.

Password Reset Mechanisms: Most online accounts feature a password recovery option for use in case you forget your password. Though these are sometimes referred to as "security" questions, in reality they are convenience questions for forgetful users. Numerous accounts have been hacked by guessing the answers to security questions or answering them correctly based on open source research, including the Yahoo Mail account of former Vice Presidential candidate Sarah Palin. The best way to answer these questions is with a randomly generated series of letters, numbers, and special characters (if numbers and special characters are allowed). This will make your account far more difficult to breach through the password-reset questions. If you use a password manager, the answers to these questions can be stored in the "Notes" section of each entry, allowing you to reset your password in the event you become locked out of your account.

If you are prompted to enter a password "hint", we recommend using purposely misleading information. This will send the attacker on a wild goose chase if he or she attempts to discover your password through the information contained in the hint. You should never use anything in the hint that leaks any personal information about you, and if you are using a strong, randomly generated password, the hint should have nothing at all to do with the password itself. Some examples of our favorite purposely misleading hints might be: My Birthday, Miami Dolphins, Texas Hold'em, or Password, none of which have anything at all to do with the password at which they "hint".

Password Lifespan and Password Fatigue: Like youthful good looks, architecture, and perishable foods, passwords are vulnerable to the ravages of time. The longer an attacker has to work at compromising your password, the weaker it becomes in practice. Accordingly, passwords should be changed periodically. In our opinion, they should be changed every six months if no extenuating circumstances exist. We change all of our important passwords much more often than that, because as security professionals, we are probably much more likely than most to be targeted (not to mention much more paranoid, as well). If you have any reason to suspect an online account, your wireless network, or your computer itself has been breached you should change your password immediately. The new password should be drastically different from the old one.

If you are using a password manager, a practice we strongly recommend, changing passwords is not difficult at all. Remembering them is a non-issue. If you choose not to use a password manager, or you have more than one or two accounts for which you prefer to enter the password manually, you may become susceptible to password fatigue. Password fatigue is the phenomenon of using the same four or five passwords in a rotation if you change them, or are forced to change them, frequently. This may be required on your company computer. This impacts security negatively by making your password patterns predictable, and exposes you to the possibility of all the passwords in your rotation being cracked.

With modern password hashing techniques, changing passwords frequently is typically unnecessary. The corporate practice of requiring a new password every 30, 60, or 90 days is a throwback to the days when passwords were predominantly stored in plaintext and there was significant risk of the entire password database being hacked. If passwords are being stored correctly, they should be secure even when the database is breached. With that being said, we are more paranoid than most and regularly change the passwords on all of our important accounts. Though it takes a bit of time and patience to update passwords on multiple sites, doing a few each week in a constant rotation can ease the tedium a bit and ensures that if one of your passwords is compromised it will only be good for a few weeks at most.

Password Recycling: When the time comes to make a new password, it is often easier just to change a few characters, especially if they are numbers, than it is to remember a whole new password. Examples include Timothy77, Timothy78, Timothy79, and Timothy80. This is known as password recycling, and unfortunately this makes your passwords very predictable. If one in the series is compromised, successive ones can be guessed rather easily. When you change passwords, the new and old ones should be totally unrecognizable from each other. You should never reuse a previous password.

Online Password Checkers: There are dozens of online password checkers that offer you a field into which you may type your password. The password will then be analyzed and you will be told how long it would take to crack the password using brute force. These sites can be useful, and give you an idea how strong your password might be. Additionally, by entering a password and then modifying it slightly, you can instantly see the effect that small changes can make. As an example, add a semicolon and a space and see how much harder it makes the password to crack. You should be aware that password checkers have access to the passwords that you give them. For this reason, you should never give a password checker one of your real passwords. You have no control over how, or if, they capture the password, and no control over how it is stored. Additionally, it is being transmitted over the internet where it is vulnerable to interception. The closest you should come to testing your actual password is to test one that is similar in structure.

You should also be aware that password checkers do not paint an entirely accurate picture. Password testers are based on the premise of brute force, and some will allow you to select the number of passwords tested per second. If your password is based on personal information about you that can be used in a custom dictionary attack, all bets are off. The password may be broken in a matter of minutes. Likewise, if you are using a password that has made it into a more common dictionary, your password may be broken in mere seconds.

Don't let password-checking websites give you a false sense of security about your password. There are two password-checking websites that we use and recommend. The first is **https://howsecureismypassword.net**. We like this site for its simplicity, its instant feedback, and for allowing the option to choose the number of passwords tested per second. The other is **www.passfault.com**. Passfault does not give instant feedback (you must click "Analyze" each time you want to test a password), and it does not allow you to choose the number of passwords tested per second. However, it does allow you to choose between classes of password-cracking machines. The reason we like Passfault is that it does offer much more detailed feedback about what is wrong with an entered password, and it displays dozens of categories of potential password weaknesses.

Online Password Generators: Just as there are online password checkers, there are also online password generators. We do not recommend using any of these. Instead, use the one in Password Safe or KeePass. The reason we strongly advise against using online password generators is that you have no idea what the site is doing behind the scenes. Are they recording the password along with your IP address? It is impossible to know, and there are too many other better options out there for creating randomly-generated passwords.

Two-Factor Authentication

These days, one does not have to specifically follow security news to know that password compromises happen with shocking regularity. The Wired cover story about the hack on Mat Honan in late 2012 fully underscores the weaknesses in passwords. Mr. Honan is also an excellent case study in the folly of using the same password across multiple accounts. When one of his passwords was hacked, it led to the compromise of several of his accounts. Passwords are becoming a weaker method for securing data. Passwords can be brute-forced, captured during insecure logins, via key-loggers, or lost when sites that do not store passwords securely are hacked.

There is a method of securing many accounts that offers an orders-of-magnitude increase in the security of those accounts: two-factor authentication (TFA). Using TFA, each login requires that you offer something other than just a username and password. There are several ways TFA can work, and there are three categories of information that can be used as a second factor. The three possible factors are something you know (usually a password), something you have, and something you are (fingerprint, retinal scan, voice print, etc.). A TFA scheme will utilize at least two of these factors, one of which is almost always a password.

Text/SMS: With your cell phone designated as a second factor, you will enter your username and password to login. Before being allowed access to the account, you will be presented with another prompt asking for your one-time code. This code will be sent via text/SMS message to your mobile phone. Upon entering the code, which is typically 6-8 digits, access to the account will be granted.

It is possible with this scheme (and most others) to set up "trusted" computers. For example, you may wish to forego the second factor each time that you login on your home computer. In our opinion, this is a convenience that we can live without, even though it is a bit onerous to unlock our phone each time we log into an email or other online account. If you choose to set up trusted computers, be very selective about which ones you trust. The only computers you should even consider trusting are those that never leave the confines of your home. It should go without saying you should never trust a public computer.

Using the text/SMS scheme of two-factor authentication is a major security upgrade, but it is not as good as the next option we will discuss: the dedicated authenticator app. Text/SMS two-factor can be defeated if your phone's texts are forwarded to another number. This may happen if your service provider account is hacked, or if a phone company employee is a victim of social engineering and allows an unauthorized person to make changes to your account. This may seem like a very sophisticated and unlikely attack vector, but several well-documented cases of this attack have occurred. This illustrates an excellent reason to make your phone number private as outlined in Chapter Eleven. The text/SMS system can also fail if you do not have phone service and cannot receive texts.

App: Another option for smartphone owners is a dedicated two-factor authentication app. One such app is the Google Authenticator (available for Android and iPhone). With the app installed on your phone, you will visit the site and enter your username and password. Next, you will open the app, which will display a six-digit, one-time code for that account (this code changes every 30 seconds). You will enter the one-time code to login. Setup for the app is slightly more complicated than setting up text/SMS, but is not terribly difficult.

Once the app is installed on your phone, you visit the site for which you wish to setup TFA. The site will present a QR code (a modernized bar code) that you scan within the app, which links your phone to the account, and adds an entry for the account into the app. Google Authenticator works for a number of sites, including Amazon Web Services, Dropbox, Gmail, Facebook, Microsoft, WordPress, and more. Another smartphone application that can be used in lieu of Google Authenticator is called Authy. Authy is very similar to Google Authenticator, but we prefer it largely because it can be passcode protected and has a slightly more user-friendly interface.

Though we generally consider app-based tokens more secure than text/SMS systems, it is important to be aware that they are not invulnerable. While an attack on your phone or account could get some of your login tokens, the capture of the token that is transmitted to your app could allow an attacker unlimited access to all your two-factor codes indefinitely. We consider this unlikely, unless you are being targeted by a very sophisticated attacker.

Google Authenticator

The "Google Authenticator" protocol gets a bad rap with some privacy enthusiasts because of its connection with Google. While the name "Google Authenticator" is the name of a Google app, it is merely a colloquialism for the popular TFA protocol. The true name of this protocol is TOTP-OATH (Time-based One-Time Password Algorithm/Initiative for Open Authentication). If you are using an app that uses the "Google authenticator" protocol it is very unlikely that information is being shared with Google. Rather, the developer or website implementing the technology is using the common name for the protocol for the sake of name recognition.

Hardware-based TFA: Some very specialized devices exist specifically to provide a second factor. One such device is the Yubikey. The Yubikey is a small device that resembles a USB flash drive. When using the Yubikey for authentication, you simply plug it into the computer, and when prompted, press a touch-sensitive button on the device. There are no moving parts to the Yubikey and it is a fairly robust device. Be aware, however, that loss or damage to the device can lock you permanently out of whatever it protected.

There are a great many websites and applications that support the Yubikey. Gmail, LastPass, Password Safe, PayPal, WordPress, and even full-disk encryption for TrueCrypt and VeraCrypt encrypted devices are just a few of the implementations supported by Yubikey. The biggest drawback of the Yubikey is that each device is only good for one account within an individual service. Another drawback of the Yubikey is that it cannot be backed up. If you lose your Yubikey you are permanently locked out of whatever it protected. However, we crave this level of security. If you plan to store all of your passwords in LastPass, enforcing TFA with a Yubikey will protect you well.

The LastPass password manager has a very original and very effective system of hardware-based two-factor authentication. It is called "The Grid" and we have yet to see it offered anywhere else. When you set up TFA on the LastPass account using this method you are given a grid which you can download in .pdf format. The grid consists of letters A through Z across the top and 0-9 down each side, with a random character at each coordinate. After logging in, you are presented with a pop-up dialogue that requires you to enter four characters from prescribed coordinates on the grid.

We like this system because of its sheer simplicity. Someone with very little technical background or know-how could implement this and understand its use. Further, because it requires no electronics and no cellular signal, this system is allowed in even the most secure working environments and can be carried anywhere in your wallet. If you print it and retain only a hard copy, it would be very difficult to compromise, even if your computer became infected. We would love to see a system like this implemented in many more applications as a "low-tech" option.

Bad Example: An example of poorly implemented two-factor authentication was the scheme that was used by a popular free email provider (this system has recently been changed, thankfully). After entering your username and password, you had the option to receive a code by SMS or email, or to answer a "security" question. Answering the security question bypasses the second factor (something you have) and replaces it with an additional "something you know" token. The problem here is that an attacker has the ability to compromise the password. If an attacker can compromise the password it is fairly reasonable to assume he or she could also compromise the answers to the security questions. By implementing a faulty scheme like this, the email provider made only an incremental upgrade. In our opinion, they gave its customers a false sense of security in exchange for the effort of setup and use.

This chapter is by no means inclusive of all methods of two-factor authentication. There are numerous other methods for implementing two-factor, including fingerprint readers, smart cards, and even USB-connected retinal scanners. Implementing two-factor makes you a great deal more secure than a password alone can (even a good password), and you should enable it everywhere it is supported.

Securing Online Accounts

Online account security concerns us greatly. This concern is largely the result of two facts. First, most online accounts contain some personal information including financial information or other sensitive data like your home address, mailing address, telephone number, etc. The second reason we are deeply concerned by online accounts is that they exist on servers that we do not personally control. They are enemy territory. Existing on the internet, these sites are vulnerable to attacks against us personally, attacks against the site the account is held with generally, and other, more general forms of spillage.

Online data stands a statistically much greater chance of being exploited than data-at-rest on your machine, and for this reason, we take some special pains and considerations to ensure the security of online accounts. Some of these techniques have been covered elsewhere in this book. We will cover some other best practices for online accounts and make you reconsider the information you are putting online, whether through email, social media, other accounts, or into cloud storage.

Common to All: Basic Best Practices

Do You Really Need an Account? Many online accounts that you are asked to create are unnecessary and time-consuming. Some services require an account. Before you set one up, we strongly recommend considering the potential downsides. You should also carefully consider what data you are willing to entrust to a website. An online dating site may request a great deal of data and periodically invite you to participate in surveys. Of course, it will also ask you to upload photographs. We urge you to use caution when doing so because it is a near certainty that any information you put on the internet will one day be compromised in some manner. Consider these factors before you sign up to create an account with a service.

Use Accurate Information Sparingly: When signing up for a new online account, consider what information is really important and necessary to the creation of the account. When you sign up for an email account, does it really need your true date of birth? Probably not. E-commerce sites require your address to ship packages to you, but do they need your real name? Perhaps they do. When you create an online account with your bank, do you need to use complete and accurate information? Yes, you probably do.

When creating online accounts carefully consider the information that service or site really needs and do not give more information than necessary. Thoughtfulness is what we intend to encourage. If you are using completely accurate information it is collected and sold to marketers which is damaging to privacy. If someone is attempting to hack your account and they have accurate information about you it is more likely they will succeed. With that in mind, let's reconsider the above examples.

Though it might seem counterintuitive, some of these sites need far less information than you would imagine. Email accounts don't need your true birthday or gender. Though your birthday may be collected to ensure you are of age to view certain content, the primary purpose of collecting such data is help them to build a profile on you. E-retailers need your home address but they don't necessarily need your real name as we will see in Chapter 10. Again, this information is collected so it can be used in a profile that is sold to data marketers. On the other hand, some sites do require fully accurate information, and this underscores the need to be thoughtful. It is imperative to use accurate information with some sites such as those used for online banking. Using false information on a bank account could be a crime and could result in you being locked out of your account.

In the months before the writing of this book, two popular "hook-up" sites, Adult Friend Finder and Ashley Madison, were hacked. Very private details about users' sexual proclivities and preferences were leaked in these hacks. Unfortunately, the hack could not have been prevented by users employing good passwords, two-factor authentication, and other security best practices. However, users could have protected themselves by using anonymous usernames, false profile details, and masked email addresses through services like 33Mail, notsharingmy.info, and Blur.

Check the Status of Existing Accounts: An early step in securing online accounts is to ensure they have not been breached. There are a couple of services that will offer you a bit of insight into this by allowing you to cross-reference your email address against lists of hacked accounts. **Breachalarm.com** (formerly shouldichangemypassword.com) allows you to input your email address, which it then cross-references against a list of hacked accounts. If your account has been hacked, change the password immediately. Notify your friends and family that you will be changing your email address and then migrate as quickly as possible to a new email account. Before closing the hacked one, delete all the emails, contacts, calendar entries, and other personal information from it.

Haveibeenpwned.com is a similar site that checks both email addresses and usernames against lists of known-hacked accounts. The site is relatively new and maintains a database of breached accounts. When you enter your email address or username it is cross-referenced against a blacklist of leaked usernames and passwords. If you find that your account information has been leaked, you should change the password on the account immediately, and perhaps close it if at all possible. Keep in mind that services like these only track large breaches and should not be considered conclusive proof that your account is safe. However, checking your email address through one of these services will give you some peace of mind that you are OK in the wake of big breaches.

Multiple Email Accounts: All of the techniques described above merely obscure your username and make it difficult for an attacker to locate your online accounts. If they all forward to the same address, the compromise of that one address could lead to a total compromise. An individual's primary email account is typically the linchpin of anyone's online security posture. Almost any website account that individual has will feature a password reset mechanism that forwards to this account.

Further, the email provider will also have a comprehensive picture of the "real" you if all the emails from all your online accounts forward to the same inbox. The best (but most time consuming and potentially frustrating) practice is to use multiple email accounts and assign only one or two online accounts to each email address. Admittedly this takes some patience and dedication and is not for everyone. At a minimum we recommend that you transition to a primary email account that does not scrape your messages for advertising purposes. These accounts are discussed in more detail in Chapter Three.

Get Rid of Unused or Untrusted Accounts: If you have old online accounts that are no longer used, close them down if possible. Some websites that can help you do this are KnowEm (**www.knowem.com**), a page that helps you find all the sites on which you have created accounts, and online resources that help you close those accounts such as Account Killer (**www.accountkiller.com**), WikiCancel (**www.wikicancel.org**), and Just Delete Me (**www.justdelete.me**). Account Killer and Just Delete Me will give you the links and helpful hints for removing online accounts and they also rate sites on the difficulty of deleting their accounts. It is a good idea to check this out before you build an account in the first place.

Before closing an account, we encourage you to rid the account of as much personal information as possible. Many services will continue to harvest your account for personal information, even after it has been closed. Before closing the account, login and replace the information in as many data fields as possible. Replace your name, birthday, billing information, email and physical addresses, and other fields with false information.

Unfortunately, some sites do not allow you to completely close an account. If you cannot delete an account, you can still take steps to protect your information. Log into the offending site and replace as much information as possible with disinformation. This will ensure that even if these old, unused accounts are breached they will not leak any sensitive information about you. Accounts that you are closing or filling with inaccurate information can also present a disinformation opportunity. You may wish to couple your real name with a false address, or vice-versa. Disinformation will be discussed at length in Chapter Sixteen.

Only Log in on Trusted Platforms: We strongly recommend that you never log into a website that contains any information about you from a machine that you do not personally control. The risks of doing so are high. It is very unlikely that the owner of that computer is as secure as you are and the computer may be infected with malware that could capture your login information.

Before you sit down and log into a website on an untrusted platform, ask yourself if you really need to login or if it can wait until you get back home or to your office. If you cannot wait, consider alternate strategies. For example, if you really need to print a file that is in your email, consider forwarding the file to a friend and having him or her print it for you. If you do log into a site from a public or untrusted computer, uncheck the "remember me" box during login. This option keeps you logged in by placing a cookie on your computer but it is too easy to forget to manually log off (especially on a public computer). We also strongly recommend that you change your login credentials as soon as you get back to your primary computer. The account you logged into from the untrusted machine should be considered compromised until you do so.

Bank Accounts

The table displayed in a moment shows a list of popular banks and some of the security features they offer. Banks that do not offer two-factor authentication were not considered for inclusion on this list. You will notice that not all of the banks mentioned meet all of the criteria we define as ideal. It is up to you to weigh these factors and select the bank that offers the features that are most important to you. The factors that are included on the table are:

- **Two-Factor Authentication**: We both refuse to bank with an institution that does not support two-factor authentication. This is both from a philosophical stance (we do not wish to support companies that do not take user security seriously) and a practical one (we are worried about our own accounts). With the prevalence of breaches occurring on a daily basis financial institutions have no excuse for not implementing this as a standard feature. If your bank does not support two-factor authentication, choose one that does.

- **Maximum Password Length**: Bafflingly, several financial institutions that we have seen in the past have severe password limitations. One bank that a client used disallowed passwords longer than eight characters. This is completely unacceptable on an account that protects such sensitive information. We would prefer unlimited-length passwords but we have not yet found this to be the case with online bank accounts.

- **Changeable Usernames**: We prefer to use banks that allow us to choose a random username. Because of the sensitivity of these accounts we prefer to use a "real" email address when creating these accounts. We do not like being forced to use this address as our username, though. Banks that allow us to create a random username and change it at will are preferred.

- **One-Time Card Numbers**: Very few banks offer this, but this is an incredibly useful feature. One-time card numbers allow you to use a credit card number for each purchase you make. This obscures your true credit card number, ensures that if the number is captured in transit it cannot be re-used, and (somewhat) limits the amount of information that is collected about that card number to a single purchase.

- **Photo Debit/Credit Cards**: Though this does not pertain to online accounts we do believe it is a high-quality security measure that is worth mentioning.

- **Alias Credit Cards**: Chapter 10 will detail how to obtain an alias credit card and how it is useful for protecting your privacy. Though there is nothing illegal about this, many financial institutions are hesitant to allow it. We believe having a credit card in a second name is an important step to protecting your privacy and we prefer banks that are amenable to the practice.

Cloud Storage Accounts

Cloud storage has become immensely popular in recent years (though trust in them has perhaps waned slightly, post-Snowden). Dozens of companies offer cloud storage services, allowing you to exchange the small monthly or annual fee you pay for a space on their server to store your files, and bandwidth over which you can upload and download those files. Cloud storage is tantalizingly convenient. You can upload a document to your cloud account from your work computer, download and edit it on your home computer, view it from your smartphone, or share it with another person or group of people.

BANKING SECURITY FEATURES							
	Ally Bank	Bank of America	Chase	CitiBank	HSBC	US Bank	USAA
Two-factor authentication	Y E, SMS	Y	Y	Y	Y HT	Y	Y HT, SMS, ST
Max Password Length	?	?	32	?	?	?	4/32*
Random Username	?	?	Y 32 char	?	?	?	Y 20 char
Changeable username	?	?	Y	?	?	?	Y
Single-Use Card Numbers	N	Y	N	Y	N	N	N
Photo Debit/ Credit Cards	N	Y	N	Y	N	N	N
Alias Credit Card	?	N	Y	?	?	N	N
E = Email, HT = Hardware Token, SMS = SMS/Text Message, ST = Software token (app), *USAA only allows a 4-character "PIN" when two-factor authentication is enabled. If TFA is disabled a 32-character password is permitted.							

Cloud Storage Considerations

We are asked weekly about the security of cloud storage accounts. Many people worry that their data will be viewed by unauthorized people or hackers. We believe that most of these services are very secure when applying the correct security techniques. However, there is another concern that trumps security: ownership. Some cloud storage providers technically own the content that is stored. The lengthy terms of service agreements that none of us can truly understand will explain each company's stance on uploaded content. Before you commit to any service that is offering free storage of your business' documents, ensure that you retain the ownership of any content. Aside from ownership, the use of your data is also a concern. Consider the following two portions of Google Drive's terms of service from December 2015.

"You retain ownership of any intellectual property rights that you hold in that content".

This sounds good. Your content is owned by you. Google will not steal it and take ownership. However, the next portion makes us uneasy.

"When you upload, submit, store, send or receive content to or through our Services, you give Google (and those we work with) a worldwide license to use, host, store, reproduce, modify, create derivative works, communicate, publish, publicly perform, publicly display and distribute such content".

This tells us that Google has the authority to take anything you upload, personal or business related, and use it however they wish. Technically, they could share your content with any of their partners, change your content, and publish it through any channel. While we suspect that this is designed for future Google products, the scope is not defined and could extend far further than one would expect. We maintain our personal documents on our computers synced to redundant backups.

Making these services even more enticing is the fact that most offer a small amount of storage for free, generally 2-5 gigabytes, which may be a sufficient amount of storage for home users. However, this convenience comes at a cost. Anything stored on a server or device that you don't control is vulnerable to the terms of the provider. Cloud storage operators, if inclined, may inspect, edit, or delete (intentionally or accidentally) your documents as long as doing so does not violate the terms of the user agreement. All of these things have happened. Further, if you store files with a cloud storage provider that does not provide secure storage, it negates a lot of the hard work you have done in securing your own system. A hacked account could result in the spillage of sensitive data.

The greatest concern we have with files stored in the cloud is that they will be accessed by an unauthorized party, whether an employee of the provider (either for "legitimate" or illicit purposes in the case of a rogue employee), or a hacker who has gained unauthorized access to your account or the cloud provider's servers. This may sound slightly far-fetched, but as this book was being written a large data breach occurred that exposed nude photographs of several A-list celebrities. All of them had their accounts hacked, and some of them had "deleted" the photographs in questions months earlier. For these reasons, we use cloud storage only minimally and only for completely non-sensitive data. However, if you require this service, use the best practices discussed earlier in this book (obscure usernames, strong passwords, TFA) as well as those discussed below. Further, we will recommend what we feel to be the most secure providers and best practices.

BitTorrent Sync: BitTorrent Sync isn't truly a cloud-based service. BT Sync is a peer-to-peer file sharing service that allows you to sync multiple devices without ever uploading your data to a cloud storage provider. Though this information does flow from one device to another via the internet (where it is potentially vulnerable to intercept), it is not stored on an external server. BitTorrent Sync requires that one of your devices always be on, and online, if you wish to use it as a cloud service. There are numerous tutorials that show you how to build your own cloud storage with a network-attached storage device, a computer that you can leave on, and even with a Raspberry Pi (a very small, minimalistic computer processor). If you go this route you may wish to look further into also building your own encrypted virtual private network through which you can access the device. The major downside of a setup like this is that your "cloud" is (most likely) in your home, so if you house burns down or falls victim to a natural disaster, you have lost one of the major advantages of cloud storage. On the other hand, it is probably far more secure than placing it with a true cloud provider.

SpiderOak: SpiderOak is perhaps the most recommended cloud storage provider among the security conscious. This is primarily due to SpiderOak's "zero knowledge" claims. According to their website, SpiderOak has no access to (i.e., zero knowledge of) your data. Further, all data that is uploaded to SpiderOak's servers is first encrypted on your device before being uploaded. SpiderOak does deem it necessary to make users aware that logging in via the internet or on a mobile device, rather than from the SpiderOak desktop application, does place your password on SpiderOak's servers for the length of the session. SpiderOak claims that the password is encrypted and is destroyed on logout. We do not find this ideal, but we do appreciate their transparency. One other major downside of SpiderOak is that they do not offer two-factor authentication for free accounts. If we were storing documents in the cloud, we would find it incredibly important to make the account as difficult to get into as possible. SpiderOak does offer a limited two-factor authentication system for paid account holders. SpiderOak is available at **https://spideroak.com**.

DropBox and Google Drive: DropBox and Google Drive are far more popular alternatives to SpiderOak. Both are usable across most platforms, both offer excellent security by way of strong encryption, have HTTPS connections when uploading and downloading, allow very long passwords (99+ characters), and support two-factor authentication. DropBox offers 2Gb of free storage, while Google Drive offers 15Gb of free storage. Further, if sharing files with others is a priority, both of these providers enjoy the immense advantage of popularity. With convenience comes a cost. Reading through the privacy policies of both Dropbox and Google, it is clear that your data can be accessed at their discretion. If you opt to store data with a cloud provider, we recommend understanding and implementing the cloud storage best practices that follow. Dropbox is available at **https://dropbox.com**. Google Drive is available at: **https://drive.google.com**.

Read the ToS and Privacy Policy: The terms of service are an important part of any online service that the vast majority of users fail to ever examine. This document should always be read carefully, as it clearly outlines what the provider can do with your information. If reading through the legalese is too time consuming, there is a website that can help: **https://tosdr.org**. TOSDR (which stands for "Terms of Service, Didn't Read") attempts to simplify the terms of service from many popular websites into a small amount of easily understandable information, along with a letter grade (A through F).

Limit what you Store: You should carefully consider the items you store in the cloud. We have no problem with cloud storage if it is only used to conveniently access non-sensitive information. If the information you store would not leak data about you and does not contain information that would be financially or personally damaging, the risk is minimal. This is a very high bar to pass, as just about anything would leak some information about you.

Encrypt Before Uploading: Even though cloud storage providers now take pride in the encryption they offer, it is very likely that they possess the encryption keys. This could give them access to your data. For this reason, it is a good idea to encrypt files locally with your own encryption before uploading them. If you use Windows, we recommend encrypting with CryptSync (Chapter Thirteen). TrueCrypt/VeraCrypt, 7-Zip, or GPG would also work equally well. This ensures that if the provider or a hacker does access your data, they will only be able to access an encrypted version. Admittedly, this likely makes your files inaccessible from your smartphone or other computers without the software necessary for decryption, which defeats much the convenience inherent in cloud storage. It still serves you well if the primary intended purpose of the account is as an offsite backup.

Email Accounts: Though we generally recommend against using free, mainstream email providers, we realize that there are many that will still choose to do so. Because of this it is important to point out that while Google has a very poor reputation in the privacy community, its security is almost without equal. Google accounts can be protected with very long passwords (up to 99 characters) and excellent two-factor authentication. Google is incredibly responsive, letting you know when your account has been accessed from a new device, IP, or browser. Google even records your recent logins so you can review them for suspicious activity, which is admittedly yet another privacy concern.

If you do choose to use a Google account to access Google products including Chrome, Gmail, Google Drive, YouTube, etc., we recommend that you minimize the amount of information that is collected about you. To do so you must first log into your account. Next, click on your avatar in the upper-right side of the page and select "Account" from the fly-out menu. On the next screen select "Privacy Checkup". This will open a list of four options that allow you to somewhat control your privacy on Gmail accounts. They are "Choose what Google+ profile information to share with others", "Help people connect with you", "Personalize your Google experience", and "Make ads more relevant to you".

First, we recommend opting out of Google+ completely. Under "Help people connect", you should uncheck both boxes that allow Google to share information about you based on your phone number. If the phone number in question is the real number associated with your cellular service provider, click the "Edit Your Phone Numbers" button and change it to an anonymous number (for more information on anonymous numbers see Chapter Eleven). On "Personalize your Google experience" you should review all of the options and pause the history that Google stores about you. These include Web & App Activity, Location History, Device Information, Voice and Audio Activity, YouTube Search History, and YouTube Watch History. Finally, under "Make ads more relevant to you" click the Manage Your Ads Settings". This will take to you another page where you can turn off targeted advertisements.

Modifying these settings in a Gmail account helps but you should not let it give you a false sense of security. Besides encrypting your email which will be covered later in this book, nothing you do will prevent Google from having access to your email. This content will be collected and collated into meaningful profiles about you, which will then be sold to various third-parties.

E-Commerce Accounts

E-retailers have an excellent opportunity to collect information about their customers. Online stores are happily given your full name and home address, your credit card number, and your date of birth. This is highly prized information to advertisers who will use this information to collate you into groups based on your age, the wealth of your neighborhood, the types of things you shop for online, and other information. We recommend using accurate information sparingly as discussed earlier in this work, as well as the additional best practices listed here.

Shop Reputable Sites: Though we hate to encourage you to use the big-box online retailers at the expense of smaller, independent retailers, they do typically offer excellent security. These large retailers characteristically have a lot more to lose if a breach occurs and more money to throw at the issue before it becomes a problem.

Check Out as A Guest: If you are using a site that you will not likely use again check out as a guest to avoid creating an account if at all possible. If you are required to create an account, do not save your credit card information. Though not a guarantee, this may somewhat limit the information that site maintains about you. More accounts equate to a larger attack surface, and more databases containing sensitive personal information. If you are shopping with a smaller retailer that offers the option to use a digital wallet service like PayPal, please consider this. PayPal offers excellent security features and supports two-factor authentication. The biggest benefit of using a service like this is that you don't have to enter your credit card or bank account information to the site with which you are transacting, and PayPal can serve as a single, unified payment service. An even better option than PayPal is Blur, which is discussed at length in Chapter Ten.

HTTPS: When shopping online, ensure that the site you are using is encrypted (https) on any page requesting credit card information. Though it is relatively rare to find a site that still permits transactions over insecure connections, they do still exist. Be especially aware of this when purchasing from less reputable websites. Firefox displays a padlock to the right of the URL bar when a secure connection has been made. A grey padlock indicates the site has been verified and the connection is encrypted. A green padlock means the same, and that an extended verification has been conducted by Mozilla to verify the authenticity of the site.

We realize that this chapter was massive compared to most chapters in this work. Our goal is to help you create a secure digital foundation that will allow you to take advantage of the upcoming methods in order to achieve complete privacy and security. Next, we must tackle social networks.

CHAPTER SEVEN
SOCIAL NETWORKS

With the explosion of social networks, many data mining companies are now collecting content from public profiles and adding it to a person's record. Overall, society has made it acceptable to provide every level of personal detail to the corporations that own these networks. We have been trained to "like" or "favorite" anything that we find enjoyable or feel pressured into identifying with. These actions seem innocent until we discover the extent of usage of this data. Think about your online actions another way. Would you ever consider spending time every day submitting personal details to online survey websites? Further, would you consider doing this for free? Would you sit down for an hour each day with a complete stranger and answer invasive questions about the details of your life and your likes and dislikes, knowing that he was going to sell this information?

Essentially, when you create a Facebook account you are agreeing to work as unpaid survey-taker, photographer, and writer. When you "like" a site you are adding to Facebook's trove of data about you. When you install the Facebook app on your phone you often give Facebook permission to access your location data, letting the service track you everywhere you go. When you upload photos to Instagram you are actually giving them, in perpetuity, to Facebook who can use them for almost any purpose whatsoever. When you update your status, submit a photo, or comment on Facebook you are voluntarily giving them data they can resell or reuse in almost any legal way. This is in addition to the fact that all your posts, status updates, likes, and other actions are used to build an incredibly accurate profile about you. Your photos are used in facial recognition software so accurate that Facebook could conceivably build a near-perfect 3D model of your body. Facebook exemplifies the axiom that if a product is free, you aren't the customer. You are the product.

The other danger of social networks and other services that rely on data collection is that they never forget. While you can delete your Facebook or Google account, the information that you have submitted to the service will always be retained in some form. While Google may not keep the entirety of your emails, your profile will be saved for potential future use. While using some of these services, teenagers and adults are making irreversible decisions.

Before you learn how to remove your social network data from the companies that sell it, you must first clean up your social network profiles. Otherwise, the data companies will eventually collect the data from your profile and create a new database on you. The level of difficulty with the privacy strategies will depend on how much information you have already made available.

There are hundreds of social networks. The largest networks will be discussed in this chapter. You should visit any social network where you have created a profile. Even if you think that there was no personal information provided, take a look at both the public page visible to anyone on the internet and the "private" page visible only to friends. Evaluate the information that could be gathered about you and then log into the social network and see what information was provided when you created the account. Make note of all of this and consider the next three topics.

Privacy Settings

Most social networks provide an option to protect your personal details from the public. This is usually in the form of privacy settings that you can customize. These settings allow you to specify who can see the content of your profile. This can determine who can see your messages, photos, current location, employer and alumni information, friends and family, and other details. You can usually specify that either the public can see everything, or that certain details can only be viewed by people that you have classified as "friends". Facebook also provides another option of "Friends of friends". This means that people that you do not know can see your information if they know someone that you have classified as a friend. Modifying these settings to restrict who can see your data is advised. But, it can also create a false sense of security and encourage you to post sensitive content. Here are a few of things to consider about privacy settings.

These settings only prohibit the public from seeing the content. The content is still visible to the company that owns the social network. When you created the account, you agreed to a long list of legal terms called the terms of service. These terms probably discussed how the company that owns the social network can do whatever they want with the data that you provide. While these networks may be careful not to share your private data now, no one knows what will happen in the future.

Privacy settings can also be incredibly confusing. Some larger social networks may have dozens of privacy settings and hundreds of combinations of settings. This can make choosing the most private and secure options difficult. Privacy settings are subject to change. Facebook is notorious for updating its privacy policy to allow more and more of your data to become less and less private. Frequently, when the privacy policy changes many of your privacy settings will change. When these automatic changes occur, they will not be in the interest of privacy. They will be to the benefit of the social network and will make as much of your information public and accessible as possible.

It is common to read in technology news sources about people that break into other people's accounts to steal information. Celebrities are continually having their accounts compromised by self-proclaimed "hackers" for both fun and profit. If someone wants your data bad enough, and has the money to fund an expedition to retrieve your data, there is a criminal ready to complete the task.

Finally, there are many legal ways to retrieve data that is believed to be private. We have demonstrated during live training how content from "hidden" social network profiles can be located through simple search techniques, like those described in Chapter Four. Many people take a quick glance at their profile and are satisfied that only those with approved access can see their content. They are often wrong.

We believe that any time you post anything to the internet, you must assume it is for public view. Even if you have your privacy settings locked as tight as possible, you should accept that there is a possibility that someone else could get your data. If the content you are uploading to your private page would also be acceptable for public view, then you can proceed. However, if the photos of you drunk the night before would embarrass you if anyone but your friends saw it, you should not take the chance. Privacy settings will not always save you. Therefore, we do not explain specific privacy settings. Instead, we will focus on information removal and proper account deletion.

Content Removal

If you have looked at your profiles and identified personal data that you no longer want on the internet, you can remove it. There are too many different social networks to provide instruction for the removal of specific information. The process is usually fairly easy. If you have trouble, conduct an internet search for the answers. Ultimately, any information that you provided to your profile can be removed. The exception may be your name on certain sites. If you find something that you cannot remove, choose to update the information and insert blank spaces or disinformation.

Most likely, it will not be your profile that contains information that worries you. It will probably be the profiles of your children and other relatives. Many teenaged children have no concern about privacy and the dangers of online information. Many will post hundreds of photos from their daily activities that will expose every intimate detail of their lives. There is nothing legal that you can do to modify this information on your own. Often, a calm yet stern talk with your children will start the process of cleaning up the profiles.

Account Deletion

By now, you may be considering completely removing all of your social networks. This process is not as easy as you would think. Social networks want your profiles and, more importantly your eyes on their advertisements. Facebook's home page does not inform you how to delete your account. Actually, no social network that we are aware of does this. It is very important to delete your accounts in a specific manner to ensure that the data is removed. The process to do this on several popular networks will be explained here.

Facebook

If your Facebook content is public, there are several data mining sites collecting everything that you post including comments, photos, and friends. The first layer of privacy that you should implement is appropriate privacy settings. Recently, Facebook made this process much easier than before. After you log into your account, click on the "down arrow" in the upper right corner of the page. Choose the "Settings" option and select "Privacy". In the section "Who can see my stuff?", you can edit your desired settings.

You will now have four choices of how you want to protect your data. The first choice, "Public", allows anyone to see all of your information. This is not advised. The second option, "Friends", allows only the people that you have identified as your friends to Facebook. This is a slightly more secure option. The third option of "Only me" is designed to to make your posts completely private and only visible by you. The last option allows you to customize different areas of your profile so that different people can see different types of content. We only recommend this for advanced Facebook users. If you are going to use Facebook, select the "Friends" option. More importantly, make sure that the subjects listed on your friends list are people you really know and trust. Again we reiterate that if you put it on the internet, do not be surprised when it becomes public.

Many people have decided to completely delete their Facebook profile. They have discovered that this process is not as easy as it should be. Additionally, a Facebook account cannot be deleted right away. There is a "waiting period" of fourteen days. After the account is deleted, photos may remain on the Facebook servers for months or years. These photos are the legal property of Facebook. This may sound discouraging, but the sooner you begin deleting and stop adding additional information to Facebook, the better off you will be. If you are ready to pull the plug, the following are the proper steps.

- Log into your account and delete all of the content that you can. This includes all photos, messages, and interests. If you find something that cannot be deleted, replace the current data with bad information.

- Navigate to **http://www.facebook.com/help/delete_account**.

- Click on the "Delete My Account" button. This will technically deactivate your account in two weeks. If you log into your account any time within that period, your account could be reactivated.

- You will immediately receive an email from Facebook confirming the request.

- If you log into your Facebook account, you should receive a notification of a pending deletion. You can cancel or approve this request, but this step is not mandatory.

Why We Do Not "Like" Anything

We previously discussed methods of identifying a person's "Likes" on Facebook regardless of their decision to display them publicly in their profile. This was part of the pre-assessment conducted earlier. Other people can locate the items, businesses, pages and other "things" that you like on Facebook. We encourage people to refrain from clicking the like button anywhere. Consider the following scenarios.

- Courts have allowed the introduction of a person's interests from social networks as part of both criminal and civil cases. Imagine that you are the defendant in a civil dispute in reference to a traffic crash and your likes are "fast cars", "street racing", and "marijuana". None of this may have had any impact on the incident, but you will appear guiltier from the association.

- Attorneys have used a person's interests from online activity to create "jury appeal". Imagine that you are going through a bitter divorce proceeding and custody dispute. The opposing attorney presents the judge with your likes of a specific brand of beer, your favorite type of semi-automatic pistol, and your previous support of a politician that opposed the presiding judge's seat. While none of these interests are morally wrong, they definitely do not help your case.

- Many people jokingly like inappropriate topics on Facebook. We have seen police officers that "Like" prostitution pages, military members that associate with anti-military propaganda, and politicians that thought it was funny to click "Like" on pages associated with derogatory statements about mentally disabled individuals. The actions were done in jest, but the consequences of discovery are harmful.

- Finally, there is the consideration of first impressions. Before you meet for that first date, you are likely to conduct some online ~~stalking~~ research. What happens when the other person looks at your page? Will he or she know that you were not serious when you clicked "Like" for the Facebook fan page for the dentist that killed the protected lion in Zimbabwe?

Facebook Tagged Photos

If you possess a Facebook profile, anyone can post a photo of you to his or her own profile and "tag" you in the image. This will identify you in the photo by name and connect the viewer directly to your own Facebook page. Facebook gives you the ability to not only remove this tag, but you can also request removal of the entire photo. The following instructions will guide you through the process.

- Click on the down arrow in the far upper right of your profile while logged in to your Facebook account. Select "Activity Log".

- Click "Photos" in the left column. Select the images that you would like to remove the tag from.

- Click "Report/Remove Tags" at the top of the page and select "Untag Photos" to confirm.

- If you would like the photo completely removed, choose the option "I want this photo removed from Facebook". This will send a message to the user that posted the photo indicating your desire to remove the image. This is not mandatory to the user, but most people comply with this type of request.

Twitter

Deleting your Twitter account is fairly straightforward. Go to your settings page. On the bottom of the account tab, there is a "Deactivate my account" link. Click it, and confirm. Before you take the easy route, we encourage you to consider a few things.

If you have a Twitter profile with personal posts associated with it, there are dozens of websites that have collected all of your data and reproduced it. Deleting your account will not remove the posts that are replicated on third party websites. Investigators are often presented a message on a suspect's account that says "Account deleted". This is usually due to the suspect learning that he or she is being investigated and the account is deleted out of panic. When they find this, they just go to a website such as Google and and pull up the user's posts within cached results. The next tactic will add an additional layer of privacy to hide your tweets.

Before deleting your account, remove every message that you have ever posted. Eventually, many of the third party websites that collect Twitter data will re-scan your profile and update the messages that are displayed on their site. Often, this will overwrite the information that is currently displayed with the current messages, which will be none. We prefer this over simply deleting the account. Also, when you delete your account, someone can open up a new account with your profile name after 30 days. With this method, you still have control of your account, there are no personal messages associated with it, and sites that collect your Twitter posts will collect your empty profile. Active Twitter users often have thousands of messages on their account. Removing each message individually can be very time consuming. Instead, consider an automatic message deletion option that will do the work for you.

Twit Wipe

This service will remove all messages from your Twitter profile. In order to do this for you, the site will need your username and password for your Twitter account. Before you provide this information, make sure that the password for your account is not associated with any other accounts. For example, if you use the same password for Twitter and your bank account, you do not want to provide anyone or any service that information. The chances of Twit Wipe disclosing this information are minimal, but do not take the chance. Change your password on Twitter to something unique. After you have a unique password for your account, navigate to **twitwipe.com** and log into your Twitter account. Confirm that you want the site to delete all of your messages and click the link for "Start Wiping". This can often take up to an hour. When the process is complete, and you have verified your messages are gone, change your password back to the original password of your choice on Twitter.

Google

We have a love/hate relationship with Google. We believe that it can be a great resource for anonymity when used appropriately and Google's security is almost peerless. However, it can be very invasive when used with your real name and contact information. We will discuss the various ways to use Google products throughout this book. In this section, we will only discuss removal considerations.

The bad news is that Google stores absolutely everything. While there are scenarios that allow you to remove specific content from public view, the data continues to impact the overall disclosure of your account. The items that you post on Google products such as YouTube, Google+, and Google Photos will always have an association with your account. Consider the following test that we conducted.

We created a new Google account and obtained a new Gmail address. We then accessed this account from a new Android device and added five email addresses of people that we knew to the contacts of the phone. We opened the Google Play store and immediately received information identifying the apps that these people use, their reviews of these apps, and the apps that they like. We expected this to happen as it is standard Google "sharing". We immediately removed the contacts from our device, logged out of the Google account, rebooted the device, and logged back into this same account. While the contacts had been removed, Google remembered that we once knew these people and continued to allow us to see these types of data about them. Google never forgets.

Before proceeding, think about how this could impact you. It is likely that you have a Google account associated with your real name. It is also likely the primary account is connected to your phone if you use an Android device. With Android, you have probably downloaded numerous apps and possibly rated them or marked some as favorites. If this applies, anyone that has your email address in their contact list can see this information about you. Further, if a person has communicated with your email account in any way, the information described here will populate their Google Play and Google+ profiles. Google also knows the names, phone numbers, and email addresses of your friends and family through your Gmail account or Android phone. If you have emailed photos of yourself to any of these people Google knows what you look like. If you have emailed "adult content" or your intimate thoughts, Google knows that, too. Based on your email account Google knows about your health problems. It knows about the wild weekend you had with your college friends, and if you are having an affair. Google knows what your interests and hobbies are, where you like to eat, and what movies you have seen lately. The more Google services you use, the more accurate and detailed this information becomes. While we are not worried about Google "coming after" us, we are concerned with what such a large amount of data represents. A rogue Google employee may use this data for nefarious purposes as has happened before. Though their security is excellent, Google could be hacked. This information could be accessed by any law enforcement agency in the country. Worse, we have voluntarily and legally released this information to Google to use as they see fit by our acknowledgment of the Terms of Service.

Therefore, we believe that any Google account that has been used in your real name, and connected to your real contacts, will always know and share more about you than you realize. We do not believe that you can sanitize these accounts to a state of anonymity. We can only recommend that you remove as much content as possible, and then consider alternative services. While we have both used Gmail accounts associated with our real names in the past, we no longer use any Google services for personal communication. Chapter Nineteen will identify more secure alternatives. For now, we should focus on content removal from non-email based services from Google.

YouTube: The only way to delete your YouTube account is to delete your Google+ profile. Before you take this action, you should delete your YouTube Channels. These contain the videos, comments, messages, playlists, and history within your YouTube account. The following steps will allow you to remove these containers.

- Sign into your Google account and navigate to **youtube.com/account_advanced**.

- In the top right, click your account, then YouTube settings. Under the Account Settings, select Overview. Under each channel's name, select Advanced.

- At the bottom of each channel, select Delete channel and confirm.

This may take a few days to completely propagate. After you have confirmed that your channels have been removed, proceed to delete your entire Google+ account.

Google+: Google began integrating services into Google+ without user's consent. This has led to much confusion about how the social network should be used and has encouraged most users to seek alternatives. However, much of your personal details are likely present on some layer of this service. The directions below will completely close your Google+ profile.

- Navigate to **google.com/account** and select Data tools in the menu.

- Under the Account management section, click Delete Google+ profile.

Google Photos: The Google Photos app has been described as a way to upload and view all of your photos from any device. This obviously stores your content on the internet and is prone to leakage. Many people installed the app and decided it was not optimal for them. Unfortunately, simply installing the app allows Google to begin collecting your photos. Many people assume that deleting the app from your device will stop this behavior and remove your content. Upon deletion of the app, Google retains the photos that were synced. Further, it continues to collect your photos and add them to your profile unnoticed. The steps below will stop this behavior and remove your content from their servers. We can think of little else as private as your personal photos.

While these steps eliminate the photos from Google's live data set, it does not remove them from the Google archive. Users can restore deleted photos within 60 days of removal. However, if you do not take any action to reverse these steps, the data should be unavailable after the 60-day period.

- From a computer, navigate to **photos.google.com**.

- At the top left corner of each photo, click the select icon. You can hold down the shift key to select an entire range.

- At the top right corner of the page, click the trash icon. This will move all selected photos to trash, which will completely disappear after 60 days.

- From your device, choose Google Settings and select Google Photo Backup. This location within your Settings menu will vary by the version of Android being used. It can often be found under Accounts. When located, toggle the switch to Off.

You should revisit your photos page a few days after you take these actions to ensure that new photos are not being shared. You may want to take a few test photos from your device and monitor closely.

Google Contacts: The contact information in your Google Contacts database is used by Google to associate you with the people you know. It is shared with every Google service and you cannot stop that. While Gmail is not a social network, it has several similarities. It is heavily integrated into Google's other services. We believe that you should think of the data in your contacts as a "Friends" list instead of an address book. Google uses this to disclose information about you to anyone that possesses your address in their list, similar to the earlier example.

This important data should always be exported before removal. You may regret simply deleting your contacts when needed later. We will export them in a way that they can be later imported into another provider. The following steps will create a backup of the content and then remove it from Google's databases. This should only be conducted when you are ready to leave Google as an email provider.

- Navigate to **google.com/settings/takeout** and click the Select none button.

- Enable the switch to the right of the Contacts option.

- Click Next at the bottom and follow the prompts.

This will create a small file in vCard format that will contain all of the data stored in your contacts. It can be used later to import this content into another email provider. You may want to take a moment and download all of the types of content from your Google account. There is never any harm in possessing a locally stored backup in a properly encrypted container as described in Chapter Thirteen.

Google Now: This service is a voice activated personal assistant similar to Siri for the iPhone. Regardless of your opinion on the benefits of this technology, we would like to acknowledge the data collected from you when used. It should be noted that this data is only visible to Google, you, or anyone who has compromised your account through legal or extralegal means. The following directions will identify the content being collected, remove undesired data, and disable future recording.

- Navigate to **google.com/settings/accounthistory**. Disable all options.

- When prompted, follow the prompts to delete the stored history of each service.

Google Account Removal

Some people simply want to delete their entire Google account. If you choose this option, we still recommend removing individual pieces of content using the previous methods. We do not believe that every reader should completely delete their Google accounts. Doing so will eliminate the ability to forward incoming email to a safer address. It may be sufficient to remove all content possible and forward all incoming email to a more secure alternative. If you do not log directly into the account in any way, you prevent new data from being created from your usage. This is the route that we took. We each had Gmail accounts associated with our real names and our previous phones. We eliminated all content throughout the Google architecture, forwarded our incoming messages to our new email provider, and never logged in again. Google collects minimal data from the incoming messages. These emails decrease weekly as people notice your new address from outgoing messages. However, some dedicated privacy enthusiasts may want to take it a step further.

If you no longer need the Gmail account associated with your Google profile, deleting the entire profile will eliminate all related data from Google's active environment. It may take a few weeks to purge out of all networks. In our experience, we were able to recover deleted data within 60 days of individual removal. However, we were unable to reactivate an entire deleted account. The following steps will eliminate all of your Google data associated with an individual account.

- Navigate to **myaccount.google.com**. In the Account preferences section, select Delete your account or services. Choose Delete Google Account and Data. Review the options and check both boxes at the bottom of the page. Choose Delete Account.

We should disclose one last time that this action is not reversible. Regardless of your certainty of these actions, we encourage you to download all of your Google content from their takeout website at **google.com/settings/takeout**. We can think of no logical reason to skip this phase of the process.

Instagram

Instagram makes account deletion easy. There is no need to remove individual posts or content. The following steps should permanently remove your entire profile from the internet.

- Navigate to **Instagram.com/accounts/remove/request/permanent**.

- Select any option from the dropdown menu explaining the reason for deletion and click "Permanently delete my account.

MySpace

MySpace users have been steadily leaving the service for more advanced networks such as Facebook and Twitter. These users leave behind an abundance of data that is being collected by dozens of data mining companies. If you have ever created a MySpace page, you should consider completely deleting the profile to keep your photos, messages, and contacts from being passed around in public view. The official process is to log into your account, click on "Settings", and select "Delete Account". You can visit the MySpace privacy page at **https://myspace.com/pages/privacy.** In our experience, this account removal process does not work. The request is ignored and nothing changes. However, we have found the following techniques effective.

- Log into your MySpace profile and click the control panel and then "Profile". On this page, click on the "Basic" tab and change your year of birth to a year 12 years before today. This will make you appear to be 12 on your profile.

- The URL of the page that you are on will reveal your user number. It may look something like "http://www.myspace.com/4024450". Write down this number.

- Send an email to the law enforcement legal compliance division's account at compliance@support.myspace.com. Type "Underage User" in the subject line. Include a message similar to "My 12-year-old daughter has a MySpace profile stating she is 12. She is receiving unwanted contact from adults. Please remove this account immediately".

- As a last resort, log into your account, delete any photos, and replace them with inappropriate (but legal) photos of your choosing. Contact MySpace via email and complain about the page content. They should remove it quickly.

While these methods are deceptive, they have worked. You are not breaking any laws by using these techniques on your own profile. MySpace should delete the profile immediately without question as a precaution. You should check your profile often to ensure the content has been removed.

LinkedIn

Many people have successfully used LinkedIn to gain employment and communicate with others in their industry. Most people who use this social network supply personal information to their LinkedIn profile including employment history, education, contact information, and various details that are often placed on a resume. We are most concerned with LinkedIn's terms of service that basically allow them to do anything they want with your content. Consider the following excerpt from their TOS as of December 2015 that outlines the permissions given to them.

"A worldwide, transferable and sublicensable right to use, copy, modify, distribute, publish, and process, information and content that you provide through our Services, without any further consent, notice and/or compensation to you or others".

If you are not comfortable with giving them practically unlimited rights to your entire profile, the following steps should remove your account from the internet. They will still likely posses your data provided up to this point, but it will eliminate any further data leakage.

- Log into your account. Hover over the photo or photo placeholder of the account and select "Privacy & Settings". Click the "Account" link near the bottom of the page and navigate to "Helpful Links" and then "Close your account".

- Complete the Account Closure form and confirm the account that you want to terminate. LinkedIn will try a few times to convince you to keep your account open.

When you successfully complete this process, you will be notified that an email will be sent confirming the deletion of your account. This may take up to a week.

Many people report that the account deletion confirmation never arrives. If this happens to you, submit a help center request. Navigate to **help.linkedin.com/app/ask**. The website may automatically direct you to the help home page. If this occurs, you will notice access to the "Contact Us" link at the top of the page is blocked until you search for an answer. Simply search any term. Then after the results are displayed, you are allowed to click the link to "Contact Us". Complete this form with your information and an account deletion request. Be sure to include your profile number, which can be found in the address (URL) of your profile. In the address http://www.linkedin.com/profile/view?id=300972, the profile number is 300972.

Photo Storage Sites

A combination of cheap digital cameras and free online storage of photographs has made an enormous amount of personal information available to the public. Social networks and photo sharing websites encourage you to upload all of your photos and send the links to all of your friends and family. Many people have a false belief that only people that possess the direct links to the photos can see them. This is not true. Every one of these sites has a search function embedded into all of the pages that allows anyone to search for pages that may contain photos. The obvious risk here is that your personal photos will be seen by complete strangers. These strangers often include internet predators looking for images of children. With numerous photo sharing websites existing over the years, we often forget about older content existing on sites that we have abandoned. The next concern is called the Exif data.

Exif Data

Every digital photograph captured with a digital camera possesses metadata known as Exif data. This is a layer of code that provides information about the photo and camera. All digital cameras write this data to each image, but the amount and type of data can vary. This data, which is embedded into each photo "behind the scenes", is not visible within the captured image. You need an Exif reader, which can be found on websites and within applications. Keep in mind that most social network websites remove or "scrub" this data before being stored on their servers. Facebook, for example, removes the data while Flickr does not. If the image has been compressed to a smaller file size, this data is often lost. However, most photo sharing sites offer a full size view. The easiest way to see the information is through an online viewer.

Jeffrey's Exif Viewer

We consider Jeffrey's Exif Viewer (**regex.info//exif.cgi**) the online standard for displaying Exif data. The site will allow analysis of any image found online or stored on a drive connected to your computer. The home page provides two search options. The first allows you to copy and paste an address of an image online for analysis. Clicking "browse" on the second option will open a file explorer window that will allow you to select a file on your computer for analysis. The file types supported are also identified on this page.

The first section of the results will usually provide the make and model of the camera used to capture the image. Many cameras will also identify the lens used, exposure settings, flash usage, date and time of capture and file size. This is a lot of data to share with the world.

Scrolling down the analysis page will then identify the serial number field. This is most common in newer, costlier digital cameras and may not be present in less expensive cameras. These cameras will identify the make, model, and serial number of the camera inside every photo that they capture.

ExifTool

As we express constantly on these pages, we typically prefer local solutions over cloud-based solutions. ExifTool is a simple, lightweight tool that will quickly and easily display the Exif data contained on photographs. It runs in portable mode and does not require you to permanently install the application. To view Exif data for a photo simply open ExifTool and drag the photo onto the command line interface. A list of all available Exif data will be displayed. This tool can be used to see what metadata needs to be removed from the photo, and to verify that it has been removed before uploading. ExifTool is free and available by visiting **owl.phy.queens.ca/~phil/exiftool**/. A graphical user interface (GUI) that makes ExifTool easier to use, especially for bulk photos, can be downloaded at **http://u88.n24.queensu.ca/~bogdan/**.

A serial number of a camera associated with an image can be valuable data. This can help someone associate photos that you "anonymously" posted to the internet directly to you. For example, if a stalker found a photo that you posted on your Twitter feed that you took with your camera, he or she may be able to identify the serial number of your camera. If the stalker then finds a photo and suspects that you took it but posted anonymously, he or she can see if the serial numbers match. We bring this up to explain the next threat.

Stolen Camera Finder

This site (**www.stolencamerafinder.co.uk**) was designed to help camera theft victims with locating their camera if it is being used by the thief online. For that use, you would find a photo taken with the stolen camera, and drop it into the site for analysis. This analysis identifies a serial number if possible. If one is located, the service then presents links to photo-sharing websites, such as Flickr, that contain photos with the same serial number. This can locate photos that you may not want to take credit for.

Camera Trace

An additional site that provides this service is called Camera Trace (**cameratrace.com/trace**). Type in the serial number of a camera and the site will attempt to locate any online photographs taken with the camera. This service claims to have indexed all of Flickr, Twitter, Twitpic, Panoramio, and 500px.

GPS

Many new SLR cameras, and almost all cellular telephone cameras, now include GPS. If the GPS is on, and the user did not disable geo tagging of the photos in the camera settings, you will get location data within the Exif data of the photo. This field will translate the captured GPS coordinates from the photo and identify the location of the photo. Further down an Exif results page, the site will display an image from Google Maps identifying the exact point of the GPS associated with the photo. All Android and iPhone devices have this capability.

Cropped Photos

Another piece of information that can be located from the Exif data is the presence of a thumbnail image within the photograph. Digital cameras generate a small version of the photo captured and store it within the Exif data. This icon size image adds very little size to the overall file. When a user crops the image, this original smaller version may or may not get overwritten. Programs such as Photoshop or Microsoft Photo Editor will overwrite the data and keep both images identical. Other programs, as well as some online cropping tools, do not overwrite this data. The result is the presence of the original and un-cropped image within the Exif data of the cropped photo. You can now see what the image looked like before it was cropped.

It is possible to delete or manipulate this Exif data. If you have a situation where it is necessary to upload photos to the internet, you may want to consider removing this metadata. This process is often referred to as "scrubbing" a photo. There are several ways to accomplish this.

If you have a computer that uses Microsoft Windows as an operating system, you are ready to edit this data immediately. Locate an image on your hard drive, right-click the file name, and select "Properties". This will present a new window with a tab titled "Details". Click on this tab and review the information. If the data attached to this image contains information that you do not want to share with the world, click on the link "Remove Properties and Personal Information". This will allow you the option to remove specific data from the image. I recommend choosing the "Select All" button to be sure that all of the Exif data is removed. If you are using a different operating system, there are several free applications that will remove this data, as well as online services. Again, we prefer local tools since they do not require us to transmit our photos to the cloud.

Exif Remover

This website (**verexif.com/en/**) allows you to upload a digital image and either view or remove the metadata attached to it. Click on the "Browse" button, locate the photo you want to edit, and click "Remove Exif". You will be presented with a new download that will contain your image without the Exif data embedded. ExifTool will also allow you to remove this data without touching the internet.

BatchPurifier

BatchPurifier is a very simple local application for Windows computers. Open the application and drag the appropriate photos into the GUI. Click Next, and on the Filters Selection screen you can individually choose the items to be removed from the photos or click the "Select All" button. This will select all possible Exif items for removal. Click Next and on the following screen choose either a name and location for the new, Exif-free files, or choose "Overwrite existing files". We generally prefer the latter option. On the next screen choose "Purify". New versions of your files will be written, without the accompanying metadata. BatchPurifier Lite is free and will clean JPEGs only. The paid version will remove metadata from many other file types, as well. Both the free and paid versions are available at **http://www.digitalconfidence.com/batchpurifier.html**.

Deleting Photo Sharing Accounts

Has this information motivated you to delete your photos uploaded to photo sharing networks? The following is a list of the most common services used in past years to upload and share photos. Many of these are no longer popular, but any content uploaded is still present today. If you do locate photos that need to be removed, you must log into the account that was used to upload them. If you did not create the account, you will need to contact the friend or family member that did.

You may find that your account settings on these photo sharing networks block your images from public view. I urge you to use caution with this restriction. In my experience, privacy settings only keep out the honest people. Hackers know how to bypass these and steal your content. Always assume that anything posted to the internet is public. Always choose strong privacy settings, but do not rely on them. Consider removing any undesired photos from the following accounts.

500px	Fotki	Ipernity	Photobucket	Snapfish
Bayimg	Fotolog	jAlbum	Pinterest	TinyPic
Dayviews	GifBoom	Lafango	Pixabay	Vhoto
DeviantArt	Imgur	Panoramio	Shutterfly	yfrog
Flickr	Instagram	Phanfare	SmugMug	

What is so bad about online photos?

Neither of us have photos on the internet. This is a very conscious decision based upon our views of privacy. We can think of many reasons why you might not want photos online, and the following may justify our harsh stance.

- Most private investigators will conduct a photo search before initiating any type of surveillance. If your adversary has hired a P.I. to tail you and document your activity, the absence of a public photo makes it a bit more difficult.

- Media outlets constantly scour the internet for embarrassing photos of subjects involved in the hot story of the day. We have seen journalists ignore respectful photos of someone in the news because of an unfortunate event and instead choose to show the most inappropriate option available.

- The photos available of you can be taken out of context. The image of you jokingly appearing unconscious at the bar years earlier may be used against you when you are seeking a position at a conservative company.

- Finally, you cannot take them back. We must assume that anything posted to the internet stays there forever in some form. Decisions today to post images online cannot be reversed later when desired. Proactive policies on removing current photos, and eliminating future images, might benefit you drastically some day.

Google Maps

Unless you live in a very rural area or at the end of a mile-long private drive, a street view of your house is probably on the internet. Google has been taking 360 degree photos from every street in the country for years. People can then use the Google Maps website to see images of a residence or business. This often identifies personal and work vehicles, physical security vulnerabilities, and occasionally family members standing in the yard. Many people assume that there is nothing that can be done about this. Removing these images is quite easy.

- Navigate to the Google Maps website and type in your home address. There will be a red marker on the map hovering over your house. Click on this marker and look at the options in the popup menu. If there is a street view of your house, this option will appear in this window. Click on the Street View link to open a new view which can be moved and zoomed with the mouse.

- On this new view, manipulate the image so that you can see your house on the screen. On the lower left portion of the image, there is a link titled "Report a problem". Click on this link and view the resulting page.

- The first section of this page asks "Why are you reporting this street view?" Select "Privacy Concerns", then "My House", and then "I have found a picture of my house and would like it blurred". In the next section, enter your privacy concern which can be "I have found a picture of my house and would like it blurred". Enter your anonymous email address and make sure that the red box on the image below is surrounding your house. Complete the word verification and click "Submit".

We have heard about both success stories and failures. Some people have reported that they added one of the following lines in the description window to obtain immediate removal.

"Photo identifies a building used for home-schooling students". We like this one. Most likely, you have taught a child something in your home at some point. Technically, you were home-schooling.

"Photo identifies physical security vulnerabilities of the building". This one is a great catch-all as well. Every building has a physical vulnerability such as a door lock, windows, or attic vent. Your home would qualify for this.

"Photo identifies home of a covert police officer targeted by violent criminals". For the law enforcement community, this seems to get their attention. If you believe that you would not qualify as a covert officer, think again. Have you ever been involved in a work situation off duty or in civilian clothes? That sounds covert to us. If you have not, report some speeders on the highway to your immediate supervisor while off duty and "under cover". You now qualify. You will immediately receive an email confirmation from Google and a removal confirmation within 48 hours. Check and verify that the image has been removed or blurred.

Blogs

An individual blog is a website where a user can publish personal content. These are often compared to a diary kept in public view. They are popular with teens and young adults. Often, the site will include text, photos, and videos. The text is usually personal and occasionally discloses information that is later undesired. Items that were posted publicly by a naïve teenager often become regrets by that same adult later seeking employment. The most common free blog services are provided by Tumblr, Blogger, WordPress, and Blog. The method of deleting a blog is different on each service and is outlined below.

Tumblr

This Yahoo owned service is now the most popular blogging website. Millions of users upload billions of posts for the world to see. Some of this is innocent, some intrusive, some illegal, but all removable. The following steps will permanently remove your account.

- Log into Tumblr at **tumblr.com** and visit your settings page from the left corner.

- Scroll to the bottom and choose Delete account.

Blogger

Blogger, owned by Google, does not give you the option to delete your blog after it has been published. There are no options in your account settings that allow you to close your account. Instead, you must take a manual approach.

- Log into your Blogger profile. This will be the same credentials used to log into your other Google accounts, and you should be automatically logged in if you are already signed in to any Google service. You should be directed to your Blogger Overview page. If not, click on "My Blogs". Click on "Posts" on the menu on the left of the page. This will present every post published on the blog. Select each box next to each post and then click the trash can icon.

- Edit your profile to remove any personal information stored there. For required fields, you can enter false information. To access this content, click on your username in the upper right corner of any blog page. This will present a menu with an option of "Account Settings". Click this and remove or edit personal data.

- Change your username on Blogger to something not related to you. We recommend a string of random characters. This will prevent any traces of your old blog from being associated with you.

WordPress

Similar to Blogger, WordPress will not let you delete your account. They will allow you to delete any individual blogs though.

- Log into your WordPress profile page and click on the "My Blog" tab. This will provide a list of all blogs that exist in the account. Click on the "Dashboard" link under each blog.

- Highlight the "Tools" option on the left menu. This will present a link titled "Delete Site". The next page will ask for a reason for this action. Choose the last option of "Permanently delete the blog name and all content". Check the box to confirm this action and click the button to execute the removal.

- Check your email account that was used to originally create the blog. You will receive a verification email that will include a link to confirm the removal. Repeat this process for any other blogs in the account.

Blog

Until recently, the only option for removing a personal blog on this site was to submit a help ticket and request removal from customer service. You can now complete this on your own account.

- Sign in to your account on **blog.com**. On your dashboard, click "Settings" and then "Delete Blog". This will present a large button titled "Delete My Site Permanently". You will receive an email at the address that you used when creating your account. Click on the verification link in this email to confirm the deletion.

Everything Else

There are hundreds of social networking websites. They each have their own method for proper account deletion and few of them make these instructions easy to find. The websites Account Killer (**accountkiller.com**), Just Delete Me (**justdelete.me**) and WikiCancel (**wikicancel.org**) offer detailed instruction on deleting hundreds of different accounts. If you have a rare site that is not mentioned here, conduct a search on a couple of search engines and you are likely to find everything you need. Many of you will find that you have never opened a social network account, yet there are many personal details out there about your family. This is often posted by parents, siblings and children. You will not be able to take direct action against an online profile that you do not have access to. If you want the data removed, you will need to approach the friend or family member that posted the content.

CHAPTER EIGHT
PERSONAL DATA REMOVAL

The removal process of your information is usually easy, with a few exceptions. Most services will offer you a website to request they remove your details. These direct links are often hidden within fine print or rarely visited pages. Our goal in this chapter is to take the research out of the removal process and simply tell you where to start. Many of the links listed here are long and easily mistyped. We encourage you to visit the resources section of our websites. As mentioned before, the link called "Privacy" will have everything you need.

The book "Hiding from the Internet" outlined specific details of the data removal process for each service that was mentioned. It also included screen captures displaying the process. Since its original release in 2012, many new data collection companies have surfaced. Instead of explaining each step of the process for every service, we decided to compress this information throughout this chapter. We did not include any screen captures in order to provide removal details of every service that we could locate within the space limitations of the chapter. This section should be used as a workbook.

Each removal summary will display several pieces of information about each service that we have identified. The following structure outlines the data that is displayed throughout this chapter. The final line will have blank forms for you to document your work and successful removals.

Service: The name of the service　　　　**Category**: The type of website
Website: The website of the service
Removal Link: The direct link for online removal, if available
Privacy Policy: Page containing detailed instructions
Email Address: Any email addresses that will reach an employee responsible for removal
Requirements: Any special requirements, such as a copy of an ID or written request
Notes: Any special instructions
Date: (date of request)　　**Response**: (response received)　　**Verified**: (confirm removal)

The "Date" field should list the date that you submitted the removal request. The "Response" should include any details received from the service after your submission. The "Verified" option should be used to "check-off" that service after you have confirmed that your details have been removed. Repeat the process using initials for family members and friends. All resources are listed in alphabetical order for easy reference.

The data supplied in the email address field could be used for unsuccessful removal attempts. If the official removal process for that service does not meet your needs, we recommend sending an email to the company. We have tried to locate email addresses of employees that appear to be responsible for removal requests. We suggest the following message be sent from the anonymous email address that you created earlier.

> I have been unsuccessful in removing my personal information from your website. Per the information provided from your legal privacy policy, please remove the following details from your service.
>
> Full Name (As appears on their service)
> Physical Address (As appears on their service)
> Telephone Number (ONLY if it appears on their service)
> Email Address (ONLY if it appears on their service)

This chapter is displayed within five unique sections:

People & Telephone Search: Free websites that expose your home information.

Public Data Brokers: Companies that sell your data for public use.

Non-Public Data Brokers: Companies that sell your data for private use.

Data Marketers: Companies that collect and sell your interests for targeted marketing.

Ancestry Records: Services that display family information provided by users.

At the end of each section, we present the workbook portion that will help you issue your data removal requests. We recommend pursuing data removal in the section order presented. The most important may be people search databases.

People & Telephone Search Engines

When a person wants to locate your home address, telephone number, family information, or associations, he or she will probably visit an online people directory website. These sites give anyone with internet access a view into your personal details. When we were young, the only option for this type of information was a phone book or community roster. If the subject of interest paid for an unlisted number, we were out of luck. Today, an unlisted number and address mean nothing to the internet. Other sources, such as tax data, social networks, resumes, and marketing databases, fill in the gaps. The people and telephone search websites listed at the end of this section are mostly free to access. They create revenue by enticing visitors to pay for premium data in the form of a complete background check. These premium services are often disappointing.

Deleting Inaccurate Information

During your information deletion process, you are likely to locate inaccurate data. You may find a previous address or addresses where you no longer reside. Many privacy advocates encourage people to leave this information online to protect real addresses. This is an example of disinformation. We do not recommend leaving any information online that was ever accurate. While the expired data may not be a privacy issue, it can create a serious security problem.

Many services will require you to complete a questionnaire to confirm your identity. Common examples would be when you open a new bank account online or request a credit report. The questions generated during this automated process are validated through your current credit report and personal profile. These questions are designed to be difficult to answer by anyone except you. The questions usually reference previous addresses and the precise amount of specific bills. The following example illustrates how leaving your previous addresses online can jeopardize your identity.

An identity thief decides to open a new credit line in your name. He has already obtained your full name, date of birth, and Social Security number from various sources. He completes a form on a credit lender's website and is asked two security questions to verify the identity. Your security questions likely include a previous residence street and current home mortgage holder. This type of verification is common on financial websites. The multiple choices make it easy to guess the correct answer, but an educated thief will conduct a quick search. Searching the victim's name on Spokeo identifies a previous residence addresses with the numbers masked. The same search on Spokeo would also reveal your relatives, one of which is most likely your mother. He could then use that information to find her maiden name. As this example illustrates "mother's maiden name" is a very insecure mechanism for verifying identity but it is still commonly used by banks and other financial services.

This scenario is far too common. This is why we recommend erasing all information from public view. An old address on a reverse search website can haunt you later. If you find information associated with you that has never been correct, you should leave it. If a people search website identifies your residence as a location where you have never lived, this can be beneficial. Disinformation is an effective privacy layer.

Do Not Call Registry

This is the most common opt-out request conducted by people. It adds your telephone number to a database of numbers that are passed on to telemarketing companies from the government. The companies are forced to remove these numbers from their automated systems used for telemarketing. This should stop unwanted sales calls and add an extremely thin layer of privacy for you. You can register landlines and cellular numbers, and it is recommended that you register all numbers that you own.

- Navigate to donotcall.gov and click the "Register a Phone Number" button. Identify up to three telephone numbers that you want removed from telemarketers' databases. Provide your anonymous email address and click "Submit". Verify the information and again click "Submit".

- Check your inbox. You will receive a separate message for each number that you registered. Click on the link in each message to confirm the removal request. You will be forwarded to confirmation that the number was entered into the registry.

Nomorobo

While the Do Not Call Registry will likely stop many of the undesired calls that you receive from telemarketers, it is not perfect. As a backup, consider registering with Nomorobo at **nomorobo.com**. You must provide your type of connection (cell, landline, VOIP), service provider, and telephone number. You must also provide a working email address, such as your anonymous personal account created earlier. Some carriers are not supported yet.

Landline Telephone Numbers

Telephone number directories are generally split into two categories, landline and cellular. The way that landline data is acquired is much different than cellular data. Much of the landline data is obtained from the companies that create phonebooks and city directories. This data originates with the telephone companies that provide the service. If you have a landline telephone at your house in your name, this information is available to the public. If your number is unlisted, that does not mean that it is not in public databases. In fact, most people with unlisted numbers are listed in the online directories mentioned in this chapter. This is because public information, such as voter records and tax data, leak telephone numbers into public databases. If your number is not listed as private, you should request this option with your telephone service provider.

During this contact with the telephone company, we recommend that you update your contact information with them. Once you have established service with the telephone company, there is no further need for them to verify your details and check your credit. You can now basically change your information to whatever you want. Obviously, the address of service must stay the same. However, you can change your billing address to your post office box address. This will eliminate your home address from a database that is shared for marketing purposes. Your bill will now be sent to the post office box.

Next, consider changing the name on the account. This cannot be a complete change, but changing a portion of the name will make your listing more difficult to find. For women, the easiest change would be your last name. Calling the telephone company and notifying them of a last name change is common. There is no verification process. If you are married, you may want to change it to your maiden name. If you are not, tell them you recently were married and give them your mother's maiden name. While this may seem like you are providing unnecessary personal details, maiden names usually pass identity verification. For men, consider a change of the spelling. We have found success with conversations using the following template.

"Hello, my name is Michael Bazzell, and I have service through your company. This really is not that big of a deal, but your contact information for me has my name spelled completely wrong, and I would like to finally correct your records. You have my first name as "Mike", but it is actually "Michael" spelled M-I-C-H-E-L. My last name is spelled B-A-S-I-L. Could you correct the record?"

These corrections are made immediately and verified. Now, the listing has your first and last name spelled incorrectly. You may wish to obscure your details even further by making incremental changes. For example, the follow month your wife or girlfriend could call and state the following: "my name is actually Michelle Basil. I know this is not a big deal but could you correct the spelling of my first name? The correct spelling is M-I-C-H-E-L-L-E".

Now the name on the account is both misspelled, and of the opposite gender. Anyone researching your location will have difficulty finding this listing. Through persistence, creativity, and subtle, incremental changes you can eventually modify your name to something entirely different. If you receive a representative who will not change your name, hang up and try again. It is very likely that you will get a different operator. Through trial and error, you are almost certain to find one who would be willing to change your name in the system.

Companies will probably acquire this data and continue to make new databases. This will not have a negative impact on you since your last name is spelled differently or changed completely. It may even help you create disinformation by making it look like a different person lives at your physical address if you have not yet migrated your bill to a PO Box. You should now focus on removing the correct data from the internet.

Cellular Telephone Numbers

There are fewer cellular number directories than landline directories. There is no official White Pages-style of phonebook for cellular numbers. That does not mean that the numbers are private. Many companies are attempting to create databases of cellular numbers and make them available to the masses. There are several methods they use to collect your number.

All of these databases rely on someone supplying a cellular number to them. Usually, this is you. When you use your cellular number as a contact for anything official, you take the chance of this number becoming public information. For example, when you sign up to win the new car at the mall and supply your name, number, and address, that information gets added to a large database. When you locate and print online coupons, you are often required to provide your personal information including a telephone number. This content also gets added to various databases. The advancements in technology allow for immediate identification of a telephone number to determine if it is a landline or cellular number. This identification can also be added to the database. Later chapters discuss how you should protect this information in the future. Next are the methods for removing your cellular number from databases.

Caller ID Databases

You probably know that when you call a landline telephone number from your home landline service, you pass along the caller identification (caller ID) information about your account. If your home phone is registered in your name, your name will appear on the caller ID screen of the receiving telephone. Many people do not realize that the name associated with your cellular telephone is also provided to the receiver's caller ID. Most cellular companies now announce your name and number when you call landline telephones. You cannot stop this data from being transmitted, and this practice is acceptable to the telephone companies because you are generating the contact by placing the call. Only a few years ago, this would have been fairly safe. Today, anyone can look up your cellular number.

There is an abundance of reverse caller ID service providers that will allow anyone to identify the owner of a number for less than a penny. One service that currently offers a free trial of this type of query is Who Calld. Navigate to **whocalld.com** and search your cellular or landline number. If you do not see your name, click the "Update" button.

You will likely see your name and cellular service provider displayed publicly. Attempting the same search at numerous reverse caller ID providers will also likely present your name as associated with your cellular number. There is no point in contacting these providers and requesting removal. While some have this option, most do not. Additionally, your data will be repopulated soon by your cellular provider or another third party company. Instead, you should consider modifying the subscriber information on your account. The following true scenario should help guide you through your own process.

Michael's Experience

I conducted a search for a relative's number through seven unique reverse caller ID services. All of them accurately identified her name as associated with her number. With permission, I logged into her online billing account and viewed her details. She was one of five members of a family plan with AT&T. Not only was AT&T providing the information of the subscriber, but also each individual name associated with each number on the family plan. I changed this relative's name to "A. Unknown". Within seven days, I conducted another query on her cellular number. The caller ID information associated with it was updated to "A Unknown".

Justin's Experience

I conducted a search for a friend's telephone number. I found that half of the online databases had her name listed correctly, while the other half had a different name that I will call "David Brown". This name was consistent across all of the listings so I assumed it was the former owner of that number. With permission I logged into her Verizon Wireless account and changed her name on the account to that of the former account holder. Within fourteen days I conducted another search. All the queries returned either "David Brown" or "D Brown". Her name was no longer associated with this number in any of the online databases.

You can likely log into your own online portal for your cellular account. If you are on a family plan, attempt to change the name as it appears for your individual number. If you are not within a family plan and have only one number on the account, attempt to change the name associated with the bill. Some services allow this activity through their website. If yours does not, consider calling them and specifically ask to change the information associated with your caller ID.

Other Online Directories

New websites promising accurate reverse telephone number information appear regularly. Some of these stick around and achieve slight growth, but most disappear or become unused. Those that are useful tend to become acquired by larger data companies. You should routinely conduct a search of your telephone number on Google and Bing to view the results. If you find too many spam results, try placing quotes around the number. If you find a website that has posted your personal information, start snooping around and try to find a link titled "Privacy" or "Terms of Service". These links often identify the procedure for removing your information. If you cannot find such a process, there is one last thing to try.

Most data mining websites, including telephone directories, have established some type of policy that prohibits children from posting their information. If this information is identified by the company, a manual removal is conducted immediately. As an example, assume that you found your telephone number and address on the website cellrevealer.com. This site offers mediocre reverse cellular telephone number lookups. They do not have any sort of removal option and provide no opt-out instructions. However, at the end of their privacy policy is the following content.

"We are in compliance with the requirements of COPPA (Children's Online Privacy Protection Act), we do not collect any information from anyone under 13 years of age. Our website, products and services are all directed to people who are at least 13 years old or older".

COPPA is an act passed by congress in 1998 which can be found in its entirety online. It was created to place parents in control over what information is collected from their young children online. The Rule was designed to protect children under age 13 while accounting for the dynamic nature of the internet. The Rule applies to operators of commercial websites and online services directed to children under 13 that collect, use, or disclose personal information from children, and it applies to operators of general audience websites or online services with actual knowledge that they are collecting, using, or disclosing personal information from children under 13. Basically, it makes it illegal for a website to knowingly display any personal information about children under the age of 13. This is one reason you see many social networks enforce an age limit.

You can use this to your advantage. If you have a child under the age of 13 in your home, this may be a way to force websites to remove your information. Let us explain by providing two different scenarios.

Scenario # 1: Your child is eight years of age and lives in your residence. You conducted a search of your cellular telephone number on cellrevealer.com which identified your name and address. On occasion, your child uses this telephone number to communicate with friends and family. Therefore, it is fair to say that cellrevealer.com currently displays information that identifies a cellular telephone number used by a child under the age of thirteen and associates the number with the child's home address.

Scenario # 2: You have no children, but you have a niece that is ten years of age that occasionally visits your house. When she is there, she often uses your landline telephone to stay in touch with her parents. You located your landline telephone number listed on numberguru.com which identified your home address. Therefore, it is fair to say that numberguru.com currently displays information that identifies a landline telephone number used by a child under the age of 13 and associates the number with the child's current location.

Sending the following email to any contact email address on the website should generate immediate action.

"It has come to my attention that your website displays information that identifies a cellular telephone number used by a child under the age of 13 and associates the number with the child's home address. This is a violation of the Children's Online Privacy Protection Act (COPPA). I request that the following information be removed from your database immediately".

This probably sounds sneaky and misleading. Only you can decide if protecting your privacy is worth any ethical dilemmas. In our collective conscience it is more unethical to collect personal information from people and broadcast it to the world for a profit than to use legal loopholes to have your own information removed. This tactic could be applied to other websites that disclose information such as home addresses, social network data, personal interests, and friends or associates. In our experience, few companies will decline a request such as this. They are more afraid of being sued than eliminating a single entry.

Everything Else

By the time that you read these words, much will have changed in the world of digital privacy. Michael began documenting methods for information removal in 2011. It was much more manageable then and changes rarely occurred. Today, new data collection websites seem to appear daily and the existing sites change their removal process often. No written work like this can remain timeless in our digital age. This portion is designed to aid you with any future issues that you discover which jeopardize your right to privacy.

Privacy Policies

You will likely encounter new personal information websites that are not listed in this book. During your Pre-Assessment in Chapter Four, you may find unique online information about yourself that you want removed. When an opt-out process is not obvious on the website, always look for a privacy policy page. These are often linked from the very bottom of the home page and the link is commonly in small print.

The privacy pages often contain very detailed text about how the company receives and shares the personal information that it collects. It will usually discuss how it uses cookies on your computer to collect further details and what your options are for disabling this technology. Many of the techniques that we have shared in this book come directly from privacy pages of the businesses discussed. Look for specific instructions to opt-out or remove your information through these pages.

Some websites possess a privacy policy page but do not link to it from their home page. This fulfills the requirement to offer an opt-out process, but makes it difficult to locate the page with instructions. A specific query on Google or any other search engine should assist you. While researching everify.com, we immediately noticed that there was not an obvious opt-out process or privacy page, but eventually learned that these details were stored within a small

"Legal" link between several other unrelated links. Instead of clicking through a lot of irrelevant content, you can conduct the following search on Google.

Site:everify.com "Opt-out"

In this example, "site:everify.com" instructs Google to only search one specific domain. It will ignore any other websites and bring all results relevant to your search. The "Opt-out" within quotation marks informs Google to only display results that have that exact phrase within the page or document. The actual result of this search is a PDF document that is exactly what you would need to complete their removal process. The following searches may be helpful. Replace everify.com with the website from which you are trying to remove your information.

Site:everify.com "privacy page"
Site:everify.com "privacy policy"
Site:everify.com "privacy"
Site:everify.com "opt out"
Site:everify.com "removal"
Site:everify.com "legal"

Email Messages

Some services will not offer an online form or document for personal information removal. They may force you to contact them directly with your request. For many companies, this fulfills their obligation to offer a removal option. The direct contact deters many people from proceeding with the process. An email message will often achieve the desired result.

Identifying the appropriate email address to send requests can range from obvious to difficult. Many privacy policy pages include a generic account for opt-out requests such as privacy@eburesu.com. This is likely an account that is monitored by many different people. We list these in the workbook section as we find them. Some services do not publicly list the most appropriate address, so you will need to take a couple of additional steps in order to locate a helpful address.

Email Assumptions

Most companies have a standard format for all of their email addresses. This will often include a combination of a last name and first name at the business domain, such as john.smith@eburesu .com. These companies usually also have a standard account that is set up to receive requests for removal of information, such as privacy@eburesu.com. Any time you find a company that does not include an obvious removal process for your personal data, consider sending an email to several possible accounts. In the case of eburesu.com, you could send a removal request to the following accounts.

remove@ebureau.com
removal@ebureau.com
optout@ebureau.com
opt-out@ebureau.com
privacy@ebureau.com
legal@ebureau.com
info@ebureau.com
questions@ebureau.com
contact@ebureau.com
support@ebureau.com
admin@ebureau.com

Some of these email addresses will likely not exist and you will receive a message delivery error. Often, you will be fortunate in delivering at least one message to someone that can help. If you want to be more precise about this tactic, you could test the email addresses first.

Email Verification

Mail Tester (**mailtester.com**) is a free service that will allow you to immediately test an email address to determine if it is valid. The response will confirm that an email server exists, that it is functioning, and that the designated email address is real. A valid email result should be all green in color while any presence of red indicates a bad address.

LinkedIn

If you have submitted email messages to the standard accounts such as remove and privacy and did not get any results, you may consider contacting key employees directly. The best way to identify the appropriate contacts is through LinkedIn (**linkedin.com**).

For example, assume that you have completed the information removal process at EBureau, but your information was never removed. You now want to reach out to a real human for assistance. The following steps will likely receive a response from an employee.

- Conduct a search for "EBureau" on LinkedIn. Many of these will not display the name of the person, and will only display "LinkedIn Member". Some will display the name of the employee.

- Attempt to identify an employee that possesses an important role at the company. Our search displayed the profile of a senior vice president of EBureau. Unfortunately, the name is redacted, but you can still identify it with some internet investigation.

- Open the profile and right-click on the photo. Choose the option to copy the image location, which is sometimes referred to as the image URL.

- Connect to **images.google.com** and click on the small camera icon within the search field. This will display a new window. Paste the URL or address of the LinkedIn image and click "Search by image". It identifies another identical image which identifies the individual as Mic O'Brien.

- Alternatively, search Google for the terms "Vice President EBureau" and document any employee names discovered.

- Determine the email format of employee addresses at the company. Search for "@eureau.com" with the quotation marks to identify any email addresses publicly visible. A search result identified a website announcing an EBureau event that includes contact information. These details announce that Anna Haire's email address is annahaire@eureau.com. We can now assume that the email format is first name + last name @eureau.com.

- Combine the employee names that you discovered with the domain of @eureau.com and test them with mailtester.com. This will display a result confirming micobrien@eureau.com is valid. You now have the email address of a senior vice president at the company.

- Repeat this process for numerous employees and send each a polite request for action in regards to your removal request.

Fax Requests

Many businesses will publish a facsimile (fax) number on their public websites. While these numbers may not be the appropriate reception for removal requests, the message will be received by an employee who may forward it to the person responsible for the information. Conduct the following steps in order to identify the fax numbers of a business.

Perform a Google search for the name of the company and the word fax, both within separate quotation marks. Our search identified a valid fax number of 320-534-5020 for that business.

Direct Telephone Call

If all else fails to get you the results you desire, consider making a telephone call. This has been the least effective method in our experience. However, we have on occasion spoken to very helpful employees who were willing to help us remove our information. Since most people do not choose this method, employees are fairly surprised to get a call for a removal request. Search through the target business' websites, and conduct searches for the company name and the word "phone".

Additional Privacy Information

We learn new information about our privacy, and lack thereof, every day while we conduct research for our own purposes. One of the best resources for extremely current content is the Privacy page on Reddit. We encourage you to visit and bookmark the following website for the most vital information about the state of privacy: **reddit.com/r/Privacy**.

Online Removal Databases

On the following pages, we have tried to identify the most common online databases that reveal personal details about you. We have found that removing information from these services has the most impact on enhancing your overall online privacy. Listing every service that may have information stored about you is not feasible. Fortunately, there are several websites that maintain a list of removal options. You can always find a current list of Opt-Out instructions for most data vendors at the following websites.

www.inteltechniques.com
www.computercrimeinfo.com
www.justdelete.me
www.privacyrights.org/online-information-brokers-list
www.abine.com/optouts.php

While this book maintains a focus on removal from the most prevalent data collection companies, you may find your information on smaller, unlisted websites. If you do, there is probably a direct link to a page to assist with the removal process.

It is now time for you to attack the invasive websites that disclose your private information to the world. Turn the page and begin your adventure.

Service: **10 Digits**   **Category**: Telephone Search
Website: 10digits.us
Removal Link: 10digits.us/remove
Privacy Policy: 10digits.us/privacy/
Email Address: mail@10digits.us
Requirements: Online submission
Notes: Online removal tool will complete the process.
Date: _____ **Response**: _____ **Verified Removal**: _____

Service: **411**   **Category**: Telephone Search
Website: 411.com
Removal Link: None
Privacy Policy: www.whitepagescustomers.com/data-policy/
Email Address: support@411.com, support@whitepages.com
Requirements: Online submission
Notes: Remove entry from whitepages.com
Date: _____ **Response**: _____ **Verified Removal**: _____

Service: **411 Info**   **Category**: Telephone Search
Website: 411.info
Removal Link: 411.info/manage/
Privacy Policy: 411.info/privacy/
Email Address: support@411.info, admin@411.info
Requirements: Online submission
Notes: Online removal tool will complete the process.
Date: _____ **Response**: _____ **Verified Removal**: _____

Service: Addresses   **Category**: People Search
Website: addresses.com
Removal Link: addresses.com/optout.php
Privacy Policy: www.addresses.com/terms.php
Email Address: support@addresses.com, admin@addresses.com
Requirements: Online submission
Notes: Online removal tool will complete the process.
Date: _____ **Response**: _____ **Verified Removal**: _____

Service: **Advanced Background Checks**   **Category**: People Search
Website: advancedbackgroundchecks.com
Removal Link: advancedbackgroundchecks.com/optout-form.pdf
Privacy Policy: www.advancedbackgroundchecks.com/privacy
Email Address: Unknown
Requirements: Postal mail submission
Notes: Print and mail online form.
Date: _____ **Response**: _____ **Verified Removal**: _____

Service: **Anywho**   **Category**: People Search
Website: anywho.com
Removal Link: None
Privacy Policy: corporate.yp.com/privacy-policy/
Email Address: ypcsupport@yp.com, press@yp.com
Requirements: Online submission
Notes: Select profile and choose "Remove Listing".
Date: _____ **Response**: _____ **Verified Removal**: _____

Service: **DOB Search**   **Category**: People Search
Website: www.dobsearch.com
Removal Link: Embedded into results
Privacy Policy: www.dobsearch.com/privacy.php
Email Address: support@dobsearch.com
Requirements: Online submission
Notes: Search your name and click "Manage my listings" at bottom. Follow instructions.
Date: _____ **Response**: _____ **Verified Removal**: _____

Service: **Email Finder**   **Category**: People Search
Website: emailfinder.com
Removal Link: www.emailfinder.com/EFC.aspx?_act=Optout
Privacy Policy: www.emailfinder.com/privacypolicy.shtml
Email Address: Unknown
Requirements: Online submission
Notes: Online removal tool will complete the process.
Date: _____ **Response**: _____ **Verified Removal**: _____

Service: Free Phone Tracer   **Category**: Telephone Search
Website: www.freephonetracer.com
Removal Link: freephonetracer.com/FCPT.aspx?_act=Optout
Privacy Policy: freephonetracer.com/FCPT.aspx?_act=PrivacyPolicy
Email Address: privacy@ freephonetracer.com
Requirements: Online submission
Notes: Online removal tool will complete the process.
Date: _____ **Response**: _____ **Verified Removal**: _____

Service: Infospace   **Category**: People Search
Website: infospace.com
Removal Link: infospace.intelius.com/optout.php
Privacy Policy: support.infospace.com/privacy
Email Address: support@infospace.com, info@infospace.com
Requirements: Online submission
Notes: Online removal tool will complete the process.
Date: _____ **Response**: _____ **Verified Removal**: _____

Service: Lookup   **Category**: People Search
Website: lookup.com
Removal Link: lookup.com/optout.php
Privacy Policy: www.lookup.com/privacy.php
Email Address: optout@lookup.com
Requirements: Online submission
Notes: Online removal tool will complete the process.
Date: _____ **Response**: _____ **Verified Removal**: _____

Service: Lookup Anyone   **Category**: People Search
Website: lookupanyone.com
Removal Link: None
Privacy Policy: www.lookupanyone.com/privacy-faq.php
Email Address: support@lookupanyone.com, info@lookupanyone.com
Requirements: Fax submission
Notes: Send your custom opt-out request form via fax to 425-974-6194
Date: _____ **Response**: _____ **Verified Removal**: _____

Service: MyLife
Website: www.mylife.com
Removal Link: None
Privacy Policy: www.mylife.com/privacy-policy/
Email Address: privacy@mylife.com
Requirements: Email submission
Notes: Send email with removal request.
Date: _____ **Response**: _____ **Verified Removal**: _____

Category: People Search

Service: PeekYou
Website: peekyou.com
Removal Link: www.peekyou.com/about/contact/optout/
Privacy Policy: www.peekyou.com/privacy
Email Address: support@peekyou.com
Requirements: Online submission
Notes: Online removal tool will complete the process.
Date: _____ **Response**: _____ **Verified Removal**: _____

Category: People Search

Service: PeepDB
Website: peepdb.com
Removal Link: None
Privacy Policy: www.peepdb.com/privacy.html
Email Address: info@peepdb.com
Requirements: Online submission
Notes: Locate your info and click on the "Remove This Listing" at bottom of page.
Date: _____ **Response**: _____ **Verified Removal**: _____

Category: People Search

Service: People By Name
Website: peoplebyname.com
Removal Link: www.peoplebyname.com/remove.php
Privacy Policy: www.peoplebyname.com/privacy.php
Email Address: support@peoplebyname.com
Requirements: Online submission
Notes: Online removal tool will complete the process.
Date: _____ **Response**: _____ **Verified Removal**: _____

Category: People Search

Service: People Finder　　　　　　　　　　　　　　**Category**: People Search
Website: peoplefinder.com
Removal Link: peoplefinder.com/optout.php
Privacy Policy: peoplefinder.com/privacy/
Email Address: support@peoplefinder.com, info@peoplefinder.com
Requirements: Online submission, email verification
Notes: Online removal tool will complete the process.
Date: _____ **Response**: _____ **Verified Removal**: _____

Service: People Finders　　　　　　　　　　　　　**Category**: People Search
Website: peoplefinders.com
Removal Link: peoplefinders.com/manage/default.aspx
Privacy Policy: www.peoplefinders.com/privacy.aspx
Email Address: support@peoplefinders.com
Requirements: Online submission, email verification
Notes: Select your profile, click "This is me", then "Opt-out my info".
Date: _____ **Response**: _____ **Verified Removal**: _____

Service: People Lookup　　　　　　　　　　　　　**Category**: People Search
Website: peoplelookup.com
Removal Link: None
Privacy Policy: www.peoplelookup.com/privacy.php
Email Address: support@peoplelookup.com, info@peoplelookup.com
Requirements: Fax submission
Notes: Send your custom opt-out request form via fax to 425-974-6194
Date: _____ **Response**: _____ **Verified Removal**: _____

Service: People Search Now　　　　　　　　　　　**Category**: People Search
Website: peoplesearchnow.com
Removal Link: www.peoplesearchnow.com/optout-form.pdf
Privacy Policy: www.peoplesearchnow.com/privacy
Email Address: support@peoplesearchnow.com, info@peoplesearchnow.com
Requirements: Postal mail submission
Notes: Complete form and mail to listed address.
Date: _____ **Response**: _____ **Verified Removal**: _____

Service: **People Smart**   **Category**: People Search
Website: peoplesmart.com
Removal Link: www.peoplesmart.com/optout-go
Privacy Policy: www.peoplesmart.com/privacy-policy
Email Address: privacy@peoplesmart.com
Requirements: Online submission
Notes: Online removal tool will complete the process.
Date: _____ **Response**: _____ **Verified Removal**: _____

Service: **Phone Detective**   **Category**: Telephone Search
Website: phonedetective.com
Removal Link: www.phonedetective.com/PD.aspx?_act=OptOut
Privacy Policy: www.phonedetective.com/PD.aspx?_act=PrivacyPolicy
Email Address: privacy@phonedetective.com
Requirements: Online submission
Notes: Online removal tool will complete the process.
Date: _____ **Response**: _____ **Verified Removal**: _____

Service: **Phone Number**   **Category**: Telephone Search
Website: phonenumber.com
Removal Link: None
Privacy Policy: www.whitepagescustomers.com/data-policy/
Email Address: support@phonenumber.com, support@whitepages.com
Requirements: Online submission
Notes: Remove entry from whitepages.com
Date: _____ **Response**: _____ **Verified Removal**: _____

Service: **Pipl**   **Category**: People Search
Website: pipl.com
Removal Link: pipl.com/directory/remove
Privacy Policy: pipl.com/privacy
Email Address: support@pipl.com
Requirements: Online submission, email verification
Notes: Must enter the required URL with your name as explained on the page.
Date: _____ **Response**: _____ **Verified Removal**: _____

Service: Poedit   **Category**: People Search
Website: poedit.org
Removal Link: toppeoplefinder.com/remove.aspx
Privacy Policy: toppeoplefinder.com/privacy.aspx
Email Address: Unknown
Requirements: Online submission
Notes: Select profile, copy URL, click "Removal Request" at bottom of page.
Date: _____ **Response**: _____ **Verified Removal**: _____

Service: Public Records 360   **Category**: People Search
Website: publicrecords360.com
Removal Link: publicrecords360.com/optout.html
Privacy Policy: www.publicrecords360.com/privacy.html
Email Address: optout@publicrecords360.com, privacy@ publicrecords360.com
Requirements: Postal mail submission
Notes: Complete opt-out form and email with ID to optout@publicrecords360.com.
Date: _____ **Response**: _____ **Verified Removal**: _____

Service: Radaris   **Category**: People Search
Website: radaris.com
Removal Link: None
Privacy Policy: radaris.com/page/privacy
Email Address: support@radaris.com, info@radaris.com
Requirements: Online submission, email verification
Notes: Select your profile; click "Information control" then "Hide Information".
Date: _____ **Response**: _____ **Verified Removal**: _____

Service: Reverse Genie   **Category**: People Search
Website: www.reversegenie.com
Removal Link: None
Privacy Policy: www.reversegenie.com/privacy.php
Email Address: support@reversegeniwe.com
Requirements: Postal mail or fax submission
Notes: Follow online instructions at www.reversegenie.com/data_optout.php
Date: _____ **Response**: _____ **Verified Removal**: _____

Service: **Reverse Phone Lookup**   **Category**: Telephone Search
Website: www. reversephonelookup.com
Removal Link: reversephonelookup.com/remove.php
Privacy Policy: www.reversephonelookup.com/privacy.html
Email Address: support@reversephonelookup.com, info@reversephonelookup.com
Requirements: Online submission
Notes: Online removal tool will complete the process.
Date: _____   **Response**: _____ **Verified Removal:** _____

Service: **Sales Spider**   **Category**: Business Search
Website: salespider.com
Removal Link: None
Privacy Policy: www.salespider.com/index.php?privacy=1
Email Address: support@salespider.com
Requirements: Online submission
Notes: Locate profile and select "Delete this profile".
Date: _____   **Response**: _____ **Verified Removal:** _____

Service: **Search Bug**   **Category**: People Search
Website: www.searchbug.com/tools/reverse-phone-lookup.aspx
Removal Link: None
Privacy Policy: www.searchbug.com/privacy.aspx
Email Address: support@searchbug.com
Requirements: Online submission
Notes: Follow online instructions at www.searchbug.com/help.aspx?WHAT=people
Date: _____   **Response**: _____ **Verified Removal:** _____

Service: **Spokeo**   **Category**: People Search
Website: spokeo.com
Removal Link: www.spokeo.com/optout
Privacy Policy: www.spokeo.com/privacy
Email Address: support@spokeo.com, customercare@spokeo.com
Requirements: Online submission, email verification
Notes: Online removal tool will complete the process.
Date: _____   **Response**: _____ **Verified Removal:** _____

Service: Super Pages **Category**: Telephone Search
Website: www.superpages.com
Removal Link: None
Privacy Policy: www.superpages.com/about/privacy.html
Email Address: support@superpages.com, info@superpages.com
Requirements: Online submission
Notes: Select profile and choose "Remove Listing".
Date: _____ **Response**: _____ **Verified Removal**: _____

Service: SwitchBoard **Category**: People Search
Website: switchboard.com
Removal Link: switchboard.intelius.com/optout.php
Privacy Policy: www.switchboard.com/privacy_central
Email Address: info@switchboard.com, support@switchboard.com
Requirements: Online submission
Notes: Online removal tool will complete the process.
Date: _____ **Response**: _____ **Verified Removal**: _____

Service: That's Them **Category**: People Search
Website: thatsthem.com
Removal Link: thatsthem.com/optout
Privacy Policy: thatsthem.com/privacy
Email Address: Unknown
Requirements: Online submission
Notes: Online removal tool will complete the process.
Date: _____ **Response**: _____ **Verified Removal**: _____

Service: Top People Finder **Category**: People Search
Website: toppeoplefinder.com
Removal Link: toppeoplefinder.com/remove.aspx
Privacy Policy: toppeoplefinder.com/privacy.aspx
Email Address: Unknown
Requirements: Online submission
Notes: Online removal tool will complete the process.
Date: _____ **Response**: _____ **Verified Removal**: _____

Service: US Identify   **Category**: People Search
Website: usidentify.com
Removal Link: None
Privacy Policy: www.usidentify.com/company/privacy.html
Email Address: privacy@peoplesmart.com
Requirements: Postal mail submission
Notes: Send custom opt-out form to address on privacy policy page.
Date: _____ **Response**: _____ **Verified Removal**: _____

Service: US Search   **Category**: People Search
Website: ussearch.com
Removal Link: ussearch.com/privacylock
Privacy Policy: ussearch.com/about/privacy
Email Address: cservice@ussearch.com, social@ussearch.com
Requirements: Online submission and fax report
Notes: Online removal tool will generate form. Fax form to 425-974-6242.
Date: _____ **Response**: _____ **Verified Removal**: _____

Service: W9R   **Category**: People Search
Website: w9r.com
Removal Link: None
Privacy Policy: www.w9r.com/about/privacy.html
Email Address: support@w9r.com
Requirements: Online submission
Notes: Locate profile and select "Opt out or remove".
Date: _____ **Response**: _____ **Verified Removal**: _____

Service: White Pages   **Category**: Telephone Search
Website: whitepages.com
Removal Link: None
Privacy Policy: www.whitepages.com/data-policy
Email Address: support@whitepages.com
Requirements: Online submission
Notes: Locate profile, click "Edit", create anonymous account, delete as desired.
Date: _____ **Response**: _____ **Verified Removal**: _____

Service: Yasni   **Category**: People Search
Website: yasni.com
Removal Link: None
Privacy Policy: yasni.com/privacy
Email Address: info@yasni.com, support@yasni.com
Requirements: Remove data from the original source
Notes: No removal option, but will identify sources of data. Will refresh occasionally.
Date: _____ **Response**: _____ **Verified Removal**: _____

Service: Yellow Pages   **Category**: Telephone Search
Website: www.yellowpages.com/reversephonelookup
Removal Link: None
Privacy Policy: corporate.yp.com/privacy-policy/
Email Address: ypcsupport@yp.com, press@yp.com
Requirements: Online submission
Notes: Select profile and choose "Remove Listing".
Date: _____ **Response**: _____ **Verified Removal**: _____

Service: Zabasearch   **Category**: People Search
Website: zabasearch.com
Removal Link: None
Privacy Policy: zabasearch.com/privacy.php
Email Address: info@zabasearch.com, response@zabasearch.com
Requirements: Fax submission
Notes: Send your custom opt-out request form via fax to 425-974-6194.
Date: _____ **Response**: _____ **Verified Removal**: _____

Service: ZoomInfo   **Category**: Business Info
Website: zoominfo.com
Removal Link: None
Privacy Policy: www.zoominfo.com/business/about-zoominfo/privacy-center
Email Address: info@zoominfo.com, support@zoominfo.com
Requirements: Online submission, email verification
Notes: Click "Is this you?" in your profile. Signup and delete desired details.
Date: _____ **Response**: _____ **Verified Removal**: _____

Public Data Brokers

Data brokers collect public information like names, home addresses, purchase histories, credit card activity and other sensitive data. They create large databases and then sell copies to other companies. It's mostly marketing companies that are interested in this information, particularly those that do online targeting. But most will sell the data to anyone that will pay. Some of the companies mentioned in the previous section are technically data brokers. Since their primary purpose is locating people, they were isolated from those in this section. The companies mentioned in this section collect and sell much more interesting data about you.

Aside from the basics needed to locate you, these data brokers, sometimes called information brokers, go deeper into your life to build a profile on you. Their databases include your DMV records, property records, voter records, weapon permits, internet search history, online comments, online aliases, shopping history, court history, and much more. Most of this is also geo-coded, which provides your location when the information was gathered. This is all done thanks to the advancements in technology and the internet. These companies take this data and package it into a profile that can be easily analyzed and used to target more products and services toward you. Removing your information from these databases will be similar to the methods discussed earlier.

Much like the previous section, these instructions are presented in workbook format. If anything ever seems unclear, refer to the privacy policy link. As a reminder, always consider the following tips.

- Never use your real email address. Use the new anonymous address that was created earlier. Most of these services will allow you to use your 333Mail forwarding address.

- Only provide information to these services that they already know. If you find your name and address on one service, it is safe to assume that they all know it, but do not voluntarily provide it.

- For those that require a postal mail submission, be sure to include all documentation required per the privacy page listed for each service. If you fail to include any mandated information, they will deny your request. They are not required to notify you of this denial.

- Take notes as you work through this process. Use a pencil or photocopy these pages for additional future use.

Turn the page and begin your removal of personal data from public data brokers.

Service: **Accutellus**   **Category**: Public Data Broker
Website: accutellus.com
Removal Link: accutellus.com/opt_out_request.php
Privacy Policy: www.accutellus.com/terms.php
Email Address: Unknown
Requirements: Online submission
Notes: Online removal tool will complete the process.
Date: _____ **Response**: _____ **Verified Removal**: _____

Service: **Address Search**   **Category**: Public Data Broker
Website: addresssearch.com
Removal Link: addresssearch.com/remove-info.php
Privacy Policy: www.addresssearch.com/privacy-policy.php
Email Address: support@addresssearch.com
Requirements: Online submission
Notes: Online removal tool will complete the process.
Date: _____ **Response**: _____ **Verified Removal**: _____

Service: **Axciom**   **Category**: Public Data Broker
Website: www.acxiom.com
Removal Link: www.isapps.acxiom.com/optout/optout.aspx
Privacy Policy: www.acxiom.com/about-acxiom/privacy/us-products-privacy-policy/
Email Address: consumeradvo@acxiom.com
Requirements: Online submission
Notes: Online removal tool will complete the process.
Date: _____ **Response**: _____ **Verified Removal**: _____

Service: **Been Verified**   **Category**: Public Data Broker
Website: www.beenverified.com
Removal Link: www.beenverified.com/faq/opt-out/
Privacy Policy: www.beenverified.com/privacy
Email Address: privacy@beenverified.com
Requirements: Online submission
Notes: Online removal tool will complete the process.
Date: _____ **Response**: _____ **Verified Removal**: _____

Service: Complete Investigation Services   **Category**: Public Data Broker
Website: www.cisnationwide.com
Removal Link: cisnationwide.com/optout.html
Privacy Policy: cisnationwide.com/privacy.html
Email Address: support@cisnationwide.com
Requirements: Fax submission
Notes: Fax required documents to 888-446-1229.
Date: _____ **Response**: _____ **Verified Removal**: _____

Service: Confi-Chek   **Category**: Public Data Broker
Website: confi-chek.com
Removal Link: None
Privacy Policy: None
Email Address: support@confi-chek.com
Requirements: Postal mail submission
Notes: Send opt-out form to PO Box 110850, Naples, Florida 34108.
Date: _____ **Response**: _____ **Verified Removal**: _____

Service: Core Logic   **Category**: Public Data Broker
Website: www.corelogic.com
Removal Link: None
Privacy Policy: www.corelogic.com/privacy.aspx
Email Address: privacy@ebureau.com
Requirements: Online submission
Notes: Online removal tool will complete the process.
Date: _____ **Response**: _____ **Verified Removal**: _____

Service: Data Detective   **Category**: Public Data Broker
Website: datadetective.com
Removal Link: www.datalogix.com/privacy/#opt-out-landing
Privacy Policy: www.datalogix.com/privacy/
Email Address: Unknown
Requirements: Fax submission
Notes: Fax required documents under "Opt Out Policy" to 617-993-9946.
Date: _____ **Response**: _____ **Verified Removal**: _____

Service: Datalogix   **Category**: Public Data Broker
Website: datalogix.com
Removal Link: None
Privacy Policy: www.interactivedata.com/privacy-policy/
Email Address: support@datalogix.com
Requirements: Online submission
Notes: Follow instructions under "Choice" section of removal link.
Date: _____ **Response**: _____ **Verified Removal**: _____

Service: EBureau   **Category**: Public Data Broker
Website: ebureau.com
Removal Link: www.ebureau.com/privacy-center/opt-out
Privacy Policy: www.ebureau.com/privacy-center
Email Address: Unknown
Requirements: Online submission
Notes: Online removal tool will complete the process.
Date: _____ **Response**: _____ **Verified Removal**: _____

Service: Instant Check Mate   **Category**: Public Data Broker
Website: instantcheckmate.com
Removal Link: instantcheckmate.com/optout
Privacy Policy: www.instantcheckmate.com/privacy_policy/
Email Address: privacy@instantcheckmate.com, support@instantcheckmate.com
Requirements: Online submission
Notes: Online removal tool will complete the process.
Date: _____ **Response**: _____ **Verified Removal**: _____

Service: Intelius   **Category**: Public Data Broker
Website: intelius.com
Removal Link: www.intelius.com/optout.php
Privacy Policy: www.intelius.com/privacy.php
Email Address: privacy@intelius.com
Requirements: Online submission
Notes: Online removal tool will complete the process.
Date: _____ **Response**: _____ **Verified Removal**: _____

Service: **Interactive Data**   **Category**: Public Data Broker
Website: interactivedata.com
Removal Link: None
Privacy Policy: www.interactivedata.com/privacy-policy/
Email Address: Investor.Relations@interactivedata.com
Requirements: Postal mail submission
Notes: Send opt-out form to address on privacy page.
Date: _____ **Response**: _____ **Verified Removal**: _____

Service: **LexisNexis Direct Marketing**   **Category**: Public Data Broker
Website: www.lexisnexis.com
Removal Link: www.lexisnexis.com/privacy/directmarketingopt-out.aspx
Privacy Policy: www.lexisnexis.com/privacy/
Email Address: privacy.information.mgr@lexisnexis.com
Requirements: Online submission
Notes: Online removal tool will complete the process.
Date: _____ **Response**: _____ **Verified Removal**: _____

Service: **LexisNexis People Locator**   **Category**: Public Data Broker
Website: phonedetective.com
Removal Link: None
Privacy Policy: www.lexisnexis.com/privacy/
Email Address: remove@prod.lexisnexis.com
Requirements: Postal mail submission
Notes: Follow instructions at lexis-nexis.com/clients/iip/removingInfo.htm
Date: _____ **Response**: _____ **Verified Removal**: _____

Service: **Tower Data**   **Category**: Public Data Broker
Website: www.towerdata.com
Removal Link: dashboard.towerdata.com/optout/
Privacy Policy: www.towerdata.com/company/privacy_policy
Email Address: privacy@towerdata.com
Requirements: Online submission
Notes: Online removal tool will complete the process.
Date: _____ **Response**: _____ **Verified Removal**: _____

Non-Public Data Brokers

In Chapter Three, you created a general opt-out request form for submission to companies. A second form, the "extended form", was mentioned which would include additional information that would qualify you to have further data removed. This data is often called non-public data. Such data is often shared with both government and private agencies. None of the methods in this chapter will prevent law enforcement from seeing your records. However, the techniques will help prevent your data from leaking into databases that can be bought by banks, lawyers, medical organizations, and credit agencies. We believe it is only a matter of time before these databases are breached and shared publicly.

These methods are not for everyone and the removal process is much stricter. The companies that sell this data allow people to have their information removed only if certain criteria are met. While each company offers specific wording on the requirements, the basic idea is that a person must fit into **one** of the following circumstances:

- The person is a judge, public official, or member of law enforcement in danger

- The person is the victim of aggravated identity theft

- The person is at risk of immediate physical harm

At first glance, you may think that you would not meet these requirements. The criteria are actually quite broad and many people can honestly declare that they fit into one of these statements. The first category is the most defined.

Judges: If you are a documented judge on a local, state, or federal level, you definitely meet the requirement. This also includes retired judges.

Public Officials: Many city, county, state, and federal employees are "public officials". There is a good chance that whatever your duties are, you have a presence in the public. Elected officials or those that provide information to the public are the easiest to declare. If your position has ever required you to speak to the press, disclose information to the public, or respond to public inquires, you are a public official. It will ultimately be up to you to determine if you meet this definition.

Law Enforcement: A substantial portion of this book's audience is law enforcement. Whether you are a part-time or full-time officer or agent, as long as you are sworn by your local agency, county, or state, you fit in this category. This also includes retired officers and agents. Recently, many companies have added a requirement that the person making the request be in a position of "immediate danger". Personally, we believe every law enforcement officer is in immediate danger. These companies may not have that opinion. We will provide optimal wording for your request in just a moment.

The grey area is with those that are previous law enforcement but did not retire. We believe the Law Enforcement Officers Safety Act would apply here. This act establishes the meaning of a "qualified retired law enforcement officer" as it relates to the ability to carry a concealed weapon. It states that if a person was a police officer for a minimum of ten years and separated from service in good standing, the person qualifies for this definition. Therefore, if you meet this condition, we believe that you qualify for this data removal.

Though military members do not fall into any of the protected categories we have helped military members successfully suppress their records in these databases. They did so by providing a letter, on command letterhead, from the battalion- or squadron-level commanding officer requesting removal. The letter was polite and expressed the commander's concern about individuals in his unit (listed by name and with other identifying information required for removal) that he felt were under extraordinary risk because of their operational history. He requested that these records be suppressed for reasons of operational security and personal safety. Your results may vary but it is worth attempting if you have a supportive command.

Aggravated Identity Theft: With the number of identity theft cases on the rise every year, more of you are now technically victims of this crime. Some of these cases are much worse than others. People that have had homes and vehicles purchased illegally in their names by criminals are obviously victims of identity theft. The FTC defines identity theft as a serious crime that "occurs when your personal information is stolen and used without your knowledge to commit fraud or other crimes".

Have you ever received a telephone call from your credit card company notifying you that someone is using your name and credit card number for unauthorized purchases? Have your friends told you that they received an email from your account telling them that you are stuck in another country and need money to get home? Has a disowned relative tried to open a credit line in your name to feed a drug habit? The examples are endless, but they all involve a situation where someone's personal information is stolen and used without their knowledge to commit fraud or other crimes.

For some of these services, identity theft alone is not enough to qualify for removal. You must be the victim of aggravated identity theft, which is an enhanced form. It occurs when someone knowingly transfers, possesses, or uses, without lawful authority, a means of identification of another person in the commission of particular felony violations. Basically, this occurs when someone uses false identification to commit identity theft against you. When this happens, you may never know about it. Therefore, we believe it is plausible that someone might be using identification in your name. We will discuss that further in a moment.

Ultimately, you must determine if you fit into this category. If you are ever the victim of identity theft, report it to your local police, and obtain a copy of the report. Most data companies require proof. In our experience, local police departments that take a report of identity theft from a citizen rarely follow-up on the complaint. The offender is likely from another state or another country where they have no jurisdiction.

Physical Harm: A person at risk of physical harm is allowed to have information removed from public access. We believe an argument could be made that any person is at risk of physical harm, but these companies do have some guidelines. Most want proof of this claim in the form of a police report identifying you as the victim of a violent crime or a copy of an order of protection issued by a court. Domestic abuse victims should have no problem meeting this requirement.

If you believe that you meet any of the criteria, you should create an extended opt-out request form. Basically, this is all of the information included on the basic form created in Chapter Three, but with a new section identifying how you meet one of the requirements. The data company may respond with a denial of your request, but this will not harm anything in your report. Many people have reported that sending a duplicate request after receiving a letter of denial resulted in a successful removal. Most likely, the person fielding requests is an entry level employee with little experience or authority in handling requests that vary from the norm.

To create the extended opt-out request form, open the basic opt-out request form that you created in Chapter Three. Remove the information that allowed for the entry of a URL of data found online. That will not be needed for these requests. In place of this section, you need to supply exactly how you fit into one of the qualifications mentioned earlier.

If you are a member of law enforcement, you could add a paragraph above your driver's license that states the following:

> "I am a full-time sworn police officer in the state of _____ that is actively conducting investigations of violent subjects. This assignment has put me in immediate danger of physical harm. The attached letter from my supervisor confirms my position and assignment".

If you are the victim of domestic abuse, a statement similar to the following could be added:

> "I am a victim of domestic violence that has been reported to the police and prosecuted by the courts. I continue to fear for my safety. I have attached a copy of a police report/order of protection for verification".

If you are a public official, maybe a parking enforcement employee for the city you live in, you could state the following:

> "I am a full time parking enforcement official for the city of _____. This work as a public official has created a hostile working environment and I am often targeted by the public. The attached letter from my supervisor verifies my employment and assignment".

If you are the victim of aggravated identity theft, a statement similar to the following could be added:

> "I am the victim of aggravated identity theft. I have enclosed a police report filed in reference to this incident. It is believed that the offender(s) in this incident are representing themselves as me and likely possess identification in my name".

Including a police report verifying your claim is extremely helpful. This may not be feasible for you. We have had mixed success when including an affidavit signed by the victim. Many people believe an affidavit is something only created by law enforcement as part of a criminal trial. Anyone can create an affidavit. It is simply a written statement voluntarily made by a person under an oath or affirmation administered by a person authorized to do so by law. A notary public can declare your signature on an affidavit as authentic.

We recently had a client that was being harassed by an ex-boyfriend. The moment that she changed her telephone number, he would call her on it. After she moved to a new apartment, he showed up outside her door. He sent her borderline threats to every email address she possessed and created several social network profiles in her name containing slanderous comments. The local police could not identify a specific crime within his harassment that would qualify for authorization of state charges. Instead, she created an affidavit. It read similar to the following.

> I am currently the victim of daily stalking by a former boyfriend. I have contacted the police. An investigation has been initiated. I have been threatened via various forms of communication including in-person, telephone, and electronic mail. The suspect in this incident has created an environment where I physically do not feel safe. I suspect that he is accessing information about me through non-public databases. These details have likely aided him in his attacks toward me.

This affidavit was printed and signed in front of a notary public. The notary confirmed the signature and stamped the document with a state issued seal. This was enough to proceed with a data removal request. The request was authorized and a removal confirmation letter was received within weeks. Your mileage may vary with this technique. The worst case scenario is that your request is denied.

You need to create a statement that is accurate for your situation. Be prepared to verify this claim through a police report, affidavit, or letter from your supervisor. We recommend that you gather as much supporting documentation as possible. If you have traveled to non-industrialized countries and believe your information could have been stolen during your travels, include photocopies of your visas or passport stamps. If you have had to cancel three credit cards over the last four years, get a letter from your creditor identifying each instance. The more thorough and prepared you are, the better your chances of success. Only you can determine if you are eligible for the removal of your private information. You are now ready to submit requests for removal. Figure 8.01 displays a completed form for law enforcement. Your version should accurately reflect your situation. Note that the grey redactions must be visible on your copy. This would include address and date of birth. The following pages include non-public data brokers that accept removal requests.

Date____________________ Company____________________

I request to have my name removed from your public and non-public databases. Here is the information you have asked me to include in my request:

Name: ____________________

Mailing Address: ____________________

Social Security Number *(If Required)* ____________________

Date Of Birth *(If Required)* ____________________

I am a full-time sworn police officer in the state of Illinois that is actively conducting investigations of violent subjects. This assignment has put me in immediate danger of physical harm. The attached letter from my supervisor confirms my position and assignment.
Thank you for your prompt handling of my request. I have also included a redacted copy of my driver's license below to prove identity.

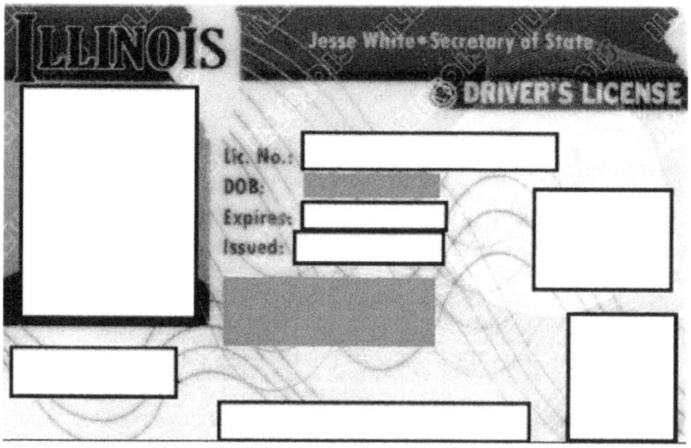

Figure 8.01: An extended opt-out request form.

Service: **Infopay/EVerify**   **Category**: Non-Public Data Broker
Website: everify.com
Removal Link: www.everify.com/opt_out_form.pdf
Privacy Policy: www.everify.com/legal.php
Email Address: privacy@cisnationwide.com
Requirements: Postal mail or fax submission
Notes: Print form, complete, and mail to listed address or fax to 888-446-1229.
Date: _____ **Response**: _____ **Verified Removal**: _____

Service: **LexisNexis/Accurint**   **Category**: Non-Public Data Broker
Website: lexisnexis.com
Removal Link: lexisnexis.com/opt-out-public-facing-products
Privacy Policy: www.lexisnexis.com/en-us/terms/privacy-policy.page
Email Address: privacy.information.mgr@lexisnexis.com
Requirements: Online submission
Notes: Online removal tool will complete the process. You can upload digital documents.
Date: _____ **Response**: _____ **Verified Removal**: _____

Service: **TLO**   **Category**: Non-Public Data Broker
Website: tlo.com
Removal Link: None
Privacy Policy: www.tlo.com/privacy.html
Email Address: CustomerSupport@TLO.com, TLOxp@transunion.com
Requirements: Email submission
Notes: Send completed extended opt-out form and documentation to both email addresses.
Date: _____ **Response**: _____ **Verified Removal**: _____

Service: **Westlaw**   **Category**: Non-Public Data Broker
Website: www. thomsonreuters.com
Removal Link: static.legalsolutions.thomsonreuters.com/static/pdf/opt_out_form.pdf
Privacy Policy: thomsonreuters.com/en/privacy-statement.html
Email Address: westlaw.privacypolicy@thomsonreuters.com
Requirements: Postal mail submission
Notes: Print form, complete, and mail to listed address. Include extended opt-out form.
Date: _____ **Response**: _____ **Verified Removal**: _____

Data Marketers

Data marketing companies sell personal data to businesses that want to sell a product or service. They collect information about you that assists them with matching these businesses to the most appropriate audience. These businesses include a wide range of organizations that sell everything from soda to mansions. The goal of data marketing companies is to identify people that are most likely to buy the specific product or service that a business is selling. When they do, they profit from this information and continue to build databases of your interests.

These marketing databases are less likely to be viewed by the general public than the databases discussed so far. Instead, they are bought, sold, and traded by private organizations that want to determine exactly how to entice you to buy something. You probably experience the effects of this every day.

For example, if you have a vehicle made in 2007, you will start to receive extended warranty options on that type of vehicle in the mail in 2012. Your name, address, phone number, and vehicle information is in a database sold to companies that provide vehicle warranty services. The package is purposely meant to look like an official manufacture warranty, and the intent is to make you believe that you should buy this warranty in order to keep your vehicle protected. Instead, these warranties are often provided by companies that will be difficult to contact when needed.

If you are shopping on the internet and researching a specific pair of shoes, your computer stores data that identifies your shopping history. This information is passed to other websites that you visit. You may start to see shoes similar to those that you were looking at earlier begin to appear in advertisements on various pages as you browse the web. The goal of these ads is to determine what you are most likely to buy, and forward you to a website that will pay a premium for this information.

These are just two examples of the many ways that marketing companies try to keep track of what you are doing. It is common for companies such as these to have a complete profile on you that reveals more about your interests and buying habits than your closest friends and family are aware of. Similar to the earlier example of a department store knowing that a minor was pregnant before the family knew, businesses such as Amazon and Proctor & Gamble are using data to sell you more products.

If you enjoy receiving mailed advertisements, telephone calls, and emails encouraging you to buy specific products, you should skip this section. If you feel that this is an invasion into your privacy and are tired of being targeted for a profit, then this section will help eliminate this practice on you.

DMA Choice

DMA Choice is an online tool located at **dmachoice.org** developed by the Direct Marketing Association to help you manage your postal mail and email advertisements. DMA Choice represents about 80% of the total volume of marketing mail in the United States. This website allows you to create an account and specify what types of mailing databases you want to be included in. Further, it allows you to specify if you want to be removed from an individual company's list or all of the different company's lists. To do this, you must create a free account which requires you to provide your name, home address and a valid email account. You must then identify individual companies that have your information and request removal from their databases. Another option is to request removal by category such as catalogs, magazines, donation requests, political mailings, and credit offers. This process is time consuming and still allows companies to collect your data if you had any type of relationship in the past.

There is an alternative solution. DMA Choice has two rarely used options that will remove a person's information from the databases of all companies associated with DMA Choice. It will also remove personal information from companies that have an existing relationship with the person requesting the removal. This could include credit companies that you have had a loan with in the past or retail stores where you had previously subscribed to a mailing list. These databases are referred to as their "Deceased Do Not Contact List" and "Do Not Contact for Caregivers List". Since we do not want to encourage people to fake their own death, you should use the caregiver's list option.

- Navigate to **www.ims-dm.com/cgi/dncc.php** and complete the online form. In the "Primary Name" section, provide your name and address only. If you receive mailings under another version of your name, such as Michael or Mike, add that name as well.

- In the "Information About You" section, you must provide the name of your "caregiver". Most likely, you do not have an official caregiver, but you do not need one for this unofficial request. We recommend that you provide the name of your mother or father. After all, they were your legal guardian while you were a child. If your parent is still living, he or she probably provides care to you in some form on occasion. If your parents are deceased, you can still put their name on this form. There is no verification process. Provide your anonymous email address where appropriate.

- Under the name of your "caregiver", there are five questions you must answer as your caregiver would answer. These are formalities of DMA Choice, and will not be verified. Only one question needs to have an answer of "Yes" to meet the minimum qualification.

Catalog Choice

If you find yourself bombarded with unwanted catalogs and advertisements in your mailbox, you are probably on many marketing lists as a valued shopper. The following instructions can be used to eliminate these mailings and remove your information from their databases. You must cancel with each individual company, but Catalog Choice makes this easy to do from one interface. If you do not receive unwanted catalogs, there is no need to complete these steps.

- Navigate to **catalogchoice.org** and click "Sign Up Now". Supply your initials instead of your name, a password, and your anonymous email address. Be sure to un-check the option to receive email from them.

- On the next page, assign a nickname to your home address. This could be "Home". Leave the "Company Name" blank and add your actual home address. Click "Save new address" when finished.

- You will receive an email from Catalog Choice. Open this message and click on the link inside the email. This will confirm your anonymous email address as active.

- When you receive unwanted mailings, log into this site and select "Find Companies". Search for the company name and view the removal options. Usually, you will only need to click the "Submit Request" button at the bottom. This will send a notification to the desired company to remove you from all distributions.

- Since most companies remove the entry by address, your name is never required. If the company does require a name, they will see your initials that match the initials of the name that is in your profile. This will satisfy the requirements of the company removing you from their database.

- Occasionally log into your account and click the "Your Choices" menu option. This will display the current status of your removal requests. When a company confirms the removal of your information, this page will display notifications.

We have used this successfully on several occasions. It usually works better than contacting the company directly. You do not need to submit a reason for removal; the default option is "Prefer not to answer".

The following section can be used as a workbook for eliminating your personal details from various data marketers. Many marketers can be avoided by simply using a secure web browser with privacy extensions as discussed in Chapter Two.

Service: Catalog Choice   **Category**: Data Marketers
Website: catalogchoice.org
Removal Link: None
Privacy Policy: www.catalogchoice.org/privacy
Email Address: support@catalogchoice.org
Requirements: Online submission
Notes: Online removal tool will complete the process.
Date: _____ **Response**: _____ **Verified Removal**: _____

Service: DirectMail   **Category**: Data Marketers
Website: directmail.com
Removal Link: directmail.com/directory/mail_preference/
Privacy Policy: www.directmail.com/privacypolicy/
Email Address: donotmaillist@directmail.com
Requirements: Online submission
Notes: Online removal tool will complete the process.
Date: _____ **Response**: _____ **Verified Removal**: _____

Service: DMA Choice   **Category**: Data Marketers
Website: dmachoice.org
Removal Link: www.ims-dm.com/cgi/dncc.php
Privacy Policy: www.dmachoice.org/static/privacy_policy.php
Email Address: ethics@the-dma.org
Requirements: Online submission
Notes: Follow instructions on removal link.
Date: _____ **Response**: _____ **Verified Removal**: _____

Service: Epsilon-Main   **Category**: Data Marketers
Website: epsilon.com
Removal Link: None
Privacy Policy: www.epsilon.com/privacy-policy/
Email Address: optout@epsilon.com
Requirements: Email submission
Notes: Send email with "Removal" as the subject. Include name and address.
Date: _____ **Response**: _____ **Verified Removal**: _____

Service: Epsilon-Abacus   **Category**: Data Marketers
Website: epsilon.com
Removal Link: None
Privacy Policy: www.epsilon.com/privacy-policy/
Email Address: abacusoptout@epsilon.com
Requirements: Email submission
Notes: Send email with "Removal" as the subject. Include name and address.
Date: _____ **Response**: _____ **Verified Removal**: _____

Service: Epsilon-CFD   **Category**: Data Marketers
Website: epsilon.com
Removal Link: None
Privacy Policy: www.epsilon.com/privacy-policy/
Email Address: dataoptout1@epsilon.com
Requirements: Email submission
Notes: Send email with "Removal" as the subject. Include name and address.
Date: _____ **Response**: _____ **Verified Removal**: _____

Service: Epsilon-Shopper   **Category**: Data Marketers
Website: epsilon.com
Removal Link: None
Privacy Policy: www.epsilon.com/privacy-policy/
Email Address: contactus@shoppers-voice.com
Requirements: Email submission
Notes: Send email with "Removal" as the subject. Include name and address.
Date: _____ **Response**: _____ **Verified Removal**: _____

Service: Haines & Company   **Category**: Data Marketers
Website: haines.com
Removal Link: None
Privacy Policy: None
Email Address: criscros@haines.com, info@haines.com, custserv@haines.com
Requirements: Email submission
Notes: Send email with name and address and request to be removed from all databases.
Date: _____ **Response**: _____ **Verified Removal**: _____

Service: **Infogroup**   **Category**: Data Marketers
Website: infogroup.com
Removal Link: None
Privacy Policy: www.infogroup.com/privacy-policy
Email Address: contentfeedback@infogroup.com
Requirements: Email submission
Notes: Send email with "Opt-Out" as the subject. Include name and address.
Date: _____ **Response**: _____ **Verified Removal:** _____

Service: **Publishers Clearing House**   **Category**: Data Marketers
Website: pch.com
Removal Link: None
Privacy Policy: www.pch.com/privacypolicy
Email Address: privacychoices@pchmail.com
Requirements: Email submission
Notes: Send email with name and address and request to be removed from all databases.
Date: _____ **Response**: _____ **Verified Removal:** _____

Service: **Vallasis/RedPlum-Main**   **Category**: Data Marketers
Website: redplum.com
Removal Link: redplum.com/tools/redplum-postal-addremove.html
Privacy Policy: www.redplum.com/info/privacy
Email Address: wecare@vallasis.com
Requirements: Online submission
Notes: Online removal tool will complete the process.
Date: _____ **Response**: _____ **Verified Removal:** _____

Service: **Valpak/Cox**   **Category**: Data Marketers
Website: Valpak.com
Removal Link: www.coxtarget.com/mailsuppression/s/DisplayMailSuppressionForm
Privacy Policy: www.coxtarget.com/privacy_policy.html
Email Address: legal@coxtarget.com
Requirements: Online submission
Notes: Online removal tool will complete the process.
Date: _____ **Response**: _____ **Verified Removal:** _____

Ancestry Records

We believe that online ancestry records are often overlooked by privacy enthusiasts. These family history websites seem innocent and educational on the surface. However, many of them expose details about you that should not be in public view. This often includes your full name, date of birth, address, and complete family history. Many of these services are available only to paying members, but removing your data is free. The following details should help you eliminate any unwanted information.

Service: Ancestry   **Category**: Ancestry Search
Website: ancestry.com
Removal Link: None
Privacy Policy: www.ancestry.com/cs/legal/privacystatement
Email Address: support@ancestry.com, customersolutions@ancestry.com
Requirements: Email submission
Notes: Send message to both email addresses requesting specific information removal.
Date: _____ **Response**: _____ **Verified Removal**: _____

Service: Archives   **Category**: Ancestry Search
Website: archives.com
Removal Link: archives.com/?_act=Optout
Privacy Policy: www.archives.com/privacy
Email Address: privacy@archives.com
Requirements: Online submission
Notes: Online removal tool will complete the process.
Date: _____ **Response**: _____ **Verified Removal**: _____

Service: Family Search   **Category**: Ancestry Search
Website: familysearch.org
Removal Link: None
Privacy Policy: familysearch.org/privacy/
Email Address: DataPrivacyOfficer@ldschurch.org
Requirements: Email submission
Notes: Send message to email address requesting specific information removal.
Date: _____ **Response**: _____ **Verified Removal**: _____

Offensive Mailings

The United States Postal Service (USPS) offers a rarely used form to prohibit specific types of mailings from being delivered to your home. It is called a prohibitory order and was created to prevent adult content from reaching an audience of children. The Prohibitory Order program provides a deterrent to continued mailings by a specific mailer advertising a product or service you consider erotically arousing or sexually provocative. Submitting this order will cause the USPS to demand the removal of your information from the database of the company that mailed the content. It is up to you to determine if content is arousing or provocative, and the power of this form should not be abused.

This method is targeted toward those with children. Police officers have used this technique to eliminate unwanted erotic mailings initiated by vengeful suspects. Families have used the form to stop adult content requested by mischievous friends of their children. Once any adult content is received at a home, it is very likely that the address will be added to several other adult content databases for future mailings. This form will also add the address to a database of addresses not wishing to receive adult advertisements.

- Navigate to **about.usps.com/forms/ps1500.pdf** and print the form. Complete all requested information and attach the original mailing that you find inappropriate. Deliver the form and offensive mailing to any post office.

Online Coupons

Many companies are embracing the idea of online coupons. These coupons can be printed from the internet and redeemed in stores like any other printed coupon. These appear to be very beneficial for the consumer. A person can conduct a brief search on various coupon websites for a specific product. When a coupon is located, it can be printed and applied to the sale of the product. Unfortunately, many people are not aware of what is happening behind the scenes with most online coupons.

Most of today's online coupons use special bar codes that help identify information about the life of the coupon. Each of these online coupons has a unique serial number embedded into the bar code. This can allow a company to track the date and time it was obtained, viewed and redeemed. It can also identify the store where it was used and the original search terms typed to find it. This is all reported back to the original source of the digital coupon. Retailers are combining this data with information discovered online and off, such as your age, sex, income, shopping history, internet history, and your current location or geographic routine. This creates a profile of the customer that is more detailed than ever. This profile can also include the other products purchased during the transaction and form of payment.

If you choose to use printable coupons, you have no choice but to give up some privacy. Here are some suggestions if you want to continue receiving these deals.

- When prompted for personal information, supply an alternate name. These details are seldom verified by the coupon delivery system.

- Log out of any social networks, especially Facebook, while researching and printing coupons. Companies will collect your profile data to associate you with the coupon and purchase history.

Loyalty and Reward Cards

Large stores such as Safeway and Vons offer a loyalty card, sometimes referred to as a reward card, to shoppers for instant savings on products. These stores offer "members only" sales that discount specific products for customers who have a membership card. If a customer does not have a card, the full price is charged instead of the sale price. This business model encourages a customer to favor a specific business for discounted items. Further, the business now possesses a large pool of information about customers.

Since customers are required to disclose their name, address, phone number, date of birth, gender, and email address to receive a card, stores can create an individual profile of your habits. This profile can include the items you buy, dates and times of purchases, form of payment, and location of purchase. They can also analyze the data and determine how often you buy a product, the amount you will spend on a product, and your overall value to the business. This data helps them individually target you with advertisements and track your redemption. The data can then be shared with other companies, law enforcement, private investigators, attorneys, and anyone else that will pay or use the courts to obtain the data.

We still encourage people to use these cards. In Chapter Sixteen, we will explain how these programs can be beneficial for the purposes of disinformation. We provide the following suggestions when using any type of rewards or loyalty program that relies on physical cards to redeem savings:

- Immediately stop using your current loyalty cards. Apply for a new card as needed at the customer service area of the store.

- Provide an alternate name on the application for the card. Provide a real mailing address, but not yours. The address should exist. We recommend supplying the address of the store from which you are requesting the membership. If the store requires you show identification, tell them that you just moved and the address on your license is inaccurate.

- Most loyalty cards insist on a telephone number. This number can be used to access your account in case you lose your card. Provide your anonymous telephone number created in Chapter Three This could be 867-5309 with your own area code..

- Trade your loyalty cards with other people whenever you get the chance. It confuses the shopping profiles stored about you. Explain the privacy concerns to friends and family and encourage them to swap cards with you. We have not found success in approaching strangers with this method. It tends to generate skepticism and a complaint to the store manager.

These techniques will stop a large portion of the marketing projected toward you. None of these methods will remove your information from every marketing database. There will still be occasional evidence of your details being sold to another company. Chapter Seventeen will identify methods to notify you if this happens.

Chapter Nine
Credit Companies

Credit companies collect a lot of information about you. They obviously know your name and personal details. Since they are providing you with a line of credit, they are entitled to know where to find you if you do not pay them. Unfortunately, they do not keep this information to themselves. They share their data with other creditors and various data mining companies. This important chapter should apply to everyone reading this.

Credit Opt-Out

Under the Fair Credit Reporting Act (FCRA), consumer credit reporting companies are permitted to include your name on lists used by creditors or insurers to make firm offers of credit or insurance that are not initiated by you. These are the pre-approved credit and insurance offers you receive in the mail. The FCRA also provides you the right to opt-out, which prevents consumer credit reporting companies from providing your credit file information to businesses.

Through this website, you may request to opt-out of receiving these offers for five years. If you want to opt-out permanently, you can print a form that you must send through postal mail. If you choose to opt-out, you will no longer be included in offer lists provided by consumer credit reporting companies. The process is easy.

* Navigate to **optoutprescreen.com** and click the button at the bottom of the page labeled "Click Here to Opt-In or Opt-Out". On the next page, choose the second option of "Electronic Opt-Out for Five Years"

* Complete the online form and click "Confirm". You will receive an immediate confirmation. This action will need to be repeated every five years.

Fraud Alert

We want to begin discussion about this topic by stating that we never recommend a fraud alert. However, they are very popular. Therefore, we will explain the benefits and then direct you to a better option. A fraud alert is an action that you can take to protect your identity from being used by criminals for financial gain. You can place an initial fraud alert on your credit report if you think that you have been the victim of identity theft. This is a good idea if you see any suspicious activity on your credit report. It can also be used if your wallet or purse has been stolen, if you've been a victim of a security breach, or even if you revealed too much personal information online or over the telephone. A fraud alert means that lenders must take extra precautions to verify your identity before granting credit in your name.

Anyone can place a 90-day initial fraud alert in their credit report. This alert can be renewed in 90-day intervals indefinitely. To request the alert, you need to contact only one of the three credit bureaus. The chosen bureau will notify the others. The following links forward to the online forms to complete the request for a fraud alert. While you only need to complete one of these, we recommend completing all three if you are a victim of identity theft. In our experience, Experian provides the smoothest process. If you decide to pursue a credit freeze, which will be discussed in a moment, do not complete the fraud alert process.

- Experian: https://www.experian.com/freeze/center.html

- Equifax: https://www.alerts.equifax.com/AutoFraud_Online/jsp/fraudAlert.jsp

- TransUnion: https://fraud.transunion.com/fa/fraudAlert/landingPage.jsp

The alert should be activated within 24 hours. You should receive a confirmation in the mail within a few days. If you do not receive this confirmation within one week, place another alert. When activated, your name will be removed from all pre-approved credit and insurance offers for two years. Instructions for removing the fraud alert will be included with the documentation sent to you via postal mail.

You can also obtain an extended fraud alert which stays on your credit report for seven years. To qualify, you must provide a police report or other official record showing that you've been the victim of identity theft. You will receive two free credit reports from each of the credit bureaus every 12 months in addition to the free copies anyone can obtain yearly.

Fraud alerts are not foolproof. A lender can see the fraud alert when a query into your credit is conducted for the purpose of opening a new line of credit. When the lender observes this alert, the lender should contact you by phone to verify that you really want to open a new account. If you are not reachable by phone, the credit account should not be activated. However, a lender is not required by law to contact you even if you have fraud alert in place. Many criminals who will open new fraudulent accounts will seek friends and family that are associated with lending companies to process the request. When this happens, the fraud alert does nothing. Most criminals will not attempt to open an account with a reputable institution that would acknowledge the fraud alert and take extra precautions. If you would like to have real credit protection, you should consider a credit freeze.

Credit Freeze

During our training sessions, people often ask about paid services such as Lifelock and Identity Guard. They want to know how effective they are at protecting a person's identity. These services can be very effective, but you pay quite a premium for that protection. A more effective solution is a credit freeze. This service is easy, usually free, and reversible.

A credit freeze, also known as a credit report freeze, credit report lock down, credit lock down, credit lock, or a security freeze, allows an individual to control how a U.S. consumer reporting agency is able to sell his or her data. This applies to the three big credit bureaus (Equifax, Experian, and TransUnion). The credit freeze locks the data at the consumer reporting agency until an individual gives permission for the release of the data.

Basically, if your information stored by the three credit reporting bureaus is not available, no institution will allow the creation of a new account with your identity. This means no credit cards, bank accounts, or loans will be approved. In many cases if someone tries to use your identity but cannot open any new services, they will find someone else to exploit. We can think of no better motivation to freeze your credit than knowing that no one can open new lines of credit in your name. This does NOT affect your current accounts or credit score.

A credit freeze also provides a great layer of privacy protection. If companies cannot gain access to your credit report, they cannot identify you as a pre-approved credit recipient. This will eliminate many offers mailed to your home. This will also remove you from various databases identifying you as a good credit card candidate. Credit freezes are extremely easy today thanks to State laws that mandate the credit bureaus cooperation. This section will walk you through the process.

The first step will determine whether your credit freeze will cost you any money. The fee for the freeze is $10 for each of the three bureaus. While this is well worth the protection, most states have a law that entitles identity theft victims a waiver of this fee.

Currently, each of the three credit bureaus voluntarily waive this fee for victims of identity theft. A large portion of this book's audience has had some type of fraudulent financial activity. This may be an unlawful charge to a debit or credit card or something more serious such as someone opening an account in your name. If you have had any fraudulent charges or activity, contact your local police to obtain a police report. Request a copy of the completed report including the case number.

Complete three packets that will be sent by certified mail. One will go to each of the three credit bureaus. Each packet will include the following:

- A letter requesting the credit freeze including the following information:

Official request for freeze
Full name
Full address

Social Security number / Date of birth

- A copy of your police report if you have one.

- A recent pay stub or utility bill.

- A photocopy of your driver's license or state identification.

Send this packet to each of the following credit bureaus:

Equifax Security Freeze
PO Box 105788
Atlanta, GA 30348

Experian Security Freeze
PO Box 9554
Allen, TX 75013

TransUnion
Fraud Victim Assistance Department
PO Box 2000
Chester, PA 19022-2000

If you do not have a police report and do not want the $10 fee waived, you can complete the entire process online at the EACH of the following three sites:

- Equifax: **www.freeze.equifax.com**

- Experian: **experian.com/freeze/center.html**

- TransUnion: **freeze.transunion.com**

The following is an example of a TransUnion credit freeze request.

TransUnion
Fraud Victim Assistance Department
PO Box 2000
Chester, PA 19022-2000

January 1, 2016

To whom it may concern,

Please accept this letter as an official request for a Security Freeze on my TransUnion credit file. Per your instructions, I have included a photocopy of my driver's license and recent pay documentation. Below are my details.

John Patrick Doe
1234 Main Street
Chicago, IL 61234
321-54-9876
December 1, 1980

I further request waiver of any fees due to my recent status as an identity theft victim in the State of Illinois. I have attached a photocopy of my police report.

Within a few weeks, sometimes sooner, you will receive a package from each of the bureaus confirming your credit freeze. This confirmation will include a PIN number that you need to keep. This number will be required if you ever want to temporarily or permanently reverse the credit freeze. After sending our requests via certified mail, and receiving the confirmation of delivery, we received a response from TransUnion within three days, Equifax within four days, and Experian within eight days.

If you want to reverse the credit freeze, you can do so online at the previously mentioned websites. A temporary reversal would be done to establish new credit such as a credit card or loan. Be sure to generate this temporary reversal prior to the loan request, otherwise your loan may be denied. A permanent reversal will completely stop the freeze, and your account will be back to normal.

Beginning in 2015, we also started recommending establishing a credit freeze with Innovis. If you have had a credit freeze in place for at least three years, this may not be mandatory. However, our opinion is that we should all take advantage of all protections provided to us. The method is the same and you should submit your letter to the following address. You can also establish the freeze online for free at **www.innovis.com/personal/securityFreeze**.

Innovis Consumer Assistance
PO Box 26
Pittsburgh, PA 15230-0026

Even if you are constantly opening new lines of credit or using your credit to purchase real estate often, we highly recommend a credit freeze. The very small effort it takes to temporarily lift a credit freeze for new lines of credit is worth it. It is the most effective way of stopping people from using your identity for financial gain. Lately, people are reporting that their underage children are becoming identity theft victims. A freeze could be applied to them as well. Generating a credit freeze on your child now will protect them until you request removal. This could protect your children from the temptation in high school and college to open new lines of credit.

Credit Options

There are some techniques regarding credit cards and lines of credit that you can apply to further protect your privacy and security. Credit companies do not promote these methods because the actions make it difficult for them to make more money from you. You may get resistance as you apply these techniques, but do not give up. You have every right to control your information.

Unused Accounts

When you obtain your free credit report as outlined earlier in this chapter, you should pay special attention to each line of credit. If you observe an old account that you have not used in years, consider closing the account. Usually, these dormant accounts do not cost you any money, but they do not help you either. This open account contains your personal information that can be sold and traded to other organizations.

Closing unused accounts will generally not affect your credit score. The only time this would apply is with your oldest credit account. One way that your credit score is determined is by the amount of time that you have had a line of credit in good standing. If you have had an unused credit card for ten years, that would help your credit score. If you close this account, and your next oldest account is two years, this may hurt your credit score. If you have any open account that is older than the accounts you are closing, your score should not be negatively affected.

Closing these unused accounts will also add security to your credit. Any accounts that you have open make you vulnerable to identity theft. The fewer accounts you possess; the fewer accounts can be compromised. Criminals often target dormant accounts that may not be watched as thoroughly as current accounts. Having multiple unused accounts can make it difficult to monitor for unauthorized transactions.

Michael's Credit Freeze Experience

After your credit freeze is in place on all three credit bureaus, you may want to test the system. In May of 2013, I decided that I was overdue for a test of my own credit freeze. The following are details of what I had to go through while attempting to obtain a new credit card with an active credit freeze in place.

May 27, 2013: I navigated to a website that was offering a great rewards point bonus for new members of a specific travel credit card. It was a very legitimate company that I have held credit with in the past. Even though I had a credit freeze in place, I thought that this company may use our previous relationship as a way around the freeze. This seemed like the best company to test my freeze with. I completed the online application and was told that I would receive an answer via postal mail soon.

May 29, 2013: I received a letter from the credit card company stating that they could not offer me a card. They advised that I had a credit freeze in place and that I would need to remove the freeze before my application could be processed. They identified TransUnion as the credit bureau that they ran my credit through. The freeze worked. This would stop the majority of criminals from accessing your credit. In order to continue the test, I contacted TransUnion and conducted a temporary credit freeze removal over the telephone. It was an automated system and I only had to provide the PIN provided earlier.

May 30, 2013: I contacted the credit card company via telephone and advised them that the credit freeze had been removed and that I would like to submit my application again. I was placed on hold for a few minutes. The representative stated that she could still not offer me the card. While the freeze had been removed, there was still an extended alert on my credit file and there was not a telephone number for me attached to the account for verification. Basically, TransUnion automatically added this extended alert to provide another layer of protection when a freeze was ordered due to fraud. The representative advised that I should contact TransUnion. I contacted them and was told that I should add a valid telephone number to my credit profile. Before I was allowed to do this, I had to answer four security questions about historical credit accounts, addresses, vehicles, and employers. After successfully answering these questions, I was able to add my cellular number to my account. I was told the changes should take place within 24 hours.

May 31, 2013: I contacted the credit card company and advised of my actions taken. She advised that she would not be able to pull another copy of my credit for 14 days. This was policy and there was no way to work around this due to the fraud protection rules in place.

Michael's Credit Freeze Experience (Continued)

June 15, 2013: I contacted the credit card company again and requested a new pull of my credit report. The credit freeze was still temporarily disabled until the end of the month. The new credit request was successful, and the representative could see the extended alert and a telephone number for contact. She placed me on hold while she dialed the telephone number on file. My cellular phone rang and she verified with me that I approved of the new credit request. I approved and switched back to the other line with her.

June 19, 2013: My new credit card arrived.

This was an interesting experience. I had never tested the system with the intent of actually receiving the card. I had occasionally completed credit card and loan offers in the past for the purpose of testing the freeze, but I was always denied later in writing. This reinforces the need to have a current telephone number on file for all three credit bureaus. This entire process took just over two weeks. Any criminal trying to open an account in my name would have moved on to someone else. This same chain of events would have happened if I were trying to buy a vehicle, obtain a personal loan, or purchase real estate. Even routine tasks such as turning on electricity to a home or ordering satellite television service require access to your credit report. A credit freeze will stop practically any new account openings in your name. While I became frustrated at the delay in obtaining this card, I was impressed at the diligence of the credit card company to make sure that I really was the right person. My credit is now frozen again and I am protected at the highest level.

Several readers have been impacted by the huge breach at the Office of Personnel Management (OPM). Many of you have now received an official notification if your records were part of the breach. If you have ever held a clearance, or applied for one, you are likely a victim. The response from OPM is to offer temporary free credit monitoring. Unfortunately, if you already have a credit freeze in place, you cannot participate in the free coverage. Why? Your credit freeze is blocking the legitimate service from monitoring your activity. We believe that this speaks volumes about the effectiveness of a credit freeze. Aside from hackers, credit monitoring companies cannot see the details of a frozen account. We urge you to never remove a credit freeze in order to allow any free credit monitoring.

Many of these third party credit monitoring services also induce people to provide even more information than was leaked in the original breach. For example, ID Experts (the company that OPM has paid $133 million to offer credit monitoring for the 21.5 million Americans affected by its breach) offers the ability to "monitor thousands of websites, chat rooms, forums and networks, and alerts you if your personal information is being bought or sold online". However, in order to use this service, users are encouraged to provide bank account and credit card data, passport and medical ID numbers, as well as telephone numbers and driver's license information.

We can see no reasonable purpose for ever giving any company more personal information in order to protect that same data. What happens when they get breached? On a personal note, we were both victims of the OPM breach. We are not worried. We have credit freezes in place, and they have been tested. We have no automated credit monitoring. Are we still vulnerable? Of course, we all are. However, we are both much more difficult targets.

Account Information

Credit companies share your home address to other companies. We highly recommend changing your address with your credit companies to your post office box or commercial mail receiving agency (CMRA). These mail drops can include commercial chains such as The UPS Store or locally owned mailing shops. This can be done by calling the number on the back of the card, but we suggest completing the process online. Calling the company and giving them the information may not help. The operator may simply add a new address to the account and not actually change the address of the account. If you have a login to access your account online, there should be an option to update your account. You then want to change your mailing address. If you do not have online access to the account, you can request access through your credit company's website.

Secondary Credit Card

Credit card companies will issue additional cards at your request. These cards possess the same account number as the primary card and all charges will be applied to the primary account holder. These cards are often requested by parents to give to their children for emergencies. Any time the secondary card is used, it is processed as if the original card had made the purchase. Since the secondary card is part of an account that has already been verified, there is no verification process to obtain the additional cards.

To request an additional card, you should contact the credit card company by calling the telephone number on the back of the card. Tell them that you want a duplicate card in the name of a family member. You can request an additional card in any name that you want. You will be warned by the credit company that you are responsible for any charges, and the new card will be sent out immediately to the address on file for the account. If you do not want this new name associated with your home address, be sure to update your address on file with the credit company as explained previously. I recommend confirming that the new address is active before ordering additional cards.

Many readers of the first edition of Hiding from the Internet reported difficulty in obtaining a secondary card from traditional banks, such as Bank of America or U.S. Bank. We have found this technique to work best with traditional credit card companies. We have had great success, even recently, with several Chase cards. This technique will usually not work with debit cards.

There are a few ways that you can take advantage of this additional card. Both of us have a credit card in an alternate name that we created for this single purpose. We keep the card with us, alongside our true name credit and debit cards. We now have a choice of which name to use when making a purchase. We try to pay with cash whenever possible, but many scenarios exist where cash is not accepted.

Michael's Caution on Secondary Cards

In 2011, I conducted an experiment. I called my credit card provider and requested an additional card in another name completely different from mine. A new card arrived promptly with the alternative new name, and my original account number. I began using this card for alias purchases, which were charged to my account. In thirty days, I conducted a detailed online search through premium resources for my address that I use for the bill. The fictitious name I had provided was now associated with my address. I was astonished and concerned.

While we will expand on ways to effectively use this technique, we urge you to only request a secondary card in an alias name after you changed the billing address to a PO Box. This will prevent the alias name from being directly associated with your home address. We must never be naïve and assume that this technique gives us complete anonymity. The credit card company will still know that you made the purchase. Our point is that anyone can track you on the internet through your credit. The following methods will not replace the privacy of cash, but will eliminate much of the information available to the general public. This chapter is important for other concerns besides privacy. These methods will offer a new layer of security to protect you from identity theft and fraud. The advantage, as you will see in the following examples, is that the company of purchase will not know your real name.

Hotels

Obtaining a hotel reservation is very difficult without a credit card. Some will reserve the room without a guarantee that it will be available. Some will refuse the reservation without a valid card number. Lately, many hotels and third-party booking services apply the entire charge for the visit at the moment of the reservation. When you arrive, you must provide the card at the front desk to be scanned. Even if you have prepaid you will likely be required to present a credit card for "incidental purchases" such as meals in the hotel's restaurant. This collects the data about the cardholder and attaches it to the sale. There are two main reasons for applying this technique while at hotels.

When you stay at a hotel, there is a lot of information that the business can analyze about you and your stay. The amount you paid, the length of your stay, any amenities you purchased, and the distance you travelled from home will be stored in your profile. This will all be used to target you for future visits. Worse, it will be shared with other hotels in the chain that can benefit from the data.

A more serious concern is for a person's safety. If you are the victim of a stalker or targeted by someone who would physically harm you, it is not difficult for them to find out the hotel where you are staying. The easiest way would be to contact every hotel in the area where you will be traveling. The following conversation with a hotel operator will usually divulge your chosen hotel.

"Hello, I made a reservation there a while back and I need to add an additional day to my stay. I may have put the reservation under my wife's name, Laura Smith. If not, it could be under my name, Blake Smith. I'm afraid I do not have the reservation number; can you find the reservation without it? It is for next week".

The operator will either be unable to locate your reservation or confirm that an extra day was added. The call that gets the confirmation will identify where you are staying. A more high-tech approach could be conducted through the hotel's wireless internet. Many hotels require you to log into the wireless internet before you use it. This usually requests your last name and room number as verification that you are a valid guest. Some amateur programming can create a script that will attempt to log in with your last name and each room number of the hotel until the attempt is successful. This not only confirms the hotel you are staying at, but exposes the room number you are in. This can be a huge security concern.

You can use your new alternative name to create your hotel reservation. Since you are not committing any type of financial fraud, this is legal. You will be providing your legitimate credit card number and will pay the charges through your credit statement. Upon arrival at the hotel, hand this card to the receptionist. You may be asked for identification. In my experience, stating that your wallet was stolen and you only have the credit card because you keep it in the car is sufficient. If this does not work, have your travel partner show identification to meet the requirement. This information will most likely not be added to the reservation. We recommend persistence that you do not have an ID. Very few hotels will turn down a paying customer with a credit card in hand. We find that being polite and understanding always works better than acting agitated.

In 2014, we encountered a hotel chain that has made it absolute policy that the customer supplies both a valid credit card and photo identification in order to rent the room at check-in. We have found that the following two scenarios bypass this requirement almost every time.

First, create a rewards card with each of the hotel chains that you plan to use. When you check in, immediately give both your credit card (alternative name) and your rewards card (also in your alternative name). If you travel often and have an elevated status on your rewards card it is very rare that you will encounter any resistance upon check-in. If you detect a stubborn receptionist that appears determined to follow the corporate rules, you can act like you are in the middle of a very important call. Usually, the receptionist will continue with the process just to get rid of you.

When you arrive at a hotel, always hold the door open for anyone else entering and allow them to check in first. This is not merely being polite; it also allows you to determine what resistance you will be up against when it is your turn. Knowing the attitude of the employee may aid you in creating the most appropriate pitch.

If the previous trick does not work, we have found that having an identification card in your alternative name to be very helpful. We would never condone obtaining a real or fraudulent government identification card in your alias name. Not only is that illegal, but completely unnecessary. Instead, you can create your own "club", of which you are the founder (as your alternative name of course).

For example, you may be very interested in rock climbing. You could start your own organization titled "The Greater Houston Climbing Gym", the "Fort Lauderdale Health and Fitness Center" or the "Lower East Side Athletic Atrium". Now, you may choose to create an identification card for the members of your new club. In this example we used gyms because it is common for them to provide members with photo IDs. This could be completed in Microsoft Word and may include a photo of you. Your local print shop will happily print this on a nice paper stock and laminate it for you. The following should work well at the check-in of your hotel.

"I'm sorry, I left my license at the gym, can I show you my gym membership card until I go back to get it? You can call the number on the back to confirm".

What phone number should you put on the back of the membership card? We will present some ideas in Chapter Eleven.

Events

Many events, concerts, and various forms of entertainment now require a credit card for attendance. Most events allow the purchase of tickets through a single vendor. The tickets must be purchased either online or via telephone and mailed or picked up at the ticket area of the event. When you purchase tickets, you are usually required to give all of your personal information including full name, home address, home telephone number, and date of birth. With your secondary credit card, you should only provide the name on the card, and your post office box if the tickets will be mailed. There is no verification on any additional information. Ultimately, the company just wants to be paid for the tickets. Any other information they collect gets passed on to databases for the marketing division.

Utilities

In Chapter Eight, we discussed how to modify your name on your utility bills by making subtle changes over time. Here we will offer another technique.

Michael's Utilities Experience

In 2011, I assisted a colleague that was receiving very serious death threats to him and his family. It was serious enough that he moved his family to a new home that he purchased in a business name. He was having issues obtaining services to the residence without providing his complete personal information including a Social Security number for a credit check. He had reached a dead end with the cable company responsible for internet access in the area. They refused to provide internet service to a business name in a residential area. With his permission, I contacted the cable company on his behalf and reached a fairly polite customer service representative. My friend had already obtained a secondary credit card in another name on his primary account.

I advised the representative that I wished to initiate new service at my residence. I provided the address and the name on his new card. When she asked for a Social Security number, I informed her that I had been advised to never give that out over the telephone and requested an alternative way to verify my identity. As expected, she stated that I could place the monthly charges onto a credit card and warned me that the charges for the entire month would be applied immediately. I agreed to that and provided the card number. This eliminated the need for them to conduct a credit check. They now had a credit card number on file for automatic billing for the upcoming month. If the charges failed to go through, they would be able to disconnect service.

This method will not always work. we have been declined by one representative only to be approved by another with an immediate second call. Persistence often pays off. Power providers and water companies are less likely to accept automatic credit card payments. Fortunately, they are usually willing to bill the customer in a business name. This will be further explained in the next chapter.

Legalities

You may be reading this and thinking that there is no way this could be legal. It is absolutely legal as long as you are not using this method to commit fraud. The card is attached to your account, and you are paying the bill. It is not identity theft because you are not claiming to be a specific person. If you were using someone else's Social Security number and opening credit lines with their information, then this would be illegal. You must only apply this to your own account that you have authority over. Additionally, you must always follow these rules:

- Never provide your alternative name to any law enforcement or government official.

- Never open new credit lines with your alternative name.

- Never generate any income with your alternative name.

- Never associate any Social Security number with your alternative name.

- Never receive any government or community benefits in your alternative name.

- Only use this name to protect your privacy in scenarios that a credit card is needed.

Prepaid Credit Cards

If you are not ready to jump into using an alternative name, a prepaid credit card may be better for you. A prepaid credit card is not a true credit card. No credit is offered by the card issuer. Instead, the customer purchases the card by paying the entire balance of the card upfront. A prepaid card with a balance of $500 would cost the customer $500 plus a small fee. This card can now be used anywhere that traditional credit cards are accepted. When the balance of the card is spent, the card is no longer accepted. These cards can be purchased at many retail stores.

American Express

For the best economic value, we recommend the American Express prepaid cards. They occasionally offer to waive the fee associated with the card and that's when we stock up. Further, they offer a business gift card that you can customize. Navigate to **americanexpress.com/gift-cards** and choose the "Custom" option. This will allow you to choose the quantity, dollar amount, and two lines of custom messages. These messages will appear directly below the credit card number where a person's name usually appears. You can get as creative as you want, but remember that American Express will manually approve or decline each submission. We have found the following to pass any scrutiny.

Peter Smith (Any Name)
Travel Adventures LLC (Any Business)

Peter Smith (Any Name)
Business Travel Card (Any Purpose)

The Estate of Peter Smith (Any Entity)
Account # 85367 (Any Number)

Cards that possess some sort of customization often pass scrutiny more than those that do not. A benefit of this card is that your name is in no way associated with it. You can provide any name you want when making a purchase. When the company you are dealing with applies the name to the card for the purpose of charging the account, the prepaid card company disregards any name submitted. The card company knows that this is a prepaid card and allows any name to be used. In this example, American Express will need a real name and credit card to complete this transaction and send a gift card. This may be invasive for many readers. The next technique should solve this issue.

Vanilla Visa/MasterCard

For the most private prepaid card, we recommend the Vanilla Visa and MasterCard options. These do not require any personal information and can be purchased at numerous stores with cash. After purchasing the card, it is ready to go for any in-person purchases. If you want to use it for online purchases, you only need to register it through the Vanilla website. This registration will ask you for your postal code. You can provide any code that you want, but it should match the code that you will be providing on any orders. We have had numerous experiences with these cards and have found the following to be helpful.

- You can change your postal code at any time on the Vanilla website. You may change this as you make online purchases using different physical addresses.

- You can purchase card increments up to $500. We suggest purchasing larger denominations to avoid numerous cards with small leftover balances.

- You can purchase cards in Canada and then use them in the United States. You will pay a small conversion fee, but the extra layer of privacy is nice in some cases. You can change your postal code from a Canadian code to U.S. code at any time. Some use this technique when purchasing online services such as VPNs.

- Any name and physical address entered during an online order will be accepted.

We often use prepaid cards when traveling. If one gets lost or stolen, we do not need to worry about unauthorized access to our true credit accounts. If the card information gets "skimmed" by a dishonest employee of a business we visit, the damage will be minimal. Any purchases we make will be completely anonymous and we will not be subject to future marketing attempts.

We recently had a client who wanted to purchase a completely anonymous VPN service and Blur account. He wanted to use an alias and have no connection from him to these services. After establishing proof that he did not want to do this for malicious purposes, we offered to help. While on a business trip to Toronto, one of us stopped at a grocery store and purchased a Vanilla Visa with Canadian cash. We activated this card while connected to a local hotel Wi-Fi and supplied the postal code of that hotel. We used the card to purchase the VPN services and Blur subscription while on this network. We provided the credentials to the relieved client. This may be overkill to most readers. However, to someone in fear of his life, the scrutiny to both privacy and security is justified.

Virtual Credit Cards

When you make purchases online, you are at risk of your credit card getting compromised during a database breach. These thefts are so common that they rarely make the news. A criminal can obtain thousands of card numbers at one time by breaking into a business's servers. If your number is in the database, you will probably be a victim within hours. To avoid this, you can use virtual credit cards. A virtual credit card, sometimes referred to as a temporary credit card or throw away credit card, is a credit card number that is generated by your credit card issuer on your behalf for temporary use. You do not actually get a physical credit card with this number. You simply use the number for an online transaction and then it expires.

Any time that we need to order something on the internet from a questionable source, we use this option. Many of our clients provide these numbers for free trials that require a credit card. If the company tries to apply an unauthorized charge, it will be declined. Some banks, such as Citi and Bank of America, offer this free virtual number service. You should contact your credit card company to find out the options available to you. If it is not, we highly recommend the service Blur.

Blur

Blur (**abine.com**) was mentioned earlier in the preparation chapter and is one of our favorite new privacy enhancing services. It is a premium service that provides masked email addresses, telephone numbers, and credit card numbers. If you are serious about privacy, and desire the conveniences of credit card transactions, a private credit card number is vital. Blur's masked credit cards work the same way that a banks' virtual cards function. It is very similar to a prepaid credit card. When you wish to make a purchase online, you log into Blur and create a new masked card. Blur will generate a unique credit card number complete with expiration date and CCV. You can use any name you like with the card and use Blur's Boston address as the billing address. Be aware that to use a Blur card you must know the total purchase price, including taxes and shipping, and create a card for at least that amount. Some online retailers will not display the total price including shipping, handling, and taxes, until you have already entered a credit card number. In these instances, we recommend estimating the total and padding the estimate when creating your Blur masked card. For instance, if you are purchasing a book for $19.99 the total with taxes and shipping should not exceed $30.00, so create your masked card in this amount. Any unused balances can be refunded.

This allows you to make purchases online without giving out your real credit card number that could be stolen in transit, spilled in a data breach, or otherwise compromised. It also limits the amount of information your credit card company has about your shopping habits, and helps to prevent merchants from building accurate data profiles about you. We use this service every time we make a purchase online. The following details outline a typical use scenario. Assume that your goal was to purchase a VPN service for $69.95, pseudo-anonymously, but use your real credit card.

- Create a premium Blur account and pay for the service with a Vanilla prepaid credit card. Do not add this prepaid card as a credit card into your Blur Wallet. This is only for the payment for the service. Use your secondary credit card alias as your name for the account and provide a non-existent physical address. The prepaid card will successfully charge with any billing address. The reason you should consider making the initial payment to Blur using a prepaid card rather than your secondary card is that Blur will always keep a record of your initial purchase. However, any cards that you add for payment purchases once you have Blur can be removed and these records will be purged.

- Provide a 333Mail email address to Blur for contact and login credentialing.

- Add your secondary credit card to the Blur wallet. This will be your actual credit card number as assigned to your secondary alias name. This will be used by Blur to charge any purchases for masked credit cards.

- Log into Blur and create a new masked card. Give the card a descriptive name you will remember and choose an amount of $69.95. Blur will display your new prepaid credit card number, expiration, and verification code. Your real credit card will be charged exactly $69.95 plus a $2.00 fee from Blur

- Purchase the VPN, or any other goods or services, with this new prepaid credit card number. If required, provide Blur's Boston physical address which will be visible on the new masked card in your account. You can provide any name to the provider, as any option will successfully charge to the Blur number.

You now have the new service that you desire, and the provider of the service knows nothing about you. The masked credit card number used is now invalid, and your real credit card was charged $69.95 by Blur. Your credit card provider does not know what you purchased. The VPN service provider believes you live in Boston and does not know your name. If the service tries to charge a renewal fee to that credit card number, it would be declined. You will not have any surprises and do not need to worry about cancellation to avoid recurring fees. There are two basic strategies to use with Blur; single and continuous.

Single: Each time you need to make a purchase online, create a Blur masked card for the exact purchase amount. The card will expire immediately after use. The benefits here are unique numbers for every purchase and precluding any unauthorized purchases. The negative aspect is the need to access your Blur account, create a new card, and pay a small fee each time you wish to make a new purchase.

Continuous: Create a Blur masked card in a generic amount such as $200. Use this number as you would a prepaid card and make small purchases until it is depleted. If there are a few dollars remaining on the masked card, simply refund it back to your credit card through Blur. The benefit with this method is that you always have a prepaid credit card number available for immediate online purchases. The concern is the ability for unauthorized charges and an association of all purchases through the single credit card number.

Occasionally, an online merchant will want to verify that the credit card being used was not stolen. They may want the complete billing address associated with the account or the issuing bank's address and telephone number. If this happens, Blur allows you to provide their verification information. The billing name and address associated with all masked cards is Abine, Inc, 280 Summer Street, Boston, MA 02210. The telephone number associated with that billing address is 617-345-0024. The bank issuer of the cards is Wex Bank.

Prior to August 14, 2015, we applied both methods to our privacy strategies. We would create unique numbers for every online purchase when possible. The masked card was in the exact amount of purchase. We also maintained a handful of prepaid Blur numbers that carried a balance for immediate availability while traveling. However, Blur's policies changed on that date. As of this writing, Blur charges $2.00 per masked number for cards with a value up to $100.00. An additional 1.5% is charged to cards with a value above $100.00. Blur also charges $5.95 monthly to any open cards with a balance after 30 days. Therefore, we have adjusted our strategy for Blur masked cards. When we need to make a purchase, we continue to create a new masked number in the exact amount of the purchase price. If we expect to make any additional purchases within the next 30 days, we make the total value of the masked card $100.00. That will leave a balance to the card without any additional fees. If we do not deplete the balance within 30 days after the creation, we refund the remaining balance to our secondary credit card on file. With this method, the total expense for the service is $2.00.

We have seen some minor issues with Blur. A client recently made a purchase through a smaller online merchant using a Blur credit card number and billing address. However, he was shipping the item to an alias name at a friend's house. After thirty days the package had not arrived, even though the merchant had sent a shipping confirmation email. Upon contacting the merchant our client learned that as a matter of policy the company only ships to billing addresses to "prevent fraud". Our client contacted Blur who explained the issue to the merchant. The company sent a new item to the shipping address. Situations like this are very rare in our experience. However, if you do purchase through a small operation you may want to contact them before completing your purchase to ensure that they will ship to an address other than the billing address. Another issue that may come up occasionally is in the interest of fraud protection. Justin made a purchase with a moderately-sized specialty retailer during the writing of this book. The alias he used on the order form and shipping address was the name of the female who lived in the house where the package would be shipped. Within an hour of placing the order Justin received a call from the merchant asking to speak to the female. They were doing due diligence and ensuring the purchase was not fraudulent which we admire. However, because he had locked himself into ordering with a female's name, Justin had no choice but the tell the caller that "Heather" was not home and would call back. He then had to explain the situation to Heather, have her call the merchant back, and assure them that the order was not fraudulent. This created a somewhat awkward scenario that could have been avoided by using a male name that he could have then verified himself.

At the time of this writing, a premium Blur membership costs $39.99 per year, $59.99 for two years, and $79.99 for three years. Blur occasionally offers lifetime memberships at a reduced rate. We encourage to contact them and ask about upcoming promotions. According to Blur, the surcharges on masked cards are actual expenses passed down from the credit card companies. In most uses, this will still be more affordable than the standard $5.95 fee that is associated with most physical prepaid cards. Blur currently allows you to connect a banking account to your Blur account. This allows for masked cards at no cost. If you want to go this route, we prefer Privacy.com, which is explained next.

Privacy (privacy.com)

This new service is very similar to Blur, but does not accept or provide credit card numbers. Instead, you connect your bank account to your online profile and Privacy generates debit card numbers at your request. By default, the numbers can be tied to only one merchant and contain no balance. Your account is not debited until actual use. You can select the "Burner" option to close the card number after the first use, which is beneficial to avoid forgotten recurring subscription fees. You can also close a card at any time to eliminate future transactions. You can provide any name or billing address to purchases made with Privacy card numbers. If "Discreet" billing is chosen, Privacy will not disclose the merchant name to your bank, and your statement will only display "Privacy.com".

The biggest benefit of Privacy is the cost (free). The drawback of Privacy is that you must connect it to your actual banking account. This provides a solid association between you and your purchases. However, the merchants will not know your true identity. We believe this is a great solution for ongoing expenses such as internet services. Providing a Privacy debit card number to iTunes or Google will shield you at no cost. When we consider Blur's rising cost to generate new and unique card numbers, we are beginning to migrate many purchases toward Privacy.

Utilities and Residential Services

As a reminder, you can have all of your bills delivered to your post office box. We recommend contacting each credit and utility company that you have service with and request a mailing address change. The service will still be provided to your home, but the database of customers will list your address as your post office box. If this database is sold, traded, or compromised, the information will not identify your home address and landline telephone number. This can help keep you off marketing lists. It will also help hide your residence from public view of data mining company reports. Later chapters provide more ideas for your own custom strategy.

LEVEL TWO:
INTERMEDIATE

Level Two of this book will pick up where Level One left off. It will discuss how to make anonymous purchases through several mechanisms. We will teach you how to purchase a telephone anonymously, so even if your metadata is leaked it will not be in your true name. We will explain the threats against mobile phones and how to defeat them. It will cover how to encrypt all of the data on your computer. It will walk you through how to redundantly encrypt all of your internet traffic, and explain the reasons why doing so are important to achieving and maintaining your privacy.

We believe that this tier of privacy and security applies to the majority of our readers. While we wish that the majority of Americans would embrace this level of privacy for the good of the country, it will never happen. If you have completed the techniques described in Level One and chosen to pursue this level, you should congratulate yourself; you are likely in the 95th percentile of privacy- and security-focused individuals. If you intend to move beyond this level, a thorough mastery of the techniques discussed here is essential.

CHAPTER TEN
ANONYMOUS PURCHASES

The previous chapter explained the importance of a credit card in an alternate name. We rely on this technique during much of our travels. However, this is no longer reserved only for traveling. On a daily basis, we all make purchases that require credit cards or personal information. The days of living solely on cash are almost gone. While it is still possible, and many people do it, it has become increasingly difficult. Many toll roads no longer accept cash. If you do not have a digital pass attached to your front windshield, you will be billed at the address attached to your vehicle registration. Most airlines will no longer accept cash for in-flight purchases. You must have a credit card.

This chapter will explain various ways to protect your privacy while maintaining the convenience of making non-cash purchases online and in person. Before outlining these techniques, we feel obligated to examine how convenience is inversely proportional to privacy and security. The more convenient something is the more personal privacy and control of your identity you are probably sacrificing. Credit and debit cards are one such convenience. With cash you have to make time to visit an ATM, carry bills, and manage change. All of these inconvenience factors are compounded if you make multiple small purchases throughout the month.

Despite its inconveniences, making these multiple small purchases routinely is precisely the reason you should use cash when available. Though it is certainly more convenient to swipe a credit card for purchases than it is to use cash, it also creates a tangible, searchable record of each transaction. Your purchases record a wealth of data about you including your location and movement, interests, hobbies, and a plethora of other information. Some will say this data is protected and only visible to those with proper authority. We counter that argument with whatever data breach is in the headlines while you read this chapter. Further, history has proven that those with proper authority often abuse their power.

A client of ours did not fully realize the extent to which his personal pattern of life was spelled out in black in white until he bought his first home. One of the requirements for the loan application was to submit three months of statements for all bank and credit accounts. He was very disheartened when he had to submit statements for several accounts that looked something like the following.

Date	Transaction Description	Amount
07/01/15	Debit – Local Grocery Store #1	$17.35
07/01/15	Debit – Local Grocery Store#2	$31.53
07/02/15	Debit – National Coffee Chain near Work	$4.88
07/02/15	Debit – Convenience Store near Work	$2.37
07/02/15	Debit – Lunch Restaurant near Work	$12.72
07/02/15	Debit – Gas Station	$43.68
07/02/15	Debit – Local Grocery Store #2	$8.19
07/03/15	ATM Withdrawal	$60.00
07/04/15	Debit – National Coffee Chain near Work	$4.88
07/04/15	Debit – Big-Box Department Store	$81.41
07/04/15	Debit – Local Dinner Place near Home	$27.12
07/04/15	Debit – Large National Bookstore	$27.19
07/05/15	Debit – Fast Food Place near Work	$6.01

Years prior, he had subscribed to the philosophy that plastic is easier to use, and somehow inherently better, than paper. What he did not realize was that he was sharing a ton of personal details about his life with others. With the information above which only covers a period of five days, he reveals where he shops for groceries, where he gets coffee and eats, and where he gets gas. If this information is multiplied by six to accommodate the entire month even more information is revealed. Details such as the frequency of eating out, getting coffee, or visiting the bookstore are revealed. If this information is coupled with the retailers' records, we could know exactly what he buys and how often. Within a few months, we could begin to predict not only where he shops, but what he buys and the meals that he consistently orders. Though there was nothing "shady" on his cards, it was more than a little embarrassing to share such granular level of detail about his life with strangers.

He realized that he had been sharing all of this information with his bank and creditors for several years. Additionally, many stores where he shopped kept a detailed record of the items he purchased based on his credit card number. Some stores even tout this as a convenience measure, allowing you to get a refund without receipt based on your credit card. In reality, this information helps them send targeted advertising to you. Have you ever used the self-checkout at the grocery store and received coupons printed immediately after purchase? If you look closely at the items that are promoted in these coupons you will probably notice that these are based on your credit card's shopping history.

Purchasing with cash offers much more anonymity. Unless you are purchasing something that requires you provide your real name, purchases with cash are about as close to anonymous as you can get. With most purchases, there is no paper trail, no bank statement, and no record of your life and activities. If he had it to do over again, he would have made some changes in his personal habits. His account statements would have reflected the same period of time a bit more succinctly similar to the following.

Date	Transaction Description	Amount
07/01/15	ATM Withdrawal	$500.00
07/08/15	ATM Withdrawal	$500.00
07/20/15	ATM Withdrawal	$500.00

You will notice that if he had used cash, this brief statement covers a period over four times as long as the above example, while still being eight lines shorter. Not only is this statement more compact, it also reveals very little about him. It does not reveal where he buys his groceries or the location his favorite coffee, lunch, and dinner restaurants. You cannot see his culinary preferences. It does not associate his name to any of his purchases.

We attempt to use cash as much as possible but realize that we will never be able to fully eliminate credit cards from our lives. Air travel, rental cars, and hotels require credit cards. We still find ourselves in locations where we don't want to pay exorbitant ATM fees, and end up using a credit card. But we use it a lot less, which is what we are truly advocating. Use more cash and less plastic. This reduces the amount of information about yourself that you give over to your bank, your lenders, or anyone curious enough to swipe a statement out of your mailbox.

There are significant and compelling reasons to keep your purchase history anonymous. Your purchases reveal almost everything about you. The sporting goods you buy (or don't buy) probably say a lot about your level of physical activity and fitness. The books you read reveal a lot about your personality including your religious beliefs, your political leanings, your sexuality, and the things you are passionate about. The foods you buy, the restaurants at which you eat, the frequency with which you eat at them, and the alcohol and tobacco products you consume reveal a lot about your health. This may one day very soon be used to calculate your health and life insurance premiums.

Using cash isn't bulletproof, and it won't make you totally anonymous. But it will lower your digital signature, offer you a lot more anonymity, and make an attacker's job a bit harder. Every little bit helps. For those situations that do not allow cash purchases, we have some ideas that will decrease the invasive tracking of your buying habits.

Online Purchases

Do you remember a day when you would go to the grocery store for all of your food, the hardware store for replacement parts, and the department store for household goods? For many people, this has all been replaced by online retailers such as Amazon and EBay. Even artwork and specialty crafts are now sought through websites such as Etsy. You can avoid these types of companies and still get what you need with cash at physical stores. However, you will miss out on the convenience and affordability of online shopping. This section will guide you on maintaining your privacy while using these services.

Amazon

We begin with Amazon because it is one of the largest online retailers. We place orders through Amazon weekly and never jeopardize our privacy during the process. If you are already using Amazon and have an account created, we recommend that you stop using that account and create a new one. The details that you provide are very important. Before discussing the appropriate methods, please consider an actual scenario.

A client had recently moved to a new rental house to escape a dangerous situation. She had nothing associated with her real name at the address. The utilities were still in the name of the landlord. She used a PO Box for her personal mail. She was doing everything right. She created a new Amazon account and provided the name of her landlord and her home address for shipping purposes. This way, her packages would arrive in the name of the property owner and she would stay invisible. She made sure that her name was not visible in any part of the order.

When prompted for payment, she used her real credit card in her name. She verified one last time that her name was not present anywhere within the actual order or shipping information. Her item, a pair of hiking shoes, arrived in the name of the landlord. Her real name was not referenced anywhere on the package. Within thirty days, she received a piece of mail that made her stomach drop. It was a catalog of hiking equipment addressed to her real name at her address. The company that accepted the order through Amazon was given her name as attached to the credit card. Therefore, the company added her to its catalog delivery list.

All of her hard work was ruined from this one mistake. Within another thirty days, she started receiving other junk mail in her name. Within ninety days, she found her name associated with her address online. This was her only slip. The lesson to learn here is that you can never tie your real name to your address if you do not want that association to be public.

The following steps will mask your real identity from your Amazon purchases. This technique can also apply to other online retailers. Create a new account with the following information.

- **Name**: Use the name that you want your packages shipped to. This could be the former resident or landlord at your address, or a complete alias.

- **Email Address**: You must provide an email address for your new Amazon account. We recommend using a forwarding email service such as 33mail.com as discussed earlier. If your 333Mail username is "privacy", you can use an address of amazon@privacy.33mail.com. This new Amazon account will never be associated with your real name, and it will not be connected with any of your real email accounts.

- **Credit Card**: If you have a Blur account, create a new masked card and title it Amazon. Add a balance to it with at least $100. Supply this masked card number to Amazon and provide the alias name that you want to use for deliveries. Use the Boston address provided by Blur for the billing address. If you do not have a Blur account, you could use your alternate credit card number, expiration, and security code. This number will be the same number on your real credit card, so be sure that this number is not in use on any existing Amazon profiles. Blur is recommended.

- **Address**: If using Blur, provide your shipping address as desired. This may be your actual home if you do not have a better place for deliveries. If you do not have a Blur account, provide the PO Box that you used for your credit card billing address. You can alter this information after the account has been verified. In the settings of the account, you can add a new address for shipments. We have used our real home addresses in the past for deliveries. Because the name on the shipment is not a real name, we do not see this as a privacy concern. We believe it helps establish that someone else lives at your residence, and provides great disinformation. You should scrutinize any option that you choose and make sure that it is appropriate for your scenario.

This method should protect you from any association between your name, your purchases, and your home. You could likely use this new Amazon account for all of your purchases and have no problems. However, we encourage you to take things a step further and apply a bit more paranoia to your plan. We create a new Amazon account after each Blur card has been depleted. If we add a $200 Blur masked card to our account, and then use those funds over a period of five orders, we do not add a new masked card to our Amazon account. Instead, we close the account and create a new one. If there is a small amount of money remaining on the Amazon masked card, we refund it through Blur back to a credit card. This way, Amazon does not have a single record of all transactions. Additionally, each Amazon account is in a new alias name for both shipping and billing. It will add disinformation to your address and will confuse your delivery person. The only drawback to this is if you subscribe to their Prime membership. You may want to create one account to be used with those benefits, such as free streaming movies.

Amazon Gift Cards

An alternative strategy for purchasing anonymously on Amazon is to use their gift cards. These are available for sale at many retailers including drug stores such as CVS and Walgreens, grocery stores, and even hardware stores such as Home Depot and Lowes. They can be purchased in amounts up to $2,000.00, require no additional activation fee as prepaid credit cards do, and some retailers require that you pay cash for them. Using these cards is incredibly simple. Create a new Amazon account, navigate to your payment settings, and add the gift card. When you have used up your gift card balance of $25, $50, or even $500, open a new Amazon account providing your real shipping address and a false name. Now order items from Amazon as you normally would. This creates disinformation rapidly. Within 30 days of making a purchase on an alias account, you might begin receiving junk mail at your home address in that name.

One minor disadvantage to this strategy is that you may end up abandoning a small balance of a few dollars on each account which can add up to a substantial amount over time. We attempt to mitigate this as much as possible by carefully calculating our last few purchases to use the maximum amount of the balance possible. If there is under $5.00 left on the account it can typically be used to purchase a movie or Kindle book (see the next section). Taken to the extreme, you could use this technique to make a new Amazon account, complete with a new name at your shipping address, for every purchase you make.

Kindle and Other E-book Readers

You may be reading this book right now in digital form. If so, your reading device is likely sharing a lot about you to the service that supplies your books. If you are using a Kindle, Amazon stores the following about you in your profile:

- Books that you have purchased

- Books that you have read

- Books that you have searched from the device

- The last page read of any book in your account

- Any annotations, highlights, or markings within the book

- Speed at which you read any book

Some will argue that this is not a big deal. Those people probably did not make it this far into this book. We believe that this is a very big deal. Per the Electronic Frontier Foundation (EFF), this data is shared upon request with law enforcement, civil litigation attorneys, and other Amazon services. If you are involved in a lawsuit, your reading habits, including the date and time that you read a specific chapter, are available to the case. If that happens, they become public record. Imagine that you are in a child custody dispute or a bitter divorce. If you have been reading books about privacy and security, moving to a foreign country as an expatriate, or brewing beer, these titles may be used to paint you as shady or unfit. It may be argued that you were reading privacy books to conceal an affair. Your interest in a book about living overseas may be construed as you planning to flee the country to avoid child support obligations. A book about brewing beer at home may be painted to make you look like an alcoholic.

Amazon obtains this data when you connect your device to the internet. This happens over the internal Wi-Fi or cellular connection within the unit. The easy solution is to turn the connection off. However, this is also how you obtain new books and have them sent to your device. We encourage you to withdraw from this type of data collection by using the following techniques. We will assume that you are purchasing a new Kindle, but the steps can be applied to existing units. Please note that only a new Kindle will give you complete anonymity. Any existing device already possesses your personal information.

- Purchase a new Kindle from Amazon using a new account created in an alias name. Pay with a masked Blur credit card for added privacy. Never attach this account to your real name or address. Ship the device to your PO Box. Register the device with this account and use any alias name for the Kindle.

- Turn the device on while outside of the range of any public Wi-Fi. This could be in your home if your wireless router is secured with a password. Immediately place the Kindle into airplane mode which will disconnect any wireless connections. Never disable airplane mode.

- Order any books for this device from the same Amazon account that purchased the Kindle. The books you purchase will only be accessible on this specific unit. Change the default option of "Deliver to Kindle" to "Transfer via Computer". Your Kindle will be listed on the following screen. Select "Deliver to:"

- A file with the extension of AZW will be downloaded to your computer. Connect your Kindle to your computer via a USB cable. You should see your Kindle listed as a new drive. Copy and paste the book into the Documents folder of the Kindle. Unplug the device and you can now read this book without invasive tactics.

If the Kindle never leaves airplane mode, you will not share any data from the device. Further, the Kindle cannot retrieve new advertisements to place on your home screen. If your device has never touched the internet, there will never be any ads. Amazon will know the books that you have purchased, but will not know who you are. They will not know the details of your reading and annotating. They cannot target you with ads similar to books that you like. If you plan on purchasing a Kindle, we recommend creating a new Amazon account, and using this account only for Kindle related book purchases.

EBay & PayPal

EBay and PayPal, which are owned by the same company, can be trickier. EBay will apply some minor validation to the data that you enter and will require a valid form of payment to make a purchase, such as your alternative name credit card. PayPal will also require this valid form of payment and will request a Social Security number that will only be used for income reporting. We have had mixed success with using alias names. The following information may be useful.

- EBay will accept an alias in order to create an account. You can also use a 333Mail email address. You do not need to use your real name.

- EBay will accept masked credit card numbers generated from Blur. The billing address must be Blur's address in Boston. Any other address will fail verification.

- PayPal will allow you to create an account using an alias name and address. The address must actually exist, and library addresses do not appear to be blocked. They appear to accept 333Mail email addresses, but not NotSharingMy.info accounts.

- PayPal will accept Blur masked numbers if you provide your home address as the Boston address for Blur. They will not accept all prepaid cards. The address on file at PayPal must match the address on file for the prepaid card. We have found the Vanilla prepaid card to work on one occasion but not a second. This will be trial and error.

- PayPal will not accept "Load Money" PayPal gift cards if you have not verified your identity and provided true financial information. Avoid purchasing these as you will not be able to use them anonymously.

- If you want to sell items on EBay and/or accept payments through PayPal, you will need to provide a valid Social Security number and banking information. We believe you would be better suited using Craigslist and accepting cash only.

Everything Else

For the most part, any online retailers simply want to be paid. If the credit card that you use is valid and matches the shipping name and address of the purchase, the order should go through. There is not much other validation when you complete the sale. There is no reason that you should not be able to use your alternate name credit card for all of your purchases.

Eventually, your UPS, FedEx, or USPS delivery person will start to believe that you are named the alternate name on your card. Some have called us our alias names during deliveries.

BitCoin

No discussion of anonymous purchases would be complete without mentioning the infamous cryptocurrency Bitcoin. Bitcoin became widely known when the online drug marketplace Silk Road received media attention. It is still widely known today as a way to make anonymous purchases. Bitcoin still offers one of the most robust anonymous digital purchasing solutions available.

Bitcoin offers perhaps the most anonymous form of digital payment available, but its use can be a bit daunting. Before you can begin using Bitcoin, you must acquire some Bitcoins to use. Though it is possible to "mine" Bitcoins by putting your computer to work solving extremely complex mathematical problems, this is unlikely to be successful unless you have an incredibly powerful array of computers dedicated to the task. Instead, this will discuss the process of purchasing Bitcoins.

- The first step you must take to use Bitcoin is to setup a digital wallet. Your digital wallet can be either an application on your computer or an online service. If you choose to use a desktop wallet, we recommend Armory which can be downloaded at **https://bitcoinarmory.com/**. Though we generally prefer host-based applications to online services, there are some benefits to online Bitcoin wallet services. First, the desktop applications can take up a serious amount of disk space. Next, to purchase a Bitcoin you must actually find a seller and coordinate the purchase. Online wallets require only minimal disk space and simplify the purchase process by placing you in the middle of a digital confluence of Bitcoin buyers and sellers. If you choose to do so we recommend using Coinbase because of its intuitive interface and robust security. Coinbase is available at **https://www.coinbase.com/**.

- The next step required to use Bitcoin is to link a bank account to your digital wallet. Though it may seem counterintuitive, linking a bank account is an essential step to using Bitcoin, and the anonymity built into Bitcoin will protect your banking information. This is the banking account from which money will be taken to purchase Bitcoins. After submitting your account information, it may take several days for the account to be verified and linked.

- Once your account has been verified and linked you can purchase Bitcoins. To make a purchase in Coinbase, click the "Buy/Sell Bitcoins" link. Choose the number of Bitcoins you would like to purchase and the appropriate amount will be withdrawn from your bank account to pay for them. The price of Bitcoins fluctuates wildly, so know what you are paying for before you commit to a purchase. Once you have purchased Bitcoins, it may take several days for them to be transferred to your wallet.

After your wallet has been set up and you have some BitCoins to spend, what do you spend them on? More and more online services are now supporting Bitcoin. Many privacy- and security-focused services support Bitcoin. These include VPNs (see Chapter Fourteen) and premium email providers. You can purchase computers and digital accessories from Dell, Newegg (**http://www.newegg.com/**), and Tiger Direct (**http://www.tigerdirect.com/**). You can also obtain content hosting from WordPress or prepaid hotel reservations through Expedia. The online retail giant Overstock.com now accepts Bitcoin as a form of payment, and even Microsoft supports Bitcoin for the purchase of some software and service.

Store Purchases

Any time that we make a purchase that requires delivery, we never use our real name. Doing so would add the name and address to various online websites from which we have previously removed them. The additional benefit is that this disinformation that we provided will now be associated with our home addresses. It will confuse data marketing companies about the actual tenants.

Remember, we are keeping everything legal because we are not causing any financial fraud. All of our purchases are billed to a credit card number that is assigned to us. We will pay the bills as agreed with our credit card company. These transactions will not financially affect anyone else.

Many purchases will ask that you to fill out a warranty card. We have purchased items as large as refrigerators and as small as coffee pots that include a "Warranty Registration Card" in the package. We strongly advise against filling these out with accurate information. Your receipt is a legally-accepted proof of purchase for the item. The warranty registration card is merely an attempt to lure you into providing personal information that can be sold. Warranty cards also offer an excellent opportunity to create disinformation which will be covered in Chapter Sixteen.

One big lesson in regards to in-person purchases is that you always have a name, address, and telephone number memorized at checkout. If paying by secondary credit card in an alias name, you should use that name if asked. However, the physical address and telephone number provided during an in-store purchase is not verified with the credit card being used. This is collected for that store's internal marketing database and will likely leak out to third parties. Take a moment now and start thinking about the address and telephone number that you would give out if asked.

Many businesses will demand this information from you as a customer. In a blog post, JJ Luna shared his experience with purchasing a new pair of glasses at an optometrist. He was paying cash, but they insisted on collecting his home address and telephone number. He argued that the cash sale did not require that information, and they refused to serve him. He walked out without the glasses. While we certainly respect his response, there may be situations that you face that will not allow you to simply walk away. Instead, always have an address and telephone number ready. Later chapters present many examples of safe information that you can use to protect your privacy while functioning in today's society.

Online Payment Methods

The world has changed drastically when it comes to cash purchases. Prior cash transactions for Girl Scout cookies in front of a grocery store have turned into credit card processing by children. Several new services have made it incredibly easy to accept credit cards for payment at any time. PayPal, Square, and others have introduced free credit card readers that attach to any smartphone. They then use the phone's internet connection to process the payment through secure servers. While this has not helped the fight to preserve the anonymous option of cash, we can still use it to our advantage. If you want to make a purchase from someone that accepts these forms of payment, you are not required to use an actual credit card. The focus of these readers is the ability to swipe a card for payment. However, the owner can also accept a virtual credit card as payment. Consider the following two scenarios.

You are at a mechanic, art festival, or used musical instrument shop and you want to make a purchase. The items that you want to buy exceed the amount of cash that you possess. The seller has a Square credit card reader connected to his iPad and can accept credit card payments. Advise him that you want to use a gift card that you received via email. The seller can type the credit card number, expiration, and security code into the Square app on the device to accept the payment. A physical card is not required. When you give him a masked credit card number issued by Blur, you can associate any name with the purchase. If the purchase is a high dollar amount, you may be required to present the billing address of the card. When using Blur, you would give the company address of 280 Summer Street in Boston. We have used this address so often that we likely receive postal mail there.

You have identified an item that you want to buy on Craigslist. The seller will accept PayPal as a form of payment and can either swipe a credit card through the PayPal reader of accept a transfer of funds from your account. Instead, ask the seller to issue you an invoice from within the PayPal account. Give an email address connected to your 333Mail account. You will immediately receive an invoice via email from PayPal for the exact amount. Use a masked credit card from Blur to complete the transaction without creating a PayPal account. When prompted, simply choose to pay by credit card.

We believe that our society is going to see more adoption of electronic payment and fewer opportunities to buy with cash. While disappointing, we must go with the flow. Knowing your options ahead of the transaction will prepare you to stay as private as you can. Being prepared with an alias and virtual credit card will take you a long way.

Michael's Experience

In 2012, I purchased a new refrigerator. The large home improvement store that had the best price won my business. They also offered free delivery to my home. I sat down to complete the purchase with the salesperson when the questions began. In order to sell and deliver a refrigerator, I had to provide my name, home address, telephone number, cellular telephone number, work telephone number, credit card information, and a secondary contact person. Obviously, my address was necessary, but I am hesitant to provide the rest. Later in the book, you will read about the ways that data marketing companies learn information about you and resell the data. This is one of the primary ways that you are targeted for future purchases. As soon as you provide this information, it is added to an internal database and resold to other companies. The following is how I handled the situation.

- **Name**: I advised that this purchase was for my father, so I would like the delivery in his name. I then provided a very specific name such as John Coolman. Why Coolman? The last name Coolman will remind me of my "cool" refrigerator. I choose a name like that because I want to monitor where the data provided to the salesperson is sent. In a few weeks, when I receive a mailing from an advertiser to John Coolman, I will know where that company received the information.

- **Address**: I provided my home address for the delivery. Because this was not associated with my real name, and I needed to tell them where to go, this was acceptable.

- **Telephone Numbers**: I advised that there is no telephone at the house but I will be available on my cellular number at any time. I then provided my Google Voice account.

- **Payment**: I used my alternate name credit card.

- **Secondary contact and work number**: I assured the salesperson that I would be available and a secondary contact or work number was not necessary.

This may all seem very basic and like common sense, but think about what took place. I kept the purchase anonymous with my alternative name credit card. I added another layer of privacy by placing the delivery in a generic name. That generic name will never be used by me again and will help me identify where that store shares my information. I will not personally be targeted with offers of extended warranty protection. My real name will not be added to the database of large product purchases that will receive future promotional offers. Finally, I have a receipt that will suffice for any issues with the product.

Services

You will likely be asked to provide a credit card as a deposit when you reserve a company for any type of high value service. This may include home maintenance, satellite television, or movers. Many of these will not accept prepaid cards and will insist on a hold on funds within the credit card account. For these situations, we always recommend using your secondary credit card in an alias name. The following example illustrates the importance of not using a card in your name with home services.

A client was relocating to another state to escape an abusive ex and to take on a new job. She was renting a small apartment near her new employer that included all utilities. She knew not to attach her name to anything regarding her new address. She contacted a popular home moving company and scheduled them to arrive at her current home, pack her belongings into a moving truck, and deliver them to her new address. As you can imagine, this presented a unique situation. They rightfully needed her current address and new address. They also insisted on obtaining her name, credit card number, and a telephone number at which they could reach her at during delivery. She panicked and hung up without giving them any details. She then called us.

If she had completed the order, there would be a very strong trail from her current address to her new address. We suspect that within weeks, she would receive targeted advertising in her name at her new address offering typical services to a new resident. Many moving companies supplement their revenue by sharing customer databases with non-competing services that cater to new residents. This data could easily leak to online people search websites. We decided to help her by facilitating the entire moving process on her behalf.

We chose U-Haul as the most appropriate mover for her situation. Her relocation was substantial, and the mileage fees alone for a moving truck were outrageous. When adding the fee for two movers to facilitate the transfer, the quote was several thousands of dollars. We completed the order for the move in three isolated phases. For the sake of this scenario, assume that she was moving from Miami to St. Louis.

We scheduled U-Haul to deliver two moving U-box containers to her current home. These are large wooden crates in which you can store your belonging before they are shipped by a semi-truck and trailer. U-Haul required a valid credit card so we provided our client's secondary credit card in an alias name. This order also included pickup of the full containers and storage at the Miami U-Haul headquarters. The boxes were delivered by the local Miami U-Haul provider closest to her home.

She had friends help her fill the containers and we called U-Haul to come and pick them up. They were transferred and stored at the Miami headquarters awaiting further instruction. Customers are allotted 30 days of included storage before additional fees are introduced. We called the Miami U-Haul and provided the order number and alias name. We requested that

U-Haul deliver these containers to the St. Louis storage facility. We were given the rate for this service and a deposit was charged to the card on file.

The 333Mail email address on file received a confirmation that the containers had arrived in St. Louis six days later. They were stored there awaiting further orders. The storage fees were covered as part of our original contract. Through the U-Haul website, we identified a reputable moving company that offered to transport U-box containers to the final destination and unpack the contents. We added this to our current open contract and provided a destination address of a post office within the new city that she was moving to. This was the last piece of information that was given to U-Haul. We authorized U-Haul to release the containers to the moving company.

We called the independent moving service that would be picking up her containers and delivering them to her new apartment. We provided the order number and her alias name. We stated that the original order had a placeholder address because we did not know the new address that we were moving to. We then gave this company her actual address and she met the movers there to direct them with the move. She possessed the release code that allowed the moving company to close the contract and be paid by U-Haul.

At the end of this move, we paid for the following services using the client's secondary credit card.

- U-Box drop-off at original location

- U-Box pickup at original location

- U-Box storage for one month

- U-Box delivery from Miami to St. Louis

- Independent moving company delivery to new residence

- Independent moving company empty container return fee

Out of curiosity, we input similar beginning and ending addresses within the U-Haul website moving calculator. Our method was the exact same price as if we had given U-Haul everything they needed in one step. In our method, U-Haul does not know her real name or her current address. For full disclosure, they know that she likely lives near St. Louis. There is very little value in this information to U-Haul. The independent moving company knows her new address, but they do not know her name or where she moved from. If her U-Haul account were to be breached, her address would appear to be a local post office.

We trained her to have small talk answers ready for the movers. She was to say that she is staying in St. Louis with her husband while he was assigned there by his employer and then returning to California where she came from. We later asked her how that went. She stated that she simply did not answer any of their questions and they stopped talking to her altogether. We liked working with her.

Her first purchase at the new apartment was DirectTV satellite television service. She placed the call for the order through a Google Voice number and provided an alias name with her real address. She asked for paperless billing and requested her credit card be automatically charged prior to each month of service. She again provided the secondary credit card in her alias name. Because she was enrolled in automatic billing to a valid credit card, there was no approval process or credit check. Most services will bypass this requirement by enrolling in a type of auto-pay option.

Justin's Experience

Sometimes unplanned occurrences can offer excellent opportunities for privacy. Such was the case at my rental house when I woke up to find that the propane tank was unexpectedly empty. This created a problem for me, and not just because I had no hot water. My landlord paid for all utilities except propane. However, I had been assured by the landlord that it was full and I would not need to worry about it for the duration of my lease, after which he would have it refilled and I would reimburse him. To further complicate the issue, the landlord lived in another state. I would have to find a way to get the tank filled, pay for it, and not associate my name with that address.

I called the propane company and explained my situation. Unfortunately, they required that I have an account, even though I was paying in cash. I thought I may have a way around this, though. I told the lady I would set up my account online and get back to her. I promptly went to the propane company's website and filled out the registration form using a fake name. I provided no credit card information. I called back and told her to schedule the delivery. She pulled up my account and noted, "Mr. Morgan, you have no credit card on file. How would you like to pay for this?" I informed her that I would be paying in cash. When the delivery driver arrived he handed me an invoice and I handed him cash to pay for the propane. For the remainder of my stay I received statements and promotion flyers from the propane company addressed to Dexter and Rita Morgan.

Internet Service

We believe that the most import utility or service that you can anonymize is your home internet connection. Possessing internet service at your home address in your real name jeopardizes your privacy on two levels. Many providers use their subscriber list for marketing and it often ends up in the hands of other companies. This will eventually make your home address public on the internet and associated with you. This is possible with any utility or service that is attached to your home address. However, your home internet account shares another layer of your life that you may not realize.

Internet service providers (ISPs) create the connection required for you to have internet access. In its simplest terms, a cable or phone company possesses a very large connection to the entire internet. It creates its own connections to its customers (you). This might be in the form of a cable modem connected to the main connection coming into your house. This allows you to connect to the entire internet through your ISP. Therefore, the ISP can monitor your online activity. Other chapters explain how to mask this traffic with virtual private networks (VPNs) and other technologies. However, you cannot stop the ISP from seeing the amount of traffic that you are sending and receiving, the times of the day that you are online, and details of the devices that you are connecting to their system.

Those that use other technologies discussed in this book will likely be protected from the invasive habits of ISPs. However, people make mistakes. You might forget to enable your VPN or it might fail due to a software crash. You might have guests that use your internet without practicing secure browsing habits. Consider the following scenario.

Every day, numerous people receive a dreaded letter from their internet service provider. It states that on a specific date and time, your internet connection was used to download copyrighted digital material. This is usually in the form of movies or music. This practice usually occurs when law firms monitor data such as torrent files that are commonly used to share pirated media. They identify the IP address used for the download, contact the provider of the IP address, and demand to know the subscriber information. The providers often cooperate and share your details. You then receive a notice demanding several thousands of dollars in order to avoid a lawsuit. Not paying could, and often will, result in legal proceedings. There are numerous cases of people who have lost the lawsuit and have been ordered to pay much more than the original asking amount.

We are not encouraging the use of the internet to obtain files that you do not have the authority to possess. We also do not advocate fishing expeditions by greedy lawyers looking to take you down. We see another side of the problem. What if someone uses your Wi-Fi to commit these acts? What if malware or a virus conducts activities that are seen as infringing? While our first solution is to use the methods discussed in Chapter Fourteen, we believe a good backup to this issue is to simply have an anonymous internet connection. These methods will only work if you have gone to the extent of residing in an anonymous house as explained in the expert level at the end of this book. If you have not, or are not going to that level, it does not hurt to apply these methods for a small layer of protection. The following is a true example from a recent client.

Our client had recently moved into his new invisible home. He was renting, and nothing was associated with his real name. The electricity and water were included in the rent and associated with the landlord's name. However, there was no internet access included with the rent. Our client contacted the telephone company to take advantage of a deal for DSL internet service at a promotional rate of $24.99 per month for two years. He did not need anything faster than this access, and liked the price. He gave an alias name and the real address for the service and was quickly asked for a Social Security number (SSN), date of birth, and previous address. He tried his best to convince the operator that he did would not give this out, and she politely stated that their policy is to conduct a brief credit check before providing access. He gave up and terminated the call.

He emailed us asking for guidance. While we had dealt with similar issues for ourselves and others in the past, it had been a while since we had tested our methods with all of the providers. In exchange for us helping him without any fees, he agreed to share his experiences for this book.

We first contacted the telephone company offering the DSL connection. Before giving any personal information to the operator, we politely asked about the signup policy and what type of credit check would be conducted. We were told twice that a "soft pull" would be conducted based on the SSN of the customer. This was to ensure that there were no outstanding bills from previous connections and to simply verify the identity of the customer. While telling our sad story of identity thefts, harassment, and threats to our lives, we pleaded for a way to obtain service to no avail. Part of the issue here was that a two-year contract was required, and they wanted to be sure that they would get their money. There was nothing to obtain here.

We searched for other service providers and found two possibilities, Charter Spectrum cable access and various satellite internet options. Due to speed and cost, we wanted to avoid the satellite option. We contacted Charter and verified the service connection to the residence. They had a high speed connection of 60 Mbps offered at $59.99 per month. We assured them that we had never had Charter in the past, and asked if there was an introductory price similar to the DSL offer that we quoted. As usual, the representative came up with a lower offer. He acknowledged a new customer offer at $39.99 (taxes included) per month for up to one year. We accepted that and knew that our client could likely negotiate that cost down through threats of cancelling when the time came.

We provided our client's address, an alias name that had already been established and associated with a secondary credit card, and requested automatic bill pay through credit card. We were told that we could set up the automatic payment ourselves after the account had been established. This was even better. We got to the end thinking things were too smooth when the personal questions arrived. He needed our SSN in order to complete the process.

We had dealt with Charter in the past and were able to bypass this requirement so we started testing the situation. We first stated "Oh wow, I was not prepared for that. You see, I was recently the victim of identity theft and the police told me I was not allowed to give out my SSN until the investigation was complete". The operator was very sympathetic and placed us on hold briefly. He then asked for simply a date of birth in order to conduct the query. We continued to resist and stated "I think that would be the same as giving you my SSN. I will give you my credit card right now, can I just auto pay?" We were then greeted with something we did not expect. The operator stated "The system demands at least a year of birth, can you give me that?" We took a second to evaluate the risk and provided a year of birth that was not accurate. This seemed odd to us because there is not much the operator could do with that limited information. However, it was enough to get to the next screen. He now needed an email address for the account details and monthly electronic billing. It is always important to have this alias email account ready before any calls are made. He finished the order and the call was terminated.

Three days later, Charter arrived at his house and installed the service. They provided a modem, and charged $29.99 for installation. Our client had his secondary credit card ready, but he was never asked for it. Charter literally conducted the installation, activated the service, and left without collecting any form of payment. The next day he received an email notifying him of a payment due. He created a new account on the Charter website and provided his secondary credit card for the payment. He then activated automatic payments to that card and enabled the paperless billing option. Today, he continues to receive great internet service from Charter and pays his bills automatically to his secondary card. Charter does not know his true name. He has committed no fraud. He is a loyal customer and will likely pay Charter for services for the rest of his time at this residence. Charter did not require any contract and he can cancel any time. We were pleasantly surprised.

We thought that this may be a fluke. Maybe we were lucky with that operator. We decided to test the system again. However, this time we would contact all of the providers. We decided to contact each major internet provider through two separate calls and document the results. Our goal was to identify the personal information requirements for each provider in order to activate service to a residential home. The following describes our findings. Please note that your experiences may differ.

We started with Comcast. We assumed that they would be the worst to deal with. This is probably due to years of negative publicity in reference to horrible customer support. They were actually quite pleasant. We stated on two calls with two different employees that we wanted internet service but would not provide a SSN. The first employee stated that a SSN was required for a "risk assessment". We inquired on ways to bypass this requirement and discovered that Comcast will eliminate this requirement and risk assessment if the customer pays a $50 deposit. The deposit would be returned after one year of paid service.

The second employee also stated that a SSN was required for a "risk assessment" and that there was no way to bypass this. We mentioned the $50 deposit, and after a brief hold were told that the deposit would eliminate the requirement. We have had two clients since these conversations that have confirmed that Comcast will provide service to any name provided as long as a credit card deposit of $50 was provided. We consider this a fair compromise. Comcast also did not require a contract of any specific length of service.

We contacted many of the most common internet service providers in the United States. We asked a series of very specific questions in order to identify those that would allow an account to be created in an unconfirmed name. The table that follows this section displays our results. The categories of the table are explained below.

SSN Required: If the provider requires a Social Security number (SSN), they will likely perform a hard credit check. This will associate your real name with the address of service (your home).

DOB/DL Required: If the provider requires a date of birth or driver's license number, this is also a strong indication that a check will be conducted. This is likely a risk assessment at the least, and will also attach your name to your home. Using anything but your real full name will result in a denial of new service.

Contract Required: This indicates whether the provider requires you to sign a contract for service. This usually locks you in to a set period of time before you would be allowed to cancel. This is not a concern as far as a commitment to service. However, signing a false name here could get you into trouble in civil court. We discourage using any name aside from your own on any binding contract.

Deposit Required: This field identifies the deposit required in order to bypass the credit check mandated by most companies. Paying this amount, as well as the monthly service fee, ahead of service will often eliminate the requirement of a verification check of your name. We welcome a deposit requirement in lieu of providing personal details.

Credit Check Required: This column identifies the companies that absolutely require a full credit check. We have found no way to bypass this requirement with the providers listed. This will certainly connect your name to your address and will be present through online resources.

Your experiences may vary from ours. Overall, most internet service providers stated that a SSN and credit check were required for service at first. When pushed on alternative options, many acknowledged that this information was not required. We found that the following two questions gained the best results when talking with a sales representative.

- I was recently the victim of identity theft and was told to no longer disclose my SSN. Is there any way I can purchase your services without giving you my personal details? I will pay the deposit.

- I reviewed your website offer details and I want to purchase internet service though your company. I will be paying automatically by credit card in order to forego giving you my SSN or DOB. Thanks!

We encourage you to be persistent and do not give in to the sales tactics. Overall, the person you talk to wants to complete the sale. Hopefully, this chart will help you choose an internet provider that values your privacy. Later in this book, we will discuss strategies for making all of your utilities anonymous.

Provider	SSN Required	DOB/DL Required	Contract Required	Deposit Required	Credit Check Required
AT&T	No	Yes	Yes	No	Yes
CenturyLink	No	No	Yes	$75	No
Charter	No	No	No	No	No
Comcast	No	No	No	$50	No
Cox	No	No	No	$40-$65	No
DishNet	Yes	Yes	Yes	N/A	Yes
EarthLink	No	No	No	Varies	No
Frontier	Yes	Yes	No	N/A	Yes
Verizon	No	Yes	No	No	Yes

Incoming Mail

Your purchases prior to reading this book are likely to have an impact on the mail that you receive today. After you complete the data removal process in this book, pay close attention to the mail that you receive at your home. Each piece should be categorized as either junk or important. If it is junk, refer to Chapter Eight and eliminate the mailings through Catalog Choice or DMA. If the mailing is something important that you want to continue to receive, contact the sender and change your address to your post office box. If you have an online account for the company, attempt to change this yourself through their website. Any mail that you send out should always have your post office box address instead of your home address.

If you receive advertisements in the mail addressed to your name at your home address, you may want to contact the sender and ask to be removed from the mailing list. In our experience, this seldom works. Reputable companies may honor your request. However, many companies simply ignore it. When you believe this happens, we recommend calling and changing your address. Consider the following actual scenario.

We had a client who had a taste for expensive vehicles. He had purchased a few over the years, and he was now targeted heavily by a large local dealer. He had eliminated most of the mail to his name at his home address, but this dealer sent him a flyer, letter, or invitation every week. He called and politely asked to be removed from the database. This never worked. Finally, he called and stated the following.

"Hi, I have been shopping for a car at your dealership, and I have received some great offers.

I just moved and I want to make sure I don't miss the next big sale. Can you update my address?"

The dealership happily updated his file to include the new address that he provided. The address that he provided was that of a competing dealership located one town over. The receptionist that answered the phone had no clue.

Post Office Box Issues

There are occasions when companies will refuse a post office box as a mailing address. This has nothing to do with the deliverability of mail to the address. They just want your home address to add to your profile. Therefore, they have rules in place that will reject your box number in an online form submission. The only times that a physical house address must be verified are when you are establishing a new line of credit or completing official government paperwork. Any other company should only receive your post office box address. There is a way to usually force it.

Assume that your address is PO Box 9985, Chicago, IL 60601. There must only be one box with that number in that zip code. When your online form refuses to accept your address, enter it in reverse order. Enter it as 9985 Box, Chicago, IL 60601. The post office will know that any mailings to this address should be sent to your box. This format should meet any requirements in an online form. You may notice that some generic advertisements are addressed in this reverse format.

Vehicle Servicing

Having your vehicle serviced will usually result in your information entering advertising databases. Whether it is an oil change at a national chain or a repair at a local dealership, your information is being collected. This will eventually result in related advertisements at your home and direct marketing toward your preference in vehicles. An average visit makes the following information available.

- Full name, home address, and home telephone number
- Cellular telephone number for pickup notification
- Make, model, year, mileage, registration, VIN, and maintenance history of vehicle
- Services provided and services declined
- Estimated warranty expiration

This is the type of information that companies such as TowerData and Epsilon use to build custom profiles on you. This is why you receive mailings from auto dealers and warranty providers at specific times. Staying out of this system is difficult, but not impossible.

Your best option is to locate a trusted individual to service your vehicle either in a small shop or home. It is more affordable, service is usually superior, and you leave no trace. If you must visit a repair shop or dealer, never provide your real name and address. Use alias information. Payment can be made with your secondary credit card in your alternate name. You should also be careful not to leave your vehicle registration or insurance information in the vehicle when you drop it off. These documents are often referenced by auto service personnel to capture your data. Is this overkill? Maybe. Use your best judgment.

Package Deliveries

Internet shopping offers cheap prices and global access to products. You have probably ordered a product from an internet company such as Amazon or Netflix. When you supply your home address for these deliveries, the information will be added to marketing databases. These databases will probably only be used for internal marketing from one company, but the data may eventually be sold to other collectors. The best solution is to provide your post office box address for deliveries. Further, be sure to remove your residence address from your profile through the online retailer. If you have a mailbox that is not large enough for the delivery, you will receive a notification of a package available for pickup at the counter.

Another option is to have packages delivered to your workplace. This may not be appropriate for everyone. If you are a victim of domestic violence and you do not want anyone to know where you work, you should not choose this option. If you are a government employee, public official, or have a job with any public presence, there is probably no harm in using a work address. A package left inside a workspace is more secure than one left outside an empty home. Additionally, there will likely be someone available to sign for a package during business hours.

Food Deliveries

Ordering pizza or Chinese food does not necessarily compromise your privacy. You must disclose your address for the delivery, but you do not need to provide your real name. If you want to keep your home address private and unassociated with your name, always obey the following rules:

- Never provide your real name or telephone number. Always use an alternate name.
- Never call from your landline telephone. It will identify your name.
- Never rely on caller ID blocking to protect your information.
- Order online through the company's website when available.
- Always pay with cash.

Michael's Age and Identity Verification Strategy

There will be times when you are "carded" in order to verify a minimum age. This may be at the grocery store when you purchase alcoholic beverages or to gain access to an "over 21" area at an event. For most situations, I do not mind displaying my driver's license. The employee is only looking at your birth date and no information is being collected into a system. This is not always the case. Recently, I attended an event at a local casino. Upon entry, everyone had to show identification for age verification. If you frequent the casino often, the player's card will escalate you through this process. Since I do not participate in these programs, I was stuck in line. I watched my friend ahead of me display his license which was scanned into a card reader by a gaming agent. The computer displayed my friend's driver's license photo and information. I had no doubt that his information had just been added to this chain casino's database. He was allowed to pass. As my paranoia kicked in, I pretended to receive a cellular call and got out of line to retrieve a forgotten item from my car. When I returned, I walked through the line without showing my license and personal address. How did I do it? I displayed my passport.

Passports are accepted practically everywhere as proof of identity. They contain your name, date of birth, place of birth, and a photograph. A passport contains a unique number assigned to you that can be used in place of a driver's license number. This number is much more difficult to trace by the private sector. A passport has never contained a home address. Further, instead of carrying around a large passport that does not fit in your wallet, you can apply for a passport card. This card is only good for land or sea travel between the US and Canada, Mexico, the Caribbean, and Bermuda but is accepted nearly everywhere as federally-issued identification. Like a passport it does not contain your home address. It lists only your full name, date and place of birth and passport information.

I contacted my friend a few months later and inquired about the casino. I asked if he ever receives advertisements and offers from them. He replied that he gets coupons and announcements from them in the mail. After thinking for a moment, he said that he also gets mailings from other casinos owned by the same company. He verified that he had never signed up for anything through the casino. They must have used the data from his driver's license. I suspect that the data collected will eventually find its way to a company that will not keep it private.

Any time you need to provide proof of your name or age, consider showing your passport. While it can be scanned in the same manner as a license, very few establishments have the hardware devices to do this. Banks, hospitals, airports, and hotels are familiar with passports and should never offer resistance in their use.

CHAPTER ELEVEN
ANONYMOUS TELEPHONES

Cellular telephones are digital trackers in our pockets monitoring and recording every move we make. They are beacons announcing our locations, conversations, contacts, and activities to companies outside of our control. Do we use cell phones? Absolutely. Can we reclaim our privacy without ditching the convenience of a computer in our pocket? Yes, and we will explain our methods in this chapter.

We believe that having an anonymous cellular telephone is very high on the list of vital steps to take in order to obtain true privacy. Even if you implement every tactic explained in the next chapter about phone security, your device is always tracking you. If the device is on and connected to either a cellular tower or Wi-Fi connection, it is collecting and sharing your location information. The moment you place a call or send a text, you have updated a permanent database of these details attached to your account. Some will argue that these details are not publicly visible and only obtainable with a court order. While in a perfect world this is true, we do not live in a perfect world. There are many scenarios that could leak your entire communications history to the world.

The most common scenario would be a data breach. We hear every day that a new database of customer information has been stolen and released to the wild. What is to prevent that from happening to a cellular provider? We also know from widely publicized reports that some government agencies overstep the scope of data collection from both Americans and non-Americans, often including telephone records. We have seen several civil legal battles incorporate cellular records into the case after submitting a subpoena to a provider. We have even heard of rare instances where a Freedom of Information Act (FOIA) request was submitted for cellular records of government employees.

Regardless of your situation, we believe that you have a great deal of data to lose by using a standard cellular telephone setup. This chapter will explain many ways of maintaining privacy while remaining connected to the world. Near the end, we will each share our current telephone strategy and the following chapter will provide details of securing your device.

The most common way to possess a cellular telephone is through a contract with a major provider. This typically happens when you visit a provider's kiosk or store and are given a free phone. While this sounds like a great excuse to upgrade, you are committing to multiple years of service though this carrier. Privacy through this method is practically impossible since the provider will mandate a financial check on you using your Social Security number. Your phone, bill, and call details will be stored forever and connected to your name. This can all be avoided, but at a cost.

The rest of this chapter will assume that you are ready to change your cellular strategy. If you are currently stuck in a contract, you may want out of it. If you are no longer committed to the original contract terms, you are ready to ditch the service. Either way, it is time to break away from the comfortable options provided by the carriers.

First, we need to acknowledge that many readers are stuck in a contract and do not have the option of simply stopping the service. We understand that and want to help you eliminate that monthly bill. Every provider is different, but we believe it is always possible to force a company to release you from the contract. The following methods should be evaluated for your specific needs. Choose one that is most appropriate for your situation and attempt the technique. The worst that will happen is that you will be told "no".

Changes to Contract Terms

If your cell carrier changes the terms of the contract you signed, you can cancel your contract without paying any early termination fees. Many states require cell phone companies to give customers advance notice of contract changes which could increase the cost or extend the length of the contract. These cell phone companies must get consent from their customers before increasing the cost or extending the length of contract. Contact your provider and request a copy of the contract that you originally signed. In a separate call, to a different representative, request the current contract terms for your plan. If the price, coverage, or usage limitations have changed, you can likely demand release from the contract. This method became very popular when Sprint changed their terms of service in 2008. Any customer that signed a contract before that date had the legal right to cancel the agreement without penalty. Providers are very aware of this trick, and will likely resist. However, persistence usually pays off. Third party services such as **cellbreaker.com** can assist with this technique. As always, if you create an account with CellBreaker you should use anonymous information.

Changes to Coverage

Most cell providers' coverage areas are quite extensive, but there will always be gaps in service. If you move to an area with little or no coverage, you may be able to get out of your contract. Keep in mind that most cellular service providers don't want to let you go, so they may offer you a mini antenna or tower for your home. This will often boost your signal enough to give you reasonable coverage. You can often use your provider's coverage maps to identify areas with weak reception. Stating that you have recently moved to an address within this non-existent coverage area will occasionally lead to termination without penalty. Currently, AT&T and T-Mobile have policies to release you from contract if you move to an area without service.

Document and Report Bad Service

We believe that anyone reading this section has suffered numerous dropped calls, awkward delays during a conversation, and the occasional absent signal. Complaining to the carrier and documenting these complaints can assist when you attempt to break your contract. You should always see if you can get your wireless provider to come around to your cause. They won't want to lose you as a customer, but most companies will make some kind of exemption if you talk to the right person and have a good reason. If you are a soldier who is being deployed, or you've lost your job and are unable to continue paying your contract, they'll usually let you out or work with you on a compromise.

However, don't expect to just call up and have the first person you speak to solve your problem. You may need to call back several times or escalate your issue. Consider using the company's social media channels to your advantage, or go straight to the top and contact corporate executives.

Sell Your Plan

There is likely someone out there looking to get out of their plan and into a new one, and they may be interested in buying yours. You can choose to swap with them, or just sell your plan to them directly. Sites such as Cellswapper or Trade My Cellular attempt to make this painless. This doesn't violate your terms of service because the other party is fulfilling the terms of your original contract. Again, if you sign up for such a service attempt do so as anonymously as possible.

Last Resorts

There are also doubtlessly a few individuals reading this book who are nearing the end of their contract term, or who can wait a few months. Riding out the remainder of your contract is an option, as is paying an early termination fee. If you are only a few months away the early termination fee may be an affordable option for you. Regardless of how you do it, moving to an anonymous phone will not happen as long as you are on a contract. Getting off of a subsidized contract is essential, otherwise the steps in the remainder of this chapter will be useless.

We will now assume that you are free of any contract for cellular service and are ready to jump into a completely anonymous phone. Many people will mistakenly think that any pre-paid phone will protect you from intrusive provider practices. In reality, it is not that simple. Going to the local grocery store and purchasing a device with 100 minutes and 500MB of data using cash may feel private. However, there is much more to consider if you want to enjoy your new device and associated plan. The majority of pre-paid users possess inferior devices and over-pay for the limited service that they receive. We aim to correct all of that.

The Device

First, you will need a proper telephone. We never recommend any devices that are marketed toward pre-paid buyers. These are always the unpopular models that no one else wants. They are slow, have poor battery performance, and will only meet the minimum hardware requirements to function. Additionally, they are overpriced. At the time of this writing, a local grocery store was selling an Android smartphone for $149 that was available on eBay for less than $60. Either way, it was not a powerful device. Instead, consider a used phone.

Searching your local Craigslist.org community will identify hundreds of used devices for sale. You will need to be careful. Many of these are stolen, some are broken, and others are counterfeit. We recommend filtering these results until you are only left with the following.

- Devices that include the original box, cables, and manuals: This is an indication of a one owner phone that is not likely stolen property. A person that keeps those items probably takes good care of their property.

- Sellers that have recently upgraded: Many people must have the latest and greatest devices and upgrade the moment a new version is available. While you can never believe everything that you read on Craigslist, this is an indicator of a decent phone.

- High prices and old posts: Many people believe the value of their used equipment is higher than what others are willing to pay. Seeking phones that were posted over three weeks' prior at a high price will usually reveal people desperate to sell. Make a reasonable offer and you will be surprised how many people accept.

You may already have an unused device collecting dust. Usually, when you upgrade a phone, you are allowed to keep the old unit. You could use a device that was previously attached to your name and account, but we urge caution in this. Financially, it makes sense to use a device that you already have. Unfortunately, providers never truly forget what you have used. If you decide to use a phone that was previously attached to an account in your name, please know that the history will continue to be available.

Your device possesses an IMEI (International Mobile Station Equipment Identity) number that is transmitted to the carrier. When you activate an old phone, even as a pre-paid, that number could still jeopardize your privacy. This may seem extreme, and it may not be important to most readers. If you want to completely start over and not contaminate your new communications device, you should obtain a unit that has no association to you.

If you are not concerned with the trail left to the cellular provider, then you can re-activate an old device. Only you can decide which is appropriate. We ask that you consider the following question. Will anyone ever ask your cellular carrier for a list of every phone that you have owned or used? By "everyone" we include hackers, friendly government agencies, enemy government agencies, the media, and general public after the next big data leak. In the most basic terms, your cellular telephone that was used in your real name is permanently attached to you. There is no way to break this connection. This device tracks your location at all times and reports to your provider. That data is stored forever. Therefore, we believe that now is the time to activate a new device with a new account.

We encourage privacy enthusiasts to start fresh with different new or previously-owned devices from strangers. You could also organize a swap with someone else that you have no official connection with. New non-subsidized phones are becoming more affordable while offering a level of privacy unavailable through a traditional contract. This might be a good time to try a different operating system. Android versus iPhone is a matter of personal preference. We have used both, and will outline our current devices, plans, and strategies for anonymity at the end of the next chapter. You should use what you are most comfortable with. Both can be made secure and anonymous. We will also discuss the privacy- and security-focused BlackPhone later in this chapter.

If you are looking for an extremely affordable solution, you might consider the various "Mini Card Cell Phones" available at online retailers such as Amazon. These miniature telephones usually cost $20 or less and are the size of a credit card. They do not contain touch screens, cannot use data plans, and do not work with apps. They can only make and receive calls and texts. We have used these as "burner" phones in hostile environments. The lack of data usage and internet access creates a fairly secure phone for minimal communication. These are almost always based on GSM networks and nano SIM cards, and the carrier plans for these phones are minute compared to those of modern smartphones.

Factory Restore

Regardless of the operating system, previous owner, or current state of the device, you should conduct a factory restore. This eliminates all personal data from any previous user and replaces the phone's operating system in the identical state as the day it was first purchased. This will ensure that there are no unique configurations that could jeopardize your privacy. The process for this will vary slightly by device. However, the following general practices should obtain the desired result.

- **Android**: Settings > Backup and Reset > Factory Data Reset > Reset Device

- **iPhone**: Settings > General > Reset > Erase All Content

- **Windows Phone**: Settings > About > Reset Your Phone

Rooting Android

Rooting is an optional process that gives you the power of full functionality of your Android device. It allows you to delete programs that could not be deleted normally and suspend processes that could normally not be accessed. We believe that this can be important for functionality, battery life, and privacy. However, this also makes the device much more vulnerable to malware and monitoring implants. Before you consider rooting your device, please read the next chapter. It will identify major security weaknesses that may change your mind.

Each model of Android is unique and has a preferred method of rooting. Rooting will allow you to dive deeper into a phone's sub-system. Essentially, it will allow you to access the entire operating system and be able to customize just about anything on your Android. With root access, you can get around any restrictions that your manufacturer or carrier may have applied. You can run more apps, you can over-clock or under-clock your processor, and replace the firmware. The process requires users to back up current software and installing a new custom ROM (modified version of Android).

One of the most obvious incentives to root your Android device is to rid yourself of the bloatware that is otherwise impossible to uninstall. You will be able to set up wireless tethering, without paying extra, even if it has been disabled by your carrier. A lot of people are tempted by the ability to completely customize the look of their phones. You can also manually accept or deny individual app permissions.

There are essentially three potential cons to rooting your Android.

- Voiding your warranty: Some manufacturers or carriers will use rooting as an excuse to void your warranty. It's worth keeping in mind that you can always un-root. If you need to send the device back for repair, simply flash the original backup ROM you made and no one will ever know that it was rooted. In our scenario, the warranty has likely expired

- Bricking your phone: Whenever you tamper too much, you run at least a small risk of bricking your device. The obvious way to avoid it happening is to follow instructions carefully. Make sure that the guide you are following works for your device and that any custom ROM you flash is designed specifically for it. If you do your research and pay attention to feedback from others, bricking should never occur.

- Security risks: Rooting introduces some security risks. Because of this Google refuses to support the Google Wallet service for rooted devices. For our purposes, this will not be an issue.

Two recent rooting programs that have garnered some attention in the past year are Towelroot and Kingo Root. Both will root your device in a few minutes. However, both rooting programs are not compatible with every Android device. Searching these applications will present a list of compatible devices. If your phone is not compatible with the apps, you'll have to spend a little time researching ways to root on the Android forums. The best place to start is XDA Developers Forum. Look for a thread on your specific device and you are sure to find a method that has worked for other people. It's worth spending some time researching the right method for your device.

Cellular Service

After you have performed a factory reset and rooted your new device, you are ready to activate it on a cellular network. For complete privacy, we only recommend prepaid plans. Subsidized contract plans require a real name or credit check but prepaid plans generally do not. Every major U.S. provider offers these types of plans. The following list compares the most affordable advertised services offered at the time of this writing. After, we will discuss a better option.

Service	Price	Minutes	Text	Data
AT&T:	$45	Unlimited	Unlimited	1.5GB
Sprint:	$35	Unlimited	Unlimited	1GB
T-Mobile:	$40	Unlimited	Unlimited	Unlimited*
Verizon:	$45	Unlimited	Unlimited	1GB
*Speed limitations on data				

T-Mobile "Hidden" Plan

Privacy advocates have known about a hidden pre-paid plan at T-Mobile for a while. This plan, sometimes called the "Wal-Mart Plan", is not available at T-Mobile stores or kiosks. You will not find it advertised on billboards. In fact, it takes effort to locate the plan online. The plan gives you unlimited text and data, and 100 minutes of talk time, per month, for $30. The talk time may seem low, but that will not matter once you have your device properly configured for free unlimited calls. The following instructions will guide you through the process of obtaining a great anonymous phone plan at an unbelievably low cost.

- Ensure that you have a cellular telephone that is T-Mobile friendly. This device needs to support the GSM network. Most iPhone and Samsung Galaxy models will work as will phones that have previously been registered with AT&T. You should check the T-Mobile website before you commit to this plan.

- Obtain a T-Mobile SIM card. Stores and kiosks will not offer you a card without committing to a plan. The T-Mobile website will send you a free card, but will require you to buy a more expensive plan. A third party online order is your best option. At the time of this writing, several vendors on Amazon were offering a T-Mobile SIM card starter pack, including a $30 credit, for $24.99 - $30.95. This is the best deal that we have found. Use the method explained in the previous chapter to create an anonymous Amazon account before ordering.

- Insert the SIM card in your device and turn on power. Have the SIM card serial number and the phone's IMEI ready. On a computer, navigate to the T-Mobile prepaid activation site and enter these details. On the next page enter your anonymous information. You can provide any name and address that you choose. This will not be verified. We recommend a common name and address that does not exist. Finally, it's time to choose the plan. Choose the $30 plan with unlimited text, data, and 100 minutes of talk time. Follow the activation prompts and you should possess an active phone.

- If you can make calls but cannot use data, manually enter the T-Mobile APN settings. Navigate to **https://support.t-mobile.com/docs/DOC-2090** for specific instructions for your device.

You should now have a fully functioning, and fairly anonymous, cellular telephone. You should have fast 4G data, and the ability to install or uninstall any apps. However, this device is not ready for completely anonymous use. As mentioned previously, your phone is always tracking you, your calls and texts are being logged, and the data that you send is being monitored. You will need to make some modifications to the way that you use a cell phone. The following is an actual plan, from start to finish, that we executed for a client.

An Actual Sample Strategy

Our client demanded an Android device. First, we purchased a used Samsung Galaxy S4 on Craigslist. It was listed at $125, and the ad had been posted over 30 days prior. We offered $75 and obtained the device at that price. We conducted a factory reset and rooted the phone. We removed all Samsung and Verizon bloatware. We purchased a T-Mobile SIM card and activated the hidden plan as discussed in this chapter.

Next, we secured the data traffic by installing a Virtual Private Network (VPN). These will be explained in much greater detail in Chapter 16. Basically, it encrypts the network traffic, whether through cellular or Wi-Fi, for all data transmitted to or from the device. For this specific installation, we chose VyprVPN as the provider. This will prevent the cellular provider from having the ability to intercept the data or implant data packets with tracking codes.

The hidden T-Mobile plan includes only 100 minutes of talk time. For many, that is plenty. Most use the unlimited text and data for communication. However, it is important to have options for placing outgoing calls and accepting incoming calls that do not count toward this limit. In order to subsidize voice calling features, and add another layer of anonymity, we added two additional free telephone lines to the phone.

Google Voice

First, we installed the Google Voice app. Many readers just cringed when they read that line, but hear us out. Yes, we know that Google analyzes all of our data and uses it to generate targeted ads. We also suspect that Google stores every bit of data possible from its users. However, they offer a free product that will work well for our needs. Google Voice was discussed early while preparing for your journey into anonymity. The account referenced earlier is only to be used during the removal stage when needed. We created this second account for the sole purpose of making calls.

We created a new account while connected to a public Wi-Fi at a library, used the name of an alias, and selected a number from a different area code. Will Google still collect data on this account? Yes. Will they know it is you? No. Not if you are careful. If you use a VPN at all times on the device, Google will only know the IP address of the VPN provider and not your cellular provider's IP address. This is an important technique that will be explained further in later chapters. You can use the Google Voice app to send and receive unlimited text messages. Please note that while you can delete messages within the app, it does not delete them from the "Trash". You will need to access this account from a web browser in order to properly delete messages from the account.

Hangouts Dialer

Next, we downloaded the Google Hangout Dialer app. This will allow you to make free calls from your device, using your data connection, without sacrificing any talk minutes. The calls will appear to come from your Google Voice number. The VPN will prevent Google from knowing where you are or which internet connection you are using. This solves the problem of free outgoing telephone calls, but not the issue of incoming calls. If someone calls your Google Voice number, they will either be forwarded to your real cellular number (not recommended), or voicemail (recommended). This will vary based on your user settings. Instead, we will use another service to fill this void.

Groove IP / Ring.To

We installed GrooveIP to the Android device. This app, with the help of a Voice Over IP (VOIP) service called Ring.To, will give you unlimited free calls to or from your device. While installing the app is very straight forward, creating a new account can be a bit tricky. The most important rule with this technique is to conduct all actions over the device. Navigating to the

Ring.To website and creating an account will typically result in failure. You can successfully create the account, but it will default to a premium paid account that you do not want. Instead, simply launch the GrooveIP app and follow the prompts to create a new account within the application. You will need to provide an email address that you can access and any desired alias name.

The email address that you choose must be associated with the telephone that you are using during registration. Navigate to Settings > Accounts > Add Account and provide the email credentials of the anonymous account that you will be using. In our experience, Gmail accounts work best. We created a Gmail account in an alias name, associated it with the device, completed the GrooveIP setup, and finally disconnected the Gmail account through these same settings. Before disconnecting the email account, you will be allowed to choose an area code and select a free telephone number within GrooveIP. This number will be assigned only for your use.

This phone can now open the GrooveIP app and place unlimited outgoing calls. These calls will appear to come from the new number assigned to the device. The calls will not use any of the cellular provider's minutes, and they will use the data connection to complete the call. If the app is open, the phone can accept incoming calls to this new number. There is no access to text messaging for this number.

We should summarize our current setup at this point. We have a cellular phone that is registered to an anonymous alias. The phone never makes or receives any calls through the carrier. A Google Voice account is attached to the device and that number can be used to make unlimited outgoing calls through the Hangouts dialer. A third telephone number can be used for incoming and outgoing calls through the data connection and GrooveIP. There are three individual telephone numbers at the user's disposal at any time. None of them are associated with a real name.

Many readers are likely wondering if they can have multiple numbers through these services on the same device. The answer is yes. You can log out of your Google Voice account at any time and log into another account. You are only limited by the number of accounts that you can successfully create. This also is true for GrooveIP. If you can successfully create an account through the GrooveIP app, using a new email address associated with your device, you can switch between the accounts and possess several potential cellular numbers. The headache will be the logging in and out process each time but this can be eased through the use of a password manager.

All of these services are free. There are also paid options that are very affordable that may give you a better layer of anonymity. These include popular services called Blur and Burner. Our client wanted numerous options at all times, so we installed both to the device.

Burner

Burner allows you to create semi-anonymous, disposable phone numbers. These numbers can send and receive calls without requiring you to give out your real phone number. If you need to make a call or give out a number, you set up a new burner. You can choose your area code and "size" of the burner you need. The size is determined by how many days it lasts before self-destructing, how many texts and voice minutes are allowed, and whether or not it can send and receive photos. The burner will be created and you can then send and receive calls at this number.

Our client can now use Burner while selling an item on Craigslist or some other classified ad service, giving a number to a new acquaintance or romantic interest who is not yet fully trusted, or signing up for a service that requires a valid phone number. These are all good opportunities to give out a number that can easily be terminated. If you wish to terminate the number before it expires, you can simply "burn" it on command. Alternatively, if you run out of texts or minutes or want to keep the burner longer, you can always replenish it inside the app.

One minor problem that we have repeatedly encountered with Burner is that it is very difficult to answer an incoming call. When you answer the call, you are greeted with a voice prompt that asks you to press "1" to accept the call. All of this takes time. Typically, when we receive a call on a Burner number, the other party has hung up by the time we finally answer. However, one area that Burner is extremely useful in is for receiving incoming text messages. If you want to set up a new email address, Amazon account, or other service that requires a working text capable number, you can quickly set up a Burner number. This provides a decent layer of privacy between your true number and the account. This is the primary reason we choose to include this app.

It is important to note that the makers of Burner, Ad Hoc Labs, explicitly acknowledge in their privacy policy and terms of service that they will comply with law enforcement requests for information about the use of their product. They also acknowledge that they maintain only limited information. What it does offer is a thin layer of privacy for everyday situations when you don't want to give out your real number or one of the other, more durable options you have set up on your device.

Burner is a free app and comes with one free burner that is active for seven days. You can burn it sooner or extend it if desired. Burner uses your phone minutes rather than data, and can send and receive calls and texts. It also accepts voicemails. 25 Burner credits can be purchased within the app for $11.99. Burner lines cost from 3 to 8 credits each depending on the length of time they last. All burners will self-destruct after a given length of time if they are not renewed.

Blur

Blur was mentioned earlier when explaining masked email addresses and credit card numbers. Another privacy related service they offer is masked telephone numbers. This feature allows you to create a phone number with which you can send and receive calls. When you create a masked phone number, it forwards calls to your real phone number (or Google Voice or Silent Circle number), protecting the "real" number. There are a couple of minor downsides to this service. Although you can change the number to which your masked number forwards, there is a $7 charge to change the masked number itself. In order to place an outgoing call you must use the Blur app or login through your web browser. You will then receive a call from your Blur number. Once Blur has established a connection with you, Blur places the call to the third-party you are calling. It is not the most elegant solution but it could be used for things like verification and two-factor authentication text messages.

For most of Blur's services there is no additional charge, but the Masked Phone charges a very reasonable fee of one cent per incoming call, one cent per minute the call is connected, and one cent per incoming text. Currently Blur's Masked Phone service does not offer outgoing text messages. Your premium account will include a $3.00 balance to cover these charges.

It should be noted that none of these solutions provide any type of encryption. Providers of these services could likely see content of your calls. In Chapter Twenty, we will identify encrypted solutions, both premium and free, that will give you that extra layer of security.

At this point, our client is ready for fairly anonymous telephone calls and text messages. The traffic is encrypted through a VPN. However, standard searching on the device could easily be captured by Google. Google wants to know what you search in order to build a dossier on you. This information will help with targeted ads. If intercepted by someone, this data could expose sensitive details about you. Please pause for a moment and think about everything you have ever searched on the internet. Chapter Two explained a browser extension called Disconnect Search that eliminates this intrusion. That service has an app that will do the same thing. We installed this app on our client's home screen and directed him to use this as he would use Google.

This phone provided a private environment for standard communication. The client could make outgoing calls from one of three anonymous numbers. He could receive calls from two different numbers. He could send and receive text messages from two unique telephone numbers. The next chapter will identify the security measures that were implemented to make it secure from any intrusions. It will also outline the exact strategies that we use to possess private and secure devices.

Balance Refilling

In the previous example, our client chose to use T-Mobile as his cellular provider. The Amazon starter pack with SIM card also provided him his first month of service. At the end of that month, he will need to refill his account. Regardless of the carrier that you choose, it is important to refill the account balance as anonymously as possible. There are several ways to this.

- The easiest and most anonymous way is to purchase renewal cards with cash. These are often found on the end of an aisle in a store. There is usually a large rack of what appears to be gift cards for various cellular providers in increments of $30-$100. After purchasing, the card is activated and the credit can be transferred to your account online.

- The way recommended by most carriers to reload your balance is through an online payment via credit card. This can be acceptable if using Blur to mask your identity. We believe that cash in person trumps this option.

- If choosing T-Mobile, you could purchase additional SIM starter packs. Each of these includes the $30 credit that can be applied to an existing account. This method is often more affordable than cash when you consider the taxes added at checkout. Also, this idea may have more value when you read about our next client.

Wi-Fi Only

You may have noticed that the majority of the services that we recommend do not necessarily require a cellular service provider. They only require internet access through cellular data or Wi-Fi data. If desired, you could eliminate the activation of cellular service and rely on wireless internet. The pitfall in this plan is that your device will be useless for communication when you cannot find open access.

We always keep two devices operational at all times. Our primary device possesses cellular connectivity and the secondary device only contains a Wi-Fi connection. While the setup for the secondary device is very similar to the primary unit, there are a few differences.

- Our secondary phones never attach to a wireless internet connection that we use with our primary devices or laptops. This prevents us from creating an association between the two devices. If we logged into two Google Voice accounts, on two unique devices, from the same network, Google would now know that we are the same person on both accounts. This may seem like overkill, and may not apply to your desired level of privacy.

- The secondary device possesses a Google account that was not created on a network connection that our primary devices access. Again, this creates a trail to the primary unit. We use public Wi-Fi to create, activate, and connect these accounts directly from our secondary devices. While this seems careless in regards to security, it is optimal for secondary devices that you do not want associated with your real identity.

- The secondary phone remains turned completely off until needed. It is always in airplane mode with the Wi-Fi enabled. All location services are disabled. These actions prevent your movements from being collected and stored.

- Finally, for the truly paranoid, we always turn our primary devices off before turning the secondary device on. We also confess that we do this while in motion so that the secondary device is not turned on at the same location the primary was powered down. Again, this prevents Google from knowing that we may be the same people using these two accounts.

iPhone

We have had clients that prefer to use an iPhone instead of Android. Apple has taken a very pro-privacy, pro-security stance on behalf of its users and the overall security of the iPhone is excellent. Apple does not monetize bulk data, and apps must be approved before inclusion in the curated App Store. Though some bad apps have been allowed into the app store, malware for non-jailbroken iOS devices is virtually non-existent. Further, most of the benefits of jailbreaking are in the interest of user experience and do not improve privacy or security. We believe iOS is the most secure mainstream mobile operating system on the market and modifying it has a negative net impact on privacy or security. This comparison between iOS and Android will be explained more thoroughly in the next chapter.

Had our client preferred an iOS device, a similar end result could have been achieved. Google Voice is supported on the iPhone through Google's own Google Voice app and through more functional third-party apps like GV Mobile+. Unfortunately, GrooveIP is not available on iOS devices. However, a user has the option of using multiple Google Voice accounts on a single device if he or she is willing to log in and out of multiple accounts. Additionally, iOS users can use Burner to provide unlimited inexpensive, disposable numbers.

As we have mentioned previously, privacy is not cheap. If you are willing to pay, there are numerous other apps that allow you to have a second phone line on your iPhone. Our favorite is called Line2. Line2 is a voice-over IP (VOIP), cross-platform app. You can use it on your iOS, Android, Mac, or Windows device. Line2 works over 3G, 4G, LTE, and Wi-Fi. The downside of Line2 is the cost of $9.99 per month.

iCloud/iTunes

Choosing to use an iOS device will also necessitate having an iTunes and iCloud account, without which you will be unable to download applications. Apple does not monetize data. The iAds program through which app developers can monetize apps can be opted out of, but we still prefer to store as little information in the cloud as possible. For this reason, we back nothing up to iCloud. To gain full use of an iTunes account you will have to provide a credit card number, but in the interest of setting the account up as anonymously as possible we recommend the following technique:

- Do not provide any real information to Apple when setting up the account. Choose an alias name that you are comfortable using for some time.

- Log into Blur and create a masked credit card number in a small amount or go to a brick and mortar retailer and purchase a prepaid credit card. The amount is up to you but we recommend a minimum $10.

- Use this credit card number to purchase an app, song, or other product from Apple. This will establish the card as valid.

- Go to a brick and mortar store and, using cash, purchase an iTunes gift card in an amount you will not exceed in the immediate future; we recommend approximately $25 if you are a very light user of iTunes and $100-200 if you are an average to heavy user of the service.

- Maintain a gift card balance. As long as you do not use or exceed the balance iTunes should never attempt to withdraw money from your credit card, preventing you from needing to purchase a new masked card.

Extreme Anonymity

We recently had a client in a unique situation. He was a high level CEO that believed sophisticated hackers were targeting him at the direction of a competitor. He had received several text messages with links to malicious websites attempting to compromise his device. It was vital that his daily telecommunications were anonymous. He was not technologically sophisticated and did not desire third party applications to make calls over data. His request was very simple at first. He wanted an anonymous cell phone for data and text. He would be making no voice calls. The additional demand was that he wanted to be issued a new telephone number and account every month, and would never use the same data plan for more than 30 days. He believed that having a new number every month would make it more difficult to target his account.

- We created a Blur account for him and attached a secondary credit card in the name of an assistant that could receive mail at a PO Box.

- We created twelve masked Blur credit cards with a balance of $30.95 each.

- We created twelve Amazon accounts in the assistant's name. With each account, we ordered one T-Mobile SIM starter pack using a different masked Blur card for each purchase.

- We obtained a slightly used iPhone that would work on the T-Mobile network.

- When the SIM starter packs arrived, we labeled them each by the month that they would be used. Every 30 days, the client would allow the prepaid account to expire. He would then insert the next card and follow the very simple instructions to activate the next SIM card. He would repeat this process every 30 days.

- Every time his plan expired and he activated a new card his phone number would technically change. But because he was using VOIP solutions and never gave out the T-Mobile number to anyone, the change was completely transparent to his contacts. The only additional step he had to take was to log into his Google Voice account and change the number to which his Google Voice number forwarded.

We respect that there are privacy flaws with this plan. T-Mobile would be able to see the hardware information (IMEI) from the device and would know that this was likely the same person each month. However, they have no reason to look. Is this overkill? Quite possibly. However, the cost was minimal. It would have been the same price to purchase the first card and refill the balance monthly as it was to issue a new SIM card every month.

An additional benefit is that each account that expires can be refilled within five months of expiration. In other words, you can allow your balance to deplete at any time. The account will stay there for you up to five months in a dormant state. At any time, you can reactivate the account by adding the standard $30 monthly usage fee. Your same telephone number will be activated on that SIM card. We know of no traditional cellular plans that will allow this type of flexibility.

With this plan, you could own a new cellular number and online account every month. If you use VOIP services as your primary number, this would have no negative impact on your daily communications. If you open numerous social network accounts that each require a unique cellular number for verification, this method has huge potential. It would allow you to provide your actual cellular number while knowing that it will be disconnected in one month. We are not personally comfortable with this because the number is attached to a device that knows your location for the past month. It will depend on your level of paranoia.

The Complete Reset

Our favorite clients are those that want a complete reset of their entire communications strategy. They realize that they have been sharing intimate details with huge corporations and jeopardizing their privacy every time they looked at their phone. They understand that every movement of theirs over the past several years has been tracked, logged, and preserved thanks to the device carried in their pocket or purse. While the previous examples illustrate good privacy protocols, we had a client that wanted to take it further. The following scenario occurred in early 2015. The sharing of this content was approved by our client in hopes that it may help someone else.

"David" was a government employee under attack by a group of very sophisticated hackers. He was confident that his personal email account and cell phone had been compromised at some point because sensitive details about an investigation were leaked during a trial which were only present in private email messages. He met with us and provided his device.

We analyzed his personal cell phone and discovered several suspicious text messages that appeared to contain malicious website links. David believes that he may have clicked one of these many weeks earlier. We observed that he used Gmail as his personal email account and his email address included his real name. A quick search online found this email address present on many websites. We also confirmed that he used his personal cell number on his Facebook page and that it was visible to any "friends". These presented two very large attack surfaces.

We informed him that he should never again use this telephone, number, or email account ever again. Attacks will likely continue toward these accounts and he must assume that the device is compromised. David was ready to commit to starting over but had a few reservations. He asked that he could still somehow see any communications going to his old accounts while being safe with only new accounts associated with a new device. We began our assignment.

We purchased a brand new telephone for David. He insisted on a device that had never been assigned to anyone else. We chose the third edition of the Motorola "Moto G". This phone had a stock Android operating system, minimal bloatware, and is unlocked for any GSM network. It was also only $179 without any contract. We purchased the device through Amazon, with an account in an alias name, using a pre-paid Blur credit card attached to another alias name, shipped to a mail drop registered to a friend with a very common name.

We activated this device with an anonymous T-Mobile SIM starter pack purchased previously with Vanilla Visa prepaid cards. We refer to these SIM packs as "Shelf SIMs". We usually have about 30 ready to go at any time. This presented him with a brand new phone and private cellular number. Neither is connected to him in any way. The activation was completed from a café in another city on a Wi-Fi connection through a VPN. The phone was registered to a generic name.

The Android phone must be connected to a Google account in order to properly function and connect to the Google Play store for apps. We created a generic Google account through another anonymous internet connection that had no association with his real name. This account will never be accessed from a computer. The attack surface of this device is extremely minimal because there is no affiliation with David.

We exported the entire contents of David's Gmail account and then deleted all messages within the account. If the hackers still had access to this account, the data is gone. He chose a new non-Gmail email provider and we imported all of his messages into that account. We installed the official Android application for that email provider and connected his account. All of his email was now available to him on his device without any connection to the old account. However, any outgoing messages were now routing through the new email address.

David expected that he would need any email still being received at his previous Gmail account. We set up a rule within his old Gmail account to forward all incoming messages to a new 333Mail account created for this purpose (explained earlier). The 333Mail account was configured to forward these messages to David's new personal email account. If hackers were able to access David's old Gmail account, they could see the forwarding address. If a Google employee was ordered to find any forwarding information, the 333Mail account is all that would be seen. The 333Mail address does not compromise David's new email address. We set up a rule within David's new email account to forward all messages from 333Mail into a folder titled "Caution". This would remind him to be careful when viewing these messages.

David requested that his contacts be imported from his old phone into the new device. This is where we drew the line. If we were to import the hundreds of contacts from one account into another, we would create an obvious connection between the accounts. Google would begin to recommend apps based on his "friends" and would know a lot about David. We asked him to revisit his contacts while logged into his Gmail account through a laptop. He discovered that Google had been automatically populating information into his contact list every time he sent an email to someone. Google then used data from Google+ to create profiles on each contact. David had over 4,000 people in his Google contact list.

The current view of Google Contacts does not isolate intentional contacts from automatically populated profiles. Fortunately, the previous version of Google Contacts allows this separation. While viewing the current version of these contacts, we navigated to https://www.google.com/contacts/u/0/?cplus=0#contacts. This loaded the previous version of the contacts database which includes "My Contacts" and "Other Contacts". In David's scenario, the "My Contacts" included 217 people while the "Other Contacts" included over 4,000 people.

We first exported the entire contact list before taking any action. On this previous view page, we chose "Other Contacts", then "More", then "Export". We exported all categories of contacts into a standard CSV file. This could be later imported into an email client if a contact's information was needed.

We then deleted the entire "Other Contacts" category and allowed David time to consider the remaining 217 contacts. Many of these were people that he no longer communicated with. We encouraged him to only save the contacts that he would need to communicate with via phone from this new device. These should only be close friends and family that he would be comfortable reaching out to if he needed some type of help. The final list included 28 people. We then exported only this list for import into the new device.

Before import, we opened this exported spreadsheet file with Microsoft Excel. The file was organized into columns including first name, last name, mobile number, and others. We focused on the name sections and asked David if possessing the full first and last name was vital to him. Since he was being heavily targeted by sophisticated criminals, we encouraged him to not include the full names of his contacts in his phone. If he were compromised again, this information could put others in danger. He agreed to use only initials for most of the contacts. For those that would create duplicate initials, he chose a city to help identify the options. One example might be T S (Denver) while another is T S (NYC). While the name of the friend is not disclosed, he would know right away which contact he desired.

This technique may have brought out a laugh or an eye roll when read. We agree that it might be overkill for some readers. However, our entire contact lists on our devices contain absolutely no names. We believe that this method decreases future attack surfaces while protecting both ourselves and our contacts. It prevents Google or other services from extracting any details provided by us to their profiles on these people. While we crave the dated methods of storing contacts into a flip phone without internet access, we accept the digital world that we live in today. David's personal life with his friends and family is now more secure by changing his phone habits.

David had previously used Google Calendar for all of his appointments. He stated that it was crucial to maintain this setup. His configuration had two calendars. The first was the default personal calendar and the second was marked "Private". He stated that he only wanted the personal calendar, so we exported the iCal file and properly deleted all of the entries. Through his Google account, his personal calendar was now empty. However, there were several sensitive entries associated with the "Private" calendar. David asked for a few minutes to look through these in private.

David returned and said that he did not need the "Private" calendar and that he had deleted the entries. When asked for clarification, he confirmed that he had "Unsubscribed" from the calendar and that it was no longer visible. Unfortunately, this does not delete anything from Google. That calendar was still present in their system and the content was visible to anyone at Google. This put David into a slight panic. Fortunately, there is always a way around these things.

This calendar was associated with the same Google account as his Gmail. We had David's entire Gmail account backed up as a 5GB file. We expanded the data and conducted a search for group.calendar.google.com. Every Google calendar has a unique ID that ends in that address. We quickly located an email message notifying David of a change to an entry in the "Private" calendar. These are common when appointments are entered and later changed. They are considered notifications. Within that message was an attachment titled "Attachment1.3". This was a small text file with data similar to the following.

ORGANIZER;CN=Private:mailto:u8%rsg79dqbdtvjdi88&6@group.calendar.google.com

The unique address listed after "Private" is the ID for that calendar. We connected to his old Google account, clicked "Settings", clicked "Calendars", clicked "Browse Interesting Calendars", clicked "Add a friend's calendar", and provided the address in the attachment. This populated all of the "Private" entries back into his calendar. This was proof that unsubscribing to a calendar does not delete any data. In the settings for this calendar, we chose "Permanently delete this calendar". The data was now gone.

David had previously used a Google Voice account for all of his text messaging. We configured his account to forward all incoming messages to David's 333Mail account. This will allow him to see any incoming texts through his new email account in the "Caution" folder. If he chooses, he can reply through his new Google Voice account.

We created the Google Voice account while in the café mentioned previously. Google demanded a valid telephone number in order to activate the account. We told the barista that we were trying to connect to a webinar, but that we needed to validate the connection. We asked if we could use their phone to accept a brief incoming call in order to enter a code to prove that we were human. We were allowed and gave Google Voice the number of the café. Google presented a code on the screen and the café phone rang. We answered, entered the code when prompted, and then possessed an active Google Voice account. All we had to do then was to select a new phone number.

We then changed the password and enabled two-factor authentication on both the old and new Google accounts. David should rarely need to access either. The Gmail and Calendar accounts were free of any personal data. David stated that he would never use the telephone number assigned to his new device. Instead, he would use GrooveIP for incoming and outgoing calls and his new Google Voice number for text messages to the trusted people in his life. It will be very difficult for anyone to determine the phone that David uses every day. Tracking him through this device is not likely.

If David were worried about physical monitoring of his device while in the vicinity of his location, we would encourage appropriate security habits. We have instructed other clients to turn the telephone completely off while traveling close to their home. In one scenario, a client always turned her phone off at a specific landmark on her way home from work. The next day, she would turn it back on at that same landmark while on her way back to work. If anyone were to identify and scrutinize her cellular account, it would have no location information about her residence. Additionally, she never needed her phone while at home. She used an anonymous Google account for all phone calls from her computer.

We took great care in the actions executed for David. More importantly, we were careful to avoid taking any actions that could compromise the situation. Instead of focusing on the details that were performed, it may be more vital to review steps that were NOT taken.

- The Google accounts were not created on the same computer as the client's real accounts. Google cannot use browser fingerprinting to pair the two.

- The Google accounts were not created using the same IP address of personal accounts. IP logs would not compromise the accounts.

- The Google accounts were never accessed from the same connections as personal accounts. IP logs at Google would not disclose the connection.

- The telephone account was not activated using internet connections associated with the client. The cellular provider cannot associate the account to the client.

- The telephone was not connected to any accounts associated with the client. Neither the cellular provider nor Google has any connection to the client.

- The telephone was never connected to any Wi-Fi access points associated with the client. Google cannot use their Wi-Fi database to make the association.

- Various personal accounts were not imported into the new telephone. Google cannot use historic data to associate the new phone with our client.

Is this all overkill? Some may think so. However, our experience supports our paranoia. We have witnessed investigations involving Google and other similar companies. They know more than you think. They know that you have multiple Gmail accounts under various names. They record this activity and will disclose all of your related accounts if given an appropriate court order. More concerning is when their data is compromised during a breach and all collected information is exposed. Some may read this and think that it will never happen. We are sure that the 32 million subscribers to the marital affair website Ashley Madison assumed they were protected as well. They were not.

Outgoing Telephone Call Concerns

When you make a telephone call, the receiver can identify you by your caller ID. Since this is common knowledge, many people dial "*67" before the telephone number to hide their identity. This causes the caller ID display on the receiving end to display "Unknown Caller" or "Blocked Call". This does not work at large companies. If you attempt to block your caller ID when calling a toll free number, your information will not be blocked. Large companies have telephone systems that will still display your name and number regardless of masking attempts. Because of this, you should be careful when calling large businesses. If you call from your landline telephone, your information will automatically be populated into the company's database. You will now be more susceptible to receiving calls from the organization. If you call from your cellular number, your number will be collected, but not your name. When you discuss your account with the business, your number will be added to your customer profile. If this concerns you, consider these alternatives.

- Place the call from a pre-paid cellular telephone (Chapter Eleven).

- Place the call through a VOIP service such as Google Voice (Chapter Eleven) or Silent Phone (Chapter Twenty)

- Contact customer service through internet services such as email or website chat.

- Request a call from the company to your anonymous number through email.

Telecommunications for the Deaf Options

Most large companies have a system in place for accommodating deaf customers. This may include a Text Telephone (TTY) or Telecommunication Device for the Deaf (TDD). Previously, a user needed to possess an expensive device in order to connect to these services. Today, free websites such as ttycall.com will facilitate the calls directly with no hardware. Additionally, there is no caller ID to be obtained from the communication. In our experience, contacting customer service through this option results in a less intrusive conversation. Some may frown on us recommending that people without hearing disabilities use services specified for them. We counter that with our belief that increased usage of these systems will result in additional resources allocated to the service.

Why can't I give my cellular number to close friends and family?

During our trainings, we have learned that most users possess a single cellular telephone number and use it for all voice communications. We believe that this is very inappropriate behavior if privacy is desired. The following will identify the four main concerns.

Attack Surface: As said before, if your publicly known number is your actual cellular number, you have created a direct link to your cellular account. If this account is compromised, it contains data about your historical locations and communications. It is also possible for anyone having access to your mobile phone account to set up SMS forwarding. They could use this to forward your two-factor authentication tokens to their device to get into other online accounts. If someone only knows your VOIP number, it is not always possible to associate that number with a cellular account. By using a VOIP number, you have created a layer of protection from revealing your cellular account.

Dynamic Number: If you rely on VOIP methods for communication, you can easily activate a new cellular account at any time without notification to your contacts. You can change cellular providers, hardware, and calling plans at will, and never have to update your information with anyone. You can link the known VOIP number to any cellular plan without anyone noticing a difference.

Verification Mechanism: In some cases your phone number is a verification mechanism. For example, if you call your bank you may be told "we see you are calling from the primary number on your account" and face fewer security questions as a result. It is possible for someone who knows your cellular number to spoof it and call the bank, pretending to be you. We recommend using a VOIP number with your financial institutions, too, but a different one than you give friends and family. If you only give this number to banks it will be very difficult for anyone to find.

Account Privacy: The most vital reason for never giving your true cellular number out is to keep it private. In past years, there were no cellular number lookup websites or publicly available databases of all cellular owners. Today, this exists. You also need to be aware of sites such as TrueCaller. This is a crowd-sourced telephone directory that will display a real name for most cellular numbers. It works as an app that a person installs on their device in order to see caller ID information when receiving a call. What most people do not realize is that the app also collects all of your contacts, including name and number, and adds them to the live online database. As of this writing, one of our disconnected government issued cellular numbers can be searched on this website to reveal the true name associated. This is because someone that we know downloaded TrueCaller and unknowingly shared all of their contacts with the world. Further, they are sharing your true cellular number and name with either Google, Apple, or Microsoft, depending on the device operating system. Their account likely syncs several times every hour. Can you hold complete trust in the security and ethics of any large corporation? We believe not.

We often encounter skeptics that ask us "What is wrong with having a contract for cellular service like everyone else?" Our response includes several levels of concern, most of which have been outlined in this chapter. Overall there are two main vulnerabilities. The first is associated with privacy and the second security.

As we have explained in this chapter, you lose all privacy when you register a phone in your real name. Because of the subsidies offered to you in the form of discounted phones, you will be required to also disclose your DOB and SSN for credit checks. Your identifiers, phone, account, number, calls, texts, location, traffic, and overall usage will be forever stored. It will be disclosed to anyone that possesses a court order for the data. It can be extracted by any rogue employee of the provider. Criminal hackers will access any data from illegal breaches.

For those that do not care to protect this data, or subscribe to the "I have nothing to hide" mentality, we offer the following. As we write this paragraph, T-Mobile has announced that 15 million customers' data were exposed during a breach through Experian, a vendor they use for credit checks. This means that 15 million T-Mobile customers that used their real information are compromised. Their names, addresses, account data, and SSN's are now in the hands of unknown hackers. We see no scenario where this is not a concern. While we have T-Mobile accounts, we have no worries. The accounts have absolutely no information about our true identities. They do not possess our names, addresses, SSN's, or credit card numbers.

Additionally, there are several news sources citing a new vulnerability in Android that allows the device to be compromised by simply receiving a malicious text message. This message contains specific coding that infects the phone with minimal input from the user. We believe that by eliminating the telephone number of your device from your attack surface, you are well protected from this issue. If you never give out your actual cell number, and only use the text message alternatives that we have described, you will not fall victim to this attack. No one will know the number that they need to target. In the worst case scenario, you will receive these messages within accounts such as Google Voice. Without going directly to your stock messaging app on your phone, these attempts are useless.

This chapter may have quickly turned into an advanced level for many readers. We believe that knowing about all of your options will help you make the most appropriate decision for your situation. What works well for a domestic violence victim might not be enough for a targeted special operations individual.

At the end of the next chapter, we will disclose our current configurations for our primary and secondary devices. "Justin's Strategy" will outline some additional ways to optimize an iPhone for privacy and security while "Michael's Strategy" will focus on Android devices.

CHAPTER TWELVE
SMARTPHONE SECURITY

To call a smartphone a "phone" is a bit of a misnomer. With the increased technology being poured into these devices a phone is no longer "just a phone". In fact, the telephonic functionality of such a device is usually a third or fourth consideration, and is not the most frequent or most common way in which such devices are used.

Today's smartphone is an incredibly compact, marvelously powerful computer that is carried on a daily basis, and also happens to be able to place and receive calls. For most of us the collective time spent snapping and reviewing photographs, texting, streaming music, reading e-books, playing games, and browsing the internet far eclipses time spent actually talking on the phone. We believe it is important to realize this distinction and to think about smartphones differently than "just a phone", and to understand that this conceptualization has serious security implications.

Why is this distinction important, and how does it impact security? Many still view their phone through the "just a phone" lens and put very little effort into securing it. But with all of their uses, smartphones are now a part of our everyday lives and reflect this daily inclusion more each year. With the Internet of Things becoming a reality, smartphones are now linked to our real, physical worlds in ways that were unimaginable just a few decades ago.

The threats arrayed against smartphones are also increasing. Because they are used everywhere and contain increasingly large chunks of personal information, smartphones are more dangerous than ever. Fortunately, securing them is getting somewhat easier. Both Apple and Google have taken steps to make privacy and security easier, but there are still many ways this can be compromised. There are many improvements that can be made. Ultimately it is up to the individual user to take control of his or her own security and privacy to the extent possible.

This chapter will examine the threats against smartphones, of which there are many. It will also discuss how to take your anonymously purchased and registered phone and secure it against these threats.

Smartphone Threats

There is no perfect secure solution to any security problem, and making your phone completely secure against the threats they face is an impossible goal. The only way to be completely secure is to forego having a phone at all, an idea that becomes more attractive to us with each passing day, even as it becomes less and less realistic. With the knowledge that a mobile phone can never be completely secure should come the realization that a smartphone is a security and privacy compromise regardless of the measures you take.

Before you can begin the process of securing your device, it is important to understand the threats arrayed against it. With this knowledge you can assess your own threat profile and the threats from which you wish to defend yourself. The primary threats facing smartphones can be broken down into three broad categories: metadata collection, traffic interception, and hardware exploitation.

The widespread collection of millions of Americans' metadata was the first of the Edward Snowden revelations that was published by the Guardian during the early summer of 2013. The fact that this information was collected was extremely alarming to those within the security community, but was met by many Americans with the thought of "so what, they aren't listening to my calls". So what is metadata and why is it alarming?

Metadata: Metadata is data about data. In the context of a telephone conversation, metadata would not include the content of the call, the actual conversation. Metadata would include such information as who placed the call, to whom it was placed, and how long the conversation lasted. Where text and SMS messages are concerned, metadata would include who placed the text and to whom, how often the two text each other, and how many texts are generated during a conversation. Metadata about text messages and telephone calls can be used to link you with others and to draw conclusions about your level of association.

Historical location data is also a form of metadata that can be collected from smartphones. Combined with call and SMS data, this information amounts to an alarming body of information. Anyone with this data can see where you went, how long you stayed there, who you talked and texted with, when you left, and where you went after that (as well as all of this data for everyone with whom you interacted). If every individual were legally compelled to carry a personal tracking device at all times, revolt would ensue. In spite of that we still pay hardware manufacturers and service providers hundreds or thousands of dollars per year for the privilege of carrying a tracking device in our pockets.

This is because a phone (whether smart or dumb) is, first and foremost, a tracking device. In order for the phone to function correctly it must be able to connect to nearby service towers. These tower connections or "check–ins" are the most common way mobile phones are tracked and can be used for both near-real-time (NRT) and historical data. Cell providers can access your location data now and forever through your use of their towers. Law enforcement may do so through warrants to obtain the tower data, or through cellular site simulators. Smartphones may also be tracked through a number of other means as well. Most smartphones utilize an internal global positioning system (GPS) to provide mapping and other location-specific services. The GPS data may be shared by a number of applications and transmitted back to numerous third-parties. Other technologies such as Wi-Fi and Bluetooth may also allow their location (and that of their owners) to be tracked, often with extremely high levels of precision.

Location tracking may not seem like a big deal or it may seem so beyond the pale that few will worry about it. However, location tracking can reveal a great deal of very sensitive personal information about you. It can reveal with whom you meet, where you meet, and for how long. Location tracking can reveal what church you go to, how often you go, or whether you go at all. It can reveal your interests and hobbies as well. Do you visit gun stores, marijuana dispensaries, adult-themed shops or clubs, or other niche locations? Do you attend politically-oriented conventions, speeches, or protests? Do you attend alcohol or drug-addiction recovery meetings or clinics? Have you had a one-night stand lately?

If you took your phone with you (and it is a near certainty that you did), your cell service provider knows all of this about you. The stores and shops are mapped, and the trysts can be extrapolated from the confluence of two phones in the same location overnight. Some of the apps on your device know where you've been, too. In all likelihood, so does your device's hardware manufacturer. Though none of these things may seem especially provocative or embarrassing to you now, how would you feel if this data was breached? How will you feel about those actions in 10 years? Data storage is cheap and it is unlikely that any of this information will ever be forgotten.

Traffic Interception: Traffic interception is the practice of capturing the actual content of your phone calls, texts, and emails. While traffic interception is a major concern for individuals traveling overseas or those who work on exceptionally sensitive projects (such as the military and intelligence communities), it is also still a concern for the average individual. Cell site simulators have placed the ability to intercept voice and data traffic in the hands of even small local police departments. And as security guru Bruce Schneier reminds us, "Today's NSA secrets become tomorrow's PhD theses and the next day's hacker tools".[1]

Cell Site Simulators

Cell site simulators are devices that, as the name suggests, masquerade as legitimate cell phone towers. These devices are useful only in a relatively small area, but they emit a very powerful signal that forces all the phones in that area to connect to the simulator rather than legitimate towers. Once connected these devices collect metadata about every device in the area, not just the target's. They can capture the content of phone calls, texts, emails, etc.

Hardware Exploitation: Hardware exploitation is taking data directly from the device through physical access. It is hardly news that smartphones store impressive quantities of data (up to 128 Gb in the case of the iPhone). A smartphone may contain or be able to access tens of thousands of emails, thousands of photos, personal and intimate text messages, logins, web browsing history, call histories, and more. The loss of a device can potentially give all of this information away to anyone who bothers to look, which will almost certainly be someone. Like so many problems in the security world, the best solution to hardware exploitation is

---

[1] https://www.schneier.com/essays/archives/2015/02/cyberweapons_have_no.html

encryption. Well-implemented encryption and a strong passcode are the surest defense against this type of exploitation.

Another potential avenue through which your hardware may work against you is camera and microphone hijacking. Sometimes this is a feature, not a bug. In the case of some smartphones with voice-recognition capabilities, the phone may "listen" constantly, even when you are not using the voice recognition feature. This information is recorded, saved, and analyzed. Your camera and/or microphone can also be compromised by malware that allows the attacker to turn one or both on at will. Microphones may be hijacked by government agencies by calling into the phone in a way that does not make the phone show any signs of being on or operating, but leaves the line open so an eavesdropper can hear everything within earshot of the device.

Choose Your OS

Between us, both Android and iOS devices are well represented. In the past both authors have typically demurred when asked to weigh in on which OS is more private or secure, but we do not feel we can do this any longer and will make a firm recommendation. Before we weigh in with one operating system or the other there are some facts that are worth comparing. First, we will examine some statements from both Apple and Google and make an assessment of each's general views on privacy and providing customers with privacy. Next we will discuss data aggregation and monetization, malware prevalence on the two platforms, and finally encryption of data-at-rest and data-in-motion.

General Stance on Privacy: Apple's policy on this is pretty clear, per Apple's "commitment to your privacy", signed by CEO Tim Cook:

> "Our business model is very straightforward: we sell great products. We don't build a profile based on your email content or web browsing habits to sell to advertisers. We don't 'monetize' the information you store on your iPhone or in iCloud. And we don't read your email or your messages to get information to market to you".

Google's stance on privacy is equally clear. Said former Google CEO Eric Schmidt:

> "…A person has no legitimate expectation of privacy in information he voluntarily turns over to third parties".

The bottom line: Apple is a hardware company, interested in selling you, its customer, more products. Google is an advertising, data-aggregation, and marketing company interested in selling you, its product, to more customers. This should make our position on these two companies clear.

Data Aggregation and Monetization: We don't need to explain in great detail the vastness of Google's data collection apparatus. Google Search/Image Search/Patent Search/News,

Gmail, YouTube, Google Calendar, Google Drive, Google Voice, Google Plus, Google Books, Google Docs, Google Translate, Google Chat, Google Groups, Google Hangouts, Google Sites, Google Alerts, Google Maps, Google Street View, and Google Earth are just a few of the "free" services designed to entice you to put more, and more granular and detailed, information into the Google data stream. Google also controls a number of advertising services, including AdMob, AdSense, AdWords, AdWords Express, Double Click, Google Grants, etc. Google is now also involved in the Internet of Things, purchasing Nest, a manufacturer of internet-connected thermostats and smoke detectors for $3.2 billion. Why would an advertising company purchase a thermostat company for such a huge sum? Because it can record when you are at home, when you are sleeping, how active you, and other information that it aggregates along with your other information to build a more detailed advertising package about you.

Perhaps the single most detailed collection platform in Google's inventory is the Android-equipped phone. Your Android phone (make no mistake about it, it's really a Google phone) can record your location, periods of wakefulness, frequency of movement, Wi-Fi connections and passwords, physical movement at an incredibly detailed level, correlation with other devices, and a host of other detailed information that it shares with Google. Some of this can be opted out of to some extent, but it's still a Google-powered handset, and Google put the software on the open market for a reason. Do you have privacy-related concerns about using a Chromebook? If so you should probably re-think your Android phone.

Apple does allow some app developers to collect and sell data to advertisers. However, it is minimal compared to the scale and scope of what Google does. We again point out that Apple is a hardware company and Google is an advertising company. This data collection is done in a very limited manner through an initiative called iAds, and it is possible to opt out of them. This is not to downplay Apple's data collection. We still don't like it from a privacy perspective and you shouldn't either. When compared with the immensity that is Google, there isn't much of a comparison. In fairness, Apple does still collect a lot of data and this is not a good thing, even if it doesn't package and sell it. Large repositories of data are dangerous because they are desirable targets for hackers and governments alike. All other things being equal, we still prefer the company that does not package and sell our data as a primary revenue stream.

Malware Prevalence: A smartphone is a computer and is subject to the same malware threats as computers. The commonality of malware for the two devices is incomparable. In 2014 the Cisco annual security report estimated that an astonishing 99% of mobile malware was targeted at Android devices. There is little evidence to suggest this trend has changed dramatically in the intervening two years. Though Apple is not immune to malware, it still makes news when Apple products are found vulnerable to it. As an example of this, Zerodium recently offered a $1,000,000.00 bounty for a remote jailbreak vulnerability for iOS 9. Only one team (of three possible) actually collected. Root access exploits for Android devices are far more common, and don't make national news when they are found. As another indicator, Zerodium also publicly posted a pricing chart for remote exploits. Nothing ranked higher in pricing (up to $500,000.00) than iOS. By comparison, Android exploits only fetch up to $100,000.00. Much of the malware problem with Android is due to the lack of routine, direct updates of the operating system and the inclusion of unvetted applications in the Google Play store.

Much of the malware issue can be lain at the feet of operating system integrity, or the operating system remaining intact and being kept up to date. This is a major problem for Android handsets. Google released Android as an open-source project and as a result it can be freely modified. Hardware manufacturers modify the OS to suit their needs, and service providers such as AT&T and Verizon modify them even further. However, updating is the real issue with Android. When Google pushes software updates they typically don't go directly to the device. Instead they have to to work their way again through hardware manufacturers and service providers before reaching the end-user device.

The Apple OS, on the other hand, is designed for a particular set of hardware and is not modified. Further, and perhaps more importantly, updates are pushed directly from Apple to all handsets. This means that a significantly higher percentage of iOS devices get updated quickly. A number of articles highlight this trend. Most cite statistics retrieved from mixpanel.com. Within 72 hours of its release, a higher percentage of iOS users had upgraded to the latest OS version (iOS 9) than Android users had in the previous nine months (to Android 5/Lollipop). At the time of this writing approximately 75% of iOS users are running the latest version of the OS compared to only 44% of Android users who are running the latest OS. At the time of this writing, iOS 9 has been out for under three months while Lollipop has been available for more than 12. Even the brand new Blackberry Priv, a phone marketed around privacy and security, ships with an outdated operating system.

If you are one of the few Android users with an updated operating system, the herd immunity has been breached. Android exploits are profitable because they are so successful (and because Android enjoys a larger market share). As a result, you may become the victim of malware in the future during a gap before you have updated your OS. This is an incredibly important consideration, especially if you are running a rooted Android phone. The compromise of your operating system can give an attacker access to the metadata and content of all communications conducted over the device as well as location data (historical or Near Real Time (NRT)), camera and microphone access, and more.

Installing an application on a device gives it an incredible amount of privilege. Regardless of whether you use an Android or iOS device, it is only as private and secure as the applications you choose to install on it. If you install the Facebook app on your Blackphone and allow it to to have access to your location, contacts, calendar, camera, and microphone, you have chosen to compromise your own privacy and your choice of operating system is irrelevant. With that being said, there is a difference between the level of trust we place in the apps we download from the App Store and Google Play. Apple's App Store is a so called "walled garden", into which only vetted applications are allowed. Curating apps in this manner prevents many potentially malicious apps from even being accessible to the user, let alone executed. This is not to say that the App Store is perfect. Privacy and security compromising code does occasionally get through. Much to everyone's chagrin, Apple is incredibly opaque about the vetting process for applications and what black and whitelisted criteria they look for.

Apps for Android devices face no such scrutiny. Anyone can create an Android app, and anyone can download and execute any Android app from nearly any source. Couple this with an outdated OS and the potential for abuse is staggering. Because the App Store is curated, fewer apps are available to Apple users than Android users, but this argument is beyond the scope of this work.

With that being said, we will cover both Android and iOS operating systems in this work. We understand that many users are locked into contracts with Android phones, have Android devices for work, or may simply just prefer them. For this reason, the following sections will list potential vulnerabilities that need to be secured, as well as the techniques to secure them for both Android and iOS.

BlackPhone 2

This chapter cannot be complete without mentioning the BlackPhone 2. This device, brought to you by the Swiss privacy company Silent Circle, takes security and privacy to a whole new level. It was designed with privacy enthusiasts in mind. Every decision made in its development prioritized privacy and security. For full disclosure, we were given a demo unit direct from the company for testing. For further disclosure, the price of a new unit is $799. What do you get for that?

First, this GSM-capable phone is not associated with any carrier, is completely unlocked, and does not contain any bloated undesired apps. When you consider that an unlocked iPhone is over $700, the price of the Blackphone 2 seems appropriate. The most vital piece of the phone is the custom operating system called Silent OS. It is a heavily modified version of Android that allows you to manipulate the most granular permissions settings of all apps. This gives you a level of privacy control that far exceeds that of regular Android phones. When you make a call, send a text, or initiate a videoconference, your communications travel encrypted across Silent Circle's private cloud VPN. Any man-in-the-middle attacks would be worthless.

Silent Circle has secured the Blackphone 2 handset all the way down to the chip level. The company partnered with Qualcomm to create a chip that can be securely partitioned. This allows the user to set up unique "Spaces" that keep work and personal usage separate. Each space has its own privacy settings, its own app permission settings, and its own allocation of system storage. The device currently ships with 32GB of internal memory plus an empty micro SD card slot. Regular Android 5.0 allows users to create separate spaces in the OS, but the Blackphone 2 keeps each space entirely separate at the chip level. This gives you complete control over the permissions and security options for each space. The phone is fully encrypted by default upon initial boot.

The "Security Center" settings panel on the Blackphone 2 offers complete control of individual permissions of all installed apps. The OS does an audit of an app's code during installation in order to identify all of the different bits of data and pieces of hardware the app wants to access. This gives you complete control of every possible permission. This would allow you to prohibit apps from accessing specific types of data. Uber is a great example. This app provides an alternative to traditional taxi services and allows you to request a ride over the phone. While the ride service can be great, the permissions required to use their app is dreadful. It requires you to share your contacts, messages, and other sensitive data with Uber. Silent OS allows you to block each of these permissions without blocking the vital services needed to function. You can now share your location with Uber, but block all other intrusive requests.

We also liked the randomized keypad for the screen unlock code which prevents you from leaving physical evidence, such as fingerprint oils, on your screen. Static keypads could be used to make logical guesses at your unlock code. Purchase of the phone includes one free year of subscription to Silent Phone. This is the company's secure communications service that lets you call, text and chat through Silent Circle's private VPN. The app is also available for Android and iOS users without this device. The service outside of this free year is $10 per month.

Usage Note

Due to the extreme variations in Android builds the exact instructions covered here may or may not be applicable to your device. The devices used during the research and writing of this book were purchased unlocked and have minimal added applications from the manufacturer. The mobile devices used in the writing of this book were:

Motorola Moto G (2014/2nd Generation) running Android 5.1/Lollipop
Motorola Moto G (2015/3rd Generation) running Android 6/Marshmallow
Blackphone 2 running Silent OS
iPhone 6 running iOS 9.2.

OS and App Updates

Keeping the operating system and applications on your mobile device up to date is just as important as it is on your home computer. OS and application updates are patched to add more function. In nearly all cases they also patch known security vulnerabilities.

Android Devices: Open Settings and scroll down to "About Phone". Select the first option on this page, "System updates". This will query the hardware manufacturer's site to see if an update for the phone is available. If an update is available follow the instructions and allow it to download and install.

To update applications on your Android phone, visit the Play Store. Click on the hamburger at the top, left side of the screen. When the fly-out menu appears, select "My Apps and Games". This will display a list of the applications you have that are waiting to be updated. You can tap the "Update All" button at the top of the list, or update each individually.

iOS Devices: A badge will typically be displayed on the settings icon when an update is available. If you suspect an update is available but do not have a badge on the Settings icon, you can search for and update manually. Open Settings and scroll down to "General". Select the second option on this page, "Software Update". This will query Apple to see if an iOS update is available. If an update is available follow the instructions and allow it to download and install.

Application updates are made available for iOS devices through the App Store. You have the option to have app updates download and install automatically or on demand. Open Settings and scroll down to iTunes & App Store. Under the section labeled "Automatic Downloads" is an option for Updates. Toggling this setting on will allow updates to download and be installed automatically, ensuring they are installed at the earliest possible convenience. If you toggle this setting off you will instead see a badge on the App Store icon the next time an update is available, allowing you to see what it is and download and install it at a time and place of your choosing. If you have chosen the latter option, you can also manually check for updates by opening the App Store, going to the "Updates" tab, and pulling down and release.

Encryption and Passcodes

This section is one of the most important to the physical security of a mobile device. Apple has used very strong full-disk encryption (AES) on iOS devices since iOS 3 and the iPhone 3GS. To take advantage of this encryption, you must passcode-protect the device. On most Android devices you will still have to choose to encrypt the device.

Android Devices: Android devices offer four options for protecting your device and you should implement one of them before encrypting your device. To do so, open Settings, Security, and Screen Security. The options available to you are None, Swipe, Pattern, PIN, and Password. We strongly recommend a PIN or password. Even though the pattern lock is better than no security, it is very poor security. The pattern is frequently left visible on the screen of the device and research has shown that most pattern users create their patterns very predictably. We also recommend enabling the "Require PIN to start device". This provides additional protection against resetting the device.

When you set up PIN or password protection on your device you will receive a message asking "When your device is locked how do you want notifications to show?" There are three options: "Show all notification content", "Hide sensitive notifications content", and "Don't show notifications at all". We have used all three of these options and in our experience almost any notification content reveals information about what apps are on your device. Because of this, we choose to hide all notification content. It is our belief that when the phone is locked it should reveal absolutely nothing about us to a potential attacker. The name of apps on your device could be potential attack vectors. They could reveal the dating sites and social networks you participate in and other information that is best kept private.

We strongly recommend you do not allow the Smart Lock feature. This feature allows the device to make decisions about when to unlock. It can be set to unlock when it recognizes other devices (Bluetooth devices or NFC tags), when it recognizes your face, or when you are carrying the device with you. Smart Lock is a convenience feature, not a privacy or security feature.

After you have set up your PIN or password you are ready to begin encrypting your Android device. Under the Security settings scroll to "Encrypt". If your device is already encrypted it will be indicated here and you need to take no further action. Tapping this icon will open a warning that tells you about the encryption process. Before you click through, ensure that your phone is plugged into a charger and that your battery is at fifty percent or higher. Because of the risk of the phone becoming inoperable if the encryption process is interrupted, the operating system will not let you continue without ensuring there is adequate power to begin the process. If you have a lot of data on your device, it may take an hour or more to encrypt your phone. If it is brand new with nothing on it, the device may only take a few moments. Your device will dictate whether or not you can encrypt your Micro SD card storage. Many Android phones will not allow you to do so. If this is the case, we do not recommend using this storage for anything sensitive.

If your Android build permits a provision to wipe the device after a set number of incorrect passcode attempts, you should enable it. If you are using a strong passcode, this will reduce the possibility of your passcode being defeated through brute force or by simple guessing to nearly nil.

iOS Devices: When you are initially setting up an iOS device, configuring a passcode is one of the very first steps you should take. Scrolling down you will see "Turn Passcode On". However, before you do this, we recommend toggling the "Simple Passcode" option to "Off". This will require you to enter a passcode that is longer than four characters. Though it may not seem like it, even a five-character passcode offers substantially better security than the four-character "Simple" passcode. With the Simple Passcode enabled there are only 10,000 possible passcodes on the device (0-0-0-0 through 9-9-9-9), a relatively small pool of potential passcodes from which to guess.

When the Simple Passcode is disabled, the phone will not reveal how many characters are in the passcode and a small increase in the length of the passcode can pay dividends. Just increasing the passcode to six characters increases the possible passcodes from 10,000 to 1,000,000. Further, each additional character adds exponentially more complexity to the passcode. By disabling Simple Passcode, you are allowed the option of using letters and special characters in addition to numbers, increasing the difficulty of guessing your passcode significantly.

The downside to using letters and special characters in your passcode is the keyboard. When you use these characters your lock screen will feature a full keyboard. On an iPad this is not likely an issue, but on the iPhone it can be difficult to enter the password quickly. This is why some users, including us, opt to use numbers only. When only numbers are entered into your passcode, you are presented with the larger, easier-to-use (especially when in a hurry) numerical keyboard. This certainly sacrifices complexity, so we recommend using a very long numerical passcode. The passcodes that we use are over 20 characters in length and use each number at least once. Using each number minimizes the chances that your passcode can be discovered by looking at fingerprints on the screen.

After setting a passcode on your iOS device, the next option for consideration is "Require Passcode". This option sets the length of time after the phone's display shuts down before a password is required. Setting this option to "Immediately" allows positive confirmation that the device is locked as soon as the display shuts off.

The Touch ID on iOS devices is very popular but there are a couple of reasons we hesitate to recommend it. The first is that it is has been defeated (at least in tests) by a fake fingerprint. Security researchers have demonstrated bypassing Touch ID with a printed copy of a photograph of a fingerprint. The fingerprint was physically lifted off of the screen of the very iPhone that was being hacked. The second potential vulnerability in this is that in the United States you typically cannot be legally compelled to give over your password, but you can be required to give up your fingerprints. Neither of these are likely a serious concern to most people. If you do use Touch ID to unlock your iPhone we recommend only registering one or two fingers on each hand, and preferably not the ones you typically touch the screen with, minimizing the chance that the correct fingerprint could be captured on the screen of the device.

One final setting that we strongly recommend enabling under iOS's Touch ID and Passcode menu is the "Erase Data" function. This function will wipe the phone and restore it to factory defaults after ten incorrect passcode attempts. If you are using a long, strong passcode this reduces the chances it will be broken by brute force or simple guessing to nearly nil. If you are (justifiably) concerned about the possibility of your phone being inadvertently wiped by your children, a malicious prankster, or your own fumbling hands, there are some protections in place. After five incorrect passcode attempts the phone will begin to enforce time penalties (ranging from one minute to one hour) before another attempt can be made. If your phone is wiped it can be painlessly restored from an iTunes backup, assuming you back your device up regularly.

Wi-Fi

Wi-Fi should be turned off when you are not connected to a network that you trust. When your device is not connected to a network and Wi-Fi is on, it constantly sends out probes searching for all networks that it "knows". Knowing a network means that you have previously connected to that network and have not manually removed it. These probes can be identified and can set you up for an evil twin attack.

An evil twin attack occurs when an attacker sets up a rogue Wi-Fi access point that masquerades as a legitimate access point. Unsuspecting users will connect to it, not realizing that all traffic transmitted over it is being intercepted. If the attacker conducts this attack in real time, he or she can make it more effective by making a network with the same name as a network your phone knows. By capturing your phone's probes he or she can see these networks and quickly set up a malicious network of the same name. Your phone will automatically connect to that network when it recognizes the name, and all your traffic will be routed through that network.

Leaving Wi-Fi on can also allow an attacker to discover a great deal about your pattern of life in the real world. He or she can see which Wi-Fi access points you have connected to and map these networks using websites like wigle.net. If you connect to a typical number of Wi-Fi networks and these probes are captured, a quick analysis will likely reveal where you live, work, and the coffee shops, stores, and bars that you frequent. Several national retail stores have been caught using unique sets of Wi-Fi probes to track customers around stores to identify their shopping behavior.

To avoid this, we recommend keeping Wi-Fi off when you are not actively using it. At home, for instance, we will enable Wi-Fi long enough to download podcasts, application updates, and other bandwidth intensive data. We then immediately turn it off. It is very easy to forget to turn it off when you leave your home or office. Not only does leaving Wi-Fi on have security ramifications, your phone's constant searching for a signal can drain your battery rapidly.

Android Devices: On both Android and iOS devices you can toggle Wi-Fi on and off through the control center. There are some other issues with each platform that you should be aware of and take steps to mitigate.

When you are finished using a wireless network that you will never use again, you should remove the network from the list of networks in your phone. Unless you have gone in and deleted them individually, every Wi-Fi network that you have ever connected to is still remembered and searched for by your phone. If you have had your phone for a couple of years, or have rebuilt new phones from previous backups, there may be scores of Wi-Fi networks on your phone which make your device unique and reveal a lot about your pattern of life. You should keep your list of networks brief. If you have a large number of networks stored on your device, the device sends out probes looking for all of them. It only takes a few network probes (in many cases only one or two) to identify your device as unique.

To delete networks from your device open Settings and tap Wi-Fi. Tap the overflow button (the three stacked dots in the upper, right side of the screen) and select "Saved networks". Select the network that you wish to remove and tap "Forget". This network will no longer be probed for by your device.

Disable the setting "Scanning always available". As described in the phone's settings, this "allows Google's location service and other apps to scan for networks, even when Wi-Fi is off". This means that Google can track your location even when Wi-Fi is turned off. It also means that your device can be seen on any network that is passively listening for Wi-Fi probes.

iOS Devices: When you are finished using a wireless network that you will never use again, you should remove the network from the list of networks in your phone. One complaint that we have about iOS is that it never forgets a wireless network and doesn't let you remove that network manually if you don't remove while connected to it. This means that every Wi-Fi network that you have ever connected to is still remembered and searched for by your phone. If you have had your phone for a couple of years, or have rebuilt new phones from previous iTunes backups, there may be scores of Wi-Fi networks on your phone which make your device unique and reveal a lot about your pattern of life. If you wish to remove them (and we strongly recommend you do), you can reset all network connections. Be aware that this will remove all of your Wi-Fi networks as well as any credential-authenticated VPNs that you have set on your device. If you have been careless with Wi-Fi up to this point, it is not a bad idea to start fresh. To do this, go to Settings > General > Reset > Reset Network Settings. You will be required to enter your passcode and confirm this decision.

In the future, it is a good idea to reduce the networks that your phone remembers. Because iOS remembers all networks by default and does not let you retroactively forget them individually, you must remember to forget them while you are still connected to the network. This will prevent your phone from probing for that network in the future, but it also means that your phone will not automatically connect to it. This slight inconvenience is worth it. To forget a network, connect to it, and navigate to Settings > Wi-Fi and select the Wi-Fi network to which you are connected. On the next screen scroll down to "Forget Network". An additional dialogue will ask you to confirm your decision. It is imperative that you forget the network while you are connected to it. It is easy to "forget to forget" the network, so we recommend being very selective about the networks to which you connect.

Bluetooth

Bluetooth presents challenges similar to those presented by Wi-Fi. Bluetooth can be used to track your location to a very high degree of accuracy (though only over short distances from a receiver). Bluetooth traffic can also be intercepted and though the security protocols for Bluetooth have gotten better, it can still be broken by a sufficiently skilled attacker. Because of its susceptibility to attacks like Bluebugging, Bluejacking, and Bluesnarfing, Bluetooth should be turned off when not actively in use. Bluetooth can be toggled on and off by accessing the control center in both Android and iOS devices.

Cellular

Cellular data is the primary communications pathway for mobile phones and tablets that have a cellular data plan. By default, many applications and services on your device will want to access or use your cellular data. Allowing all applications and services to use this data has two potential consequences. Most prosaically, this uses the expensive data that your pay for each month. From a security standpoint, access to a communication pathway allows the application a way to transmit and share data in the background without your knowledge or explicit consent. Though it may do more good on some apps than others, we prefer to restrict the ability to use cellular data to only those applications and services that truly need it.

Android Devices: Turning off cellular data is an all-or-nothing proposition in Android. You can disable it completely but you do not have granular control over individual applications. You can do so by opening Settings and choosing "Data Usage". Under this tab you have the option to toggle Cellular Data off globally. We should note that SilentOS, a custom Android operating system on the Blackphone 2, allows you to toggle the permissions of each app individually.

iOS Devices: Navigate to Settings, select "Cellular" and scroll down to the applications that are displayed. By default, most of the applications you have installed on the device will be permitted to use cellular data. You should disable this for every app that does not require a communication pathway to perform its desired function. This is largely up to your uses of the applications you have, but think critically about each one. Optionally you can toggle cellular data off globally in this menu.

For example, you may consider disallowing the App Store from using cellular data. Even though you will doubtlessly wish to download apps, you may prefer to wait to do so until you have a Wi-Fi connection. This is because apps are relatively large files and just a few can use a significant portion of your data plan. Other applications like Photos have the option to use cellular data. Because we do not use any sharing of photos through iCloud (or anything else), we recommend disallowing cellular data for that particular application. For some apps it may be necessary or desirable for you to allow cellular data. Maps is a good example of an application for which you may wish to enable cellular data. Without the ability to use cellular data the Maps app cannot retrieve imagery or plan routes except when you are connected to Wi-Fi.

Airplane Mode

Airplane mode is designed to allow you to turn off all transmit and receive capabilities (interfaces) inherent to the phone with the touch of a single button. This allows the device to be used on aircraft without risk of interfering with the aircraft's navigation and communication systems. Placing the device in airplane mode eliminates all communication, including your ability to send and receive texts, phone calls, emails, or anything else requiring a cellular or data connection.

Airplane mode may be useful for privacy and security in certain instances: if you want to disable all transmission from the phone (when having a sensitive conversation, for instance) you can do so easily with the push of a single button. It can be used to defeat location tracking by Apple, Google, or any of the apps that are installed on your phone. We are big proponents of using airplane mode frequently. As a word of warning, this is not a one-hundred percent solution. As long as the phone has power applied (even if it is turned off), it may be accessed by entities with the requisite technology (i.e. nation-state adversaries) and should not be relied upon to fully protect you. To toggle airplane mode on or off in either an Android or iOS device, open the control center and tap the airplane icon.

Location Services

The absolute best practice would be to disable Location Services entirely but there are negative security consequences to that. With Location Services completely disabled, the phone cannot be tracked if it is lost or stolen. iOS offers very granular control over what applications request access to your location data. We recommend leaving Location Services on and individually selecting apps and services that can access this data. You should limit these applications to the smallest number of apps possible. This is a very vivid example of the adversarial relationship between security and privacy. Enabling Location Services for everything is very convenient, but has a huge negative impact on security and privacy.

Android Devices with 5/Lollipop or Earlier: In the older versions of the Android operating system, location services is a global setting that is either on or off. There is no granularity of control. Users should keep location services turned off as much as possible. This setting can be toggled on and off in the control center.

Android Devices with 6/Marshmallow and Later: The latest version of Android offers users flexibility to give apps and services permission to use location services individually. To do so, open Settings and the Apps. Tap the gear icon in Apps to open "Configure apps". Next, tap "App permissions". Scroll down to Location. This will display a list of the applications that have requested permission to use your location data. We recommend that you only allow the minimum possible number of applications.

iOS Devices: Opening the Location Services menu allows you to disable Location Services globally or individually by application or service. Location Services relies on the device's internal GPS, cell tower locations, and Bluetooth and Wi-Fi hotspots to determine your location. Limiting Location Services is not a panacea and will not make your phone untraceable. Rather, minimizing Location Services is an attempt to minimize exposure by limiting the number of times your real-time and historic locations are captured and transmitted and the places they are stored.

The next option is Share My Location. This setting allows you to share your location with anyone in your contacts for one hour, one day, or indefinitely. Again, this necessarily requires that your location be tracked, recorded, stored, and transmitted, creating yet one more record of your physical movements.

Below Share My Location are apps that have requested location data. The only applications that we allow to access location services to our data are Maps (While Using) and the Find my iPhone lost device app (Always). All other applications are set to Never. It is important to question whether an application needs your location data. For example, does the Camera app really need to know where you are? We say it does not, and enabling this feature allows your photographs to be geo-tagged. Before allowing a service or application to access your location data you should ask yourself how it benefits you.

Below the list of applications is a sub-menu called System Services. Tapping this will open a new screen of system services that request location data. You can turn Location Services off for all of these system services except Find My iPhone (if you use it). Even though some services (like Cell Network Search and Setting Time Zone) have a legitimate need to access location services, they can, and will, still update correctly without being enabled in Location Services.

At the bottom of this display is the Status Bar Icon option and we recommend enabling it. This will place a small icon in the status bar of the phone that indicates several things depending on the color of the icon. Solid purple means an item has recently used your location, gray means an item has used your location within the last 24 hours, a purple-outlined icon means an application is using a geofence. A geofence is a geographical boundary. Siri uses a geofence when she reminds you to take out the trash as soon as you get home. Leaving this on can give you an idea of the services that use your location data and when it is being used.

Lost Device Applications

Lost device applications allow you to track your device if it is lost or stolen. Unfortunately doing so may be a devil's bargain. This ability requires that you also enable location services. There are a few things to take into account when installing or enabling one of these applications on your device. Consider the following:

- What is the likelihood you will lose your phone? Though it is certainly a possibility for each of us, some are at more risk than others. If you are in a low-risk category you may be comfortable foregoing this option.

- Cost/benefit analysis? On iOS devices you can enable location services for this application only. Unrooted Android devices running 5.1 Lollipop and earlier have no such luxury. Enabling a lost-device application on an older Android device also means permitting location services globally. Weigh the cost of doing so against the potential benefit and risk of your device being lost or stolen. In most cases like this, we believe the cost outweighs the benefit.

- Remote wipe functionality. One added benefit of many lost-device applications is the ability to wipe your phone remotely if it is lost or stolen. We believe this is the single biggest benefit of these applications.

Android Devices: Android devices can easily be tracked by logging into the Google account with which they are associated. This works even if you do not have a lost device application installed on the device. After you have logged into the device, conduct a Google search for the following terms: "where is my phone". Google will open a map and attempt to find the last location of your device. It will also give you access to your Android Device Manager. Once you have located your device you can track its location, play a sound, remotely lock the device, or erase all its content and settings.

It is important to note that the Android Device Manager will not be able to locate your device under the following circumstances: when both location and Wi-Fi connectivity are disabled, if your device is not signed in to a Google account, or if the phone is turned off. You should carefully consider whether the benefits of being able to track a lost device outweigh the data collection that occurs when location services are enabled globally or not.

iOS Devices: Though there are a number of third-party iOS applications that perform lost device tracking, none of them include a remote wipe capability. We recommend using the OEM "Find My iPhone" service. The Find My iPhone application does not need to be installed on your device to work. You can access it from any device where you can log into your iCloud account. However, it must be enabled on your device. To enable Find My iPhone, open your device settings and tap iCloud. Scroll down to and tap the last option, Find My iPhone. Toggle the Find My iPhone option on. This will necessitate allowing location services.

Find my iPhone allows you to track your device, remotely wipe it, and place it in "Lost Mode". Tracking your lost device must be done through another device or computer from which you can log into your iCloud account. We recommend securing this account with a strong password and two-factor authentication since anyone accessing it will have near-real time access to your location data. If you are tracking your lost device, you can see its location and have it play a sound. While in your iCloud account you can also place your device in Lost Mode.

When placed in Lost Mode you can lock the phone (even if it did not previously have a passcode) and display a custom message on the lock screen, such as where you can be contacted. If you choose to enter a number into the custom message, the finder can call you at that number, from your iPhone, but still have no access to your phone's contacts, history, or other data. If all else fails and you cannot locate your phone, you can remotely wipe the data on it and restore it to factory defaults, ensuring that no one will have access to the data that it contains.

Exif Data

Chapter Seven discussed how metadata within photos, often called Exif data, could potentially identify sensitive data within the image files. This has become fairly common knowledge. However, many people become careless when distributing video files created on mobile devices. The following details were extracted from the hex data of a video file that we created on an iOS device.

Format: MPEG-4
Format profile: QuickTime
File size: 1.00 MB
Duration: 10s 712ms
Recorded date: 2015-12-15T17:46:36-0500
Make: Apple
xyz: +19.369528-81.40232038.8890+161.000/
Model: iPhone 4S
com.apple.quicktime.software: 6.1.3

As you can see, anyone that possesses this video file would know our phone make and model, the operating system installed, and the GPS location of the image capture. Free programs such as MediaInfo make this collection process automated. We believe that two specific policies regarding videos will prevent extensive data leakage.

First, disable any location gathering options on your mobile device as described in the next section of this chapter. Overall, disabling location services within the system settings as well as the camera settings will prevent location data from appearing within this metadata. Next, use caution when sharing any videos. There is nothing that you can do to stop metadata from being inserted into your videos. Possession of these videos on your encrypted device has minimal consequences. Sending a video via email, text, or file transfer will preserve all metadata and allow the recipient to view the details. We know several stalking victims that disclosed this data unknowingly. While most video sharing websites extract metadata from the videos available online, they often retain the original content with preserved metadata.

App Best Practices

Applications are one of the huge benefits of owning a smartphone. We have both known some individuals who have seriously weighed the availability of several specialty apps in their selection of device. Applications are a double-edged sword and can present some security challenges of their own. Apple's "walled garden" approach to applications is a boon to security. It is not a perfect solution but overall the process seems to work pretty well. Everything allowed into the App Store must be vetted by Apple security engineers before being approved for inclusion in the App Store. This means that apps obtained in the app store can be used with a fairly high degree of trust that they contain no malware, backdoors, or other security issues. As we have mentioned above Android applications are extremely common attack vectors for various forms of mobile malware. If you use an Android device the considerations below are extremely important for your continued privacy and security.

Consider Apps Carefully

The biggest thing you can do from a privacy standpoint is limit the number of applications that you install on your phone to the absolute minimum. Each additional application you install on your device introduces new potential vulnerabilities. Before installing a new app, ask yourself if you really need it. The functions of many applications can be replicated on your web browser and do not truly require a dedicated app. If you decide that you do need a particular application, do your due diligence. See what it does in the background and read its privacy policy.

Additionally, you should consider whether or not it is a good idea to allow certain capabilities on your mobile device. Though it is certainly convenient to have a mobile banking app or a password manager at your fingertips, it is also somewhat risky. If you lose the device, you have also potentially given up banking information and credentials for all of your accounts. This should be a very real concern if your device has a weak passcode or password. You are also transmitting banking data through your phone's data or Wi-Fi connection not only when you are using the app, but when it is running in the background before, during, and after your use of the app. While these conveniences are nice to have, there are probably few situations in which you will find yourself where you cannot possibly wait to get home and check your bank account on your computer.

Review App Permissions

You should verify the permissions that each app on your device is allowed access to is actually needed for the function of that app. Though changing global settings should enforce these settings for each application, it is not a bad idea to view the settings for each app individually. The most dangerous of these settings are Location Services, Contacts, Photos, Microphone, and Camera. Some applications may have a legitimate need for access to these functions that may not be readily apparent. For example, two-factor authentication apps often request access to the camera. Though this may not seem necessary the app does need the ability to scan QR codes when setting up two-factor authentication on a new account. Regardless, when in doubt deny the permission and if it interferes with the function of the app, you can temporarily or permanently allow it in the future.

Applications that have no need whatsoever may request permission to access your camera, microphone, and contacts. The infamous "Flashlight" app that collected contact information is a good example. There is no reason an application that does nothing more than light the screen should have access to contacts or any other sensitive information. One particularly useful tool for vetting applications is called Clueful. Clueful is a product of antivirus company BitDefender and analyzes popular apps and shows you what they do in the background. Searching an app on Clueful can tell you if the application uses your unique device identifier (UDID) or an anonymous identifier, tracks your location, uses data analytics, sends usernames and passwords encrypted or unencrypted, accesses your contacts, modifies your calendar, and more. Clueful for Android devices is available as an application and is known as Clueful Privacy Advisor. Clueful for iOS is not a true application and does not need to be installed on your device. Rather Clueful is a web-app which must be accessed through your device's internet browser at **www.cluefulapp.com/#**. For ease of access, however, you may install the website to the homepage of your phone where it can be accessed with its own icon.

An Intrusive Application Example

Every time that you install an application, you are asked to agree to the amount of data that the application will have access to on your device. Most people agree to these terms without reading the details. This can expose you to great risk of divulging your personal information. There are many examples of these sneaky applications on the internet, but we will only document one here.

TrueCaller is an app for Android and iPhone telephones. It is marketed as an application to provide phone number search and spam blocking features. You can set a list of people that you do not want to communicate with, and the software will forward these callers to voice mail without bothering you. Further, it will display the caller ID of many callers even if they are not in your contact list. Their website claims that the service will identify over 2 billion incoming telephone numbers. This includes both landlines and cellular numbers. This level of identification is impressive, which made us investigate how they collect cellular number information.

TrueCaller collects contact information from the telephones that it is installed on. When you install the application, it reports your entire contact list to a server. These entries are then added to a master database. If you had a friend's private number stored in your telephone as "Brad O'Neal", the number and name assigned to it are now in the database. If you install this application, and he calls you, the application will tell you that his name is "Brad O'Neal" without already having his information stored. It will further identify personal details such as employer and a photograph if available from a public source such as LinkedIn. This is referred to as crowd sourcing. The hundreds of thousands of users that installed this application gave possession of their contacts list to TrueCaller to do whatever they want. How did they legally do this? The permissions required from the application should give the answer.

Every application on the Google Play store must document the permissions required from the device to function. These are the areas of information that the application can have access to. When you install the application, you will be asked to approve or reject these permissions. If you reject them, the software will not install. The following permissions were extracted directly from TrueCaller's Google website. This application is allowed to:

- Read your contacts
- Modify your contacts
- Know your approximate location (network-based)
- Read your text messages (SMS or MMS)
- Directly call phone numbers
- Reroute outgoing calls
- Read the contents of your USB storage
- View Wi-Fi connections
- Read phone status and identity

Some of the items on this list explain how this company can legally copy your contact list and add it to their database of numbers and names. You give them permission to do this when you agree to these terms. Now everyone in your contact list has lost the privacy of their cellular and landline numbers. Also, any of your friends that installed this application have now shared your contact information that is stored in their telephone. If this were not bad enough, the service will also let anyone type in a telephone number and display the caller ID information stored on the database. It eliminates the need for you to call someone for them to identify your number.

We do not mean to pick on TrueCaller. There are thousands of applications that require you to grant similar permissions. I recommend that you read the permissions that you are granting to every application that you install. If something looks wrong, do not install the application. In my experience, the applications that offer any free service to interact with your telephone calls, text messaging, caller ID, or contact list are extracting all information from your telephone. It is not worth jeopardizing the privacy of you or your friends and family. If you navigate to truecaller.com, you can search the database of collected caller ID information. If you were to type in the cellular number assigned to my previously issued government phone, you would receive a result of "Mike Bazzel". This tells us that someone in that former government circle installed this app on their device, and spelled "Bazzell" wrong.

Android Devices with 5/Lollipop or Earlier: On older Android devices, there is little that can be done to restrict applications' permissions without rooting the device. The user can navigate to Settings, Apps, and App Info where scrolling down will show the apps permissions, or use Clueful Privacy Advisor to show what permissions will be requested before installing the app. If you have rooted the device, you can download an app called App Ops that will allow you to manually control all of the app's permissions.

Android Devices with 6/Marshmallow and Later: On Android 6/Marshmallow and later, control of app permissions is integrated into the OS. To access these permissions open Settings and open Apps. Tap the gear icon on the Apps screen, and once you are in "Configure apps" tap "App permissions". This will open a list of features that your apps have requested permissions for including body sensors, calendar, camera, contacts, location, microphone, phone, SMS, and more. Selecting any one of these items will show you the apps that have requested permission to use the data. Deny any app that does not have a compelling reason to access the requested function or data set.

iOS Devices: Open Settings, and scroll down until you reach the settings for each app. Tapping any app will allow you to turn on or off access to any of the functions it has requested including Background App Refresh, Camera, Cellular Data, Contacts, Location, Microphone, and Notifications. Turn off any of these that are not necessary for the performance of the app's designed function.

Passcode or Password Protect Apps

Many applications allow themselves to be individually passcode protected. This allows you one extra layer of security if your passcode is breached, or if you share your phone with others. Be aware that this does not necessarily encrypt data (though on certain applications it may). If not, your data will not be protected against a forensic examination.

Backups

Backing up your personal data is important. Backing it up on a smartphone that is in constant danger of being stolen off a bar, dropped in a toilet, forgotten in a taxi, or stepped on by a horse (all of these are real life examples that we have personally witnessed) is at least as important. Of course, the ideal strategy is to store as little data on your phone as possible. Not only is there less data for you to lose, there is less that is potentially falling into someone else's hands and less data that is potentially being exfiltrated by your apps, malicious software, or by your operating system. Of course, we also understand that a phone is really a computer and most of us desire to use the computer to near its full potential. For this reason, you should maintain a backup so you can restore your data in the event your device fails or is physically removed from your life.

Android Devices: Android devices offer less flexibility for backups. You have the option to either not backup, or backup to Google servers. We find both of the options distasteful. If you must backup we recommend using an anonymous Gmail account as your Google Play account and limiting the personal information supplied in the account. It would be nearly impossible to completely anonymize this data; even the presence of your home Wi-Fi network in the backup could reveal who you are.

If your Android device is rooted, our preferred option for backups is Titanium Backup. This application allows you to create backups of your device locally, without submitting them to the cloud. The backup can include all apps, all data stored in those apps such as calling history and SMS messages, and most of the phone's settings. Titanium Backup backs all of this information up to your device's SD card storage. It is very likely that the SD card would be lost or damaged with the phone itself, so we recommend having two SD cards. One should stay in the phone and one in a safe location. You could also backup the SD card to a computer or other media. This also allows you to strongly encrypt these backups. Always use a very strong password for the backup.

iOS Devices: You have two basic options when backing up iOS devices. You can backup your data or some portion thereof to your iCloud account or you can back it up locally to "This Computer". Naturally we prefer the second option. When backing up with iTunes you are creating a full system image of the phone including all settings, messages, call history, photos, apps, podcasts, music, and other data. If your phone is lost, stolen, or irreparably damaged you can restore a new device from this backup with all of the exact same settings. iTunes also offers you the ability to encrypt your backup. We recommend doing so even if the backup is stored on a full-disk encrypted computer as the contents of your phone reveal much more granular details about your day-to-day activity.

Jailbreaking iOS Devices

Previously in this book we have mentioned rooting Android devices. There are some security compromises with rooting. When rooted you can use apps like Titanium Backup that are not available to stock Android users. You are also able remove hardware manufacturer and service provider bloatware that is constantly running on your phone and transmitting information about it. You have additional options that were not previously available. Rooting is a fairly advanced skill and is not for the casual user. If you do choose to root your device, we encourage the use of alternative operating systems like CyanogenMod. This version of Android is frequently updated and is reputed to be very secure though the installation can be problematic for less experienced users. For more information on CyanogenMod visit **www.cyanogenmod.org**.

Jailbreaking is the process of "privilege escalation" on iOS devices. Jailbreaking allows the user to have root access to the phone and make changes that are not allowed in the OEM version of iOS. Jailbreaking can be tantalizing because jailbroken phones are much more malleable. Their user environments can be changed, features can be added or taken away (such as customizing the Control Center, etc.). However, there are some very good reasons not to jailbreak your iPhone or other iOS device. In spite of this ability to customize, jailbreaking introduces many vulnerabilities. First, it allows many unvetted, third-party apps to be installed on the device. Ironically this is a huge reason people decide to jailbreak in the first place. Third-party apps are not inspected or curated by the App Store and may contain viruses. This is not to say that the App Store's vetting process is perfect ("bad" apps have gotten in), but they do not have root permissions which pose a much greater threat. As much as we understand the desire to tinker, modify, and hack your devices, we strongly caution against jailbreaking. We strongly believe iOS is the most secure mobile operating system on the market. As we mentioned previously, Apple has done an admirable job at securing the OS, and jailbreaking negates many of these protections.

A Final Strategy for Smartphone Security

Sometimes, the best solutions are the simplest. We believe that one extremely powerful, yet simple idea, is to turn your device off when not in use. Compare your smartphone to your computer. Do you shut down your computer when not in use? Do you leave it on all night every night? We need to view smartphones as computers, which they are. While you sleep or work away from your device, it is constantly communicating with several servers. It is exchanging information about your contacts, messages, and activities with numerous data collection sources. On many devices, the audio noise occurring near the unit is being recorded as a "feature" for use within apps. You may have followed our methods of having an anonymous phone. This will provide an amazing layer of security, but it will not stop the data transmissions about your alias.

If you shut your device completely down, or at at least place it in airplane mode without any active connections, you prevent this data from escaping. You may choose to simply turn your phone off at night. If you use it as an alarm, disable the cellular, Wi-Fi, GPS, and Bluetooth connections. You may choose to take this to another level and shut down your device while traveling. We like both of the following strategies.

- When traveling toward your residence or workplace, turn the device off within five miles. This will prevent your cellular records from profiling these important locations. When leaving your residence or workplace, turn the device back on after passing the five-mile radius.

- If you travel extensively, turn your device off before arriving at an airport and back on when needed away from the airport in the new city. This will create a wild pattern and chaos will appear normal in your profile. If your records are ever compromised or monitored, and your device is turned off routinely, this will appear normal to the viewer.

Remember that even with a VPN on your device, it is still connected to a cellular provider. You cannot prevent them from knowing the location of the device if the cellular connection is established. Possessing a device completely in an alias name cannot stop the companies from tracking the device, but they will have no idea that you are the owner. The next pages will identify our individual configurations which may inspire you to create your own strategy.

Michael's Mobile Communications Strategy

Primary Device
Hardware: BlackPhone 2   **Operating System**: SilentOS (Android 5)
Carrier: T-Mobile   **Plan**: $30 "Hidden" Prepaid, 100 Talk, Unl. Text & Data
Primary Alias Incoming/Outgoing Calls: GrooveIP
Secondary Alias Outgoing Calls: Google Voice (Hangouts Dialer)
Secure Personal Incoming/Outgoing Calls: Silent Circle / Signal
Primary Alias Text Messaging: Google Voice
Secure Personal Text Messaging: Wickr / Silent Text / Signal
Secure Personal Email: ProtonMail
VPN: PIA   **Password Manager**: Keepass   **Encryption**: SilentOS Default
Connection Strategy: Airplane mode or power off at night and within 5 miles of residence

Notes: I alternate between two T-Mobile SIM cards. When I am home for an extended period of time, I use my primary SIM. When I prepare to travel for extended time, I allow the primary to expire and I activate the secondary SIM. This way, I am still paying the typical $30 monthly fee, but I can switch the accounts every other month in order to avoid tracking of every movement. There is crossover from home to travel, but an analysis of any one of these accounts would be missing a lot of data about me. Of course, knowing both of my accounts would tell the full story. Each account is in a different alias. One is always paid by Blur masked numbers, and the other only with cash refill cards.

Secondary Device
Hardware: Samsung Galaxy S3   **Operating System**: Android KitKat (Rooted)
Carrier: None   **Plan**: None (Wi-Fi Only)
Primary Alias Incoming/Outgoing Calls: GrooveIP
Secondary Alias Outgoing Calls: Google Voice (Hangouts Dialer)
Primary Alias Text Messaging: Google Voice
Secure Text Messaging: Wickr / Signal
Secure Email: ProtonMail
VPN: PIA   **Password Manager**: None   **Encryption**: Android Stock

Notes: This phone is turned off at all times unless needed. I carry it with me while traveling when I need to make or accept a call or text while acting as an alias. This device is used for Uber and other invasive apps when necessary while traveling.

Justin's Mobile Communications Strategy

Primary Device

Hardware: iPhone 6S   **Operating System**: iOS 9.2

Carrier: Various   **Plan**: Various

Primary Alias Incoming/Outgoing Calls: Google Voice (non-personal use only)

Secondary Alias Outgoing Calls: Silent Circle

Secure Personal Incoming/Outgoing Calls: Signal

Primary Alias Text Messaging: Google Voice

Secure Personal Text Messaging: Signal/Wickr

Secure Personal Email: ProtonMail

VPN: PIA   **Password Manager**: STRIP   **Encryption**: iOS Default

Connection Strategy: Combination of leaving device at home when going out, turning off, or placing in airplane mode in an attempt to create unpredictability.

Notes: Because the iPhone is capable of operating on both CDMA and GSM networks I alternate between a variety of providers including AT&T, Sprint, Straight Talk, and T-Mobile. Because I nearly always have a Wi-Fi connection, I only need a limited phone plan and go with the smallest and most economical prepaid plans available. Because all my personal and business communications are made through apps like Signal and Silent Phone I have no need to maintain the same telephone number for any extended period of time.

Secondary Device

Hardware: iPod Touch   **Operating System**: iOS 9.2

Carrier: None   **Plan**: None (Wi-Fi Only)

Primary Alias Incoming/Outgoing Calls: Google Voice

Primary Alias Text Messaging: Google Voice

Primary Secure Voice: Signal

Secure Text Messaging: Wickr

Secure Email: ProtonMail

VPN: PIA   **Password Manager**: STRIP   **Encryption**: iOS Default

Notes: I purchased this lightly used, latest-generation iPod Touch from Craigslist. I paid more for it than most used devices of similar age and condition but am confident it is not a stolen device. I keep it turned off at all times when not in use, it is never connected to my home Wi-Fi network, none of the accounts on it are associated with true name personal accounts, and it is on a completely separate iTunes/iCloud account. This means that I had to pay for some apps twice but I am ok with that.

I like that this is an iPod rather than a phone; that means a SIM has never been associated with it and it does not even have an IMEI, making me that much more anonymous. Without GSM or CDMA architecture to work with it is that much more difficult to track my location. The phone company doesn't get any of my data, either, which I really dig.

CHAPTER THIRTEEN
COMPUTER SECURITY: DATA-AT-REST

This chapter will detail the protection of data-at-rest. Data-at-rest is the information that is stored on your computer's hard drive or on removable media when it is not being used or transmitted, which is most of the time. In the event your computer is lost or stolen, accessed by an unauthorized person, or malware is scraping your personal files, encryption will prevent any information from being compromised. This chapter will cover some basics of encryption, encryption programs, and some best practices for effective employment of encryption.

Encryption Basics

Encrypting sensitive data is one of the single most important steps users can take in the interest of securing sensitive personal information. Unfortunately, it is also something that many users seem very hesitant to do. To the uninitiated it seems like a lot of work, and may even seem to be a sign of paranoia. Though encryption does require a very minor shift in how users think about their data, it isn't a great deal of work to set up initially. After it is installed and running it is almost completely transparent to the user.

Before we move into the specifics of the encryption programs it is important to discuss the two broad categories of encryption that are used to protect data stored on a computer. They are file-level and full-disk encryption. We believe that it is important to understand the benefits and limitations of each, and to use each where appropriate.

File-Level Encryption: File-level encryption allows you to create a file "container" that encrypts all the files within it. When you "close" the container, all the files within it are encrypted, restricting access to anyone who does not possess the correct password. This is perhaps the most commonly implemented type of encryption employed by the average user. Both of us use file-level encryption for some applications but consider it generally inferior to full-disk encryption.

Full-disk Encryption: Full-disk encryption (FDE) offers the ultimate security for the data on a computer's hard drive. Full-disk encryption means that the entire hard drive, including all files, the operating system, applications and programs, and anything else on there is encrypted when the computer is turned off. The only portion of the hard drive that is left unencrypted is the boot loader, a very small portion that allows the computer to accept the entered password and begin the boot process upon startup.

Most users assume that file-level encryption is sufficient as long as all versions of sensitive files are encrypted. Unfortunately, this is fairly inaccurate. While using your computer, it stores various versions of files such as saved "recovery" versions, records of filenames that you have accessed, internet browsing history, and a great deal of other sensitive information, the majority of it without your permission or knowledge. If your computer is unencrypted, this information can be exploited to reveal sensitive information about you. This information may reveal the names, sizes, and even the contents of your most sensitive encrypted files. For example, if you edit a Microsoft Word document, it will automatically create an AutoSave version that can be recovered in the event your computer crashes or you accidentally close without saving. Unless you specifically change the location to which this file saves, it is written unencrypted to your hard drive in a nebulous location that is not always easy for the average user to locate. Full-disk encryption prevents this kind of leakage from being accessed and exploited.

Encryption of the entire hard drive is beneficial for several other reasons. Full-disk encryption is the most transparent form of encryption. After the user initially enters a password and the computer boots, it functions as it normally would. And if your computer is lost or stolen, no information can be recovered from it. When a thief or attacker turns the device on a password prompt will appear, and the computer will not boot up until the correct password is entered. If the hard drive is removed and plugged into another device as an external hard drive, or if the computer is booted with another operating system like a bootable DVD (two common techniques to get around operating system passwords), all of the data on the computer will still be encrypted and inaccessible to the attacker.

Though some users possessing some familiarity with encryption consider full-disk encryption overkill, we firmly believe it should be the standard. Full-disk encryption is the simplest form of encryption to use. Though setup may be a bit more daunting, the simplicity of its day-to-day use (especially in comparison to file-level encryption) far outweighs the hassle of encrypting it in the first place. Once installed and running, FDE only requires a single password (when booting). It is totally transparent from then on, and offers total protection whenever the device is powered down.

Users should also recognize there are downsides to everything, and FDE is no exception. There is a degradation in system performance when using any form of encryption because the computer must decrypt everything on-the-fly as it is used. We have found this reduction in processor power to be minimal, though your circumstances may vary depending on your processor speed, the encryption algorithm you use, and some other factors. Power users who depend on their devices for processor-heavy functions like video editing or graphic design may find this slow-down noticeable but the overwhelming majority of users will not.

Full-Disk Encryption on Removable Storage

Full-disk encryption can apply to system and non-system drives alike. System drives are the hard drives upon which the computer's operating system resides and from which it runs; non-system drives are other disks that are connected to the computer such as auxiliary internal or external hard drives, SD cards, and USB flash drives. If you do not enable full-disk encryption for your system drive we highly recommend enabling it for your non-system drives and devices, especially those with which you travel. USB flash drives are notoriously easy to lose, and the loss of one containing sensitive data can be extremely damaging.

Encryption Algorithms: There are three encryption algorithms that are used with the programs that will be discussed in this chapter. They are AES (Advanced Encryption Standard), Serpent, and Twofish. AES is currently the United States Government's only approved algorithm for the protection of classified information. The algorithm that underlies AES was selected by the National Institute of Standards and Technology (NIST), in a contest to transition the US Government to a new, improved algorithm from the elderly and inferior 3DES (Third Generation Data Encryption Standard). After selection by NIST the AES algorithm was further vetted by the National Security Agency (NSA) before being certified for the protection of classified information in 2003. Currently there are no known workable defeats for AES.

Serpent and Twofish were both finalists in the AES competition, and both are very strong algorithms. While some of the programs discussed below will allow you to use cascaded algorithms (i.e. AES encrypted by Serpent, which is then encrypted by Twofish), AES is currently susceptible to no known defeats, and is widely believed to be more than sufficient. While we leave it in the hands of the user to decide which algorithm he or she trusts, we add a morsel of food for thought. Cryptanalysts are probably much busier working on defeats for AES than they are for Serpent or Twofish because of the ubiquity and popularity of AES. For this reason, we consider using all of the algorithms for different things. AES could be used for full-disk encryption, Serpent for file-level encrypted volumes, and Twofish for Password Safe databases. If a vulnerability is discovered in any one of these algorithms, we still have a good degree of protection provided by the others.

Verifying File Integrity

Verifying the integrity of a computer program before installing and using it is incredibly important, especially for security software. Verifying the program ensures that it has not been modified. While a modified or look-alike version of more conventional software is almost certainly an attack vector for malware, modified versions of security applications are typically more insidious. A security application that has been modified will probably have no immediately obvious indicators that it has been tampered with. The program will function normally, and appear to do all of the things it was designed to do. The changes made to it will be visible only to someone closely examining the source code. The purpose for such a modification would be to weaken the security it offers or insert a backdoor. This is unacceptable if you are truly relying on a security program to keep your data safe.

The simplest way to ensure you are getting the original, unmodified version of the application is to verify its checksum. Every file created in Windows (or any other operating system) has a checksum. A checksum is simply the product of all the 1s and 0s of a program when hashed through a cryptographic algorithm. Hashing produces a reliable output code that will be of a consistent length, and will not change, no matter how many times the program is copied, moved, or renamed, as long as its underlying source code remains the same. If even the slightest modification has been made to the code, the checksum will also change drastically. The example below shows the difference even very subtle changes to the word "hello" can make when this text is hashed using the MD5 hashing algorithm. Even though only one letter has been changed in each example of the word, you will notice that the output product for each is drastically different:

hello: 5d41402abc4b2a76b9719d911017c592
Hello: 8b1a9953c4611296a827abf8c47804d7
hellO: 06612c0d9c73d47a7042afd7024d7c82

If you download a program and the checksum is not what it should be, you should not rely on that software. To verify a checksum, you must have access to a known good checksum to compare it with. This checksum should not come from the same website from which you downloaded the program. If you have been redirected to a look-alike site from which you are tricked into downloading a modified version of the program, it is reasonable to assume that the checksum on that site reflects their modified version of the software. A better option would be to get the checksum from a trusted, unaffiliated, third-party site. It is also important to use a checksum that has been calculated using a hashing algorithm that is secure.

Windows: The program we recommend for verifying checksums in Windows is the CHK Checksum Utility. This program runs in portable mode and does not need to be installed. To verify a program using CHK, open the application and simply drag the .exe or .msi file to be verified into CHK's interface. It will appear in a list view in the interface, and display the name of the file, the file type, the file's size, the checksum (SHA1 by default), and a path to the file.

CHK supports fourteen different hash functions including MD5, SHA-1, SHA-224, SHA-256, and SHA-512. If you wish to change the hash function, open the "Options" pull down menu and select the function you prefer (we recommend SHA-256 or SHA-512). Once the program has been imported and calculated by CHK, retrieve a verifiably good checksum to compare it with (again, preferably from a disinterested third-party site). In CHK, right-click on the file and select "Verify". This will bring up a new window into which you can paste the checksum and click "OK". If the two checksums match, a green check mark will appear beside the application in the CHK interface. If there is a conflict and the two checksums do not match, a red "X" will appear.

If this happens and the two checksums do not match, double-check your work. Ensure that the checksum you are using is from the same hash that CHK is set to use. For example, ensure you did not copy the MD5 hash, but set CHK to test SHA-1 hashes. If the two hashes are not from the same algorithm, go to "Options" and change the algorithm. If the algorithms are the same, ensure that you copied the entire checksum. If you still get an error, something is wrong with the application and you absolutely should not trust it (especially if it is a security application). The CHK Checksum Utility is free and available at **http://compressme.net/**.

OS X: Verifying a checksum in OS X will require that you use the terminal. To access the terminal, navigate to Applications > Utilities > Terminal. A terminal window will open. Type in "shasum" followed by a single space. Next, drag the file into the terminal window and press enter. A SHA-1 checksum will be displayed by default, but SHA-256 and SHA-512 algorithms are also available. To use them will require entering some additional text into the terminal. To use SHA-256 type "shasum" followed by a space; next, type –a followed by a space, and the drag the file into the terminal window. If you wish to use SHA-512 enter "512" instead of 256. The commands should look like this:

SHA-1:   shasum /user/Macbookpro/desktop/filename
SHA-256:   shasum –a 512 /user/Macbookpro/desktop/filename
SHA-512:   shasum –a 512 /user/Macbookpro/desktop/filename

After you have typed the command in and hit enter the OS will return the appropriate checksum (depending on algorithm chosen). You must visually compare this checksum with a known good one.

Full Disk Encryption Utilities

Full disk encryption is an absolute necessity and as we have mentioned previously it is perhaps the easiest and most transparent encryption to use. This section will cover the excellent cross-platform TrueCrypt/VeraCrypt, as well as platform-specific full-disk encryption utilities: BitLocker, FileVault II, and LUKS.

TrueCrypt/VeraCrypt

Until May of 2014, TrueCrypt was the de facto encryption program du jour for individual and home users. TrueCrypt offered very robust encryption, was exceptionally feature-rich, and was fairly user-friendly. TrueCrypt could be used for both full-disk and file level encryption, could support various two-factor authentication schemes, was available for Linux, Mac, and Windows, and was totally free. Unfortunately, the developers of TrueCrypt decided that they would no longer support the program and dropped it in a rather public and alarming manner. The TrueCrypt homepage (**TrueCrypt.org**) was redirected to a warning page that advised, "WARNING: TrueCrypt is not secure as it may contain unfixed security issues". The site then went on to detail the procedure to migrate data to a different encryption program. In conjunction with this warning, one final version of TrueCrypt, version 7.2 was (and still is) offered. This version is not useful for encryption purposes as it only allows users who had previously used TrueCrypt to decrypt their files if need be.

In spite of this, both of us stuck by TrueCrypt for some time. Even though the future of the program was uncertain, TrueCrypt was one of the few encryption programs available that had been independently audited (the audit was crowd-funded and nearing completion when developer support was dropped). Both of us independently decided to continue using the program until a major vulnerability was discovered, because competing encryption programs are abundant but none have been independently audited.

Unfortunately, two privilege escalation vulnerabilities were discovered in TrueCrypt in September of 2015 that make us uncomfortable continuing to use or recommend TrueCrypt in Windows and both of us have since migrated to VeraCrypt. VeraCrypt is a fork of TrueCrypt and is almost identical in appearance and function. Some functions have been changed "behind the scenes" that make VeraCrypt more secure than TrueCrypt (assuming they have been implemented properly), but the biggest benefit is that bugs in the code are patched. This is not the case with TrueCrypt, which will never again be patched. VeraCrypt is free and available at **https://veracrypt.codeplex.com/**.

VeraCrypt can be used on Windows, Mac OS X, and Linux platforms. Once you have downloaded, verified, and installed VeraCrypt, you will find that it is an incredibly feature-rich encryption program. VeraCrypt offers the ability to create file-level encrypted containers (called "volumes"), hidden volumes (which are built inside standard volumes and offer a layer of plausible deniability), and full-disk encryption for the system drive and non-system drives. It is also capable of encrypting a partition or entirety of a USB flash drive or hard drive. Further, with VeraCrypt you can use two-factor authentication for volumes (using keyfiles), choose any of three very strong encryption algorithms or use them in combination, and even create a hidden operating system on your computer.

VeraCrypt is incredibly well documented, and the 161-page VeraCrypt User's Guide that is included in the download of the program does a very thorough job of explaining how to use all of the functions available in the program. For this reason, we will not duplicate this effort here. To access the VeraCrypt User's Guide, open VeraCrypt, click the Help drop-down menu, and click the first option: User's Guide.

How We Use VeraCrypt: Our preferred method of using VeraCrypt is to use both file-level encrypted volumes and full-disk encryption. This belt-and-suspenders approach gives us peace of mind that our data is secure no matter what. The following will explain our recommendations for how it is used.

First, full-disk encrypt your computer using a platform-specific utility (we use FileVault II on our MacBooks). If you choose to use VeraCrypt to full-disk encrypt, select "Create Volume", and "Encrypt the system partition or entire system drive" option in the VeraCrypt Volume Creation Wizard. Consult the VeraCrypt User's Guide for exact instructions on how to proceed from here. As previously discussed, this will protect all of the contents of your entire device if it is lost or stolen. Be aware that in order to fully encrypt your hard drive, VeraCrypt will prompt you to burn a "VeraCrypt Rescue Disk" onto a CD. Though there are ways to bypass the requirement to burn an actual disk, we highly recommend completing this step. This rescue disk contains volume header information for emergency use. In the event your encryption becomes corrupted, you can boot from the disk, enter the correct password, and the encryption can be repaired, once more allowing you access to your files. It is a common misconception that this disk contains the password. It does not. If you forget your password, the VeraCrypt rescue disk will not let you back into your device.

Next, build an encrypted volume (or series of encrypted volumes if you desire compartmentalization) that is large enough to store all of your sensitive documents. We recommend storing not only credit reports, work documents, résumés, and other obviously sensitive information, but family photographs and other seemingly innocuous files as well. Though typically not considered "sensitive", these items can reveal a great deal of information about you and your family including your interests and hobbies, your patterns of life, and valuables that you possess in your home. On our computers everything gets stored in a VeraCrypt volume. This volume may be quite large, but this won't be an issue as long as you have space on the hard drive. Once all of these items are secured in a VeraCrypt volume, verify the contents, ensure you didn't miss anything, and delete the unencrypted versions (see Chapter 21: Secure File Deletion).

Using two layers of encryption like this may seem superfluous to some. This method offers two advantages. First, it allows you to dismount the VeraCrypt volumes that contains your sensitive documents, and safely step away from your device for a short time. Second, if multiple users have access to the device (a family or roommates using a common computer, for instance), it allows you to store items privately that you do not want the other users to access. Finally, by using very strong, very different passwords on the full-disk and volume-level encryption, you have the peace of mind of knowing that to recover all your sensitive files an attacker will be forced to break two passwords. This will require an unacceptably long period of time.

VeraCrypt Favorites: One extremely useful feature of VeraCrypt is its ability to designate volumes as "Favorites". Favorites allow you to mount all your favorite volumes at once if they share a password. It will consistently assign them to the same drive letter each time they are mounted and allow you to give them a custom name. We find all of these features extremely helpful and always mount two VeraCrypt volumes at a time (primary and backup). Giving them custom names helps us quickly discern the difference. Another benefit of being able to mount all Favorites at once is that you only have to enter one password to mount them.

One final useful feature of VeraCrypt Favorites is the ability to assign a consistent set of behaviors to mounted Volumes. These behaviors can be customized to meet your needs. The list of behaviors that can be assigned to each Favorite volume include mounting as read-only or removable medium and opening Windows Explorer when the volume is mounted. As is the case with all other features of VeraCrypt, more thorough explanation is contained in the

VeraCrypt User's Guide. To access the Favorites menu in VeraCrypt, click the "Favorites" drop-down menu and click "Organize Favorite Volumes…".

An Example of Justin's "Favorites" In Use

This is an example of my Windows setup. Being able to consistently and easily mount volumes to the same drive letter each time is extremely helpful in setting up a number of other features on your computer. Even though they are independently encrypted, I store my Password Safe databases inside a VeraCrypt volume because of the disproportionate amount of damage that would be done if they were compromised. When I open Password Safe, it attempts to open the database from the last location from which it was opened. If I am careless and mount my VeraCrypt volume to a different drive letter each time, I would then have to manually navigate to the database. This is inconvenient and time consuming, and can be completely avoided by mounting volume(s) as Favorites. I also set up Microsoft Office to store auto-saved versions inside a VeraCrypt volume, which is mapped according to a drive letter. If this drive letter changes, the program will force me to manually choose the save location each time it is opened. The most important reason I use Favorites is for my backup system. CryptSync, my preferred backup utility for Windows (which will be discussed later in this chapter) will not work correctly if the original and duplicate volumes are mounted to incorrect drive letters.

Protecting Encrypted Volumes in OS X: An excellent reason to use TrueCrypt or VeraCrypt favorites in OS X is to prevent the files within these volumes from being accessed by Spotlight Search. Spotlight is Apple's search assistance program that sends searches and some results to Apple. Simple searches are also shared with Microsoft's Bing. We do not like the thoughts of our our encrypted contents potentially being searched and indexed by Apple.

Fortunately, you can mark certain file locations as unsearchable to Spotlight. To prevent files from being indexed in Spotlight, first mount your TrueCrypt or VeraCrypt volumes. Next, open "Spotlight" in System Preferences. Click on the privacy tab and you will see a list of locations that Spotlight is not allowed to search. At the bottom of this list click the "+". A Finder dialogue will open that allows you to navigate to the location of your choice. Select your encrypted volume(s). Since all of the files stored on our computers are in an encrypted volume we have very few files to add here. If all of your files are not stored in an encrypted volume you should also mark these locations as unsearchable through Spotlight.

Keyfiles: The ability to use keyfiles is an often overlooked feature of VeraCrypt. Keyfiles serve as a second authentication factor for volumes and can increase the security of encrypted volumes significantly. When mounting a volume that uses keyfiles, the user must enter the correct password and select the correct keyfile(s) that are associated with that volume. Keyfiles are simply files such as photos, videos, executable programs, text documents, PDFs, or any other type of file. If you have difficulty selecting a keyfile, VeraCrypt has a built-in keyfile generator. When creating a volume or changing a volume password, you can elect to use keyfiles by checking the "Use Keyfiles" checkbox. From now on you will have to add these keyfiles each time you mount the volume.

Keyfiles increase security by requiring both the correct password and the correct keyfiles to mount the volume. You can add as many keyfiles as you want. We have successfully added as many as fifty keyfiles. An attacker attempting to open your volume would have to know the password as well as the fact that the volume requires keyfiles, and what those keyfiles are. Further, the attacker would require access to these files. If you store them in the cloud or on a USB flash drive that you carry in your pocket, access to them could be very difficult for an attacker to acquire. Below we will discuss some other encryption options. This is not because of any uncertainty around TrueCrypt or VeraCrypt. Indeed, they are two of the few independently audited encryption options out there, and we still trust them as fully as anything else despite the lack of future support.

Keyfile Safety

A number of encryption programs support keyfiles, and though any file type can be used as a keyfile, we recommend exercising extreme care when selecting one. We prefer to use a file type that cannot easily be modified (such as a .jpeg or .mp4) rather than ones that can easily and thoughtlessly be altered (such as .docx or .txt). If the file is modified in any way, there is a very good chance that it will no longer be recognized as the required keyfile and you will subsequently be unable to get back into your VeraCrypt volume. We much prefer to use image or video files that are not easily changed. Further, we strongly recommend backing up keyfiles. Backup keyfiles can be stored on a USB flash drive, in the cloud, on another machine, or in your email inbox, but if so, they should probably be concealed among a number of other innocuous files.

BitLocker (Windows)

BitLocker is Windows' OEM full disk encryption utility. BitLocker allows the encryption of both system and non-system drives, utilizes AES-128 or 256 encryption, and is very easy to implement. BitLocker is only available on the following top-tiered editions of Windows.

Windows 7: Enterprise and Ultimate Editions
Windows 8/8.1: Pro and Enterprise Editions
Windows 10: Pro and Enterprise Editions

Making this feature exclusive to the more expensive versions excludes millions of home and personal users. This is unfortunate. BitLocker is extremely easy to use. It is available directly from the right click context menu. We cautiously recommend BitLocker if you have a version of Windows that supports it. We urge caution only because we greatly prefer applications that are independently audited and not provided by Microsoft.

DiskCryptor (Windows)

One program that is touted as an alternative to VeraCrypt is DiskCryptor. It offers some, but certainly not all, of the functionality of VeraCrypt. DiskCryptor is a free and fully open-source program that offers full-disk encryption for system and non-system devices and partitions. DiskCryptor does not offer file-level encryption but does support the use of keyfiles and the AES, Serpent, and Twofish algorithms. For what it is worth, we have worked with DiskCryptor and feel comfortable considering it our full-disk backup solution in the event that a serious vulnerability is discovered in VeraCrypt.

DiskCryptor is incredibly easy to implement. After downloading and installing it, open the simple interface which shows a list of drives attached to your computer. To encrypt a non-system drive, select the drive you would like to encrypt by clicking on it. Click "Encrypt" and a new dialogue will appear. The first option in this new dialogue is to select the encryption algorithm. The same options that are available in VeraCrypt are available in DiskCryptor. It includes support for AES, Twofish, Serpent, and cascaded versions of all three. The next option is the wipe mode. This will overwrite any data on the drive to permanently delete it before encrypting (for more information on overwriting, see the next chapter). The three overwrite options are the DOD 3- and 7-pass methods, and the Gutmann method. There is also the option to skip the overwrite altogether by selecting "None".

Clicking "Next" will advance the dialogue to the next screen where you will be prompted to input a password. Here DiskCryptor offers a built-in password checker. The password checker lets you know what character types are used in your password and gives you an indication of its strength with a vertical bar graph that rates your password as Trivially Breakable, Low, Medium, High, and Unbreakable. We would not consider any password unbreakable but this is a nice feature that is based on the length and complexity of the password. Like VeraCrypt, DiskCryptor also supports the use of keyfiles as a second authentication factor.

After selecting the encryption algorithm, wipe method, and password, clicking "OK" will begin encrypting the disk. This may take some time depending on the size of the disk and the speed of your processor. Selecting a wipe method will add significantly more time (up to several hours). Once your drive is encrypted using it is a simple matter. Plug it into your PC and open DiskCryptor. When the drive is recognized by DiskCryptor click "Mount", enter the password, and add any necessary keyfiles. The drive is now mounted as a virtual drive and will appear as a hard drive in My Computer in the same way mounted VeraCrypt volumes are mounted as virtual drives. When you are finished working with the files on the drive dismount it by clicking "Unmount".

There are several additional options that can be selected in DiskCryptor's "Tools" menu, such as backing up the header for a volume, changing a volume's password, benchmarking, and encrypting a CD. There are also several options under "Settings" that let you customize some of the functions of the application including whether it begins at startup and how volumes are unmounted. DiskCryptor also allows you to set hotkeys for several functions such as Mount All, Force Unmount All, Wipe Passwords, and Blue Screen. Though not a full-fledged replacement for VeraCrypt because of its inability to conduct volume-level encryption, DiskCryptor does offer an uncomplicated interface, simple volume creation, and strong encryption. In addition to encrypting your system's hard drive, it can also be used to fully encrypt external media such as SD cards or USB flash drives. One downside with DiskCryptor is that when full-disk encrypting your system drive, DiskCryptor places severe limits on your password (0-9, a-z, and A-Z only), DiskCryptor is free and open source and available at **https://diskcryptor.net/wiki/Downloads**.

FileVault II (OS X)

One of our favorite features included in Mac computers is FileVault II (referred to hereafter simply as FileVault). FileVault is a built-in full disk encryption utility that uses AES-256 encryption. Enabling FileVault is incredibly simple, and it is included standard with every Apple computer. If FileVault is turned off, you can use the following steps to turn it on.

- Open your Mac's System Preferences.
- Click the Security & Privacy icon in the System Preferences window.
- Click the FileVault tab.
- Click the lock icon and enter an administrator name and password.
- Click the "Turn On FileVault" button.

If you have more than one user account (one as Administrator and one or more as Standard Users), you can select which of these can decrypt the machine and turn it on. We recommend that you consider two Administrator accounts. Only one of these should decrypt the machine from a powered-down state. You should use a very long, very strong password on this account, since that is also your decryption password. You will only enter this long password upon initial boot.

To prevent you from entering this very long password each time you need to perform an administrative task, such as install a program or change a global setting, you should have a second Administrator account. Once the machine is decrypted, you can log into this account and perform administration tasks without being burdened with an onerously long password. Having only one account with permission to decrypt the computer creates a smaller attack surface against your disk encryption. Fewer passwords exist that can decrypt the powered-down machine. We recommend against allowing more than one account to decrypt the computer. Your user and Administrator accounts can be managed by opening System Preferences > Users & Groups.

FileVault requires you to create a recovery key and gives you two options through which to do so. The recovery key is an emergency, 24-digit string of letters and numbers that can be used as a recovery option should you forget your password. The first option is to store the recovery key in your iCloud account. If you needed to access it, you would log into iCloud using your credentials. The second recovery option is the most secure. Your device will display the 24-digit series of letters and numbers. This code is not stored with Apple or in your iCloud account. It is your responsibility to keep it safe. Neither of us record this recovery key anywhere because its compromise means the compromise of the entire machine. Rather, we each simply remember our password. If you do choose to store the recovery key, do so in a strongly encrypted location and not on the encrypted hard drive that it is intended to recover.

Linux Unified Key Setup (LUKS)

The Linux Unified Key Setup comes standard with most Linux operating systems. Setup is prompted upon initially installing the operating system. Because of the sheer number of Linux distributions and subtle differences in each one (and the hardware they run on) we will not offer specifics in this volume. You should conduct an internet search for exact instructions on your distribution.

File Level Encryption Utilities

As we have discussed earlier, we are strong proponents of encrypting everything. The ability to encrypt individual files is an important one. If you have extremely sensitive files, it would be wise to encrypt the files themselves, even if they are stored on an encrypted hard drive or in an encrypted VeraCrypt volume. Additionally, if you are transmitting a file through email you may wish to encrypt it first. The following three utilities will allow you to do so. Unfortunately, encryption utilities like this are hard to find and there are no simple universal encryption platforms that allow you to quickly encrypt a file or files.

If you are using any of these methods to transmit messages through insecure channels, you must have a way to first exchange the password. This is the fundamental problem with symmetric-key encryption. If you send the password through any insecure channel you should consider it, and the document it protects, to be compromised.

7-Zip

Though typically considered a compression program that allows you to "zip" files into the much smaller .zip file format, 7-Zip also offers the ability to encrypt individual files. If you have a small number of files that you would like encrypted without having to create an encryption volume, 7-Zip is a good solution. Additionally, the ability to encrypt files individually allows you to create layers of encryption. You can encrypt the file, place it within an encrypted volume, and assuming you have used different passwords on each layer of encryption, have a double-layer of encryption over your most sensitive files.

7-Zip uses AES-256 encryption. In addition to encrypting the files, it also offers the ability to encrypt the filenames. This is a very important feature as filenames can reveal information about the contents of the files themselves, making 7-Zip a great tool for use when uploading to the cloud or anywhere else the files may be visible to a third-party.

To use 7-Zip, download and install the application. Once installed, 7-Zip can be used to encrypt individual files via the right-click context menu. Select the file you wish to encrypt and right-click on it. From the context menu select "Add to Archive". This will bring up an additional dialogue which will give you a number of compression protocols. This dialogue will also allow you to enter a password. Entering a password will automatically create an encrypted copy of the file. If this is the only version of the file you wish to retain it is important to delete the original securely as described in the next chapter.

To open a file that has been encrypted using 7-Zip, right click on the file. From the right-click context menu select 7-Zip. In the context menu a fly-out menu will appear. Select "Extract Here". You will be prompted to enter a password. When you enter the password an unencrypted version of the file will be extracted. If you modify the file, the encryption process must be repeated. This is not the most convenient solution but automated processes like CryptSync (discussed below) make 7-Zip much more user-friendly. 7-Zip is free, open source and available at **http://www.7-zip.org/**.

Microsoft Office 2007+ (Windows, OS X)

Microsoft Office allows users of the suite the ability to encrypt documents individually. Though this solution can be somewhat onerous (you must enter the password for each and every document you open), it prevents Microsoft Office documents from being written to the hard drive unencrypted, even as an AutoSave. Earlier versions of Microsoft Office used an encryption algorithm that was trivially broken by brute-force. However, with the introduction of MS Office 2007, Microsoft implemented AES-128 encryption that remains very secure. Enabling this option on a given document is incredibly simple. Open the document and navigate to File (or click the Office button). In the backstage, select "Encrypt Document with a Password". Enter your chosen password and the document is now encrypted and can be stored or transmitted.

Adobe Acrobat Pro

One of our preferred techniques for sending especially sensitive files, even when sending them within an encrypted email ecosystem, is to save them as a PDF and encrypt them natively with Adobe Acrobat's native encryption. Adobe Acrobat Pro allows you to encrypt documents up to AES-256 if using Version X or later. Adobe allows two levels of password protection. One limits the ability to open the document to those possessing the password. The other option allows you to limit editing to those with the permissions password.

To encrypt a PDF, open the document and click on the File option in the toolbar. From the fly-out menu select "Preferences". The preferences dialogue will contain six tabs. First, select "Security". Within this dialogue choose the pull-down menu that is, by default, on "No Security". This will allow you to choose Password Security or Certificate Security. If you routinely work with digital certificates this may be the preferred option for you but this work will cover only password security. After you choose password security you will advance to the next screen where you will be allowed to "Require a password to open the document" and/or "Restrict editing and printing of the document". Input your password. In the lower portion of the pane is an option to choose the version of Acrobat your recipient is using. If he or she is using a version of Acrobat newer than version 7 you have the option to use AES-256 encryption. Acrobat 7 and earlier versions can only use AES-128.

After you have input your passwords you will be required to confirm them. It is also important to note that these changes will not take effect until you save the changes to the document so be careful not to transmit the document before saving. Open the File menu and click Save. Your file is now encrypted and may be emailed, uploaded to the cloud, or stored for safe-keeping.

Preview (OS X)

Mac's built-in Preview application can encrypt certain types of files including PDFs. To encrypt a PDF using Preview, open the File dropdown menu and select "Export as PDF" (El Capitan/OS X 10.10) or "Save As…" (older versions of OS X). A new dialogue will appear allowing you to choose the location to which you wish to save the new file. At the bottom of this dialogue check the box labeled "Encrypt". If this box is not visible click the "Show Details" button; this should open an expanded dialogue of options including Encrypt. Enter the encryption password and save. This will not encrypt the original document, so you must delete it securely through another method as discussed in Chapter Twenty-One.

LibreOffice (Windows, OS X, Linux)

LibreOffice (formerly OpenOffice) is a free and open source suite of productivity software that attempts to replicate many of the functions of Microsoft Office. Though it is available cross-platform it is most commonly used on Linux operating systems. To encrypt the contents of an LibreOffice document, open the File dropdown menu. Select "Save As" and ensure that the "Save with password" box is checked.

Backups

Anyone reading this book should already understand that backups are a critical component of a thorough information security posture. In the event a hard drive fails (as has happened to us before), your computer is lost, stolen, or irreparably damaged, or you mistakenly overwrite data, you have a copy. It goes without saying that backups should be encrypted at least to the level of the original data being backed up. In our opinion, if it's worth backing up, it's worth backing up twice. Neither of us use traditional full-image backups that record all the settings and applications on our computers. Though it would take some time and effort, if one of our computers crashes we can easily restore all of the programs on it. All we are truly concerned with when backing up are the documents and photographs that cannot easily be replaced.

Windows 7

The program we use for backups in Windows is CryptSync. Intended primarily for use with cloud storage, CryptSync is free and allows you to make copies of pairs of folders. For example, if you want a copy of My Documents to go to a DropBox account, you open CryptSync and choose "My Documents" as the original folder and your DropBox folder as the destination folder. CryptSync will create a copy of My Documents in your Dropbox folder, and keep it updated as you make changes to files in My Documents. Another major benefit, and the main reason we choose CryptSync is that it will also encrypt the copy that is sent to the destination folder using 7-Zip or Gnu Privacy Guard (GnuPG). Both 7-Zip and GnuPG utilize the AES-256 encryption algorithm and 7-Zip offers the advantage of compressing files if this is a concern for you. If you are storing data in the cloud, we highly recommend you encrypt it first. CryptSync is an excellent tool for such encryption. CryptSync will even encrypt your file names if you so choose, because the names themselves can reveal information about the contents of the file.

This is not quite how we have employed CryptSync. As you now know, we do not use cloud storage. We use CryptSync to synchronize the master VeraCrypt volume on our hard drives with a full-disk encrypted USB flash drive. To some, encrypting twice like this may seem heavy-handed, but we do not consider it to be. These backups are stored on USB flash drives which, as we have previously pointed out, are extremely easy to lose. We like knowing that our most sensitive, personal files are doubly encrypted with drastically different passwords for each layer of encryption. If the USB drive is lost, we can sleep peacefully with the knowledge that no one has access to our files. Further, not all of these backups are in our physical control.

To set this system up, open CryptSync and choose the drive letter to which your VeraCrypt volume is mounted and designate it as your original folder. This necessitates that you always mount the volume to the same drive letter. In VeraCrypt, assign this volume as a system favorite so it will always mount to the same drive letter. Next, mount your fully-encrypted USB flash drive to its appropriate drive letter and assign it as a favorite. Now, open CryptSync and click the "New Pair…" button. Assign your primary VeraCrypt volume as the original folder and the encrypted USB drive as the destination folder. You can allow CryptSync to run in the background but we have found some issues with this. Our preferred technique is to open the application at the close of our work session and click "Sync files and exit". CryptSync is free and available at **stefanstools.sourceforge.net/CryptSync.html**.

OS X

Our preferred file backup utility for OS X is FreeFileSync. This is a free and open source program used for file synchronization. It is available on Windows, Linux and OS X and works very similar to other backup solutions mentioned up to this point. FreeFileSync works by comparing one or multiple folders on their content, date or file size and subsequently synchronizing the content according to user-defined settings. We have found this to be the fastest backup solution for OS X. When properly saving configuration files for each backup operation within the data being backed up, the jobs complete very quickly. Complete instructions and software download can be found at sourceforge.net/projects/freefilesync/.

Other Backup Utilities

There are numerous other backup utilities out there that will do full system image backups. Most of them require a paid subscription and we do not find them necessary. Full disk image backups offer you the ability to restore your computer (or a new one) to its condition at the time of the last backup. However, they take a long time to run and slow your system down while doing so. We find that we do not need this level of protection, but if you do we recommend you choose one that encrypts the backup with AES, Serpent, or Twofish encryption. If your backup utility does not allow you to encrypt the backup natively, ensure that it will allow you to create backups to a hard drive that is encrypted with a separate encryption utility like VeraCrypt or DiskCryptor. Regardless of which backup utility you use, use something. The loss of precious data is not something we would wish on anyone.

Considerations for Air Gaps

The end of this chapter is a good time to address some considerations for running an air-gap. There is not enough information here to merit a dedicated chapter, but this information should be addressed and it should be addressed before moving on to the data-in-motion considerations we will begin discussing in the following chapter.

What Is an Air Gap? The concept of running an air-gapped computer is relatively simple: Keep a literal air gap between the computer and an internet connection (the term "air gap" is older than the concept of Wi-Fi). The machine should never be connected to the internet, greatly reducing chances of being infected, hacked, or otherwise exploited. In practice, maintaining an air gap is extremely difficult. Running one does not make a computer completely invulnerable to attack, but it does make a computer significantly safer than one connected to the internet, all other things being equal.

The first consideration and question you should ask yourself is, "Do I need an air gap?" Though we do not discourage air gaps at all, they are extremely tedious to do correctly and obviously require the expense of a second machine (one that can access the internet, and the other one that cannot). For journalists, high-profile executives, individuals entrusted with trade secrets, and the extremely security conscious the answer to the question above may be "yes". If you require extraordinary security, an air gap affords it. There are several best practices that must be followed when using an air-gapped computer, which will allow it to provide the full measure of security necessary to warrant the inherent inconvenience and expense of having one.

Purchase Anonymously: Maintaining an air-gap is serious business, and if you really need one you need it to work correctly. If you have examined your personal circumstances and determined that an air-gap is a necessity for you, you should make the purchase as anonymously as possible. If the device is not associated with you because no one knows you purchased the machine, there is far less risk of it being targeted personally. When you purchase the computer, pay cash at a big-box store. There is privacy in the large numbers of devices they sell, and you won't be remembered. However, there are certainly security cameras in the store to record you being there. If you are truly worried about that, have someone make the purchase for you. Again, we will indulge any level of paranoia. If you connect the computer to the internet during the initial setup process or to download your software, don't do so from your home Wi-Fi connection or a VPN that is already associated with you.

Install Minimal Programs: The fewest possible number of programs should be installed on an air-gapped machine. As mentioned in Chapter One, more applications on a machine represent more potential attack vectors and more potential risk. We recommend an encryption program, a general cleanup tool like CCleaner or Bleachbit (discussed later) and the absolute minimum number of utilities that you need. This may include a PDF reader, word processing application, and printer software. These programs may need occasional updates. When they do, do not connect the machine to the internet to update them as this defeats the air gap. Rather, burn the necessary update files to a disk as described below.

Use Optical Media to Transfer Files: An air-gapped machine is not very useful if files cannot be transferred to and from it. Unfortunately, it is difficult to safely transfer these files with anything other than optical media. Flash drives and USB hard drives are not a secure method of transferring files to or from your air-gapped machine. The primary insecurity stems from the fact that it is impossible to tell when they are being read from or written to. Though many USB flash drives have an LED that lights up or blinks when reading or writing is occurring, they don't distinguish between the two. If you are reading a file from a USB flash drive the light will be on. However, you have no idea if malware is simultaneously writing a file that will be transmitted when you connect that same USB device to a computer with an internet connection. Though this may seem far-fetched, if you are someone who really needs an air gap, it is a real threat. Air gaps are not impenetrable, and jumping the air gap with media is one way they are defeated.

Instead of using USB devices to transfer data to an air gap, burn a CD/R or DVD/R. Preferably, use the smallest capacity you can find that will hold the files you need to transfer. It would be difficult for files to be written secretly to an optical disk, as you will hear the disk drive spin up when a read or write occurs. It is possible that files being exfiltrated by malware from an air-gapped device (or malware being infiltrated to it) could be written at the same time as the files you are burning. If you use a disk that is just big enough for what you need to move, you leave little space for the hazardous files. If you are not moving enough data to fill up a disk, move some random data to fill the disk to capacity, regardless of which way your data is moving across the air gap.

Encrypt: When using optical media to transfer files across the air gap, you will be unable to delete the files when finished. However, if the disks and the files on them are encrypted with strong passwords, you shouldn't need to. If you are still worried about it, destroy the disks by microwaving or shredding them. If you are extremely paranoid, do both.

Physically Disable Connectivity: Connecting an air-gapped computer to the internet via wired or wireless connection can negate the entire purpose of maintaining an air gap. You should also strongly consider physically disconnecting the Wi-Fi card. Wi-Fi may be turned on by accident, or it may be turned on as part of a malicious attack. Should your machine become infected, malware may silently turn on Wi-Fi selectively to exfiltrate files off of the machine or insert additional malware. If your computer is equipped with Bluetooth, it too should be disabled. If you are concerned about your air-gapped computer being physically connected to the internet by your teenager in search of a device on which to watch a video, you can tape over the Ethernet port or fill it with a non-conductive epoxy. If this sounds like an extreme measure, it is. Our air-gapped computer will never be connected to the internet, even when it is retired, so we are unconcerned about permanently removing its connectivity capabilities.

Air Gap Jumpers

As we have mentioned earlier, an air gap does not mean a system is impenetrable. There are still malware programs that can "jump" the air gap and either insert destructive malware onto, or exfiltrate data off of, an air-gapped computer. Two such examples are Stuxnet, a joint U.S./Israeli application used to successfully attack an Iranian nuclear facility and "agent.btz", a program that jumped U.S. military air gaps and was suspected to be Chinese in origin. Fortunately, such attacks are extremely sophisticated and are extremely unlikely to be employed against the average home user. If you have been targeted or are in a high-risk occupation that necessitates the use of an air gap you should be aware of these threats and not take best practices lightly.

Setting up and maintaining an air gap is not a simple affair, nor is it an extremely inexpensive one. While we do not discourage anyone from attempting to achieve the highest level of security he or she may desire, air gaps aren't for everyone. If you are seriously concerned with the protection of your sensitive data, a well-maintained air gap is perhaps the most secure option available to you.

CHAPTER FOURTEEN
COMPUTER SECURITY: DATA-IN-MOTION

Data-in-motion is information that is in transit from one device to another. This data is vulnerable to a number of potential exploits. Your traffic may be intercepted by "legitimate" entities to serve you advertising information, ensure you are complying with the Digital Millennium Copyright Act, insert tracking codes into your data packets, or for other reasons. On the other end of the spectrum, data may be intercepted by an attacker. A malicious actor may sniff (intercept) your packets, set up a man-in-the-middle attack, or launch an evil-twin attack, depending on what you are most vulnerable to. One of the most important steps you can take to protect yourself is to encrypt all of your data-in-motion to the extent possible. This is possible through a number of methods including Secure Sockets Layer (SSL) and Transport Layer Security (TLS), high quality, modern Wi-Fi encryption protocols, and the use of Virtual Private Networks and the Tor network. These factors working together can protect that data while it is in motion from one place to another.

SSL and TLS

Two protocols, Secure Sockets Layer (SSL) and Transport Layer Security (TLS), are the first line of defense in securing your data-in-motion. These two encryption protocols rely on asymmetric encryption. This is a form of encryption where the site to which you are connecting and your computer negotiate an encryption key for the information they will exchange. Websites encrypted with SSL or TLS are "HTTPS" sites, and are considered secure. In addition to websites, connections to mail clients, online calendars, data transferred between devices, and other services like Voice Over Internet Protocol (VOIP) and instant messaging applications are frequently encrypted with one of these protocols.

Transport Layer Security is an upgraded version of the aging SSL protocol and provides very robust encryption for data-in-motion. Most reputable sites should employ TLS, though some sites still rely on SSL 3.0. Despite the differences in the two protocols, many still refer to both generically as "SSL", making things somewhat confusing. (In order to simplify here, we will refer to all such connections as SSL/TLS). Until early 2014, security experts considered SSL/TLS to be fairly secure if implemented properly, but a litany of vulnerabilities was revealed in these protocols in recent years.

One of these vulnerabilities was known as "gotofail", and was specific to Apple's products. The vulnerability was patched in iOS 7.0.6, then a few days later in OS X Mavericks 10.9.2. Shortly thereafter, the HeartBleed bug was discovered twice within two weeks by independent researchers. In very early 2015 it was revealed that a Wi-Fi provider on airlines was intentionally issuing fake SSL certificates. Though these connections were initially encrypted, they could be decrypted by the Wi-Fi provider. In late 2014, the Superfish adware was discovered being installed as OEM software with some Lenovo laptops. In November of 2015 a program called eDellRoot was found to be included with many Dell laptops. Much like the in-flight Wi-Fi provider, Superfish and eDellRoot used a self-signed certificate to tamper with the encryption on supposedly secure connections for the purpose of sending customized advertisements to users.

When using a site that is encrypted with SSL/TLS, it is a good idea to check the certificate of the site if you have any question whatsoever about its authenticity, or maybe even if you don't. Clicking on the padlock icon (shown during encrypted connections) just to the left of the address bar of Chrome, Epic, Firefox, or Safari will display a small amount of information about the site you are visiting. Clicking the "More Information…" button will bring up an additional dialogue. The "Security" tab in this dialogue will display some technical details about the connection, including whether or not the connection is secure, whether or not the site is leaving a cookie on your computer, and if you have visited the site previously today. In the bottom portion of this view are some technical details about the security of the connection.

Clicking on the "View Certificate" button will open an additional window that will provide very detailed information about the certificate. There are a couple of things you should look for here. First, the "Issued To" information should match the name of the organization that owns the website you are visiting. For example, if you visit https://bankofamerica.com, the Issued to Common Name should be Bank of America. Next, the period between the issue date and expiration date of the certificate should be for one year. Most certificates are only issued for one year and you should proceed with caution if a certificate is valid for longer.

Finally, the certificate should be issued by a reputable certificate authority (CA). There are a limited number of CAs, and while this list is not comprehensive, some of the most popular CAs are Symantec (which includes VeriSign, Thawte, and GeoTrust), Comodo, GoDaddy, Avast! Web/Mail Shield, GlobalSign, and DigiCert. Be aware that some very large organizations (Google, for example) have internal certificate authorities. Though it takes a lot of time and patience, checking the authenticity of a certificate before you input your authentication credentials on any website is a good idea. If you do not do so on all sites, you should definitely consider going to the trouble when you are connected to an untrusted internet connection like public Wi-Fi, since SSL/TLS connections still offer a decent layer of security despite the highly publicized exploits against it.

The vulnerabilities and exploits discovered in SSL/TLS are demonstrative of the need to be cautious about relying on a single point of failure in a security system. SSL and TLS encryptions are a good first layer but should not be relied on totally. A good defense-in-depth will have multiple, strong, overlapping layers of security. If one of these layers fails, as has been the case with SSL and TLS many times, the other layer(s) will still provide some security. One of the strongest layers you can add to your defense to protect your data-in-motion is to use a Virtual Private Network.

Virtual Private Networks

A Virtual Private Network (VPN) provides a good mix of both security and privacy by routing your internet traffic through a secure tunnel. The secure tunnel goes to the VPN's server and encrypts all the data between your device and that server. This ensures that anyone monitoring your traffic before it reaches the distant server will not find usable, unencrypted data. Privacy is also afforded through the use of a distant server. Your traffic that exits the VPN's server does so in plain text (or ideally, still encrypted with HTTPS if you are visiting an SSL/TLS capable site) en route to the destination site, but it is mixed in with the traffic of scores or hundreds of other users. This makes it much more difficult to distinguish your traffic from all the rest. Also, because your traffic appears to be originating from the VPN's server, websites will have a more difficult time tracking you, aggregating data on you, and pinpointing your geographic location.

Virtual Private Networks are not a perfect anonymity solution. It is important to note that VPNs offer you privacy, NOT anonymity. The best VPNs for privacy purposes are paid subscriptions with reputable providers. Though some providers take anonymous payment in the form of Bitcoin or prepaid gift cards, it is difficult (though not impossible) to create an account with one of these providers without associating yourself in some manner. This will be discussed in some detail later. If you log into an account that is associated with your true identity this login can be associated with your VPN account. Additionally, if you use the VPN from your home's internet connect, the VPN provider will be able to capture your IP which can be used to identify you.

There are several excellent paid VPN providers out there and we strongly recommend them over free providers. Free providers often monetize through very questionable means, such as data aggregation. This compromises one crucial benefit of a VPN: privacy. Paid VPN providers monetize directly by selling you a service. Reputable providers do not collect or monetize data. Paid providers also offer a number of options that will increase your privacy and security. The first option you should pay attention to is the number of servers they have.

Exit servers: Most reputable VPN service providers will have a number of geographically remote servers from which your traffic will exit. When you visit a website your traffic will appear originating from the VPN's server IP. VPN services with a number of servers to choose from give you the ability to distribute your usage over a number of servers. They also give you the ability to switch servers if one is exceptionally slow, as may be the case depending on the number of users on that server and your distance from it. Further, if you are traveling to a country that has internet restrictions and you cannot access certain sites, connecting to a VPN server in another country can allow you to bypass these geographic restrictions. When using a VPN, ensure that you patch the WebRTC vulnerability in your browser (see Chapter Fourteen). This vulnerability allows websites that you visit to capture your true IP address despite the use of a VPN.

Encryption: Another set of options a good VPN provider will offer is the ability to choose between a variety of encryption and tunneling options. These will typically include OpenVPN, IPSEC, L2TP, and PPTP. This versatility is desirable because although most VPN services will work well cross-platform (Windows, Linux, OSX, Android, iOS, etc.), some devices may not work with certain protocols. Further, some VPN providers even sell routers or allow you to set up your own with their VPN software built-in. This allows all of your home's traffic to be protected with a VPN connection. This is helpful, as not all devices (such as smart TVs and gaming systems) have the ability to have VPN software installed. Though most VPN providers offer several options for encryption we recommend you use the OpenVPN protocol where available. Though Justin has previously recommended using IPSec, recent months have demonstrated some successful pre-computation attacks against the IPSec protocol. We now believe OpenVPN to be the most secure protocol currently available for virtual private networks.

A good VPN service provider will offer a totally transparent privacy policy about the information they collect on your usage. The best ones will retain only minimal records, and although bound by law to cooperate with warrants and other legal instruments, if they do not store your information, they cannot turn it over. Minimal logging is actually used by most VPN providers to improve connection speed, performance, reliability, troubleshoot customer problems, and protect the service from abuse such as spammers, port scanners, and the execution of DDoS attacks across the service. It is important to realize that paid providers are also vulnerable to financial and legal pressure from their host-nation governments to cooperate with measures that may compromise security for all users.

We also fully recommend that you, as the user, conduct your own research and find the provider that works best for your situation. There are also times when it may be appropriate to have several different VPN services simultaneously. You may wish to have one on which you do personal tasks like banking and email, and another across which you do internet browsing that you would not wish to be associated with your true name or identity. You may also wish to use different VPN service providers from time to time to limit the amount of information that could possibly be collected by a single provider, rogue employee working at that provider, or government agency with a backdoor into their servers. For this reason, we have listed several VPN providers that meet all of the criteria list above, and that we personally recommend are (in alphabetical order):

- AirVPN: **https://airvpn.org/**
- IPVanish: **https://www.ipvanish.com**
- Private Internet Access: **https://www.privateinternetaccess.com/**
- PureVPN: **https://www.purevpn.com**
- VyprVPN: **https://www.goldenfrog.com/vyprvpn**

Two other factors that are definitely worth considering when choosing a VPN are bandwidth restrictions and speed limitations, both of which can be annoying. It is also possible to build your own VPN. If you have a computer at your home that can be left on and used for little else, you can create your own, free VPN with software that is native to Windows 7. Linux and Mac both offer to do this as well. If you do not have an old computer to use as your VPN server, you can purchase a Raspberry Pi (a very small computer costing only $35) to function as your VPN server. However, this is not our preferred option. Though it encrypts all traffic from your computer to the VPN portal at your house, it does not protect anything leaving your home, which would still be vulnerable to Wi-Fi sniffing, packet inspection by your internet service provider, tracking, and other forms of interception and monitoring. If you are only concerned with protecting your signal when using public Wi-Fi hotspots or for securely accessing files on your home computer or server remotely this may be sufficient for your needs.

We consider VPNs to be an incredibly important part of an overall privacy and security strategy and are willing to pay for them. Running a virtual private network costs money. It incurs a large cost in bandwidth since it must accommodate at least the amount of bandwidth its customers are using, and bandwidth is not cheap. It also must setup and maintain its front-end applications, implement crypto, and many other functions that cost money. For this reason, we are very skeptical of free VPN service providers. How do they make their living?

There are two good examples of "free" VPNs that were actually paid for, not with cash, but with your privacy and security. One is Onavo Protect (available on Google Play and iTunes). Onavo advertises free VPN service that even says in its description on iTunes that it "as part of this process, Onavo receives and analyzes information about your mobile data and app usage". This is absolutely true – they do analyze your data and usage. What they don't tell you is that Onavo is owned by Facebook and that by using the VPN you are giving Facebook access to all of this data. Another notable offender in this category is VPN Defender which is owned by the data analytics firm Smart Sense, a subsidiary of data analytics powerhouse App Annie. Of course App Annie made no formal public announcement that they were releasing a VPN application; we are confident our readers can figure out why they chose not to. Unfortunately, packet inspection is not the only malicious use for a disreputable VPN service.

Another major offender of "free VPN" service is Hola. Hola offered a free Chrome add-on that allowed you to bypass regional restrictions through its VPN. What Hola didn't tell its users (you will notice we did not say "customers") is that their unused bandwidth was being sold behind their backs. Not only was their bandwidth being sold, it was being sold to hackers and criminals who used this excess bandwidth in several DDoS attacks. Users of Hola were seriously abused because they elected to use a free VPN service rather than research and pay for a reputable service. VPNs are not an instance of "anything is better than nothing" security. Under the right set of circumstances, using the wrong VPN can potentially be far more damaging than using none at all.

VPN Setup: The first step in setting up your VPN will be choosing your provider. After you have settled on the provider the next step is to subscribe to their service. Most VPN services offer monthly plans with price breaks for purchasing several months or one year at a time. We recommend you pay for your VPN service using one of the anonymous purchase options listed in Chapter Ten. After you have purchased the VPN you will have to set it up on your computer.

Though the specifics vary somewhat, each virtual private network will have a similar setup process. You will download their application and install it on your device (including mobile devices). You will likely be required to enter your login credentials into the application before it will connect. Most of these applications have some settings that can be modified to optimize your experience. WiTopia, for example, allows you to choose your default server and encryption algorithm, and force an automatic connection anytime you connect to insecure Wi-Fi. Private Internet Access has an option called "Internet Kill Switch" that will disable all internet access on your computer if the VPN connection is lost. This prevents you from accidentally transmitting plain-text data. The specifics of these applications vary, but we encourage you to research providers and find the one that has the features you desire.

After your VPN application is installed you can now browse privately. Each time you start up your computer or wake it from sleep you should ensure that connecting to your VPN is one of the first steps that you take, if a connection is not automatically established. Even if you do not plan to browse the internet you should ensure that all outgoing traffic is protected. This is because the applications on your computer are constantly "calling home" and some sensitive data may be passed through these unseen connections.

VPNs on Mobile Devices: It is strongly recommended that you run a virtual private network on your personal mobile devices including phones and tablets. Your devices constantly emit information from your applications, to the hardware developer, and mobile service provider. If this information is intercepted locally by a malicious party, it could reveal sensitive personal details. A VPN will ensure that this traffic is routed through a secure tunnel, however.

There are two different "categories" of virtual private networks for mobile devices: credential-authenticated and certificate-authenticated. The difference is in how you connect to the VPN. With a credential authenticated VPN your connection will be established and verified using your login credentials, usually a username and password. Additionally, these VPN connections must be installed manually on your device. The major downside to this type of VPN is that it will not always stay connected to the VPN server. This is bad for two reasons. First, if you pick up your phone after it has gone to sleep you may forget to reconnect to the VPN server. Additionally, in the interim between connections your device is sending plaintext information in the background that can be intercepted and exploited.

The alternative is a certificate-authenticated VPN. This type of VPN will typically require that you install an application on your mobile device. The application will install a certificate that is unique to your VPN account and will be used to establish your connection to the VPN server. The biggest benefit to this type of VPN is that it will automatically establish your VPN connection, greatly reducing the chance that you will forget to connect before browsing or transmitting other types of traffic. Some VPNs even offer an "internet kill switch" that will restrict most types of data traffic from being sent or received until the VPN connection is established and secure. Private Internet Access is a VPN that provides such a feature.

Regardless of which type of VPN you choose; we strongly encourage you to use one on your mobile device(s). Mobile devices transmit at least as much sensitive data as your laptop, even if you do nothing overtly sensitive on them. Most VPN providers will allow you to connect three to five devices to the same account. Obviously this correlates those devices to the same owner. If maximum privacy is your goal you may wish to setup different VPN accounts for different devices.

Enhanced VPN Privacy: If you do desire a stronger level of privacy than a "standard" VPN setup affords there are some steps you can take to make your VPN more private. You will notice we did not say it will make you "anonymous". If you access a true name account with it, you should assume that it is now tied to your true name. Depending on your threat model even accessing an account that you have ever accessed from the same IP as your true name account can pierce your privacy. You can still be browser-fingerprinted. You can be exploited through Java and Flash. Cookies on your machine can still leak data from one browsing session to the next. A pseudo-anonymous VPN can create an excellent privacy layer but it does not create true anonymity.

Each of these steps will require additional expense and effort, and a tremendous effort will be required to maintain this privacy. To have a pseudo-anonymous VPN you must first register for it anonymously. This is a difficult part; the internet connection from which you register it can compromise your privacy. Paying for a VPN may be somewhat easier. You can pay for some VPNs by using gift cards, purchased for cash. Most major retailers' gift cards, such as Amazon, Barnes and Noble, Chili's, or REI, are accepted by Private Internet Access who cashes them in through a gift card clearinghouse. Most VPNs now also accept BitCoin. After you have registered your pseudo-anonymous VPN you must exercise extreme caution to maintain this privacy. This is probably a complicated step for most of our readers.

Wi-Fi Security

As was pointed out in the introduction to this book, security and convenience are inversely related. Wi-Fi is an undeniable convenience. Negating the need for a physical cable, Wi-Fi allows us to access the internet from just about anywhere at just about any time. Intrinsic to this convenience, however, is a great deal of insecurity, especially when compared with wired internet connections.

Wi-Fi is nothing more than a radio transmission that carries data packets between your computer's Wi-Fi card and the wireless router. Because of this anyone with a capable radio can "listen" in on your traffic. Simply listening in by capturing your packets as they travel to and from your computer is called sniffing. Sniffing requires some specialized (but free) software and a Wi-Fi card that can be placed in promiscuous mode (the ability to "listen" to all Wi-Fi traffic while not broadcasting). USB Wi-Fi antennas that can be purchased very inexpensively and require only very little technical know-how.

While some of the techniques we will discuss below are changes made to your operating system, the majority of this chapter will deal with securing your wireless signal and best practices when using Wi-Fi. Before continuing with the security of Wi-Fi we will digress for just a moment to talk about how it is exploited.

Wi-Fi Exploitation

While we do not recommend sniffing strangers' Wi-Fi traffic, capturing packets is not terribly technically demanding and can even be beneficial. Seeing first-hand how Wi-Fi is exploited can underscore the point of how insecure Wi-Fi truly is and help you understand the importance of good encryption. Sniffing your home network is also a good way to see what vulnerabilities you have. If you are interested in learning how to do this, you will need the following:

- Software. There are various Wi-Fi sniffing programs and many of them are free. Using them often requires using a Linux operating system. Kali Linux is a penetration-testing specific Linux operating system that comes with an incredibly capable suite of Wi-Fi exploitation tools built-in.

- Hardware. The only specialized hardware you need is a promiscuous-capable Wi-Fi card. These are available online for as little as $30 on Amazon.com. As long as your computer has an optical drive or you can boot from a USB flash drive you will not need a new computer. Kali can be booted from optical or USB flash media.

- Technical know-how. Though hacking Wi-Fi is relatively simple it does require some specific knowledge. The graphic user interfaces for most of the programs consist mostly of a command prompt, so good working knowledge of Linux command line is necessary, though most of these commands can be found online.

Wi-Fi Security Measures

Wi-Fi should be turned off when your computer is not actively connected to a network, and the computer should not be set to connect automatically to networks. When your computer is not connected to your network (e.g. when you are traveling), it will actively search for networks it is set to automatically connect to. This searching is not passive. Other computers can detect this searching, and see the name of the network(s) with free software. If your networks are all being broadcasted through probes it is trivially easy for an attacker to set up an "evil twin" or "rouge access point" attack. To execute this form of a man-in-the-middle attack, an attacker will set up a network that has the same name as one of your trusted networks. When your device recognizes this name, it will connect to the rogue network automatically (unless you have disabled automatic connections) allowing your traffic to be routed through his or her device and potentially compromising it. Even SSL/TLS-encrypted traffic is vulnerable to a technique called "SSL Stripping". If, on the other hand, you have disabled automatic connections, the names of your stored networks will not be available to the hacker. Even if they were, your computer would not connect to them automatically.

Wi-Fi Settings in Windows

To set your Wi-Fi networks to manually connect, navigate to Control Panel >> Network and Internet >> Network and Sharing Center, then select Manage Wireless Networks. You should see a list of all the networks your computer remembers.

Next, right-click on each network that you need to change from an automatic connection to "Manually Connect", and select "Properties". In the Properties dialog, uncheck the following boxes: "Connect automatically when this network is in range", "Connect to a more preferred network if it is available", and "Connect even if the network is not broadcasting its name (SSID)". This will ensure that your computer is not broadcasting requests for known networks and protects you against several types of Wi-Fi exploits.

Define the network as Public: When connecting to a Wi-Fi network, Windows will ask you if you would like to define the network as Home, Work, or Public. Each of these settings gives the network different privilege sets, with the most secure being Public and the least secure (but the one with the most accessibility) being Home. A "Home" network in Windows is one with a great many sharing permissions enabled, allowing other devices on the network to access any shared folders on your machine. To prevent this, always define the network as "Public", even if it is your home network.

Remove the network or set to manually connect: If the network is one that you will probably not use again in the future (or not use frequently), you should remove it from the list of networks Windows "remembers". To do so, navigate to Control Panel > Network and Internet > Network and Sharing Center, then select Manage Wireless Networks from the menu bar on the left. Right-click on the network you wish to delete and select "Remove network".

Wi-Fi Settings in OS X

To access the Wi-Fi settings in OS X open System Preferences and click Network. You can disable Wi-Fi globally from this menu by clicking the button labeled "Turn Wi-Fi Off". This will disable your Wi-Fi card at the hardware level. You must then close the System Preferences if you wish Wi-Fi to remain turned off following a reboot of your computer.

To make additional changes to your Wi-Fi settings click the lock icon and enter your Administrator password to enable changes. The first option you should examine is the "Ask to join new networks" checkbox. If this setting is not enabled your computer will connect to open Wi-Fi hotspots without your consent. Next, click the "Advanced" button. This will display a list of your "Preferred Networks". You can prioritize your networks here by dragging them into the preferred order. You can also remove networks here. Unlike Windows, OS X computers do not allow you to choose to manually or automatically connect to selected Wi-Fi networks. Your Mac computer probes for every network that it remembers anytime Wi-Fi is turned on. Because of this we recommend you adopt some combination of the following strategies:

- Remove Wi-Fi networks that you do not commonly use. If you never forget networks and frequently access different Wi-Fi hotspots you are greatly increasing your attack surface. The probes that are sent out as your machine searches for networks reveal information about you and may set you up for an evil twin attack.

- Turn off your computer's Wi-Fi unless you are actively connected to a network and using it. Remember that if you disable Wi-Fi through System Preferences you must close the System Preferences pane for that setting to survive reboot. Even if this is the strategy you choose we still recommend minimizing the networks your computer remembers.

- Another option is to uncheck the box reading "Remember networks this computer has joined". From now on your computer will not remember, or search for, any networks other than those listed in you preferred networks. You can choose to selectively remember networks. When you connect to a new Wi-Fi hotspot simply check the "Remember this network" box when you are prompted for the password.

- The safest option is to remember no networks at all. Your computer will not probe for any networks, greatly lowering your attack surface. The downside to this is that you will have to re-enter the password for protected networks every time you join them. If you choose this path we recommend creating a "Wi-Fi" category in your password manager. This will allow you to quickly copy and paste the password when you wish to connect.

Little Snitch: Little Snitch is a firewall application for OS X that focuses on outgoing internet connections. We love this application because of its incredible capabilities. Little Snitch allows you to monitor each and every outgoing connection on your computer. When Microsoft Office or Adobe Acrobat or even OS X attempts to call home, Little Snitch will know about it, and in turn make you aware of it. When an application attempts to access your computer's camera or microphone, Little Snitch will step in and allow you to confirm or deny this access. We like Little Snitch not only because it lets us see when connections are attempted hundreds of times per day, it also allows us to block these connections.

Little Snitch offers an extreme level of granularity. You can set up rules to block any or all of the scores of connections that your computer routinely attempts in the background. Some of these connections may be necessary for its smooth functioning, however. Setting up Little Snitch can be a bit daunting, but we recommend a simple strategy. We recommend that you err on the side of blocking everything, and then go back and allow some permissions if you experience a problem. When you install Little Snitch and allow it to run you will get a pop-up each time a connection is attempted, along with a prompt to allow or deny the connection. As you allow or deny these connections Little Snitch will "learn" how you wish to handle certain types of connections and begin to create rules.

Little Snitch also allows your machine to behave differently on different networks. For example, you can set up a home network that allows some routine maintenance like applications "calling home". You can also set up work and public networks where only the minimum necessary outbound communications are allowed.

Though Little Snitch is primarily focused on outgoing connections, it can also monitor and manage incoming connections. Because of this we do not feel it necessary to run the OS X Firewall when using this application. Little Snitch is not inexpensive but we consider the cost to be completely justified for the service it provides. Before committing to the full purchase price of Little Snitch, you can download the demo mode to ensure that it works on your system and accomplishes your goals. At the time of this writing Little Snitch costs $35 and is available at **https://www.obdev.at/products/littlesnitch/index.html**.

Basic Router Setup

When setting up your home's network there are some basic steps you can take to make your account much more secure than the average account. Some of these settings will require that you be physically connected to the router via an Ethernet cable.

Change management account credentials. The first step you should take when setting up your home's network is to change the management account credentials. This account is the account you log into to change the router's settings. Anyone having access to it can turn off your encryption, view your usage logs, or take other malicious actions. The default credentials that are preset on the router are openly available information and could allow anyone connecting to your network to make changes to your router. To change these settings, log into your router by typing the router's internal Internet Protocol (IP) address into the address bar while connected via a wired or wireless connection to the router. The internal IP address for most Linksys routers is 192.168.1.1, while most D-Link and NetGear routers use an IP of 192.168.0.1. This will bring you to the administrator login page. If you have never changed your router's login credentials they are probably set to the default. Conduct an internet search for the default username and password, then change these credentials immediately using a randomly generated username and a good, strong password.

You can also make it more difficult to change the settings on your router by changing the IP address used to log into it. Login credentials can be defeated, so this step makes it more difficult for an attacker to connect to the router. The IP address can be changed to anything between 192.168.0.0 and 192.168.255.255, but ensure you remember what you change it to. As soon as this change is saved and takes effect, you will need the new IP to log back into the router to make additional changes.

Disable remote management. Remote management gives you the ability to log into and change the router's management system without physically accessing the router or being connected to the router's network. When this function is disabled you may be required to physically connect to the router with an Ethernet cable to log into the management account. Though slightly inconvenient, you shouldn't have to make changes to the router very often and the security upgrade is well worth it.

Encrypt the signal. Next, encrypt the wireless signal using WPA2-PSK encryption. There are several options on many routers for encryption, including WEP (Wired Equivalent Privacy), WPA (Wi-Fi Protected Access), and WPA2 but the only one you should consider using is WPA2-PSK. WEP has been broken for years and is extremely easily defeated through an attack known as a "statistical attack". WPA has serious vulnerabilities, especially with its Temporary Key Integrity Protocol (TKIP). WPA2 is a re-engineered version of WPA offering AES encryption and the greatest security for wireless networks currently available. If your router does not offer WPA2-PSK (Pre-Shared Key) (802.11n) upgrade your router as soon as possible. Do not neglect to assign a good password to your network. Though it may take some time and effort to enter the password on your devices, it only has to be done once.

Change your SSID. You should also change the SSID, the name of your network that is broadcast to your devices. Though it is possible to (and some recommend this) hide the SSID, this is a fairly ineffective technique. Wi-Fi sniffers (programs designed to detect and exploit Wi-Fi networks) can easily find hidden networks. Instead, rename the network with a name that does not leak information about you.

Renaming your network is an excellent opportunity to provide some disinformation about your home. There are websites that map every known wireless network (https://wigle.net is a good example). Anyone seeing your true name attached to a network can make a reasonable assumption about the location of your residence, while false name on these websites could obscure your home address. Instead of naming your network something personally relatable to you like "NicoSellNet" or "NSell_Wi-Fi", use an alias like "Smith_Wi-Fi" or something generic like "FamilyNetwork". If anyone is looking for your house based on Wi-Fi networks, this will make it more difficult to locate.

Opt-out of Wi-Fi mapping. Wi-Fi networks are now mapped in tandem with other street mapping efforts such as Google Street View. This means that if your network name is collected, it can be looked up as an overlay on a map. This allows anyone to map your location, based on your Wi-Fi networks, by capturing the SSID that your computer broadcasts when searching for a network to connect to. To prevent your home network from being mapped (at least by Google), an option you can take is to terminate your router's SSID with the suffix "_nomap" (for example: Luna_wifi_nomap). This is the opt-out for Google's Wi-Fi network mapping. Any router SSID containing this suffix will not be included on Google map overlays that display Wi-Fi networks. Alternatively, assign your Wi-Fi network an SSID that creates disinformation as described in the previous paragraph.

Disable Wi-Fi Protected Setup (WPS). Wi-Fi Protected Setup is a convenience feature that is intended to make it easier to connect to a wireless device. Rather than entering the password when connecting to an encrypted network the user can physically push the WPS button on the router or enter a six-digit WPS code when connecting for the first time. Unfortunately, the WPS protocol is broken. No matter how strong the password on your network is, cracking the simple six-digit WPS code can grant access to the network. Disable WPS completely, even though it makes logging into your network more time consuming (though again, you only have to do this on your home network on initial setup and when you change the password).

Turn off the signal when not in use. In the setup menu for most routers, you can elect to turn the router's signal off between certain hours and on certain days, at times when everyone in your home is typically asleep or everyone is gone, for example. Unless you rely on wireless IP cameras or other Wi-Fi devices as part of your physical security system, there is no need to leave your router on when you are going out of town; simply unplug it. Powering the router off lowers its profile; the less time it is on and broadcasting, the smaller its attack surface.

Scan your home network: Though this does not pertain to router setup specifically, it is a good step to take after setting up your home router. Our antivirus application of choice (Avast Free Antivirus) can conduct a home network scan. It will test to see if your devices are visible from the internet, check router security configurations, and ensure that your wireless signal is encrypted. You can run this scan on any network to which you are connected to give you an idea of the security of the network before you use it to transmit sensitive information.

MAC filtering. One security measure that is sometimes touted but is largely ineffective is MAC filtering. A MAC address (Media Access Control) is a number unique to your device, analogous to its electronic ID. Filtering MAC addresses allows connections only from devices on a "whitelist" (a preapproved list of trusted devices). While MAC filtering is good in theory, it is very easily defeated through MAC spoofing, a technique used by attackers to capture your MAC and assign it temporarily to their device. This technique is not especially difficult to do, especially by anyone with the ability to crack your (WPA2) encryption. Additionally, MAC filtering requires you to log into the router and update the whitelist each time you need to connect a new device.

A technique that is allowed on many routers similar to MAC filtering, though slightly less onerous, is to limit the number of devices that may connect at a given time. This is intended to keep networks uncrowded to manage bandwidth, though you will occasionally hear it listed as a security measure.

Best Practices for Untrusted/Unencrypted Networks

There are times when it may be necessary to use an untrusted, unencrypted wireless network. While ideally you would never use such a network, the convenience of such networks make them hard to resist and there may be situations in which you have no choice but to work from one. Some basic best practices when using these networks (if you must use them) can make your browsing much more secure.

Absolute Best Practice: Don't use them. Again, Wi-Fi is terribly convenient and it can be hard to resist the urge to connect and watch YouTube, download your podcasts, or log in and get some work done while you wait to board your flight. The risks of using untrusted networks are very high though. If at all possible avoid using them and instead tether your phone or better yet, wait until you can use a trusted connection. If you can wait to use the internet until you get home or at least to your hotel, where you can likely use a wired connection, do so. If not, do not enter any sensitive information (like login credentials) on that network, and follow the steps listed below.

Connect to the right network. Every day criminals and hackers set up fake wireless access points to lure the unsuspecting into connecting to them. This is often done in public spaces where dozens of Wi-Fi networks exist and a free hotspot does not raise much suspicion. With names like "Free Wi-Fi" or "Public Hotspot", these insecure connections are used naïvely by many who treat them no differently than their home network. Unfortunately, many of these are merely traps to capture login, banking/credit card, and other sensitive information. When you check into a hotel, visit a coffee shop or bookstore, or use Wi-Fi at a public library, ask someone who works there which network you should use. If two or more networks have very similar names, take a closer look at the names. If you have any doubt whatsoever, do not connect. It is worth the hassle to ensure you are on a legitimate network.

Use a wired connection if available. Many hotels offer in-room, hard-wired connections. Some coffee shops offer wired connections, too. Using a wired connection will not make you invincible, but because of the switching involved in transmitting and receiving packets it does make intercepting and exploiting your traffic much more difficult. It also reduces the likelihood of you connecting to a phony network to almost nil. Capturing Wi-Fi packets is notoriously easy and can be pulled off by even unskilled attackers, but attacking wired networks is much more difficult. There are still many exploits against wired connections, but they are far fewer in number and require far more technical know-how. Also, be aware that even if the traffic over a wired network is not being maliciously attacked, your packets are still vulnerable to inspection on the router to which you are connected, and by the internet service provider. This is a major consideration if you are working in a country where your threat model adversary is a nation-state actor who monitors the country's internet, such as Egypt,

Iran, North Korea, or the United States.

Use a VPN or Tor. Using a virtual private network or Tor (see the section concerning Tor in the next chapter) is one of the best security measures you can take if you must connect to any untrusted network, wireless or wired. While it does not prevent your packets from being captured, it will ensure your traffic is encrypted from your device to the exit server. Any packets that are captured on the local wireless network will be encrypted and therefore unusable. Using one of these measures will protect you against inspection by both the owner of the router (i.e., the coffee shop or hotel) and the internet service provider. If you have a VPN for work that you must log into to access your office's server, you can probably connect to it before accessing the internet from an unsecured Wi-Fi. Even though it will not protect your traffic from your office's IT department, it will secure your connection and prevent the packets from being captured in plaintext locally.

Do not open files. Running more applications means presenting more attack surface. When using an untrusted network, you should be exceedingly cautious about opening any attachments you download, or running any applications other than the web browser you are using on the network. This will lessen the chances of information being automatically sent by these applications over an unsecure connection.

If you will be using a certain network frequently in the future and would like to leave it as a known network, change the settings so that you must manually connect to it. To change this, navigate to Manage Wireless Networks as described previously. Right click on the network and open the properties. Uncheck "Connect automatically when this network is in range". Either of these options, removing the network or setting it for a manual connection, will prevent Windows from actively searching for that network in the future, eliminating your attack surface for evil twin attacks, and reducing information leaked about your Wi-Fi networks.

MAC Address Spoofing

Every internet connection possesses a MAC address. It is assigned to the hardware element of the connection such as the Ethernet port or the Wi-Fi chip. This is hard-coded into the boards and broadcasted to the first router connection. It is unlikely for online services, such as websites, to ever see this information. However, internet service providers, wireless hotspots, and public tracking systems collect these details at all times. There are numerous ways to spoof a Mac address. Some prefer a terminal solution with system commands. Many prefer applications that automate the process, such as the following.

Windows: Technitium Mac Changer - technitium.com/tmac/
Mac: MacDaddyX - www.macupdate.com/app/mac/25729/macdaddyx
Linux: Terminal - linuxconfig.org/change-mac-address-with-macchanger-linux-command

LEVEL THREE:
ADVANCED

We believe that the third level of privacy and security applies to many individual reading this book. It includes properly creating and executing alias names, providing disinformation to data mining companies, monitoring your real details for online leaks, disassociating your real name from your home address, using secure communication channels, properly deleting sensitive files, creating bootable operating systems on removable media, and possessing an anonymous web presence.

We realize that most of our readers will not take the steps described in this level. However, we encourage all of you to continue reading. The methods here may become useful when something negative happens in your life. For those excited about these topics, you already know that a proactive response is always better than a reactive response. Preparing your private and secure life now will be much easier than repairing any damage after an unfortunate incident.

CHAPTER FIFTEEN
ALIASES

We have mentioned legally using a secondary credit card under an alias name several times in this book. This is used in situations when disclosing your true identity is not necessary. We should now take a look at selecting an appropriate alias name and corresponding details related to this new identity. For some, this may be a simple and random thought. Some may pick John Williams as their new alias. We prefer to make an effort to intentionally choose proper details that have been thoroughly reviewed for long term use.

The most vital lesson in this chapter is to be prepared. We never "go live" with an alias name without having all information in place. This may include your alias address, phone number, email address, middle name, mother's maiden name, and other details. We have been caught off guard in these situations. We recently helped someone order anonymous internet access to their home and were asked for our email address for the automatic billing. We had not created one yet. It became awkward when we had to say "hold on" while we quickly created one. Instead, be prepared for everything. Hopefully, this chapter will help you in these preparations.

In Chapter Three, we discussed preparation for your journey into removing your details from the internet. The material focused on having anonymous email addresses and phone numbers to give out. These would be associated with your real identity in an effort to protect your private information. This chapter is much different. None of the previous work should be used here. This chapter will help you create new content that will never be associated with your real identity. It will be attached to your alias identity only.

Choosing your alias name, sometimes referred to as an alternative or secondary name, is very important. You need to be comfortable with it. You need to respond to it when called in a crowded room. Basically, it needs to be natural. We do not promote obvious names such as John Williams or Jane Smith. These sound fake. This might bring more attention than desired. Instead, consider a new version of your current name.

If you have a common first name, such as Michael or Justin, we do not see much risk in keeping that first name. Instead of Michael Bazzell, you may create a secondary identity of Michael Williams or Mike Wilson. This maintains the natural response to people calling you by your first name. The unintentional nuances that you exhibit in relation to your true identity are difficult to replicate when using a new first name. People that enter the world of covert government work may be prepared to take on a completely new identity. Most of our clients are not ready for that task. Before we can get into the details, we need to discuss things you should never do.

- Never choose an alias name of someone that you know.
- Never choose an alias name with the intent of portraying another real person.
- Never use an alias when identifying yourself to a government official. That is a crime.
- Never attempt to obtain any credit under an alias name.

Some clients, especially female victims of domestic violence, desire a completely new name. They do not want to recycle their first name and want a fresh start. We completely understand this and encourage you to do what is best for your situation. The most difficult part of selecting an entire new name is ensuring that it has no ties to you. While it may sound easy to pick a random name, try it for yourself. As you read this, mentally state your new alias without giving it much thought. The name that you just chose likely fits into one of the following categories. If it does, it should not be used.

- The full name of a famous person.
- The first name of a relative or friend.
- The last name of a fictional movie or television character.
- The middle name of a close ancestor.

This list could go on, but you get the point. We tend to pick names that have some type of meaning to us. This is bad because it might leave a trail to your real identity. We suggest you come up with names that have no relationship with your past. As of this writing, the ten most common last names in America are the following.

| Smith | Williams | Jones | Davis | Rodriguez |
| Johnson | Brown | Miller | Garcia | Wilson |

We believe that these make for great last names. They are vague enough to be difficult to search, and popular enough to appear legitimate. If you use a common last name, we suggest using a slightly more unique first name. Remember that names like Jane Smith seem fake while Alicia Smith appears to be a bit more authentic. Only you can create the alias best for your situation. We only ask for you to consider these recommendations.

After you have selected the new alias name that you will use, you need to create the digital life that will go with it. At the minimum, you need a new email address and telephone number. If you want to truly be prepared, you will also need an alias mailing address, employer, hometown, social networks, credit card, identification card, family history, and digital footprint. We will explain each in its own section below.

Email Address: This is vital. You need an email address that you can give out at any time that can be associated with your new alias. We believe that the address should include your alias name within it in order to appear more legitimate. If your alias name is Brad O'Neal, and your email address is robert911@hotmail.com, this seems suspicious. If your address is brad.oneal.5@outlook.com, this appears more authentic. The host of your email address is not very important. If you plan on incorporating a Google Voice number into this alias, it may make most sense to create a Gmail address. While we dislike Gmail's intrusive collection of your personal information within your emails, we will accept it for this purpose only. None of your communications will be associated with your real identity. You will also delete all messages in a timely manner.

Telephone Number: We believe that this is also vital. You will need a number to give businesses when you use your alias. This number should connect to a generic voicemail that you have access to. A Google Voice account will suffice for all of this. Forwarding your voicemail messages to your 333Mail account will make sure that you have immediate access to these messages within your personal email account (non-Gmail). Chapter Three explains things you need to know about creating Google Voice accounts.

Employer: You should always have an alias profession memorized and ready to deliver. Our society really enjoys small talk. When meeting people for the first time, you will likely be asked within a couple of minutes about your profession. Some are truly interested in what you do, but most are trying to appear polite because silence feels awkward. When choosing your alias profession, be careful not to violate any laws. Never state you are a police officer or a federal agent. This is a crime. It is also a crime in some states to identify yourself as a coroner, judge, paramedic, or other government employee. We highly recommend to stay away from anything close to this. We also suggest that you avoid professions that you know nothing about. Imagine that you just told the clerk at the hotel that you were a truck driver. She then tells you that her father is a truck driver and asks about your rig. You are now stuck in this lie and are on the spot. Instead, consider keeping things generic. We prefer to state we are self employed consultants, tech support, or data entry employees. This is usually boring enough to stop further questioning. We never recommend stating something too interesting. If you tell the people at the table of the conference you are attending that you are a pilot, you will now be the focus of attention.

Hometown: Similar to questioning your employment, people tend to ask "Where are you from?" If you are from a small town, and disclose this, you might be disclosing too much information. We prefer to state that we are from a large city that we know something about. If we say we are from Chicago, the next question will be "What part?" You had better be prepared. We like to pick a well-known landmark in a residential area and use that. We have a client that tells everyone he is from Chicago. When pushed for more data, he states "Two blocks from Wrigley Field! Do you like the Cubs?" This then puts the questioner in the spotlight and allows him or her to talk about themselves. This usually results in a topic change very quickly.

Social Networks: In Chapter Seven we encouraged you to minimize or delete your social networks. In contrast, we now suggest that you create some. If you are going to use an alias name with people that you might continue a relationship with, you should probably have an online presence. This does not mean that you should create profiles on ten different networks, but you should have at least two. We recommend a Facebook profile and Twitter account in your new alias name. This way, when someone tries to check up on you, there is something to see. Keep the alias personal data minimal, set your privacy settings appropriately, and occasionally post extremely generic information. On our accounts, we occasionally retweet a celebrities' comments on Twitter or respond to random people on Facebook when they post their birthday. We post just enough to seem real without divulging any real information.

Credit Card: Chapter Nine explained how to obtain a secondary credit card in an alias name. If you plan on using this name in front of other people while dining, shopping, or making any purchases with a credit card, you should be prepared to pay with the proper card in that name.

Identification Card: This gets tricky. We do not want to commit any crimes, but we may need photo identification at some point. We had a client that attended an invite-only party at a popular club. The person that invited her knew her as the alias name that she had provided on an attendance roster during a public event. At the time, she did not want to give out her real name because it was an event surrounding a controversial subject. Entrance to this party required photo ID. Fortunately, she was prepared. In her wallet with the secondary credit card, she possessed her gym membership card. Since she had registered for her gym in her alias name, and she pre-paid her monthly dues with her secondary card, they never asked for identification. They created her membership card for her after taking her photo with a digital camera. At this new event, she displayed her gym membership card to the bouncer stating "I left my DL at the gym, but you are welcome to call them to verify that". The bouncer matched her alias gym membership name to the name on the list and waived her through. She committed no crimes during this process. It is important to discuss again the importance of staying legal. Never create an identification card that appears similar to any government ID and never give an alias to any law enforcement. We will later discuss alternative ways to obtain identification in the name of an alias.

Family History: The people that ask you about your hometown and profession are likely to also inquire about your family history. Questions such as "Do you have kids?", "Do your parents still live in Chicago?", and "Do you come from a big family?" are very common. We recommend that you are prepared for this. In many situations, you might want be honest in order to remember what you have disclosed. However, this often leads to more questioning. If you say that you are from a big family, you will likely be asked if you had brothers or sisters, if you are the oldest, where they all live, and other details. This may make you uncomfortable when talking with strangers who are only trying to be polite. Ultimately, you should choose the best option for you and stick with it. We prefer minimal details. Therefore, we usually stick with simple answers followed by a question such as "I was an only child, what about you?".

Digital Footprint: This is an area that is often overlooked by privacy seekers. We tend to stop ourselves from sharing anything on the internet. However, your alias is not you. Think of him or her as the exact opposite as you. Your alias may be a social maniac that desires online fame. This can help establish your alias as a real person and really "sell" it. If you want to build up the persona of your alias online, we recommend that you consider the following avenues.

Practically everyone has a blog or media website today. We cannot generate enough content to keep up with the demand of new material. Therefore, practically every outlet accepts guest posts from readers. If you follow a blog about finance, you could likely write an article and have it posted under the name of your alias. If you have an interest in technology, there are numerous websites that will publish your original article without much scrutiny. We believe that this method establishes better credibility than a social network profile. While anyone can create either anonymously, the published content appears more legitimate. Consider the following actual example.

A client had established an alias name, email address, and social networks. He planned to use this alias while interacting with a local hackerspace. While most hackerspaces understand your desire for privacy, this one asks that you disclose your real name when interacting with members. He was uncomfortable with this because of the unfortunate negative connotations surrounding hackers and hackerspaces. He also held a respectable position at a law firm and did not want to associate his professional life with his personal interests. He has also observed the hackerspace website disclose the real names of the people that attended past events. He knew that the group would likely Google him at some point and he wanted to appear legitimate.

He sent an email to over a dozen of his favorite technology related websites asking if he could write an article explaining the details of his classic arcade machine project using the M.A.M.E arcade emulator and a Raspberry Pi device inside a refurbished arcade cabinet. Three responded right away and were happy to publish his work. He sent the well written article to all three, disclosing that he would be posting on multiple sites, and waited. A few days later, his article appeared on all three websites in the name of his alias as the author. All three were linked to his alias Twitter account in order to contact the author. If you Google his alias name today, the first two results are links to these articles. This not only helps his alias appear real, but it also declares that his knowledge coincides with membership into the hackerspace community. For those wondering, he approved this disclosure here and encourages you to try to locate his true identity.

For most people, possessing a single alias is sufficient. It gives you an alternate name to use when appropriate to protect your privacy. It is enough to get you out of awkward situations. If you are well prepared and have adapted to your alias details, the information you provide will sound smooth and authentic. We encounter situations every day that support the use of aliases. Consider the following scenario.

A large national chain of hair cutting services offers affordable cuts to a mostly male audience. When you arrive, they ask if it is your first visit. If it is, they ask for your first and last name, home address, and cellular telephone number. This is for marketing purposes and to text you when it is your turn. They then ask for your date of birth in order to give you a free cut on your birthday. They ask for identification if you want to take advantage of this. The data is searched based on the telephone number. If it is not your first visit, they will ask for your number in order to retrieve your visit history and access your data.

One of us recently visited this chain while traveling during speaking engagements. While desperate for a haircut, is was the only option on a Sunday afternoon. When prompted for this information, only a first name of John was given. The statement "I prefer to pay with cash and decline to offer any personal information" was given during all other questioning. It was a bit awkward, but worth the hassle.

Many people might scoff and say "who cares if your barber knows this information?" We do, and you should. It is not a matter of an individual knowing your birthday. Instead, it is a matter of you protecting your personal data and privacy. When you hear about that service announcing a breach of all of their customer data, you will not be concerned. When the company sells their customer database to a data mining company for a few thousand dollars, your name and home address will not appear on the internet. The small actions that we take to prevent the leakage of our personal information will have a huge impact on our overall privacy. Everything is connected.

Some people require multiple aliases. We only recommend this to those that can keep all of the details straight and have a need for additional names. Before we explain our recommendations, you should understand the scenarios when one alias is not enough. Consider the following example that was sent to us via email after reading the book Hiding from the Internet, shared with permission from the sender.

A woman was the victim of constant harassment from a former lover. He was mentally and physically abusive and a drug addict. On several occasions, she would leave their shared apartment and stay in a hotel for safety. He would call all of the hotels in the area and convinced hotel staff that there was an emergency. Through social engineering, he was able to identify her hotel room number. This created a very dangerous situation.

She finally left him permanently and moved into a new apartment in another portion of the city. She attended numerous local conferences as part of her job and often stayed overnight in the hotel that was hosting the event. She created an alias to use during these travels in order to hide from any future attempts. This worked great for a while.

She used her new alias every time that she checked into a hotel. She also used the same alias with her new book club that she joined. Eventually, the former boyfriend went to every book club meeting held at independent book stores in the area. He knew that she enjoyed these and thought he would find her eventually. When he spotted her, he likely watched from a distance.

When she left the book store, he approached the remaining members and turned on his charm. He gave the following story to one of the elderly members of the club.

"I am so sorry to bother you. I have a weird story to share, and you might think I am crazy. You see, I am a true romantic, almost to a fault. I met a woman the other day here at the store, and I will never forgive myself if I do not try to contact her again. We had so much in common, and she was so beautiful that I could not build up the courage to ask her out. I only know what she looks like, and I do not even know her name. She mentioned that she belongs to this book club, but I guess I arrived here too late. Do you by any chance know who I am talking about?"

Immediately, the woman screamed "I bet you mean Amy!" The other ladies then joined the conversation and were determined to get these two together. He left there knowing her first and last alias name, the area of her new apartment, the current book she was reading, and the details that she shared with the group about her ex (him). The harassment began right away.

We believe that readers that are in any type of physical danger should have two aliases at a minimum. One of these should be used solely during travel. It should be used at hotels and while shopping. It should not be used in any type of social gatherings or personal environments. "Amy" should have a personal alias and travel alias. They should be different first and last names and should have no obvious connection to each other. Your situation may require a third or fourth alias, but that is very rare.

Isolating these aliases within their own wallets are vital. You do not want to keep secondary credit cards in alias names in the same location. Presenting a credit card in one name while you are holding two additional in other names looks suspicious. You want to be able to immediately access any credit cards or non-government identification cards as if it were natural. While we can offer a couple of ideas, you should ultimately choose the method best for you. Hopefully the following will generate your own thoughts.

We support isolating your alias documentation in individual collections that are similar to each other but uniquely identifiable. One client found an online store that sells a "Slim Wallet". It is a bi-fold leather wallet that will hold a small amount of cash and up to four cards. It is available in several colors. He keeps three wallets in his backpack at all times. One color is his true identity with real driver's license and credit cards. He chose blue for this one as it is the wallet he will retrieve when stopped by the police for his awful driving. The black wallet is his primary alias that he uses for generic occasions. This contains a secondary credit card in his alias name which he uses for shopping, dining, and social interactions. It also contains his gym membership card and random frequent visitor food reward cards. They are all in the primary alias name. The final wallet is red and only used during travel. It contains another secondary credit card and several hotel rewards cards, all in his alias name.

Another client chooses to use binder clips as his wallets. His situation is very unique and he possesses four "wallets" at all times. Each set contains the appropriate identification cards and secondary credit cards, with a small amount of cash folded once around the cards. The small binder clip holds it all together. He knows immediately which alias is represented by the type of currency on the outer layer of the wallet. The $20 bill is the primary, the $10 bill is the secondary, the $5 bill surrounds the third, and a $2 bill covers the fourth.

You may be struggling to think of ways that you can possess identification cards in your alias name legally. We offer the following as theoretical options. Be sure to check all state and federal laws before attempting any of the following.

- Practically every hotel chain offers an online enrollment into their rewards system. This will present you with a plastic card in any name you desire. While no photo is on these, it helps create the illusion of a real person. It provides "padding" to your wallet to convince others.

- Many volunteer programs insist that you wear identification while providing your services. Zoos, museums, gardens, libraries, and attractions often have volunteer groups that provide tours, guidance, or post event trash pickup. Some of these issue photo identification to be worn around a lanyard to identify you as an authorized visitor. If you are not being paid, very few of these verify your identity. With this method, you can establish an alias, obtain an unofficial photo ID, and give back to your community all in one step. Be careful not to violate laws surrounding your access. If you are a registered sex offender required to stay away from schools, an alias does not circumvent this to allow you to help after a school event. You will get caught and arrested.

- Many travel groups issue identification cards to be used while on tours of a city. These are also usually worn around your neck in order to identify yourself as associated with that tour. We have seen city tour gatherings leading groups of people around major cities. All of them have a similar laminated card on a lanyard with their photo and name, along with the name of the tour group.

- Many large corporations provide occasional tours of their campus. In years past, this meant that you showed up and followed a line of people while learning about the features of the product made by the company. Today, you are often required to wear a visitor's pass. Many corporations now collect a digital image of each visitor and print this image on a paper label to be worn on clothing. While many of you will cringe at the thought of providing a photo of your face, we do not get too bothered by this. We are all already being monitored on CCTV. You could attend a tour, provide an alias name, and receive a business card sized label that includes your alias name, company logo, and real photo. An affordable laminator can quickly give this the appearance of legitimate identification.

One final option is to simply make your own. We hesitate to discuss this option too much in detail because people may try to break the law and create fake government ID's. Lamination machines and holograms are very affordable on Amazon and local print shops will happily laminate anything you print yourself at home. There are many templates of various styles of photo ID's online, but most are illegal. Instead of presenting you with random ideas, we prefer to separate legal and non-legal options.

- **LEGAL**: Non-government identification in an alias name can be legal. There should be absolutely no mention of any state or the word government. There should be no mention or reference to any real businesses. It should not identify you as an employee of a legitimate company.

- **NON-LEGAL**: Any false identification that displays the words city, county, state, government, police, license, driver, court, agent, et cetera is a crime. This should be obvious. Any reference to employment by any government agency is also illegal. If at any time you think that you might be crossing the line, you probably are. Please stop.

Aliases carry the unjustified stigma of being shady or criminal. In spite of this unfortunate perception, an alias itself is not illegal. As long as you do not cross the line of any sort of government identification, you can be anyone you want. It is not a crime to give another civilian a fake name. If we were to visit a Starbucks, we would not give out our real name. There is no benefit. If we entertain a group of clients at a restaurant, we do not provide our real name to the establishment. They do not need that. They only need payment for the services in the form of cash or a secondary credit card. We do not want our true identities within their databases and guest books that will eventually be breached and leaked online. While this may seem overly cautious, we are aware of the daily breaches and intrusions into sensitive data stored by third parties. We ask you to consider scenarios where using an alias name might protect you, your family, and your identity.

CHAPTER SIXTEEN
DISINFORMATION

The first edition of the book Hiding from the Internet made a brief mention of what many people refer to as misinformation. Technically, misinformation is when a person unintentionally provides inaccurate information which causes inappropriate content to be released or replicated. Most people are really talking about disinformation. This is when a person intentionally provides false or misleading information with an attempt to create inaccurate data. Disinformation is exactly what we want to do more of.

So far, this book has explained the many ways to remove your information from the internet. However, it is important to understand that it is not always possible to erase every piece of data about you. Disinformation will make that small amount of permanent data seem useless inside a stream of completely inaccurate content. We have devoted an entire chapter to disinformation techniques that we believe should be applied in some situations. This step is optional, and not suitable for everyone.

If you have been extremely successful with eliminating your online information, you may not need disinformation. However, if you have found a few services that refuse to remove your data, any websites that will not respond to your requests, or simply want to harden your overall security, disinformation may be the perfect solution. Providing inaccurate details while completing the removal processes discussed earlier will also increase your effectiveness substantially.

Before proceeding, consider whether this action is right for you. Completing these tasks will add more information about you to the internet. Since the information supplied is false, there is little privacy concern. However, this will lead to much more content available about your name. Many people like this because it creates a difficult scenario when someone tries to locate them. Some people do not like this tactic because it makes their name more visible throughout the internet. Only you can determine if this action is appropriate. Understand that it may be difficult or impossible to remove the false information that you provide.

You have learned how public records, data brokers, advertising companies, and various businesses build complete profiles on you and your family. Our main concern with these reports is the inclusion of our home addresses. Most people's home address can be found on 40 different websites within a minute. This is not only an invasion of privacy, but a danger to many people.

Michael's Experience with Hiding from the Internet

My goal with Hiding from the Internet was always to have a home that no one could associate with me. I wanted a safe location that I could feel comfortable in without looking over my shoulder. Police officers and other people targeted because of their profession will understand. After accomplishing this, I experienced an interesting moment.

In 2012, I received a piece of mail to my residence addressed to "New Resident". It was an automated welcome packet from several local businesses containing coupons for home related purchases. Basically, I had fallen so far off of the radar that data mining companies had assumed that someone else must have moved into my house. This was a rewarding feeling, but it quickly concerned me. If I was no longer likely to be living at my house, where did the data companies think I was living? I thought that too little information available about me could be causing more harm than good. This is when I became fascinated with disinformation.

A friend of mine is a private investigator. I had him look up my information through a popular data broker that he had premium access with. There were no entries associated with me for the past few years. This indicates to an investigator that I was dead, homeless, or hiding. The only recent activity was my PO Box. I retained a copy of this report and used it as a comparison for future analysis.

The first call I made was to my internet service provider for my home. This was a major cable company and I started the conversation by requesting a discount on my service. I was advised that if I extended my contract two years, I could negotiate a lower price. One of my arguments was that this was a second home and that I was hardly there. We agreed on a price, but I had two conditions. The first was that I wanted the bill and all associated records to be addressed to my full time residence. Second, I insisted that they only send me an electronic bill via email. This eliminated any need to have access to any physical mail coming from this company.

For my "full time residence", I supplied an address that did not exist in a neighboring town. I went to Google Maps, identified a random nearby street, and found the last address available. I then added two digits to that address and attempted a search for it. Google identified it as a possible address, but it could not pinpoint exactly where the house was. I wanted to provide an address that would seem realistic, but not jeopardize anyone else. I never use any information that is unique and real to another individual. Another option would have been to identify a new neighborhood being built, locate the highest number for an address on the street, and add a few digits. If you are met with any resistance, you could say that it was a brand new house.

Within 30 days, I had my friend request another report on me. This time, it indicated that I had recently moved to an address that matched the disinformation that I provided to the cable company. I considered this a success and continued with my disinformation campaign.

The remaining content of this chapter will identify possibilities that you may consider for your own disinformation attempts. They are divided into three specific groups. The options are endless, and we encourage you to email us any great ideas that you have.

- **Name Disinformation**: This will focus on providing many different names to be associated with your real address and real telephone number to make it difficult to identify the true owner of each. This is beneficial for hiding your real name from people or companies searching for information about your address or number.

- **Address Disinformation**: This will focus on associating various addresses with your real name to make it difficult for people or companies to determine which address is your real home.

- **Telephone Disinformation**: This will associate various telephone numbers with your real name to make it difficult for a person or business to identify a valid number to contact you.

Name Disinformation

In the perfect scenario of hiding from the internet, every reader will be moving soon, can purchase the home in cash, possesses an invisible New Mexico LLC for the title, and will never associate the new address with a real name. In order to be realistic, we will assume this is not the case for you. Name disinformation will create an appearance that numerous people live at your residence. This could increase the delivery of mail and advertisements to your house. However, none of it will jeopardize your privacy. In fact, it will increase your privacy quickly. At the end of this section, we will display actual results from these techniques.

Bills

Earlier, we explained how to use disinformation to have a landline telephone listing modified to inaccurate information. This technique works well on practically any service provided to a home or business. Contact the service provider, possibly your cellular telephone provider, and request a change to your billing information. Advise the representative that the account is listed under your middle name and that you are uncomfortable with that and desire it to be associated with you first name. Provide any first name that you like. Within weeks, third party companies will receive the updated information which will eventually override the real information on file. We prefer to choose a different first name for every bill.

Magazines

If you have a subscription to any magazines in your real name, you should stop that practice immediately. This data is openly shared with many companies and will quickly identify your name and home address online. Contact the magazine company and tell them that you were recently married and want the magazines delivered in your married name. Provide any last name that you desire, as long as it has no personal association with you. This works for men as well. Since same sex marriage has been so controversial lately, no magazine company is likely to challenge a man on changing his last name to his partner's.

If you do not have any magazines delivered to your home, it may be time to start. Identify a couple of popular magazines that you are interested in a subscription. Conduct a search for that magazine plus "free subscription". You may be surprised at the abundance of magazines that will give anyone a free subscription. This will often involve the need to complete a short survey. The survey can also be used as a disinformation opportunity.

The most vital part of this exercise is that you do not provide anything close to your real name. Additionally, provide a different name for each subscription. We like to relate each name to the magazine that is being requested. The following could be a guide.

Men's Health: John Sporting
Money Magazine: Tim Cashman
Wired: Alex Techie
Food Magazine: James Cook

We also encourage you not to go overboard. Please only obtain subscriptions that you will read or pass on to someone that will enjoy them. There is no need to waste the product and immediately throw them in the trash. You will also eventually get frustrated if you have several issues arriving every week filling your mailbox.

Newspapers

Similar to magazines, we encourage you to identify a single newspaper that you would enjoy receiving. Newspaper subscriber databases are unique and cater to a specific market. This subscription information will leak out slowly to third party companies. We do not recommend multiple newspaper subscriptions unless this is appropriate for your daily reading abilities.

You may enjoy reading the Wall Street Journal every day. A search online for "Wall Street Journal 39-week" will identify dozens of websites that will allow you a 39-week free trial of the paper. Complete the request and provide a unique name. We have found Mary S. Market to be appropriate. You will begin receiving your print and digital editions within one week.

Trade Mailings

Trade magazines and mailings are designed to target a specific industry or trade. These are usually free by default and generate revenue from the advertising within the publication. Visiting freetrademagazines.com will display numerous options to consider. We encourage you to be cautious with this method. Many people will load up on magazines of interest and use a false name. While this is acceptable, it does create an association with your home address to your real interests. For example, if you subscribe to seven different web design magazines, and you are a web design artist, this could lead to an accurate profile about the people that live at your home. We would only choose this option if you do not take advantage of a magazine or newspaper subscription.

Home Repairs

The time will come when you will need some professional work completed at your home. This will often happen the moment that you stop associating your real name with your home address. Use this as a disinformation opportunity.

A friend recently discovered that he needed a new roof. Calling a stranger on Craigslist and paying cash would have been acceptable for privacy concerns. However, he understandably wanted to hire a professional company and possess a valid warranty on the new roof. He had recently conducted a complete cleaning of his personal information on the internet, and was concerned that this could jeopardize his privacy.

We recommended that he identify the company that he wished to hire and ask them to provide a quote. He gave them his real address for the roof job, but provided the name of a fake contracting company that was similar to the name of his invisible LLC. If your LLC was named Particle Ventures LLC, you could provide Ventures Contracting. This allowed him to keep his real name away from the process and attach yet another type of disinformation to the address. Upon completion of the work, my friend possessed a written warranty attached to the address and not to a person. This would suffice for replacement if problems with the roof appeared. If you do not possess an invisible LLC, you could use the name of your living trust. Instead of providing the full name of the trust, leave off the description at the end. If your trust was titled The Big Adventure Revocable Living Trust, you could use The Big Adventure Contracting Company.

Remember, we are not using any of these methods to commit fraud. We are only protecting our privacy and will pay any accounts in full. For most work like this, paying either cash or with a check is acceptable. It is not likely that the name on the check will be attached to the data from the work, but it is possible. If you have an LLC or a trust, consider opening a free checking account in its name. This will not only add a layer of anonymity, but it will also reinforce the appearance of legitimacy.

Address Disinformation

This is the most vital type of disinformation if you are trying to disassociate your real name from your real address. The goal with these methods is to create an illusion that you currently live somewhere that you do not. This will make accurate name searches difficult. Before proceeding, you should have an idea of which addresses you will be providing.

Choosing an Address

This section will explain how to create at least three valid addresses that you will intentionally associate with your real name. The purpose is to show recent activity if someone was to search for you within a people search service. These services always display the most current information first. Therefore, you may want to complete as much as possible of the removal process that was discussed earlier before providing this disinformation. Additionally, you would only want to do this after you have stopped associating your real name with your real address.

It is very important not to use another individual's home address. While it may not be illegal, it is not ethical and not fair to the other person. If you are hiding from an abusive ex, you do not want to put someone else in danger when he or she decides to break into a house believing it is yours. If you are a police officer trying to protect your family from criminals seeking revenge, you should not send them to some stranger's house and let those residents deal with it. We will only choose locations that do not pose a threat to anyone.

The first address may be a place that does not exist. This is our favorite technique. Many companies possess verification software that will identify invalid addresses. These programs can often be fooled by selecting addresses in new neighborhoods. The following instructions will easily identify a new address for you.

- Conduct a Google search for "new construction city, state". Replace "city, state" with a location at least a few towns away from you. We also recommend clicking "Search Tools", "Any Time", and selecting "Past Year". This will display recent results.

- Choose a search result that connects to a real estate website that displays new homes for sale. The newly planted grass, identical houses, and same list price in each listing are also an indicator of a brand new neighborhood.

- Conduct a search on Zillow.com for the highest number visible on the chosen street. You should see a house attached to this address. Increase the address by ten or twenty digits. In this scenario, you could search 1017 Park Charles Blvd. Zillow should inform you that there is no house at this address.

- Search this new address on Google maps and confirm the house does not exist. Switch to the satellite view and confirm that there would not likely be enough land to add the number of houses necessary to create this address.

- Document this new address and use it for disinformation.

Occasionally, advanced verification software will identify a fake address as invalid. You may need to provide a real address that is listed as residential but does not belong to an individual family. One technique that we have found works surprising well is to choose a large apartment complex by searching "apartment for rent in _____". Then identify the largest one based on amenities like fitness center, swimming pool, etc. The address for the main office of the apartment complex could be used. Knowing the complex has over 100 residences, the main office is a generic address that does not endanger anyone and would not be flagged as a false address.

Another alternative is to choose the address of an emergency shelter. The residents in these are constantly changing, and most of them have 24-hour staff and security. Since many people must consider these a temporary residence, the addresses often defeat the most advanced verification services. Choosing a city and searching it online including the terms "shelter", "men's home", "women's home", and "homeless" will usually provide options. We use this as a last option.

Another address that may work are the numerous "long term" motels. There are some national chain hotels that advertise weekly or monthly rates and it is not uncommon for these to be rented by corporations who send employees to other cities on extended work trips. Most mid-sized cities also have some smaller, independently owned motels that cater to a shadier element usually consisting largely of drug dealers, addicts and prostitutes. We have found that hotels that specialize in stays of a week or longer, especially the independently owned versions, will often be accepted as a residential address. The standard Marriot, Hilton, and IHG chains will usually be flagged as commercial, and will not work for this purpose.

Public library addresses are almost always identified as commercial, but the addresses will pass standard validation. For most disinformation purposes, the address of any public building, including a library, will suffice. Now that you have some ideas for your new address, the next techniques will help you populate online records with this information.

Internet Surveys

There will never be a shortage of internet surveys. These are websites that ask you to answer numerous personal questions and offer small rewards in return. Most of them never fulfill their promise to send you money, tech devices, or Amazon gift certificates. They all collect your information, create large databases of personal details, and sell that data to marketing companies. The content associated with you often makes its way to the public visible internet.

These surveys are time consuming but effective. The content that you provide will quickly be disseminated to various public sources. Be sure to always provide your real name, but never provide your real address, personal email account, or any real information about you within the survey responses. You do not want to create an accurate profile of your interests and family situation.

Many readers will want nothing to do with this section. We completely understand this stance, especially when seeing the level of intrusive questioning that is involved. We only recommend this approach when you have been unsuccessful at removing your personal details from the internet such as the city and state you live in, your age, and family members' information.

In order to explain the appropriate way to provide disinformation through online surveys, we will demonstrate using swagbucks.com. The following instructions will walk you through the process.

- Navigate to swagbucks.com and create a new account. Provide a 333Mail address created earlier and a password used only for that website. We recommend using a specific 333Mail account such as swagbucks@nsa.33mail.com. Be sure to use a 333Mail account that will forward to you. You will need to verify this email address by clicking the option within an email sent to your 333Mail account.

- You will be given the option to "Complete Your Profile" in a popup window after email verification. Choose this option and provide your real name. This website will walk you through providing your gender, date of birth, zip code, and other personal details. Provide inaccurate responses to all of these. Within weeks, this false information will start to appear within public people search sites.

- Complete a few surveys always providing inaccurate answers. You will be prompted to complete a "Profiler" which will ask many invasive questions related to income, race, employment, education, health issues, and sexual orientation. Always provide inaccurate data. Three to five surveys should be enough to pass your name, false age, and incorrect location details to third party companies.

TV Offers

A less invasive way of populating bad information about you on the internet is responding to television offers during infomercials. You have likely seen various offers for information about devices such as medical alerts, home security systems, and reverse mortgages on both daytime and late night television. They all offer to send you an informational packet describing how they can help any situation that you are in. These are always a profitable business anticipating huge financial returns when they engage you for their services. Instead, we will use this as a way to mask our true home address.

We recently watched a commercial for a slow motorized device created to help the elderly and those with disabilities. It was a combination of a wheelchair and a moped that could move anyone around the street, grocery store, or mall. You are probably familiar with these "scooters". We each called the number and requested information. We used our real names and addresses in new subdivisions that did not exist. We do not like to use real addresses because someone will need to deal with the junk mail that is received. This way, the mailings are simply returned to the business. We purposely provided street names that we located called "Mobility Way" and "Mobile Drive".

Within 90 days, while conducting a routine query of our names on people search websites, we located entries for us on "Mobility Way" and "Mobile Drive". We now know with certainty that this company shares personal information. If someone is trying to locate us, he or she will have two more address to research and be disappointed.

Online Offers

There is no need to wait in front of a television all night with the hopes of catching a great disinformation opportunity. The internet has thousands waiting for you at all times. Searching for any of the following topics will likely present numerous websites eager to send you a free information packet. Providing your new "fake" address will get you listed in several marketing databases quickly with this false information.

Home Scooter
Time Share
Home Alarm
Lawn Treatment Service
Home Food Delivery

Please do not ever provide any real information about yourself, besides your name, to any of these services. Never provide a credit card number or any other type of payment information. You should only use this technique to create the illusion that you live somewhere other than your real home. Additionally, if you have a common name, such as John Smith, address disinformation is not likely necessary.

Be aware that paper mailings will likely be delivered from and returned to the businesses that you contact. This is very wasteful for both the business and the planet. We encourage you to only perform the actions necessary to obtain your address disinformation goal. We do not encourage you to unnecessarily contact hundreds of companies. It only takes a few large companies to make an impact on your overall address identity.

Social Networks

We usually do not promote the creation of personal social network profiles. However, they can be very useful in some cases. We once consulted a young woman that was the victim of severe harassment by a man who was a former high school classmate of hers. His unwelcome approaches caused her to move and purchase a different vehicle. She was doing well at staying off of his radar, but knew he was still looking for her. She created a Facebook page, added a couple of photos of her pet, and publicly displayed her location as a town over an hour away. While monitoring the Twitter account of her stalker, she observed him "check into" a bar in that very town, likely looking for her. While this does not solve the issue long-term, it provided enough uncertainty to confuse the stalker and waste his time.

Creating several social network profiles and including publicly visible location data can be beneficial. You can either make them very confusing by placing different locations on each profile, or place the same city on all of them to create a convincing situation. If this type of disinformation is appropriate for you, it can be taken further with the following technique.

GPS Spoofing

Most social networks allow you to share your current location at all times with the world publicly. The readers of this book will likely think that this is ridiculous. While we agree, we can also use it to our advantage. Manipulating the location information stored within social network posts can be very easy or fairly difficult. We will explain two different options to consider based on your level of technical skill.

Please Don't Stalk Me (pleasedontstalkme.com)

The easiest way to spoof your location on Twitter is to use the service Please Don't Stalk Me. This website will perform all of the necessary actions in order to provide a false location during your "Tweets". The following instructions will explain the process.

- Either create a new Twitter account or log into your current Twitter account from which you want to post messages. Confirm that you have location sharing enabled by going to Settings > Security and privacy > Tweet Location. You want to check the box that allows you to add location information to your Twitter posts.

- Navigate to pleasedontstalkme.com and allow it to connect to your Twitter profile through the "Sign in with Twitter" button.

- Enter the address or general location from which you want to appear to be posting your message. Click the "Tweet" button to post the message.

- Navigate to your Twitter profile to view the post and associated location information. The upper right marker and location confirm that the message was posted from New York City while we were really sitting in Chicago.

- If you want to test the accuracy of your false GPS information, load your profile on the website tweetpaths.com by entering your Twitter username.

Providing false location information to your Twitter posts can be extremely effective for disinformation purposes. While we usually encourage people to stay away from social networks, this can be helpful. If you are trying to convince an abusive ex that you now live in a new area, frequent posts with false location data from that area can be very convincing. If you want your family and friends to believe that you are vacationing overseas, this technique should fool them and allow you some peace and quiet in your own home.

Please use caution not to divulge any accurate personal details. Always remember that the content that you post to the Twitter servers will likely be present forever and can never be completely removed.

Web Browser GPS Data

The previous technique is great if you only need to fool someone through Twitter. It does not work for other services. We can emulate a GPS location within our web browser and allow the browser to share this with any website. This will cause social networks to broadcast our current location, which we can control with misleading information. This can quickly confuse anyone that is stalking or harassing you. The following instructions will walk you through the entire process of providing false location data to a Twitter profile and posts.

- Download and install the Chrome web browser. This free browser works on all operating systems and will often provide a faster internet browsing experience. Navigate to google.com/chrome and follow the directions.

- Launch Chrome, click the menu in the upper right corner, highlight "More Tools" and select "Developer Tools". This will launch a new window on the side of your screen. Strike the "ESC" key on your keyboard which will launch the necessary console at the bottom right. Click the word "Emulation", then "Enable Emulation".

Click "Sensors" on the left menu of this window. Select the "Emulate geolocation coordinates" checkbox and enter any GPS location that you desire.

- Close the developer tools console by clicking the "X" in the upper right corner of the tools box at the bottom of your screen. You should now only see the web browser page.

- Navigate to Bing Maps (bing.com/maps) and click the icon next to "Click to center the map on your current location". Your browser will likely ask you if you want to share your location. Accept this request and the map should identify that you are at the location that you provided.

- Connect to any network that you want to use to broadcast a false location. You should connect to the mobile versions of the services you want to fool. Instead of facebook.com, you should connect to m.facebook.com. Adding "m". or "mobile". in front of most websites will take you to the mobile version which will ask for location information.

Be aware that this technique does not hide or change your IP address. Websites that you visit will still know this information and may be able to determine your approximate real location. This should only be used for purposely posting false location data through social networks. Always test this procedure with a non-sensitive account to validate the result.

> **Michael's Address Disinformation Results**
>
> I consulted a government employee that was being harassed by a federal prisoner that he had arrested. The prisoner threatened to find his family and kill them in their sleep when he was released from prison. With permission, I began a disinformation campaign for him. He had a unique name and lived in Chicago. Before the process, searching his name in Spokeo identified two locations. One was his home and the other was his workplace. After removing these entries, which was discussed earlier, I helped populate false information through the techniques discussed here. The current result when searching his name displays over 20 possible addresses, and none of them relate to his actual home.

Telephone Disinformation

Receiving unwanted telephone calls from telemarketers can be annoying. Calls from them to random numbers are unavoidable. However, targeted calls specific to you can be extra frustrating. You have already learned how to eliminate public record of your telephone number. You may now want to populate disinformation to prevent a person or business from discovering your true home or cellular telephone number.

Identifying New Numbers

Before you can provide the false telephone number information with hopes of it being attached to your name within public databases, you must select some appropriate numbers. Most importantly, you never want to provide a false number that belongs to another individual. That is not only rude, but it can also jeopardize that person's right to privacy from unwanted callers. Instead, focus on telephone numbers that either do not exist or belong to services that are never answered by an individual.

Busy Numbers

Our favorite telephone numbers for disinformation are numbers that are always busy and cannot be answered. These were once abundant, but many of them have now been assigned to customers. There are still two large groups of telephone numbers that will always be busy when dialed. The following sets of numbers should work well.

909-661-0001 through 909-661-0090
619-364-0003 through 619-364-0090

The 909 area code serves the Los Angeles area of California and the 619 area code serves the San Diego area. These were early line numbers when service began in this area and the numbers should not be assigned to any customers. Since these are not toll free numbers, they should not be flagged as non-residential. Because numbers are ported so often, possessing a number in another area code should not raise any suspicion. When you give someone a number that is always busy, it does not create the appearance of a fake number. These may appear to be real to a person that would otherwise question the validity of a given number.

Disconnected Numbers

There are plenty of unused numbers that announce "disconnected" when dialed. Most of these are temporary and will be assigned to a customer at some point. The following range of numbers all announce a "non-working number" when dialed. The area code serves Pennsylvania. Giving one of these numbers to a person or business can reinforce a desire to not be contacted.

717-980-0000 through 717-980-9999

Always test the numbers that you choose before using. The following table displays a useful chart of the "busy" numbers with an area next to each to document the numbers used and specific application of each. You could use this to keep track of your disinformation.

909-661-0001	_____	909-661-0031	_____	909-661-0061	_____
909-661-0002	_____	909-661-0032	_____	909-661-0062	_____
909-661-0003	_____	909-661-0033	_____	909-661-0063	_____
909-661-0004	_____	909-661-0034	_____	909-661-0064	_____
909-661-0005	_____	909-661-0035	_____	909-661-0065	_____
909-661-0006	_____	909-661-0036	_____	909-661-0066	_____
909-661-0007	_____	909-661-0037	_____	909-661-0067	_____
909-661-0008	_____	909-661-0038	_____	909-661-0068	_____
909-661-0009	_____	909-661-0039	_____	909-661-0069	_____
909-661-0010	_____	909-661-0040	_____	909-661-0070	_____
909-661-0011	_____	909-661-0041	_____	909-661-0071	_____
909-661-0012	_____	909-661-0042	_____	909-661-0072	_____
909-661-0013	_____	909-661-0043	_____	909-661-0073	_____
909-661-0014	_____	909-661-0044	_____	909-661-0074	_____
909-661-0015	_____	909-661-0045	_____	909-661-0075	_____
909-661-0016	_____	909-661-0046	_____	909-661-0076	_____
909-661-0017	_____	909-661-0047	_____	909-661-0077	_____
909-661-0018	_____	909-661-0048	_____	909-661-0078	_____
909-661-0019	_____	909-661-0049	_____	909-661-0079	_____
909-661-0020	_____	909-661-0050	_____	909-661-0080	_____
909-661-0021	_____	909-661-0051	_____	909-661-0081	_____
909-661-0022	_____	909-661-0052	_____	909-661-0082	_____
909-661-0023	_____	909-661-0053	_____	909-661-0083	_____
909-661-0024	_____	909-661-0054	_____	909-661-0084	_____
909-661-0025	_____	909-661-0055	_____	909-661-0085	_____
909-661-0026	_____	909-661-0056	_____	909-661-0086	_____
909-661-0027	_____	909-661-0057	_____	909-661-0087	_____
909-661-0028	_____	909-661-0058	_____	909-661-0088	_____
909-661-0029	_____	909-661-0059	_____	909-661-0089	_____
909-661-0030	_____	909-661-0060	_____	909-661-0090	_____

Store Giveaways

One of the quickest ways to associate a false telephone number with your real name is to enter various contests. You have probably seen a brand new vehicle parked inside your local shopping mall. A box next to it likely contained blank pieces of paper asking for your name, address, and telephone number with promises that someone would win the vehicle. Have you ever known anyone that won a vehicle this way? We do not. Instead, these gimmicks are often used to obtain a great list of potential customers that might be interested in automobiles. This content is often combined with other contest data and sold to numerous companies. Eventually, the provided information is attached to you through a marketing profile that may follow you forever.

In years past, we have always laughed at the idea of entering these contests. Today, we never pass up this opportunity. We always provide our real names, our false addresses from the address disinformation section mentioned earlier, and one of the "busy" telephone numbers listed previously. We like to use different numbers every time and watch for any online associations to us from these numbers. We then know which contest companies are selling our information.

Shopping Cards

Most grocery stores have a shopper's card program that provides discounts on merchandise. These are portrayed as opportunities to save money for being a loyal customer to the brand. In reality, these cards are closely monitored to learn about your shopping habits. This data is used to create custom advertising and offers. The only benefit of joining this program is the savings of the items that you purchase. The risk of joining is the guaranteed profile that will be created about you and sold to interested parties. You can enjoy the benefits without jeopardizing your privacy. This is a great opportunity for telephone number disinformation.

Practically all of the stores that utilize this type of savings program allow you to access your account by the telephone number that you provided during registration. You are not required to provide or scan your shopper's card. You can simply enter your telephone number to obtain the savings and attach your purchases to your profile. We have found the following telephone number to work at most stores.

867-5309

This number may not look familiar, but say the number out loud. This was the title of a song by Tommy Tutone in 1982 that gained a lot of popularity. This number is currently assigned to customers in most area codes. In fact, it is often sought after by businesses due to the familiarity. We never use this number with services that may try to contact me. Instead, we only use it when we register a shopping card at a grocery store.

If we are shopping in Chicago, we use an appropriate area code such as 847. If you ever find yourself at a Safeway store anywhere in the world, you can use 847-867-5309 as your shopper's card number and it will be accepted without hesitation. If you find that this number does not work at another chain, you should consider requesting a shopper's card and provide it as your number.

We provided a real name, the disinformation address discussed earlier (which does not exist), a Chicago area code, the 867-5309 number, and a specific email address at my 333Mail account. We will never use that email account again, and will know which company provided the information when we receive unwanted email at Safeway@nsa.33mail.com. We can now provide 847-867-5309 as our member number when we shop at Safeway. Most importantly, you can too.

As a community service, we create new accounts at every store that we can in the number of 847-867-5309. The more strangers that use this number during their shopping, the more anonymous we all are. The data collected by the store will not be about one individual. Instead, it will be a collective of numerous families. If you locate a store without a membership with this number, please consider activating your own card with address disinformation.

Within weeks, this information will be associated with your real name. It will add an additional layer of anonymity by making any present legitimate information difficult to find and harder to prove accurate.

Rewards Cards

Chapter Fifteen discussed a method of using hotel reward programs to help convince a receptionist to accept your credit card in your alternate name. These programs can also be used to spread disinformation for your benefit. Many companies that offer reward programs share or sell the collected data to other interested businesses. If you have an account with a chain of luxury resorts, they are likely to sell your information to credit cards that cater to business travelers. If you are a rewards member of a fast food chain, they are likely to share your details with other food and retail companies. While some privacy advocates warn you to stay away from these traps, we encourage you to embrace them with disinformation.

Rental Vehicles

We travel often and find ourselves in a rented vehicle monthly. We joined various rewards programs in order to obtain substantial discounts and upgrades. We always provided our real name because a driver's license was always required to complete a transaction. However, the address and telephone number was never verified during the signup process. Every time that we would rent a vehicle, we were asked if we were a rewards member. We always advised yes, but stated that we did not know our membership number. The most common response was "What is your telephone number?"

Like many other programs, most car rental rewards clubs can access your account by telephone number. The telephone number is heavily associated with your name and a great opportunity to provide disinformation. The details that you provide will likely become visible either publicly or to data marketing companies. Providing your real name, disinformation address, and one of the telephone numbers discussed earlier will help create an inaccurate profile and may help eliminate your real telephone number that is currently on file with other companies.

You do not need to actually use any of the services that you register with. All of them allow you to join their rewards program before you make any reservations or purchases. The information below will take you directly to the online application process for some of the popular vehicle rental companies.

Enterprise: enterprise.com/car_rental/enterprisePlusCreateAccount.do
Hertz: hertz.com/rentacar/member/enrollment/contact-details
Thrifty: thrifty.com/BlueChip/Enrollment.aspx
National: nationalcar.com/index.do?action=emcIndex.do&type=uszl-withnav-header
E-Z Rentals: e-zrentacar.com/rewards/money_main

Caller ID Apps

Mobile apps such as TrueCaller are discussed in Chapter Twelve. They collect the contacts from your device and add them to a huge database that anyone can search. You can use this to your advantage. If you have an unused smart device, conduct a hard reset to remove all personal data. Connect to Wi-Fi and add your real telephone number to your contacts but provide a random name. Install every caller ID app that you can find and agree to the permissions. This will identify your real number as someone else's. If someone searches your number on the website, they will receive a result with a random name. While not always foolproof, this can add a small layer of disinformation to your overall strategy. This could be completed for every VOIP number that you use. You could also provide disinformation for your family's numbers without them knowing. Maybe your child needs this assistance.

> **Michael's Phone Number Disinformation Results**
>
> A college student of mine once told me that her ex-boyfriend was constantly harassing her through telephone calls and text messages. She had changed her number once, but he was eventually able to find the new number through the internet. With her permission and assistance, we embarked on a telephone disinformation campaign before she changed her number again. Eventually, Spokeo and other services associated her name with three of the "busy" numbers, her email address with a 333Mail account, and her home address with a non-existing building. She was now ready to change her number for the last time, and keep it out of any public databases.

General Tips

- Consider always providing disinformation that will help you identify the leak of data when you find it. For example, if you request information from a reverse mortgage company with a goal of name disinformation, you should use a name that will remind you of this company, such as "Joe Reversi". When you receive unwanted mail at your residence attached to this name, you will know the original source.

- A benefit of disinformation involving companies that cater to a specific demographic is that your residence will now be associated with the same category. Requesting reverse mortgage information or a medical alert quote will likely indicate that older adults live at your residence. This can help mask your real interests.

- Never use your real name or alternative credit card name in association with your real address or telephone number. The goal here is to generate inaccurate details in order to help mask any real data that you cannot remove.

- Remember that it will be difficult to remove disinformation that you provide about yourself. If you have very little online information identifying your personal details, these techniques may not be appropriate for you. However, if there is an abundance of accurate details that you cannot remove, it is better to add bad information in order to hide the real content.

Several people have expressed concern to us about the risks of removing all personal information from the internet. Their thinking is that if there is no information about you it could be a red flag that could cause you to come under suspicion. This creates a conundrum: if members leave all their personal information on the internet, their spouses and children could be exposed and placed in danger. This is becoming even more important as we are starting to see targeted terrorism and doxing of personnel within the borders of the United States. Alternatively, doing so may compromise their status by giving them a digitally "different" profile. We agree entirely with this logic. However, we disagree with the suggestions we have heard for solving this problem. Most of these suggestions are to essentially do nothing and take a more passive posture on social media. This is not our approach.

Our solution is to remove all real information to the maximum extent. We believe you should make your home, your vehicles, your children, and your spouse as difficult to identify as possible. Only then will you be able to sleep soundly at night, secure in the knowledge that you and your family are a difficult target to locate. However, we do not believe you should stop here. Our opinion is that disinformation in this case is as good as real information. If the person reviewing it finds five separate records of your "home" online, the scrutiny will likely end there.

Chapter Seventeen
Future Monitoring

Now that your information is out of public view, you must continually monitor the entire internet for any new information that may surface. Recent studies have identified over 55 billion web pages in existence. The hard way to do this would be to scour Google every day looking for anything new identifying your information. Do not worry, this monitoring can be automated.

Google Alerts (google.com/alerts)

Google is a very powerful search engine. It can identify areas where your personal information, such as name and home address, are on display in a public website. Manually searching every week or month is a burden. Google Alerts can automate this search and send you an email when any new results appear. This free service will basically notify you when your information has appeared on a public site.

- Log into your new personal Gmail account. If you do not have a Gmail account, navigate to **gmail.com** and create a new free account.

- Determine the exact searches of your personal information that would return appropriate results. This will vary depending on how common your name is. If your name is unique, such as Jeremiah Dressler, and you live at 4054 Brenner Street in Biloxi, MS, you should create the following alerts.

"Jeremiah Dressler"
"Jeremiah Dressler" "Brenner"
"4054 Brenner" "Biloxi"

- The quotes should be included in the alert. If you have a child named James, you should add the following alerts.

"James Dressler"
"James Dressler" "Brenner"

- However, if you have a common name, you will need to add more data. If you do not specify the exact search that you want, you will receive too many false positives for pages that are not about you. If your name is Brian Johnson, and you live at 1212 Main in Denver, CO, you should create alerts that are specific to you. These should include interests, a workplace, or associations. The goal is to search for the perfect amount of data to identify your public personal leaks without receiving irrelevant data. You will need to manipulate these searches until you achieve only the results that are about you.

"Brian Johnson" "1212 Main" "Denver"
"Brian Johnson" "volleyball" (a specific interest)
"Brian Johnson" "Denver" "Johnson Ford" (workplace)
"Brian Johnson" "Denver" "Colorado AARP" (association)

- If your landline telephone number is 314-555-1234 and your cellular number is 713-555-9999, you should add the following alerts.

"314-555-1234"
"314" "555-1234"
"713-555-9999"
"713" "555-9999"

These specific search terms will attempt to locate information placed within websites that match the terms inside quotes. For example, if a person search site created a new profile in the name of Jeremiah Dressler, Google would pick up on this and let you know. If a reverse telephone directory listed the term "Jeremiah Dressler" and the street of "Brenner" in the same page, this service would alert you. The quotes mandate that a result is only returned when those words are next to each other on the page. The telephone number examples would identify a website with your number even if the area code was separated from the rest of the number.

- Navigate to **google.com/alerts**. Supply the first alert that you want to create. The result type should be "Everything", frequency should be "As-it-happens", results should be "All results", and the delivery should be to your Gmail address. As you create the alert, you will see the current search results in the right column. Click "Create Alert" when complete and continue to add alerts.

- Click on the "Manage your alerts" button and review your alert settings. Here you can modify or delete an alert that you have created.

With a properly configured set of Google Alerts, you can be notified in real time as Google finds information about you and your family. You are not limited to these examples. We have alerts in place for our websites and books. If any website links to our websites, or someone is discussing our other books, we can be notified and provided a link to the source.

Google Analytics (google.com/analytics)

This book has discussed how websites track you and collect information about your internet searches and history. You can use this same technology to track people that are looking for information about you. You can know when someone searches for you on Google, where they are located, and what they were researching in order to find you. This may sound expensive and difficult. The easiest way to apply this tracking technique is to create a free website and add Google Analytics.

- Navigate to **sites.google.com** and log in with your Gmail account information. Click the red "Create" button to start a new project.

- Provide the name of your site. This should be your real name. Contrary to the rest of this book, you want people to find this website. For the site location, supply your real name without spaces. If that name is taken, add generic information to the end of the name. If your name is Chris Johnson, "ChrisJohnson" will probably already be in use. Try "ChrisJohnsonHomeAddress". This will make more sense in a moment. Select the "Create" button to generate a new generic website.

- Click the small icon that looks like a pencil. This will allow you to edit your new website. For this site's purpose, change the title to "YOUR NAME's Home Address". Obviously, enter your real name. In the content box below it, type any names that you think people would search to find you. If you have a fairly unique last name, include different spellings of the name with the full and shortened versions of your first name. Also include "telephone number" and "phone number". Note that you should not actually place your number here, only a reference to it. Click "Save" when you are finished. Continuing from the example above, when someone conducts a Google search for "Chris Johnson home address" or "Christopher Jonson phone number", this new site will be in the results. If you have a common name, you may want to consider adding any term that is very public about you that would help with this bait, such as the name of your spouse or the high school you attended. It is important that you not include any information that would identify your home or children. You only want to make it easy for someone to find this page through a search.

- Navigate to **google.com/analytics**. Select "Create an account" and click the "Admin" tab in the upper right portion of the screen. This will present a page with a button labeled "+ New Account". Click this button. In the "Account Name" field, type your real name. In the "Website URL" fields, select http:// and then type the location of your new website. This will be the name you used earlier without spaces. In the example, we used "ChrisJohnsonHomeAddress". If this was your example, your website would be sites.google.com/site/ChrisJohnsonHomeAddress. If you have trouble with this, go back to the website that you created. When you can see the website, look at the address bar. It will display the exact URL of your site. Agree to the terms and click "create account".

- On the next page, ignore everything and click "save". At the top of this page will be your new Google Tracking ID. It will look like UA-33333333-1. Select this entire ID and copy it.

- Return to your new Google website. Select the "more" button and click "Manage Site". In the "Statistics" portion of the page, check the box labeled "Enable Google Analytics for this site". Paste in the number you previously copied. Click the red "Save" button. It may take up to 24 hours for Google to add the analytics to your site.

- Navigate to **google.com/webmasters/tools/submit-url**. Enter the entire website address of your new site. Continuing from the previous example, it would be sites.google.com/site/ChrisJohnsonHomeAddress. Click "Submit Request". This notifies Google and requests that they scan your website for keywords to be added to their search index. This will make the website appear in a search result when someone is trying to locate you. It may also take up to 24 hours to be activated.

In summary, this process created a free website with limited information about you in plain view. This will only be your name and possibly some other content that is not private to you. Since you added Google Analytics, you can track the visitors to this site and learn information about them. This will often identify why a person is trying to find you. You should now visit your analytics site and see what you find. There is an abundance of data available about the visitors to your website. Most likely, you will have very few visitors, if any at all. When you do receive visits, the Google Analytics portal will let you browse the data collected from the visit.

Analytics Reports

Now that you have Google Analytics installed and monitoring your website, you are ready to view reports about visitors.

- Navigate to **google.com/analytics**. Sign in to your Google account and select the name of your website. This will present an overview page of traffic to your site. If you see that there were no visitors, then you know that no one was at your site for the past 30 days. There is nothing else to see here. However, if you have visits, continue to the next step.

- In the left menu, click "Demographics" in the "Audience" section. Click "Location" and view the map to your right. This will identify the locations of people visiting your website. The dark green states have had the most visits and the white states have had no visits. Clicking on a state will open the state view and identify which cities have visited your site. This will never disclose the name of the person searching for you, but knowing the city and state the person is in could be helpful.

- In the left menu, click "Traffic Sources" and then "Overview". This will present a summary of how people found your website. This will probably all be through search traffic. Scroll to the bottom of the page and view the data in the lower right portion. These are the exact searches that were typed into Google.

This will be an important area to monitor on your website. If someone does visit your page, you can identify the terms that were typed to find you. A search of your name may not concern you. However, a search of "Mike Bazzell home address" from a location of a past stalker should raise your interest. The following true story may shed light on why this process is important.

Michael's Experience with Analytics

In 2010, I was asked to assist with creating a Google Analytics site for a client receiving serious death threats. He suspected it was the family of a federal prisoner that he had testified against. A few months after the analytics were active, someone from Minneapolis, MN conducted a search on Google for my client's name and the term "address". A quick search of the suspect on the Federal Bureau of Prisons website verified that the suspect had just been released from federal custody. He had been housed in Minneapolis, MN. This was an early notification that this suspect had not forgotten about my client.

If you have been the victim of harassment or stalking, you should execute your own bait website. We also believe that law enforcement should consider using analytics now instead of waiting until a problem arises.

CHAPTER EIGHTEEN
GOVERNMENT RECORDS

Government records contain some of the most sensitive pieces of information about you. Information about your finances are contained in your tax records. Data about your date and place of birth and parents, is contained in your birth certificate. Your place of residence is purposely recorded by the city, county, and state you will live in. The politicians you support financially and vote for are present in these records. If you have a permit to carry a concealed handgun, this information is recorded. In some states, it is considered a matter of public record, along with your home address.

Opting out of most of these records is not possible. The government will not allow you to simply remove the record of the purchase of your house. Though this would certainly enhance your privacy it would make it much more difficult for your city, county, and state to collect taxes on you. The strategies for dealing with these types of records may vary from state to state, and from town to town within a given state. There is no single, check listed approach that we can offer that will work in every jurisdiction in the United States. Consider this chapter as a set of guiding principles rather than a collection of guaranteed techniques.

Public Records

While reading this book, you have probably found your home address, telephone number, and family member's names on the internet. Most likely, this data was collected at some point from public information. From there, it has spread to dozens of websites and marketing lists. In order to prevent your information from reappearing on these websites, you must make some changes to your public profile.

Some of the most vital information that you should protect from public view is data that everyone has legal access to. If you think that your date of birth, divorce records, voter records, traffic offenses, and civil litigation are protected, you are wrong. This is all public data and there is nothing stopping individuals and private companies from collecting your information and selling it to anyone that wants it. This is not the end of the chapter though. Just because something is a part of the public record, it does not mean that you cannot make it difficult to find. This chapter will help you reverse some of the damage that is already out there, but your future actions are more important.

Property Tax Records

We believe that the most important data to consider in reference to privacy is your property taxes. Most likely, you own a home and you pay yearly property taxes. These may be incorporated into your house payment. Your property taxes will likely be in your or your spouse's name, or maybe both. This single record will announce your home address to the world. The numerous people search sites that were discussed in Chapter Eight rely on these records to locate people and charge a fee to disclose your location. Having an unlisted telephone number does not hide this data. There are two approaches to fixing this problem, and we recommend applying both.

Data removal

Because the tax records are public, you cannot expect the information to be removed from public view. However, you can request that the information is removed from the online database. Each county has a database that stores the property tax records. Most of them make this data available online through the county website. The companies that have been discussed here know how to collect all of that data and add it to their own data set. This data is more reliable in locating people than telephone directories or social networks. You cannot remove the records yourself. You will need to contact the county in a very specific way.

- Conduct a search on the internet for your county's property tax database. If you live in Cook County, Illinois, your search may look something like "Cook County IL property tax search". For most counties, this will display some type of database that can be searched by name, address, or parcel number. Search your own information and make note of the parcel number and a telephone number for the Clerk's office.

- Telephone your County Clerk's office and politely make the following request:

"I have noticed that my personal information and address are visible on your property tax website. I realize my property tax records are public records and must be made available to anyone that wants to personally view them, but I would like to have the online records removed. I have recently discovered several websites that have extracted the information from your database and made it available for the purpose of locating people".

- Continue the conversation and include any other reason to enforce the removal request. This can be any of the reasons identified in Chapter Eight that may make you more vulnerable to danger. The following are four examples.

> "I am a (choose one) police officer / public official / community leader and possess a higher risk of danger from the community".
>
> "I have been the victim of identity theft and I am removing my personal information from data mining companies in order to prevent further criminal activity"
>
> "I have been a victim of a violent crime and fear for my safety. The ability to locate me based on your online records has increased the danger of bodily harm"
>
> "I have been the victim of threats and harassment. The ability to locate me by searching your online database places me in immediate danger of bodily harm".

Choose your response wisely. You may be asked to provide proof of your claim. Subjects that attend our training sessions have notified me that proof of their statements were never requested. Some attendees have stated that they received great resistance in these telephone calls and were occasionally told that the request was impossible. If this happens, call again and request the Information Technology (IT) division. Repeat the above process to them. Most likely, a computer professional will be the person that will ultimately be responsible for removing the information. Attendees have confirmed that this second call was successful.

Removing your information from this online database is a huge victory. However, this does not hide your address from the public completely. It also does not remove your information from companies that have already obtained the data. The previous chapters should help with that. It will prevent data mining companies from getting easy access to it, but someone can still find you with a personal visit to the County Clerk's office. Most likely, a helpful employee would even conduct the search for them and offer to write down or copy the information. Our recommendation is to never have your property taxes in your name.

Ownership Change

If you plan on living in your current home for the next several years, you may want to consider legally changing the owner of your residence to a living trust. This will also change your property taxes to the name of the trust. Before you do this, you must establish a living trust for yourself and your spouse. The full details of establishing a living trust are far beyond the scope of this book. There are many great books that will help you accomplish this, and many people complete the process without the guidance of an attorney. Here are a few of the benefits.

- You can place any assets in a living trust including real estate, investment accounts, and personal property in your home.

- Having all of your assets in a living trust can keep your assets out of probate, which provides a great layer of privacy.

- It will give you complete control of what happens to your assets when you die without making the details public.

- The trust can be amended at any time or completely revoked.

- You can name your trust anything you want. It does not need to include your name, and I do not recommend identifying yourself or your family in the name of the trust. It could even be "Hiding from the Internet Living Trust".

After you establish a living trust, you can contact the County Recorder in your county to change the ownership of your property. In one county we recently contacted, the fee was $41.

New Ownership

If you are planning on purchasing a new home or making any permanent move, this is a huge opportunity to make it practically impossible to be located. This method is only for those of you that are truly committed to being invisible from the public. The general idea of this process is credited to J.J. Luna, the author of the book *How to be Invisible*. This book is considered by many to be the definitive guide to removing yourself from public view. The fourth edition was released in 2012. The basic premise of this specific method is the following:

- Purchase an official LLC from a registered agent in New Mexico. These are never publicly associated with your real name, but you own the business.

- Purchase your new home using the LLC as the owner. The LLC can also purchase vehicles and other property.

- Never associate your name with the house you live in. Personal mail should be delivered to a PO Box. Utilities should be in the name of the LLC.

If you are at all intrigued by these possibilities, purchase Luna's book immediately. The methods are completely legal. If you are in any way targeted by the public, such as police officers or victims of harassment, this will guarantee that you will have a home to be safe in.

Internal Revenue Service

You have likely heard about criminals filing false tax returns and claiming unauthorized refunds from identity theft victims' filings. This has become a multi-billion dollar problem for the IRS. It is obvious that your tax records are not completely protected, and you have no choice but to allow storage of your details such as SSN, DOB, address, and income. However, you can control some data provided. You can also eliminate unauthorized filings. We recommend that everyone consider the following as mandatory practice.

- File before the fraudsters do it for you. Your primary defense against becoming the next IRS scam victim is to file your taxes at the state and federal level as quickly as possible. This is usually the second or third week in January. It does not matter whether or not the IRS owes you money. Thieves can still try to impersonate you and claim a refund.

- File IRS form 14039 and request an Identity Protection (IP) PIN from the government. This form requires you to state you believe you are likely to be a victim of identity fraud. We believe that all Americans have been impacted by incidents that could lead to ID theft. This form can be found on the IRS website.

Voter Registration Records

If you are a registered voter, your home address is visible to the public. Most likely, there is a database on your county's website that will list every registered voter's home details for the entire county. It identifies a person's full name, home address, dates voted, and political affiliation. Data mining companies know about these and use them to collect information about you. Removing this information is vital to protecting your privacy.

- Navigate to **www.blackbookonline.info/USA-Voter-Records.aspx** and select your state. On the next page, select your county. This will forward you to the online voter database for the county you live in. Some counties do not have online access yet.

- Search for your name in the database. If you locate your records, it will probably identify both your residence address and a unique number associated with your voter record. Make note of this number. It will also likely display each date that you have voted in either local or national elections.

- Contact your County Clerk's office and request to add your voter registrations information to the "Address Confidentiality Option". This can be done at the same time you request the removal of your property tax information from the online database. This option was originally designed to help participants keep their home address secret. Most people that take advantage of this program are victims of violent crime, harassment, or identity theft. If this request is denied, request an address change and provide your PO Box information.

If you cannot find an online database, this does not mean that one does not exist. Some counties have removed this database from public view but continue to share it to data mining companies and political campaigns. If you are a registered voter, you can be assured that your information is in this database. While we encourage every American to vote, many people have expressed interest in being removed completely from voter registration databases because of privacy concerns. This is possible with the following instructions. Please be warned that this will eliminate your ability to vote unless you register again.

- Navigate to the site **http://www.eac.gov/election_management_resources/ voter_registration_cancellations.aspx** and click the link for "Election Dictionary for Cancellation Notices".

- This will present a Microsoft Word file that includes every county in the U.S. Locate your office and contact them stating that you have moved, registered to vote in another county, and need to be removed from their database.

We have found that adding the information about moving to another county to be vital. When only requesting to be removed, some counties refused. However, removal is mandatory if you are registered to vote in another county. They have no practical way of verifying this information. We should state again that this will eliminate your right to vote unless you reinstate your registration. Doing so will require you to disclose your name and home address. It will also add these details to the live database for publishing. Please choose wisely.

Military Recruiting Databases

Section 9528 of the No Child Left Behind Act of 2001 requires all school districts to release student names, addresses, and telephone numbers to all military recruiters. If you do not want military recruiters to add your child to their recruiting database, you can demand that the school not release the information. This removal option is a part of the Family Educational Rights and Privacy Act (FERPA), but is rarely offered.

- Navigate to **leadps.org/images/content/479/Military_OPT-Out.pdf** and print the form. This form only requires the school name, student name, student signature, and parent signature. Figure 18.01 displays a portion of this form.

- Deliver this form to any schools that your child attends.

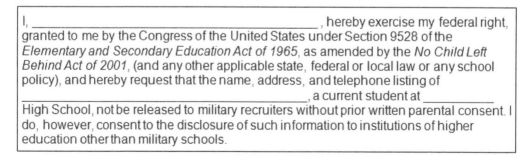

I, _____ , hereby exercise my federal right, granted to me by the Congress of the United States under Section 9528 of the *Elementary and Secondary Education Act of 1965*, as amended by the *No Child Left Behind Act of 2001*, (and any other applicable state, federal or local law or any school policy), and hereby request that the name, address, and telephone listing of _____ , a current student at _____ High School, not be released to military recruiters without prior written parental consent. I do, however, consent to the disclosure of such information to institutions of higher education other than military schools.

Figure 18.01: The removal options of a FERPA form.

Aristotle (Aristotle.com)

This website relies on public records to assist in political campaigns. This includes voter records and county data. If you located your personal information on any county website, Aristotle has your data for sale. A removal request is accomplished through email.

- Use your new personal email account and create a message to remove@aristotle.com. In the body of the email, state that you request "Any and all information associated with the following person removed from all online and offline databases maintained by Aristotle". Include your full name and home address.

Court Records

Civil and criminal court records are public information. Anyone can visit their county court and search local court cases on county owned computers. Most courts have uploaded this live database to the internet. A quick search on a county's court database identified profiles by subject name which included civil cases, traffic offenses, misdemeanors, and felonies. There is very little that you can do about information in your profile. You should visit the following website and select your state of residence.

blackbookonline.info/USA-County-Court-Records.aspx

Select your county and visit the county's online court database. Search your name and verify any cases that you are involved in. If you have only one offense, you can contact the state's attorney's office for your county and request an expungement form. If the expungement is approved, the details of the event will be removed from all court databases. This will not remove the data from any private websites that possess a copy of the archive. Below is a list of websites that provide court records for a small fee. If you want to be sure that your expunged case is removed from these websites, visit the link for contact information. Contact each site and inform them that their database discloses details of an expunged case. You should receive no resistance in removing the data.

BCS Backgrounds	https://usabackground.com
Complete Backgrounds	completebackgroundchecks360.com/privacy.html
Court Records	http://www.courtrecords.org/2011/privacy.php
Court Registry	courtregistry.org/index.php?xpath=privacy
Court Click	courtclick.com/terms.php
Criminal Pages	criminalpages.com/optout/
Criminal-Records	criminal-records.org/privacy.php
Data Detective	datadetective.com/privacy.php
Detective Unlimited	detectiveunlimited.com/privacy-policy.html
Public Backgrounds	publicbackgroundchecks.com/privacypolicy.aspx

Privacy Act Requests

The Privacy Act of 1974 establishes a Code of Fair Information Practice that governs the collection, maintenance, use, and dissemination of personally identifiable information about individuals that is maintained in systems of records by federal agencies. You have the right to request your own record. If your files contain anything classified or deemed inappropriate for release, they will be redacted. We have found the following letter helpful for a successful response containing your personal files, followed by three agencies that you may want to contact. This can also be sent to the FOIA division of any federal agency.

> This is a request for records under the provisions of the Freedom of Information Act and the Privacy Act. Please process this request under both statutes to release the maximum number of records. I request copies of all personal files, correspondence, or other records.
>
> My full name: My place of birth:
>
> My date of birth: My Social Security number:
>
> Under penalty of perjury, I hereby declare that I am the person named above and I understand that any falsification of this statement is punishable under the provisions of Title 18, United States Code (U.S.C.), Section 1001 by a fine of not more than $10,000 or by imprisonment of not more than five years, or both; and that requesting or obtaining any record(s) under false pretenses is punishable under the provisions of Title 5, U.S.C., Section 552a(i)(3) as a misdemeanor and by a fine of not more than $5,000.

Information Coordinator
Central Intelligence Agency
Washington, DC 20505

Federal Bureau of Investigation
Records Dissemination Section
170 Marcel Drive
Winchester, VA 22602-4843

United States Secret Service
FOIA / PA
245 Murray Drive, Building 410
Washington, DC 20223

Concealed Carry Permits

Most states in the US allow the issuance of concealed carry handgun permits to qualified citizens. The laws in each state vary and it is up to you to know your own state's regulations regarding legal concealed carry. Each state also varies in how it handles the information of concealed carry permit holders. In some states this information is considered a matter of public record and may be requested by the media or by individual citizens through a Freedom of Information Act request. The accompanying chart shows each state's stance on protecting the privacy of concealed carry permit holders. The extent of the information to which these states will give out, and to whom they will give it, also varies state-to-state. If you have questions about your own state's laws regarding your privacy as a concealed carry holder consult the applicable law, also listed in the chart.

Notes about the following chart:
1. KY; only names are made available
2. NE; concealed carry permits not considered a public record
3. OH; only available with a public interest statement from a journalist
4. TX; confirmation of individual names only
5. VA; available at local but not state level
    Not listed: Vermont; does not issue concealed carry permits.

State	Public/Private	Applicable Law
Alabama	**PUBLIC**	Alabama Public Records Law
Alaska	PRIVATE	Alaska Public Records Act
Arizona	PRIVATE	Arizona Public Records Law
Arkansas	**PUBLIC**	Arkansas Freedom of Information Act
California	**PUBLIC**	California Public Records Act
Colorado	**PUBLIC**	Colorado Open Records Act
Connecticut	PRIVATE	Connecticut Freedom of Information Act
Delaware	PRIVATE	Delaware Freedom of Information Act
Florida	PRIVATE	Florida Sunshine Law
Georgia	PRIVATE	Georgia Open Records Law
Hawaii	PRIVATE	Hawaii Uniform Information Practices Act
Idaho	**PUBLIC**	Idaho Public Records Act
Illinois	PRIVATE	Illinois Freedom of Information Act
Indiana	**PUBLIC**	Indiana Access to Public Records Law
Iowa	**PUBLIC**	Iowa Public Records Act
Kansas	**PUBLIC**	Kansas Open Records Act
Kentucky	**PUBLIC**[1]	Kentucky Open Records Act
Louisiana	PRIVATE	Louisiana Sunshine Law
Maine	**PUBLIC**	Maine Freedom of Access Act
Maryland	**PUBLIC**	Maryland Public Information Act
Massachusetts	PRIVATE	Massachusetts Public Records Act
Michigan	PRIVATE	Michigan Freedom of Information Act
Minnesota	PRIVATE	Minnesota Data Practices Act
Mississippi	**PUBLIC**	Mississippi Public Records Act
Missouri	PRIVATE	Missouri Sunshine Law
Montana	**PUBLIC**	Montana Public Records Act
Nebraska	PRIVATE[2]	Nebraska Public Records Law
Nevada	**PUBLIC**	Nevada Open Records Act
New Hampshire	**PUBLIC**	New Hampshire Right to Know Law
New Jersey	PRIVATE	New Jersey Open Public Records Act
New Mexico	PRIVATE	New Mexico Inspection of Public Records Act
New York	**PUBLIC**	New York Freedom of Information Law
North Carolina	**PUBLIC**	North Carolina Public Records Law
North Dakota	**PUBLIC**	North Dakota Open Records Statute
Ohio	**PUBLIC**[3]	Ohio Open Records Law
Oklahoma	PRIVATE	Oklahoma Open Records Act
Oregon	PRIVATE	Oregon Public Records Law
Pennsylvania	**PUBLIC**	Pennsylvania Right to Know Act
Rhode Island	**PUBLIC**	Rhode Island Access to Public Records Act
South Carolina	**PUBLIC**	South Carolina Freedom of Information Act
South Dakota	PRIVATE	South Dakota Sunshine Law
Tennessee	**PUBLIC**	Tennessee Open Records Act
Texas	**PUBLIC**[4]	Texas Public Information Act
Utah	PRIVATE	Utah Government Records Access and Mgmt Act
Virginia	**PUBLIC**[5]	Virginia Freedom of Information Act
Washington	PRIVATE	Washington Public Records Act
West Virginia	**PUBLIC**	West Virginia Freedom of Information Act
Wisconsin	PRIVATE	Wisconsin Open Records Law
Wyoming	PRIVATE	Wyoming Sunshine Law

Chapter Nineteen
Communications Security: Email

Ladar Levinson, founder of the now-defunct Lavabit encrypted email service once stated "If you knew what I do about email, you probably wouldn't use it". Email is not as private as many of us have long assumed it to be. For decades, the assumption around email is that it is essentially a private communication between two parties. The analogy that is commonly drawn is that email should be like a letter mailed between two parties: the email is sealed by the sender and opened by the recipient with the understanding that any given email could be selectively opened by a third party. This myth has largely been dispelled by the Snowden leaks, and many average individuals are now much more aware of the lack of privacy inherent in email communication. In reality, email is less like a letter sealed in an envelope and more like a postcard that anyone along the way can read.

Email is accessible to many parties between the recipient and the sender, including law enforcement and intelligence agencies, the email service provider, and malicious third-parties. For all intents and purposes, email should be treated by the sender as a matter of public record. We assume as a matter of course that every email sent through a mainstream provider is read by someone other than the intended recipient (or at least scanned by several computers). As a result, we are very hesitant to send anything via these channels that we would not wish to read alongside our names in the news.

There are two basic categories of "secure" email. The first is what most people typically think of when they imagine email encryption: emails that are encrypted end-to-end between the sender and recipient and are not accessible by the mail provider. This is what we consider to be the safest and most secure form of encrypted email, even though this form of email is typically more complicated to use. We call this category "End-to-End Encrypted Email". The second category of email encryption is less secure; the emails themselves are not necessarily encrypted end-to-end. All emails stored with such a service, including those in the inbox, sent, draft, and trash folders, are stored encrypted on the provider's servers. They are not "scraped" for marketable data and their contents are safer from prying eyes. We refer to this category of email as "Securely Stored Email".

End-to-End Encrypted Email Options

One of the huge problems with encryption for email is the problem of key exchange. It would be simple to encrypt a file with VeraCrypt or 7-Zip and email it to another party, but it would be difficult to exchange the password for that file without sending it unencrypted in some form or fashion. Sending the password in plaintext (whether through email, text message, voice phone call, snail mail, etc.) would leave it vulnerable to interception and compromise the integrity of the entire system. At best, it leaves all participants with some level of doubt about the security of the system. Meeting in person to exchange the key would perhaps be the safest method of symmetric key exchange. This may not be possible and is rarely feasible. Because of the problem of key exchange, email encryption typically relies on a wholly different encryption model than that used to protect data-at-rest. This encryption model is known as asymmetric or public-key encryption.

Asymmetric encryption solves this problem rather elegantly by using a pair of keys. Instead of a single key that is used to both encrypt and decrypt, such as the symmetric keys used by VeraCrypt, an asymmetric keypair consists of a public key and a private key. Each has a separate and distinct purpose. The public key is used to encrypt messages to the recipient, and the private key is used to decrypt the same message. For example, if Michael wanted to send an encrypted email to Justin he would download Justin's public key. Michael would then use Justin's public key to encrypt the message to Justin. When Justin receives the email he must have his own private key and password to decrypt the message. When Justin responds to Michael, he will encrypt his response using Michael's public key. The response can only be decrypted using Michael's private key.

Because the public key can only be used for encryption, it is not secret. Public keys can be posted on websites and blogs, hosted on purpose-built key servers, or emailed freely. The interception of the public key makes no difference as it cannot be used to decrypt anything. The private key, on the other hand, is secret and should be very closely guarded. The private key can be used to decrypt anything encrypted with the public key. The compromise of a private key means the compromise of all your incoming messages that were encrypted with your public key, including all historical communications until you revoke it with a revocation certificate.

This system of asymmetric encryption has been around for many years. Unfortunately, it has traditionally been unwieldy and difficult to implement. Until recently, email encryption has required a complicated process to set up and use. While this was not necessarily a problem for the security conscious and technically literate, it was difficult to convince anyone else to implement encryption. Email encryption requires participation on the part of both sender and recipient. For years, email encryption was implemented only by very few security-conscious users. Fortunately, a new breed of encrypted email providers has proliferated. These new providers automate much of the encryption process.

We believe that the automation of encryption is important. One of the most commonly used forms of encryption for internet traffic is the HTTPS protocol. It is so commonly used because it is transparent to the user and requires no technical skill or effort on the part of the user. It just happens in the background and the overwhelming majority of internet users don't even notice it. The easier encryption is to use, the greater the number of people that will actually use it. Our favorite among these new providers that are leading the way in automating email encryption is ProtonMail.

ProtonMail: At the time of this writing, ProtonMail is still in beta but looks extremely promising. ProtonMail is a new service that automates much of the process of asymmetric key encryption and places strongly encrypted email within the reach of even average users and has a number of exciting features. The best of these is the one that is not even seen: strong PGP encryption between ProtonMail users for the body of the message and any attachments. Because all emails sent within the ProtonMail ecosystem are encrypted, ProtonMail cannot scrape emails for advertising or any other purpose.

When a user sets up a ProtonMail account, a keypair is generated for him or her and stored within ProtonMail. From that point, any email that is exchanged with another ProtonMail user is encrypted using these keypairs. ProtonMail still provides security against these keypairs being stolen by requiring the user keep two passwords. One of these passwords is the login password to the account and the other is required to use the private key and decrypt messages. The second password is used only once per login and the extra step is worth the added security. All messages that are stored on ProtonMail's servers are encrypted and accessible only with the decryption password.

The two-password system offers some advantages over competing providers. If a user loses both the login and decryption passwords, the account can be reset. All mail in the mailbox will be lost because it can no longer be decrypted. However, the user will still retain his or her email address. Tutanota, which is discussed later in this chapter, uses only a single password but has no access to it. This would result in total loss of the account and email address if you lose your password.

ProtonMail also provides the ability to set destruction time for messages from one hour up to six days, after which the message will be deleted from the inbox of both recipients and ProtonMail's servers. However, there is one slight issue with this. If the email is replied to, a copy of the message is saved in the "sent" folder of the original recipient. Like other ephemeral (i.e. temporary) messaging systems that we have discussed, ProtonMail and similar services are designed to be used with people you trust.

ProtonMail also allows you to encrypt emails to "outside" users, or users who do not possess a ProtonMail account. The recipient of such an email will receive a link that will allow him or her to decrypt the email with a pre-arranged password. However, this creates the problem of key exchange. ProtonMail offers some other security and privacy-related features including the ability to record login time and date information, and the IP address from which the event occurred. This allows users to verify that their account has not been accessed from an unknown IP address. These logs are stored within users' mailboxes and are not accessible without the decryption password. If you wish to turn them off, that is an option as well.

At the time of this writing, 1-GB ProtonMail accounts are free. Paid options offering additional features such as mobile applications, two-factor authentication, aliases, the ability to use custom domains, and additional storage will be available sometime in early 2016.

ProtonMail is available at **https://protonmail.ch**.

Tutanota: Tutanota is very similar to ProtonMail. It automates the PGP encryption process for both body and attachments of emails. It also offers many of the features found in ProtonMail, including the ability to encrypt attachments to outside users and set a self-destruct time on messages. Tutanota's cryptographic implementation is free and open source and open to independent audit. It also offers paid tiers that support aliases (numerous organic email addresses that forward to a single account), custom domains, and expanded storage options.

We both admit to a bias toward ProtonMail, though this is subject to change at a moment's notice as systems are upgraded or security vulnerabilities are discovered. This bias is for two primary reasons. First is the password issue. Tutanota does not have dual passwords. If you lose your password, you have also lost your account and your email address. The second is the lack of a search or the ability to store drafts in Tutanota. The absence of these features makes it unsuitable as a primary email provider.

Tutanota is still a far superior option for privacy and security over mainstream email providers and we do not discourage anyone from using it. Redundancy is good, and both of us have Tutanota accounts created and ready should a vulnerability be discovered in other systems and an immediate switch becomes necessary. For more information on Tutanota and to setup an account, visit **https://tutanota.com**.

Mailvelope: If you wish to implement this system manually, a new browser add-on called Mailvelope has greatly simplified the process of asymmetric encryption and puts email encryption within the grasp of casual users. Mailvelope is available for Chrome and Firefox and is fully integrated with Gmail, Microsoft, Yahoo and GMX email accounts. Once Mailvelope has been installed on your browser, clicking its icon will allow you to open its options. You must open these options and generate a keypair before using Mailvelope to encrypt your emails.

To generate a keypair, open the Mailvelope options. On the right side of the screen, select "Generate Key". Several fields will appear, the first being Name. Enter the name that you wish to have associated with that key. We generally recommend using the name that is on the email account you intend to use with the key because this name will be visible to others using the key. Next, enter the email address with which the key will most commonly be used. Though you can use this keypair with any email address you wish that information will also be available to recipients of your public key.

Below the email address field select "Advanced". This will give you the option to select your desired key length. The default key length is our preferred length of 4096-bit. If you are working with a legacy system and require a shorter key length, be warned that although 2048-bit keys are considered plenty strong by today's standards, computer power is constantly increasing and new attacks on encryption are constantly evolving. We always prefer to go with the strongest key possible. Generating a 4096-bit key requires slightly more time than generating a smaller key. In our opinion, this is time well spent. In practice, it is only a couple of minutes. The last field that must be completed before generating your keypair is the password field. You should use a very strong password for your keypair. Once you have selected a password it can never be changed. For this reason, we probably go overboard. The passwords for our keys are randomly generated and in excess of 100 characters but we have little concern that they will be broken. If you are using a password manager, this should be a painless step as the manager does all the work for you.

After you have generated your keypair, we recommend saving it to a secure location. Mailvelope stores your key ring, which is your personal keypair(s) and the public keys of everyone with whom you correspond, using Mailvelope in the local storage of the browser. If anyone has brief access to your computer in the decrypted state, they can access all of your keys, public and private. Because your keys are only stored here, if your system crashes and you have to rebuild, you will also have lost all your keys. Storing a copy locally in your encrypted file that you backup regularly will ensure that you don't lose them.

To save your keys, open Mailvelope options. Right above your Key Ring (the list of keys you possess) is a blue button labeled Export. Clicking this button will reveal a number of options including Display public key, Send public key by mail, Display private key, Display keypair, and Display all keys. To download your keypair, click on the Export button and select Display keypair, and then click Create file. Save this file in an encrypted location. When you have exchanged keys with others, use the Display all keys option to save all of their public keys. We recommend doing this each time you exchange keys with someone to ensure your database is up to date.

Once you have generated your keypair and saved it to an encrypted location on your hard drive, the next step is to share your public key with others and import theirs. To share your public key, you can copy it and paste it into the body of an email or download it as an .asc file that can be sent as an attachment. Regardless of which of these two methods you choose, be absolutely certain you are sending your public key only. Sending you private key once would compromise the integrity of all past and future communications using that keypair.

When you receive a public key from another person, Mailvelope will usually recognize it as such. Immediately upon opening the email, Mailvelope will superimpose a blue box with a key over the body of the email. Clicking this blue box will automatically import the key. If Mailvelope does not recognize it as a key, or if you receive it in some other manner, it can still be imported. First, copy the public key. Next, open Mailvelope options and click Import keys. Paste the key into the field provided, then click Submit. If the key is valid Mailvelope will recognize it and import it.

Once you and others with whom you intend to communicate have shared keys you are ready to send and receive encrypted emails. When you log into your Gmail, Hotmail, Yahoo or

GMX email account and click the "Compose" button to create a new email you will notice an icon in the composition window that looks like small envelope. Clicking this icon will open a new composition pane where you will type the content of your message. Typing it in this pane prevents the content of the message from being readable by the email provider.

When you have finished composing your message, click the "Encrypt" button in the lower right corner. A dialogue will appear with a drop-down menu allowing you to select the public key you wish to use to encrypt the message. Select the recipient's public key and click "Add". Next, click "OK" and the dialogue will disappear. Finally, click "Transfer" and the encrypted text will be transferred back to the mail provider's compose pane. Your message is now encrypted and ready to be sent.

When you receive an encrypted message, Mailvelope will recognize it as such. The message will appear superimposed with an envelope and a lock; your mouse pointer will look like a key when you hover over the message. Clicking this icon will prompt you to input your password. Entering the correct password will allow the message to be decrypted.

It is important to note that metadata about your communications is not encrypted. The email addresses with which you are communicating are visible, as are subject lines. For this reason, it is imperative not to place any sensitive details in the subject line. One major drawback of Mailvelope is that it currently does not support the encryption of attachments. Be aware that any attachments to an encrypted email will remain unencrypted. Mailvelope is free and open source and available through **https://www.mailvelope.com/**.

Full Manual Encryption Options: Mailvelope is not the sole option for manually encrypting email and despite our enthusiasm for ease in encryption there are reasons you may wish to go "old school". There are a number of other options available and we would be remiss if we did not mention them. As mentioned earlier in this chapter, ProtonMail offers free email accounts that are automatically encrypted using PGP (Pretty Good Privacy) and enjoy the tremendous benefit of requiring no working knowledge of public key encryption, and Mailvelope makes a good entry-level PGP solution. However, because both are in-browser crypto, both are vulnerable to Java exploits and other remote attacks against the browser. Further, neither of these options currently allow you to generate a revocation certificate. A revocation certificate allows the user to revoke his or her keypair. Upon revocation any historical or future messages encrypted with that keypair will no longer be accessible. By implementing manual PGP encryption users are given the opportunity to take email encryption out of the browser and enjoy the protection of a revocation certificate.

Probably the most prevalent and popular option for full-manual email encryption for years was and still is the Thunderbird/Enigmail/GPG combination. Thunderbird is nothing more than a desktop email client and is a product of Mozilla. Thunderbird performs like many other email clients (such as Outlook) and allows you to use the POP3 email protocol, which downloads your emails from the server to your device where you can access them at your leisure without an internet connection. Thunderbird is free and available for Windows, OS X, and Linux at **https://www.mozilla.org/en-US/thunderbird/**.

After installing Thunderbird, you will be prompted to set it up with an email address. Though we are firmly against the use of Gmail in almost all other scenarios, this would be an excellent use of Gmail: an email account that is for encrypted communications only. If all communications are encrypted, they cannot and will not be scraped for advertising data or other privacy-compromising purposes, and Gmail's security is absolutely top-notch. To set up the account you will be required to input your username, password and the email account's server details. If using Gmail with two-factor authentication you should generate an application-specific password for Thunderbird in your Gmail account's security settings. If you are using a mainstream provider like Gmail, Microsoft, or Yahoo, this information will be retrieved automatically.

You will also be given the option of IMAP (Internet Message Access Protocol) and POP3 (Post Office Protocol). While IMAP will allow you to view messages from anywhere on any device, POP3 will download these messages to your computer and delete them from the server (Gmail, for example). POP3 is the option we recommend. Even though we are only using this account for encrypted communications and they will persist on Google servers for some time (7-30 days), we still prefer to delete them as soon as possible. Be aware that if you have a large number of emails in the account you must also have space for them on your local storage device.

After you have added your primary email account or accounts (you can add as many accounts as you like to Thunderbird) you can now use it as your email client. You no longer need to go to Gmail's website and log into the account; instead, just open Thunderbird. Before you can begin encrypting emails you will need to take a couple more steps. The next is to download GPG (Gnu Privacy Guard). GPG is a software suite that, among other things, provides the encryption for this setup. GPG for Windows, Mac, and Linux is available through **https://www.gnupg.org/download/index.html**.

After you have installed GPG you will have to install an add-on to Thunderbird called Enigmail. Thunderbird add-ons are small programs that add additional functions like the add-ons we discussed for internet browsers. Enigmail is a Thunderbird add-on that allows Thunderbird to use the encryption provided by GPG. To install Enigmail, navigate to Thunderbird's menu icon in the upper right of the interface (the hamburger) and open the dropdown menu. Select Add-ons and search for "Enigmail".

After Thunderbird has been set up, GPG has been installed, and Enigmail has been added, you are almost ready to begin encrypting emails. Before you can send an encrypted email, however, you must generate a keypair. The Enigmail Setup Wizard will walk you through the process of generating a public and private key, as well as a revocation certificate. The revocation certificate can be used to render the encryption key invalid in the event the encryption key is compromised. After these steps are complete you can begin sharing your public key and sending and receiving encrypted mail.

A major benefit to this system over Mailvelope is the ability to encrypt attachments. Though technically sophisticated users will have no problems with it, a major drawback to this system is the time and effort it takes to learn it, set it up, and use it. We use this system and have for years, but have failed in convincing more than a handful of people to use it on a regular basis. We are much happier showing our friends Mailvelope (or better yet, ProtonMail) and much more successful at getting them to actually use it.

If you are interested in using this system rather than relying on Mailvelope, ProtonMail, or Tutanota, numerous tutorials are available online and we will not attempt to duplicate them here. Perhaps the best written tutorial we have found online is part of the Electronic Frontier Foundation's Surveillance Self Defense series of articles and is available at **https://ssd.eff.org/en/module/how-use-pgp-windows-pc**.

Securely Stored Email Options

The email services listed in this section will not encrypt your emails end-to-end. They will, however, store your emails in an encrypted state on their servers. Neither of these services will scrape your email content for advertising data, nor sell your information to anyone. Both of them offer features that make them appropriate for business- and power-users.

FastMail

FastMail is a very interesting email provider. With the exception of being free (it is not), FastMail is very comparable to Gmail in the rich set of features it offers. It also offers many features that Gmail does not. FastMail allows you to use custom, domain name-based emails, the integration of multiple email accounts, and it supports business users as well as individuals. One of the biggest benefits of FastMail is that although they offer many of the convenient features of Gmail, they monetize directly and do not scan your email content or build profiles about you. FastMail has a very transparent privacy policy, does not store deleted emails past one week (if configured), and does not sell user data to advertisers.

FastMail has a couple of authentication options. The Yubikey can also be used as the sole authentication token, allowing you to login from public computers without typing a password into the keyboard. The passcode is transmitted directly from the Yubikey. Though this service is not invulnerable it may be worth considering if you frequently use public computers to access your email account. This feature would totally bypass key loggers and allow you to login with at least some confidence that your credentials are safe (we still recommend against logging into personal accounts from computers that you do not physically control). The Yubikey can also be used as a second authentication factor for FastMail accounts. FastMail also supports two factor authentication through OATH TOTP (Google Authenticator/Authy).

Another incredibly interesting feature offered by FastMail is the ability to create and use aliases. These aliases are alternate email address that allow you to send and receive mail from without revealing your master email address/username. Aliases allow you to have multiple email addresses at your disposal.

There are two things additional to note about the security of FastMail. Because of these two simple reasons we are hesitant to fully and unreservedly recommend FastMail. The first is that passwords are capped at 50 characters. Though this may seem a very liberal limit it still causes some reluctance on our part; we generally prefer to use much longer passwords. The second security factor that gives us a great deal of pause is the two-factor authentication implementation. Though FastMail does allow TFA it does so in an odd fashion. To enable it you must first create a "master" account that is ONLY password protected. You may then create additional accounts that are protected with both a password and a second factor. We dislike this because the master account can bypass the second factor if compromised. To protect the master account, we recommend choosing a randomly-generated username for the master account, changing the password frequently, and never sending an email from this address. Instead, send emails only from an alias (or aliases). FastMail is available on a paid basis at **https://www.fastmail.com/**.

Kolab Now

Kolab is a Switzerland-based email service provider that has gained popularity as of late and markets heavily to privacy-minded users. Kolab is a paid subscription service. Because they monetize directly, Kolab does not scrape data to sell to marketing companies. Further, we like to use providers who advertise privacy as a selling point. If they are caught violating customer privacy their entire business model is in jeopardy which gives them very good incentive to do the right thing. Kolab Now supports both personal and business accounts. Business accounts are slightly more expensive but support custom domains and multiple users.

Just as Gmail is a tradeoff between security and privacy, so is Kolab. While Kolab offers excellent privacy, its security could be better. Kolab does not (at time of writing) offer two-factor authentication. For this reason, we strongly recommend using very long passwords (100+ characters) and changing them frequently. This minimizes the chances of your password being hacked and ensures that if it is it will only be good for a short period of time (though all the historical emails stored in the account would be compromised in the event of a breach). Kolab Now email is paid and available at **https://kolabnow.com/**.

Not Recommended

There are a large number of email providers that claim to be secure. In large part this is true; these services are almost certainly both more secure and private than mainstream email providers. On the other hand, most of these services have also given up their keys to the U.S. Government and/or created backdoors. Backdoors in cryptosystems that are only available to a single party are technically impossible. It is very likely such a backdoor is being exploited by other parties as well. Further, as we have mentioned elsewhere in this book, we have strong doubts about the U.S. Government's ability to protect its own secrets. For this reason, the possession of encryption keys by the US Government makes their security questionable. Though we are advocates against mass surveillance, our bigger fear is that the government will be hacked or otherwise lose control of these keys and compromise the security of all users.

We also highly recommend you shy away from proprietary cryptosystems. The systems we prefer and have mentioned here tend to use widely available, vetted PGP encryption, or other open-source cryptography. The systems that we recommend above, while not perfect, come very close. On the other hand, the systems we recommend *against* have backdoors or violate some basic principles such as those found on the EFF's Secure Messaging Scorecard. Insecure providers such as these include CryptoHaven, Hushmail, and StartMail. Stay away from them!

Designing Your System

So which one of these options do we use? Since there is not yet a "one-size-fits-all" email encryption solution we use a combination of some of the above to meet our needs. First, both authors maintain ProtonMail accounts and have set up accounts for most of their technically-challenged friends, family, and even a few business contacts. This ensures that almost all of their personal communications are end-to-end encrypted and stored encrypted on the provider's servers. Is it the strongest encryption available? No, but it is much stronger than the alternative of freely giving information to mainstream providers whose business model is data collection, and it is very easily implemented by anyone. Next, we both use full-manual encryption via Thunderbird/Enigmail/GPG. This *is* the strongest encryption available, but sets a very high technical literacy and patience bar that few are willing to take the time to learn. This setup is used with anyone with the know-how and patience, and is always used between us when extremely sensitive information must be emailed. Finally, both authors employ an unencrypted provider that offers secure storage. This account is used for business purposes where a custom domain must be used and where correspondents must use unencrypted corporate or government systems anyway.

This system is not perfect and requires that each check multiple email accounts throughout the day, but it is not overly onerous. To communicate directly with either of us via email you will need to implement one of the end-to-end encrypted email solutions.

Friend Don't Let Friends Use Gmail

When you send a message to an acquaintance, colleague, family member, friend, or lover who uses Gmail, even from your ultra secure, encrypted email account, you become a Gmail user. When you place data into the Google ecosystem, your data is collected and associated with your name, even if you do not have a Gmail account. The quote that we presented earlier by former Google CEO Eric Schmidt was not in reference to Gmail users. It was in reference to people who are not Gmail account-holders but sent email to Gmail accounts. Though we are picking on Gmail, the same can be said for Hotmail, Yahoo, and other mainstream email providers. The ones who do not monetize services directly or monetize primarily through hardware sales must make their money in some other way. This way is nearly always through advertising.

Gmail is an excellent product with excellent security, and even businesses rely on its powerful features. If there are individuals with whom you share intimate personal details, trade secrets, or other sensitive information, do not do so over Gmail if at all possible. It would be an extremely hard sell to convince many people to leave Gmail. How do you avoid using Gmail when others insist on it?

Our mutual friend Jason illustrates an extremely proactive and elegant solution to this problem and privacy advocates would do well to follow his example. Jason went to the trouble of setting up a ProtonMail account for every single member of his family. This took a great deal of time and dedication on his part; he had to request the accounts, set them up, and then distribute them to the appropriate family members. Once it was done, enforcing compliance took some more work. But now that his system is up and running nearly all of Jason's email traffic is not only out of Gmail, it is all also end-to-end encrypted. Jason even maintains several "shelf" ProtonMail accounts that he passes out to new acquaintances who do not yet have one.

One other word of warning: just because someone is using a custom domain does not mean he or she is NOT using Gmail. Both of us have, at one time or another hosted websites with custom email domains. These domains were administrated through Google Apps, meaning the email was all sent through Gmail, giving Google access to all of the content and metadata of those messages. Though you can see the user's true email provider by looking at the email's header, we recommend the following: do not send email to anyone who does not offer a provision for encrypting with PGP (whether through Mailvelope or manual PGP), or who does not have a FastMail, KolabNow, ProtonMail, or Tutanota email address.

CHAPTER TWENTY
COMMUNICATIONS SECURITY: VOICE AND TEXT

Protecting your personal voice and text communications is an incredibly important step in achieving true privacy. Though the thought of all of your voice and message traffic being intercepted may seem incredibly paranoid and unlikely, recent news articles have indicated that it certainly is not. Though metadata collection was the first privacy bombshell to burst, it did not end there. We advocate encrypting the maximum amount of voice and message traffic possible. Fortunately, encrypting voice and message traffic is a fairly simple affair. In most cases it requires nothing more than installing an app, modifying your own behavior, and that of the people with whom you talk and text.

Most mobile telephone calls that occur on LTE (Long Term Evolution) networks are already encrypted by default. In fact, LTE encryption is one of the most successful cryptography implementations ever in regards to user compliance. It is completely transparent and requires no user input whatsoever – it just happens. The problem with LTE encryption is that it has avowed backdoors for use by law enforcement, intelligence, and other government agencies. Unfortunately, due to the technical nature of "backdoors", this vulnerability is also available to anyone else able to discover and exploit it. Depending on your threat model, LTE encryption may be sufficient for your needs, but we strongly recommend implementing stronger, intact encryption protocols, even if no specific threat exists against you.

We also strongly encourage each reader of this work to convince as many friends, family, colleagues, clients, and anyone else to use these apps. When more of us use these products, we create noise for each other. If only one of us uses a particular encryption product, it is easy to single that user out and massive amounts of resources can be dedicated to exploiting that user's communications. When we all encrypt as much of our communications as possible, surveillance must become targeted again, and a good deal of our privacy is restored. We also believe that we can reach a point where these apps are "mainstream" and not considered uncommon or different, even among "common" users. So please, convince others to use these apps.

Most of the applications listed here are produced by security-focused companies and do not collect data about their users beyond what is necessary to create accounts or process financial transactions. This chapter will discuss products that will replace your plaintext voice and texting apps. We will also discuss some native iOS apps that are already encrypted that you may not be aware of. Finally, we will discuss an application that can replace instant-messaging style apps.

All of the applications here utilize your device's data or Wi-Fi connection rather than your service provider's calling minutes or texting plan. This has the benefit of reducing the data your wireless service provider is able to collect about your calling and messaging habits by cutting them out of the loop completely. It also allows you to use your device even when you do not have cellular service as long as you have a Wi-Fi connection. Depending on your service provider, coverage plan, and your personal habits, you may be able to reduce your phone's calling and texting plan and send the majority of your calls and texts from your home's Wi-Fi. With the exception of iMessage and FaceTime, all of the applications mentioned here are supported by both Android and iOS.

Convincing Others to Use Encryption

Since encrypting your communications requires participation from both ends of the call or text, it is essential that you get others "on board". Both of us have spent some time getting our friends and family into these cryptosystems and now the vast majority of our personal and professional communications are encrypted. How do we convince others to participate? Both of us have a fairly successful strategy for getting others to use these apps, even if they care little about privacy. Though there is no single answer for getting everyone to use encryption, we have found a combination of techniques that works fairly well.

- **Meeting New People**: When we meet someone with whom we exchange contact information we give them several encrypted options and tell them to get in touch via "one of these". If they are truly motivated they will typically take the necessary steps.

- **Friends and Family**: Though this may sound a bit cold-hearted, we simply refuse to respond to others who will not use encrypted communications. This is usually all it takes to get friends and family to migrate to these options.

- **Misdirection**: On occasion we have attempted to convince someone to migrate to an encryption program and are met with either boredom ("Here he goes again"), laziness ("That stuff is too hard for me"), or outright hostility ("You mean I have to install another app? Why can't I just text you like a normal person?"). We have found that some very subtle misdirection can help convince these individuals to use encryption products. For example, Justin recently visited a foreign country for work. He told one resistant individual, "Download this app. I won't have cell service but it works over Wi-Fi, so we can still talk". She downloaded the application and they used it during the entirety of the trip. Once the trip was over he simply kept communicating with her on it rather than reverting to more conventional texting. By pointing out that the app was useful for talking over Wi-Fi, he focused on a feature of the app that was beneficial to her. If you are not planning a trip out of the country, you can use the same technique by telling your friends and family that you have poor cellular reception at your home.

- **One More Thing**: You should choose one or two apps that have a strong security track record and with which you are reasonably satisfied, and stick with them. If you are attempting to convince non-technical or disinterested individuals to download a new app every couple of months, they will quickly become frustrated and lose interest. This is not to suggest that you cannot or should not migrate to something new if a serious vulnerability is uncovered, but changing for the sake of change will not help your cause of influencing the disinterested.

Over time, some infrequent correspondents may simply forget to use the encrypted option. If this is the case, we respond to the original text or message on the encrypted app. This is all the reminder that is typically necessary. If the incoming communication is a phone call, it will be declined and we will immediately return the call from the encrypted option. Within a few weeks you can have most of your circle using encrypted communications options. Besides encrypting all of your personal communications, this also has an added benefit. We have found that when most people install an encrypted communication app they are usually pleasantly surprised to see that a few other friends are already on there, and will sometimes immediately send their friend a text message on it. This is good for us all. As more people use these programs, the more ubiquitous and mainstream they will become. This makes it easier for us to convince others to use them and creates more "noise" for us all.

Signal

Signal Private Messenger is a free application, and our new favorite encrypted communication solution. Signal supports both voice calls and text messaging in a single app and is incredibly easy to use and convince others to use. There is no complicated setup, no username or password to create and remember, the app is incredibly intuitive, and resembles native phone and texting applications. Signal uses your phone's Wi-Fi or data connection. Signal has replaced the legacy apps RedPhone and TextSecure for Android and merged them into a single platform. To use Signal, simply install the application. You will be prompted to enter your telephone number for verification. The app will verify the number by sending you a code that you must enter into the application. No other personal information is required or requested.

If you allow Signal to access your contacts, it will identify the ones who have Signal installed. There is one slight downside to the way Signal identifies its users. In order for others to contact you via Signal they must have the telephone number you used to register the app in their contacts. This requires that you give out this number to others with whom you wish to use Signal. For this reason, we recommend setting up a Google Voice number that is used only for Signal, and giving that number out to friends, family, and business contacts that are likely to use Signal (or be persuaded to in the future). Even though the Signal app warns that Google Voice numbers are not supported for verification we have had multiple successes using Google Voice for this purpose. This is not a guarantee, but if you are denied we recommend that you keep trying. If you are not planning to change your number or transition to Google Voice, then you should register Signal with your existing number.

Signal's interface is almost disconcertingly simple. Tapping the "+" icon in the upper right of the interface is a list of your contacts who have Signal installed. Tapping one of these contacts will open a new message to that contact. From there you can send a text message, photo, video, or tap the handset icon to initiate a voice call. In the search bar on this screen you may input a telephone number, which Signal will then search to see if the number has the app installed. Once a call is initiated a more typical phone interface is displayed with some standard phone options to mute the call or use the phone's speaker.

The call interface will also display two random words; the words displayed will change with each phone call but should match on both handsets involved in the call. These words are used to ensure the call is not being tampered with by a man-in-the-middle. If an attacker were to successfully get in the middle of a call each handset would establish a key with the attacker rather than the corresponding handset, and each phone would display different authentication words. We recommend always validating these words at the beginning of each conversation made over Signal, and especially before engaging in sensitive communications.

The messaging portion of the application is likewise incredibly simple. Messages are composed and sent like they are in any other messaging application, and attaching a file is as simple as tapping the paperclip icon beside the compose pane. Signal also supports group messaging. At the time of this writing Signal also offers a beta desktop version. This version interfaces with the user's handset to display synchronized messages across all devices and allows users to make voice calls and send instant messages from a desktop computer.

Signal does not offer anonymity. Because it uses your mobile number to register you will be associated with the account. Even if you use an anonymous number to register the account consider the contacts to whom you provide this number. If they put you in their Android phone's contact list by your full name this information will likely be transmitted to Google and dozens of other apps on their device. Signal also does not obscure your metadata: who you talk to, when you talk to them, and for how long. It merely protects the content of the message.

Signal is one of the best privacy-enhancing applications available (especially considering its cost) and we strongly encourage its use. Signal is funded by donations and grants, and much of the work in developing and maintaining the app is done by volunteers. Signal is free and available in the App Store and on Google Play, and at the time of this writing a desktop version of the application is in beta. For more information on Signal visit at their website **https://whispersystems.org/blog/signal/**.

A Word of Warning on Message Ephemerality

Message ephemerality has been sold to us as a way to prevent others from having permanent access to our messages. Snapchat was the first widely-publicized ephemeral messaging system and became popular with adolescents who could "sext" each other, supposedly without the recipient being able to create a permanent copy of the image. Snapchat told users that the image would be available for a short period of time, after which it would be deleted. We were to learn only later that messages truly weren't deleted, and ephemeral messaging is flawed.

You should never send a message to anyone that you would not trust to have permanent access to that message. These systems should only be used with those you trust and you should only transmit content you trust in your recipient's possession. There are various ways the message could be captured and stored by the recipient. The messaging system could be deleting images or texts insecurely and they could persist on the device, as was the case with Snapchat. On an iOS device the user could take a screenshot (iOS developers are prohibited from disabling screenshots), as could any desktop-environment user of the app. And on any device the recipient could take a photo of his or her screen with another camera. So what is the value of ephemerality?

The real benefit of ephemerality is this: if an attacker has access to your device he or she will not recover months' worth of communications. Unlike standard text messaging applications which may store years of data, ephemeral messaging systems rarely allow you to store messages longer than a week. Understanding the limitations of these messaging systems is important to their correct employment.

Silent Phone

Silent Phone is probably one of the most widely publicized encrypted voice applications in existence. Its parent company, Silent Circle, is well-known in security and privacy circles for their custom BlackPhone handset. Fortunately for privacy-minded users, the Silent Phone app that affords the BlackPhone its encrypted calling capability is also available on Android and iOS handsets. The app is free to download, but you must pay for a subscription before you can use it. The legacy app Silent Text was recently merged into Silent Phone so users now have access to encrypted phone calls and messaging within a single app. Unfortunately, we have found little use for the messaging function since it can only be used between Silent Circle subscribers. We have had very little success convincing anyone to add $10 per month or more to their phone bill.

Silent Circle offers several subscription plans. The first and least expensive at $10/month is called "Silent Suite". Silent Suite allows you unlimited voice and text communication with other Silent Circle users, and rather than a phone number you receive a username. For Silent Suite to be of much use at least some of your contacts must use it, too, since it can only be used to contact other Silent Circle users. When using Silent Circle with other Silent Circle users, calls and texts are placed from username-to-username. We have found that for a minor increase in cost the Silent World offerings are much more flexible.

Silent World: Silent Circle's Silent World (formerly known as Out-Circle Access) offerings permit you to call landline and mobile numbers, not just other Silent Circle subscribers. Silent World also gives you a telephone number that allows you to receive incoming calls from any landline or mobile number. While the usefulness of subscriber-to-subscriber calling is dubious for our purposes, we really like Silent World. Now we have a new incoming and outgoing phone number that works in most countries.

The other major benefit of this number is encryption. When you place a call with Silent Phone using this plan it first goes to a Silent Circle server where an encrypted connection is established. Traffic between the server and the person you are calling is not encrypted so this is not an ideal model, but it does ensure that if you are within range of a cell site simulator your communications will not be intercepted in plaintext. Silent World plans are offered in increments of 100, 250, 500, and 1,000 minutes, and incoming calls are free with all plans. These plans begin at $15 per month. There are two minor downsides to using Silent Phone as your primary number. First, it does not accept voicemail, nor can it receive text messages, except from other Silent Circle users. To prevent others from attempting to send texts to this number we typically list it as a landline.

The call quality on this app, whether calling another subscriber or using Silent World, is excellent. Silent Phone can be used on your cellular data plan or over a Wi-Fi connection. Silent Phone also offers the ability to video chat and has all of the standard phone functions (mute, speaker, etc.). The app is available in the App Store and on Google Play. To subscribe to Silent Circle, navigate to Silent Circle's website at **https://silentcircle.com**. We have absolutely no financial interest in Silent Circle or the sale of Silent World subscriptions.

Wickr

Wickr is a free app that, in addition to being available for both iOS and Android, can also be used as a desktop messaging application on Windows, Mac OS X, and Linux operating systems. After downloading the Wickr app to your device you must choose a username and create a password. Wickr asks you for no personal information whatsoever during setup. Once the username is set up users can message each other through the very intuitive interface. Wickr can also be used to securely send pictures, videos, voice messages, and attachments from Dropbox and Google Drive. According to the company's privacy policy Wickr messages are only stored on the Wickr server in an encrypted state, and then they are only stored until the message has been delivered, after which they are erased from the servers.

Wickr is considered an ephemeral messaging service because your messages are deleted from both the sender and recipient's devices at a set interval of your choosing (see the section on Default Destruction below). You should be aware, however, that iOS users do have the ability to take screenshots of your text messages and photos, and anyone using the app in a desktop environment can take a screenshot. Wickr has found an inventive solution to this. When someone takes a screenshot in iOS everyone in the conversation is alerted to it and receives a copy of the screenshot. It is not a perfect solution but as Wickr points out, the app is intended to be used with people you trust. Also remember that if a user is on a desktop computer no screenshot protection exists.

The security of Wickr is incredibly good. When you send a message via Wickr it is encrypted locally on your device, with a unique, randomly-generated, asymmetric key for each and every message. When the message is sent the key is destroyed. The message is encrypted in transit to the recipient and decrypted locally on his or her device only where it is then forensically destroyed upon expiration. All data-at-rest and data-in-motion are encrypted with AES-256 and as Wickr's website puts it, "your messages are encrypted and secured during their entire lifespan". Wickr is very security- and privacy-focused and offers a number of settings to allow you to customize the app to your security needs.

Account: The Account setting displays your Wickr ID and allows you to terminate the account. This will completely delete the account and all messages and contacts contained within. This screen will also show you the devices that have connected to your account, allowing you to suspend a device if it is lost or stolen, or if you didn't log in from that device.

ID Connections and Friend Finder: Through ID Connections you can allow your contacts to see that you are on Wickr. You can assign phone numbers and email addresses; anyone with your phone number or email address in their contacts can see that you have Wickr, view your username, and message you. This can leak information about you, but if you want your friends to be able to locate you on Wickr this may be beneficial. Wickr only has access to encrypted representations of your contacts, and no access to the unencrypted versions, so you will not leak your friends' information. Since they do not know who your contacts are, they will never sell your information, and do not send invitations to your contacts. This is also spelled out in their privacy policy.

Secure Shredder: This setting is a deletion function that can wipe the free space on your device and make deleted items unrecoverable.

Auto Logout: This allows you to choose the interval that the Wickr application will stay open before requiring the password to unlock. You may choose to never lock the application (not recommended) or choose an interval between five seconds and eight hours.

Block List: You may block users from contacting you on this screen. Alternatively, you may choose to whitelist users, only allowing individuals you trust to message you while simultaneously disallowing everyone else.

Default Destruction: From this screen you can choose the length of time a message is displayed (after it is opened) before it is deleted. Destruction may be between three seconds and six days, and each conversation may be customized with a unique destruction interval. Unique destruction intervals are useful; if you wish to send an extraordinarily sensitive message you may likely choose to make the destruction interval very short. On the other hand, if you are sending directions, lists, or other very detailed information you may choose a much longer destruction interval than you normally would.

There are two other features that Wickr offers that are worth mentioning. The first is the ability to verify your contacts' identities through a process known as key verification. When you execute this process you and a correspondent exchange unique cryptographic keys and import them. Wickr will use these keys in the future to ensure that messages are being sent from a trusted device. To initiate this process, go to the Friends tab. Tap the icon for the friend you wish to verify. A new dialogue will appear with several options (Favorite, Block, Delete, and Advanced). Tap on the Advanced icon (which looks like a key), then select Send Verification Request. The recipient can verify him or herself by sending a key via text message or email, or through a video message (video being the most certain) and you will be prompted to do the same in return. Verified contacts appear with green icons, contacts to whom you have sent a verification key appear with a yellow icon, and unverified contacts have a red icon.

The other feature worth mentioning is Wickr's camera access. When you take a photograph through Wickr on your mobile device (which requires allowing it access to the camera setting) the photograph is only saved in Wickr. This means it will not show up in the phone's native photos application and is not stored on the device. This is a terrific feature for taking and transmitting sensitive photos without fear that they will be discovered forensically on your device or inadvertently uploaded to Google Drive, iCloud, or some other service. Wickr is free and available in the App Store and through Google Play. For more information on Wickr visit **https://wickr.com**.

iMessage and FaceTime

If you are an iOS user, you enjoy a tremendous benefit over non-iOS users, at least when messaging other iOS devices. Both FaceTime and iMessage are strongly encrypted by default. FaceTime is Apple's voice- and video-telephony application that allows you to conduct voice calls and video chats from your iOS device or OS X computer. iMessage uses neither the SMS nor MMS protocols. Messages are transmitted over cellular data or Wi-Fi. This offers the benefit of being able to use iMessage on various platforms that do not have cellular data plans such as iPods, iPads, and MacBooks. Further, using iMessage does not create a record of your messages with your wireless service provider, limiting the amount of metadata they have access to (though Apple certainly has access to it). iMessage is strongly encrypted using AES encryption, greatly minimizing the risk of your messages being readable if they are intercepted.

Like Signal, Silent Phone, and Wickr, Apple uses asymmetric encryption to encrypt messages between iOS devices. When you initially open the iMessage application an RSA-1280 bit keypair is created and public keys are stored on Apple's key server. The keys are then encrypted using AES. The presence of your public key on the key server is how iPhones identify each other as capable of sending and receiving iMessages. When you send a message to another iMessage user your keypair is used to encrypt the communication, it can only be opened by your device and any recipient's devices. Your keypair is tied to your iCloud account. This is how a single user can access the same messages across all of his or her devices.

One downside of iMessage is that it can only be used between two iOS or Mac users. If your friend has an Android or Windows phone, your messages to him or her will be sent via unencrypted SMS or MMS. Another major downside of iMessage is that Apple's encryption is not open to an independent audit. Still, we prefer this over totally unencrypted communications or communications with avowed backdoors.

Cryptocat

Cryptocat is a simple instant messaging system that allows extremely secure chat conversations between multiple parties. Cryptocat was available as an add-on for Chrome, Firefox, Opera, and Safari, and as an app for Mac for use in the desktop environment. Currently, Cryptocat is offline and being re-worked, but we like it so much still feel it is important to include it in this volume. Cryptocat differs from other applications we have discussed here because it is not used in the same way that "text" messaging applications are used and is optimized to be friendlier for IM-style communications. Cryptocat is intended to be a secure alternative to services like Google Chat and Yahoo Messenger, while being more accessible to non-technical users than services like Pidgin Off-The-Record Messenger.

Cryptocat is extremely simple to use. After installing the app, you must coordinate a chat with another user. First, you and the person with whom you wish to chat must agree on a conversation name. The conversation name should be considered sensitive information since anyone who has it could join the conversation. There are various ways you could arrange the names of your conversations to make them obscure such as creating a password using diceware (as discussed in Chapter 6), and transmitting the conversation name to all participants through another secure medium like Signal.

Next, you must choose a nickname. The nickname can be anything you wish, but we recommend choosing nicknames that each participant will recognize. Each user can see the nickname of everyone who joins the conversation, so your username should be distinctive but not something that an imposter could guess. After you have settled on a conversation name and nicknames, input them into the appropriate fields and click the connect button. Your conversation will be created. When the other participant joins you can begin your conversation. Your communications will be end-to-end encrypted using the Off-The-Record (OTR) protocol and only stored locally on your devices.

Cryptocat does not require that you set up an account, username, or password, or any other information that may be used to identify you. You must only know the conversation name and the nicknames of the other participants, and these elements can (and should) change with each new conversation. When you are finished with your conversation simply disconnect from it. All content and logs of the conversation (which are only stored locally on participating devices) will be deleted. Cryptocat does not conceal or obscure your IP address, so you should use it with a VPN when possible. At the time of this writing Cryptocat is not currently available but it is being rewritten. For more information on the status of Cryptocat visit **https://crypto.cat/**.

Not Recommended

In this chapter we have recommended only a tiny percentage of messaging apps, many of which claim to provide encryption, privacy, and security. There are a number of messaging apps on the market that advertise themselves as ephemeral or secure. Unfortunately, many of them are not. Various apps of this type are on the market and new ones seem to arrive each month. Before trusting an ephemeral messaging application with your sensitive communication and media, do your due diligence. We trust apps like Signal and Silent Text because they have been thoroughly vetted. They are open to independent review and have undergone a recent code audit. When in doubt, check with a reputable watchdog like the Electronic Frontier Foundation's Secure Messaging Scorecard which is available at **https://www.eff.org/secure-messaging-scorecard**.

The Secure Messaging Scorecard gives indicators to how secure a given messaging system is based on seven factors, and does so in an easy green check mark/red caution sign format. The factors considered on the Secure Messaging Scorecard are:

- **Is the message encrypted in transit?** This is important for obvious reasons.

- **Is the message encrypted in a manner that prevents the provider from seeing it?** It is entirely possible for a provider to encrypt your messages in transit (protecting them from local attacks against you) while still leaving them the ability to view the messages. This compromises security because if they can access the messages, they can turn them over to law enforcement and intelligence agencies, they are accessible to rogue employees, and the company itself may be hacked and your information leaked. Further, the very presence of a backdoor is a security concern because it may be used by an actor other than the provider.

- **Can you verify contacts' identities**? This protects you from having a conversation with an imposter who is posing as the intended recipient and revealing sensitive information.

- **Are past communications secure if your keys are stolen?** This is possible in some systems, but not possible in others. Encrypted email using typical public key encryption is an example of a system where the compromise of your keys could lead to the compromise of historical communications.

- **Is the code open to independent review?** Closed cryptosystems that are not open to independent review are less trusted than systems that are open to review. If the code is not open to review, users must blindly trust that the provider is following through on any security claims that are made.

- **Is security design properly implemented?** Self-explanatory.

- **Has there been any recent code audit?** Code audits are necessary to validate the implementation, and are only possible when the code is open to independent review. Ideally, a code audit would occur each time an update was made to a secure messaging application, but this is not always feasible due to the time and expense involved. When possible, select programs that have undergone a recent code audit.

We will not repeat the results of this scorecard here, but we will encourage you to take a look at it. Using this scorecard, you should take a look at any messaging systems you currently use. If you find that the ones you currently use are not up to your security standard, consider switching (and getting your friends to switch) to ones that do. There are quite a few messaging systems out there that are very secure, including some that we have not previously mentioned here including Chatsecure/Orbot, SureSpot, Telegram (when using "secret chats"), and Threema.

Why does this all matter?

You may be reading at this point and questioning our level of paranoia. Do we believe that spies are listening to our telephone conversations from a van outside of our homes? No. Do we think that cellular provider employees are reading our text messages as we send them? No. Are either of these possible? Absolutely. We believe that our obligation to defend our privacy extends beyond encrypted email. Many of you send and receive more text messages than emails on a daily basis. We would like to present four specific scenarios that should justify our demand for encrypted text and voice communications.

We give cellular providers unlimited access to our telephone calls and text messages transmitted over their networks. The vast majority of these communications are never viewed and the metadata is stored forever. However, a rogue employee can absolutely intercept cellular records including text message content. While the chances of this happening are low, there is always the possibility. We are confident that these abuses happen daily. By only using secure solutions, you take the content away from the cellular provider and thereby eliminate that attack surface.

Several reputable sources have documented the government's access to cellular metadata and content. While we support the desire to be safe from terrorism, we do not want our content to be part of the mass collection. We have observed mass surveillance fail at protecting us from attacks. We do not believe that the NSA is specifically watching our daily communications and doubt that they have any interest in what we say. However, what happens when the government is hacked? The storage of our personal content could be compromised. If that sounds fictional, please research the Office of Personnel Management (OPM) hack where every background investigation of every person with a government clearance was released. We do not believe that the government is equipped to protect the data that they collect. Therefore, we will protect it ourselves.

We believe that it would be quite easy to be the victim of misrepresented data. While many might view their cellular records as innocent and unimportant, this data can be manipulated in order to view you in a bad light. We have witnessed attorneys, investigators, and employers scrutinize cellular records looking for any evidence that can support their claim. This might be a divorce attorney trying to prove that you were in contact with someone suspicious. It could include an investigator making the case that you were acting in conflict with a current contract. Your supervisor may decide to find proof that you were using a company device for personal purposes. They can all use your activities to support their personal agenda. You can stop them. While it may seem unimportant now, protecting your communications might be the most important step that you take before an unknown future incident.

Finally, we are concerned about inappropriate or incorrect court orders. Our government backgrounds should convince you that we support the prosecution of criminals. However, mistakes are made. There are several documented events where errors were present on court orders and incorrect houses were searched, telephones were monitored, and overall accounts were collected. Humans will always make mistakes. Encrypting your content will remove your personal communications from unnecessary scrutiny. While it is rare, government employees have abused their powers to monitor communications without probable cause. We believe that most readers would be surprised at the number of judges who do not thoroughly read the orders that they are signing. Why not just "opt-out" of the entire communications collection process?

CHAPTER TWENTY-ONE
SECURE FILE DELETION

Being able to securely delete files that are no longer wanted or needed is an important aspect of computer security. If your device is fully encrypted this is less of concern as no files, deleted or otherwise, will be recovered from your device as long as your password remains uncompromised. You may still desire to sanitize a computer prior to reselling, donating, gifting it, or trashing it, and if you do not have full-disk encryption thorough deletion is especially important. You may just prefer to know everything is gone once it has been deleted, as we do.

First, it is important to understand that there are two types of memory in a computer. The first and most commonly referenced is non-volatile and is technically referred to as "storage". This is the computer's hard drive and it contains data that is intended to be saved permanently. The other type of memory (which is correctly called "memory") is Random Access Memory (RAM). RAM is considered volatile memory, or memory that dissipates and is lost when the computer is shut down.

A computer's RAM is used to store temporary files, open programs, open files for use in on-the-fly encryption applications like TrueCrypt and VeraCrypt, run virtual machines, and a host of other things for which some short-term storage is needed. Fortunately, the data contained in RAM is typically unrecoverable within a few moments of the computer being shut down. Under certain conditions (typically very cold conditions) the information in RAM can be recovered hours later but this requires a very sophisticated (and expensive) attack. Because of this, we worry very little about what is stored temporarily in RAM unless facing very sophisticated adversaries such as nation-state actors. Under normal room temperatures, if you remain with your device for an hour after shut down, the chances of any data being recovered from it is vanishingly small.

We are much more concerned, however, with the security of the information that is stored on a computer's hard drive. The storage in a hard disk drive (HDD) is persistent by design – it is where files are saved and intended to be stored for hours, weeks, or years. Unfortunately, this information can also be difficult to get rid of when it is no longer needed or wanted. When using most operating systems the most common way of deleting a file is to select it and hit the Delete key which sends the file to the Recycle Bin or Trash. When the Recycle Bin or Trash is emptied the file is presumed to be gone forever.

Unfortunately, this does not actually remove the file from the hard drive. Deleting a file in this manner simply removes the information that the operating system uses to locate it. The operating system then allocates the space on the hard drive where the file resides as "free space". The file is still almost totally intact on the hard drive until it is overwritten with new information. Though it would not seem like it, it can take an extremely long time for the entire file to actually be overwritten. In the meantime, as long as the file remains intact it is easily recovered from your hard drive, even by a novice.

HDD vs. SSD: Before we move further into this discussion it is important to note that erasure techniques do not work as well when permanently removing individual files on solid-state drives (SSDs). SSDs store data in an entirely different manner than traditional spinning-disk HDDs, and in a way that does not lend itself to easy and effective overwriting of individual files. This is not to suggest that secure file deletion applications are entirely ineffective, but merely that they are less effective and will likely leave some percentage of any given file on the disk in recoverable state. While individual files are difficult to fully delete, a full wipe of SSDs will work as well as one conducted on a HDD. If you have a device with an SSD, full-disk encryption is your primary means of data erasure. Though we do not wish to downplay the importance of FDE for all computer users, it is especially important for SSD users.

Recuva (Windows)

Recuva is a freeware program for Windows computers that allows you to recover deleted files. Recuva is a very simple, user-friendly application that does a remarkably good job considering its cost. Why do we mention a file recovery application in a chapter devoted to ensuring your files are never recovered? We recommend running Recuva before running a secure file deletion software for two reasons. First, if you have been using your machine for a while you will likely be surprised to find all the previously deleted files that still reside on your hard drive. This can help underscore the need for secure methods of file deletion. Second, running Recuva can occasionally give you an indication as to whether or not you need to perform some of the steps listed below, like wiping your free space.

Recuva Warning

Only run Recuva on a computer that you personally own and on which you are the sole adult user. Running this program on a computer that you share with roommates, romantic partners, or co-workers may reveal information that they do not desire you to see, and that you almost certainly do not want to see. Both of us have personally witnessed (and experienced) some embarrassment when helping friends who have accidentally deleted data. As the desired file was being searched for plenty of others often surfaced (usually JPEGs) as the friend looked on in horror. Justin also used Recuva during his tour in Iraq to recover hundreds of compromising photos on public computers on military bases.

To use Recuva, install the application or download the portable version. Recuva must be run with Administrator privileges. If you are working from a user account (which you should be) you will have to log in as an administrator or right-click the application and select "Run as Administrator". After entering your Administrator password, you will be presented with the Recuva Wizard. Click Next, then select the radio buttons for the file types for which you wish to search. The most comprehensive of these, and the one we typically choose, is "All Files".

This is the most exhaustive search and will net the most results. Click Next again, then you will select a location to search. We recommend choosing the "In a specific location" option and selecting an entire hard drive. If you are doing a pre-assessment on your own computer this will most likely be your C drive. Click Next once more, and on the following screen check the "Enable deep scan" box, then click Start. This will begin the scan.

Recuva will now scan the selected location for files. This may take some time depending on how much free space is on your hard drive. Once the program finishes its work the results will be displayed and you will have the option to restore or delete each file. This should give you a good idea of your need (or lack thereof) to wipe free space with the programs discussed below. Recuva is free and available at **http://www.piriform.com/recuva**.

If your computer is subject to a true forensic attack the tools used will be much more sophisticated and capable than Recuva. First, a bit-by-bit copy of your entire hard drive will be made to preserve the original. With the fresh copy, each file will be carved from the hard drive and examined at the bit level. Even small fragments of files may reveal sensitive information under these conditions. If this attack fails to reveal any information, more sophisticated techniques may be used, such as a laboratory attack. During a laboratory attack your hard drive will be disassembled and examined under a forced electron microscope depending on your threat model and your adversary's capabilities. At this point it is important to make clear the following: if you are subject to such a forensic examination, you have probably made some very serious and very well-financed adversaries who may be able to retrieve the desired information through other avenues. Secure deletion may not save you. We still like to take a redundant approach to security, though, and feel much safer knowing that we have increased the difficulty of extracting files from our machines.

Secure File Deletion Basics

The surest way to get rid of unwanted files is known as "secure file deletion" or "data erasure". When a file is written to your hard drive, it is written as a series of ones and zeroes. These ones and zeroes are transcribed to the disk by flipping magnetic switches; one direction for "1", the other for "0". A secure deletion program will overwrite these files with a random series of ones and zeroes, obscuring the original information. Just as there are numerous encryption algorithms, there are also numerous overwrite patterns. Most of the programs we will discuss offer the ability to do a single pass of pseudorandom data, or one pass of randomly generated ones and zeroes. They will also offer much more complex algorithms, including a 3-pass, 7-pass, and the infamous Gutmann 35-pass. These more complex algorithms do not merely write 3, 7, or 35 passes of pseudorandom data. Rather, they work in intricate, well-defined patterns as shown in the chart below.

Name	Passes	Description
Single	1	One pass of pseudorandom data
DOD 5220.22-M (8-306. /E)	3	All 0s, all 1s, one pass pseudorandom data
RCMP TSSIT OPS-II	7	All 0s, all 1s, all 0s, all 1s, all 0s, all 1s, pseudorandom data
Schneier Method	7	All 1s, all 0s, five passes pseudorandom data
Gutmann Method	35	Passes 1 – 4: Pseudorandom data Pass 5: 01010101 01010101 Pass 6: 10101010 10101010 Pass 7: 10010010 10010010 Pass 8: 01001001 01001001 Pass 9: 00100100 00100100 Pass 10: 00000000 00000000 Pass 11: 00010001 00010001 Pass 12: 00100010 00100010 Pass 13: 00110011 00110011 Pass 14: 01000100 01000100 Pass 15: 01010101 01010101 Pass 16: 01100110 01100110 Pass 17: 01110111 01110111 Pass 18: 10001000 10001000 Pass 19: 10011001 10011001 Pass 20: 10101010 10101010 Pass 21: 10111011 10111011 Pass 22: 11001100 11001100 Pass 23: 11011101 11011101 Pass 24: 11101110 11101110 Pass 25: 11111111 11111111 Pass 26: 10010010 10010010 Pass 27: 01001001 01001001 Pass 28: 00100100 00100100 Pass 29: 01101101 01101101 Pass 30: 10110110 10110110 Pass 31: 11011011 11011011 Passes 32-35: Pseudorandom data

For most purposes, a single overwrite will be sufficient to make your data unrecoverable to all but the most sophisticated attacks, and it is very doubtful that more passes really make much of a difference. What is not a doubt is the time they take. For each pass the computer has to generate that same amount of data. For example, if you are overwriting one gigabyte of data with a 7-pass overwrite, the computer has to write 7 gigabytes of data to the hard drive. Not only does this take time, it also exerts wear and tear on the hard drive (which has a finite life cycle). For the vast majority of overwriting purposes, we rely on a single pass overwrite.

There are three other factors to consider when discussing file deletion and data remanence. They are cluster tips, alternate data streams (ADS) and MFT Free Space. Alternate data streams and MFT free space apply only to Windows computers. Cluster tips refer to small, unused sections of a "cluster". Files are stored on the hard drive in small units known as clusters and a file will usually take up more than one cluster. If a file takes up 5.3 clusters, the sixth cluster will have 0.7 (or 70%) free. This last 0.7 of a cluster is the cluster tip. This cluster tip may contain some sensitive, recoverable information from a previous file and should be overwritten along with the rest of the file. The erasure programs presented in this chapter allow the overwrite of cluster tips.

Alternate data streams exist only in Windows systems with the NFTS file structure. Alternate data streams are small "sidecar" files that accompany some original files. They frequently contain metadata about the file. For example, in Internet Explorer ADSs are used to store favicons in website shortcut files. Because of the information they may contain, ADSs should be deleted along with the original file. All of the deletion programs we will discuss for Windows below offer the ability to delete alternate data streams.

The Master File Table or MFT exists only in Windows systems with NFTS file structure which includes nearly all Windows systems. The MFT contains a huge array of metadata about every single file on your computer including file name, creation date, size, access permissions and other information. If you are securely deleting a file you will also want to securely erase any indictors of it from the MFT. The ability to wipe MFT free space ensures that any files that have been deleted insecurely and have left traces on the MFT will be cleaned up. All of the deletion programs we will discuss for Windows below offer the ability to wipe the free space on the Master File Table.

File-level encryption offers some defense against data recovery, too. Unfortunately, there are numerous data leaks in the Windows operating system. Anyone gaining access to your machine would very likely be able to recover scads of metadata, partial file fragments, registry entries, and other information that could be used to piece together your sensitive information. This is yet another reason we are so adamant about full-disk encryption.

Encryption-as-Erasure

As awareness of full disk encryption becomes more pervasive, the corporate world is taking notice. More and more companies are full-disk encrypting computers and FDE is being considered by some as a form of data erasure. The concept behind encryption-as-erasure is this: if a full-disk encrypted computer is lost nothing can be recovered from it, even under sophisticated attacks so the data has effectively been "erased". This logic is yet another reason we are such strong advocates for full-disk encryption. We still recommend taking pains to erase files securely, though, on the off chance that your encryption is compromised or your password is broken. As we mentioned previously in this chapter, if your hardware is equipped with a solid state drive rather than a hard disk drive, encryption-as-erasure is your most effective form of erasure.

Targeted File Deletion Utilities

Targeted file deletion is the selection of a file or set of files to be deleted. Targeted file deletion utilities allow you to delete the selected file and that file only, and do so quickly and easily.

Eraser (Windows)

Eraser is our preferred program for the targeted, secure deletion of selected files on Windows machines. When we use Windows machines, every file we delete is permanently and securely deleted with this application. Eraser is incredibly easy to use, offers a number of features, and does an excellent job of permanently deleting files. The first step after installation is opening Eraser and modifying the basic settings.

To modify the basic settings in Eraser open the application. The interface is very streamlined, with only three options: Erase Schedule, Settings, and Help. Click the Settings icon. The first item in the settings is the checkbox allowing Eraser to be integrated into Windows Explorer. This will ensure Eraser is available via the right-click context menu. The next section concerns the secure deletion settings. The dropdown menus for "Default file erasure method" and "Default drive erasure method" contain a comprehensive list of options, depending upon your desired overwrite method. By default, Eraser makes the default file erasure method the most secure option (Gutmann's 35-pass), while the default drive erasure method is a single pass (due to the length of time taken to wipe free space). Select the method of your choice.

Scrolling down Eraser will offer a number of other options. First ensure "Force lock files to be unlocked for erasure" is checked. This will reduce the incidence of errors when you attempt to erase a file that is locked. Eraser also allows you the option to replace deleted files with pre-selected files for the sake of "plausible deniability". Were anyone to forensically examine your computer there would be a file where the deleted file had previously been, making it less obvious that a file had ever been deleted from that location.

The Erase Schedule option allows you to plan erases at specific times: immediately, on restart, or recurring. A recurring erase would be an excellent means of cleaning your machine if you generate a large number of files in the same location(s) on a daily basis that all need to be deleted at the end of the day. You can designate a target (targets may be files, files in a folder, the recycle bin, unused disk space, or a drive or partition) that gets cleaned automatically. The task can be set to run at a specific time daily, weekly, or monthly, or only on certain days of the week, though extreme care should be taken when selecting files that will be deleted automatically. If Eraser is allowed to run in the background on startup its most useful functions can be accessed directly from the right-click context menu. This is incredibly convenient and the three functions you will use most commonly are:

Erase: This is the simplest yet most useful function in the application. The Erase function allows you to quickly delete a file. To access this function simply select the file, right click on it, and select "Eraser". Two options will appear: Erase and Secure Move. Select "Erase" and the file will be securely deleted with the overwrite algorithm you chose when setting up the program's settings.

Justin: "Think Before You Delete"

While I was writing Your Ultimate Security Guide: Windows 7 Edition I made a huge mistake. I should note at this point that you should exercise caution when using secure deletion software, especially when deleting multiple files at once. Once a file is gone it is gone for good and there is no recovering it. While writing the Windows book I had each chapter in a separate Microsoft Word document. After I transferred them all to a single document I used Eraser to get rid of the individual files. Unfortunately, there was one chapter that I had overlooked when copying the text over. Somewhat ironically, it was this chapter. I was unable to recover it and was forced to rewrite the entire chapter from scratch. Needless to say I do not wish this to happen to you.

Secure Move: Another useful feature of Eraser, Secure Move, allows you to copy a file to a new location and get rid of the original in a single function. When you select a file and choose "Secure Move", Eraser will ask you where you would like to put the new file. Navigate to that location, and click "OK". Eraser will then make a copy of the file in the new location and delete the old copy using the default overwrite algorithm.

Erase Unused Space: Eraser offers the option to erase the unused space on a drive. This ensures that if files have previously been deleted insecurely they will not remain recoverable. Cleaning unused space can take a very long time if you have a lot of it and depending on what overwrite algorithm you use. Not only is overwriting large amounts of space time consuming, but each additional overwrite also puts wear on your hard drive. We recommend doing this only occasionally. You may wish to wipe your free space once every few months to ensure you have not accidentally deleted a file insecurely, but if you are consistently deleting files securely with Eraser this is probably unnecessary.

Eraser is free and available at **http://eraser.heidi.ie/**.

Secure Empty Trash (OS X)

Many Mac computers have a very simple, very effective, pre-installed application called "Secure Empty Trash" that will securely overwrite files without the need for an additional third-party application. You can empty your trash securely on demand by clicking Finder in the top toolbar and selecting "Secure Empty Trash". This function will perform a seven-pass overwrite of the targeted files, permanently purging them from your system.

You can set up your Mac computer up to always delete files securely. To do so click on "Finder" and select "Preferences". Go to the Advanced tab where there is a check box labeled "Empty Trash securely". You will no longer have the option to merely "Empty Trash" in the Finder menu, only the option to "Secure Empty Trash". If your Mac computer does not have the Secure Empty Trash function do not worry. Due to the ineffectiveness of overwriting files on SSDs this feature is being phased out of Mac computers that have internal solid state drives.

Mac computers also come with the organic ability to wipe free space or format entire non-system HDD/SSDs or removable media. There are three overwrite options available including Zero Out (which writes all zeroes in all positions on the available space), a three-pass option, and a seven pass option. To access this feature open Applications>>Utilities>>Disk Utility. Once in Disk Utility select the drive on which you wish to wipe the free space or format totally and click the "Erase" tab at the top of the pane. If the drive is a system drive you will only be able to erase free space. If it is a non-system drive you can click "Erase Free Space" or "Security Options…" which will let you choose the overwrite algorithm for fully wiping the disk.

The options available in OS X's Finder and Disk Utility are sufficient for our needs and we do not add another dedicated file deletion software to the OS. It is nice to have these features built directly into the operating system because we don't have to go download the applications. Much more importantly having these applications on our machine does not look out of place and is not alerting because all Mac users have these same programs as well.

General System Cleaning Utilities

Utilities in this category allow you to clean a wide array of files that you probably don't even know exist. These tools serve the dual functions of ensuring that these files that probably contain some sensitive information are forensically removed, and that your system does not accumulate digital "clutter" that will slow it down over time.

CCleaner (Windows, OS X, Android)

This is one of our absolute favorite applications and one that we each use several times a day. CCleaner is not designed to be used for deleting an individual, targeted file but is a user-friendly general cleanup software. CCleaner (formerly known as "Crap Cleaner") cleans up much of the accumulated detritus of your operating system. As you use your computer numerous files are created by the OS. They record what files you open, what programs you use, your internet browsing history, recent places to which you navigate and a wealth of other information. Obviously, this information would be of large benefit to anyone conducting a forensic analysis of your machine and it is a good idea to keep these files to a minimum.

CCleaner will securely erase these files, but there is also a more practical reason to use CCleaner.

Many of these useless files that accumulate are created by the OS in an attempt to speed up your system. Pre-fetch data, for instance, is designed to help the computer "remember" which files you access frequently so it can bring them up quickly. While this works well in theory, over time the accumulation of all this data ends up slowing the system down (we have seen CCleaner remove as many as 8 gigabytes of data from exceptionally "dirty" systems). Because of the large volume of junk CCleaner removes running it regularly may also improve your system performance drastically, especially on aging machines or machines that have never been cleaned.

CCleaner is remarkably easy to use. First, download and install the program. Once the program is installed open it, and on the left side there are several icons: Cleaner, Registry (Windows only), Tools, and Options. Before actually cleaning your system click the Options icon. This will present a list of selections, the first of which is Settings. Click Settings next. The settings menu will contain the basic settings you can manipulate in CCleaner. Since this chapter is dedicated to data erasure we will focus on the Secure Deletion settings.

First, select the "Secure file deletion (slower)" radio button. On Windows machines this will open up some new options that are unavailable by default. They are Wipe Alternate Data Streams and Wipe Cluster Tips; both should be selected. Just above these options is a drop-down menu allowing you to select the number of desired overwrite passes. For CCleaner we typically select a single pass, or the Simple Overwrite option. If you desire a more thorough cleaning you may select from any of the other options, keeping in mind that more passes will increase the time taken to run the cleaning process of this application. Finally, (for Windows machines only), at the bottom of these settings select "Wipe MFT Free Space". The Master File Table (MFT) is a list of all the files on a Windows system. As files are deleted, space in the MFT becomes free. That space can contain information about files that were previously on the system, which will ensure these filenames are not recoverable from the MFT.

After changing these settings return to the main screen by clicking the Cleaner icon in the left pane. Just to the right of this pane there will be two tabs containing options that can be selected. These are the items that CCleaner will delete when it is run. The first tab is the operating system (Windows or Mac OS X). We recommend checking every option here with the exception of Wipe Free Space (where available) as we prefer wiping free space with Eraser as outlined above. Be forewarned that if you are storing passwords insecurely on your machine (in your browser, for instance) they will be lost. The second tab contains options that are specific to applications installed on your machine and we recommend selecting all of these options.

After modifying the erasure settings and selecting the items to be cleaned, CCleaner is now ready to go. In the lower right corner of the interface select "Run Cleaner". CCleaner will warn you that you are about to permanently delete files from your system. Check the "Don't show this message again" box and click "OK". If you have never run CCleaner before this may take a significant amount of time, up to several hours in extreme cases. We recommend running CCleaner daily and do so just before shutting our computers down each time. This ensures our systems are cleaned at least once every day. If we are working on certain tasks on the internet and do not wish to be tracked from one activity to the other, we will run CCleaner between sessions to ensure that no cookies were left behind from the previous session. By running CCleaner so frequently it never takes more than a few seconds to finish, and is totally worth the security and privacy it offers.

The other option for Windows that CCleaner offers is the Registry Cleaner. We recommend running this function occasionally. Each time you install, uninstall, or modify a program, random bits of that program are left behind in the registry. Not only does this create a trail of the programs that were once installed on your machine, over time it can slow your computer down, too. The registry cleaner is very simple and requires no changes in any settings. To use it click the "Registry" icon in the left pane. On the bottom of the interface click the "Scan for issues" button. This will scan the registry for stray bits of data. When this process has completed click the "Fix selected issues" button at lower right.

Before actually fixing the issues, CCleaner will as you if you want to back up changes to the registry. If this is the first time you have used this feature and have hundreds of issues to be fixed, backing up the registry in its current configuration is probably not a bad idea. If the cleaning creates instability in your system you can revert back to the pre-cleaning copy of the registry. Though it is incredibly unlikely you will experience any issues, it is a good idea to back up the registry just in case. Create this copy and save it in a location where it won't be forgotten (like your desktop or your primary encrypted volume). Next, click "Fix all selected issues". You may have to run this several times, as fixing the first set of issues may reveal others. Keep running this until there are no more issues to resolve. The CCleaner registry cleaner only needs to be run every month or after installing, uninstalling, updating, or otherwise modifying a program.

Not only will CCleaner keep your system clean, it will also keep your system running smoothly. CCleaner can also be used to remove programs from startup and has a very capable uninstaller through which you can uninstall unwanted programs. CCleaner is free and available at **http://www.piriform.com/ccleaner**.

CCEnhancer (Windows)

Though CCleaner is a very thorough program, CCEnhancer can greatly increase its abilities. Produced by a third party, CCEnhancer is a portable application (it does not need to be installed to work) that downloads a small file that it then imports to CCleaner. This file contains data needed for CCleaner to clean dozens of other programs and adds hundreds of options to programs cleaned natively by CCleaner.

To use CCEnhancer, download the application. When working in a Standard User account, right- click the CCEnhancer.exe file and select "Run as Administrator". Upon entering your Administrator password, the application will open. Click "Download Latest" and CCEnhancer will begin downloading the most updated .ini file. When it is finished you will be asked if you want to open CCleaner. When CCleaner opens, it will take a moment to "think" as it imports the options available in the .ini file. When CCleaner imports these options you will have hundreds of new application items that may be cleaned by CCleaner, as well as options to clean applications that are not cleaned by CCleaner alone.

CCEnhancer only needs to be run occasionally. After you have run it once, the expanded cleaning options will always be present in CCleaner. You should run it once a month in case there are any new additions to the .ini file. CCEnhancer is free and available at **https://singularlabs.com/software/ccenhancer/**.

BleachBit (Windows, Linux)

BleachBit is our preferred general system cleaning utility for Linux operating systems. BleachBit's interface is functionally very similar to that of CCleaner but is much more basic and streamlined. One thing we like about BleachBit is that each checkbox for items to be cleaned displays a description of what it does. After you have installed BleachBit or executed a portable version, check all of the applicable boxes. Above the list of items to be cleaned are two buttons: Preview and Clean. Preview will show you a detailed list of everything that is to be removed. Scrolling to the bottom of this list will show you the total number of files and the amount of disk space that will be freed. Clicking clean will prompt a pop-up warning that asks you to confirm your decision to permanently delete files.

BleachBit is also our preferred option for targeted file deletion on Linux machines (it works well on Windows, too). To target a file for deletion, go to the top right of the interface and click on "File". You will be presented with the option to Shred Files, Shred Folders, Wipe Free Space, Shred Settings and Quit, or Quit. While most of these options should be self-explanatory at this point in the chapter, Shred Settings and Quit is interesting because it allows you to obscure your use of BleachBit. This is perhaps most effective when the application is run in portable mode from a removable device. Clicking Edit from the top of the interface will allow you to open BleachBit's preferences, all of which are self-explanatory.

The downside of BleachBit is that it cleans fewer applications than does CCleaner. BleachBit only cleans the system, organic Windows features like Internet Explorer, third party browsers (Firefox and Google Chrome only), in addition to deep scanning for temporary files. It will not clean the same comprehensive list of applications that CCleaner will. Bleachbit also offers no option to use multiple overwrites; the BleachBit file shredder only does a single pass which is plenty, unless perhaps your device is undergoing a laboratory attack in which case overwriting probably will not help you anyway.

We also like this option for Windows because it will clean some items that CCleaner will not and Windows creates a tremendous amount of digital exhaust. On one basic machine running Windows 7 Professional we installed CCleaner and ran CCEnhancer. We ran CCleaner with every single option selected (except Wipe Free Space) and received a clean bill of health for CCleaner. We then opened Bleachbit and clicked "Preview" which still found 8,693 files totalling 1.48 GB to be deleted. However, when we ran BleachBit before we ran CCleaner, we still found that CCleaner cleaned some files that BleachBit did not. We recommend using both because they offer overlapping and independent capabilities. BleachBit is free and available at **bleachbit.sourceforge.net**.

Wickr (Android, iOS)

The secure messaging application Wickr also offers an option to wipe the free space on your device's storage. Though deleting solid state storage is difficult this is an excellent way to keep your device clean. To access this option open Wickr. Go into the settings and open "Secure shredder". The secure shredder has four options for automatic shredding: Never, Slow, Medium, and Fast. Wickr will automatically wipe your free space periodically. This wipe will occur more frequently if you select "Fast" and less frequently if you select "Slow". You can also choose to do a manual overwrite at any time by tapping "Shred Now".

Darik's Boot and Nuke (DBAN) (Windows, OS X, Linux)

If you have reached the end of your relationship with a computer or its hard drive and wish to ensure that nothing whatsoever will be recovered from it, we recommend using Darik's Boot and Nuke (DBAN). DBAN is technically a bootable operating system that, upon startup, will wipe your entire hard drive completely. It is truly the "nuclear option", and one that should be used sparingly, as nothing will be left behind on your hard drive. No files, no applications, no settings or operating system—nothing. To use DBAN, download the bootable file and burn the .iso to a disk. You must burn it as a bootable disk.

When the disk has finished burning, insert it into the optical drive of the target machine and boot from the disk. Upon booting the disk, you will be presented with several choices. Typing F2 will tell you more about DBAN, typing F3 will give you a list of quick commands, and typing F4 will show you the DBAN RAID disclaimer. Pressing the Enter key will allow you to run DBAN in the "interactive mode", which allows you to select certain options. Typing "autonuke" into the command prompt will begin the autonuke process, which is fully automated. The program will begin wiping your hard drive with default settings and show you a progress bar. At this option menu we recommend pressing Enter, the option to customize the wipe. This will allow you to choose drives and erasure methods. DBAN supports single passes (a choice of all 0s or pseudorandom data), the DOD 5220.22-M three pass method, the RCMP 7-pass method, and of course, the Gutmann 35-pass method. DBAN is free and available at **http://www.dban.org/**.

Managing Data Leakage

Windows 7/10: As we saw in the section on BleachBit, Windows stores an incredible amount of information and metadata about your computer usage. Productivity software stores copies of files in seemingly random locations. Windows tracks the programs you use and how often you use them. Documents are pinned to the task bar to make them easier to retrieve. All of this information and much, much more makes up what we refer to as "leakage" and can paint a fairly accurate picture of what you do on your computer and the files contained in its hard drive. Though the surest method of protecting this data is a good combination of full-disk encryption and secure file deletion, there are steps you can take to (somewhat) control how much of this information is saved in the first place. The steps mentioned here are by no means exhaustive; the applications you need to modify will vary greatly depending on what is running on your machine. There are a few settings you can modify in Windows that will be universal, however.

With the security measures already in place (full-disk encryption and a comprehensive system of secure file deletion) these steps may seem redundant. We really like redundancy though, especially where security is concerned. If someone manages to access your computer in an unencrypted state, it would be preferable to have less information, even if leaked information, available to them. And if your secure deletion applications are not working properly for some reason (you have done something wrong, the program has been compromised or has a bug, etc.), you can still have some confidence in the knowledge that there is very little information there to exploit.

The first of these steps is the list of recently used programs and documents that is pinned temporarily in the Windows Start menu. By default, your most recently used applications and files are kept on top in the Start menu so you can access them quickly and easily. Anyone seeing these can probably make assumptions about the type of work you do on your machine, as well as seeing file names if they have enough visual access. To limit this information, open the Start menu and right-click inside it. Select Properties, and click "Start Menu" on the ensuing window. In the middle of the window is a box labeled "Privacy". Uncheck both of the options in this box: "Store and display recently opened programs in the Start menu" and "Store and display recently opened items in the Start menu and the taskbar". These items will no longer be displayed.

Microsoft Office: A suite of applications in Windows that leaks data purposely is the Microsoft Office Suite. This is done through the AutoRecover functions that are intended to save a copy of your work in the event your computer's power is interrupted. This is great for productivity—we have had similar instances throughout the writing of this work and were extremely relieved to have an automatically saved copy of our work to which we could revert. However, this is a problem for the security of these documents generally. Even though we have only stored these documents in encrypted volumes, the unencrypted AutoSave versions are still here and recoverable in plaintext.

To avoid this, you can choose the location where these versions are saved rather than relying on the default, nebulous location provided by Windows. To do this, open Microsoft Word and select the "File" tab on the ribbon. From the menu on the left side of the application, select "Options". This will open the "Options" dialogue. Within this dialogue click "Save" to display the options for automatically saving the document.

You have the option to choose how often the file is saved. The more often you save it, the less work you will lose if you lose power, but this can also slow your machine down by overtaxing RAM. We recommend choosing a middle-of-the-road option of five to ten minutes for saving frequency. We enabled the "Keep the last auto-saved version if I close without saving" during the writing of this book because of the large amounts of information being changed on a daily basis, but for more casual use you may not want to enable this. Next, and most importantly, are the "AutoRecover file location" and "Default file location" options. For both of these, we use a custom location: a folder named "Microsoft AutoSaves" that is located inside an encrypted volume. This ensures that all of our AutoRecover versions and documents we have saved to the default location are encrypted.

Again, this list is not comprehensive, but it should get you thinking about the applications you run and what they save in the background. If at all possible, make your default and automatic save locations an encrypted volume to prevent sensitive files from being written to the hard drive in plaintext. Think similarly about data-in-motion. If you use a mail client, you may want to look in the settings too see what connections are being made, what information is being sent automatically, and whether these settings can be changed.

OS X: Another potential source of data leakage that secure file deletion will not repair is Mac's ability to backup local documents to your iCloud account. We know of several instances where an individual has been caught in an extra-marital affair because of messages and other compromising data being backed up to a shared iCloud account. There are also numerous instances of an individual being prosecuted because of information that was collected from his or her iCloud account through legal measures. Though we wish to assist neither cheating spouses nor criminals, these techniques could also be used to collect sensitive information about you. Your iCloud account could be hacked as happened to scores of celebrities within the last two years, a rogue employee could access it, or large amounts of data could be spilled in a breach. Your data could also be intercepted as it is transmitted to Apple's iCloud servers.

Secure file deletion techniques will not help you in this instance, but we feel a warning belongs in this section. Thousands of individuals are leaking large amounts of personal data to the cloud through this mechanism, many of them unwittingly. We have urged you previously in this book to carefully consider the content you upload to the cloud and we will again do so. Information stored in the cloud represents a massive increase in your attack surface and should be weighed carefully against the risk of spillage. In this chapter we are much more concerned with information that is unwittingly being transmitted to the cloud. If you have a Mac computer, you should confirm that you are not sharing more information with iCloud than you wish to. To review your iCloud settings, open your computer's System Preferences and click the iCloud icon. The safest way to operate is to simply log out of iCloud. This will prevent anything from being shared with the cloud storage provider. However, logging out prevents you from being able to use certain functions like Find my Mac. If you are logged in you should carefully review the items selected for backup to iCloud and deselect anything that you do not wish to be backed up.

Justin's Experience

Secure file deletion may seem like an overly paranoid step but I contend it is necessary. If a file is no longer needed there is no reason it should reside on the hard drive for months or years. This is especially true if you intend to gift, donate, or even trash the device. Before I began working on this book I worked on a very secure military installation. One day while walking by a dumpster, I happened to notice a desktop PC had been thrown away. Naturally I pulled it out. Upon further inspection, I realized it was a personal computer that someone had brought to work to throw away.

I took the computer home, found a power cable for it, and powered it up. I was shocked at what I found on the machine. The individual who trashed his computer in a dumpster had not deleted anything off the hard drive, nor was anything encrypted. The information still on the machine included his scanned military ID, thousands of family photographs, and other personal information. He was fortunate that the computer was found by me and not someone with more malicious designs. I did him a favor and ran DBAN on the machine before disposing of it properly.

This story should serve to underscore the importance of this chapter and the need to delete files properly. Deleting a file (insecurely) through the Recycle Bin does not make the file go away any more than throwing a computer in a dumpster makes it disappear. It is still there and you are relying only on the hope that no one will go looking for it. By attempting to limit the amount of information that is saved without your knowledge or consent and deleting securely on a regular basis you can have the peace of mind that little (if anything) could be recovered off of your device.

CHAPTER TWENTY-TWO
STATELESS OPERATING SYSTEMS

We believe that every computer should have a selection of removable operating systems ready to boot at any time. While optical media such as compact discs will be discussed later, creating bootable USB devices is the easiest and most robust solution. The general premise of this method is to create a USB drive that can be used to boot an entire operating system from itself. It requires no access to the primary hard drive, and cannot read or write data to it. It is completely isolated from your important data. It will not leak any usage details to your regular system. There are many scenarios that support the use of a bootable USB. Please consider the following.

You may encounter situations where you consciously, but uncomfortably, allow others to access your computer. The most common scenario could be when someone with poor security habits wants to use your device to browse the web. A friend, coworker, or relative may ask to use your laptop in order to quickly research a purchase or obtain directions to a restaurant. Telling this person that you do not want to allow this will likely cause an awkward silence. However, giving them your laptop that has been booted to a secondary USB drive has minimal risk. The password to this new operating system could be disclosed when requested. Your friend can browse the internet all day and never see one private piece of your data.

You may want an operating system that you know is always clean of any malicious software or viruses. Typical browsing behavior on a daily basis is likely to bring in some type of unwanted software onto your device. Many of you are likely using a computer that possesses an operating system that has been installed and running for several years. While your antivirus software has identified known risks, there is simply no way of knowing about the unknown variants of malicious applications. This new USB device can contain a complete operating system that has never been used for any private activity. There is no contamination from previous use. The following instructions will give you a private operating system that masks your primary operating system. It will have absolutely no negative impact on your daily computer use. We will explain the process for both Windows and Mac computers.

First, we encourage you to use the techniques already discussed in this book to ensure that you have full disk encryption enabled on the primary hard drive. This prevents the new alternate operating system from having access to that data. When booting to the new device, it will not have the ability to decrypt the primary device. Next, you need to choose the proper USB flash storage device. We highly recommend only using USB 3.0 devices and ports. If your computer does not have a USB 3.0 port, this method will be painfully slow, and likely unusable. Most laptops created in the past three years have this feature. The benefit of USB 3.0 versus 2.0 is speed. The 3.0 drives can be read at over ten times the rate of the 2.0 devices.

The correct USB flash storage drive is as important as the appropriate port. While USB 3.0 is a standard, not all drives function at the same speeds. You will find very cheap devices that are technically 3.0 drives, but barely function above 2.0 speeds. You will also find extremely expensive drives that operate at nearly the same speeds as internal hard drives. Your situation and budget will determine the most appropriate drive. All of our testing for this section was completed using Sandisk Ultra Fit USB 3.0 drives. We chose these as the best option for several reasons.

Price: These drives are very affordable at $11 (32GB) and $20 (64GB). While we appreciate the speed of some devices at 400MB/s read and write, we do not like the $100 cost.

Size: We believe that a micro USB device is vital. These drives fit into the USB port and are almost flush with the computer. They can sit in the ports permanently if desired and will likely be undetected. Figure 22.01 displays the desired Sandisk drive in use. While obviously present, it will not break during travel and does not appear suspicious.

Speed: This drive is not the fastest available USB device. However, it possesses the best speed in its price class and physical size. We have successfully used this drive to boot multiple operating systems without any obvious lag or delay. The listed speeds are 130MB/s (read) and 40MB/s (write). Our tests revealed actual speeds of 115MB/s (read) and 30MB/s (write). All are suitable for our purposes.

Availability: These devices are very popular and readily available. Our test drives were purchased from Amazon, but we have seen them at Best Buy in the past.

Figure 22.01: A Sandisk Ultra Fit USB 3.0 device in use.

Now that you have your USB 3.0 drive and port ready to go, you need to create the bootable device. Your method will vary depending on your primary operating system. We will explain both Mac and Windows options in detail. The following should explain each category. At a minimum, you would only need to choose one of these paths. At a maximum, you may want to execute all for the most options.

Mac Computers - OS X: This will allow you to create a bootable USB device that will only work on a Mac computer. It will boot an entire Mac OS X operating system from the USB drive and will not impact the permanent system on the internal hard drive. Any changes that you make while in the USB operating system will be preserved. This is the ideal choice for Mac users.

Mac Computers - Linux: This will allow you to create a bootable USB device that will only work on a Mac computer. It will boot an entire Linux operating system from the USB drive and will not impact the permanent system on the internal hard drive. Any changes that you make while in the USB operating system will NOT be preserved. This will provide a clean operating system on each use with no contamination from previous sessions. This is ideal for situations where you do not want to save any data or history and do not have access to a Windows machine.

Windows Computers - Linux (Single System)

This will allow you to create a bootable USB device that will work on both Windows and Mac computers. It will boot a single Linux operating system from the USB drive. This will not have any impact on the permanent system on the internal hard drive. Any changes that you make while in the USB operating system will NOT be preserved. This will provide a clean operating system on each use with no contamination from previous sessions. This is ideal for situations where you do not want to save any data or history. It is the simplest option for Windows users.

Windows Computers - Linux (Multiple)

This will allow you to create a bootable USB device that will work on both Windows and Mac computers. It will boot a menu that will present three Linux operating systems. Any system can be chosen and each will boot from the USB drive. These will not have any impact on the permanent system on the internal hard drive. Any changes that you make while in the USB operating system will NOT be preserved. This will provide a clean operating system on each use with no contamination from previous sessions. This is ideal for situations where you do not want to save any data or history and want multiple system options.

Windows Computers - Linux (Multiple with Persistence)

This will allow you to create a bootable USB device that will only work on Windows computers. It will boot to a Linux Ubuntu operating system. This will not have any impact on the permanent system on the internal hard drive. Any changes that you make while in the USB operating system WILL be preserved. This is ideal for situations where you DO want to save any data or history.

Mac Computers - OS X

The following instructions will download the Mac OS X operating system onto your Mac device, install it to a USB drive, and configure the system to boot from the device. It will appear identical to any other live OS X operating system on your computer.

- While in your primary system, connect your USB drive.
- Open Disk Utility within the Utilities menu of your applications.
- Select your USB drive and click partition.
- Choose Partition Layout and select 1 Partition (Mac OS extended Journaled).
- Provide a name for the drive (can be random) and click Apply.
- Choose GUID partition Table and click OK then click Partition.
- Download the latest OS X Installer file within the Mac App Store (Search "OS X").
- Navigate to the Applications folder and copy the OS X installer to your desktop.
- Execute the OS X installer, but do not install to your primary hard drive.
- Click the Show All Disks button and select the USB drive. Click Install.

Your computer will restart upon completion and may automatically delete the OS X installer within the applications folder. The copy on your desktop will still be present in case you want to create multiple USB drives. You may consider placing a copy of this installer on another portable drive as a backup. After finishing installation, your computer will reboot into the version of OS X that you installed to the USB drive. Your computer will now automatically boot to this device every time it is powered on. In order to boot to your primary hard drive, you would need to hold down the Option button and then select the appropriate drive.

We believe that this is the optimal option for Mac users. If the USB device is not present in the system, it will likely not boot to the primary (private) operating system without a second reboot. If the drive is in the port, it will boot to this alternate operating system (public). If you were asked to power on your laptop, it would boot to this new version of OS X which knows nothing about you. You could now let someone use your computer (booted to the USB drive) and their activity will not ruin your good browsing habits. However, you are not quite done yet.

Boot into the USB device and apply a strong password that is not the same as your primary operating system. This will now prompt for a password on boot. Disclosing this password will create the illusion of cooperation and "nothing to hide". It will show that you trust the person that you are disclosing this data to and will not jeopardize any real content. This new device is now functional, but is a bit too clean. It may seem suspicious when a person notices that there is absolutely no personal information present. We recommend creating a few word processing documents and placing them on the desktop with names such as "To-Do", "Tasks", and "Work Stuff". Inside these documents, you could paste text from various news articles in order to appear legitimate. You should also open a web browser and visit a few random sites. You might even change your wallpaper in order to appear personalized.

We also maintain a second OS X USB boot drive with a standard installation of OS X on it. We use this when we need to reset master passwords to vital services. Since we only use this on safe websites and on rare occasions, we feel confident that this image does not contain viruses or malicious software. We also use this image when accessing important financial websites. Overall, we want a safe image that can be trusted. Daily internet browsing, even on a Mac, is likely to bring in bad software at some point. We isolate the operating system that we use daily (primary internal hard drive) and the image that we use for sensitive data (USB boot drive). We ask you to consider if this strategy may benefit you. Many security gurus recommend purchasing a tablet or netbook solely for interaction with financial services. We think that you can use your current computer, but with a clean operating system running straight from a USB drive. This will be a fraction of the cost. You could install a Virtual Private Network (VPN) on all drives for further protection.

You might not want this new USB device to boot by default. If you want to switch back to the default OS X primary operating system, navigate to System Preferences, select Startup Disks, and choose the desired default boot volume. You should evaluate the best boot method for your situation. Our preferences will be explained in a moment.

Mac Computers – Linux

If you would like to have a Linux operating system on a USB drive, and you do not have access to a Windows computer, you can create a bootable device using only the OS X operating system. The following instructions will create a Linux drive that will not store any data between uses. While you can choose any variant of Linux you desire, these steps will focus on Ubuntu. These instructions will require a working knowledge of the OS X terminal and the commands used. If you have access to a Windows computer, skip these steps and choose the simpler solution offered in a moment.

- Navigate to **ubuntu.com/download** and download the latest Ubuntu Desktop operating system. You must choose the 64-bit option.

- Navigate to **sevenbits.github.io/Mac-Linux-USB-Loader,** download the Mac Linux USB Loader application, and launch the software.

- Click the Create Live USB option. A finder window will appear. Select the Linux Mint ISO file that you downloaded earlier.

- Choose the destination USB drive that you would like to overwrite and click next.

- Choose the appropriate Distribution Family. If using either Mint or Ubuntu, choose the default Ubuntu option. Accept any other defaults.

- Click Begin Installation and allow the process to complete.

Windows Computers - Linux (Single)

If you are strictly a Windows user, this is likely your best option. The following instructions will download a Linux ISO file, install it to a USB drive, and configure the system to allow you to boot from the device. Our steps will install the TAILS operating system, but any Linux install file could be used, such as Ubuntu or Mint. If you know that your computer possesses a 64-bit processor, you should choose that option. If you plan on booting this drive from a Mac computer, you must have the 64-bit operating system. Overall, choosing the 64-bit option at all times will likely work best. The created bootable operating system stores absolutely no data about your activity. When you shut the system down, it forgets everything. This is a way to be sure that the operating systems that you are using are free from malicious files. While we will need a Windows computer to create this drive, the final product will also boot on a Mac computer.

- Navigate to **tails.boum.org** and download the latest TAILS version in ISO file format.
- Insert your desired USB drive.
- Download the Rufus application at **https://rufus.akeo.ie/**.
- Execute the program and choose the physical USB drive that you want to create.
- Choose a partition scheme of "MBR ... for BIOS or UEFI Computers".
- Click the button similar to a CD and choose the TAILS image.
- Click "Start" and allow the process to complete.

The result is a drive that will boot to the TAILS operating system. If you have smaller drives or multiple devices, we prefer this solution. Your USB drive is now ready to be used as a boot drive. You will need to ensure that your BIOS of your Windows computer is set up to boot from USB before the internal drive. On most computers, hitting either the F2, F10, F12, DEL, or ESC buttons repeatedly when you first turn on your computer will present this menu. While each computer is unique, a search on Google for "Enter BIOS (your computer model)" will present the answers you need.

Windows Computers - Linux (Multiple)

The following instructions will create a USB device that will boot a selection of multiple Linux operating systems. While it is possible to boot a native Windows operating system from a USB drive, the successes are rare. We found this action to be completely unreliable. The following steps will download the required software, create a bootable USB drive, copy the appropriate files, and finalize the process.

- Navigate to **pendrivelinux.com/yumi-multiboot-usb-creator/** and download the YUMI Multiboot program. Decompress the files into a new folder titled YUMI on your desktop. This will be your working directory.

- Navigate to **tails.boum.org** and download the latest Tails version.

- Navigate to **ubuntu.com/download** and download the latest Ubuntu Desktop operating system. Choose the 64-bit version if your computer supports this.

- Navigate to **linuxmint.com/download.php** and download the first version under "Download Links". Choose the 64-bit version if your computer supports this.

- Place all of the downloaded files in the YUMI folder.

- Insert your USB 3.0 boot drive into your computer and Launch YUMI. Accept the terms on the first screen and apply the following settings to the setup screen.

- Under Step 1, choose the new USB device (be careful). In Step 2, Select TAILS from the dropdown menu. In step 3, browse to your YUMI folder and select the TAILS ISO file. Figure 22.02 displays this menu. Click Create and accept the defaults. When prompted about adding another image, choose "yes".

- Under Step 1, choose the new USB device (be careful). In Step 2, Select Ubuntu from the dropdown menu. In step 3, browse to your YUMI folder and select the Ubuntu ISO file. Click Create and accept the defaults. When prompted about adding another image, choose "yes".

- Under Step 1, choose the new USB device (be careful). In Step 2, Select Linux Mint from the dropdown menu. In step 3, browse to your YUMI folder and select the Mint ISO file. Click Create and accept the defaults. When prompted about adding another image, choose "no".

- Keep the YUMI folder and files for future drive creation if desired.

Once you have completed all of these steps, you have two options ready for you at all times. You can either insert the USB drive and boot to a clean operating system or remove the drive and boot to your internal hard drive. The scenarios discussed previously all apply to this new drive. Upon boot, you will be presented with a menu and an option of Linux Distributions. Choosing this will display the three operating systems that you added to your device. Inserting this USB drive into your Mac computer will also allow you to boot directly to these same options. For Mac users, immediately hold down the Option key until you see a boot option with an orange disk graphic. This is the USB drive.

Windows Computers - Linux (Individual with Persistence)

The previous instructions created a boot device that would not store any changes from your usage. It is great when you want to be sure that your computing environment is clean from malicious software every time that you use it. However, you may desire the ability to save your changes. You might want to install add-ons to your browser or store files within the operating system. You can create a USB boot drive that will store any changes as a normal operating system would. This will only work on Windows computers. The following instructions will create an Ubuntu operating system with "persistence". Persistence is the ability to store user information within the bootable device.

- Navigate to **http://unetbootin.github.io/** and download the UNetbootin program. Decompress the files into a new folder titled USB on your desktop. This will be your working directory.

- Navigate to **ubuntu.com/download** and download the latest Ubuntu Desktop operating system.

- Place the ISO file that was downloaded in the USB folder.

- Insert your USB 3.0 boot drive into your computer and Launch UNetbootin.

- Click the checkbox next to "Diskimage" and browse to the downloaded Ubuntu file.

- Below this, enter the number of megabytes (MB) that you want to designate to stored data. This will vary according to the size of the USB device. Overall, take the entire size of the drive, subtract 4 GB, and type the remainder here. If you had a 16 GB flash drive, you would assign 12,000 MB in this field.

- Finally, choose the physical USB drive that you want to create and click OK.

This system is ready to boot and stores all changes. If you update the operating system while booted to this USB, those updates will be present when you return. If you change the look and feel of the operating system, those changes will stay present. If you install any applications or save any data, you will have this content the next time you boot into this USB. However, please note that any malicious software that enters the system will also remain. While Linux malware is rare, it does happen. If you have a specific Linux setup that you want to maintain without the worry of collecting unwanted data, please consider the next advanced option.

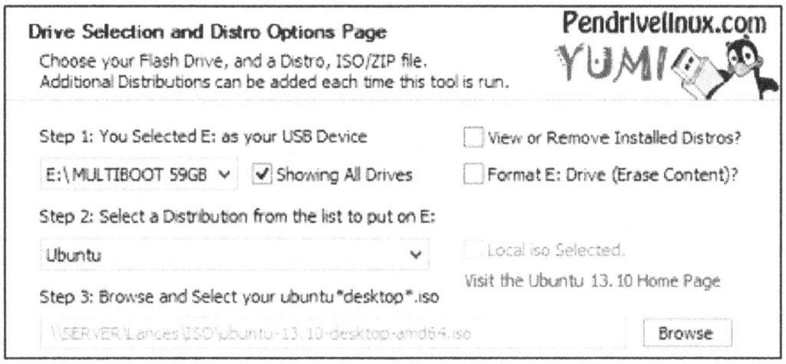

Figure 22.02: A YUMI build menu.

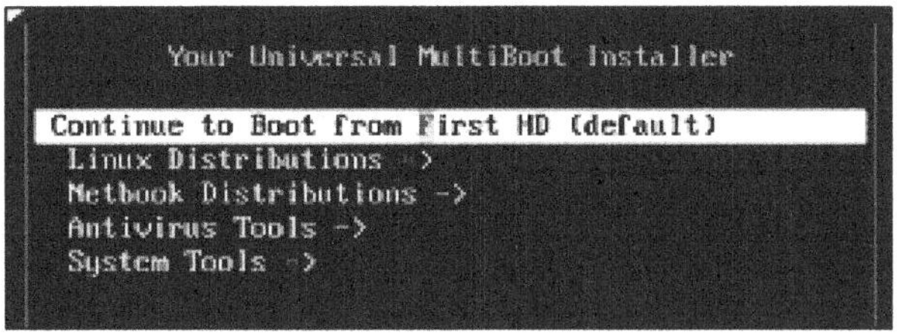

Figure 22.03: A YUMI boot screen.

Figure 22.04: A Rufus build menu.

Windows Computers - Custom Linux Build

This will be the most technical option and is most appropriate for tech savvy individuals. It was not listed in the previous categories because of the technical steps that will need to be taken. However, it is worth the time and energy to place this method into practice. It will allow you to boot into an interactive Linux operating system, make changes and customize software, and then preserve that state onto a bootable USB device. This new drive will always boot to the exact conditions that you created and will not store data from your individual sessions. It will allow you to create the exact environment that you want to use on a daily basis without allowing contamination from each occurrence. This will be explained better with actual use scenarios later.

Windows Computers - Custom Linux Build (Without Persistence-Advanced)

This option gives you the convenience of a bootable operating system that contains custom configuration while maintaining the security of a stateless environment. You can add any software that you desire and change the look and feel as appropriate. You can then "lock down" these changes and create a drive that will never save any future data. It can be used as a daily web browsing environment without fear of incoming malicious software. The following steps may seem complicated. However, the possibilities from this method are endless. This selection will require an understanding of the Linux operating system and terminal commands. If this sounds foreign to you, you could skip to the next topic without the need for this knowledge. If you are up for a challenge, continue with the following instructions.

- Choose a Linux operating system for your USB drive. These instructions used Mint, which is a distribution based on Ubuntu. It is known for looking similar to Windows and having an overall familiar feel. You can download both a 32-bit and 64-bit version of Mint at **linuxmint.com/download.php**. We always recommend the 64-bit.

- Choose a method to boot into Linux. This could be a live USB boot drive as explained in the previous method, a virtual machine as explained earlier in this chapter, or a permanent install on a computer hard drive.

- Modify the operating system in any way desired. This may include custom Firefox browser add-ons, changing the desktop background, adding software programs, or removing unwanted applications. You may even consider including specific files that you will need in the future such as documents or media.

- Install Systemback by entering the following commands in a terminal session (black box).
    sudo add-apt-repository -y ppa:nemh/systemback (this may require password)
    sudo apt-get update
    sudo apt-get install systemback

- Execute the Systemback program by clicking the icon under Menu > All Applications > Systemback. If you use an OS other than Mint, your location may be different.

- Click the right arrow in the lower right corner as seen in Figure 22.05. This will present the second page of options as seen in Figure 22.06.

- Click the Settings button and enable the "Create Live ISO images automatically" option as seen in Figure 22.07. Click the Back button when finished.

- Click the "Include" button as seen in Figure 22.06. Select any folders that you want present in your final USB device. This is where you would select the folders that contain programs or files that you will need each time. Figure 22.08 displays this menu with folders for Desktop, Documents, and Videos selected. Your standard operating system files and programs are already included by default. Click the Back button when finished.

- Click the left green arrow as seen in Figure 22.06 to return to the main menu seen in Figure 22.05.

- Click the "Live System Create" button as seen in Figure 22.05. This will present a menu to generate your new custom Linux ISO as seen in Figure 22.09. If you included folders in the earlier step, enable the "Include the user data files" option.

- Click the "Create New" button and the program will begin building the file system.

The final product will contain two files. The first will end in the file extension ISO and will be used for the next part of the process. The second file will end in .sblive and will not be used. Both will be deleted after we are finished making our drive. Before we proceed, we should understand what is happening here. When you boot your Linux operating system, even if from a live USB, you are allowed to make changes. If booting from USB, these changes disappear the moment you shut down. The new ISO file that Systemback is creating includes all of the changes that you made in between booting the system and creating the new ISO. We now need to copy this ISO onto another USB device and make it bootable. The following instructions will create a USB drive that should maintain all of your custom settings.

- Click OK to the announcement that the process is complete. You will see a new version of Figure 22.09 that now looks like Figure 22.10. Notice the new image in the upper right box. The box in the upper left will identify the location where your image is saved.

- In the terminal, type sudo fdisk -l l. This will display all of the disks currently connected to your Linux system. Insert a blank USB 3.0 drive and in the terminal, type sudo fdisk -l again. This will display all of the disks connected and you should see a new device. This is your USB drive. Make note of the name. In Figure 22.11, you can see that ours is called /dev/sdb1. This will be the target for our new custom system.

- In this same terminal window, navigate to the folder that stores the ISO that you created. If you did not change the default location, these are in the "Home" directory. Type "cd .." without the quotes to navigate one step back to this directory. If you type ls and hit enter, you should see the contents of the directory. Figure 22.12 displays this test result. You can see the ISO file and the original SBLIVE file that we created.

- In our example, we would type the following command into the same terminal window. Note that your command will be different because of your file name and USB drive specification differences.

  sudo dd if=systemback_live_2015-12-09.iso of=/dev/sdb1

This will now write a very large file to the USB device. This can take several minutes depending on the speed of your machine. In most cases, it should take less than 30 minutes. The final product is a USB device that can be inserted into any Linux, Mac or Windows computer. It will boot to the Linux Mint operating system and will appear exactly as you customized it. When you shut down the system, it will store none of your data created during that session. When you restart, it will appear exactly the same every time. Now that you understand the techniques of creating bootable operating systems on USB drives, please consider how you might use them. We carry several of these drives at all times. Our bags usually contain a variant of the following:

- A MacBook Pro laptop set to boot first to external USB flash drive.
- A 32GB USB drive with encrypted OS X install and fake personal files.
- A 32GB USB drive with encrypted OS X install and no data.
- A 32GB USB drive with TAILS, Ubuntu, and Mint OS's.

The first drive remains in the computer at all times while the computer is off. If we were requested to access data on the computer, it would only boot to this public drive. Replacing this drive with the second device would present a clean OS for sensitive work such as financial activity. The final drive would be used to boot into TAILS for complete anonymity or a Linux OS for a known clean image. This setup prevents us from accidentally booting to our OS with sensitive information. If anyone were to have access to our laptops, they would boot into this public OS. If we were forced to give out the password to the OS, we would not jeopardize any sensitive data. The following scenarios may help identify a valid purpose for you to switch to this method.

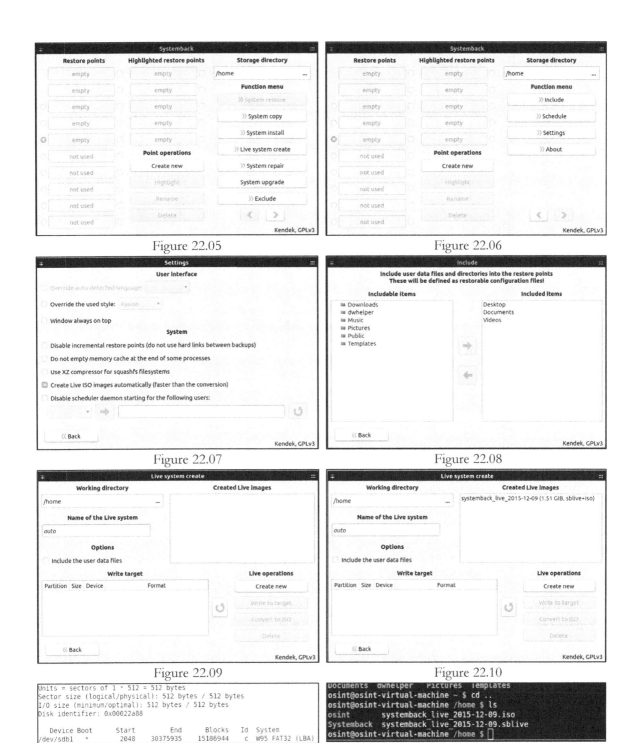

Figure 22.05

Figure 22.06

Figure 22.07

Figure 22.08

Figure 22.09

Figure 22.10

```
Units = sectors of 1 * 512 = 512 bytes
Sector size (logical/physical): 512 bytes / 512 bytes
I/O size (minimum/optimal): 512 bytes / 512 bytes
Disk identifier: 0x00022a88

   Device Boot      Start         End      Blocks   Id  System
/dev/sdb1   *        2048    30375935    15186944    c  W95 FAT32 (LBA)
```

Figure 22.11

```
Documents   dwhelper   Pictures   Templates
osint@osint-virtual-machine ~ $ cd ..
osint@osint-virtual-machine /home $ ls
osint           systemback_live_2015-12-09.iso
Systemback  systemback_live_2015-12-09.sblive
osint@osint-virtual-machine /home $
```

Figure 22.12

The Care-Free Teenager

You have created the perfect secure laptop and agonized over every setting and decision. You do not visit questionable websites and do not download pirated software. You trust that your system will protect you the best that it can from malicious activity. Then one day, your nephew asks to use your computer to play on the internet. You want to tell him "no" but do not want to face the criticism later. Instead, you have a USB drive ready to go. You plug it in, boot to the removable drive, and hand it over. If your device is already set to boot to USB by default, a reboot of the computer while you are away should have no impact. After the nephew is finished, shut the machine down and remove the flash drive. Nothing that he did impacts your private operating system. Since you have full disk encryption enabled, he could not access your files if he tried. You may want to label this USB drive and reserve it for future use.

Law Enforcement Investigations

We believe that there are two huge hurdles that law enforcement faces when conducting online investigations. The first is conducting internet searches on a clean computer and the second is preserving the environment of the investigation. We believe that the majority of investigators are ignoring both, but this USB boot method might solve the issues. Many law enforcement agencies struggle financially and do not have access to computers designated for online investigations. We have witnessed smaller departments use the same system to write a police report and then browse a suspect's Facebook page. We have also witnessed departments use older Windows XP machines for their online investigations. We believe that both of these scenarios represent extremely risky behavior. If a Linux USB drive was used, the system would not be as prone to viruses and it would not connect to sensitive data on the network.

Windows 10 Considerations

Some Windows 10 users have reported great difficulty booting to Linux USB drives. For some machines, you must disable the safe boot setting. While this seems to allow the ability to use stateless USB drives in some cases, we have heard of machines that still refuse to boot with this method. We have had the best success using Rufus to load the ISO files using the "MBR … for BIOS or UEFI Computers" option. The following instructions will disable Microsoft's safe boot option, which may increase your success with stateless USB drives on Windows 10.

- In Windows 10, navigate to Settings >> Update and Security >> Recovery >> Advanced Startup and click "Restart Now".

- Upon reboot, select Troubleshoot >> Advanced Options >> See more recovery options >> Disable Safe Mode.

- Reboot with BIOS re-enabled.

Michael's USB Boot Daily Usage Strategy

I currently view my MacBook Pro as my primary business computer. I use it during my trainings and presentations. It contains all of my digital training material on the encrypted internal hard drive along with several virtual machines. I also use it to maintain my web based business email. It is my entire business world and the contents are synchronized to an encrypted USB drive. However, it is not used for personal issues. I have two OS X 64GB Sandisk Ultrafit drives ready to boot to the latest Mac operating system. Each of their uses are outlined below.

USB Disk One: This is my primary personal operating system. I use this to connect to any financial institutions. My personal documents are stored on an encrypted container within this drive that also includes FileVault's full disk encryption. My KeePass password management database is on this drive. My documents backup to a Transcend 64GB SD card that fits flush into the SD slot. It also possesses full disk encryption and the documents are within an encrypted container. I never browse to any questionable websites. I rarely browse the internet at all. This is for sensitive matters. I use this drive for my personal communications through encrypted email (ProtonMail) and messaging (Wickr). Every action that is personal to me, but does not involve my business, happens on this drive. It is safe from malicious software.

USB Disk Two: This is my "junk" drive. This is my environment when I want to browse to suspicious websites during research for my training events. It allows me to test unapproved applications without jeopardizing the security of my important operating systems. It is an environment where anything goes. I would never connect to anything in my real name on this drive. I also keep an encrypted clone of my business laptop on this drive.

Aside from Mac operating systems, I use three additional drives for Linux devices.

USB Disk Three: This is a 32GB Linux Mint drive with a 4GB persistence volume. I use this to test Linux software that is used during my advanced training sessions. It is another environment that I can use to install Linux apps and retain the settings.

USB Disk Four: This is a 16GB Linux TAILS drive without persistence. As you have previously learned, this gives me a clean system every time and helps me mask my true identity.

USB Disk Five: This final disk is a custom Linux Mint OS on a 16GB drive without persistence. It is my investigation drive and includes a custom version of Firefox with numerous add-ons. I have an Android emulator that allows me to test mobile apps and exploit the data within them. Upon reboot, none of my activity is stored.

All of these drives are with me at all times. The first two are encrypted and offer nothing of value. The others simply have nothing of interest on them. If my laptop was stolen or broken, I can be back to normal in minutes. The drives are never left in my laptop unattended.

Justin's USB Boot Daily Usage Strategy

My primary laptop is a MacBook Pro. Though most of the specifications like RAM and processor speed have been maxed out, the internal SSD is only 128 GB. I like this because it saves me a few dollars ($200 less than the 512 GB drive and $700 less than the 1 TB model) and because I don't use the internal storage anyway. When I get the computer I log into the native OS, encrypt it, turn Wi-Fi off, and log back out. My computer is now merely a host for several removable devices.

I run my operating systems from 128-GB SanDisk Ultra Fit USB 3.0 flash drives. Running a machine off of a USB drive does cause a slight performance hit that is noticeable but not totally unworkable. There is another huge benefit to running this model, too: no matter what hardware I am on I have the same desktop, the same settings, the same password database, same VPN connections, everything. I could lose my computer tonight, buy a new one tomorrow, and absolutely nothing would change for me.

The operating systems that I use most commonly are, in order, OS X, Xubuntu, and TAILS. There are a few other penetration testing and privacy distros that I play with occasionally, but those three are the real workhorses. Though I have been a diehard Windows user - and advocate - for many years, I find the privacy abuses that are organic and non-optional in Windows 10 to be a personal deal-breaker and will no longer use Windows with the exception of teaching live events.

For storage I rely on a couple of solutions. For my primary OS X operating system I store a select few files directly on the OS drive, and all others on a doubly-encrypted Transcend JetDrive Lite SD card. Because these are my important, personally-sensitive files I back this entire drive up to a 128-GB Kingston Data Traveler that is always on my person. For other operating systems I store files on one of a couple different full-disk encrypted USB flash drives. If these files become so important that I fear losing them they will eventually make their way onto my Transcend and Kingston drives. All of my drives are doubly encrypted. They are first disk encrypted with FileVault and then volume encryption (sized to accommodate available space) is added with VeraCrypt.

I do maintain some other hardware for training sessions, testing, writing about other operating systems, and as hosts for virtual machines. I have to work with Windows quite frequently as well, especially when working with military and government clients, so I do maintain a dedicated Windows machine that (currently) bounces back and forth between Windows 7 and 10. These boxes are never used for anything personal. They never connect to my home Wi-Fi network, they never touch my "real" accounts, and they never store anything personally sensitive about me.

Stateless OS from Optical Media

Another option for stateless operating systems, and one that is more secure, is the use of an operating system that runs from optical media (DVDs). Many smaller laptops no longer come with optical media drives (including MacBook computers), but external optical drives are available for around $25 through Amazon.com. The other major limitation to running a stateless operating system from external media is that the OS must be small enough to fit on a DVD. Most DVDs will hold around 4.5 GB so this means that you are primarily limited to Linux operating systems. This limitation should not be insurmountable; if you are looking for this level of security you are probably running Linux anyway.

The huge benefit of running an operating system from optical media rather than a USB flash drive is that once you write the OS to the DVD, the operating system itself cannot be altered. This means that your operating system can never contract a virus or other form of malware, and the operating system's security cannot be modified to make you an easier target. You may create a USB drive with an operating system that does not have "persistence" and does not store any information or record any changes from session to session. Very sophisticated adversaries, however, may still have the ability to modify the OS without your knowledge. If your threat model indicates you need to take this level of precaution running the OS from optical media is the safest and surest method.

Virtual Machines

Virtual machines (VMs) are "computers" that run within a program on your computer. A virtual machine is just that: a computer (machine) that has been virtually constructed from files. The major benefits of VMs are similar to those of stateless operating systems. A VM runs virtually and does not affect the host system, so anything you do during that session is destroyed when you close the VM. VMs allow you a convenient way to use multiple operating systems for different tasks without rebooting your computer to load each new OS. Additionally, you maintain access to your host operating system while running a VM, allowing you to bounce back and forth between systems in real time without rebooting. Since these operating systems are running virtually they can be started and terminated at will from your keyboard. You can even have multiple VMs running at the same time.

At this point you may be wondering why you would wish to do this. There are numerous benefits that VMs offer, however. When running a virtual machine, you do not have to worry about your computer becoming infected with malware because if it is you can simply close the VM and your machine will reset back to the settings you began with. A clean virtual machine can make you much more difficult to track online by eliminating unique browser fingerprints and giving you a clean operating system with minimal applications. Virtual machines can be used to test applications before you allow them to run on your "real world" system. There are numerous other benefits to VMs and we use them extensively.

Virtual machines are a significant increase in security over using your native operating system. However, you should be aware that virtual machines are not as safe or secure as true stateless operating systems. A very specific family of exploits exist called "VM Escape" that can allow malware to "jump" from the sandbox created by the virtual machine and infect your host system. While exploits like this are rare and expensive they do exist. If you require maximum security against sophisticated threats, a true stateless operating system is a much better option. With that being said, we still strongly recommend installing at least one virtual machine to be used for casual internet browsing.

Virtual Box: There are multiple options for executing virtual machines on your device. VMWare and Parallels are the most common premium solutions. For this instruction, we will only focus on Virtual Box. This completely free program is easy to install and works on all major operating systems. Volumes could be written about the features and abilities of Virtual Box. Installation and download instructions can be found at **virtualbox.org**. Because Virtual box is so rich in official documentation we will not cover specifics of setup here. For full details visit **https://www.virtualbox.org/wiki/End-user_documentation**.

CHAPTER TWENTY-THREE
WEB PUBLISHING

You may expect this chapter to simply advise against any type of publishing of online content. This is not the case. We both possess multiple websites, own several domains, publish to blogs, and have a minimal online presence. We respect the requirement for activity on the internet in order to maintain a business or generate income. Some may use the internet as a tool to complement their professional life. This may apply to attorneys, aspiring politicians, software developers, or physicians.

While not appropriate for everyone, running a web-based business actually has some great privacy advantages over traditional employment. The biggest benefit is the lack of a requirement for you to expose your personal details to an employer. Most companies will demand government identification, a verified home address, your SSN and DOB, as well as a complete history of your previous employment. While this step alone might seem invasive, the potential attacks after that company is breached could be devastating. We must again reference the OPM breach. If you create your own online business as a source of primary or secondary income, you control the data that is made public. While we will reserve the huge repository of information regarding the establishment of a private business for a future volume of this series, we hope that you will consider the option of working for yourself. This chapter will provide insight to the ways your data is leaked through online publishing.

This chapter is not only for those desiring self employment. It is likely that you have a legitimate purpose for publishing some type of content to the internet. Whether it is your own website hosted on a domain that you own or a blog hosted on a third party service, you should be very cautious of the registration process. Many people realize that their details are publicly viewable after the damage is irreversible. This mostly applies to domain registration which is where we will begin.

Domain Registration

Delivering online content through your own website hosted through your own domain can be very satisfying. It also gives you compete control of your website, the data collected, and the data shared. We both host all of our own content. This gives us the option of offering transparent privacy policies that assure our visitors that we are not tracking them or collecting their information. The first step of hosting your own website is to register the desired domain name. The process for this will vary based on the service that you use to register the domain. We will only focus on the privacy aspects of registration.

Every registered domain is required by The Internet Corporation for Assigned Names and Numbers (ICANN) to include the following information for the primary registrant and technical, administrative, and billing contacts if not the same as the registrant.

Full Name
Full Address
Telephone Number
Email Address

Many readers will assume that one could simply provide false information and move on to the next step. Unfortunately, it is not that easy. The email address that you provide must be valid and retrievable by you. The remaining information will likely never be verified. However, if a complaint is received by ICANN about your registration, they will require you to verify the supplied information or update to valid details. While this is rare, we do not suggest blatantly lying about your information.

Every domain registration service will allow you to change your registration information at any time. However, this does not protect previously supplied details. An example of this can be seen on the website whoisology.com. This website extracts domain registration data and stores the historical changes. The domain name inteltechniques.com is currently registered to a PO Box in Washington, D.C. However, it was previously registered to a physical address in Alton, IL. While the record was updated, there is nothing that can be done about the previous entry. It is publicly visible forever. We have had many clients contact us to inquire about the process of removing this data. The unfortunate answer is that this cannot be undone. Therefore, it is vital to register the domain properly the first time.

If the website content is publicly attached to your real name, we see no issue with registering the domain in your name. The address should never be your home or workplace. It should never be anywhere that you could be located routinely. PO Boxes are allowed here, but we suggest caution there as well. We do not recommend using the primary PO Box that you use for bills and personal correspondence. You are likely to begin receiving unwanted advertisements. While not a privacy issue, it can be annoying. Our bigger concern is directed toward the routine collection of mail at this address. If you visit your PO Box daily or weekly, it would not be difficult to be located during this process. This may not be important to most, but it is to those that desire ultimate privacy. Personally, we do not want to provide a private investigator, process server, or stalker all of the information needed to find us through public domain registration data. We also do not recommend using the address of your employer. You have other options.

The first is a secondary PO Box. We both have one. They are only used for situations where we never expect to receive any mail, but might be required to verify ownership. We never physically check them. They are in rural towns and cost about $50 per year.

The next option is to pay for private registration. This allows the company that you registered the domain through to act as the contact. They are the public face and will forward any inquiries directly to you via email. Our concern here is two-fold. You are required to share your true contact information with the domain registrar. What if they get hacked? Second, these services are facing scrutiny from ICANN and there is a solid possibility that these masking services will be banned in the near future. It would not surprise us if they are forced to share historic contact details. We do not recommend this route.

A final solution is to simply use someone else's address as the contact. We do not recommend picking a random stranger out of a phone book. Instead, consider the address of the provider of your domain. If you registered for a website domain through GoDaddy, use their address. We believe that you have that option as their customer. If ICANN tries to reach the owner of your domain by contacting GoDaddy, you can be reached via email. However, using the same address as provided on the godaddy.com domain registration, 14455 N Hayden Rd Suite 219, Scottsdale, AZ, is not wise. It may raise a red flag. A quick search on the internet reveals that GoDaddy's Global Technology Center is located at 2150 E Warner Rd, Tempe, AZ. A GoDaddy customer may choose to use that. We believe that you meet the requirements of the registration by providing your real name, GoDaddy's address, a forwarding email address (333Mail), and a VOIP number.

Search Engine Control

When discussing the topic of search engines indexing your website, most people will do anything they can to convince Google, Bing, and others to collect as much information as possible. They hope to have a high ranking and for their website to appear first in a search result. The strategies for this Search Engine Optimization (SEO) are beyond the scope of this book. Instead, we will discuss the opposite. We want to make our website as private as possible while maintaining a healthy presence within search engine results.

Websites possess special instructions to search engines in the form of a small file stored at the root of the website called robots.txt. This text file contains specifically formatted written instructions to the search engines that crawl your website. It will allow you to block specific content from being reported, restrict archiving permissions, and other desired requests. The following will explain the options, and we will display an ideal robots.txt file.

First, you must store the file at the proper location. It should be at the base of the domain, formally known as the root folder. As an example, you can view the robots.txt file by adding a slash and the file name after any domain. Below are a few examples, one more interesting than others.

inteltechniques.com/robots.txt
google.com/robots.txt
tripadvisor.com/robots.txt

We will create a new file in any text editor and save it as robots.txt. The first decision to make is the extent that you want search engines to look through your website. If it is all public, you may include the following line.

User-agent: *
Disallow:

The first line uses an asterisk (*) to indicate that this rule applies to any and all search engines. The second line is empty after Disallow indicating that it does not request to block anything. Everything is allowed. If you do not want the search engine to look at your website or include any links to it, you would include the following line of text.

User-agent: *
Disallow: /

The option of a forward slash (/) indicates that you want to disallow everything on the site. If you wanted to only block a folder titled "Private" on your domain, the text would be the following.

User-agent: *
Disallow: /Private/

If you had a single file on the root of your website, such as private.html, that you did not want any website to index or include in search engine results, you would include the following.

User-agent: *
Disallow: /private.html

We never recommend this specific strategy. While search engines will not display a link to that page, anyone could view your robots.txt file and navigate straight to the desired content. You may have specific types of files to protect, such as those ending in .aspx. You could add the following to protect that content.

User-agent: *
Disallow: /*.aspx$

The asterisk (*) and the dollar sign ($) indicate that all files with that extension should be avoided. If you wanted to only prevent Google from indexing your content, but wanted any other search engine to proceed, you could include the following.

User-agent: Googlebot
Disallow: /

We do not recommend citing any specific search engines. We believe that it is all or nothing. Either you block all engines or you block none. This prevents the creation of a robots.txt file that contains errors or contradictions.

While these techniques are important for control of your website data that is present on search engines, we have a much more vital consideration. When your website is indexed, it is also collected and archived. Google, Bing, the Wayback Machine, and others capture a snapshot of your page and offer it as a cached file. As an example, consider the website fbi.gov. You have several options for viewing this content. Typing fbi.gov into a web browser will present the live site as it appears today. Searching Google for fbi, clicking the downward facing green arrow next to the first result, and clicking "Cached" will present a copy of fbi.gov that was recently captured by Google. Repeating this process on Bing will produce the same results. If fbi.gov were to shut down today, you could still acquire the copies collected by Google and Bing.

The Wayback Machine goes a step further. It not only collects website data similar to Google and Bing, it allows users to see all of the content collected. Searching fbi.gov on archive.org/web discloses that the Wayback Machine has collected the contents of the fbi.gov website over 6,000 times since 1996. Clicking any result allows you to view the website as it appeared on any given date. In contrast, repeat the previously mentioned steps on the domain inteltechniques.com. You will notice that Google, Bing, nor the Wayback Machine possess any cached copies of this website. This is due to a single entry of text with the robots.txt file of that website. The following prevents websites from collecting, or caching, the content.

User-agent: ia_archiver
Disallow: /

As a final example, assume that you have a website that you want to be indexed by all search engines. You want people to be able to search for you and your content. However, you have a folder titled "Hidden" that you do not want crawled. Finally, you do not want search engines to store copies of your data and make them publicly viewable forever. The following would be your robots.txt file.

User-agent: ia_archiver
Disallow: /

User-agent: *
Disallow: /Hidden/

We believe that you should consider this proactive approach rather than a reactive approach. As you can see, the internet never forgets. If you find yourself in the spotlight due to an unfortunate event, your entire web presence will be scrutinized. While you can take down your website, you cannot immediately remove the data collected during search engine indexing. If you forbid engines from caching your data in the beginning, you have much more control of the available views at all times.

If a search engine has already collected and exposed undesired content from your website, you do have options for removal. There are two basic strategies, and we will explain both for Google and Bing. The first idea is to delete the content and ask the search engines to re-scan your site. When they do, and see that the data is no longer present, they will eventually remove the dead link and the attached cached file. This is the easiest approach and does not require an account. The following will explain the steps for Google and Bing.

Google: Navigate to **www.google.com/webmasters/tools/submit-url** and enter your domain. They should re-index within two days.

Bing: Navigate to **www.bing.com/toolbox/submit-site-url** and enter your domain. They should re-index within one day.

With this method, you are at the mercy of Google and Bing's response. This is not immediate, and they may not respond to your request. The next options require more work and setup, but also receives a better response.

Google: Navigate to **www.google.com/webmasters/tools/home** and create an account. You will need to add a verification file to your website host which can be removed when complete. Navigate to **www.google.com/webmasters/tools/url-removal** and select the search results from your website that you want to remove.

Bing: Navigate to **www.bing.com/toolbox/webmaster** and create an account. You will need to complete the verification process to prove that you own the domain. Choose "Block URLS" within the "Configure My Site" section and enter the pages that you want immediately removed.

After you have achieved the desired results, we recommend that you remove any files that Google or Bing had you place on your website. While this does not give these services direct access to hidden data, it does allow more in-depth tracking of visits and content.

If your website has been on the internet for a while, and the Wayback Machine possesses several copies in its collection, you can remove them all. Simply add the "User-agent: ia_archiver" line mentioned previously to your robots.txt file. When the Wayback Machine crawls your site, it will see this command and complete two actions. It will identify your site in its database of domains to exclude from search and will remove all stored entries from its archive. Depending on the overall popularity of your site, this should happen within a week.

Blog Posts

If you operate or hope to operate a blog, and are reading this work, it is very likely that you wish to do so anonymously. Though we do not recommend breaking the law we do recommend that you set up your URL as anonymously as possible utilizing the steps described earlier in this chapter. Once you have established your URL and completed the other steps necessary to setup your blog you must continue to operate with security best-practices in mind.

Strip metadata from photos: As we mentioned in Chapter Seven, you should be aware that any photos you post will contain metadata. If you post photos on your anonymous blog that you have taken with the same camera that you use for more public purposes, the anonymous blog could be correlated with your public presence. We have found that very few blogging platforms or content management systems automatically strip metadata from uploaded photos so it is important that you do it beforehand. We discussed several techniques to remove this metadata. Another low-tech but extremely effective way to ensure that no metadata from the camera is uploaded is to upload a screenshot of the image. To do so open the image on your computer's screen and record a screen capture. If you are using Windows, you can use the Snipping Tool for this. Mac users can press CMD+Shift+4 to select an area to capture.

Be careful what you say: With modern analytic software it is possible to identify a writer just by his or her grammatical "signature" and stylistic tics. This is known as "forensic linguistics". For example, throughout this work Michael places only one space after a period at the end of a sentence, while Justin uses two. This was corrected in editing but is demonstrative of how something so simple could be used to identify you. Though it is unlikely you will face an adversary who will run a forensic linguistics analysis against you, you should still be careful what you say in a public forum.

Obviously you should avoid providing specific details of your life. If you are blogging about something it is highly likely you are passionate about that topic. It is also very likely that most of those who know you are aware of this passion. Where possible make small changes that would obscure facts about you that would reveal you as the blogger. For example, if you are single you may want to hint that you are married, and it may be a good idea to be somewhat misleading about your age, the region of the country that you live in, etc. You should also remember that the internet never forgets. Do not write or post anything on a blog that you would not want to see alongside your name in the newspaper in the future.

Hide your IP: We recommend always logging into your content management system through a VPN or the Tor network. Not only does this protect the information that is transmitted over your connection, it also provides a decent level of privacy by protecting your IP address. Your IP would otherwise be available to the CMS, your domain registry, and numerous other parties.

If you would like even more privacy you can schedule your post to become public at a later date and time. Most content management systems including WordPress and SquareSpace (two of the most prolific CMSs) allow you to schedule posts to be published at a future date and time. For example, you may login through a VPN and write your post, and then schedule it for two weeks in the future. In two weeks when the post becomes public, your trail is likely very cold and could only be traced by the most sophisticated of adversaries.

Be aware of account correlation: If you have more than one blog, website, or other online outlet and wish to keep them separate, you must fully firewall them from each other. For example, assume that you run a blog under your true name for professional reasons, and a blog about a personal topic under an alias, and do not wish the latter to be traced back to you. Do you use Google Analytics? Do you use Amazon Associates or other affiliate programs? If so, using the same account on two sites will correlate them with each other. Numerous "anonymous" bloggers have been exposed because they used the same Google Analytics account on both attributed and non-attributed blogs or websites.

You should also be careful about correlating websites to your personal email account. When you register your domain, you should also set aside the time to create an email account that is dedicated solely to your online presence. The correlation of your personal email address with your private blog may eventually unmask you, especially if correspondence through the website is expected.

Create your content offline: When generating content for a blog or website, you should do so while not connected to the internet. The longer you are connected the greater the risk of your true IP address being exposed. Rather, compose your text, edit your photos and videos, and prepare other content before you connect and log into your blogging platform. Once you have logged in, upload your content and make your session as brief as possible. This is a strong privacy measure if you are truly concerned with remaining anonymous and may not be appropriate for the vast majority of our readers.

Do not use your home internet connection: If you wish to do anything on the internet that is truly anonymous, you should never use your home internet connection. We doubt that most of our readers fall into this category, but it must be addressed. The inconvenience of attempting true anonymity must also be balanced with the level of anonymity you desire; if you simply wish to run a private, personal blog that people cannot easily tie to you, you may be less concerned with this. If you are a political activist in an oppressive environment or attempting to avoid similarly capable oppositions, this may be extremely important to you. As we discussed in Chapter Fourteen, even the incredibly strong protections afforded by the Tor network can be undone by a single act of carelessness online.

LEVEL FOUR:
EXPERT

If you have made it this far you are truly dedicated. You have probably spent countless hours preparing and executing the strategies outlined in the previous chapters. You have spent sleepless nights imagining your new private life. You have spent time and money and weathered the comments of those who don't understand your desire for privacy. Welcome to the "next level". We gladly welcome you to the domain of privacy that took us years to achieve. Be warned that these techniques are not for everyone. We realize a few individuals will read this out of mere curiosity. We know that a few will read on just to see how far we are willing to go. We also understand that a very select few will have the fortitude to persevere and actually go for it.

The remaining chapters in this book will challenge you even further but the reward will be well worth it. When you have become invisible and are truly digitally private and secure, welcome to our world. You are now a member of an extremely small cadre of educated individuals who have taken their privacy and security to the extreme. We will look forward to learning from your experiences in the pursuit of privacy and security. Good luck.

CHAPTER TWENTY-FOUR
OFFICIAL PHYSICAL ADDRESS

For some, this chapter may be the most important of the entire book. Unless you are a homeless transient living on cash, you are likely leaving a trail to your home address on the internet. This book has explained the steps you can take to remove and replace any information that you find about yourself online. But what if you want to start over? What if you want an official address where no one will ever find you? To obtain such an address, you may need to establish legal residency in a state that allows you to travel and live elsewhere. This address can be publicly visible and can be associated with your real name in any way that you want. Basically, this "ghost address" could be used for anything official.

The instruction in this chapter is not for everyone. Some of the techniques will be too hardcore for the typical reader. Most of the methods here will require you to do things that seem slightly abnormal. However, if you want real privacy back in your life, this chapter can get you there. Let's get started.

There are many services online that will sell you a ghost address domestically or internationally. These are basically mail drops that will forward any items to you at any other address you provide. These allow you to give out an address that is not actually associated with you or your home. While they do serve a unique purpose, we do not recommend them for being invisible. They are often very expensive and in the control of a single person or small company. If the company would shut down or the person would disappear, you would be out of luck.

These ghost addresses cannot be used to obtain a driver's license, register to vote, or renew a passport. You can never use these addresses for official government documents or official government identification. Additionally, the mail forwarding fees are usually outrageous.

A few decades ago, people often listed a post office box address on their driver's licenses. Today, that is not allowed. Instead, we must take advantage of the few remaining opportunities to have an official, yet anonymous, residence address. We promote establishing official residency at a mail drop.

Think about the number of times that you are asked for identification. Every time you check into a hotel or rent a vehicle, the name and address on your identification must match what was provided during the registration. The moment that this address is entered into any computer system, you take a chance of it leaking into other databases. Often, this leak is intentional and the company that provided the data is financially paid for the information. Casinos are well known for this type of behavior.

We believe the first step to becoming invisible is to establish an official residence that you will never live at that can be displayed on your legitimate driver's license. This will be the first task that many readers may scoff at, but we assure you it is completely legal. We have spent three years trying to locate the best method of accomplishing this, and we think we have a possible solution for some people. You could choose the path of a nomad.

Some states, such as Florida, allow non-residents to declare nomad status and become a Florida resident. This is designed for full-time travelers, such as those that live in a recreation vehicle (RV). Many of these nomads choose Florida as a resident state because they tend to migrate there for the winter. Florida agrees that the nomads do not officially reside in the state, and allow them to receive Florida driver's licenses registered to a commercial Mail Receiving Agency (CMRA or Personal Mail Box (PMB). This is unique, as most states do not allow this. Consider the following example.

Michael's Ghost Address Failure

For the past several years, we have been working on ways to establish ghost addresses. We had several failures and only a few successes. On one occasion, I approached a local businessman that owned a seven floor office building. He leased office space, and the top two floors were completely abandoned. I asked him to simply allow me to use an office number on the 7th floor that would only receive occasional mail. We agreed on a minimal fee for him to set my mail aside, and I had my first official ghost address. I had a cell phone bill sent there in my name and he signed a contract verifying that I was renting a "room" there. I excitedly drove to the driver's license facility with this proof and requested to change my address on my license. Within a minute, I was denied this request. The address was in their computer system as commercial property and no one could claim it as a residence.

This was my first encounter with the difficult task of disappearing. It seemed so simple in my mind. Apparently, I was not the first to attempt this. I was sternly informed by the DMV employee that I can only have a driver's license that listed my address where I actually lived. I knew there must be another option.

Why was it so important to me that my driver's license have an anonymous address on it? Most situations that require you provide a valid address will allow you to display your driver's license as proof of residency. Because your local DMV is so specific about the proof of residency requirements to obtain identification, other private services rely on this diligence and blindly accept that it is accurate.

First, let's identify the facts about Florida as they pertain to nomad interest.

Vehicle Tax: Florida has a 6% vehicle sales tax.

Vehicle Registration: Florida's initial vehicle registration fee is $100.00 plus $27.60 for most vehicles (under 2500 pounds).

Vehicle Inspection: Florida recently abolished the required emissions testing for vehicles. There are currently no mandatory inspections.

Vehicle Insurance: Florida has fairly high overall vehicle insurance premiums.

License Fees: A new driver's license costs $48 but only needs to be renewed every eight years. The renewal fee is also $48.

Jury duty: If you are called for jury duty in the county of your official residence, you will not be exempted solely because of your traveler status. A letter to the court identifying your current location (city and state) may excuse you, but there are no guarantees.

Concealed Carry Permits: Florida's resident permit is honored by 38 other states and is valid for 7 years. You must be 21 years of age, the cost is $112, and the processing time is 90 days. Under the Florida Sunshine Law concealed carry permit information is not considered public information.

Florida's concealed carry permit is popular among individuals who live in jurisdictions where it is difficult to obtain a resident concealed carry handgun permit. A non-resident permit can be obtained through the mail by requesting an application and fingerprint card at **www.freshfromflorida.com/Divisions-Office/Licensing/Concealed-Weapon-License**.

You will have to be fingerprinted by a law enforcement agency, fill out the application and submit it, passport photographs, and a money order for all applicable fees. You will receive your permit in the mail.

Recommended Mail Receiving Agencies:

American Home Base (Good Sam): amhomebase.com
Escapees: escapees.com
My RV Mail: myrvmail.com
St. Brendan's Isle: sbimailservice.com

As another benefit, Florida does not collect any state earnings tax from its residents. This also applies to travelers that use this state as a permanent address. Before you decide that you can live in a state that taxes income while becoming exempt in a state that does not, think again. Do not violate any tax laws. Please consider the scenarios toward the end of this chapter before you execute any plans.

The following pages outline both of our experiences with the execution of nomad status. We have had the pleasure of helping others work through their own privacy strategies and have learned a lot from the successes and failures of various methods. We hope that sharing a few of these experiences will help in understanding the process. Please note that several details were changed in order to protect the privacy of our clients. These details do not have any impact on the duplication of the efforts for your personal use. Please research your own strategy and confirm any plans with an attorney before execution.

Michael's Experiences with the Execution of Nomad Status

Overall, Florida seemed like a great choice for our first attempt at making someone invisible. It appeared relaxed about the residency requirements. I contacted a friend that was looking to relocate. He was a former police officer that was forced to resign due to constant death threats after the shooting of an armed robbery suspect who was also a high level gang member. He was fairly desperate to become invisible and was currently in the process of relocating his family from their current home. I will refer to him as "Kevin" throughout this chapter.

Kevin had not purchased a home yet and was living with his wife out of their vehicle. He had originally checked into a local hotel under his real name. He woke up one morning in his hotel room to the sound of someone trying to pick the lock of the door. He called the police but the suspect ran away before they arrived. He had no doubt that it was one of the other gang members. He was ready to go anywhere to establish new residency that would be vital to his disappearing act.

There are several companies in the state that will serve as a mail collection agency for you. Most of them will allow you to use their physical address and your personal mailbox number on your driver's license. Most of them will help guide you through the process. I reached out to all of them and asked a couple of standard questions through email. I already had the answers to these questions. I just wanted to see which of them would respond the fastest. In my opinion, that is a good indicator of customer support. In order to respect Kevin's privacy, I will not disclose which service he joined. Of all the companies that I contacted in this state, only three responded back to me.

"Company A" responded within one day. However, they did not answer my questions. They sent a canned response telling me to call them with any questions. I called right away and received no answer on the telephone.

"Company B" responded five days later and did answer my questions. I sent a follow-up question that received a response another five days later. The responses were a little slow, but very thorough.

"Company C" responded via email on the same day and answered most of my questions. They even forwarded a document to help with the process of becoming a resident of the state. I chose to pursue privacy with Company C.

Kevin gave me his credit card and complete freedom to do anything necessary. I chose the mail forwarding service that worked best for his needs and created a new account. Within a couple of days, I was informed of his new address. It appeared similar to the following.

Kevin Smith
100 Example Lane PMB 4444
City, State 56789

The 4444 referred to his individual box number. This is very similar to a PO Box, but with one huge difference. This address could be used on a driver's license and vehicle registration. I now had the first piece in place. He had an official address in another state. Any mail received at this address would be held until Kevin requested to have it packaged and sent to any other address he chose.

He was not quite ready to drive to the state and complete the difficult tasks. Therefore, I chose to start with his vehicle registration. He owned two vehicles. One was used primarily by him and the other by his wife. I started with his vehicle, which had no lien against it. I contacted the mail forwarding company and discussed my options. For $35, they would handle the entire process and Kevin would never need to physically be in the state.

I mailed the vehicle title, a limited power of attorney form supplied by Company C, and a money order for the price of the service and the registration. In his scenario, the entire cost was under $100. One week later, I requested a shipment of any waiting mail at his new mailbox to be sent to his current PO Box in his home state. Two days later, a U.S. Mail Priority envelope was waiting for him. Inside were the new state registration plates for his vehicle. The new title arrived about three weeks later.

I contacted a local insurance agent in the state that was affiliated with the same larger insurance company as Kevin's current agent. With Kevin's permission, I identified myself as him on the call. This was easier than explaining why Kevin did not call for himself. I informed her that Kevin had "moved" nearby and simply needed to transfer his current coverage from his old agent to this new agent. She asked for his new address, and I provided Kevin's new PMB address. She immediately asked if he was an "RV'er". Apparently she recognized the address and possesses insurance plans for several traveling retirees. I told her that they did not have an RV at this moment, but they will be traveling extensively.

I received absolutely no resistance. She transferred the exact coverage that Kevin currently had for both vehicles, and maintained the home insurance with his previous agent near his home. She advised that the premiums would decrease minimally, and that he would be receiving new vehicle insurance cards and a small refund. It seemed too simple. The vehicle was now registered to his private mailbox. Anyone researching his vehicle or plates would be lead to a commercial mail receiving agency and never to his home. He possessed valid insurance cards matching the registration address. This was a good start. I repeated the process and registered his wife's vehicle in the same manner as Kevin's. The only difference was that her vehicle possessed a lien. I received the license plates, but no title. The title was held by the state until the lien was satisfied. Kevin would only need to supply the state with proof from the credit provider once the vehicle was completely paid. Below are official instructions for registering and titling a vehicle in Florida.

http://flhsmv.gov/html/titlinf.html

Since Kevin was no longer employed, he wanted to start some type of online business. For his privacy, I will not disclose the type of business. I completed the process for Kevin to create a new LLC in the new state entirely online. I paid the fees with his credit card and he received the official paperwork within one week. I provided his new Personal Mail Box (PMB) address in the new state on the application and the business was registered at that address. Kevin now owned an official business in the new state. I instructed him not to generate any income with this LLC until further notice.

The process to initiate a Limited Liability Corporation (LLC) in Florida can be found at the following website.

http://form.sunbiz.org/cor_llc.html

Kevin had no desire to return to his home to collect his mail. He was now staying with a close friend several hours away. The safety issues and hassle were not worth him making any trips back to his home. We decided to immediately begin forwarding all of his mail to his new PMB. The United States Postal Service (USPS) provides a digital mail forwarding form on their website. However, I do not recommend going this route. I have spoken with several people that encountered errors with their new mail forwarding address. Instead, I recommend obtaining a paper form from any post office.

You will receive a packet with many coupons and moving offers. The only important piece in this packet is the half-page USPS change of address form. The majority of this process is self-explanatory. Enter your name, previous address, and new PMB address. However, there are a few important areas that need extra attention. The first section will ask you to designate the change of address for an individual, entire family, or business. In Kevin's case, we submitted one single form marked for the entire family. This way, any mail sent to either him or his wife would automatically be forwarded. In fact, any mail sent to his last name would be forwarded for an entire year. If you want to forward mail for another household member or business name, use a separate form for each request.

The form will ask you to state whether this move is temporary or permanent. For the purposes of privacy, I believe this should always be marked as permanent. When you enter the new address to which you want your mail forwarded, you will see an optional field labeled APT/STE/PMB. This is designed to allow you to add your apartment number, suite number, or personal mailbox (PMB) number. I never recommend placing your PMB within this box. Of the dozens of change of address forms that I have filed using this field, over half of them failed to retain the information. I suspect that data entry employees still enter this information manually. They likely rarely see this box used. Therefore, they do not think to check to see if something is in this field. Instead, I always recommend entering a new PMB address in the following format on the address line.

100 Example Lane # 4444

Every form that I have submitted this way functioned as desired. The PMB was never omitted from forwarding address. I do not recommend using the PMB identifier anywhere on this form. In Kevin's situation, we elected to have the mail begin forwarding immediately. He has never returned to his former residence. Kevin's house was vacant and listed for sale. His vehicle, insurance, and title were associated with another state. He had an official address in this new state that he could provide to any service, business, or entity. It was now time to take the plunge and make him an official resident. I requested his new mail receiving company send any waiting mail to Kevin's PO Box in his hometown. I wanted to have any vital paperwork with us during the entire trip. This package contained his new insurance cards and business paperwork.

Kevin, his wife, and I traveled to their new state. Upon arrival, we stayed in a hotel within the same county where they would be obtaining their new driver's licenses. This is mandatory for most "RV" friendly states. I spent the majority of the night reviewing the various rules associated with our plan to create new private lives for Kevin and his wife.

The next morning, we all checked out and I made sure to get a receipt for Kevin's room. This receipt must have his name and address on it. The address must match the PMB address at his new mail box. Everything looked good, so we made our way to the Department of Motor Vehicles (DMV).

I purposely picked a smaller office that had little traffic. Those occasionally offer better customer service and a personalized touch. We were immediately approached by a greeter that asked if he could assist us. I informed him that Kevin and his wife are now full time travelers and would like to obtain a driver's license in this state. This seemed very common to him and he immediately located the paperwork that they needed. This seemed like a good start. There was no hesitancy or resistance about our unusual request.

The greeter asked Kevin and his wife to make sure that they had all of the necessary documents before they went to the counter to process the paperwork. He asked them each to display their current driver's licenses in their previous state. He then asked them each for a second piece of photo identification. I had already prepared them to display their current passports. He also wanted to see their social security cards. I had not expected them to need these, but asked them to bring them in case it was required. They displayed the cards and that met all of the identification requirements. Everything was smooth until the next step.

The greeter asked for proof that the couple had spent the previous night in the state. Kevin displayed his hotel receipt including his name and new PMB address. The greeter was satisfied and then asked to see proof for his wife. I assumed that it would be obvious that they shared a hotel room and the single receipt would be sufficient. I was wrong.

I had brought a package of documents that we would possibly need. I supplied the greeter with their birth certificates, marriage license, and several other documents to prove that they were a legal couple. It was not enough. The greeter insisted that Kevin's wife also possess proof of one night's stay within the state. We advised the greeter that we would be back in twenty minutes.

We returned to the hotel and approached the desk clerk. I advised her that we had all stayed there last night and were seeking a duplicate receipt in the name of Kevin's wife. I had mentally prepared a thorough story to explain why we were making this unusual request. I was prepared to tell her that Kevin's wife was there on business and that her boss would be reimbursing her for the room. My elaborate explanation included how Kevin made the reservation and forgot to sign in with his wife's rewards account and that she would not be able to expense the stay if it was in his name. I was ready for any resistance.

Instead, the clerk told us that it was no big deal and asked what name the new receipt should be in. While it somewhat spoiled my fun, I was thrilled to have an additional receipt in her name. I was also grateful for this knowledge for future endeavors. We returned to the DMV within my promised twenty-minute time frame.

Kevin's wife proudly displayed her proof of stay, which was acceptable. He requested two pieces of documentation providing proof of the new address. I provided the contract and receipt from the mail receiving company and the vehicle insurance cards for their vehicles. All of these documents displayed both of their names. They had met all of the requirements and were advised to complete two forms. The first was a driver's license application and the second was a generic form acknowledging that they were not going to be residing full time within the state and that they would not be seeking residency within another state. It also acknowledged that they would be allowed to travel outside of the state the majority of the time.

Kevin and his wife each walked to the counter and talked with separate employees. I tried my best to watch and listen to both. They provided their paperwork and current driver's licenses from their previous state. The fees were paid and they were given their new drivers licenses from the new state. I was thrilled. As instructed, they both requested a state identification card. This seemed wise as a backup in case their licenses were lost or stolen. A flight back to this DMV would be much costlier than relying on a state ID. They would later secure these ID cards at a family member's house. They could easily be mailed if ever needed.

Kevin and his wife were now residents of a new state. This was a major accomplishment. They now possessed identification with their new address that could never be tied to any actual location. As this address gets populated within various databases, it does not jeopardize their safety or privacy. After the process, I scrutinized every detail, conversation, and of course the licenses. As instructed, Kevin provided the address in the following format.

Kevin Smith
100 Example Lane PMB 4444
City, State 56789

Kevin's wife supplied the address in following format.

Jane Smith
100 Example Lane # 4444
City, State 56789

Surprisingly, the DMV did not care if the Personal Mail Box (PMB) reference was missing. While it does not change their address, I prefer the PMB to not be present on the official ID. Some services may look at this as an unofficial address. The "#" could be a reference to an apartment, suite, or unit number. This allows for more address possibilities. The PMB cannot refer to anything different.

We next visited the mail receiving company. We wanted to get a look at the facility and collect any mail that was waiting for them. We chose to do this after the trip to the DMV in order to register them to vote in the state. It must be in this order because you need an official address in order to receive a driver's license. You must have a state driver's license in order to register to vote. The voter registration process is usually easier at the mail receiving company than at the DMV for most RV friendly states. This is usually a service that the mail receiving company provides for its members.

Kevin and his wife registered to vote via proxy and would be allowed to vote via postal mail during the next elections. Even if you do not plan to vote, I recommend registering. During the registration process, you will disclose the county and state of current voter registration. The new state will notify the previous state to remove you from their voter database. This will remove the association with your previous address and attach a new association to your new private address. We departed the mail forwarding company and drove to the airport.

I watched as Kevin and his wife confidently displayed their new licenses to the TSA agent as they navigated through airport security. Over the next few weeks, they began changing their address with their various services such as banking, investing, and credit cards. Since Kevin had a credit freeze in place, the credit bureaus must notify him if they detect an address change. Within three days, Kevin received this notification. This was a great test to verify this system was working.

I considered the entire event a success. This was a vital step to the future privacy of Kevin and his wife. They now had the freedom to travel as they desired while they planned their future. They had a secure address to use for any mail and all mail addressed to their previous home would be forwarded automatically to the PMB. They could request their mail be forwarded to any address desired including hotels, campgrounds, family and friend's houses, or even general delivery to a post office.

At the time of this writing, Kevin and his wife were true nomads. They traveled extensively and are still considering the location of their permanent home. When they decide, they are prepared to use a New Mexico LLC for the purchase of the home and all utilities. If conducted correctly, they will never need to worry about the wrong person locating their new address. Their true names will never be associated with the new address.

Soon after I assisted Kevin, another subject who wished the same treatment contacted me. Before you think that I only have friends that need to disappear, remember that I provide a lot of privacy training to various government, military, and private sector entities. Every month, I meet several people that have unique circumstances that demand careful execution of privacy strategies.

This scenario was quite different from Kevin's. This subject, who I will refer to as Mary, was practically a household name. She suffered from constant attention that was undesired. She did not necessarily feel threatened, but she wanted privacy. On several occasions, she left her home to discover news cameras on her front lawn and curious people trying to figure out if she really resided at the house. She was ready to do whatever it took to disappear.

She was single with no children. This made for another easy execution. She did not possess a vehicle and was ready to dive in. She had already identified a new home that she would be buying soon, and wanted her privacy protection plan in place before purchase.

I established an account for her at a mail receiving company in the new state. The process was almost identical to Kevin's experience. I met her at a hotel near the most appropriate DMV. The next morning, I obtained a duplicate receipt for her room and verified that the name and address matched her PMB information. We went to the DMV together and I quizzed her on the best responses to any questions about full time travel.

This time the DMV was much busier and there was no greeter. The workers did not appear very friendly and I grew more concerned as they chastised the person in front of us for not signing on the correct line. I did not think that Mary was going to do well.

At the last minute, I made a major change in our game plan. We needed a slight edge in our favor. I was worried that Mary would say something that she should not. I wanted to do the talking in case the worker became resistant. I asked Mary if she had ever had an ear infection. She looked concerned with my sanity and acknowledged that she had several as a child. I asked if she ever had a hard time hearing after a concert. Again, she confirmed this and I advised her to say absolutely nothing until further notice.

When it was our turn, I walked to the counter with Mary. I immediately advised the employee that Mary has had several ear problems and had experienced some hearing loss. I asked if I could assist and help make sure Mary understood the employee. We received no resistance and a mildly better attitude from the worker.

I handled the entire process and Mary never said a word. I provided her current driver's license from her previous state and her social security card. She did not have a valid passport so I provided her expired identification from the university she attended. For address verification, I provided the receipt from her new PMB address and a letter that I had mailed to her PMB address previously. This is when I learned of the next snag that I would hit.

The DMV employee stated that any mail sent to the address of the applicant that is used during the application process must be typed. I had hand written her name and address on the envelope and this was not acceptable. After a brief panic, I realized that I had other options. Within the envelope that was sent to her from her new mail forwarding company was a credit card application. The name and address was typed. I had previously contacted Discover and requested a printed application for a credit card to be sent to Mary at her PMB address. My intent was to see how quickly this new address would leak out to other companies. Fortunately, this worked in my favor in an unanticipated way.

I offered the proof of the previous night's stay, and the worker barely glanced at it. She seemed more concerned about keeping the line moving. Mary smiled huge for her new license and excitedly signed for her new layer of privacy. The employee quietly murmured "thank you" as we started to walk away. Mary confidently responded, "You're welcome!", as if she had regained perfect hearing. I encouraged her to start walking faster toward the exit.

Mary travels the world and it makes a lot of sense for her to have a stable location for receiving mail. Her new driver's license with an invisible address will satisfy any identification requirements without jeopardizing any privacy. She can freely announce this address privately or publicly without fear of the wrong person getting ahold of it. She later purchased a new home with cash using a New Mexico LLC and all of her utilities were registered in the same LLC name. She possesses a local PO Box for personal mail and packages. Her neighbors have no idea who she is.

Q & A

This topic often raises more questions than it answers. This next section will attempt to address those concerns and identifies the most common inquires about establishing a ghost residence. We always recommend seeking the advice of an attorney that specializes in these matters before you commit to any changes.

Q: I already live in Florida, or another state that allows nomad status. Can I use this method to replace my current official address?

A: We believe so. Since you are already a legal resident, the state should not care which address you use. You may have to explain to the DMV that you no longer live at the previous address and that you will be traveling extensively in the future.

Q: I do not live in Florida, or another state that allows nomad status. I live in another state that does not charge state income tax. Can I use this method to replace my current official address?

A: Possibly. Since the state you are primarily in does not collect state income tax revenue from you, they likely have little concern over your official residency. This can get into a grey area and you want to be sure that you are not violating any state laws.

Q: I do not live in Florida, or another state that allows nomad status. I live in another state that DOES charge state income tax. Can I use this method to replace my current official address?

A: Possibly. However, you will still need to pay your appropriate earnings tax within the state where you actually reside. Consider the following scenarios.

- If you live full time in California (or any other state that collects income tax), you cannot claim to be a Florida resident and not pay California income taxes. It will catch up to you.

- If you work full time in that state (California in this example), you will likely need an ID in that state and an address in that state for your IRS W-2 form. Some companies may not care what state your official address is in, but they will certainly withhold state income tax from your paycheck. You are allowed to live in one state and work in another. Remember that the state you physically work in is entitled to its state income tax from you.

- If you own a home in a state with income tax, and pay property taxes in that state, that state will want earnings tax from you. In this example, "relocating" to Florida may not be a wise option.

Q: I am retired and travel full-time (with or without an RV), is this method wise for me?

A: We believe it was designed for you. If you travel all over the country or world, it is fairly easy to establish residency in one of these states. As long as no other state has an interest in you financially, we believe this is one of the best actions you can take to achieve true privacy.

Q: I don't get it. How does having official identification with another address make me invisible?

A: Technically, it does not. This is the first and vital step to gaining a completely invisible life. This method provides you an official address that is acceptable to the government and every private entity. It can be given to anyone and tells no one where you live. Therefore, it is the perfect start to a path where you never again disclose your home address to any business or anyone you do not trust. When you are ready to move into a new residence, you are ready to use this new invisible address to help bypass intrusive demands for your personal information.

Q: Are there any reasons why I should not execute this type of plan?

A: Absolutely! There are many reasons that this could be a bad idea for you. We know of a person that successfully became invisible using this method and purchased a new home in a business name. When it was time for him to renew his security clearance, he failed. The background investigator could not verify any current address and had no choice but to block the security clearance. This person finally gained his clearance, but it took much more effort than previously. If you are in a position that requires you to disclose your home address for political or employment reasons, this may not be wise for you. Personally, we would consider alternative employment.

Q: What do you do if the police stop you?

A: The same thing we have always done. We stop, remain courteous, and comply with any demands. When asked for identification, we present our driver's license from the anonymous states that we each chose. If questioned, we explain that we travel all over and chose that state to be home. If pressured into disclosing where we sleep at night, we provide the last few hotels that we have stayed in nationally. The address on your license satisfies any legal requirement to drive or be present in any state. If you have broken any laws, legal paperwork can be sent to your PMB address. It can be entered on any citation, arrest form, or court documentation. In many states, every speeding ticket can be viewed on the internet. We know of one police officer that received a speeding ticket and admitted fault. He paid the fine. Within two weeks, the father of a gang member that he had recently arrested showed up at the officer's home. The father had found the address online from this citation. Your new PMB address will prohibit this from happening to you.

Q: How do I get my mail?

A: This varies. Most people that choose this option have their mail sent to any location where they will be present for a length of time. This could be a campground, family member's home, or general delivery at a nearby post office. Because we never encourage any mail to be sent in your name to your own home, we do not promote receiving your forwarded mail at your primary home. Our favorite method is to forward the mail to a hotel. We travel constantly. When we will be at a specific hotel for a few days, it is a great opportunity to have our collected mail forwarded to that hotel.

Q: Wait, you said to use an alias at hotels, how would I get my mail there?

A: Good catch. After you create your account at the PMB of your choice, you can add an additional line to the shipment such as "Hold for guest Michael Smith". You can add your travel alias and have the mail forwarded to the hotel under that name.

Is this strategy appropriate for you? Only you can decide. We only hope that this chapter encourages you to think outside the box. We also hope that it offers a sense of relief and reminds you that there are alternative options for possessing a private and secure official address. While it may not be appropriate today, later life changes may present an ideal scenario for this lifestyle.

CHAPTER TWENTY-FIVE
MAJOR LIFE EVENTS

This chapter will cover some, though certainly not all, major life events. If you encounter a life event or situation that is not explicitly covered by this situation we hope that the examples here will guide your thinking process.

Purchasing a Home

If you are planning on purchasing a home, this is a huge opportunity to make it practically impossible to be located from an internet search. Earlier chapters explained how your publicly visible property tax record will inform dozens of data mining websites of your home address. This data will be acquired by many websites and you would need to remove the data from each site. Instead, consider starting life in your new home without attaching your name to the residence.

This method is only for those that are truly committed to being invisible from the public. The general idea of this process is credited to J.J. Luna, the author of the book *How to be Invisible*. The basic premise of this specific method is the following:

- Purchase an official LLC from a registered agent in New Mexico. These are never publicly associated with your real name, but you own the business. These are very affordable.

- Purchase your new home using the LLC as the owner. The LLC can also purchase vehicles and other property.

- Never associate your name with the house you live in. Personal mail should be delivered to a PO Box. Utilities should be in the name of the LLC.

If you are at all intrigued by these possibilities, Luna's book is a good primer. The methods are completely legal. Mr. Luna provides recommended services in New Mexico that will make the process easy. If you are in any way targeted by someone, as victims of harassment or police officers commonly are, this will guarantee that you will have a home private from the internet. For more information, visit jjluna.com and select the New Mexico LLCs tab. While we will disclose our experiences with New Mexico LLC's in this chapter, we insist that you always consult with a real estate attorney before you commit to your invisible home purchase. It will be money well spent.

We have worked with many people who chose the path of an invisible LLC as the owner of their home. We have selected two common scenarios to present to you. Both may help you determine if this method is appropriate for your situation.

"John" purchased his New Mexico LLC through Luna's service. He dealt with "Rosie", the registered agent for this service. He provided a generic 33Mail email address during the purchase that forwards to his primary email account. This meets the requirement for notification by the registered agent that is included with the purchase. If a subpoena were delivered to the New Mexico agent, she could forward it via email. John would not necessarily need to give his real name to the agent. He paid less than $400 which includes three years of registered agent service. He used a Blur masked credit card. He received his paperwork and confirmed the LLC through New Mexico's business lookup website. He is now the owner of an invisible LLC.

John chose to register this business with the Internal Revenue Service (IRS). He associated the LLC with his own Social Security number (SSN). Some privacy advocates do not endorse this step. We believe that it is a smart move. It will definitely create a connection between his invisible LLC and real identity. However, this is only visible to the IRS, and is not publicly visible. We promote this for several reasons.

- The IRS will assign an Employer Identification Number (EIN). This will be required in order to open a business checking account, if desired.

- The IRS will have a record of this business name, creation date, and association with you. If anyone were to challenge the true owner of the property, this record could work in your favor.

- The LLC will never have any income, therefore there will be no taxes due.

- Legally registering this business with the IRS eliminates most appearances that you are trying to hide or launder money. This overt action may work in your favor if you are ever audited.

Creating the EIN number was conducted through the official IRS website and was immediate. He registered the business as a sole proprietor. The state of his full-time residence was not relevant. He will now include this EIN on his tax return yearly, but will claim no income. His accountant will fill in the proper information.

John now had the LLC in place and an EIN to use when appropriate. He identified the home he wanted to buy and had a real estate agent that he liked. He chose this agent after interviewing five candidates. At our recommendation, he asked the following question to each of the potential agents.

"How do I buy this home using my LLC and not providing my name?"

One agent stated that this was impossible, and she was immediately eliminated. Two agents stated that it should be no problem and that they would work it out at the closing. These two were also dismissed. One agent declared that he really did not know, and withdrew interest. The final candidate stated that it was absolutely possible, but there would be many requirements that John would need to work with. He further stated that a cash purchase would be the easiest way, that a real estate attorney should look over everything before closing, and John should not be present at the closing. We liked this agent.

John paid cash in the form of a bank money order for this modest home. He paid a real estate attorney $500 to verify that everything was in order. John gave limited power of attorney to the real estate attorney, and this person signed the appropriate paperwork at the closing on behalf of the LLC. Everything was smooth, and it was a bargain at $500. John's name was never disclosed anywhere on any paperwork. Only the LLC was identified as the owner. The LLC is not publicly associated with John. There is no trail for anyone to follow.

We respect that John is a rarity that can pay cash for a home. Therefore, we also want to tell you about "Jane" and her experience. Jane identified the home that she wanted but only had 10% of the price as a down payment. In this scenario, she has no choice but to disclose her true identity to the bank issuing the loan. She had already obtained the invisible LLC that would be used as the actual owner of the property. She did not register this LLC with the IRS, which is completely legal. She would not be using it for any income, she was the sole proprietor, and the LLC would never have any employees. Since she was obtaining a loan in her true name, there was little need for additional protection from the IRS.

When Jane met with a loan specialist, she quickly declared that this would not be a traditional loan request. She stated that she would be titling the home in the name of an LLC and that her name would not be associated with the property. She was promptly informed that this would be impossible. As we had instructed her, she politely walked out of the meeting. We had a backup plan.

We contacted five major home loan providers and scheduled a call with each for the purpose of negotiating a loan rate. We scheduled this call for the same time for each provider. We stated that the subject of the loan would also be on the call and that we were acting on her behalf. We disclosed her true identity and SSN in order for a preliminary credit check to be performed before the call. We did not disclose to any of the providers that other companies would be involved.

This gave the loan specialists an opportunity to discover that Jane was a great candidate for a loan with good credit. We provided her desired house price range, amount available for a down payment, and time frame for purchase. We never disclosed her current location, but this would not have been much of a compromise. Her name was already publicly attached to her current residence through numerous websites.

We arranged a telephone conference line that we could use for one hour. The cost was less than $15. On the date and time of the scheduled call, we contacted each loan specialist and placed them on a brief hold while we "patched in Jane". While we did bring Jane into the call, we also connected all five providers at the same time. We stated that Jane would like to negotiate the best rate possible, and would only be accepting offers during this live call. Before we opened the floor to the frustrated providers, we explained that the loan must be in the name of her LLC. We further clarified that she would be responsible for the loan and understood that she would need to co-sign at the least. We were adamant that her name would never be disclosed during the closing process. Only the LLC would be listed as the owner on the deed for the home. We acknowledged that she was the sole proprietor of the LLC and the confirmed the loan would be the responsibility solely of her as an individual.

One loan company ended the call right away. One sat quietly and just absorbed the entire situation. The remaining three presented their best offers. Two of them lowered the interest rate and began a bidding war to compete for the loan. The winner offered a rate that we were unable to find advertised anywhere. Jane was thrilled.

Many people enter a bank and plead for a home loan. We look at it differently. The bank should be begging you. You will be paying them tens of thousands of dollars in interest. We believe THEY are the employee and YOU are in charge of the process.

Obviously, there are flaws with this method. Associating Jane with the loan can be dangerous. If her details leak out, she would be compromised. With her situation, there was not much else as an option. We were not worried about the bank releasing any information. They keep financial details fairly secure. The title company that conducts the closing process was the only concern. As long as they do not know who Jane is, it should stay out of public record. We insisted that she hire a real estate attorney to review everything and sign at the closing as her limited power of attorney. She insisted on attending the closing. She attended as the attorney's intern and signed nothing.

The main lesson here is that a truly invisible home is possible. You will likely be met with resistance along the way. Do not let that deter you. When someone says that you cannot do this, find a different professional. Always remember that these people work for you, not the other way around.

If you have executed the "Nomad" method mentioned in the previous chapter, you may want to consider an "invisible" LLC in the state in which you established residency. Of the three states mentioned in that chapter, only South Dakota offers decent privacy. In order to establish an LLC, you only need to provide the identity of the "organizer" along with an address of the business. You could establish a new PMB for the business and have a nominee organize the paperwork for you. Most importantly, South Dakota does not require you to disclose the names of the LLC owners or partners. Texas and Florida require this disclosure.

While the New Mexico LLC is the gold standard, we believe that South Dakota nomad residents could take advantage of the laid back rules. Remember that these methods are for privacy only. Do not attempt any fraud.

Over the past few years, we have spoken with several readers that were not ready to make the jump into invisible LLC's. We completely understand and agree that the idea of placing your largest asset into the name of an LLC that is not registered to you can be overwhelming. Additionally, this can be difficult when there is a lien on the home. The following option does not provide the same level of privacy as an invisible LLC. However, it will help shield your real name from public records.

Many people choose to make the owner of their home a revocable living trust. This is usually not associated with privacy protection. A living trust is a legal entity that many people use for the distribution of wealth when they die. A will can be beneficial, but it is subject to probate. This means that your wishes detailed in your will are not executed until approved by the probate court. This can take years. A living trust avoids the probate process altogether.

To create a revocable living trust, you (the grantor) transfers ownership of some or all of your property to the trust. Because you make yourself the "trustee", you don't give up any control over the property you put in the trust. If you and your spouse create a trust together, you will be co-trustees.

In the trust document, you name the people or institutions you want to inherit trust property after your death. You can change those choices at any time if you wish. You can also revoke the trust completely. When you die, the person you named in the trust document to take over, called the successor trustee, transfers ownership of trust property to the people you want to get it. In most cases, the successor trustee can handle the whole thing in a few weeks with some simple paperwork.

Essentially, you can create your own revocable living trust by completing a form. There are numerous versions online or you could create one using a word processor. This printed trust identifies the name of the trust and the assets that are owned by the trust. This document should be notarized and witnessed by at least two trusted subjects.

Trusts are extremely common with home owners. Often, a retired person will transfer any property, including a home, into a trust as part of estate planning. If you are buying a new home, you should consider taking this step now instead of later. This will keep your name out of many public databases.

Before you purchase the home, you should have your revocable trust complete and active. You do not need to generate an EIN number with the IRS. You will need to give your trust a name. Most people choose something obvious such as "The Michael Bazzell Living Trust" or "The Bazzell Family Living Trust". Using personally identifiable information is not mandatory or recommended. Instead, consider something generic such as "The Private Life Living Trust" or "The Partners Living Trust". These names do not associate you with the trust.

Once you have created the trust, you need to add your assets. You cannot add cash, but you can add property, real estate, collectibles, and financial accounts. Many people with whom we consult have all of their wealth in the name of their living trust. Financial accounts will still be associated with your real name and Social Security number. This is important to prove ownership.

When you close on your new home, consider allowing your real estate agent to sign the paperwork on your behalf. Make sure he or she understands your desire to place the title for the home in the name of your living trust, and not in your name. Financial institutions are familiar with this process and should allow this during your loan process. Obviously, any loan will still be in your name.

If you already own your home, and moving is out of the question, you can transfer your home into the trust. This will require filing a quitclaim deed at your county assessor's office. This is a very standard practice that should not raise any suspicion. Your home address will still be associated with your real name on several websites, but new information that is collected will replace your name with the name of your trust. This will eliminate a lot of new entries associating you with your home address.

We want to stress the importance of consulting with a lawyer when creating your living trust. We also recommend reading any books by Nolo on the living trust creation process. The minor expense that you spend to make all of the documentation correct will pay off tenfold when you die and your heirs are left with your assets. Additionally, having the correct and accurate paperwork will aid in a smooth process when placing a home in the name of the trust.

Renting a Home

Renting can have advantages and disadvantages in regard to protecting your privacy. Some places include all utilities which is a huge privacy layer. If the utilities are already in the landlord's name, you never need to provide your information to the utility companies. Unfortunately, most rental agreements will require your full details for a background check. You may also be asked to obtain an occupancy permit. The following suggestions will get you through these roadblocks.

Avoid large complexes. Apartments and condominiums that are maintained by larger businesses have strict rules on processing applicants. You will need to pay a fee to have them conduct a complete history, criminal, and financial background check on your real information. If you pass, you will then be required to use your details for all utilities and permits. Look for homes and apartments owned by individuals. They will be more willing to accommodate a good renter.

We recommend applying Luna's method of obtaining an invisible LLC for renting. Your LLC can rent the place and pay the bills. Many renters welcome this arrangement. Receiving money every month from a business is more reliable than from an individual. People that I have consulted in similar situations have had the best results with the following techniques.

Find an apartment or home that is a prospect for rental. Notify the owner right away that the company you work for is relocating you and will be paying the rent. Provide the name of the LLC and your post office box address. Offer to pay a month in advance and have a check from the LLC ready for the deposit. Be polite and look professional.

Another option is to notify the owner that you have been the victim of stalking or harassment and you are looking for a new safe place to stay. Explain your concern about making your information public. This tends to work best for females or families with children. Overall, be courteous and respectful. Offer to pay an additional month of rent in advance in order to demonstrate your ability to make the payments.

LLC Bank Accounts

Regardless of your method of using invisible New Mexico LLC's, you will likely need a business checking account to take full advantage of this layer of privacy. While some privacy advocates discourage any use of business banking, we embrace the necessity. Using cash to order new utilities, pay your monthly mortgage, or hire labor services is not always an option. Today, it also makes you look guilty of something. We hate this, but we must accept the world we live in. Therefore, we believe it is important to possess a business checking account if you have an invisible LLC.

This is not an easy task. We have been denied more business accounts at banks than we have been successful. As with everything else, diligence will pay off in the end. Hopefully, our research will help you and your journey for anonymity.

We contacted numerous banks and credit unions with the intent of opening a business checking account in the name of our invisible LLC. The odd requirement was that we would not disclose the owner of the LLC or the SSN of the client. New federal laws post 9/11 have made this very difficult. Many bankers believe that obtaining the SSN of the account holder is absolutely required. While the bank's policy may require this, the law does not. They are only required to obtain either the SSN of the individual or EIN of the business. Convincing the bank of this is often impossible.

Most of the large chain banks that we visited absolutely insisted that the person that opens the business account must provide their true name, home address, SSN, DOB, and copies of two forms of government identification. We found local credit unions to be a bit more accommodating, but they still wanted ID and a SSN. In order to skip directly to the two initial successes, here are the best results.

During one of our training sessions, we met a privacy enthusiast that had just obtained his invisible LLC. He was ready to open a bank account and asked if we were interested in an after-class road trip. We took the bait and drove with him and his brother to an Associated Bank in his town. We developed our strategy on the drive there. We went in and sat down with a banker. Our new friend was nervous and allowed us to do the talking. Before you think we are crazy for this, know that he was employed by a federal agency that is in the same circles as those in our background. This brought a little comfort.

He had targeted this bank because his initial telephone calls led him to believe that they would not require a SSN. We stated that we wanted to open a business checking account. We provided the New Mexico LLC certificate, the IRS letter including EIN, $2,500 initial cash from the owner, and a contract identifying his brother as the "organizer" of the LLC. This was also referenced in the articles of organization that we provided. We completed some paperwork, had his brother sign the documents and allowed the banker to make copies of the documentation.

Eventually, the banker asked for the brother's SSN. We interrupted and stated that the business would only like the account associated with the EIN as provided by the IRS. Since the brother was not an owner of the business, it would be inappropriate for the brother to disclose his own SSN. To our surprise, the banker was not bothered by this. The brother had to provide photo government identification. He was prepared with his passport that did not include a SSN or home address.

It should be noted that the brother had a different last name than our friend. This was a nice layer of privacy. Only the bank knows the owner of the LLC. These bank records should stay private. They will definitely not be visible on the internet. Our friend left the bank with a new business checking account, temporary checks, and official checks on the way. He only provided a PO Box as the address of the business. He disclosed that it was a home based business and nothing else was required. The bank met its obligation by obtaining the EIN assigned by the IRS. The IRS should be content since we have now associated the banking account with the true owner in their eyes.

We believe that financial institutions in every area will be unique. Large chain bank branches in one town may be more willing to accommodate than identical banks in other cities. Your experience will likely be unique from anything that we can print. However, below is a table that displays financial institutions and our results when attempting to open business checking accounts.

Institution	EIN Required?	SSN Required?	Balance to avoid fees:
Associated Bank	Yes	No	$2,500
Bank of America	Yes	No	$3,000
Chase Bank	Yes	No	$1,500
Local Credit Union 1	Yes	Yes	$1,000
Local Credit Union 2	Yes	Yes	$1,500
Local Credit Union 3	Yes	No	$1,500
Local Credit Union 4	Yes	No	$2,500
US Bank	Yes	Yes	$1,500

Obviously, this list includes an extreme minority of available institutions. We only wanted to verify that this concept was plausible. We discovered that larger financial institutions seem to be the strictest. US Bank absolutely refused to entertain the thought of not collecting someone's SSN. We found this to be the case at three locations. Because the option was on the application, it was mandatory. Bank of America's application also included a mandatory SSN field. However, we were allowed to open an account with only an EIN. While we could not do this over the internet, a visit to their physical branch worked fine. On one occasion, we simply stated "I don't have an SSN, I only have this letter from the IRS with my EIN on it". Exactly 50% of the credit unions that we contacted allowed business accounts with only an EIN. Chase allowed us to use only an EIN, but demanded two forms of identification and all members of the business to be present. We were allowed to nominate an organizing member and she only had to show a passport and utility bill (neither display a SSN).

This resistance is likely due to policies and not interpretation of law. We encourage you to start with the smaller banks and credit unions in your area. Explain your situation and dress nicely. Speak clearly and confidently. We do not recommend that you open a business account anywhere that you already have personal accounts in place.

Anonymous Utilities

Whether you live in a house owned by an invisible LLC, home titled to a living trust, or apartment in the name of your landlord, you must take care in establishing your utilities. A previous chapter already mentioned acquiring anonymous internet service. Obtaining electricity, gas, sewer, trash, and water can bring complications.

If your home is in the name of an LLC, we encourage you to continue this appearance and assign your utilities to the LLC. When you contact each company, tell them that the home is owned by a business and that you want to set up the new account. Identify yourself as a representative of the business and declare that you will not be living at the house. If pressured, tell them that employees temporarily assigned to the area will stay here as needed. Offer to pay a deposit and sign up for automatic withdrawals from your business checking account. If they push for a SSN, offer the EIN assigned to the LLC. This should suffice.

If your property is in a living trust, you may consider an invisible LLC solely for the utilities. You can also try the prior instruction and ask the bills to be assigned to the trust. If pressured, tell them that you are calling on behalf of your grandmother and that the house is in the name of the trust. State that she insists that the bills match the deed for the home. Many people that are not familiar with living trusts associate them with elderly people near death.

If you are renting, ask your landlord if you can keep the utilities in his or her name. Offer to prepay and have a sob story ready. If he or she refuses, you could consider either the LLC or living trust methods. Most importantly, never place the utilities of your invisible home in your own name or the name of anyone close to you. This will immediately compromise your location.

We recently spoke to a potential client that had tried everything she could think of to place her utilities in an alias name. She had been denied during every attempt. While she had practically given up, we had one last idea that could work for her. With some brief coaching, she provided the following details to a well-known power company when asked for her SSN and DOB.

"I do not have a SSN. I am not a U.S. citizen; I am just here attending school full time. I have a credit card for a deposit if that helps. Do you want my Personal Identification Number?"

To be very clear, this is obviously a lie. However, we could find no state or federal laws that declares lying to a private company about utility service a criminal act. As long as your intentions are good and you pay your bills, there is no fraud in our opinion. She provided a random "Personal Identification Number" which does not exist to the operator. Her credit card was charged a $100 deposit and a small convenience fee. We considered this a fair trade.

Vehicle Purchases

The preferred way to stay anonymous throughout a vehicle purchase is to pay cash to an individual. This is not always ideal depending on the type of vehicle you want. I believe that vehicles should be the property of, and registered to, an invisible New Mexico LLC. At the very least, they should be attached to a revocable living trust. They should never be registered to your real name. This is based on years of monitoring criminal behavior and erroneous lawsuits. Consider the following true scenario.

Several years ago, I (Michael) was interviewing a criminal who had brutally attacked the driver of a vehicle that unintentionally cut him off in traffic. The victim had a faster car than the attacker and sped away before anything bad could happen. Though the victim had gotten away and felt safe in his own home, the attacker showed up at his door. A fight ensued and the victim was left permanently disfigured. During the interview, I learned that the attacker had obtained the home address of the victim through his license plate registration. These queries are only available to law enforcement and a handful of companies, so I was intrigued by how he was able to do this. He gave the following account.

After the road rage incident, the attacker was at home and furious about the event. He wanted revenge. He had written down the license plate of the victim and wanted to know where he lived. He turned on his police scanner and monitored the channel of his local police. He then called that police department and reported a drunk driver all over the road at a nearby location. He provided the actual license registration of the victim. He then listened to the police scanner as the dispatcher advised patrol units of the reported reckless driver. At the end of the dispatch, the patrol units were told the name and address of the victim according to the registration. The attacker had now heard what he needed to confront and beat the victim.

Having your vehicle registered to either an LLC or trust would save you from this type of attack. The offender would only know the name of your LLC or trust and a PO Box that receives mail. However, a trust will provide you no protection from erroneous lawsuits. Having your vehicle owned and registered to an invisible LLC will provide you an additional layer of protection. Nothing will make you 100% lawsuit-proof, but every layer can help. Consider the following.

Within 30 days of purchasing a new vehicle, data brokers know every detail about you, the vehicle, and how it was financed. If you have any doubt about this, request your personal report from LexisNexis and others as instructed in the next chapters. You should see the details of every vehicle at your residence and information about the licensed drivers. The report identifies the full name and home address of the owner. The vehicle information includes the year, make, model, VIN, weight, wheel base, base price, size of the vehicle, vehicle's registration, title number, and lien information. If you are still not convinced that this is an invasion of your privacy, consider the following.

Accident attorneys, sometimes referred to as "ambulance chasers", make a lucrative living from suing people involved in traffic crashes. Some of their clients come to them seeking damages, but an overwhelming number of lawsuits are generated by the attorney. Lawyers can go to a police department and request a copy of every traffic crash report for an entire month. These redacted reports include the names of the vehicle owners and the insurance companies providing insurance on the vehicles. The reports are modified to mask the name and home address of the subjects involved. This request must be allowed because the attorney filed a Freedom of Information request. The police department must comply. Michael has personally witnessed teams of lawyers sit in the police lobby and look through the reports for traffic crashes involving expensive vehicles owned by the driver at fault. They then conduct a quick internet search on the vehicle owners and respond to the victim's home to encourage a lawsuit.

If you are involved in a traffic crash, you cannot keep the vehicle owner's name from appearing on a public report. You also cannot hide the details about your vehicle. You can keep your name from the public version by purchasing the vehicle with your new LLC. When you buy a new or used vehicle, notify the sales person that you will be purchasing the vehicle on behalf of a business and that the registration and title should identify the business as the owner. This technique is explained in J.J. Luna's book, *How To Be Invisible*. With this method in place, the nosy lawyer will only know that your LLC owns the vehicle, and will not have a name to associate with the vehicle. If a lawsuit is filed, the attorney can make a new request for the complete report, which will identify you. However, the mass search will mask your details. Please note that this does not hide your details from the other party involved if they request a report. It also does not hide your details from the police department investigating the incident.

Senseless acts like these are reasons why we recommend purchasing and registering any vehicle as an entity and not an individual. The idea of an invisible LLC discussed earlier may not have been ideal for you when buying a home. However, you may be more comfortable with this tactic during a vehicle purchase. For many people, registering their vehicle to an LLC or trust is the gateway toward complete anonymity with all future purchases. There are several possibilities for this, and we will outline various scenarios here to give you an idea of the best formula for your needs. Each method identifies the type of purchase, payment used, and method of identity protection.

- Individual-Cash (LLC): If you possess an invisible LLC from New Mexico, this is the ideal way to go. Give the individual cash and obtain a valid title. Take the title and your LLC paperwork to a local vehicle title shop and have them complete the proper process for registering the vehicle. This type of business will be much more accommodating than the Department of Motor Vehicles (DMV).

- Individual-Cash (Trust): After you have created your revocable living trust, give the individual cash and obtain a valid title. Take the title and your trust paperwork to a local vehicle title shop and have them complete the proper process for registering the vehicle.

- Dealer-Cash (LLC): Staying anonymous at a dealership is not difficult, but it will take some diligence. Having the resources to purchase a vehicle without a loan will aid in this process. When you first meet the sales person, advise them right away that you are shopping for your boss and that the company (LLC) will be purchasing the vehicle. The dealership will facilitate the registration process and you should demand that all information is in the name of the LLC. While you cannot use a PO Box on your driver's license, most states allow the use on vehicle registration.

- Dealer-Cash (Trust): When you first meet the sales person, advise them right away that you are purchasing the vehicle in the name of your Grandma's trust. They will not know if this is true. The dealership will facilitate the registration process and you should demand that all information is in the name of the trust. Again, provide your valid PO Box and never give them your real address.

- Dealer-Loan (LLC): A dealer will not give you a loan in the name of an LLC or trust. This does not mean you cannot register the vehicle in the name of either. Complete the loan paperwork and demand that the vehicle is registered to your LLC. Inform the sales person that you will not complete the sale until you see proof that this is set up accordingly. I advise avoiding the loan process if at all possible.

- Dealer-Loan (Trust): Similar to the previous option, complete the loan paperwork and demand that the vehicle is registered to your trust. Inform the sales person that you will not complete the sale until you see proof that this is set up accordingly.

Michael's Vehicle Experience

I can speak from experience that providing your real address when you purchase a vehicle is a bad idea. I purchased a new vehicle in 2003 and provided all of my personal information. I did not know better at the time. In 2005, I began receiving numerous advertisements referencing my vehicle and offering me discounted services. In 2008, I began receiving third party warranty options since my standard warranty was about to expire. My name, address, and vehicle information was in the hands of dozens of companies.

When you buy from a dealer, you cannot stop this information from being sold. However, you can control the information that is attached to your profile. When paying cash, always provide the name of an LLC or trust, a PO Box address, and nothing else. Have a check ready for the sale that is attached to an account for the LLC or trust. Be prepared to walk away when a sales person begins pushing you for more information. They will always stop you and do whatever it takes to make the sale.

Names, Marriage, and Children

What is a name? Most people consider their name to be an intrinsic part of who they "are". We disagree with this prevailing wisdom. A name, in our opinion, is little more than a system of organization that people use to categorize each other. Your name does not have a dramatic effect on who you are, what you will become, or the successes you will enjoy or the failures you will endure in life. We contend that a name is simply a proper noun used by your friends, family, colleagues, and acquaintances to distinguish you from the others they know and recognize, and through which they verbally address you.

We make this assertion early in this section because this portion of the book will challenge you to think differently about your name and the names of your future children. If you have made it this far into this book you have demonstrated an above-average interest in privacy. You have also demonstrated an open-mindedness to a lifestyle that is non-traditional to say the least. We believe the suggestions contained in this section have a great deal of merit, and that you will think so too.

Marriage

When you get married a great deal of new information is generated about you. Though most individuals wish to proclaim their love of another to the world, this information is fraught with privacy concerns. Weddings are matters of public record and are often published in newspapers and on the internet. You should consider this before getting married. If you are a high-risk federal agent, you may be endangering your partner by publicly marrying him or her. Before getting married you should think through a few other things.

The first consideration is whether you really want to get married. Many couples live happy, successful lives without the legal bond of marriage. We are not anti-marriage and we understand the social and financial benefits of marriage. We do encourage you to seriously consider the commitment of marriage and the privacy implications it carries. If you decide to get married our advice is as follows.

Consider a strictly religious ceremony: For those who have deeply-held religious beliefs marriage may be mandatory. If you fall into this category and you are getting married for strictly religious reasons, it may make sense for you to have a religious ceremony only and forgo the legal formalities. Though you will not enjoy the financial and legal benefits of marriage you will be wed in the eyes of your faith and your privacy will remain intact.

Elope: We are strong proponents of private marriage ceremonies, at least as far as the official proceedings go. By eloping with certain criteria in mind, you can avoid the fact of your legal wedding being publicized on the internet. We understand that many people dream of a large wedding surrounded by family and friends, and we do not ask you to deny yourself that privilege. If you do wish to have a formal ceremony you still may, but we encourage you to have a very small ceremony ahead of time. Ideally it should consist of you, your betrothed, an officiant, and the smallest legally allowable number of witnesses. This private proceeding is the one that will be officially documented and legally join the two of you.

When choosing a location to which to elope there are two major factors to consider. First, it should be a city or township that does not digitize its records. There are still a few hold-out towns that do not have digital, searchable public records. This is changing and may not always be the case. We believe that if you look diligently you should be able to find such a place. Impoverished, rural towns in the deep south and the American west would be good candidates. The next major criteria to look for is a town that has no ties to either individual in the ceremony. The state in which you choose to get officially wed should not be a former residence, place of work, or place of birth of either party or any of their close relatives. It should also be a state to which neither party frequently travels for leisure purposes. This will significantly reduce the chances of a determined adversary locating the record of your marriage.

It should be noted that this may not be considered a one-hundred percent solution. Though the town in which you chose to get married may not currently digitize records this may change at some point in the future. As computers and digital storage become cheaper and more readily available an increasing number of municipalities are digitizing their records. You should not be surprised if you find that your records have been added to a state, county, or town database that is publicly available online. Even if the town in which you get married does digitize its records, you still have some protection. An adversary would have to know the state and town to search to find your record. If you choose randomly and do not leave a digital trail, the fact of your matrimony should remain somewhat private.

We consulted with a client recently who wished to have a large wedding ceremony. We advised against this. However, he viewed the ceremony as a social event that was necessary in his circles, so we got creative. First, we met him and his fiancé at an airport in a remote western state. From there we drove several hours to a very small town. We went to the courthouse during business hours, applied for a wedding license, then waited for the civil magistrate to perform the legal ceremony. Because two witnesses were required, and attaching our names to the marriage certificate as witnesses could be potentially dangerous for this individual, we asked two individuals who were at the court the attend as witnesses. One was a local sheriff's deputy and one was a clerk who worked at the courthouse. Both were happy to witness the ceremony. After this, the couple flew back to their East Coast home and began planning their "real" wedding. The real wedding was never recorded in public records because technically it never happened. Unbeknownst to the guests the couple was already wed and this was merely a social event.

Don't advertise: Do not announce your engagement or ceremony in the local newspaper. This is a custom in some parts of the U.S., and is a major privacy compromise. Once it is on the internet it will be nearly impossible to totally remove. Additionally, it may also contain a photograph of you and your fiancé. Avoiding this may be very important for your level of privacy. It is also becoming increasingly common to have a wedding website. Though these websites are claimed to be private and available only to those who have a direct link, we strongly advise against this practice. As everyone reading this should understand, nothing on the internet is truly private.

Maiden names: Generally, we recommend that both spouses keep their respective last names rather than taking a single, shared last name. This is another suggestion with which many people will take issue, but it offers some serious privacy benefits. If both spouses in a marriage keep their given last names, the couple has twice as many names to use in the future, should the need arise. If both spouses take a single name, there is now twice the likelihood that the name will be compromised.

Again, we urge you to consider the practical nature of a name, but if both individuals choose to take a shared last name, we recommend choosing the one that is the least at-risk. If both parties are at equal risk, we recommend taking the last name that is the most common. This may not always be possible; we realize that in today's hetero-normative society it is completely acceptable and far easier for a female to take a male's last name than the other way around. If you are in a same-sex relationship both partners may have the ability to take the last names of each other. This creates a nearly ideal situation: both individuals get to "start over" with new last names.

Wedding photographers: Many wedding photographers have prolific websites and social media presence. Often after shooting a wedding, a photographer will post photographs on his or her website for viewing by the attendees or for self-promotion. This is something that you should be keenly aware of when hiring a wedding photographer. The ownership and use of your likenesses should be addressed in the contract prior to engaging the photographer's services. Photography is already a crowded marketplace; if your first choice refuses to budge on this issue, a competitor almost certainly will indulge.

We recently worked with a pair of clients who, following their wedding, realized that dozens of very intimate photographs had been posted publicly on the photographer's website. At that point there was little we could do to protect the likenesses of the newlyweds. Though the photographer was agreeable to taking the photographs down the couple had lost control of their likenesses. They will never know if their photographs were downloaded, and if so, by whom. It is far easier to stop this before it happens than it is to take corrective action retroactively.

We know that this is starting to sound overly paranoid. Please take a step back and consider something. Imagine that you are thirty years in the past. You have just been married and possess an album of paper photo prints from the wedding. Would you consider making thousands of copies and giving them to complete strangers? Would you call up your enemies and offer the collection to them? Even if there was no cost associated, we assume you would not. When posting or allowing photos online, this is basically what you are doing. You are sharing your intimate moments with the world.

Wedding Registries: Wedding registries require you to give up a lot of information. First you must give up the names of both yourself and your co-registrant. You must provide an email address, telephone number, physical address, and other invasive information. Wedding registries are excellent vectors for collecting marketing information that is then sold to other companies in the wedding industry. If you register for your wedding, we obviously recommend using services like 333Mail, Blur, notsharingmy.info, and Google Voice to avoid giving out real information to the extent possible.

Unfortunately wedding registries also require that you provide a physical address to which your gifts can be shipped. Obviously it would be a bad idea to use your home address. Rather, consider using a commercial mail receiving agency or U.S. post office box. Many U.S. Post Offices will now accept FedEx or UPS packages, and certainly CMRAs will. Every USPS location has different rules regarding non-USPS deliveries, so check with your local office. Many have embraced the external sources and will now sign for packages on your behalf. Alternatively, if you are not in any particular danger, you may consider using the address of a bridesmaid or best man (with her or his prior consent, of course), your office, or another address that does not tie your name to your home address.

As we mentioned in the discussion of anonymous purchases, it is ok to have items shipped to your house as long as they are not sent in your name. This is difficult with a wedding registry, but it is possible. The couple we mentioned earlier who were formally married in a western US state managed to do it. In what seemed like a spirit of good humor they informed every invitee that they were registered as "Bonnie Parker and Clyde Barrow". The happy couple's family and friends had no problem remembering the names of the infamous duo and took it as a joke.

Naming a Child

The birth of a child poses both some challenges and some opportunities. The major challenge is that the child's birth certificate will be public record in the town or city in which he or she is born. The opportunities presented in this situation are to set the child up for success in the future. Again, the suggestions within this section will challenge conventional notions. Most of the suggestions here pertain to naming your child.

The less unique his or her name is, the greater your child's privacy will be in the future. As a thought experiment, consider which individual would be easier to locate (all things being equal): a person named John Smith, or a person named Bartholomew Lorang? Finding the *right* John Smith would take some serious investigative power. It would take time to sort through hundreds and possibly thousands of records. It would take a dedicated team of people, if a name is all they had to go from. It would take patience and dedication and resources that are unlikely to be possessed by anyone but the federal government. We offer several suggestions for how to accomplish this.

If you have a common last name you are already at a huge advantage over those who have uncommon last names. There are still steps you can take to make your child less distinguishable. Though we have lamented the emotional attachments to names in the introduction to this section, it does offer some advantages. Because names are so deeply personal to most it is unlikely anyone will ever seriously question your decision about what you named your child. Because these techniques are also sometimes employed for personal reasons other than privacy, it is equally unlikely that your child will even realize that his or her name was chosen with privacy as the primary goal.

Common usage naming: Though all parents wish to call their child by his or her name, using a "common name" is an incredibly powerful technique for protecting privacy. A very small number of people will call a child by a name or nickname that is not one of his or her given names. Though a common name is typically related to a person's first name (i.e. "Chuck" for Charles or "Bill" for William) it certainly does not have to be. Addressing your child by a common usage name from a young age can create a very strong layer of privacy around his or her true name. He or she will be known to most by the common name and few will know his or her real name.

Middle names: When naming your child, we recommend deciding on what you wish his or her first name to be and making this his or her official middle name. For example, if you wish to name your daughter Lindsay Michelle and you plan to call her Lindsay, use Lindsay as her middle name. She will be known to all of her friends, your family, her future work colleagues, etc. as Lindsay. However, on most official documentation she will use her true first name (Michelle), and this is the name that will be populated in databases. In the future if someone is searching for your child and only know her by Lindsay it will be more difficult to locate her because all of her official records are in her legal first name, Michelle.

It is also possible to give your child more than one middle name and we strongly recommend doing so. This gives you and your child options in the future; he or she will have the ability to use one of three first name/last name combinations in common usage, while still using a first name that has not been commonly used for all official documents.

Suffixes: We strongly recommend against using suffixes like JR, III, etc. Again, the desire to do so is typically emotional and the act of doing so serves little practical purpose. It does, however, make your child's name more distinctive which will make privacy more difficult for him or her in the future.

If you have an uncommon last name: While we recognize that there are emotional attachments to names, we reiterate our belief that names are merely a system of organizing people. If you have a very uncommon last name, we recommend choosing an alternate last name for the child. First, you may use your last name as the child's middle name. This would allow your offspring to carry the family name while still offering a significantly greater degree of privacy.

Another option is to give the child the last name of the spouse with the least common last name. If your last name is Piepgrass but your wife's last name is Smith, go with her last name. Yet another option, and the one that is probably least attractive to most, is to give the child the last name of a distant, beloved relative or admired figure that bears a common last name. Both of these options can be easily explained as needed. Once the child has been named it is unlikely the issue will come up and need to be explained very often. Most of your friends and family will probably just assume that your child bears your last name.

Though this may seem a bit "out there", consider the privacy benefits. In the future your child will be known to most by his or her first name and YOUR last name. Very few people will actually know his or her true last name. This is a very good situation. Anyone looking for your child, or you via your child, will begin with an inaccurate last name.

If you have already named your child: If you have already named your child with an uncommon, easily-searchable name, you may consider a name change for him or her. Though your state's laws will certainly vary, name changes for minor children are sometimes much simpler than those for adults. Children have no credit, no driving history, and no frequent flier miles to lose.

The easiest way to "change" a child's name is through common usage as we outlined above. If your child is young enough you may simply begin calling him or her by a new name. By the time the child is grown he or she will be known to all as a name that appears on no official records. Admittedly this may create the need for some awkward explanations with family and friends. Also it is up to you, and at some point the child, to avoid creating public information in that name.

Teach your children: If you take all of these steps you will eventually have to teach your children the reasons you did so. If you do not do so, they may order items in their common name to your home (or other address). They may, unthinkingly, fill out an official document using the common usage name. You must also be careful to avoid using their common usage name on any official documentation—it can be easy to overlook this when you are in a hurry.

Much of the power of a common usage name is that it is firewalled from the real name or home address. When someone searches for your child by his or her common first name and given last name, nothing should come up because ideally nothing has ever been created in that name. Similarly, associating the common usage name and given name can cause the same problems; anyone who learns of the association can now begin by searching for the real name. Once it has been compromised, many of its benefits have been lost and are difficult to regain.

Other Issues with Children

Credit reports and credit freeze: An increasingly common form of identity theft is stealing the identity of a child. This technique is increasing in popularity because the credit of a child will, in all likelihood, not be checked for years, allowing the criminal to get away with it. We recommend that you deal with this before it happens. As soon as you have requested and received your child's Social Security number you should begin monitoring his or her credit by requesting credit reports. Simply add his or her information to the list of people in your family for whom you request a credit report three times annually as outlined in Chapter Nine.

Next, consider requesting a credit freeze for the child as was explained in Chapter Nine. Depending on your state of residence, you may be required to pay for your child's credit freeze if he or she has not been the victim of identity theft. This is well worth the cost in the long run for the child.

Divorce

One major disadvantage of getting married is the potential for getting divorced. When you get divorced you are again faced with a situation that can create a great deal of information about you. The silver lining to divorce is that it may be a golden opportunity to create some new privacy for yourself. As we have mentioned earlier, relocating your residence is required to achieve total privacy. In the aftermath of a divorce, it is common for both parties to move. If you move, we recommend finding a new home to rent or purchase anonymously as described earlier in this chapter.

If you are a female who changed your last name when you got married, divorce presents an almost brand new start. You can change your name easier than males can. Further, you can likely keep your married name in common usage. We worked with a female client during the writing of this book that had been divorced for several months. She works in the criminal justice system in a major east coast city and deals with many convicted felons who know her first and last name. Due to her financial situation and employment by her state's government, being completely "invisible" was not an option for her. We did find an excellent opportunity to protect her privacy when she mentioned that she wanted to change her name back to her maiden name.

This prompted us to advise her to order as many business cards as possible before her name change back to her maiden name was official. We recommended that she keep using her married last name for official business, and set everything else up in her maiden name. This created a good degree of safety for her as none of the convicts with whom she interacted would know her real last name. It took some convincing because her married name was emotionally laden, but she eventually agreed and now enjoys much more safety and privacy.

Death

A death in the family can cause privacy concerns as well. The passing of a loved one can be a traumatic time, so we recommend dealing with this well in advance. The greatest compromises we have seen that are related to deaths are obituaries posted in newspapers and online. Obituaries can reveal a great deal of information about you including the names of your parents, siblings, spouse, and children, your relationship to the deceased, and other personal information.

To avoid this, you should plan ahead of time. You have several options. First, you may request of your family that you be unlisted in any obituaries or other family announcements. This is the most extreme option and one that may be difficult for you or your family. Next you may ask that your family use your middle name, common name, or a nickname.

A client that we worked with several years ago knew his father would pass within a few weeks. Our client was retired but faced some very severe threats due to his thirty-year career as a federal law enforcement agent. Revealing the names of his surviving mother, wife, children, and other family alongside his own was out of the question. After explaining this to his family they agreed to use a shortened version of his middle name which was Alexander. He was listed in the obituary as Alex. This provided some light protection against his entire name being found in a simple online search while still allowing our client and his children to be recognized in the obituary.

If you are not facing such grave threats but still wish to protect your privacy you have the right to request such consideration from your family. Rather than saying you are in danger you may wish to ask to be called something else because "it made him happy to call me that", or "that was my special thing with Dad". We recommend discussing this with your family now rather than in the immediate aftermath of a loss. Though this may be a difficult discussion to have, it is important to have it now. Deaths happen unexpectedly. When they are anticipated, the emotion involved can still make it hard to have such a conversation that your family may view as silly or selfish.

There are many other major life events that were not mentioned here. Hopefully, this chapter can provide some insight that could be applied to anything else that you encounter. As with most of this book, the biggest lesson here is preparation. Having all of the pieces together before a major decision will have a great impact on the outcome.

CHAPTER TWENTY-SIX
DATA LEAKAGE RESPONSE

Bad things happen. We know people who have spent many months creating their perfect invisible life only to see it jeopardized by one minor mistake. While this will likely never happen to you, it is important to be prepared. This chapter will provide immediate actions that can be taken to minimize the damage after a mistake has caused a data leak. Your scenario will likely fall into one of the following categories.

- Your home address or telephone number is posted online.
- Your photo is posted online.
- Your financial information or documents are posted online.
- Your reputation is purposely slandered online.
- Your criminal or traffic charges are posted online.

Home Information Leakage

The most common personal data that will find its way online will be your home address or telephone number. As discussed previously, this data is bought, sold, and shared by hundreds of companies. If your home is titled in your real name, this will eventually end up online. Previous chapters discussed the removal and monitoring options, but did not cover the next actions. Overall, a timely response is vital. The moment that a website possesses personal information about you, a clock is ticking until other sources acquire the live information.

The first step is to identify any opt-out resources. As discussed previously, most data collection websites will have information about the process for data removal. If nothing can be found, attempt to identify any option to edit a listing. Many sites will allow you to update your information in order to correct their records. This is the ideal time to provide disinformation. Finally, direct contact with the company may be required. Consider the following example from a client in 2014.

Michael's Home Information Leakage Example

A friend reached out to me after he discovered his home address associated with his name on a new people search website. He had already completed the process of removing his information from dozens of websites, and this one did not have an opt-out policy. I first attempted contact via email, but received no response. I then located a fax number and submitted a written request. Again, no response. I finally took more drastic action. I used an online email sending service and created a brief, yet firm demand to remove the posted information. I used the techniques discussed in Chapter Eight to identify possible email addresses of various employees of the target company. I then executed a scheduled email send option and sent one message to each employee per day until disabled. Within seven days, his information was removed. I never received an official response, but my point was made. Your mileage may vary.

Justin's Home Information Leakage Example

Several years ago my home information leaked. I had taken my vehicle to a local mechanic for routine service. At the time, my driver's license and vehicle were associated with my true home address, but I had managed to keep everything else private. Unknowingly, I left the vehicle's registration and insurance information in the glove box when I dropped the vehicle off. Several weeks later I started receiving promotional fliers in the mail the at my home addressed to my real name. Since the fliers were from the same local mechanic's shop I knew exactly where the mail had originated.

The first step I took was to directly contact the mechanic in question. I asked where they had gotten my information since I knew I had not provided it on any of their forms. They informed me that it was standard practice to record information from vehicle registration information for their records and for promotional mailings. I politely asked with or to whom they shared or sold data, and requested to be taken out off of their mailing list. They informed me that they shared this information only with their printing company who made and mailed their fliers and did not sell it to any other marketers. The individual with whom I spoke was more than happy to accommodate my request. During the rest of my stay at that location I vigorously monitored my address data and I was fortunate that, to my knowledge, it never surfaced on the internet.

There are two points to this story, the first of which is having your vehicles registered to an address other than your actual physical location is incredibly important. Your vehicle and driver's license represent huge weak points. The other point of this story is that you should take immediate action if your information is leaked. Had I waited the mechanic or print shop may have lost control of my information. Don't hesitate to contact a party like the mechanic in the story and attempt to repair the situation before it becomes a much bigger problem.

Photo Leakage

If you strive to prevent photos of yourself from appearing online, you are aware of the constant struggle. Family and friends are constantly updating their Facebook, Twitter, and Instagram feeds with photo and video proof of every facet of their lives. There are no opt-out policies on these websites. There are no removal request forms. Your only option is a polite request.

We have found that a simple request to friends and family is usually sufficient for them to delete any sensitive photos. Unfortunately, there is little else that can be done. We can only recommend that you never take a threatening tone. This will only agitate the person that controls the photo and they may become resistant. We have found one thing in common with the majority of our clients with this problem. Every one of them had been tagged because of their use of social networks. If you are not on Facebook, you cannot be tagged on Facebook. If you are not on Twitter or Instagram, you are much less likely to be seen on someone else's account.

Michael's Photo Leakage Example

In late 2015, I presented a keynote session at a large conference in the Caribbean. This 60-minute session focused on cyber crime vulnerabilities and the ways that criminals use social media information to create sophisticated attacks. An hour later, I received an email from one of my automated alerts that monitor my personal information. An attendee in the audience had taken a photo of me during the lecture and posted it to Twitter. I immediately reached out through a private message and politely requested removal. The attendee agreed and the entire post was removed. This was completed before Google had the opportunity to add it to their images database. If I did not have a monitoring solution in place, I would never have noticed the post. Google and Bing would have indexed the post and image. I would then have a more difficult time removing all traces. Monitoring is vital.

Financial Information Leakage

If you find a page in a Google search result that displays personal information about you, such as your social security or credit card number, you can request immediate removal. Google will review the request and remove the information from their search results. This will not remove the information from the website that is displaying it, but it will take the link off Google to make it more difficult to find. Even if Google removes the link from their search results, you should contact the offending website directly and request removal of your information. The following are the three scenarios that will force Google to remove a link to personal information.

- Your Social Security number is visible on a website.
- Your bank account or credit card number is visible on a website.
- An image of your handwritten signature is visible on a website.

Each of these situations can be reported through the following three specific websites:

SSN: **support.google.com/websearch/contact/government_number**

Bank or credit account: **support.google.com/websearch/contact/bank_number**

Signature: **support.google.com/websearch/contact/image_of_handwritten_signature**

Each page will instruct you to complete an online form which requires your name, anonymous email address, the URL of the website that is exposing the information, the URL of a Google results page that displays the information, and the information being exposed. Fortunately, Google offers detailed help on these pages explaining how to obtain the required information.

Bing does not offer an automated removal request. Instead, you must complete an email support request that includes your name, email address, and URL of the exposed information. You must also choose "Content Removal Request" as the reason for contact. This form can be found at **support.discoverbing.com/eform.aspx?productKey=bingcontentremoval**.

Financial Information Leakage Example

In early 2015, I was contacted by an attorney who was attempting to remove some content from the internet. He and a former business partner had developed a nasty relationship after a failed venture. The former partner uploaded numerous sensitive contracts that he claimed my client had defaulted on. He placed them on his personal website and posted malicious comments about my client. Since my client had a very unique name, a Google search revealed this undesired information within the first three results. At first, I assumed that there was nothing I could do about this expression of free speech. The documents were legal.

However, each scanned contract on this website included the signature of my client. I submitted a request to Google for removal of the link to this website. I cited their policy about linking to images of a person's signature. Within five days, the link was gone. While the presence of a signature was not the concern of my client, I used it as leverage to remove the undesired content. Sometimes you may need to look at alternative ways to achieve your desired removal results.

Locating Vulnerabilities

If you want to know whether your signature, Social Security number, credit card number, or bank account information is visible on a public website, you will need to conduct specific searches. The easiest way is to occasionally conduct a search of your account numbers and view any results. Keep in mind that your searches will only be successful if the exposed data is in the same format as your search query. Also, use an anonymous search function, such as Disconnect which is mentioned in Chapter Two. You should conduct several searches of this type of data including spaces, without spaces, and only the last four or eight numbers alone. This also applies to searches for account numbers and Social Security numbers. If you do not want to continually conduct the same searches, you could set up a Google Alert as instructed in Chapter Seventeen.

Reputation Information Leakage

We constantly receive email messages asking for help with removal of slanderous content. This is usually from business owners trying to protect their brand, individuals wrapped up in online gossip, or parents attempting to shield their children from bullies. If someone simply states an opinion about your product or business online, there is nothing you can do. If someone is spreading rumors about you on social networks, no one will take your complaint. If you find malicious comments about your child online, you can only report it to the host of the content. There are only a select few scenarios where you can force content offline.

Reputation Information Leakage Example

In 2015, we were contacted by a woman who was suffering from a bad case of stalking. Her ex-boyfriend constantly harassed her and her new boyfriend online. He posted malicious content on various websites and referenced them both by full name. He had posted so much content that some of it had made it to the front page of a Google search. At one point, the first result after searching her name was a pornographic video fictitiously claiming to be her. She had enough and wanted to take action.

These cases are sometimes difficult to tackle because of laws that protect free speech. We are obviously big fans of the first amendment, but we also believe that one has a right to take advantage of other laws and policies in order to protect a reputation. Our goal was to eliminate all malicious content from the first page of both a Google and Bing search. The following highlights our successes and failures.

The first website on her Google and Bing search results was a revenge pornography page. It displayed a pornographic video of an unknown female (not the victim) that appeared to be asleep on a bed. An unknown man (not the suspect) then sexually molests the woman while she sleeps. It should be noted that this video was likely staged and the woman was probably a willing participant. These consensual videos have become popular on commercial pornography websites. The title of the video on this page included the victim's full name. The comments made several references to her, the new boyfriend, and her family. We believe that the former boyfriend wanted the world to think that the woman in the video was our victim. They did appear very similar physically.

Removing this first link was relatively simple. We first navigated to the official Google revenge porn reporting page at https://support.google.com/websearch/troubleshooter/3111061. We selected the following options which each appeared after selection of the previous.

What do you want to do? Remove information you see in Google Search
The information I want removed is: In Google's search results and on a website
Have you contacted the site's webmaster? Yes, but they haven't responded
I want to remove: A pornographic site that contains a full name or business name

Does the page contain pornographic content? Yes
Does a full name or business name appear on the website without your permission? Yes
Does the page violate Google's Webmaster Quality Guidelines? Yes

We then supplied an alias email address that we created for the victim, the full name of the victim as it appeared on the web page, the address of the Google result page linking to the video, and the address of the actual video page. We submitted the request and moved on to Bing.

We navigated to Bing's simple "Report Content to Microsoft" website located online at https://support.microsoft.com/getsupport?oaspworkflow=start_1.0.0.0&wfname=capsub&productkey=RevengePorn. We provided the victim's name as it appeared on the video page, the exact address of the page, confirmation that the victim did not consent to the posting, and a digital signature.

We received a response from Bing within 24 hours and the link was removed. Google responded over 15 days later and they also removed the link. Both cited their revenge porn policies and gave no resistance to the removal. While the female in the video was not the victim, we believe that identifying the victim as the participant warranted this type of submission. Interestingly, neither service specifically asked if the requestor was actually in the pornographic video. They only required that the requestor's name be included on the page.

At this point, the Bing results page was fairly clean. The first page included legitimate LinkedIn and other social network pages under the control of the victim. However, Google was a different story. The suspect had created a post on a popular revenge pornography web forum where he linked to the previously mentioned video. Technically, this video was not present on the website, only mention of it and a direct link. This forum post was now the number one result when searching our victim's name. This page made several references to her full name and identified her in the inappropriate video. We submitted this page through the same Google reporting page and waited. We were denied the request because the page did not contain any actual pornography. The direct link did not satisfy the requirements of their takedown policy.

We took drastic action that would not be appropriate for all situations. This web forum allows any members to post comments about the videos. We created a new member account anonymously, and submitted a comment on the page in question. In this comment, we embedded an animated image in gif format that displayed a short clip of the video. This clip looped and repeats while people are reading the comment. It appears as a brief, poor quality video. We re-submitted our request to Google and the link was removed nine days later. The rest of the results on the first page of her Google search were legitimate websites that she approved. Our work was complete.

Right to be Forgotten

The right to be forgotten is a concept that was discussed and put into practice in the European Union and Argentina in 2006. Search engines began to acknowledge this option in 2014. The issue has arisen from desires of individuals to determine the development of their life in an autonomous way, without being perpetually or periodically stigmatized as a consequence of a specific action performed in the past. Basically, you have the right to "start over" in Europe. This does not apply to Americans.

Google and Bing both allow you to submit requests for content removal from search engines if you live in Europe. The removal forms can be found on their support pages similar to the instructions mentioned in the previous example. They will ask for the search results URL and a digital signature of your name. They will verify that your name appears in the results and remove anything defamatory from the index.

Until recently, we found that submitting a request from an email address that possessed a UK domain was sufficient as proof of citizenship. However, Google has become much stricter and now demands photocopied identification. We have found Bing to be more lenient. We cannot advise you on how to proceed with a request like this if you do not live in Europe. We have received many success and failure stories from other people's attempts to take advantage of this law.

Criminal Information Leakage

Many new websites have appeared that host mug shots and associated criminal information of anyone arrested in select states. This varies based on state law that allows unlimited access to this type of content. While arrest records are public data, we do not support websites that post this data in bulk. They are not doing this as a public resource. They are extortion websites that hope to benefit from your removal request. Most of these will remove your mug shot for $500. The only purpose of these sites is financial gain.

We have found removal requests to these websites to be a waste of time. Letters from lawyers will go unanswered. They simply do not care. If your mug shot appears on one of these sites, we have only found one potential solution. Your results will vary with this technique. The following example will explain the process that we took for a client.

Criminal Information Leakage Example

We were contacted by a subject that had been arrested for speeding. This may sound ridiculous, but he was speeding over 20 miles per hour above the limit, which was a misdemeanor in his state. He was booked, processed, and released on bond. The next day, his mug shot appeared on one of these extortion sites. Within a week, it had been indexed by

Google. A search of his name revealed the mug shot directly above his LinkedIn and business websites. He was devastated.

The website that hosted this image was fairly dysfunctional. It was poorly designed and only existed to make a quick buck. We placed an alert on the exact page where the client's information was hosted through a service called Visual Ping. The moment that the website went down for maintenance, we received an alert that the page had changed. We immediately submitted a request for Google and Bing to re-index our client's mug shot page, which was offline. We identified the address as missing, and both Google and Bing re-indexed it during the 24-hour maintenance down-time. The mug shot was no longer listed in his search results. If someone were to search the website directly, they could still see the photo. This is highly unlikely. It is possible that Google and Bing could re-index this live data. We have found that this usually happens when new content is posted. Since we informed the search engines that the content was missing, it will not immediately re-index that stale data.

We want to clarify that we were fairly lucky in this scenario. We took advantage of the situation. It is not a permanent solution, but it did buy some time to make an intentional decision rather than a panicked one. We take a firm stance against paying the removal fees offered by these sites. Not only does it give in to this type of behavior, but it also increases the chance of the photo reappearing. If you paid once, you will likely pay twice. Further, most of these websites are owned by the same entity.

Summary

If your sensitive details are posted anywhere online, it is vital that you act quickly. The internet is a timer counting down until your data is spread onto additional websites. Proper alerts, constant monitoring, and better sharing habits will protect your privacy long term. We respect that we cannot control the internet and that removing personal data is like playing a game of cat and mouse. However, we take our privacy seriously. We are willing to put in the effort in order to maintain our desired level of anonymity. We both have business Twitter accounts, but no posts mention anything about personality, interests, or location. Our home addresses are not connected to our names within any database, public or private. We only use VOIP numbers and never the cellular number from the provider. We use encrypted messaging apps whenever possible. While it took years, we believe that we have achieved the level of invisibility appropriate for us.

Many books about privacy will tell you that it is all or nothing. Some will say that you should abandon your friends and live in the woods or that you should never use a cell phone or the internet. We believe neither. We think that you should educate yourself and understand how data collection works. Then, decide what layers of privacy are most important to you. Finally, strategize and execute your custom plan of attack. We believe that you can establish the balance most appropriate for you.

Chapter Twenty-Seven
The Ideal Setup

This final chapter allows us to think about the perfect scenario in regards to privacy and security. It outlines the actions that we would take if money were not a factor, we had unlimited time and resources, and were allowed to completely start over with a new private and secure life. Some of this will be unfeasible for most due to cost alone. However, the ideas may spark something inside of you to take action. Every technique mentioned in this chapter is explained within this book. We hope that this final fictional selection will summarize our ultimate goal of helping you create the private and secure life that you deserve.

Residence

We will begin with your new home. You have sold your previous home and completed all of the closing paperwork. You provided only a PO Box located in the same city as your previous residence as the address on the closing paperwork. This old address was compromised and available online. You no longer have any real associations with it. You check into a hotel under your alias name and pay with your secondary credit card. You have located the new home of your dreams and you are ready to purchase it. You have already established your invisible New Mexico LLC that has no public associations to your true identity. Your real estate attorney attends the closing on your behalf and signs all of the paperwork as limited power of attorney for the LLC. Your name is nowhere on the closing paperwork. He possesses the check from the bank for the purchase amount. If you paid cash, this step is complete. If you obtained a loan, the loan is in the name of the LLC with you as the responsible debtor. Your real estate attorney verifies that your name is not on any documentation provided by the bank for the closing.

Utilities

You move into your new home. You contact the utility companies and explain that the home is owned by the company that you work for and you need to activate new service in the company name. If prompted for a SSN, you provide the EIN of the LLC. If forced to disclose your name, you use an alias. You never provide an SSN. If required, you provide a secondary alias credit card to keep on file as auto payment for the services. You order broadband internet service in an alias name and auto pay with either a secondary card or Blur masked card for extra protection. You never provide your real name to any utility companies. You will have no association with the new residence. Your internet account is in its own unique alias.

Back Story

If needed, you develop a convincing and credible backstory. You spend a month at an AirBnB rental in Albuquerque, Boston, Chicago, or Denver. You get to know the neighborhood, find a favorite bar, and learn some streets. You make contacts and learn the local idiosyncrasies and lingo. You buy a couple of hats and t-shirts for the local sports team. You visit the local attractions, learn where the parks are, and find a hole-in-the-wall diner or two. From now on when you are questioned about where you are from, you don't hesitate. You don't change your whole life story, but you also don't get into it during casual conversation.

Disinformation

You begin a comprehensive disinformation campaign. Your disinformation campaign is not only an attempt to obscure your true past, it also supports your backstory. If someone searches for you in the city that you now claim, they will find something. You make the instances of your name and address look as real as possible. For each address you have magazine and newspaper subscriptions, retail loyalty cards, and junk mail. A phone number is tied to this residence as well as your spouse's and children's names. In the meantime, you have packages, takeout food, and mail delivered to your house. You choose a generic name in which all your mail is delivered. You also pick a corresponding name for each member of your family, like Melissa, Allison, and Kevin. They receive magazines and packages, too. If anyone searches for your new address, they will find convincing evidence that the Mitchell family lives there. This name matches that of your internet service and your Wi-Fi SSID. It matches the name on your grocery loyalty cards. It matches what you have told your neighbors. If a private investigator is ever looking at your residence, he will believe the Mitchell family lives there.

Computers

Because cost is not a concern, you destroy all of your current connected devices. Your laptops, desktops, tablets, cell phones, and routers are all history. They will never enter your new home. You purchase a new wireless router with cash and properly configure the security settings. You purchase new computers with cash at retail stores. You provide alias names for the mandatory accounts and registration. You execute full disk encryption on the computers and properly encrypt all mobile devices. You create stateless operating systems for sensitive activities. Your browsers are tweaked with appropriate security settings.

Communication

You quit using non-encrypted email services and move to ProtonMail or another equivalent. You use Wickr for instant messaging and convince your friends to do the same. You purchase new cellular telephones with cash or Blur masked cards. These phones are stand-alone, are not locked to a specific carrier, and contain no bloatware. You anonymously purchase SIM starter packs online and activate the telephones from your new computers. You use your new

VPN in order to mask your IP address. The devices possess all new online accounts and nothing is carried over from your previous life.

Passwords

You have started from scratch with all your email, banking, entertainment, and other online accounts. You have preserved your contacts and other information, but will never again log into these accounts because you know that your IP may leak when you are logged in. You will not risk your hard-won privacy to save an old Gmail account. You build new accounts from the ground up. You start with a clean slate. You create only what you need and nothing more. You audit all of your passwords and identify all important accounts. You create unique passwords for each service that comply with the previous instruction. Your place all passwords in a locally stored password management program secured with a long password. You enable two factor authentication everywhere it is offered. You demand it where it is not.

Social Networks

You delete them all.

Credit

You order a secondary credit card in an alias name. This identity is used for all lodging and travel related purchases. You conduct a credit freeze through all four credit bureaus. You file an IRS Identity Theft Affidavit and receive an Identity Protection PIN. You open a Blur account powered by your secondary credit card. You stockpile Vanilla pre-paid credit cards. You pay for everything you possibly can in cash, prepaid credit cards, or gift cards purchased with cash.

Employment

You are self-employed, you pay your taxes, you obey all laws, you provide value to your community, you respect others, and you live the private and secure life that you have always wanted.

Monitoring

You hire a private investigator to track you down. He is on retainer for you, and he is your red team. If he finds you so can others, but he will not. You set up complete online monitoring of your current address and watch for any inclusions of your name. In a stateless operating system with a VPN, you occasionally search your real name to identify leakage.

Congratulations. Well Done.

CONCLUSION

To keep up with the changes in various methods of personal privacy and security, visit our websites at **IntelTechniques.com** (Michael) and **YourUltimateSecurity.guide** (Justin). All hyperlinks to the software and services mentioned in this book are available on these sites. There is a good chance that as you read this, new content has been posted about the very topic you are researching. This is also the most appropriate way to contact us.

We often collaborated from remote locations all over the world. All email communications and attachments were conducted through encrypted ProtonMail messages. All text messaging was transmitted securely through Wickr, Signal, or Silent Text. Every telephone conversation was encrypted through Silent Phone or Signal. Both computers used during this writing process possessed full disk encryption. The backups of all files were (and are) stored in encrypted TrueCrypt 7.1a containers within the full disk encrypted drives. All physical correspondence requiring actual signatures was sent to mail forwarding personal mailboxes (PMBs), hotels under alias names, and other commercial properties with no personal associations. The collaborations before final submission were in-person, outside of the United States, and without the use of wirelessly connected devices. We take our privacy seriously. We sleep well at night.

We sincerely thank the following people for all of their support, testing, patience, motivation, feedback, and overall interest in our crazy ideas. You know who you are.

T.S.
D.B.
D.S.
L.H.
J.B.
J.L.
J.R.
M.M.

Thank you for reading. Stay safe. Fight for your privacy.

Michael Bazzell
Justin Carroll

Index

58043435R00276

Made in the USA
Middletown, DE
04 August 2019